DIVERSITY AND CHANGE
IN FAMILIES

DIVERSITY AND CHANGE IN FAMILIES:
PATTERNS, PROSPECTS, AND POLICIES

Mark Robert Rank and Edward L. Kain, Editors

Prentice Hall, Upper Saddle River, New Jersey 07458

Library of Congress Cataloging-in-Publication Data

Diversity and change in families   patterns, prospects, and policies /
  [edited by] Mark Robert Rank and Edward L. Kain.
      p. cm.
  Includes bibliographical references.
  ISBN 0-13-219668-9
  1. Family.   I. Rank, Mark R.   II. Kain, Edward L.
HQ518.D58 1995
306.8—dc20   94-28524
                                                      CIP

Editorial/production supervision
  and interior design: **Joan E. Foley**
Acquisitions editor: **Nancy Roberts**
Editorial assistant: **Pat Naturale**
Copy editor: **Henry Pels**
Cover designer: **Marjory Dressler**
Buyer: **Mary Ann Gloriande**

Printed in the United States of America
10 9 8 7 6 5 4 3 2 1

ISBN 0-13-219668-9

Prentice-Hall International (UK) Limited,London
Prentice-Hall of Australia Pty. Limited, Sydney
Prentice-Hall Canada Inc., Toronto
Prentice-Hall Hispanoamericana, S.A., Mexico
Prentice-Hall of India Private Limited, New Delhi
Prentice-Hall of Japan, Inc., Tokyo
Pearson Education Asia Pte. Ltd., Singapore
Editora Prentice-Hall do Brasil, Ltda., Rio de Janeiro

Contents

Aging and Widowhood

III FAMILY PROBLEMS AND PROBLEM-SOLVING STRATEGIES

Family Problems

Family Therapy

Family Policy

Preface

The idea for this book was conceived nearly five years ago. We have taught a variety of courses pertaining to families, and throughout the semesters we have supplemented our lectures and textbook material with various articles and chapters. We were never quite satisfied with the family reader books that were available. From our perspective, some of them failed to adequately cover the issues and topics that we felt were essential. Others appeared too superficial in terms of the material that they did cover. Still others contained chapters that students found dry or difficult to read. If we wanted a family reader that was relevant, rigorous, and engaging, we came to the conclusion that we would have to construct it ourselves. At that moment, the idea for this book was born. It was our hope from the beginning that this would become a collection of readings that students would find exciting and thought-provoking, readable yet challenging, diverse and still thorough.

Each of us have professional backgrounds as sociologists. However, we also have experiences that go beyond the bounds of the sociological discipline. We have taught in departments of human development and family studies and in schools of social work. We have collaborated with researchers in economics, psychology, family studies, social work, rural sociology, and of course, sociology. In our own teaching and research we often draw upon the work of scholars in a range of fields as diverse as history, demography, anthropology, family studies, public policy, psychology, and social work. The readings in this collection represent a mix of such disciplines. We have looked across a range of academic fields to select what we feel are some of the best readings available.

Connected with this has been our intention to design a book that could be used in a number of courses, in various departments, dealing with the family. These would include large introductory courses on marriage and the family as well as a range of upper-division family courses.

SELECTING THE TOPICS AND READINGS

The strength of any anthology of readings lies in the relevance of the included content as well as the quality of the articles chosen to cover such content. We began by deciding upon the topics that should go into the reader. This was accomplished in several ways. We examined the syllabi of family courses being taught in a wide range of colleges and universities, looking at their subjects and reading material. We then went through all of the major family textbooks to see how they were organized and what topics and issues were included. Finally, we contacted dozens of faculty in the United States who were teaching family-related courses and asked them for their suggestions on what they felt should be included in a family reader. Based upon these sources of information, as well as our own teaching experiences, we decided upon the specific topics that would encompass this collection.

Next, we had to choose the articles and book chapters that would best introduce students to the specific subjects. During this process we read hundreds of articles and chapters. How did we arrive at our choices? We used several different criteria.

We began by asking, was the research that was analyzed or discussed in an article of the highest quality? In other words, we were looking for readings that were rigorous in the content of their material. We were searching for chapters that would represent the best in terms of family research.

A second criteria we relied on was readability. Were these articles or chapters well-written, accessible, and interesting? No matter how competently the research was conducted, little knowledge would be conveyed if the writing was so technical or boring that it put the reader to sleep. We insisted that the chapters be strong in both their content and in their writing style.

A third criteria was that, wherever possible, we included well-known researchers as our authors. The reason for this was that as students of the family, it was our opinion that undergraduates should become familiar with the work of key scholars in the field. In addition, the textbooks and lectures used throughout a semester would undoubtedly refer to some of these authors. By reading their works firsthand, it would make for a more dynamic learning experience.

A fourth criteria was that we wanted our readings to be up-to-date. In areas such as the history of the family or cross-cultural variation, this criteria is not quite as essential. However, on issues such as family policy or problems in the family, it is extremely important. While some of the readings in this collection might be considered "classics," most are quite recent. The bulk of the readings in this book have been published after 1990.

A fifth criteria used for selecting our chapters was that we were looking for a collection of readings that would represent a diversity of approaches. This includes methodological diversity, theoretical diversity, and political diversity. The chapters consist of a range of methodological approaches—from fieldwork, to in-depth interviewing, to survey research, to large-scale demographic analyses. Theoretical diversity includes a variety of approaches such as structural function-alism, symbolic interactionism, social exchange theory, and feminism. Political diversity encompasses both liberal and conservative perspectives, as well as those in between.

Our final criteria was that we wanted to make certain that the issues of race, class, and gender were addressed throughout the book. While the structure of the reader is organized around three themes—variation in families, the family life course, and family problems and problem-solving strategies—the centrality of race, class, and gender are found within each of those themes.

ORGANIZATION

Diversity and Change in Families is divided into three major sections. These sections, and their subsections, are found in most courses dealing with the family. However, several of our subsections, such as cultural variation, social class variation, family structure variation, and family therapy, are not often found in family readers.

We have designed this collection so that the articles can be read either consecutively or out of sequence, depending upon the structure and content of a specific class. At the start of each reading is a brief introduction. These introductions highlight several of the article's major themes and make connections and links across the readings.

The first third of the reader focuses on the topic of variation in families. In order to have a better perspective on our own families, it is often useful to examine how and why families vary. We explore this variation through historical, cultural, racial and ethnic, social class, and family structural diversity. One of the key arguments throughout these chapters is that to understand why families vary in terms of their structure and functions, we must understand the larger social, economic, and political context in which families operate.

The second third of the reader is devoted to looking at family relationships across the life course—from attraction and premarital sexuality, through marriage and childbearing, to divorce and/or old age. The manner in which relationships change over time is a critical underlying theme. The stages that span the life course are examined in detail within this section.

The final third of the reader looks at family problems and problem-solving strategies. Violence in the family, economic stress, and children's well-being are some of the problems explored. Approaches and strategies for addressing these problems are also examined—specifically, the strategies of family therapy and family policy.

Acknowledgments

We have been most fortunate to receive suggestions, advice, and assistance from many. We gratefully acknowledge the institutional support and resources provided by Shanti Khinduka, Dean of the George Warren Brown School of Social Work at Washington University. In addition, a faculty research award made by the George Warren Brown School of Social Work, Washington University, St. Louis, Missouri, provided assistance. Faculty research awards from the Cullen Foundation and the Brown Foundation of Houston also provided support for this work. We would also like to thank Elaine Walker and the Department of Psychology at Emory University, the Department of Sociology at the University of North Carolina at Chapel Hill, and the Department of Sociology and Anthropology at Southwestern University for their support and assistance.

Jan Bueckner and Scott Ward lent considerable help in the searching and locating of articles and book chapters, while Randall Cauley assisted in correspondence with faculty colleagues. The many students who have taken our family courses have provided numerous ideas and suggestions regarding potential readings for this collection. We would like to thank them all.

As mentioned earlier, we received many recommendations from colleagues around the country as to what material might be appropriate for the reader. These included suggestions from Patti Adler, Peter Adler, Margaret L. Andersen, Frank D. Bean, Felix M. Berardo, Denise Bielby, Letha Chadiha, Kenneth S. Y. Chew, Rand D. Conger, Glen Elder, Thomas J. Espenshade, Frances K. Goldscheider, Jaber F. Gubrium, Marilyn Ihinger-Tallman, Paul W. Kingston, David M. Klein, David Knox, Helena Z. Lopata, Judith Lorber, Lorraine Mayfield-Brown, Brent C. Miller, Ira L. Reiss, Ronald R. Rindfuss, Rachel A. Rosenfeld, Jerry Savells, Nancy Vosler, and Gautum Yadama.

Support from our publisher has been critical for the successful completion of this book. We sincerely appreciate the encouragement, patience, and guidance from Nancy Roberts, Joan Foley, and Wayne Spohr at Prentice Hall.

Finally, we would like to thank our own families for the support and strength that they have provided. These family members include Mark Robert Rank's spouse and daughters, Anne, Elizabeth, and Katherine; mother, Jean; and brother, Steve; and Edward L. Kain's mother and father, Mildred and Victor.

DIVERSITY AND CHANGE IN FAMILIES

The Theoretical Importance of the Family*

William J. Goode

In this introductory article, William J. Goode explores several central questions related to studying families. He discusses the emotional intensity found in families, and the ways in which kinship networks are linked with other social networks in society. He also introduces several themes which will be repeated throughout this collection. Among these themes: (1) It is frequently difficult to study families because of our preconceived notions about family life; (2) There are often differences between our "ideal" image of families, and the reality of everyday family life; (3) The family is a central social institution which serves many important functions for society; and (4) Defining "the family" can be a difficult and politically charged task.

Through the centuries, thoughtful people have observed that the family was disintegrating. In the past several decades, this idea has become more and more common. Many analysts have reported that the family no longer performs tasks once entrusted to it—production, education, protection, for example. From these and other data we might conclude that the family is on its way out.

But almost everyone who lives out an average life span enters the married

---

Source: William J. Goode, *The Family,* © 1982, pp. 1-14. Reprinted by permission of Prentice Hall, Englewood Cliffs, New Jersey.

1

state. Most eventually have children, who will later do the same. Of the increasing number who divorce, many will hopefully or skeptically marry again. In the Western nations, a higher percentage of people marry than a century ago. Indeed, the total number of years spent within marriage by the average person is higher now than at any previous time in the history of the world. In all known societies, almost everyone lives enmeshed in a network of family rights and obligations. People are taught to accept these rules through a long period of childhood socialization. That is, people come to feel that these family patterns are both right and desirable.

At the present time, human beings appear to get as much joy and sorrow from the family as they always have, and seem as bent as ever on taking part in family life. In most of the world, the traditional family may be shaken, but the institution will probably enjoy a longer life than any nation now in existence. The family does not seem to be a powerful institution, like the military, the church, or the state, but it seems to be the most resistant to conquest, or to the efforts people make to reshape it. Any specific family may appear to be fragile or unstable, but the family system as a whole is tough and resilient.

The Family: Various Views

The intense emotional meaning of family relations for almost everyone has been observed throughout history. Philosophers and social analysts have noted that any society is a structure made up of families linked together. Both travelers and anthropologists often describe the peculiarities of a given society by outlining its family relations.

The earliest moral and ethical writings of many cultures assert the significance of the family. Within those commentaries, the view is often expressed that a society loses its strength if people do not fulfill family obligations. Confucius thought that happiness and prosperity would prevail if everyone would behave "correctly" as a family member. This meant primarily that no one should fail in his filial obligations. That is, the proper relationship between ruler and subjects was like that between a father and his children. The cultural importance of the family is also emphasized in the Old Testament. The books of Exodus, Deuteronomy, Ecclesiastes, Psalms, and Proverbs, for example, proclaim the importance of obeying family rules. The earliest codified literature in India, the Rig-Veda, which dates from about the last half of the second millennium B.C., and the Law of Manu, which dates from about the beginning of the Christian era, devote much attention to the family. Poetry, plays, novels, and short stories typically seize upon family relationships as the primary focus of human passion, and their ideas and themes often grow from family conflict. Even the great epic poems of war have subthemes focusing on problems in family relations.[1]

From time to time, social analysts and philosophers have presented plans for societies that *might* be created (these are called utopias) in which new family roles (rights and obligations of individual members) are offered as solutions to traditional social problems. Plato's *Republic* is one such attempt. Plato was probably the first to urge the creation of a society in which all members, men and women alike, would have an equal opportunity to develop their talents to the utmost, and to achieve a position in society solely through merit. Since family patterns in all societies prevent selection based entirely on individual worth, in Plato's utopia the tie between parents and children would play no part, because knowledge of that link would be erased. Approved conception would take place at the same time each year at certain hymeneal festivals; children born out of season would be eliminated (along with those born defective). All children would be taken from their parents at birth and reared by specially designated people.

Experimental or utopian communities like Oneida, the Shakers, the Mormons, and modern communes have typically insisted that changes in family relations were necessary to achieve their goals. Every fundamental political upheaval since the French Revolution of 1789 has offered a program that included profound changes in family relations. Since World War II, most countries of the world have written new constitutions. In perhaps all of them, but especially in all the less developed nations, these new laws have been far more advanced than public opinion in those countries. They have aimed at creating new family patterns more in conformity with the leaders' views of equality and justice, and often antagonistic to traditional family systems. This wide range of commentary, analysis, and political action, over a period of 2,500 years, suggests that throughout history we have been at least implicitly aware of the importance of family patterns as a central element in human societies.

The Central Position of the Family in Society

In most tribal societies, kinship patterns form the major part of the whole social structure. By contrast, the family is only a small part of the social structure of modern industrial societies. It is nevertheless a key element in them, specifically linking individuals with other social institutions, such as the church, the state, or the economy. Indeed modern society, with its complex advanced technology and its highly trained bureaucracy, would collapse without the contributions of this seemingly primitive social agency. The class system, too, including its restrictions on education and opportunity, its high or low social mobility rates, and its initial social placement by birth, is founded on the family.

Most important, it is within the family that the child is first socialized to serve the needs of the society, and not only its own needs. A society will not survive unless its needs are met, such as the production and distribution of commodities, protection of the young and old or the sick and the pregnant, conformity to the law, and so on. Only if individuals are motivated to serve these needs will the society continue to operate, and the foundation for that motivation is laid by the family. Family members also participate in informal social control processes. Socialization at early ages makes most of us wish to conform, but throughout each day, both as children and as adults, we are often tempted to deviate. The formal agencies of social control (such as the police) are not enough to do more than force the extreme deviant to conform. What is needed is a set of social pressures that provide feedback to the individual whenever he or she does well or poorly and thus support internal controls as well as the controls of the formal agencies. Effectively or not, the family usually takes on this task.

The family, then, is made up of individuals, but it is also a social unit, and part of a larger social network. Families are not isolated, self-enclosed social systems; and the other institutions of society, such as the military, the church, or the school system, continually rediscover that they are not dealing with individuals, but with members of families. Even in the most industrialized and urban of societies, where it is sometimes supposed that people lead rootless and anonymous lives, most people are in continual interaction with other family members. Men and women who achieve high social position usually find that even as adults they still respond to their parents' criticisms, are still angered or hurt by a sibling's scorn. Corporations that offer substantial opportunities to rising executives often find that their proposals are turned down because of objections from family members.

So it is through the family that the society is able to elicit from the individual his or her contributions. The family, in turn, can continue to exist only if it is supported by the larger society. If these two, the smaller and the larger social system, furnish each other the conditions necessary for their survival, they must be interrelated in many important ways.

Preconceptions About the Family

The task of understanding the family presents many difficulties, and one of the greatest barriers is found in ourselves. We are likely to have strong emotions about the family. Because of our own deep involvement in family relationships, objective analysis is not easy. When we read about other types of family behavior, in other classes or societies, we are likely to feel that they are odd or improper. We are tempted to argue that this or that type of family behavior is wrong or right, rather than to analyze it. Second, although we have observed many people in some of their family behavior, usually we have had very limited experience with what goes on behind the walls of other homes. This means that our sample of observations is very narrow. It also means that for almost any generalization we create or read about, we can often find some specific experience that refutes it, or fits it. Since we feel we "already know," we may not feel motivated to look for further data against which to test generalizations.

However, many supposedly well-known beliefs about the family are not well grounded in fact. Others are only partly true and must be studied more precisely if they are to be understood. One such belief is that "children hold the family together." Despite repeated attempts to affirm it, this generalization does not seem to be very strong. A more correct view seems to be that there is a modest association between divorce and not having children, but it is mostly caused by the fact that people who do not become well adjusted, and who may for some reasons be prone to divorce, are also less likely to have children.

Another way of checking whether the findings of family sociology are obvious is to present some research findings, and ask whether it was worth the bother of discovering them, since "everybody knew them all along." Consider the following set of facts. Suppose a researcher had demonstrated these facts. Was it worthwhile to carry out the study, or were the facts already known?

1. Because modern industrial society breaks down traditional family systems, one result is that the age of marriage in Western nations (which was low among farmers) has risen greatly over many generations.
2. Because of the importance of the extended family in China and India, the average size of the household has always been large, with many generations living under one roof.
3. In polygynous societies, most men have several wives, and the fertility rate is higher than in monogamous societies.

Although these statements sound plausible to many people, and impressive arguments have been presented to support them, in fact they are all false. For hundreds of years, the age at marriage among farmers in Western nations has been relatively high (25–27 years), and though it rises and falls somewhat over time, there seems to be no important trend in any particular direction. With reference to multifamily households, every survey of Chinese and Indian households has shown that even generations ago they were relatively modest in size (from four to six persons, varying by region and time period). Only under special historical circumstances will large, extended households be common. As to polygyny, the fact is that except under special circumstances, almost all men in all societies must be content with only one wife, and the fertility rate of polygynous marriages (one man married to several wives) is lower than that for monogamous marriages. Thus we see that with reference to the incorrect findings just cited, common beliefs did require testing, and they were wrong.

On the other hand, of course, many popular beliefs about how families work *are* correct. We cannot assume their correctness, however. Instead, we have to examine our observations, and make studies on our own to see how well these data fit in order to improve our understanding of the dynamics of family processes in our own or in other societies. If we emphasize the problems of obtaining facts, we should not lose sight of the central truth of any science: vast quantities of figures may be entirely meaningless, unless the search is guided by fruitful hypotheses or broad conceptions of social behavior. What we seek is organized facts, a structure of propositions, in which theory and fact illuminate one another. If we do not seek actual observation, we are engaged in blind speculation. If we seek facts without theoretical guidance, our search is random and often yields findings that have no bearing on anything. Understanding the family, then, requires the same sort of careful investigation as any other scientific endeavor.

Why the Family Is Theoretically Significant

Because the family is so much taken for granted, we do not often stop to consider the many traits that make it theoretically interesting. A brief consideration of certain peculiarities of the family will suggest why it is worthwhile exploring this social unit.

The family is the only social institution other than religion that is formally developed in all societies: a specific social agency is in charge of a great variety of social behaviors and activities. Some have argued that legal systems did not exist in preliterate or technologically less developed tribes or societies because there was no formally organized legislative body or judiciary. Of course, it is possible to abstract from concrete behavior the legal *aspects* of action, or the economic aspects, or the political dynamics, even when there are no explicitly labeled agencies formally in control of these areas in the society. However, kinship statuses and their responsibilities are the object of both formal and informal attention in societies at a high or a low technological level.

Family duties are the direct role responsibility of everyone in the society, with rare exceptions. Almost everyone is both born into a family and founds one of his or her own. Each individual is kin to many others. Many people, by contrast, may escape the religious duties others take for granted, or military or political burdens. Moreover, many family role responsibilities cannot usually be delegated to others, while in a work situation specialized obligations can be delegated.

Taking part in family activities has the further interesting quality that though it is not backed by the formal punishments supporting many other obligations, almost everyone takes part nonetheless. We must, for example, engage in economic or productive acts, or face starvation. We must enter the army, pay taxes, and appear before courts, or face money penalties and force. Such punishments do not usually confront the individual who does not wish to marry, or refuses to talk with his father or brother. Nevertheless, so pervasive are the social pressures, and so intertwined with indirect or direct rewards and punishments, that almost everyone conforms, or claims to conform, to family demands.

Although the family is usually thought of as an *expressive* or emotional social unit, it serves as an *instrumental* agency for the larger social structures, and all other institutions and agencies depend upon its contributions. For example, the role behavior learned within the family becomes the model or prototype for behavior required in other segments of the society. Inside the family, the content of the *socialization* process is the cultural tradition of the larger society. Families are also themselves *economic* units with respect to production and allocation. With reference to *social control*, each person's total range of behavior, and how his or her time and energies are budgeted, is more easily visible to family members than to outsiders. They can evaluate how the individual is allocating his or her time and money, and how well he or she is carrying out various duties. Consequently, the family acts as a source of pressure on the individual to adjust— to work harder and play less, or go to church less and study more. In all these ways, the family is partly an instrument or agent of the larger society. If it fails to perform adequately, the goals of the larger society may not be effectively achieved.

Perhaps more interesting theoretically is the fact that the various *tasks of the family are all separable* from one another, but in fact are not separated in almost all known family systems. Here are some of the contributions of the family to the larger society: (a) reproduction of young, (b) physical maintenance of family members, (c) social placement of the child, (d) socialization, and (e) social control.

Let us consider how these activities could be separated. For example, the mother could send her child to be fed in a neighborhood mess hall, and of course some harassed mothers do send their children to buy lunch in a local snack bar. Those who give birth to a child need not socialize the child. They might send the child to specialists, and indeed specialists do take more responsibility for this task as the child grows older. Parents might, as some eugenicists have suggested, be selected for their breeding qualities, but these might not include any great talent for training the young. Status placement might be accomplished by random drawing of lots, by IQ tests or periodic examinations in physical and intellectual skills, or by popularity polls. This assignment of children to various social positions could be done without regard to an individual's parents, those who socialized or fed the child, or others who might supervise the child's daily behavior.

Separations of this kind have been suggested from time to time, and a few hesitant attempts have been made here and there in the world to put them into operation. However, three conclusions relevant to this kind of division can be drawn: (1) In all known societies, the *ideal* (with certain qualifications to be noted) is that the family be entrusted with all these functions. (2) When one or more family tasks are entrusted to another agency by a revolutionary or utopian society, the change can be made only with the support of much ideological fervor, and usually political pressure as well. (3) These experiments are also characterized by a gradual return to the more traditional type of family. In both the Israeli *kibbutzim* and the Russian experiments in relieving parents of child care, the ideal of completely communal living was once urged. Husband and wife were to have only a personal and emotional tie with one another: divorce would be easy. The children were to see their parents at regular intervals but look to their nursery attendants and mother surrogates for affection and direction during work hours. Each individual was to contribute his or her best skills to the cooperative unit without regard to family ties or sex status (there would be few or no "female" or "male" tasks). That ideal was attempted in a modest way, but behavior gradually dropped away from the ideal. The only other country in which the pattern has been attempted on a large scale is China. Already Chinese communes have retreated from their high ambitions, following the path of the *kibbutz* and the Russian *kolkhoz*.

Various factors contribute to these deviations from attempts to create a new type of family, and the two most important sets of pressures cannot easily be separated from each other. First is the problem, also noted by Plato, that individuals who develop their own attitudes and behaviors in the usual Western (European and European-based) family system do not easily adjust to the communal "family" even when they believe it is the right way. The second is the likelihood that when the family is radically changed, the various relations between it and the larger society are changed. New strains are created, demanding new kinds of adjustments on the part of the individuals in the society. Perhaps the planners must develop somewhat different agencies, or a different blueprint, to transform the family.

These comments have nothing to do with "capitalism" in its current political and economic argument with "communism." They merely describe the historical fact that though various experiments in separating the major functions of the family from one another have been conducted, none of these evolved from a previously existing family system. In addition, the several modern important attempts at such a separation, including the smaller communes that were created in the United States during the 1960s and 1970s, mostly exhibit a common pattern, a movement *away* from the utopian blueprint of separating the various family activities and giving each of them to a different social unit.

It is possible that some of these activities (meals) can be more easily separated than others; or that some family systems (for example, matrilineal systems) might lend themselves to such a separation more easily than others. On the other hand, we have to begin with the data that are now available. Even cautiously interpreted, they suggest that the family is a rather stable institution. On the other hand, we have not yet analyzed what this particular institution is. In the next section we discuss this question.

Defining the Family: A Matter of More or Less

Since thousands of publications have presented research findings on the family, one might suppose that there must be agreement on what this social unit is. In fact, sociologists and anthropologists have argued for decades about how to define it. Indeed, creating a clear, formal definition of any object of study is sometimes more difficult than making a study of that object. If we use a *concrete* definition, and assert that "a family is a social unit made up of father, mother, and children," then only about 35 percent of all U.S. households can be classed as a family. Much of the research on the family would have to exclude a majority of residential units. In addition, in some societies, one wife may be married to several husbands, or one husband to several wives. The definition would exclude such units. In a few societies there have been "families" in which the "husband" was a woman; and in some, certain "husbands" were not expected to live with their "wives." In the United States, millions of households contain at least one child, but only one parent. In a few communes, every adult male is married to all other adult females. That is, there are many kinds of social units that seem to be *like* a family, but do not fit almost any concrete definition that we might formulate.

We can escape such criticisms in part by claiming that most adults eventually go through such a *phase* of family life; that is, almost all men and women in the United States marry at some time during their lives, and most of them eventually have children. Nevertheless, analysis of the family would be much thinner if we focused only on that one kind of household. In ordinary language usage, people are most likely to agree that a social unit made up of father, mother, and child or children is a genuine family. They will begin to disagree more and more, as one or more of those persons or social roles is missing. Few people would agree that at the other extremes, a household with only a single person in it is a family. Far more would think of a household as a family if it comprised a widow and her several children. Most people would agree that a husband-wife household is a family if they have children, even if their children are now living somewhere else. However, many would not be willing to class a childless couple as a family, especially if that couple planned never to have children. Very few people would be willing to accept a homosexual couple as a family.

What can we learn from such ordinary language usage? First, that *family* is not a single thing, to be captured by a neat verbal formula. Second, many social units can be thought of as "more or less" families, as they are more or less similar to the traditional type of family. Third, much of this graded similarity can be traced to the different kinds of role relations to be found in that traditional unit. Doubtless the following list is not comprehensive, but it includes most of those relationships: (1) At least two adult persons of opposite sex reside together. (2) They engage in some kind of division of labor; that is, they do not both perform exactly the same tasks. (3) They engage in many types of economic and social exchanges; that is, they do things for one another. (4) They share many things in common, such as food, sex, residence, and both goods and social activities. (5) The adults have parental relations with their children, as their children have filial relations with them; the parents have some authority over their children, and both share with one another, while also assuming some obligation for protection, cooperation, and nurturance. (6) There are sibling relations among the children themselves, with, once more, a range of obligations to share, protect, and help one another. When all these conditions exist, few people would deny that the unit is a family. As we consider households in which more are missing, a larger number of people would express some doubt as to whether it really is a family. Thus, if two adults live together, but do nothing for each other, few people would agree that it is a family. If they do not even live together, fewer still would call the couple a family.

Individuals create all sorts of relations with each other, but others are more or less likely to view them as a family to the extent that their continuing social relations exhibit some or all of the role patterns noted above. Most important for our understanding of the family is that in all known societies, and under a wide range of social conditions, some kinds of familistic living arrangements seem to emerge, with some or all of these traits. These arrangements can emerge in prisons (with homosexual couples as units), under the disorganized conditions of revolution, conquest, or epidemic; or even when political attempts are made to reduce the importance of the family, and instead to press people to live in a more communal fashion. That is, people create and re-create some forms of familistic social patterns even when some of those traditional elements are missing.

This raises the inevitable question: Why does this happen: Why do people continue to form familistic relations, even when they are not convinced that it is the ideal social arrangement? Why is *this* and not some *other* social pattern so widespread? Of course, this is not an argument for the *universality* of the conjugal family. Many other kinds of relations between individuals are created.

Nevertheless, some approximation of these familistic relationships do continue to occur in the face of many alternative temptations and opportunities as well as counterpressures. Unless we are willing to assert that people are irrational, we must conclude that these relationships must offer some *advantages*. What are they?

Advantages of the "Familistic Package"

We suppose that the most fundamental set of advantages is found in the division of labor and the resulting possibility of social exchanges between husband and wife (or members of a homosexual couple), as well as between children and parents. This includes not only economic goods, but help, nurturance, protection, and affection. It is often forgotten that the modern domestic household is very much an *economic* unit even if it is no longer a farming unit. People are actually producing goods and services for one another. They are buying objects in one place, and transporting them to the household. They are transforming food into meals. They are engaged in cleaning, mowing lawns, repairing, transporting, counseling—a wide array of services that would have to be paid for in money if some member of the family did not do them.

Families of all types also enjoy some small economies of scale. When there are two or more members of the household, various kinds of activities can be done almost as easily for everyone as for a single person; it is almost as easy to prepare one meal for three or four people as it is to prepare a similar meal for one person. Thus, the cost of a meal is less per person within a family. Families can cooperate to achieve what an individual cannot, from building a mountain cabin to creating a certain style of life. Help from all members will make it much easier to achieve that goal than it would be for one person.

All the historic forms of the family that we know, including communal group marriages, are also attractive because they offer *continuity*. Thus, whatever the members produce together, they expect to be able to enjoy together later. Continuity has several implications. One is that members do not have to bear the costs of continually searching for new partners, or for new members who might be "better" at various family tasks. In addition, husband and wife, as well as children, enjoy a much longer line of social credit than they would have if they were making exchanges with people outside the family. This means that an individual can give more at one time to someone in the family, knowing that in the longer run this will not be a loss: the other person will remain long enough to reciprocate at some point, or perhaps still another member will offer help at a later time.

Next, the familistic mode of living offers several of the advantages of any informal group.[2] It exhibits, for example, a very short line of communication; everyone is close by, and members need not communicate through intermediaries. Thus they can respond quickly in case of need. A short line of communication makes cooperation much easier. Second, everyone has many idiosyncratic needs and wishes. In day-to-day interaction with outsiders, we need not adjust to these very much, and they may be a nuisance; others, in turn, are likely not to adjust to our own idiosyncracies. However, within the familistic mode of social interaction, people learn what each other's idiosyncratic needs are. Learning such needs can and does make life together somewhat more attractive because adjusting to them may not be a great burden, but does give pleasure to the other. These include such trivia as how strong the tea or coffee should be, how much talk there will be at meals, sleep and work schedules, levels of noise, and so on. Of course with that knowledge we can more easily make others miserable, too, if we wish to do so.

Domestic tasks typically do not require high expertise, and as a consequence most members of the family can learn to do them eventually. Because they do learn, members derive many benefits from one another, without having to go outside the family unit. Again, this makes a familistic mode of living more attractive than it would be otherwise. In addition, with reference to many such tasks, there are no outside experts anyway (throughout most of world history, there have been no experts in child rearing, taking care of small cuts or bruises, murmuring consoling words in response to some distress, and so on). That is, the tasks within a family setting are likely to be tasks at which insiders are at least as good as outsiders, and typically better.

No other social institutions offer this range of complementarities, sharing, and closely linked, interwoven advantages. The closest possible exception might be some ascribed, ritual friendships in a few societies, but even these do not offer the range of exchanges that are to be found in the familistic processes.

We have focused on advantages that the *members* of families obtain from living under this type of arrangement. However, when we survey the wide range of family patterns in hundreds of societies, we are struck by the fact that this social unit is strongly supported by *outsiders*—that is, members of the larger society.

It is supported by a structure of norms, values, laws, and a wide range of social pressures. More concretely, other members of the society believe such units are necessary, and they are concerned about how people discharge their obligations within the family. They punish members of the family who do not conform to ideal behavior, and praise those who do conform. These intrusions are not simply whimsical, or a matter of oppression. Other members of the society do in fact have a stake in how families discharge their various tasks. More broadly, it is widely believed that the collective needs of the whole society are served by some of the activities individual families carry out. In short, it is characteristic of the varieties of the family that participants on an average enjoy more, and gain more comfort, pleasure, or advantage from being in a familistic arrangement than from living alone; and *other* members of the society view that arrangement as contributing in some measure to the survival of the society itself. Members of societies have usually supposed it important for most *other* individuals to form families, to rear children, to create the next generation, to support and help each other—whether or not individual members of specific families do in fact feel they gain real advantages from living in a familistic arrangement. For example, over many centuries, people opposed legal divorces, whether or not they themselves were happily married, and with little regard for the marital happiness of others.

This view of what makes up the "familistic social package" explains several kinds of widely observable social behavior. One is that people experiment with different kinds of arrangements, often guided by a new philosophy of how people ought to live. They do so because their own needs have not been adequately fulfilled in the traditional modes of family arrangements available to them in their own society. Since other people have a stake in the kinds of familistic arrangements people make, we can also expect that when some individuals or groups attempt to change or experiment with the established system, various members of the society will object, and may even persecute them for it. We can also see why it is that even in a high-divorce society such as our own, where millions of people have been dissatisfied or hurt by their marriages and their divorces, they nevertheless move back into a marital arrangement. That is, after examining various alternatives, the familistic social package still seems to offer a broader set of personal advantages, and the outside society supports that move. And, as noted earlier, even when there are strong political pressures to create new social units that give far less support for the individual family, as in China, Russia, and the Israeli *kibbutzim*, we can expect that people will continue to drift back toward some kind of familistic arrangement.

A Sociological Approach to Family Research

The unusual traits the family exhibits as a type of social subsystem require that some attention be paid to the analytic approach to be used in studying it. First, neither ideal nor reality can be excluded from our attention. It would, for example, be naive to suppose that because some 40 percent of all U.S. couples now marrying will eventually divorce, they do not cherish the ideal of remaining married to one person. Contemporary estimates suggest that about half of all married men engage in extramarital intercourse at some time, but public opinion surveys report that a large majority of both men and women in the United States, even in these permissive times, approve of the ideal of faithfulness. On a more personal level, every reader of these lines has lied at some time, but nevertheless most believe in the ideal of telling the truth.

A sociologist ascertains the ideals of family systems partly because they are a rough guide to behavior. Knowing that people prefer to have their sons and daughters marry at least at the same class level, we can expect them to try to control their children's mate choices if they can do so. We can also specify some of the conditions under which they will have a greater or lesser success in reaching that goal. We also know that when a person violates the ideal, he or she is likely to conceal the violation if possible. If that is not possible, people will try to find some excuse for the violation, and are likely to be embarrassed if others find out about it.

The sociology of the family cannot confine itself only to contemporary urban (or suburban) American life. Conclusions of any substantial validity or scope must include data from other societies, whether these are past or present, industrial or nonindustrial, Asian or European. Data from the historical past, such as Periclean Athens or imperial Rome, are not often used because no sociologically adequate account of their family systems has as yet been written.[3] On the other hand, the last two decades have seen the appearance of many studies about family systems in various European cities of the last five centuries.

The study of customs and beliefs from the past yields a better understanding of the possible range of social behavior. Thereby, we are led to deny or at least to qualify a finding that might be correct if limited only to modern American life (such as the rise in divorce rates over several decades). The use of data from tribal societies of the past or present helps us in testing conclusions about family systems that are not found at all in Western society, such as matrilineal systems or polygyny. Or, an apparently simple relationship may take a different form in other societies. For example, in the United States most first marriages are based on a love relationship (whatever else they may be based on), and people are reluctant to admit that they have married someone with whom they were not in love. By contrast, though people fall in love in other societies, love may play a small or a large part in the marriage system.

It is possible to study almost any phenomenon from a wide range of viewpoints. We may study the economic aspects of family behavior, or we may confine ourselves to the biological factors in family patterns. A full analysis of any concrete object is impossible. Everything can be analyzed from many vantage points, each of them yielding a somewhat different but still limited picture. Everything is infinitely complex. Each science limits its perspective to the range of processes that it considers important. Each such approach has its own justification. Here we examine the family mainly from a sociological perspective.

The sociological approach focuses on the family as a social institution, the peculiar and unique quality of family interaction as *social*. For example, family systems exhibit the characteristics of legitimacy and authority, which are not biological categories at all. The values and the prescribed behavior to be found in a family, or the rights and duties of family statuses such as father or daughter, are not psychological categories. They are peculiar to the theoretical approach of sociology. Personality theory is not very useful in explaining the particular position of the family in Chinese and Japanese social structures, although it may help us understand how individuals respond emotionally to those rights and obligations. If we use a consistently sociological approach, we will miss some important information about concrete family interaction. The possible gain when we stay on one theoretical level may be the achievement of some increased systematization, and some greater rigor.

At a minimum, however, when an analyst moves from the sociological to the psychological level of theory, he or she ought at least to be conscious of it. If the investigation turns to the impact of biological or psychological factors on the family, they should be examined with reference to their *social* meaning. For example, interracial marriage appears to be of little biological significance, but it has much social impact on those who take part in such a marriage. A sociologist who studies the family is not likely to be an expert in the *psychodynamics* of mental disease, but is interested in the effect of mental disease on the social relations in a particular family or type of family, or in the adjustment different family types make to it. Since all these sciences of human behavior contribute to our understanding of the family, we should use the information as it becomes available.

Notes

1. See in this connection Nicholas Tavuchis and William J. Goode (eds.) *The Family through Literature* (New York: Oxford University Press, 1973).

2. For further comparisons of bureaucracy and informal groups, see Eugene Litwak, "Technical Innovation and Theoretical Functions of Primary Groups and Bureaucratic Structures," *American Journal of Sociology*, 73 (1968), 468–481.

3. However, Keith Hopkins has published several specialized studies on various aspects of Roman families. See his *Conquerors and Slaves* (Cambridge, England: Cambridge University Press, 1978).

The Emergence of the Modern American Family*

Carl N. Degler

Like Goode, Carl N. Degler begins his discussion of families by focusing upon how family is defined. Moving from a general definition, he traces the historical development of the modern American family from its European roots. Degler illustrates how American families have changed over time, and how the history of families in this country provides a foundation for the way in which we think about families today. His historical analysis illustrates Goode's idea that there is often a contrast between ideal and real patterns of family life. Further, he shows that historical research often challenges our myths of what family life was like in the past.

In every branch of written history, whether that of ancient Egypt, ancient China, medieval Europe, or modern America, the record shows that the family has been the vehicle through which men and women have entered upon life. In the family they have been born, there they have been trained to take a place in society as adults, and from there they go out to begin the cycle all over again with their own children. Even more significant as a measure of the antiquity and fundamental nature of the family is that anthropological studies of cultures far

---

*Source: Excerpted from *At Odds: Women and the Family in America from the Revolution to the Present* by Carl N. Degler. Copyright (c) 1980 by Carl N. Degler. Reprinted by permission of Oxford University Press, Inc.

removed in character from so-called civilized societies have turned up virtually none which lacked a family life.

What is meant by a family? It is useful to set forth the essential elements if only because the very omnipresence of the family renders it almost invisible. Because we are truly immersed in the family we rarely have to define it or describe it to one another. For our purposes here the family may be said to consist of five elements. The first is that a family begins with a ritual between a woman and a man, a ceremony that we call marriage, and which implies long duration, if not permanence, for the relationship. The second is that the partners have duties and rights of parenthood that are also socially recognized and defined. For the family has everywhere been the way in which the human being is socialized. There are several other ways to prepare children for adulthood, to be sure, but all of them are very recent in origin (orphanage, kibbutz, commune), and around none of them has a whole society yet been organized. A third element is that husband, wife, and children live in a common place. This aspect, it needs to be said, is the least universal. Anthropologist George P. Murdock in his analysis of the literature on some five hundred different cultures points out that in about one-fourth of them the father lives apart from mother and children at least for a portion of the time. But in the great majority of even those cases the distance between the houses of father and mother is slight. A fourth element in the definition of a family is that there are reciprocal economic obligations between husband and wife—that is, they both work for the family, even though the amount and kind of labor or production may be far from equal. Fifth, the family also serves as a means of sexual satisfaction for the partners, though not necessarily as an exclusive one. The striking fact is that there are very few societies known to anthropologists in which a family with at least these characteristics does not exist.

Certainly throughout Western civilization the family has exhibited all of the characteristics set forth in the basic definition. And indeed because these fundamentals are universal, the family has usually been thought of as changeless, as without a history. But when one moves beyond the skeletal definition of the family to examine it in different societies and at different times—even within the Western tradition—it quickly becomes clear that the family has changed over time and therefore, in fact, does have a history. The new field of family history has been interested in discerning both change and continuity in the long history of the family in the West.

One significant consequence of the recent historical interest in the family has been the discovery that the extended family, in which parents and their children live in the same household with their own parents, has not been usual at all. Throughout the national societies of Europe today and as far back as the Middle Ages, at least, the great majority of people has been reared in nuclear families—two parents and their offspring only. Thus a commonplace of sociology of 20 years ago that before industrialization the extended family was the characteristic unit of socialization has been shown to be without basis in fact. No more than one-fifth of all households, so far as present research can tell, has been extended in this sense, and in many societies the proportion has been much less than that. To say this, of course, does not mean that nuclear families have had no contact with grandparents or other kin. In fact, they often had a considerable amount, since kin frequently settled or clustered together. But in the day-to-day life of the family in western Europe and North America since at least the Reformation, the nuclear family has been the primary familial experience of the average person.

If the nuclearity of the family has been unchanged over the last five centuries, other aspects of the family have changed. Prior to the opening of the nineteenth century the vast majority of people in the world lived on farms or in peasant villages. And for almost all of them the family was a cooperative economic unit, with children and mother working along with husband, even though usually there was a division of labor by gender. This was true whether production was for subsistence or for sale. Even those relatively few families which lived and worked in towns acted as cooperative enterprises in their shops, inns, and other businesses. Home and work were close together, and wife and husband participated in both. Some exceptions existed, to be sure. Here and there, even in medieval times, large enterprises like shipyards, certain kinds of mines, and woolen mills (many hand-powered looms) required male workers to be separated from the family for at least a substantial part of the day or even longer. But the families in which this occurred were a negligible proportion of the population in any society prior to the eighteenth century. Especially was this true of the English colonies in North America before the Revolution. At that time well over 90 percent of the people lived outside the few cities, and the number of large-scale enterprises within the cities and towns could be counted on the fingers of two hands. This situation would change dramatically with the spread of the industrial factory system in both Europe and America after the eighteenth century.

Families in America and western Europe prior to the American Revolution were thus very much like those anywhere else in the world. Every society on the globe was then preindustrial or "less developed," to use modern terminology. Yet in two respects families in western Europe differed from all other families. They differed as to when the families began—that is, the ages of marriage—and in the proportion of the population which ever married. The age of marriage in western Europe was substantially later than in eastern Europe, and the rest of the world. Moreover, the proportion of women who never married in western Europe was at least double and not infrequently triple and quadruple that in the societies of eastern Europe.

Apparently, the western European pattern is a modern phenomenon, for the eastern European practice of early marriage and very high proportion of married people was also characteristic of western Europe in the Middle Ages and in antiquity. Why late marriages and relatively low proportions of married people emerged only after the fifteenth century in western Europe and did not develop elsewhere in the world is not known. But the economic and demographic implications of its development in western Europe are clearly important. Late marriage and a high proportion of people who never married had a direct, downward effect upon the number of children born to a family. And that, in turn, affected the ability of people to save and accumulate wealth for investment and economic growth.[1]

The British colonies in North America in the seventeenth century constituted a partial, if temporary exception to the pattern in western European societies. In seventeenth-century America, the age of marriage for women was considerably lower than in contemporary England or on the Continent. In Andover, Massachusetts, for example, the average age of marriage for women married between 1650 and 1675 was 21.3 years, as compared with the mean of 27 years in a contemporary English town. In another New England town, Dedham, the average age of first marriage for women in the late seventeenth century was 22.5 years. For women born between 1600 and 1700 in Plymouth, Massachusetts, the age of first marriage for females varied between 20.2 and 22.3. Males, on the other hand, seemed to have followed the western European pattern. The mean age of men in Plymouth in the seventeenth century varied from 27 at the beginning of the century to 24.6 at the end. In Hingham, Massachusetts, the average age of first marriage for men was 27.4 years at the end of the seventeenth century and 26.4 at the end of the eighteenth century. Throughout the colonial period the average age of marriage for men in Andover, Massachusetts, was slightly above 26 years. But even for women the average age rose in the course of the eighteenth century, thus bringing them into line with the pattern in western Europe.

At the time of the American Revolution the average age was 24 for women at Andover and 23.5 at Hingham. A study of some 250 Quaker families at the end of the eighteenth century showed a high proportion of unmarried persons at age 50, in conformity with the western European practice. Slightly over 12 percent of the males and almost 16 percent of the females in these families were unmarried. About 10 percent of colonial-period Andover women never married, a proportion that was somewhat lower than for nineteenth-century Europe, but considerably higher than any figures for the eastern European countries in 1900.[2] In sum, at the time of the Revolution, according to the somewhat limited, though consistent evidence from several colonial communities, American families exhibited the western European pattern of late marriages, and with around 10 to perhaps 15 percent of women never marrying at all.

The shift in the age of marriage for women from the seventeenth to the eighteenth century was only the beginning of the changes in the American family that are discernible around the time of the Revolution. The family was then on the verge of rather significant alterations, not only in its structure, but in its more important internal dynamics as well.

What today we speak of as the modern American family emerged first in the years between the American Revolution and about 1830. The years are not meant to be taken precisely; they simply suggest the outer limits of the period of transition from the traditional to the modern family in America. And even then the shift is uneven and slow. Yet by the 1830s one can discern quite clearly a form of family that differed in several respects from that which had prevailed prior to the Revolution. This newly emergent family in the nineteenth century exhibited at least four broad characteristics that had been absent from most families of western European culture in previous centuries.

One. The marriage which initiated the modern family was based upon affection and mutual respect between the partners, both at the time of family formation and in the course of its life. The woman in the marriage enjoyed an increasing degree of influence or autonomy within the family.

Two. The primary role of the wife was the care of children and the maintenance of the home. Furthermore, the wife, as the mistress of the home, was perceived by society and herself as the moral superior of the husband, though his legal and social inferior. The organizational basis for this relationship was that woman's life was physically spent within the home and with the family, while the man's was largely outside the home, at work. The ideological justification of this division of labor and activity will be referred to as "the doctrine of the two spheres," or "separate spheres."

Three. The attention, energy, and resources of parents in the emerging modern family were increasingly centered upon the rearing of their offspring. Children were now perceived as being different from adults and deserving not only of material care but of solicitude and love as well. Childhood was deemed a valuable period in the life of every person and to be sharply distinguished in character and purpose from adulthood. Parenthood thus became a major personal responsibility, perhaps even a burden.

Four. The modern family on the average is significantly smaller in size than the family of the eighteenth and previous centuries, a change that has major consequences for women, as well as for the family.

Because these four elements have continued to be characteristic of the family in the United States in the second half of the twentieth century, their presence among a significant proportion of the American population during the opening decades of the nineteenth century justifies our seeing the emergence of the modern family in those years.

Let us begin to look at the emergence of the modern American family in the order in which the family itself began—with the decision to marry. How was the choice of marital partner made and what was the significance of the basis of the choice? In the half-century after the Revolution the bases of marriage began to change in a decidedly modern direction. Increasingly, free choice by the partners became the basis of family formation. Today it is axiomatic that personal happiness and the affection of the two partners for each other are the only proper foundation for a marriage and the family that follows. Such a conception of marriage has not always been the way in which families were established. Affection was most unlikely to be a basis of marriage if the families of origin of the young people held large amounts of property. For to permit a marriage to take place on the basis of personal or individual preference or whim, rather than by reference to family needs and prospects, threatened a family's holdings and perhaps its long-term future. That was why European crowned heads and noble families insisted that the marriage choices of children be in the hands of parents. Lesser men and women also insisted upon it. In sixteenth-century Protestant Geneva, for instance, a man could not marry under the age of 20 without his father's consent, or, in case the father was dead, that of his mother or relative. In Catholic France, royal edicts stipulated that parental consent to marry was necessary for a woman until 25 and for a man until 30. As late as 1639 even a son who was overage in France could be disinherited if he married for the first time against his parents' wishes. Historian Lawrence Stone tells of one Michael Wentworth, who, in 1558, stipulated in his will that if any of his daughters did not accept the choice of marital partner named by his executors "but of their own fantastical brain bestow themselves upon a light person" their estate would be reduced from 100 to 66 pounds. Stone called this "powerful posthumous economic blackmail," a practice that American fathers of the seventeenth century were not hesitant to follow.[3] In Andover, Massachusetts, for instance, fathers who owned land used their control over it to influence, if not to shape, their sons' decisions about marriage. By delaying the turning over of their land to their sons, fathers could determine when and perhaps whom sons would marry.

By the eighteenth century, however, parental control over the marital choices of their children weakened. Philip Greven, who studied colonial Andover, found that by the mid-eighteenth century fathers were not using their land so frequently to influence their sons' marital decisions. A clearer measure of the decline in parental control over grown children and the corresponding improvement in the children's freedom of choice in marriage is provided by Daniel Scott Smith's study of another colonial town, Hingham, Massachusetts. Smith found that in marriages contracted before 1780 the age of the bridegroom, on the average, was almost two years higher if the father died after age 60 than it was with men whose fathers died before 60. That is, if the father lived beyond the median age of fathers at the marriage of the oldest son (60 years), then the sons' time of marriage was delayed, presumably because the fathers would not let them marry or would not give them the land necessary for the support of a wife and family. In the marriages formed between 1781 and 1840, however, the average difference in the ages of marriage of the two sets of sons was negligible—only three months. This suggests that by the last two decades of the eighteenth and the opening of the nineteenth century, a father's influence over a son's choice of decision was much less than it had been before the American Revolution. A study of Concord, Massachusetts, has come up with the same results, though using 1760 as the dividing date. After that date the difference in age of marriage was less than ten months, but before 1760 the difference was 1.5 to 2 years. Moreover, the Concord study found that prior to 1770 the eldest son was twice as likely to succeed to his father's occupation as would be expected by chance. After 1770, the other brothers were more likely to do so than the eldest son, suggesting that the father no longer was able to consider only his own preferences.[4]

In an as yet unpublished investigation of some 100 upper-class families in North Carolina between 1830 and 1860, Jane Turner Censer found that by that period almost no fathers used their power to withhold inheritance from their sons. She reported that even sons who disobeyed their fathers, usually by wasting resources, were not disinherited. Almost half of the fathers actually passed on substantial amounts of property, usually in the form of land, to their sons long before their own deaths, thus facilitating a son's wish to marry without parental influence. Finally, of the 92 wills Censer examined, only two specified a particular occupation that a son ought to follow, but even in these two cases the father added provisions to the will which permitted the son to escape having to follow his father's expectations! In short, even among very wealthy planter families in the South, who certainly had property to conserve, parental power over a son's decisions was not exercised.

Parental control over daughters similarly declined from the eighteenth to the nineteenth century. Smith, in his study of Hingham, was able to demonstrate the shift by an examination of the order in which daughters married. He began with the assumption that a father preferred to have his daughters marry in the order of birth; otherwise a prospective suitor might well think something was wrong with an unmarried older daughter. When Smith divided the marriages of daughters according to periods, he discovered that between 1650 and 1750 less than 11 percent of daughters married out of birth order. But after 1741 over 18 percent did so, suggesting a substantial increase in the freedom of choice of daughters. Censer in her study of some 100 upper-class families in North Carolina found a similar degree of freedom of choice for daughters. Of 85 women marrying between 1795 and 1865 in 25 families, 30 percent of them married out of birth order; yet these were families in which the conservation of and control over their substantial wealth certainly gave the father reasons for seeking to control marital choices as well as providing the wherewithal by which to exercise such power.

Finally, Smith advanced a third measure of the shift in parental control from between the eighteenth to the nineteenth century. He showed that in Hingham, in the early years of the nineteenth century, daughters of wealthy parents were actually marrying at a later age than those of poorer parents, though, a hundred years before, the pattern had been just the opposite. Smith's explanation was that in the early colonial period parents with money could marry off their daughters earlier than less wealthy parents simply because the rich had dowries to offer. But by the end of the eighteenth and opening of the nineteenth century, young women were making their own decisions, and were not permitting their parents to rush them into matrimony any faster than daughters of less well-to-do parents.

By the early years of the nineteenth century, parental control over the choice of marriage partners of their children was no more than a veto, as it is essentially today in the twentieth century. Parents obviously had influence, as in the case of Catharine Beecher, who broke off an engagement with a young man, even though her father, Lyman Beecher, clearly approved of the match. Her father was able to prevail upon her to reopen the relation, and in due course she made a commitment to marry the young man, but the young man's death in an accident intervened. It is nevertheless significant that Catharine never married. Even in the more traditional South, apparently, parental control was weak. Juliet Janin, writing in later life about her own betrothal in 1832 in New Orleans, explained that her suitor, because he was a foreigner, asked her father for her hand before he asked her. "In those days in N.O.," she wrote, "a girl brought up in a measure according to french usages though not coerced was apt to be influenced by . . . the wishes and advice" of her parents or guardian. This, too, was a wealthy family, but clearly considerations of family fortune were not expected to take precedence over the preferences of the young.[5]

If a parent strongly disapproved of his daughter's choice, his principal recourse was either to send her away from home or move the whole family. The second option was apparently being followed by one father in 1857, as recounted by a diarist. The diary-keeper met the daughter on a riverboat, where she showed the diarist "the pictures of her lover, from whom she had been ruthlessly torn. Her family actually came West to get her away from him," the diarist wrote indignantly. The limited role of parents and kin in marriage choices is evident, too, in Mary Robart's explanation to cousin Mary Jones of Georgia in 1855, as to why Robart's sister Louisa did not consult the Joneses when she decided to marry a widower with eight children. "Having gained Mother's consent and mine," Robart wrote, Louisa "asked no one else, as she felt she was the best judge of what would promote her own happiness."[6]

Earlier in the century, Elizabeth Southgate, vacationing at a spa far from her parents, met a young man she fell in love with, and though she did not think she could agree to marry him until he had consulted her parents, she knew that her feelings were decisive with her parents. After assuring her mother of her love for the young man, she submitted "herself wholly to the wishes of my Father and you, convinced that my happiness is your warmest wish. . . ." They checked out the young man's reputation and prospects and quickly agreed to the marriage. Even more reflective of the daughter's freedom of choice was the reaction of Mary Peirce's father to the request of Henry Poor for his daughter's hand. Poor had already obtained Mary's consent, he assured the father. Since the Peirces had complete confidence in her judgment, Peirce wrote back, "we submit the subject suggested in your communication entirely to her decision. . . ."[7]

The references to personal happiness in both Mary Robart's and Elizabeth Southgate's letters are significant, for they reveal the goal behind a couple's freedom of choice. Southgate put the matter quite baldly, she thought her suitor "better calculated to promote my happiness than any person I have yet seen." This expression of individualism, as against the collective interest of the family, was made in 1802, and with her parents' tacit acknowledgment of its rightness. The journal of Sarah Ripley of Massachusetts between 1810 and 1812, in which she recorded her movement toward matrimony, also noted that happiness was the expected objective of marriage. Although at one point her meetings with her male friend were less promising than she would have liked, she believed that "hope still soothes my heart and whispers happiness to come." Significant, too, was the fact that throughout the long courtship—five years—her father seemed to play no role at all, except to provide the job that made the marriage possible. Clearly, parents as well as children considered personal, individual happiness the goal of marriage. "There is nothing on this earth that interests me so much as that he may in all respects be worthy of her," wrote a North Carolina planter in 1838 to his son about the suitor of his daughter, "and calculated in mind and morals to make her happy. This is my greatest solicitude."[8]

When people in the nineteenth century spoke of the purposes of marriage, they were most likely to refer to "love" or affection as the basis of the attraction between marital partners and the beginnings of family formation. Love as the basis for marrying was the purest form of individualism; it subordinated all familial, social, or group considerations to personal preference. The idea of love, to be sure, was not new in the nineteenth century. The Middle Ages had certainly known of it, and the troubadours had sung of courtly love. But significantly enough, not as a basis for marriage. For as Andreas Capellanus, the twelfth-century writer, put the matter in his *Art of Courtly Love*, "Everybody knows that love can have no place between husband and wife." Or as he phrased it a little later in the same work: "We declare and hold as firmly established that love cannot exert its powers between two people who are married to each other."[9] In short, love was extramarital. The idea that love should be the cement of marriages does not figure prominently in Western marriage customs until at least the seventeenth century. Historian Lawrence Stone tells us that King Charles I and Queen Henrietta Maria were the first English royal couple to be celebrated as a domestic pair rather than as the result of dynastic considerations. Others would follow in subsequent centuries until the high point of royal conjugal love would be reached with Victoria and Albert in the nineteenth century.

More important as a sign of a new emphasis upon affection within marriage in the seventeenth century was the stress Puritans placed upon it in their sermons and writings. The Puritan conception was not so much that love ought to be the foundation or origin of marriage as that the couple could expect that time would bring love into their relationship. The Puritan divines asserted the importance of affection, intimacy, and loyalty within marriage, elements that would, of course, become central to the ideal of marriage in America in the nineteenth century. Margaret Winthrop expressed the idea in quite Puritanical terms when she told her husband, John, the seventeenth-century governor of the Massachusetts Bay Colony, that the two chief reasons she loved him were "first because thou lovest God; and, secondly, because that thou lovest me. If these two were wanting, all the rest would be eclipsed. But I must leave this discourse," she quickly interjected, "and go about my household affairs. I am a bad housewife to be so long from them; but I must needs borrow a little time to talk with thee, my sweet heart." John's affection for Margaret was no less. In an extant fragment of a letter to her he made clear that she came first in his life. "The largeness and truth of my love to thee makes me always mindful of thy welfare," he began, "and sets me on work to begin to write before I hear from thee. The very thought of thee affords me many a kind refreshment: What will then be the enjoying of thy sweet society, which I prize above all wordly comforts?" The two most popular handbooks on domestic duties in seventeenth-century England, Lawrence Stone reports, asserted that the purpose of marriage was spiritual intimacy and the avoidance of adultery and fornication outside it. Protestantism, by abandoning the Catholic ideal of celibacy, gave a new emphasis in Christianity to sexual expression, which it then tied to the family.[10]

One consequence of emphasizing affection and loyalty between spouses was an improvement in the position of a woman in marriage. Even in male-dominated Calvinistic Geneva, for example, women were encouraged to sing hymns in church and the old masculine custom of wife-beating was frowned upon. Puritans in Old and New England alike gave recognition to the individual interests of women by making marriage itself a contract, which implied equality. As a contract, rather than a sacrament, marriage could now be dissolved; thus divorce became a matter of public policy, not of religious doctrine. Even so, as John Milton found out, divorce was not easy to obtain, even for a man. But the first step in making marriage responsive to the needs and desires of individuals had been made by Protestantism. Nowhere in the Western world was a divorce easier to obtain than in seventeenth-century New England.

It is all too easy, of course, to exaggerate the ways in which the Puritans' stress upon personal affection in marriage improved the position of women. To put the proposition into perspective it is only necessary to recollect the expulsion of Anne Hutchinson from the Massachusetts Bay Colony in 1638 for presuming to preach. Yet it is worth remembering that it was the Puritans' encouragement of women's participation in church affairs that made it possible for Hutchinson to begin her teaching at all. Protestantism's part in improving the place of women inside and outside the family is best observed in the Quakers, who were, after all, a kind of latter-day Puritans. In them the implications of Puritanism reached their fullest expression. Among the Quakers, women were the religious peers of men. In fact, some of the earliest Quaker missionaries to Puritan Boston were women.

Protestantism's and Puritanism's emphases upon affection in marriage and upon a degree of autonomy for women within the family may have been strong and important, but it would be erroneous to think that the typical American marriage or family even in the eighteenth century exemplified these ideals. Yet changes were surely in process. In the years after the American Revolution there were more and more signs that affection between spouses and greater freedom for women within marriage were a growing part of family life. Lawrence Stone in his history of the family in Britain describes the emergence by the end of the eighteenth century of what might be called a marriage of companions. And though England is not America, the two countries certainly influenced one another, if only through their common language and common reading. Stone points out that by the end of the eighteenth century, sons of peers were much less likely to marry wealthy women than in earlier times, a sign of the rise of what he terms "affective individualism." The increase in the expectation of affection in marriage, Stone argues, was also measured in the upsurge in the number of romantic novels published toward the end of the eighteenth century. Between 1760 and 1779 fewer than 20 such novels were published each year. In the years 1780–89, however, the annual rate was up to almost 50; by the last decade of the century the figure reached 80 per year. Significantly, many of the novels were written by women—as they would be in the United States in the early nineteenth century. "Romantic love and the romantic novel grew together after 1780," Stone concluded, "and the problem of cause and effect is one that is impossible to resolve. All that can be said is that for the first time in history, romantic love became a respectable motive for marriage among the propertied classes."[11]

The romantic novel does not become common in America until the nineteenth century, but in the late eighteenth century examples of marriages based upon affection and future companionship are not difficult to find. John Dickinson of Pennsylvania wrote his wife of 15 years in 1784 that she was the "best of women, best of wives, and best of friends."[12] John and Abigail Adams in their correspondence often addressed each other as "friend." The rise in individual affection as a basis for marriage is also measured in a study of some 220 petitions for divorce in eighteenth-century Massachusetts. As the century advanced, the study makes clear, the number of petitions increased, even though the law, or the grounds for divorce remained substantially unchanged. More important, the grounds advanced by the petitioners shift as the century moves on. Before 1765 not a single one of the petitioners, male or female, mentioned loss of conjugal affection as a reason for divorce, though they did make other personal accusations, such as that the other party wasted goods or neglected the family. Between 1776 and 1786, however, fully 10 percent of the 121 suits in that period referred to loss of affection as a justification for divorce. "Ceased to cherish her," said one; another alleged that his wife "almost broke his heart."

Apparently this increased emphasis upon affection in marriage had an effect upon the courts and therefore upon society, much to the benefit of women. Before 1773 not a single petition for divorce by a woman in Massachusetts on the grounds of adultery by a husband was accepted by the courts, though many had been from husbands alleging such behavior on the part of their wives. In 1773, however, two women won full divorces, not merely separations, on the specific ground of adultery by their husbands. Thereafter, other women began to petition, as they had not done before, on the sole ground of adultery, and many now won their cause. In fact, the women's rate of success in divorce petitions in general went from 49 percent for the years before 1774 to 70 percent for the years thereafter. During that same period the men's rate of success advanced only from 66 percent to 73 percent. In sum, by the end of the eighteenth century, women's rate of success was almost equal to that of men, pointing to one area in which women's position in marriage, at least in Massachusetts, had come abreast of men's.[13]

Moreover, the increased use by women of the grounds of a husband's adultery clearly reflected a growing emphasis upon personal love and respect as the basis of a marriage. It was putting into practice what the Puritan writers of the seventeenth century had advocated when they opposed the double standard and defined marriage as a relationship of mutual respect, affection, and companionship. By the last quarter of the eighteenth century, funeral sermons, too, testified to the ideal of the complementarity of the marital relation and the emotional bonds between marital partners. No longer were women the Eve-temptresses against whom many divines had warned men in earlier times.[14]

Popular writings also reflected this rising emphasis upon love in marriage. A survey of some fifteen magazines published in New England during the last 50 years of the eighteenth century disclosed that romantic love was widely believed by the writers to be the heart of an ideal marriage. Indeed, the concept was so broadly apparent in the popular literature of the time that it surprised the modern sociologists who were conducting the content analysis of the magazines. They had associated the idea of romantic love with the needs and functioning of an industrial society—that is, a society in which wealth was sufficiently available to permit personal feelings to be the basis of choice of marital partners.[15]

The growing acceptance of affection as the primary ground for family formation was an important stage in the evolution of women's place within the family and in our understanding of how the family has altered over time. It is quite true, as modern observers have pointed out, that most relationships between people involve the exercise of power, and certainly the relationship of marriage is no exception. Yet once affection is a basis of marriage, the marital relation becomes significantly different from other relationships between superiors and inferiors. To begin with, unlike any other subordinate, such as a slave or an employee, a young woman contemplating marriage did have some choice as to who her new master would be. Clearly unsatisfactory possibilities could be ruled out completely, and, from acquaintance at courtship, she had an opportunity to learn who were the undesirable partners. After the marriage, the woman also had an advantage that few slaves or employees enjoyed in dealing with their masters or employers. She was able to appeal to her husband's affection for her, and she, in turn, could use that affection in extracting concessions that a slave or an employee could not. In short, by the very nature of the relation, a woman in the family of affection had more power or influence than any other subordinate one can think of. This is but another way of saying that simply because women are a sex, the analysis of the history of the family and of women must differ significantly from the ways in which we analyze the behavior of other social groups. Certainly, there are valuable analogies to be drawn between the subordination of women and the subordination of other groups, as has often been pointed out. Yet it is essential that the unique elements in the relation between men and women not be forgotten or minimized. By the same token, this caveat should not be read as an invitation to sentimentalize the relations between the sexes; that would only be retrogressive in the study of women or the family.

Marriage for love only was the ideal, and one that many young women tried to put into practice. Mollie Dorsey, in her diary written during the 1850s, epitomized the conflict between love and money as a basis for marriage when the family of origin was not wealthy and, at the same time, the way in which that conflict was probably resolved in most cases. "Aunt Eliza wonders why *I* don't try to captivate Mr. Rucker, as he is rich," Mollie wrote in her journal. Aunt Eliza had admitted that he was not as "nice-looking" as Mollie's lover Byron, "but then, he *owns a farm*, and bless my old darling, he don't own much of anything except those lots and—myself." An indication of how marriages were actually completed comes in her next observation. "My Aunt likes money, but *she* married for love," for her husband had been an impoverished itinerent minister when he asked her to marry him. Aunt Eliza's experience was recapitulated in the marriage of Mollie's sister Dora. Three weeks after Mollie was married, Dora, who was only seventeen, married a man she met for the first time at Mollie's wedding. Her mother was not "reconciled to the suddenness of the affair," Mollie admitted, but her father quietly gathered together a trousseau for Dora, and the wedding went off as and when Dora wished.

Although there is more than a suggestion in Mollie's description that Dora's decision to marry was more emotional than thoughtful, Mollie's own path to matrimony made evident that young women in the middle of the nineteenth century not only had a choice but also usually exercised it thoughtfully and with realistic expectations. There is no doubt that affection was central to Mollie's decision to marry Byron Sanford. He "loves me tenderly, truly, and...I know now that I can place my hand in his and go with him thro life, be path smooth or stormy," she wrote in her diary the night he proposed to her. She fully recognized that their relationship had not been like those depicted in the sentimental novels of the time. "We did not fall madly in love as I had always expected to, but have gradually 'grown into love,'" as the preceding entries in her diary certainly make evident.[16]

Simply because affection was a chief basis for marital choices, courtship in the nineteenth century was an important stage in family formation. At perhaps no other point in the course of a marriage was a woman's autonomy greater or more individualistically exercised. A brief examination of actual courtships provides some insight into not only how marriages were arranged but what marriage meant for women in the nineteenth century.

Contrary to what is sometimes thought about the Victorian years, courtship did not have to be formal, excessively restricted, or even chaperoned. Not until late in the nineteenth century and then only among the urban upper classes was the European practice of chaperoning at all well-known. It is true that premarital sexual relations, today so commonplace in America, were rare among all classes of Americans. Even in the eighteenth century, when premarital pregnancies reached a high not equaled until the late twentieth century, no more than 10 percent of women conceived children that were born less than nine months after the marriage ceremony. And according to the few historical studies on the subject, the proportion of bridal pregnancies in the nineteenth century was even smaller. Only among black families were premarital pregnancies proportionately high at the end of the nineteenth century. But even then, the great majority of black couples waited until marriage before conceiving children.[17] Illegitimate births were also low for all groups of society, though of course they occurred.

Means of contraception were rather well-known in the nineteenth century, but they were not sufficiently reliable to protect women from the social stigma which fell like a hammer on those whose sexual relations outside marriage were revealed by illegitimate births. Finally, it should be remembered that premarital sexual relations have not been typical of American courtships for most of the twentieth century, either.

If we leave aside premarital sexual experience as a measure of the freedom of courtship, then the Victorian courtship is far from staid. Indeed, as Alexis de Tocqueville and other foreign travelers in America in the 1830s and 1840s pointed out, unmarried women were much freer in public than their married sisters. Middle- and lower-class women moved about not only without chaperones, but also with a certain amount of abandon. Mollie Dorsey, while traveling with her family on a riverboat in the late 1850s, reported that she and a newly found female friend "have splendid times—flirt all day." It was not unusual for a young woman to accompany a young man on fishing trips, with no one else along, or to accept invitations for walks together, discussing personal matters. "I am sorry to tell you," one young woman wrote a female friend in 1822, "that I feel remarkably dull this evening having just returned from a long walk of three miles out of town . . . for I was with a gentleman who I am somewhat afraid of, as he is most appallingly sensible and intellectual, and I have been exerting every facility to say something smart." Mollie Dorsey also took a long walk; she stayed out so late with her lover that her father came looking for her. She felt "sheepish to be patrolled home," and her father's reproof "rather spoiled the romance of the thing," she complained. A young man's diary of 1861 similarly revealed young women who were hardly bashful. He told of going to a "Sewing Circle of the North Baptist Church," where he "went over the river with Miss Hutchins. 3 couples of us remained there until 1 ½ in the morning. Came up with Lizzie Green. I don't know how many kisses I had that evening, was almost smothered with sweet things." Two days later he spent an evening with a Miss Albert, who gave "me a sweet kiss before I was aware of the fact; went home with my lady. She too gave me a farewell salute." A dozen years later Anna Haskell in California told in her journal of the several boys who rather regularly came to her room at college at night, even though the practice was quite against the rules. Sometimes Anna would go off alone with one for a walk and talk. Nor was it always necessary for couples to sneak off in order to obtain privacy. When callers came to Mollie Dorsey's house, all her relatives and family quickly left the room so that the couple could be alone.[18]

Late-night courting was not limited to the new country or to forward young men. Indeed, as Lester Frank Ward's diary written during the same years in rural eastern Pennsylvania shows, courting in Victorian America could be freer than many have supposed. Again and again Ward reported that he and "his girl," as he referred to the young woman who later became his wife, kissed and caressed each other until the early morning hours. On a Monday night in 1860, when he was nineteen, he left her only "at half past three. . .amid thousands of kisses." Then on the following Wednesday he escorted her home, not leaving again until 3:00 A.M. During that stay, he reported they spent "an hour embracing, caressing, hugging, and kissing. O bliss! O love! O passion, pure, sweet and profound! What more do I want than you?"

Nor was all the initiative his. On a subsequent visit, after an absence of several days, he found her most captivated by him. "She looked at me so gently and spoke so tenderly. 'I love you,' she said, kissing me on the mouth. 'I love this mouth, I love those dear eyes, I love this head,' and a thousand other little caressing pet-names." At around 3:00 A.M., when they became sleepy, they arranged the chairs in such a way that they could lie lengthwise facing each other and he opened his shirt, placing her hand on his bare chest. She said she thought she might be doing something wrong, but, significantly, she did not stop. "As we lay in this position," he noted, "the cocks crowed." Quickly he slipped off to work, where he caught up on his lost sleep. After another equally loving visit, at 4:30 in the morning they heard her father jumping out of bed. Hurriedly they kissed and he ran home.

By early 1861 their physical attraction to one another had become so strong that it began to worry them. "I had a very affectionate time with the girl, kissing her almost all over and loving her very deeply and she *does* me." Two weeks later Ward referred to a "very secret time" with her. "I kissed her on her soft breasts, and took too many liberties with her sweet person, and we are going to stop. It is a very fascinating practice and fills us with very sweet, tender and familiar sentiments, and consequently makes us happy." They talked about their fear that "we might become so addicted in that direction that we might go too deep and possibly confound ourselves by the standards of virtue." Even when he was not with her, he dreamed about her and during the day fantasized about "kissing her sweet breasts and sleeping in her arms." A week later he characteristically, if enigmatically wrote, "I slept in her arms; yes, I lay with her, but did nothing wrong."

Yet, despite the intimacy, the relationship between them was not yet settled, for she was still seeing other young men, a practice that inevitably aroused Ward's jealousy and temporarily reduced her ardor. Gradually, after a long talk, they recognized their mutual attraction and dependence; weeping and kissing, they reestablished their old, close relation. Ward was thrown into despair some nights later when he called on her only to find that her brother was home, preventing their usual love-making. Ward managed to get a note to her asking if he could return later. To his delight she wrote back that she wanted to kiss him. When he did return, "closely held in loving arms we lay, embraced, and kissed all night (not going to bed until five in the morning). We have never acted in such a way before. All that we did I shall not tell here, but it was all very sweet and loving and nothing infamous," he assured himself. By the end of that year of rather steady courtship little restraint was left on their emotions. "When I arrived at the house of sweetness, she received me in her loving arms and pressed me to her honey-form, and our lips touched and we entered Paradise together. . . . That evening and night we tasted the joys of love and happiness which only belong to a married life." Early the next year, in 1862, they were married.[19]

Ward's diary is unusually explicit about the physical side of a mid-nineteenth-century courtship; yet even it, by late twentieth-century standards, is noticeably circumspect, suggesting the difficulty nineteenth-century people had in discussing such matters, even privately. It is worth noting, too, that the diary was originally written by Ward in French, a fact that probably accounts for his uncommon explicitness of language. But there is no reason to believe that the behavior he described was rare or exceptional.

Courtship is only one way of gaining an insight into the nature and bases of marriage in nineteenth-century America. After all, it is only the beginning of a marriage, and, in some ways, the ideal as opposed to the real expression of what marriage meant.

Notes

1. John Hajnal, "European Marriage Patterns in Perspective," in D.V. Glass and D.E.C. Eversley (eds.), *Population in History* (Chicago, 1965), pp. 101–4.

2. Philip J. Greven, Jr., *Four Generations: Population, Land, and Family in Colonial Andover, Massachusetts* (Ithaca, 1970), pp. 34, 117–20; Robert V. Wells, "Quaker Marriage Patterns in a Colonial

Perspective," *William and Mary Quarterly*, 3rd Series, 24 (July 1972), 427, 430; John Demos, *A Little Commonwealth: Family Life in Plymouth Colony* (New York, 1970), p. 193, Table 4; Daniel Scott Smith, "The Demographic History of Colonial New England," *Journal of Economic History* 32 (March 1972), 177.

3. Natalie Zemon Davis, "Ghosts, Kin, and Progeny: Some Features of Family Life in Early Modern France," *Daedalus* 106 (Spring 1977), 107; Lawrence Stone, "The Rise of the Nuclear Family in Early Modern England," in Charles E. Rosenberg (ed.), *The Family in History* (Philadelphia, 1975), pp. 45, 48–49.

4. Greven, *Four Generations*, pp. 222–23; Daniel Scott Smith, "Parental Control and Marriage Patterns: An Analysis of Historical Trends in Hingham, Massachusetts," *Journal of Marriage and the Family* 35 (August 1973), 423–24; Robert A. Gross, *The Minutemen and Their World* (New York, 1976), pp. 211n, 235n.

5. Kathryn Kish Sklar, *Catharine Beecher: A Study in American Domesticity* (New Haven, 1973), p. 36; Ms. biography of Louis Alexander Janin, Box 20, Folder 22, Janin Family Collection, Huntington Library, San Marino, Ca.

6. Donald F. Danker (ed.), *Mollie: The Journal of Mollie Dorsey Sanford in Nebraska and Colorado Territories, 1857–1866* (Lincoln, 1959), p. 7; Robert Manson Myers (ed.), *The Children of Pride: A True Story of Georgia and the Civil War* (New Haven, 1972), p. 118.

7. Clarence Cook (ed.), *A Girl's Life Eighty Years Ago: Selections from the Letters of Eliza Southgate Bowne* (New York, 1887), p. 140; see also Janet Wilson James, "Changing Ideas about Women in the United States, 1776–1825," unpublished dissertation, Harvard University, 1954, p. 141; James R. McGovern, *Yankee Family* (New Orleans, 1975), p. 59.

8. Journal of Sarah Ripley Stearns, February 2, 17, May 26, October 24, 1810, February 1, November 10, 1812, Stearns Papers, Schlesinger Library, Radcliffe College; North Carolina planter's remark quoted in unpublished paper of Jane Turner Censer presented at meetings of Southern Historical Association, November 1977. I am indebted to Ms. Censer for permitting me to use the results of her research.

9. Quoted in E. William Monter, "The Pedestal and the Stake: Courtly Love and Witchcraft," in Renate Bridenthal and Claudia Koonz (eds.), *Becoming Visible: Women in European History* (Boston, 1977), p. 123.

10. Robert C. Winthrop (ed.), *Life and Letters of John Winthrop* (2 vols., Boston, 1864), 1, 247, 292; Stone, "Rise of the Nuclear Family," pp. 26–28, 30–31.

11. Lawrence Stone, *The Family, Sex, and Marriage in England, 1500–1800* (New York, 1977), pp. 318, 284.

12. Ibid., p. 372.

13. Nancy F. Cott, "Eighteenth Century Family and Social Life Revealed in Massachusetts Divorce Records," *Journal of Social History* 10 (Fall 1976), 32; Nancy F. Cott, "Divorce and the Changing Status of Women in Eighteenth Century Massachusetts," *William and Mary Quarterly*, 3rd Series, 33 (October 1976), 586–614.

14. Ibid., pp. 599–600, 613.

15. Herman R. Lantz et al., "Pre-industrial Patterns in the Colonial Family in America: A Content Analysis of Colonial Magazines," *American Sociological Review* 33 (June 1968), 413–26.

16. Danker (ed.), *Mollie*, pp. 103, 113, 65.

17. Daniel Scott Smith and Michael S. Hindus, "Premarital Pregnancy in America, 1640–1971: An Overview and Interpretation," *Journal of Interdisciplinary History* 4 (Spring 1975), 537–70; Herbert G. Gutman, *The Black Family in Slavery and Freedom, 1750–1925* (New York, 1976), pp. 64–65, 504, Table A-30.

18. Danker (ed.), *Mollie*, pp. 7, 20, 36, 47; Mary Cogswell to Weltha Brown, April 2, 1822, Brown Correspondence, Hooker Collection, Schlesinger Library, Radcliffe College; quotations from young man's diary in Ernest Earnest, *The American Eve in Fact and Fiction, 1775–1914* (Urbana, 1974); Diaries of Anna Haskell, March 15, 1876, Haskell Family Collection, Bancroft Library, University of California, Berkeley.

19. Bernhard J. Stern (ed.), *Young Ward's Diary* (New York, 1935), pp. 10, 14–15, 18–19, 33, 35–37, 44, 80.

Death and the Family*

Peter Uhlenberg

Peter Uhlenberg is a historical demographer—he looks at families from the perspective of population change. When studying families in the contemporary United States, many people seem puzzled about why we should be interested in family life in past times. Uhlenberg's article is an excellent illustration of why examining the history of families can help us to better understand family life today. Uhlenberg focuses upon one variable—the profound impact which changes in mortality rates have had on the everyday lives of people in the context of their families. He organizes his discussion around the life course, looking at how the decline in death rates has transformed the experience of childhood, young adulthood, middle age, and old age. Uhlenberg uses the experience of three birth cohorts (people born in the same year) to illustrate how quickly these changes have transformed family life in the United States during this century.

The impact of mortality change upon family structure, although sometimes mentioned, has been seriously neglected in studies of family history. Many of the most significant changes in the American family—the changing status of children,

*Source: Peter Uhlenberg, "Death and the Family," *Journal of Family History*, 5, no. 3 (Fall 1980), 313–320.

the increasing independence of the nuclear family, the virtual disappearance of orphanages and foundling homes, the rise in societal support of the elderly, the decline in fertility, the rise in divorce—cannot be adequately understood without a clear recognition of the profound changes that have occurred in death rates. And the decline in mortality in this century has been dramatic. At the beginning of this century about 140 infants out of every 1,000 born died in the first year of life; now only 14 out of 1,000 die. In this same period the average life span has increased from less than 50 to 73. The mortality decline in this century is greater than the total mortality decline that occurred during the 250 years preceding 1900.

In searching for the meaning of aggregate statistics on death for individuals and families, we must consider the effects of a death upon the survivors. Habenstein suggests that:

> Each death initiates significant responses from those survivors who in some way have personally or vicariously related to the deceased. Inevitably, the collectivities in which the dead person held membership also react (1968:26).

The family is often the most important group in which an individual has membership and in which close relationships exist, so it is here that we should expect death to have its greatest impact. The loss of a parent, a child, a sibling, or a spouse disrupts established family patterns and requires readjustment. As the experience of losing intimate family members moves from a pervasive aspect of life to a rare event, adjustments in family structure become imperative.

If the mortality decline since 1900 has been so large and if this decline has major repercussions for the family, why has it been neglected in studies of family change?[1] One important reason is the difficulty involved in trying to measure accurately the effects of a mortality change. Suppose, for example, that we want to describe the effect of mortality upon the family position of children at various historical times. If we attempt to specify the situation in its full complexity, we must deal with the age of mothers and fathers at the birth of their children, the birth position of children, and the age-sex configuration of siblings. Furthermore, we must recognize that cohorts of individuals live out their lives in a dynamic environment in which the force of mortality is constantly changing. Even if we could construct a conceptually complex model to elaborate the detailed mortality experiences of individuals, we would not have the necessary statistics to make use of it. Nor can a retrospective survey provide the data we would need, since only survivors to the present could be interviewed.

The purpose of this article is to suggest an alternative approach by constructing relatively simple measures of how different mortality levels affect important aspects of the family. Rather than attempting to summarize the total impact of mortality upon a cohort, the present study develops hypothetical situations to provide insights into the dynamic role of death in family life. The emphasis is upon ways in which mortality impinges upon family structure, and how observed changes in mortality over this century have encouraged change in the American family.

For perspective on historical change in mortality, I will focus upon three dates in the twentieth century: approximately 1900, 1940, and 1980 (actually, 1976). At each date, the role of mortality will be considered from the perspective of individuals at four different locations in the life course. The stages of life are: childhood, young adulthood, middle age, and old age. The calculations use period life tables[2] for each date, which means that the measures do not reflect the actual experience of any cohort. Rather, the picture presented reveals the implications of mortality conditions at specific points in time. In other words, the question asked is how would mortality at the 1900 (or 1940 or 1980) level impinge upon the family experience of individuals?

Childhood

Mortality change has affected the family experience of children in three ways. First, an increasing likelihood that a newborn will survive through childhood may influence the nature of parent-child relations. Second, declining mortality in the middle years of life affects the chances of orphanhood for children. Third, changing adult mortality also alters the prospects for having grandparents alive during childhood.

Parent-child relations. There is widespread agreement that mortality levels in a society constrain attitudes and feelings that parents have toward their infant children. As Ariès writes, under conditions of very high infant and childhood mortality "people could not allow themselves to become too attached to something that was regarded as a probable loss" (1962:38; also see Blauner, 1966). As infant mortality has declined, childhood has become a more clearly differentiated stage of life, and families have increasingly focused upon children and emphasized the nurturance of children. Comparing the modern and historical American family, Skolnick concludes:

> What seems to have changed is the psychological quality of the intimate environments of family life. . . . Within the home the family has become more intense emotionally (1978:115).

Surely other factors in addition to changed mortality encouraged the deepening of emotional bonds between family members. But a look at the extent of changing survival prospects for infants since 1900 points clearly to the critical role that this change played in the increased intimacy of the parent-child relationship.

Several calculations to demonstrate the magnitude of the drop in child deaths since 1900 are presented in Table 3-1. First, the probability that an individual baby would survive his or her childhood increased from .79 in 1900 to .98 in 1976. The second calculation answers the question, what is the probability that a couple bearing three children would have at least one child die before reaching age 15? The answer is that under 1900 mortality conditions half of the parents would experience the loss of a child; under 1976 conditions only 6 percent would. But the rate of birth as well as death fell over this century. As a result, the probability of an average parent experiencing the death of a child changed even more. Women bearing children around 1900 had, on average, 4.2 children,

TABLE 3-1

Measures of Death to Children in Families: 1900; 1940; 1976.

YEAR	PROBABILITY OF SURVIVING FROM 0 TO 15	PROBABILITY OF 1 OR MORE DYING OUT OF 3	AVERAGE NUMBER OF CHILDREN PER MOTHER[a]	PROBABILITY OF 1 OR MORE DYING OUT OF AVERAGE NUMBER OF BIRTHS
1900	.79	.50	4.2	.62
1940	.94	.17	2.8	.16
1976	.98	.06	2.1	.04

[a]For 1900 and 1940 this is the average completed family size for women who were aged 25–29 at these dates. For 1976 the figure is the expected completed family size for women aged 25–29 in 1976.

Sources: U.S. Public Health Service, 1969; NCHS, 1978; Grabill et al., 1958; U.S. Bureau of the Census, 1978a.

while projections suggest that women currently bearing children will average about 2.1. Thus the third calculation in Table 3-1 shows that the probability of a child dying for parents with an average number of children for that period dropped from .62 in 1900 to only .04 in 1976. As the parental experience of having a child die changed from routine to exceptional, the simulus to invest greater emotion and resources has grown.

Orphanhood. The dependency of children upon adults for care and socialization necessitates fully developed social arrangements to deal with orphans in societies with high rates of mortality. Adoption within an extended kinship system and placement of children in orphanages were two mechanisms used to deal with the social problem of orphans in nineteenth-century America. But during the twentieth century orphanhood changes from a common occurrence to a rare event. Consequently, social institutions designed to deal with this problem have virtually disappeared. From the perspective of successive cohorts of children, the change has profoundly altered their experiences in families.

Table 3-2 contains data which show the effect of varying mortality levels upon the probability of orphanhood. Since probability of death is related to age, some assumption about the age of men and women at the occurrence of parenthood is required. Over this century the median age of women at the birth of their children has ranged from 27.2 to 25.4, and fathers have, on average, been about three years older than mothers. Therefore, the choice of a mother aged 27 and a father aged 30 for the calculations in Table 3-2 is a reasonable approxi-

TABLE 3-2

Probabilities of Parents and Siblings Dying Before a Child Reaches Age 15: 1900; 1940; 1976.[a]

YEAR	PROBABILITY OF 1 OR MORE PARENT DYING	PROBABILITY OF 1 OR MORE OF 2 SIBLINGS DYING	PROBABILITY OF DEATH TO MEMBER OF NUCLEAR FAMILY
1900	.24	.36	.51
1940	.10	.12	.21
1976	.05	.04	.09

[a] See text for specific family context of the child.

Sources: U.S. Public Health Service, 1969; NCHS, 1978.

mation to the typical experience over this time interval.[3] From the table we can read the probability of orphanhood for those born under these circumstances.

If mortality levels characteristic of 1900 persisted over time and the probability of death for the father and mother was independent, about 24 percent of the children born would lose at least one parent before reaching age 15; one out of 62 would have both parents die. Under mortality conditions existing in 1976, only 5 percent of all children would see a parent die, while one in 1,800 would lose both parents. So declining mortality has operated to increase greatly the family stability of children.

Of course, increasing divorce has had the counter influence of increasing family disruption for children. At current levels of divorce, about 36 percent of all children will experience a disrupted family (Bumpass, 1978). But the social significance of disruption due to death differs from disruption due to divorce. Current discussions of the effects of family disruption upon children should consider the very high rate of family instability that has been the historical experience of children prior to the modern era of low mortality. Further, those interested in designing social policy for the family would benefit from studying the historical ways of dealing with orphans.

In addition to the reduced probability of losing a parent during childhood, there has also been a great reduction in the probability of a sibling dying. One good example indicates the magnitude of this change. Consider the situation of a first-born child to a mother aged 27 and a father aged 30, where the parents have two additional children at two-year intervals. That is, the first-born child has siblings born when he or she is two and four. What is the probability that this child will experience the death of a sibling before reaching age 15? Under 1900 mortality conditions the probability is .36, while under 1976 conditions, it is only .04. Combined with the possibility of a parent or sibling dying during childhood, the chances of a child losing someone in the nuclear family before he or she reaches age 15 drops from .51 to .09. Since the average number of siblings for a child born later in this century is much lower than for someone born earlier, the actual experience of encountering the death of an intimate family member has declined even more dramatically than these calculations suggest. Compared to the past, children now are almost entirely shielded from the death of close relatives, except that of elderly grandparents.

Grandparents' survival. Not only did the mortality decline improve the likelihood that all members of the nuclear family would survive one's childhood, but also it increased the average number of living grandparents. Consider the probability of a child having grandparents alive if he or she is born to a father aged 30 and mother aged 27 and if both parents were similarly born when their fathers and mothers were 30 and 27 respectively. Under 1900 mortality conditions, one-fourth of the children would have all grandparents alive at birth; by 1976 it increased to almost two-thirds (Table 3-3). The probability of three or more grandparents being alive when the child was age 15 increased from .17 to .55. Thus, mortality change has greatly increased the potential for family interaction across more than two generations. The actual role of grandparents in the lives of children cannot be determined from these simple demographic data. But the

TABLE 3-3

Distribution of Children by Number of Living Grandparents When Child Is Aged 0 and 15 Under Conditions of 1900, 1940, and 1976.[a]

Year	NUMBER OF GRANDPARENTS ALIVE AT AGE 0				NUMBER OF GRANDPARENTS ALIVE AT AGE 15			
	0–1	2	3	4	0–1	2	3	4
1900	.08	.26	.42	.25	.48	.35	.15	.02
1940	.02	.13	.40	.46	.29	.39	.26	.06
1976	.00	.05	.31	.63	.12	.33	.39	.16

[a] See text for details.

Sources: Same as Table 3-2.

increased presence of grandparents suggests that statements about their declining importance in the lives of children are probably exaggerated or wrong.

Young Adults

The mortality decline since 1900 has greatly altered the prospects that a marriage between young adults will be broken by death before old age. If a man and woman marry when they are aged 25 and 22, the probability that either of them will die within 40 years after their marriage dropped from .67 in 1900 to .36 in 1976. This decline in early widowhood more than offsets the rise in divorce (Table 3-4), so that the stability of marriages during the child-rearing years has actually increased over this century. When the declining age at completion of childbearing (Glick, 1977) is also considered, the higher probability of both husband and wife surviving to the empty nest stage of life is even more marked.

With current low mortality the prospective view of married life is quite different from what it was in the past. A man and a woman marrying at the average marriage age can anticipate jointly surviving a median of 45 years, i.e., until the husband is 70 years old. The prospect of living with one person over such a long time period, especially when one anticipates significant but unknown social change, may influence one's view of marriage. In particular, it may cause higher uncertainty about whether or not the marriage can survive until broken by death. If a couple enters into marriage accepting the option of divorce as a possibility, the chances of actually ending the marriage with a divorce are prob-

TABLE 3-4

Probability of Marital Disruption Due to Death or Divorce Within the First 40 Years: 1900; 1940; 1976.

YEAR	BROKEN BY DEATH[a]	BROKEN BY DEATH OR DIVORCE[a]
1900	.67	.71
1940	.50	.63
1976	.36	.60

[a] Assuming husband is 25 and wife is 22 at time of marriage.

Sources: Same as Table 3-2; plus Preston and McDonald, 1979; Glick, 1977.

ably increased. Further, the period of time in which a divorce can occur has been lengthened. Thus it seems likely that the decreasing likelihood of marital disruption due to death has contributed to the increased rate of divorce in recent years.

Another, and more frequently noted, effect of lowered death rates upon the family behavior of young adults concerns fertility decisions. As shown in Table 3-1, the experience of having an infant or child die has moved from a common to a very uncommon event for American parents. The great variability that existed in 1900 between the number of children ever born and the number who eventually reached adulthood has disappeared. It is now possible for parents to anticipate the survival of all their children through childhood. Thus, the planning of family size has become feasible, and the need to have additional children to protect against possible loss no longer exists. A couple bearing two children can now be almost 95 percent confident that both will reach age 20. Consequently, an interesting effect of lowered mortality is the downward pressure it exerts upon fertility.

Middle Age

Discussions of the family role of the middle-aged have generally emphasized the changes involved as children leave home and as relationships with adult children are developed. Two ways of viewing the changes that occur when parents no longer have dependent children are noted by Winch (1971). On the positive side:

> With the fulfillment of the parental role and the consequent reduction of responsibilities comes the promise of a more relaxed mode of life and the ultimate leisure of retirement.

While on the negative side:

> The "empty nest" psychology implies that since the parents' job is completed, they are no longer needed. They may look forward to declining strength, declining productivity, declining health, and, usually, in retirement to diminished income.

Both of these views picture the postparental phase as a period of greatly reduced family responsibility. Clearly the average length of this segment of life has grown as the probability of surviving into old age has increased. But interestingly, the fall in mortality is also altering the nature of the empty nest stage of life. Brody (1978) has nicely captured this change when she writes, "The 'empty nests' of some of the grandparent generation are being refilled with members of the great-grandparent generation."

An increasing number of persons entering the "young-old" stage of life have parents who are still living and who are in need of substantial assistance. Older people are not generally abandoned by their children. Rather, adult children are now, as in the past, the primary care givers to the elderly in American society (Brody, 1978; Sussman, 1976). The big change has not been in norms regarding the responsibility of children to their elderly parents, but in the likelihood of a

TABLE 3-5

**Distribution of Middle-Aged Couples
by Number of Their Parents Still Alive Under
Conditions in 1900, 1940, and 1976.**

Year	NUMBER OF PARENTS ALIVE:			
	0	1	2+	Total
1900	.52	.38	.10	1.00
1940	.37	.43	.20	1.00
1976	.14	.39	.47	1.00

Source: Same as Table 3-2.

middle-aged person faced with the actual situation of having parents still alive. A quantitative assessment of the increased presence of parents for the middle-aged is given in Table 3-5.

The number of parents and parents-in-law still alive for a husband aged 55 and a wife aged 52 under mortality conditions prevailing at selected historical periods is shown. The calculations assumed that both husband and wife were born when their fathers were aged 30 and their mothers were aged 27 (which is close to the average age at parenthood over this century). As in the previous calculations, period life tables are used to capture mortality conditions at specific time periods, so the data do not reflect the experiences of actual cohorts. A shift from 1900 mortality conditions to those of 1976 implies an increase in the proportion of middle-aged couples who have living parents from 48 to 86 percent. With 1976 mortality conditions, half of all middle-aged couples would have two or more elderly parents alive.

Old Age

As discussed earlier, marital instability prior to old age has declined over this century. At the same time, the remarriage rate for those with disrupted marriages has increased. Consequently, a much larger proportion of men and women are married and living with a spouse when they arrive at old age, and a slightly higher proportion of the total older population is now married (51 percent in 1900 versus 52 percent in 1970). But while these data indicate an increased involvement of older persons in nuclear families, it is also true that average number of years that women spend in widowhood has greatly increased. The increased period of widowhood is a result of the much greater improvement in life expectancy for women than for men. The lengthening old-age period of life is increasingly divided into two parts for women: an earlier phase in which they are married and a later phase in which they are widows.

Selected values of life expectancy from life tables for men and women are presented in Table 3-6. From these values it can be seen that under the given mortality conditions, the average number of years that a typical wife can expect to outlive her husband has increased from 3.8 in 1900 to 9.7 currently. Primarily as a consequence of the increasing survival advantage of females over males, the

TABLE 3-6

Average Years of Life Remaining at Selected Ages
for Men and Women in the U.S.: 1900; 1940; 1976.

	LIFE TABLE VALUES					
Year	(1) $\grave{e}22(F)$	(2) $\grave{e}20$	(3) (1) − (2)	(4) $\grave{e}62(F)$	(5) $\grave{e}65(M)$	(6) (4) − (5)
1900	42.3	38.5	3.8	14.0	11.5	2.5
1940	49.5	43.3	6.2	15.6	12.1	3.5
1976	56.8	47.1	9.7	20.4	13.7	6.7

Sources: Same as Table 3-2.

ratio of widows to widowers over age 65 has grown from 2.2:1 in 1900 to 5.6:1 in 1976. With such a large imbalance, remarriage is clearly an option for very few of the older widows. Therefore, mortality change has created a major increase in the significance of the final stage of life for women, a period of widowhood in which few men are around. What the family experience of the rapidly growing number of older women, whose children themselves are approaching old age, will be is not entirely clear. In 1976, however, about 70 percent of the widows over age 65 were living either alone or in institutions (Metropolitan Life, 1977). Thus, a large majority of older women are now living their last years of life outside of a family context. Of course, this does not mean that they necessarily lack significant kinship links, but it does indicate that their daily life is not enmeshed in a family.

Conclusion

Declining mortality during the twentieth century has had a major impact upon the American family. The role of mortality as an independent variable producing change has been noted in the following areas:

1. Increasing survival prospects for infants has encouraged stronger emotional bonds between parents and children.
2. Decreasing deaths to adults aged 20 to 50 has reduced the proportion of children who experience orphanhood.
3. Decreasing mortality has eliminated the experience of a member of the nuclear family dying for most children.
4. Increasing survival rates has increased the number of living grandparents for children.
5. Decreasing mortality has increased the number of years that marriages survive without being disrupted by death. This change has probably contributed to the increase in divorce.
6. Decreasing infant and child deaths have allowed more careful planning of family size and have encouraged a reduction in fertility.
7. Increasing survival rates have lengthened the "empty nest" stage of the family.
8. Decreasing mortality has increased the number of elderly persons dependent upon their middle-aged children.
9. Increasing survival advantages for women relative to men have lengthened the period of widowhood at the end of the life course.

Notes

1. Several studies have discussed the significance of mortality level for the social structure (Blauner, 1966; Ariès, 1962; Habenstein, 1968), but they do not present quantitative information regarding its effect upon the family.

2. The life tables are for the U.S. white population.

3. Varying the ages of parents at the birth of the child a few years in either direction has negligible effects upon the probability of orphanhood. For example, if the mother was 25 and the father 28, the probability in 1900 would be .23 instead of .24, and the probability in 1976 would be unchanged.

References

ARIÈS, PHILIPPE. 1962. Centuries of Childhood: A Social History of Family Life. Robert Baldick, trans. New York: Random House.

BLAUNER, ROBERT. 1966. "Death and Social Structure." Psychiatry 29: 378–394.

BRODY, ELAINE M. 1978. "The Aging of the Family." The Annals 438: 13–27.

BUMPASS, LARRY and RONALD RINDFUSS. 1978. "Children's Experience of Marital Disruption." Paper presented at the Annual Meeting of the Population Association of America.

GLICK, PAUL. 1977. "Marrying, Divorcing, and Living Together in the U.S. Today." Population Bulletin 32.

GRABILL, WILSON H., CLYDE V. KISER and PASCAL K. WHELPTON. 1958. The Fertility of American Women. New York: Wiley.

HABENSTEIN, ROBERT W. 1968. "The Social Organization of Death." In David L. Sills, ed. International Encyclopedia of the Social Sciences 4: 26–28.

Metropolitan Life. 1977. "Widows in the United States." *Statistical Bulletin* 58: 8–10.

NCHS. 1978. *Vital Statistics of the United States*, 1976, vol. 2-Section 5. Life Tables. Hyattsville: U.S. Department of HEW.

PRESTON, SAMUEL H. and JOHN McDONALD. 1979. "The Incidence of Divorce within Cohorts of American Marriages Contracted Since the Civil War." *Demography* 16: 1–25.

SKOLNICK, ARLENE. 1978. *The Intimate Environment: Exploring Marriage and the Family*. 2nd ed. Boston: Little, Brown and Co.

SUSSMAN, MARVIN B. 1976. "The Family Life of Old People." In Robert H. Binstock and Ethel Shanas, eds., *Handbook of Aging and the Social Sciences*. New York: Van Nostrand Reinhold.

U.S. Bureau of the Census. 1978a. *Current Population Reports*, Series P-23, No. 70.

———— 1978b. *Current Population Reports*, Series P-23, No. 77.

U.S. Public Health Service. 1969. *Vital Statistics of the United States*: 1967, Vol. 2, Part A.

WINCH, ROBERT F. 1971. *The Modern Family*. 3rd ed. New York: Holt, Rinehart, Winston.

Prophets of Doom*

Edward L. Kain

The previous article on "Death and the Family" pointed out that when we look at information about families from the past it often challenges our assumptions about how families are changing. In this introduction to his book The Myth of Family Decline, *Edward L. Kain argues that many of today's distressed images of families are misleading. Like Uhlenberg, he suggests that we need to examine historical changes in family life in order to better understand contemporary families, as well as to make predictions about the future of family life. Kain suggests that the concept of family decline is indeed a myth, and that the "prophets of doom" are wrong largely because they lack a historical understanding of the family.*

Almost daily, the headlines scream out yet another message that seems to indicate the family is on its deathbed in modern America. News magazines include stories on unprecedented rates of divorce, frightening reports of elderly Americans (seemingly forgotten by their family and society) being mistreated and neglected in nursing homes, and children being raised in single-parent families.

Source: Reprinted with the permission of Lexington Books, an imprint of Macmillan Publishing Company from *The Myth of Family Decline: Understanding Families in a World of Rapid Social Change* by Edward L. Kain. Copyright (c) 1990 by Lexington Books.

The evening news talks about the majority of mothers working outside the home and of social movements supporting concerns as diverse as abortion rights and homosexual freedom. All these issues seem to signal that the basic institution in our society is threatened.

These challenges to the family have been met sometimes with dismay and sometimes with resignation, but in recent years they have also been met with counterattacks led by groups rallying around a battle cry for a return to the traditional family of the past. It appears that the war has begun. Those fighting in the trenches, however, are not at all certain of the outcome because there are many separate battles being waged at once.

This [chapter] is an attempt to step back from the apparent battleground of the closing decades of the twentieth century and evaluate the health of the family in the United States from a broader perspective—one that places current family life within the context of social change. Families do not exist in a vacuum, and we cannot begin to understand the quality of family life in the last decade of the twentieth century unless it is placed within historical and social context. What were American families like in the past? How have families been changing over the past century? What types of family patterns can we expect to see over the next several decades?

Unfortunately, the task of placing family life within a broader context is an assignment with many dangers. Because most of us were born into families and have spent most of our lives in the context of our own family structures, we all have some sense that we are knowledgeable on the topic of family life. It is somewhat difficult to step back from our personal experience and evaluate the institution of the family with objectivity.

To understand families in the present or the future, we must understand families in the past. We cannot possibly assess the health of family life as we near the twenty-first century unless we place it within a broader span of historical time. As individuals and as a culture, however, Americans tend not to think of contemporary issues in historical perspective. This is true not only of popular accounts of family life, but also of the work done by many family scholars as well. Like Rip Van Winkle who awoke to a world vastly different than that to which he was accustomed, we often look upon contemporary family life with dismay. Our world is changing rapidly, and many of these changes seem to challenge our very conception of family life. We long for a return to traditional values and the traditional family structure that we remember from the past.

This dismay at the current state of affairs and desire to return to the past is what I have come to label the "myth of family decline." Our image of families in the past is often based on myth rather than reality. For the past three decades, work by historians, demographers, and sociologists has begun to paint a new picture of the history of family life. Using innovative methods to explore church, family, and civil records, these researchers have discovered patterns of family experience that stand in stark contrast to the images many of us have held about the traditional family.[1]

As an illustration of this point, take the following quiz, which asks a few basic questions about family life both in the past and the present.

A Brief Quiz on Families and Change in the United States

1. Which of the following years had the highest divorce rate in the United States?
   a. 1935
   b. 1945
   c. 1955
   d. 1965

2. T F Because of the rapid rise in the divorce rate, children are much more likely to live in a single-parent household than they were a century ago.

3. T F In the past, most families lived in three-generation households. It is now much less likely for this to occur, since grandparents are put into nursing homes instead of cared for in the home.

4. What proportion of women worked outside the home in 1900?
   a. one in fifty
   b. one in twenty
   c. one in ten
   d. one in five

5. T F Over the past 100 years, fewer and fewer people have been getting married, so the number of single people has been increasing.

6. T F The high incidence of female-headed households among black families today can be traced to the impact of slavery on family life as well as to the disruption of two-parent, nuclear families among black Americans during the time of Emancipation.

7. What is the most common household type in the United States today?
   a. a single-parent family with one adult wage earner
   b. a two-parent family with one adult male wage earner
   c. a two-parent family with two adult wage earners

8. T F Very few families live below the poverty line (as officially defined by the federal government) for extended periods of time (five consecutive years).

Before I give the results to this quiz, there are two things to keep in mind: First, don't be upset if you did not score very well. I have given this quiz to hundreds of students and professionals, and the typical result is that scores are extremely low. In fact, when I gave the quiz at a conference attended only by professionals who specialize in working with and teaching about family life, most of the questions were answered incorrectly by a majority of the group! Rather than being a statement about the quality of professionals in the area of family, this reflects the tendency of our culture to ignore the past and to base opinions about our basic social institutions (family, education, economy, religion, and government) on a cultural image that often is greatly at variance with reality.

Second, I want to suggest that each of these questions illustrates a basic point. Now, for the answers to the quiz:

Question 1. Which of the following years had the highest divorce rate in the United States?: a. 1935; b. 1945; c. 1955; d. 1965. The correct answer to this question is B. No, that is not a typographical error in the book; the correct answer is 1945. Most people are very surprised that the correct answer is not

1965. "Isn't it true that divorce rates have been rising throughout the century?" they ask. This response clearly illustrates one of the first central points of this [chapter]: *We seldom have a historical understanding of family life or of the impact of specific historical events on the functioning of families.* The divorce rates in this country reached a historical peak at the end of World War II. Several explanations have been given for this: First, it is likely that a number of couples married hurriedly after relatively short courtships when the man was about to be sent off to war. Second, the stress of separation may have resulted in the development of other relationships for both the women at home and the men who were away. Third, both spouses may have changed considerably during the war years. The man who returned home from the battlefields may not have been the boy who left, and the woman at home may not have been the same girl whom he had courted and married. While it is true that divorce rates in this country consistently increased from 1950 through 1980, they did not match the peak of 1945 until the mid-1970s.[2]

Question 2. (True or False) Because of the rapid rise in the divorce rate, children are much more likely to live in a single-parent household than they were a century ago. This statement is false. Most people do not realize the profound effects on family life that have resulted from rapid declines in the mortality rate since the turn of the century. While divorce has increased throughout this century, the drastic decline in the number of parents who die at an early age (leaving widows, widowers, and orphans behind) more than offsets the increase in single-parent households that results from marital disruption caused by divorce.[3] This question reflects a second basic principle: *If an adequate understanding of family change is to be developed, we must look not only at data from the past but also at the relationships between different types of changes affecting family life.*

Question 3. (True or False) In the past, most families lived in three-generation households. It is now much less likely for this to occur, since grandparents are put into nursing homes instead of cared for in the home. This statement is false for a number of reasons. One of the most important findings of the new family history has been a challenge to the idea that the rise of the modern nuclear family (the family including only two parents and their children) is linked to industrialization and is a result of that process. Peter Laslett[4] and others have demonstrated that at least in England, the nuclear family was the dominant form of household long before the advent of industrialization. Laslett makes a strong argument for the continuity of family life over time, and suggests that in a number of ways the family in the "world we have lost" was much as it is today. This illustrates a third central point: *When we have actual data about family life in the past, it often presents a picture of family life that is drastically different from the image that is common in popular mythology.*

In fairness, I must say that Laslett's work is a reaction to most contemporary theories of the family, which ignore the importance of historical time. Unfortunately, Laslett's approach has been criticized for ignoring the dynamic nature of the family as a group. Just as the institution of the family has changed over historical time, individual families change over the family cycle. Subsequent work has suggested that while at any point in time most families in preindustrial Europe may have been nuclear in structure, if families are traced over their developmental cycle, many of them are extended for brief periods while the elder parents are still alive.[5]

Even if everyone wanted to spend part of their family cycle in a three-generation household, however, it still would not be possible for many families. First, only *one* of the children and his or her family typically lived with the elderly parents, so in every family there would be a number of siblings who would live in nuclear households. In addition, the elder generation seldom survived long enough to spend much time in a three-generation household.

Question 4. What proportion of women worked outside the home in 1900?: a. one in fifty; b. one in twenty; c. one in ten; d. one in five. If you chose answer D, you are right. Yes, fully one in five women worked outside the home in paid occupations at the turn of the century.[6] Many were employed as domestic servants and in agriculture. Others worked in textile mills and in teaching positions. Still others were employed in the new clerical sector, which was expanding as our country moved further into the industrial age.

Most people are surprised that the female labor force participation rate was that high. We tend to have an image that women only started working outside the home during World War II, and that they returned home when the war ended. The rise of female labor force participation is often seen as a recent event linked to the women's movement of the 1960s. Certainly there has been an increase in the number of women working outside the home since 1950. In reality, however, the rate of female labor force participation has been rising relatively consistently since the late nineteenth century. This points to a fourth principle: *Most of the changes occurring in families in the United States are not revolutionary but evolutionary—they are changes that have been happening gradually over a long period of time, and they do not represent a radical change from patterns in the past.*

Question 5. (True or False) Over the past 100 years, fewer and fewer people have been getting married, so the number of single people has been increasing. The correct answer to this question is false. (By now you are probably catching on to the idea that your first guess may have been wrong.) Both the popular press and sociological research in recent years has focused on the increase in singlehood.[7] This increase, however, has only been happening since 1950, a period when more people married than any other time in all of American history. In essence, there was no place for the rate of singlehood to go but up. If a longer historical view is taken, it becomes clear that the rates of singlehood today are still lower than they were a century ago. This reflects a fifth basic point: *When we do include history in our conceptions of family life, we tend to focus only on recent history and remain blind to the broader picture of social change and continuity in family life.*

Question 6. (True or False) The high incidence of female-headed households among black families today can be traced to the impact of slavery on family life as well as to the disruption of two-parent, nuclear families among black Americans during the time of Emancipation. This statement is false. While the reasons for the high incidence of single-parent, female-headed households among black Americans today may be complex, they cannot be traced to a legacy developed from the period of slavery and Emancipation. In a series of careful studies, Herbert G. Gutman[8] shows that between 1855 and 1880 as many as 90 percent of black households contained both a husband and wife or just a father with children. The matriarchal household was common neither among antebellum free blacks, nor among black families after Emancipation. The continuing myths about the causes and implications of the structure of black families illustrate another central point: *Historical causes may be built into current explanation of family life, but unless data are used to examine the validity of these historical explanations, our understanding of the relationship between historical events and family life may be seriously flawed.* I might add to this statement the general observation that when groups that are not white, male, or middle-class are concerned, our historical understanding is usually less sophisticated and more often incorrect. The new family history has involved more attention to issues of race, class, and gender—much to the benefit of our understanding of family life in the past.

Question 7. What is the most common household type in the United States today?: a. a single-parent family with one adult wage earner; b. a two-parent family with one adult male wage earner; c. a two-parent family with two adult wage earners. This question turns from the history of family life to the contemporary family in the United States. Like the questions on the history of the family, it illustrates that we may have misconceptions about families in contemporary America. The correct answer is C. By far the most common type of household in the United States today is one in which both adults work outside the home.[9] This illustrates that *no matter what family life was like in the past, in the contemporary United States the so-called traditional family is in a distinct minority.*

Question 8. (True or False) Very few families live below the poverty line (as officially defined by the federal government) for extended periods of time (five consecutive years). The statement in question 8 is true. Research using data from the *Panel Study of Income Dynamics* at the University of Michigan illustrates clearly that a very small percentage of families remain consistently below the poverty line (approximately 4 percent).[10] Rather, families move in and out of poverty as wage earners lose a job, are rehired, a divorce occurs, or additional children are born, changing the stresses upon the family budget. This clearly points to the fact that *our conceptions of the family as a static institution are inadequate, and we must think of families as dynamic groups that change over the lifetimes of the individuals who are involved.*

Many of these new findings in family history and family sociology have taken quite some time to find their way into textbooks in the social sciences—and even longer to reach the popular consciousness. Most of us still carry images of a mythic extended family of domestic bliss within our minds. It is important, however, to base our decisions about political issues related to families on reality rather than myth.

Partly because of the American tendency to romanticize the past, and partly because of the many changes in family life that seem so evident during the past several decades, it is common for social analysts to conclude that the family is, indeed, in trouble. Analyses that predict the demise of the family have come from both ends of the political spectrum. On the radical side, Christopher Lasch has suggested that the family is a failure as a "haven in the heartless world" of industrial capitalism, and he paints a gloomy picture about the future prospects of any improvement.[11] According to Lasch, the family is supposed to shield its members from the harsh realities of working life in modern society, and it has failed in this task.

Similarly, the New Evangelical Right fears that the traditional family is in serious danger. Groups like the Moral Majority preach against the sins of modern times and demand that we return to the core American values of the traditional family. The forces of the New Right have supported a variety of types of legislation that attempt to embody these so-called traditional values into the legal structure. Most notable among these attempts was the Family Protection Act, first introduced in September of 1979 by Senator Paul Laxalt. Later versions of the Family Protection Act were introduced to the House by Representative Hansen of Idaho and Representative Smith of Alabama in 1981, and Senator Jepsen of Iowa introduced a revised version to the Senate in June of the same year.[12] A full explication [of the Act] is not necessary here.[13] In essence, the goal of the legislation was to reinforce what is defined as the traditional family—based upon a mythical vision of peaceful family life under patriarchal rule, in which the husband is the breadwinner and the wife is in the home raising the children.

While certainly the most comprehensive in scope, the Family Protection Act is not the only example of attempts in the 1980s to enshrine what is perceived as the traditional family in the laws of the land. Perhaps the most visible example has been the introduction of various versions of a Human Life Amendment, which would ban or limit legal abortion. All these measures can be seen as an attempt to shore up what is perceived as the crumbling foundation of the central institution of any society—the family.

Not everyone, however, agrees with the assessment that the modern family is in trouble. Some, such as Harvard sociologist Mary Jo Bane, argue that while families are changing, they are still vigorous and "here to stay."[14] Bane provides convincing evidence that ties between grandparents and grandchildren and between parents and children have, if anything, become stronger in recent times, rather than weaker.

One reason that the debate about the health of the family is such an important concern is the rapid rate of social change in our society. Changes in our culture create many social problems, as adjustments in some parts of the culture lag behind. William F. Ogburn's concept of cultural lag provides a useful tool for evaluating this problem.[15] As we have moved in the space of a century from an agricultural economy to a postindustrial society, our social institutions have had difficulty keeping up with the massive shifts generated by technological change. The resulting social problems are at the core of many of the political controversies seen today at the national level, including civil rights for people of color, women's rights, and homosexual rights.

Not surprisingly, many of these controversies center on the family: abortion and reproductive rights; homosexuality; the changing roles of women and men; day care; and comparable worth (the idea that men and women should receive equal pay for jobs that are similar in content, not only for jobs that have the same job title). Because the family is a key institution in any society, and because the transition from agriculture to industry transforms the basic relationships between economic production and family life, many of the cultural lags demanding attention today are reflected in these national political issues.

Unfortunately, as is clear from this chapter, we are often blind to the realities of family life in the past. Our cultural images of family life in past times are difficult to change, even when data indicate the images are much more myth than reality. Like Rip Van Winkle, we long for a return to the good old days, when life was much simpler and times were happier.

We live with a myth of family decline—the notion that families in the past were stable and happy and that recent decades have seen a rapid decay of family life. [Our] central goal . . . is to paint a more accurate portrait of how families in the United States have actually been changing, so we can better understand family life in the present and in the future.

Notes

1. See, for example, John Demos, *A Little Commonwealth: Family Life in Plymouth Colony* (New York: Oxford University Press, 1970); John Demos and Sarane Spence Boocock (eds.), *Turning Points: Historical and Sociological Essays on the Family* (Chicago: The University of Chicago Press, 1978); Michael Gordon (ed.), *The American Family in Social-Historical Perspective*, 3rd ed. (New York: St. Martin's Press, 1983); Philip Greven, *Four Generations: Population, Land, and Family in Colonial Andover, Massachusetts* (Ithaca: Cornell University Press, 1970); Herbert Gutman, *The Black Family in Slavery and Freedom*, (New York: Pantheon, 1976); Kenneth A. Lockridge, *A New England Town: The First Hundred Years*, (New York: W. W. Norton & Company, 1970); and Theodore K. Rabb and Robert I. Rotberg (eds.), *The Family in History: Interdisciplinary Essays* (New York: Harper & Row, 1970).

2. For more complete data on trends in marriage, divorce, and remarriage, see Andrew Cherlin, *Marriage, Divorce, Remarriage* (Cambridge, MA: Harvard University Press, 1981).

3. See Peter Uhlenberg, "Death and the Family," *Journal of Family History* 5 (1980): 313–320.

4. See Peter Laslett, *The World We Have Lost*, 2nd ed. (New York: Charles Scribner's Sons, 1971).

5. See Lutz Berkner, "The Stem Family and the Developmental Cycle of the Peasant Household: An 18th-Century Austrian Example," *American Historical Review* LXXVII (1972): 398–418.

6. Historical data on female labor force participation in the United States can be found in a number of sources. See, for example, *The Statistical History of the United States from Colonial Times to the Present* (New York: Basic Books, 1976) and United States Bureau of the Census, *The Historical Statistics of the United States from Colonial Times to 1970, Bicentennial Edition* (Washington, DC: Government Printing Office, 1975).

7. See, for example, Peter Stein, *Single* (Englewood Cliffs, NJ: Prentice Hall, 1976). The best example of media coverage on singlehood is the flurry of popular articles that quickly appeared after a 1986 study was released projecting the rate of marriage among college-educated women. Both *Newsweek* ("The Marriage Crunch: If You're a Single Woman, Here Are Your Chances of Getting Married," June 2, 1986) and *People* ("Are These Old Maids? A Harvard-Yale Study Says that Most Single Women Over 35 Can Forget About Marriage," March 31, 1986) carried extensive cover stories examining the plight of single women. Little mention is made of where these patterns fit in historical perspective.

8. See Herbert G. Gutman, *The Black Family in Slavery and Freedom* (New York: Pantheon, 1976).

9. See George Masnick and Mary Jo Bane, *The Nation's Families: 1960–1990* (Boston: Auburn Publishing, 1980).

10. Data from the important research resulting from the Michigan Panel of Income Dynamics can be found in a number of volumes, such as Greg J. Duncan and James N. Morgan (eds.), *Five Thousand American Families—Patterns of Economic Progress* (Ann Arbor, MI: Institute for Social Research, 1979).

11. See Christopher Lasch, *Haven in a Heartless World: The Family Besieged* (New York: Basic Books, 1977).

12. For different versions of this legislation, see The Family Protection Act bill H.R. 311. 1981; The Family Protection Act bill H.R. 3955. 1981; The Family Protection Act bill S. 1378. 1981; and The Family Protection Act bill S. 1808, 1979.

13. See Edward L. Kain, "The Federal Government Should Not Foster Legislation Relating to the Family," in Harold Feldman and Andrea Purrot, *Human Sexuality: Contemporary Controversies* (Beverly Hills: Sage, 1984).

14. See Mary Jo Bane, *Here to Stay: American Families in the Twentieth Century* (New York: Basic Books, 1976).

15. See Willima F. Ogburn, "Cultural Lag as Theory" in Otis Dudley Duncan, *William F. Osburn on Culture and Social Change* (Chicago: University of Chicago Press, 1964).

The Family*

Mahmood Mamdani

The cultural and economic systems of a society exert considerable influence on a family's structure and functions. This chapter by Mahmood Mamdani is an excellent illustration of how families often operate within a traditional, rural, agrarian setting—in this case, a village in northern India. In such a setting, one of the family's primary functions is as an economic unit. Consequently, large families, an abundance of sons, patriarchal authority, strict differentiation of roles between husbands and wives and parents and children, are all highly valued and encouraged. In order to understand these family dynamics, one must look to the larger economic and cultural settings in which such families reside.

The struggle for survival and continued existence occupies the better part of an individual's time in Manupur (a village in northern India). There exists an urgency and immediacy about material interests that cannot escape even the casual visitor. Even though a little prosperity has come to Manupur within the last decade or so, for most farmers this has only meant that they can have three complete meals a day. While technological change has increased the productivity of their

---

land and labor, it has also made intensive agriculture possible and increased their workload.

Work is hard as well as time-consuming, and distractions are few and far between. Time is never allocated separately for work and for leisure: leisure is enjoyed only when the rains make it impossible to work, rest is possible only when fatigue demands it. There are no weekends; every day is a potential workday. In Manupur, life *is* work.

The rains may interrupt the activity of the men, especially the farmers, but not of the women. In fact, when a woman's husband is at home, he demands much more, and her work is increased. The major interruption in her work is pregnancy, but she assumes her normal workload up to the last three weeks of pregnancy and then limits herself to domestic work. Help is hired to do the outside work (for instance, tending the cattle) or a relative comes and helps. The woman stops work completely only a few hours before the birth; her confinement lasts no more than a week.

All but the very young and the very old make some productive contribution to the economy of the household. Older women spend their time spinning cotton into thread, a task which requires little physical labor and can be accomplished in short sittings. The thread is spun for the household or for someone who will pay for it in either money or grain.

Young girls, even when they go to school, spend their afternoons weaving mats. They make several patterns in colorful designs. A few will be used to decorate the house, while others will be sold in the village or in Khanna. Those that cannot be sold will be kept for the child's dowry. In their "free" time, young girls try to find paying tasks so that they can earn as much of their dowry as possible.

With work a total concern, even the few traditional distractions—such as festivals—have diminished in importance. Whereas the two important festivals of *Tij* and *Janmashtmi* were previously celebrated by the entire village, today only children take time out for rejoicing. Adults and young people simply add a few sweet dishes to the meal at the end of the day. In the same way, the number of visits paid to relatives outside the village (to the wife's family, for example) has been drastically curtailed. What were previously considered important social obligations have been reduced to polite social conventions. The most painful and direct effect has been on the aged. An old woman who was, as far as she could remember, in her late eighties or early nineties complained of the change, but with resignation: "Neglected today are grandparents, wells, and cows."

The family structure in Manupur is rigidly patriarchal and authoritarian. The father is the head of the family and exercises absolute control. In practice his authority might be shared to some degree, depending upon the family, with his wife, but he is at the top and the children are at the bottom. The child-parent relationship is simple: the parent commands, the child obeys. Age and experience are the yardsticks of merit and the claim to authority. A young child, however absorbed he or she may be in any form of play, will instantly stop at the most casual command of the parent.

An older man—and in Manupur that means one past his forties—who has a number of children in the house is assured a certain ease in life. When he returns from work, whatever the work may be, his youngest one will massage his head and feet, or his body, if it aches. He will bring water for a wash and a bath, and if it is very hot or humid, he will make lemon-sugar juice. Children perform a variety of small tasks that adults regard as tedious, time-consuming, and tiresome. Once in a while, a man without any small children will be seen carrying his own water from the pump or the well and cursing his fate for not having bestowed enough children upon him. Whether you are rich or poor, you are ensured these small luxuries if you have enough children.

Since the children's activity can be of considerable gain to the family, their time and their life are closely regulated by the family, more so as they become older. A young child is pampered and loved, all his needs catered to, until he is about six years old. The transition may begin at five, or even four, when children begin taking care of their younger brothers or sisters, but by six, the attitude of the elders and the life of the child have changed completely.

Older children take care of the younger ones, include them in their play, take them out in the fields in the morning and evening to be relieved, carry them on their hips when doing work, such as grazing animals. A young girl is often seen taking her younger brother or sister to school with her. Although the younger one is not old enough to attend, she takes him so she can take care of him. The school adjusts to the needs of the society, as does every institution in the village.

Darshana Kumari is 13 years old and a student in Grade eight. Her day begins at five in the morning when she gets up and makes the morning tea. Then she walks to the fields to relieve herself, taking the buffalo dung out to the dung pots. School lasts from 7:30 to 1:30. The next hour and a half is devoted to school work and the rest of the day, from 3:30 to 9:00 in the evening, is taken up with various household duties. Darshana's primary responsibility is taking care of the one buffalo. She takes it out for cleaning, grazing, and drinking. In the evening she milks it and sets some aside for making tea, a little more for making yoghurt, and the rest for making butter. After dinner she washes the dishes. Twice a week—on Sunday and Wednesday—she spends two hours washing her school clothes. Three years ago, at the age of ten, Darshana Kumari stopped spending her evenings playing with her girlfriends in the village fields. Why? "Because I had grown up. Only young ones play."

There is no adolescence in Manupur. There is only childhood and adulthood. The young in Manupur seldom display the carefree, spontaneous attitude that industrial society proverbially associates with youth. Children learn that if they are to be part of the family, they must contribute to it. Thus, children grow, not into youths, but into young adults.

The claim of the family on the lives of its children is total. Parents arrange the marriages of their children, and marriages are really a liaison between families: the primary factor is the economic position of the other family.

The fact that the family is the basic unit of work has important social implications. The discipline of work is reflected in the discipline of the family. The family is the most effective institution for maintaining discipline in society, and there are good reasons why the individual submits to family discipline. For an overwhelming majority in Manupur the financial enterprise which is its unit of work is a family enterprise and, therefore, its source of economic security. Even for those who do not work, the young and the aged, the family is the source of economic security. When a couple grows too old to work, their only shelter is among their children, and parents have a socially approved claim on the resources of their children. When no children have survived or none were born—most unusual, in either case—the parents continue to live in the family home and survive on the charity handed out by relations or other caste members. Life under such circumstances is said to be "a curse" and "most degrading."

Since daughters must always marry outside the village, security for old age depends solely on the number of sons a couple has. It is impossible for them to go and live in their daughter's household, since strong social taboos prevent even the contemplation of such a possibility. No father may take anything free from his daughter, and no brother from his sister. It is even inadmissible for a parent to spend a single night in the village where his married daughter lives.

The family also provides almost the only form of physical security. In Manupur, there are no police, or any other form of legally organized force. All conflicts theoretically go to the village *Panchayat*, which has the power to arbitrate such matters. The Panchayat, however, has no way to implement its decisions unless it calls upon law enforcement authorities from Khanna. Most important, the absence of a legally organized force means that the Panchayat has little power to maintain public peace in the community.

The need to guarantee physical security for the members of the family thus becomes one more reason parents look favorably on having a large family. Here is but one example. Puran Singh is in his fifties and has been witness or party to a number of fights; they are a significant part of his "reality." He praises God for giving him many sons, for sons bring prosperity, peace, and honor. He told me he hoped I realized that his sons were responsible for the fact that he was still alive. He scoffed at the idea of using contraceptives and added: "In these villages we have faction fights, and you win fights not with contraceptives but with men."

The factions that Puran Singh talked of have long been a feature of village life, but the social composition of these factions has changed as the social conditions in the village have changed. Previously, each faction was a *thola*, a collection of extended families, all related by blood.[1] The decline of the thola as a political institution has paralleled the decline of social ownership. The thola was based on one or another form of social property (even if it coexisted with private property) and on blood relations; the village is now a market society where private property dominates, and the faction is the *dhala*, a grouping of individual families which cuts across clan lines. Its members cooperate economically, are bound by social and ceremonial ties, and form a political alliance during village elections. When a joint family breaks up into two separate enterprises, each may join a different faction.

Although many villagers say the thola declined in importance as people became educated and less adverse to forming alliances across blood lines, dhala alliances are not in fact confined to the educated. The change has followed a change in economic organization—as the unit of work became less the joint family and more the semi-joint or nuclear family.

For the poor in Manupur, emergencies come not only as fights, but also as natural disasters. The most frequent emergency comes during the monsoon season when as many as three or four houses may be destroyed by the heavy rains. These are the dried-mud *kacha* houses, the weakest ones, the homes of the poor, which account for about 40 percent of the village. One victim of the rains one night in the summer of 1970 was Daulat, the drum beater. The next morning I found him squatting in front of the rubble that was once his house, as his wife collected their few belongings and tended their two young children. He lamented: "Look at my home. It has been wrecked by the rains. If I had enough people in my family, we could put it back together. Now I shall have to hire laborers to do it and that means putting a bandage on my stomach for quite some time to come."

When confronted with an emergency, and this includes physical violence, a villager can be fairly certain that his family members will support him, regardless of the merit of his position. This has "always been the case," and there is very good reason for it to be so. The family in Manupur is not only a group linked by ties of blood, but also by ties of money. The family is a financial enterprise, and a threat to a family member is also a threat to the family enterprise. What has changed, however, is that the relevant family unit is less often the joint family and more often the nuclear family.

We have seen again and again how children—especially sons—are vital to the people of Manupur. And so it is to be expected that religion, myth, tradition, and ritual will reinforce the belief in this necessity. A variety of mediums—song, story, proverb, or even the mere explanation of phenomena—are used for this purpose. The message transmitted is always the same: it is one's *dharma* (religious and social obligation) to have children: to desire as many children as possible is not only in the natural order of things but also an indication of virtue.

The marriage system in Manupur is exogamous. The husband stays within the village; the wife, though from the same caste, must come from outside the village. From her first day in the village, she is subtly pressured into accepting the needs of the family as more important than her personal needs, as her major and overriding obligation. She must consider herself first and foremost a mother, a source of labor power for the family. When she enters her husband's house, she touches her mother-in-law's feet with her fingers, signifying obedience and respect. Her mother-in-law responds: "May you have seven sons!" As she enters the house and greets her husband's relatives and the caste elders, they each have the same customary response: "Bathe in milk and you will have lots of sons." Folk songs, usually sung on occasions such as marriage, childbirth, or the harvest, sing the praises of the prolific mother and the fertile soil. A popular theme running through many stories is the love of the mother for the son; it is considered the purest form of human love. The mother who sacrifices for her son is said to perform the noblest sacrifice. The emphasis is upon motherhood as the supreme virtue and the most satisfying role for a woman. The message is clear: her dharma is to bear children, preferably sons.

Neither is society content with exercising mere social pressure. Severe penalties are imposed on the "barren" wife, and this includes not merely women who have no children, but women who have no sons. Discussing why a mother sometimes gives birth to a female and not a male baby, an Achuta mother commented: "It is written in Guru Nanak's *Granthsaheb* [the holy book of the Sikhs] that if you have bad karma you get more girls than boys."[2] The karma referred to here is that of the wife, not of the husband. A "barren" wife is a disgrace to the family; she is a bad omen, and she is treated accordingly. To some, she is even a "witch" who can cast evil spells, especially upon children. She can never attend the birth of a child or its celebration, and she is barred from participation in many other happy occasions. Childlessness is the main reason for divorce, and the only socially acceptable justification for polygamy.

Birth control advocates have often argued that since it is the wife who usually suffers the most from having many children (from the effects on her health of a lack of adequate spacing, from the increased demand on her time, and so on), she ought to be supplied with contraceptives she can use without her husband's knowledge. But even if the wife wants to limit the number of births, or to space them adequately, the social penalties for "barrenness" are sufficiently severe and often emphasized enough to stop even the most determined woman from following such a path.

The preference for a son over a daughter is clear, and tradition reinforces this too. It is often asserted that boys are conceived on moonlit nights, girls on dark ones. A boy is said to be conceived if sexual intercourse takes place in the first half of the night when the man is stronger, a girl if it takes place in the second half of the night when the woman is stronger.

Female infanticide, although said today to be nonexistent, was once a common practice among Punjab villagers. Even today, the preferential treatment of male over female clearly shows in the much higher infant death rate among females and in the resulting higher ratio of males over females in the general population.[3] (In most other parts of the world, females of a general population have lower death rates than males.) As *The Khanna Study* pointed out:

> Girls less than two years old had a substantially smaller chance of survival than boys of the same age; they died from the same causes, their mothers started them on solid food at the same age as boys, but their parents gave boys higher quality medical care. . .and possibly more supplementary food.[4]

As we might expect, the ratio of males to females is highest among those castes which have the greatest need for sons in their work, and is less high among the others. In *The Khanna Study* area, the preponderance of males over females is particularly marked among the farmers (1231:1000) and the least marked among other "high" service castes (1069:1000).[5]

Celebrations are kept to a minimum at the birth of a girl, but are particularly joyous if the child born is a boy. Furthermore, certain celebrations are held only after the birth of a son. The first occurs thirteen days after birth, when mango leaves are hung at the entrance of the house and a priest is invited for a meal. He sprinkles "holy" water on the mother and the male child to "purify and protect" them. Another similar celebration is held a year later. In addition, the Jajmani "clients" of the higher castes were traditionally given a gift only upon the birth of a son. And most important, the funeral pyre of a father must be lit by his son. The birth of a female child seems an occasion for silent mourning, that of a male child one for public rejoicing.

It should be emphasized that the purpose here is neither to give a static quality to the emerging picture nor to overemphasize the importance of social customs and beliefs. It is quite possible that even when society in Manupur changes, many of the songs, stories, proverbs, and customs described above will remain. At the same time, new ones will be created, ones that respond to the needs of a different society. Myth and tradition tend to survive even beyond the point of their social usefulness, but, at any point in time, there exists a measure of unity between belief and practice. It is that unity, the reinforcement belief lends to practice, that we have attempted to examine here.

Notes

1. The thola corresponds to the anthropologist's conception of a clan. It also corresponds to the *dhars* Oscar Lewis talks of in his study of village Rampur in Delhi state (see Oscar Lewis, *Village Life in Northern India* [Urbana: University of Illinois Press, 1958], pp. 113–154).

2. Needless to say, there is no such reference in the *Granthsaheb*.

3. *The Khanna Study*, p. 194.

4. Ibid., p. 195.

5. Ibid., p. 251, Table 33. This data refers to the Test and Control A population.

The preponderance of male over female babies among farmers had important implications for the institution of marriage in Manupur. When the babies came of age, the males among them far exceeded the females. The practice of polyandry developed in response to this dilemma. Only one brother married; the others shared his wife, and all tilled the land jointly. Polyandry was, by and large, confined to the poorest farmers in Manupur, to those who could promise the least "happiness" in marriage to a prospective bride. Today, however, female babies have a better chance of survival than in the past, and the preponderance of males is not as marked. As a result, more men in the village can find wives, and polyandry has diminished in importance.

Marriage in the People's Republic of China: Analysis of a New Law*

John W. Engel

Just as the economic system of a society can have an impact upon family dynamics (as seen in the previous reading on India), so too can a society's political system. A fascinating example of this is found in the People's Republic of China. John W. Engel describes how and why the communist government instituted a new law governing marriage. Traditional Chinese families were characterized by many of the traits and patterns that we saw in the previous reading. The new law was designed to break with those traditional patterns. In addition to the marriage law, the communist government has also sought to substantially reduce the high birth rates of families through the implementation of their one-child policy.

Family relationships in prerevolutionary China were guided by tradition, religion, and law for 2,000 years. In Confucian ideology, the universe had a natural order in which every person had a place and a proper role. Family organization was a critical element in the natural order. Family relationships were prescribed and taught as part of the Confucian ethical system. As a result, the traditional Chinese

*Source: *Journal of Marriage and the Family,* "Marriage in the People's Republic of China: Analysis of a New Law," John W. Engel; 46:4, pp. 955–961, 1984.

family became a model of strength and stability and the primary social and economic unit in prerevolutionary China.

A New Marriage Law for the People's Republic of China

In the twentieth century, communist revolutionaries worked and fought to create a classless socialist society in China. Their goal required redistribution of the wealth and power that were traditionally held and exercised by families. Therefore, the revolution included and depended upon change in the Chinese family. Within a year of the establishment of the People's Republic of China in 1949, a marriage law was passed that "was intended to cause . . . fundamental changes . . . aimed at family revolution by destroying all former patterns . . . and building up new relationships on the basis of new law and new ethics" (Meijer, 1971:5). Indeed, according to China's 1950 marriage law (Buxbaum, 1978; Engel, 1982; Meijer, 1971), "the feudal marriage system . . . shall be abolished. . . . The New Democratic marriage system . . . shall be put into effect." Whether a result of legislation or other factors such as economics, changes in Chinese family relationships have occurred and have been documented in the family studies literature (Huang, 1982; Liu and Yu, 1977; Rosen, 1978; Salaff, 1973; Walstedt, 1978). However, approximately 30 years after the 1950 marriage law was promulgated, China still faces serious problems (e.g., population growth) requiring continuing efforts to modify and control marriage and family life.

A new marriage law was passed in 1980 and took effect in 1981 (*Beijing Review*, 1981c: 24–27). This paper analyzes the parts of China's 1980 law that deal with marriage contracts (i.e., articles 1–8). Other sections of the law that deal with parent-child relations or divorce are beyond the scope of this discussion. Articles dealing with arranged marriage, "marriage by purchase" and dowry customs, concubinage or polygamy, marriage restrictions, rituals, and residence customs are analyzed in terms of their contexts in traditional and modern China; and implications for continuity and change are discussed. The analyses and discussion are based primarily on publications of the Chinese government and approved press and on publications of China scholars and watchers from the West.

The following articles are included in the 1980 marriage law of the People's Republic of China:[1]

> Article 1. This law is the fundamental code governing marriage and family relations.
> Article 2. The marriage system based on the free choice of partners, on monogamy and on equal rights for the sexes, is put into effect. The lawful rights and interests of women, children and the aged are protected. Family planning is practiced.
> Article 3. Marriage upon arbitrary decision by any third party, mercenary marriage and any other acts of interference in the freedom of marriage are prohibited. The exaction of money or gifts in connection with marriage is prohibited. Bigamy is prohibited. Within the family maltreatment and desertion are prohibited.

The Marriage Contract

Marriage in traditional or prerevolutionary China was a contract between families rather than a contract between individuals. Both the search for eligibles and mate selection were based on family needs and values rather than on attraction, love, or emotional involvement. Personal attraction and love between bride and groom were considered unnecessary, if not harmful, and precautions often were taken to prevent emotional involvements from disrupting family stability (Engel, 1982; Lang, 1946). Social and economic status or class was the most important criterion by which eligibles were evaluated in the matchmaking process. Arrangement of a marriage involved negotiation of a "bride price" (Parish and White, 1978), or gifts to be paid to the family of the bride, and sometimes also a dowry of furniture, clothing, or jewelry to be provided by the bride's family for use in her new home. Marriage of sons was much more important than marriage of daughters, for reasons discussed later under Patrilocal Residence Customs. Peasant or poor families sometimes sold a daughter into servitude or arranged a daughter's marriage in order to obtain a dowry, so that they could pay the bride price in an arrangement of marriage for a son.

The 1980 marriage law (Article 3) forbids "mercenary marriages" in which a bride price or dowry is paid and prohibits "exaction of money or gifts in connection with marriage." In rural areas of contemporary China, bride price payments are still common, while dowries have become smaller and less common than in the past (Parish and White, 1978). In urban areas the bride price custom continues in the form of gifts to the bride or her family, while the dowry custom has nearly disappeared (Manni, 1981). Without a dowry to balance expenses, marriage involving bride price payments can be very expensive. Wedding feasts have become more expensive, sometimes replacing the dowry as a symbol of status (Salaff, 1973). Some families go into debt to finance a marriage, but the fact that marriage brings another worker and wage earner into the family helps to reduce the burden. Sometimes marriage becomes analogous to a business investment for the future. Indeed, the popular press occasionally publishes letters from romantic young men who decry their inability to afford marriage and the businesslike nature of marriage in contemporary China (*Honolulu Star-Bulletin*, 1980).

While governmental efforts to eliminate "marriage by purchase" continue, traditional values and customs appear to be remarkably resistant to change. Changes that do occur in the future may be as much a reaction to economic conditions as a reflection of legislation and law enforcement.

Concubinage and Polygamy

The 1980 marriage law prohibits concubinage and polygamy by prohibiting "mercenary marriage" and bigamy (Article 3). Concubinage was an acceptable and relatively common method of expanding the family for the upper class in traditional China. It took some wealth to purchase a concubine and to support her and the children she produced. It appears that concubines were taken whenever a

family could financially afford to expand. Concubinage was specifically prohibited by the 1950 marriage law. In recent research Parish and White (1978) found
no evidence of concubinage in their sample and concluded that it had disappeared in modern China. Nevertheless, there is some evidence that concubinage
still exists in contemporary China. The *Kwangchow Evening News* (cited in
Parade, 1981) reported that at least 20 married men in Kwangtung Province had
taken concubines. The newspaper printed a letter from four delegates to the
Provincial People's Congress in which they complained that "in the last few years
. . . married men taking concubines has emerged . . . [as an] . . . extremely bad
influence . . . [and that] . . . the masses are indignant."

That the law must continue to prohibit polygamy suggests that the government is well aware of the tenacity of tradition and of the need for continued vigilance. The government is also practical. In Tibet, an "autonomous region" of
China where polygamy is still common, the law has been modified to allow continuation of those polygamous marriages that were contracted before the 1980
law took effect (*Beijing Review*, 1981e).

Arranged Marriage Versus "Freedom of Marriage"

The ideal marriage in traditional China was arranged by parents or by parental
representatives such as family elders, wise relatives, go-betweens, or professional matchmakers. Young people themselves had little choice in the matter and
sometimes met for the first time on their wedding day. In extreme cases, when
the betrothed man died before the wedding, the bride "had to go through a marriage ceremony with a wooden figure, a wooden or stone tablet, or a rooster"
(*Beijing Review*, 1981f:22); and then she was expected to remain single for the
rest of her life.

The 1980 marriage law legislates "freedom of marriage" (Article 3), "free
choice of partners" (Article 2), and forbids "marriage upon arbitrary decision by
any third party . . . and any other acts of interference in the freedom of marriage"
(Article 3). Similarly, the law contains the following provision:

> Article 4. Marriage must be based upon the complete willingness of the two
> parties. Neither party shall use compulsion and no third party is allowed to inter-
> fere.

While there is a trend towards increasing freedom of choice in contemporary China (Croll, 1981; Salaff, 1973), marriage arrangements in which individuals
have little or no freedom of choice still persist, particularly in the rural and more
remote areas (*Beijing Review*, 1981b). *The People's Daily* (cited in *Honolulu Star-
Bulletin*, 1981) reported the following example of "compulsion." Xu Younghua
had fallen in love with a young man; but her brother disapproved, used force to
stop her from seeing her boyfriend, and arranged for her marriage into another
family. Furthermore, it was arranged that this other family also would provide a

bride for Xu's younger brother. Xu fled from the wedding feast to her boyfriend's house, and the two of them committed suicide by blowing themselves up with homemade explosives. For his part in the tragedy, the "interfering" brother was sentenced to three years in jail. *The People's Daily*, which often serves as the voice of the government, indicated that such forced arranged marriages still occur and editorialized that readers learn from such tragedies that marriage should be based on free choice by those directly involved.

Compulsion also occurs when women are kidnapped and sold. One recent report (*Honolulu Star-Bulletin*, 1982a) indicated that in 1981 over 750 young women were abducted from their homes in the Chuxiong region of Yunnan Province and offered for sale as brides to peasants in other areas of China. Similarly, in one region of Sichuan Province, 68 abductions were reported in the first 10 months of 1982 (*Honolulu Star-Bulletin*, 1983).

In contrast to such extremes, the official ideal is for young adults to choose their own mates. Various compromises between arrangement and free choice are prevalent in contemporary China: (a) parental arrangement of marriage after consultation with the young couple, (b) arrangement by go-between on behalf of individuals, and (c) free choice with consent of parents. Despite the fact that each of these compromises potentially could involve some interference, they usually are construed as progress towards the new ideals rather than as remnants of the feudal practices that the law is designed to eliminate. Most contemporary young, urban Chinese find spouses in one of two ways: (a) a relative or friend acts as matchmaker to find a potential mate and sets up a meeting, or (b) the young person finds someone without assistance (*Beijing Review*, 1981b).

Opportunities to meet and develop relationships with eligible partners are relatively limited, so that young people still may depend upon others to "arrange" a meeting, if not the marriage itself. Professional matchmakers continue to offer their services, despite the fact that they were singled out for criticism and confiscation of fees during the 1966–1976 Cultural Revolution. Parish and White (1978) found professional matchmaking services to be available in 74 percent of their sample of villages in Kwangtung Province. It remains to be seen whether the 1980 marriage law (Article 4: "no third party is allowed to interfere") will be interpreted as forbidding professional matchmaking services. The survival of the matchmaker is, in itself, evidence of a continuing need for some kind of matchmaking service; however, there does appear to be a trend towards decreased use of professional matchmaking services and increased use of arranged introductions by friends and relatives. In the latter case, the nonprofessional matchmakers are typically expected to do much of the work of the professional, including investigation of character and family background, as well as arrangement of introductions. Recently, "marriage introduction services" have become popular in some of the communes and cities (*Beijing Review*, 1981a; Yuwen, 1981). These services appear to be encouraged by the government, probably because they are organized on a nonprofit basis and tend to foster the ideals for marriage that are set forth in the marriage law.

Dating in contemporary China, when it does occur, is often different from that practiced in Western countries. In some cases, young couples do not date until after they are engaged (*Beijing Review*, 1981b); in other cases, dating is construed to be much more serious than it is in the West. For example, the acceptance of an invitation to a movie may be interpreted as tacit agreement to eventual marriage (*Beijing Review*, 1982). Opportunities for dating couples to develop intimacy are limited by the lack of privacy that results from severe population problems, shortage of housing, overcrowding, and no personal automobiles. Young Chinese have to be very creative to find a place where they can be alone together. Nevertheless, most large cities have small parks where young couples can go at night for some limited privacy, and many do manage to fall in love and carry on romances. With the 1980 marriage law and government policies, moreover, mutual selection through dating and relationship development should become increasingly common.

Marriage Age Limits

In traditional China parents were obligated to arrange a marriage for each child as soon as the child reached marriageable age. Poor families were less able to support children and tended to arrange marriages earlier than wealthy families. Betrothal of young children was common; in some cases children were betrothed before they were born (Lang, 1946). In 1950, the communist government prohibited child betrothal and set a minimum marriage age of 20 years for men and 18 for women. A gradual rise over the years in average age at which Chinese marry has been described by Parish and White (1978), suggesting that the 1950 law was at least partially successful. The 1980 law sets even higher marriage age limits:

> Article 5. No marriage shall be contracted before the man has reached 22 years of age and the woman 20 years of age. Late marriage and late childbirth should be encouraged.

Late marriage is officially encouraged in contemporary China. The minimum age for marriage currently allowed by local registration officials varies considerably from place to place, from lower limits established by the law for the whole country to higher limits established by local governments and applied according to circumstances. For example, registration officials may enforce higher age limits for college students. In one instance, the minimum age for marriage was enforced at 28 years of age for men and 25 for women (*Time*, 1980).

Late marriage and late childbirth are critical elements in China's efforts to control population growth. Current economic conditions, including the cost of marriage and a shortage of jobs and housing, should augment governmental efforts to encourage postponement of marriage and childbirth in the future.

Marriage Restrictions

Throughout Chinese history various kinds of marriage have been forbidden. In arranging a marriage in traditional China, parents followed rules of clan exogamy. A marriage between relatives of the same surname was forbidden by custom and law (Lang, 1946). Marriage between people with the same family name had to be avoided even when they were from different clans (Meijer, 1971); however, marriages between cousins of different surnames were common (Lang, 1946). Some mixed social-status marriages also were forbidden. For example, an official could not marry a prostitute, a free person could not marry a slave, and Buddhist and Taoist monks could not marry at all (Meijer, 1971).

The 1950 marriage law prohibited marriages between people lineally related by blood but left questions about collateral blood relationships up to local custom. It prohibited marriages when one party was sexually impotent or when one party suffered from venereal disease, mental disorder, or leprosy. The corresponding article of the 1980 law states:

> Article 6. Marriage is not permitted in any of the following circumstances:
> (1) Where the man and woman are lineal relatives by blood or collateral relatives by blood (up to the third degree of relationship).
> (2) Where one party is suffering from leprosy, a cure not having been effected, or from any other disease which is regarded by medical science as rendering a person unfit for marriage.

Thus, the 1980 marriage law is more specific and restrictive in terms of prohibited relationships than the 1950 law. On the other hand, the 1980 law does not specify sexual impotence, venereal disease, or mental disorder as did the 1950 law. One can only speculate regarding whether these conditions are no longer a source of concern in contemporary China. Nevertheless, the final clause, "or from any other disease which is regarded by medical science as rendering a person unfit for marriage," leaves plenty of room for creative interpretation and application.

Wedding Rituals and Registration

The marriage rites for a primary wife in traditional China were prescribed in the ancient classics, *I Li* and *Li Chi*, and were followed with slight modifications for 2,500 years (Lang, 1946). The traditional ceremonies, following betrothal and date setting, were carried out by family members. Neither priests nor officials were necessary, since the head of the family was the "minister" of the family religion and the head of the basic administrative unit of the state. Traditional ceremonies could last several days. They typically involved a ritualistic transfer of the bride from one family to another, family religious acts, large feasts, and other wedding customs (Freedman, 1970). In the patrilocal tradition of China, the bride was not only relocating to live with her husband but also becoming a new person by giving up her place, identity, and rights as a daughter in her father's family to become a daughter-in-law in the family of her husband. In the transfer ceremonies, the bride typically was dressed in red, the color of joy and happiness, and carried in a sedan chair, followed by her dowry, from her father's household to the household of her husband's family. If households were relatively close in proximity, the wedding procession often took a longer route.

After a wedding feast, the bride was taken to the bridal chamber and unveiled by her husband (Mace and Mace, 1960). In the ideal "blind marriage," this was the first time the husband saw his wife's face. Following unveiling, a "disturbance of the room" (Freedman, 1970) or "tumult of the bridal room" (Mace and Mace, 1960) occurred, during which the bride was exhibited in her bedroom and teased by the guests. Following this ordeal, the newlyweds were left alone for the night. Sexual consummation was to occur before the third day or before the customary ritual visit to the bride's family of origin. According to Freedman (1957) the consummation was more of a virginity test than a formalization of marriage. Virginity of the bride, but not the groom, was an implied condition of the marriage contract. Failure to provide proof of virginity could result in dismissal, divorce, or reclamation of the bride price. Finally, to complete the traditional rites of marriage, the newlyweds made a formal visit to the bride's family of origin, where the bride was received and treated as a guest rather than a daughter.

Weddings in contemporary China vary considerably in the extent to which they follow tradition. Since 1950, the Chinese government has encouraged very simple, civil weddings centered around registration at a government office. Thus, the 1980 marriage law prescribes:

> Article 7. Both the man and the woman desiring to contract a marriage shall register in person with the marriage registration office. If the proposed marriage is found to be in conformity with the provisions of this law, registration shall be granted and a marriage certificate issued. The relationship of husband and wife is established when a marriage certificate is acquired.

The Chinese press depicts an official ideal in which a young couple decide to marry, go to a government office to register the marriage, and then live together with very little ceremony or expense. "Extravagant" weddings are discouraged (*Beijing Review*, 1981d). For marriage to be legal, the 1980 marriage law requires only that registration occur; however, the law gives the state and its representatives responsibility for interpreting the law in specific cases. In effect, this gives the state and its representatives the control once exercised by families over mate selection and marriage. Prior to registration, permission may have to be obtained from factories or work units. While such "modern" weddings have become increasingly common in the cities, they appear to be relatively rare in the countryside. Parish and White (1978) found that weddings in rural Kwangtung usually involved considerable ceremony and expense. Typically, both families have wedding feasts. Bicycles have been substituted for sedan-chairs, but the bride is still fetched with some fanfare and transported to her new home with her husband's family according to patrilocal customs. There is still some teasing on the wedding night before young couples can be alone together. Rural couples appear to participate in two weddings: first they register and thereby satisfy the law, and then they celebrate a wedding ceremony with their families and friends.

Patrilocal Residence Customs

According to Chinese tradition, a bride was expected to leave her family of origin when she married to live with and become a part of her husband's family. This meant that only sons (and their wives and children) would be available to continue the family's ancestor worship and to provide for parents in their old age. Therefore, daughters were valued less than were sons, and residence customs reinforced sexual inequality in traditional China. Women were kept subjugated, subservient, and dependent. Their status in society was described by the poet Fu Hsuan as follows: "How sad it is to be a woman. Nothing on earth is held so cheap" (Tavris, 1974:44). Indeed, in extreme circumstances female infanticide was practiced (Baker, 1979), and "girls were bought and sold like slaves" (Huang, 1982:775).

While great strides have been made towards sexual equality in contemporary China (Parish and White, 1978; Walstedt, 1978), the desire for sons rather than daughters is still strong among many of the people (*Honolulu Star-Bulletin*, 1982b). In a review of fertility control efforts in the People's Republic, Huang (1982) pointed out how sexual inequality interferes with efforts to reduce population growth. Parents who believe that only a son will provide for them in their old age tend not to support or cooperate with the new one-child-per-family ideal and fertility control efforts, especially when they already have one child who is a daughter. To the extent that patrilocal residence customs continue to be practiced in contemporary China, parents will want sons as old-age insurance and consider daughters to be of less value, and parents will continue having children until they have a son or enough sons to provide for them in their old age. This "feudal" way of thinking competes with and sabotages governmental efforts to encourage one-child families and to control population growth.

The 1980 marriage law provides an alternative to the traditional patrilocal residence custom that has implications for sexual equality and population control in the People's Republic. Specifically, the new marriage law states:

> Article 8. After a marriage has been registered, the woman may become a member of the man's family, or the man may become a member of the woman's family, according to the agreed wishes of the two parties.

The law encourages sexual equality by making daughters just as valuable as sons in terms of potential old-age insurance. Now daughters need not necessarily leave their families of origin when they marry. Daughters can give their parents a son (-in-law) to live with them and help support them in their old age. Furthermore, daughters themselves can be seen and valued as potential old-age insurance. This should reduce some of the motivation for having sons and some of the resistance to one-child family ideals and population control efforts.

Despite general trends toward nuclear families and away from patrilocal residences (Yunkang and Naigu, 1983), the law does not mention the Western ideal of neolocal residence (i.e., establishing an independent residence, separate from in-laws) as an alternative. While this may be a reflection of economic realities in contemporary China, it also suggests that the primary intent of this article relates to sexual equality and population control.

Conclusion

In conclusion, the success of the socialist revolution in China depends upon revolutionary change in the Chinese family. Within a year of the establishment of the People's Republic of China, a marriage law was passed that was designed to bring about fundamental changes in family relationships. Thirty years later a new marriage law was passed to replace the 1950 law. The passage and content of the 1980 law suggests that the Chinese family has been remarkably stable and resistant to change despite concerted governmental efforts to bring about change. Although China's past continues to pervade the present, changes have occurred, nevertheless. Conjugal relationships have become more important, and nuclear family structures have become more common. Instead of, or along with the family, the state now controls who, when, and how a person may marry. Changes, however, are more noticeable in urban than in rural areas; publication and enforcement of the law appear to be more successful in urban areas. The fact that a new law was designed and passed suggests that there are still problems and that there is still a great deal of work to be done before the traditional Chinese marriage system is replaced by the revolutionary ideals of the communist government.

Note

1. The translation of the law quoted in this paper was published by the *Beijing Review* (1981c:24–27). An earlier unpublished translation, by Chi-hsien Tuan of the East-West Center Population Institute, augmented interpretation and analysis of the law.

References

BAKER, H.D. 1979. *Chinese Family and Kinship.* New York: Columbia University Press.

Beijing Review 1981a. "Booming marriage introduction services." May 4:27–28.

———— 1981b. "Changes in the marriage conventions." May 4:20–22.

———— 1981c. "China's marriage law." March 16:24–27.

———— 1981d. "Extravagant weddings criticized." January 19:8.

———— 1981e. "The marriage law in Tibet." May 18:6.

———— 1981f. "Woman leader on new marriage law." March 16:21–23.

———— 1982. "Shimei youths: their spare time life." March 15:25–26.

BUXBAUM, D.C. (ed.). 1978. *Chinese Family Law and Social Change.* Seattle: University of Washington Press.

CROLL, E. 1981. *The Politics of Marriage in Contemporary China.* Cambridge, England: Cambridge University Press.

ENGEL, J.W. 1982. *Changes in Male-Female Relationships and Family Life in the People's Republic of China.* Honolulu: Hawaii Institute of Tropical Agriculture and Human Resources (Research Series 014).

FREEDMAN, M. 1970. *Family and Kinship in Chinese Society.* Stanford, CA: Stanford University Press.

Honolulu Star Bulletin. 1980. "Too many China marriages are like business deals, letter says." January 31:C-6.

———— 1981. "Lovers die in explosion." January 8:A-11.

———— 1982a. "Chinese brides offered for sale." May 16:A-24.

_____ 1982b. "Having a daughter in China can be dangerous." October 24:C-4.

_____ 1983. "A bride can still be bought in China—illegally." January 1:B-1.

HUANG, L.J. 1982. "Planned fertility of one-couple/one-child policy in the People's Republic of China." *Journal of Marriage and the Family* 44 (August): 775–784.

LANG, O. 1946. *Chinese Family and Society.* New Haven: Yale University Press.

LIU, W.T. and YU, E.S. 1977. "Variations in women's roles and family life under the socialist regime in China." *Journal of Comparative Family Studies* 8 (2): 201–213.

MACE, D. and MACE, V. 1960. *Marriage: East and West.* Garden City, NY: Doubleday.

MANNI, T. 1981. "Why new marriage law was necessary." *China Reconstructs* (March):17–21.

MEIJER, M.J. 1971. *Marriage Law and Policy in the Chinese People's Republic.* Hong Kong: Hong Kong University Press.

Parade. 1981. "Concubine comeback." June 28:9.

PARISH, W.L. and WHITE, M.K. 1978. *Village and Family in Contemporary China.* Chicago: University of Chicago Press.

SALAFF, J. 1973. "The emerging conjugal relationship in the People's Republic of China." *Journal of Marriage and the Family* 35 (November): 705–717.

TAVRIS, C. 1974. "The speak bitterness revolution." *Psychology Today* May: 43–44.

Time. 1980. "Young love and revolution." June 30: 12.

WALSTEDT, J.J. 1978. "Reform on women's roles and family structures in the recent history of China." *Journal of Marriage and the Family* 40 (May): 379–392.

YUNKANG, P. and NAIGU, P. 1983. "Urban family structures and their changes." *Beijing Review* (February 28): 25–27.

YUWEN, Y. 1981. "Finding a wife/husband in Shanghai." *China Reconstructs* (March): 21–23.

The Amish Family*

John A. Hostetler

Cultural differences in families occur not only across nations, but also within a single country. A prime example are the Amish in the United States. As John A. Hostetler notes, "The Amish are a church, a community, a spiritual union, a conservative branch of Christianity, a religion, a community whose members practice simple and austere living, a familistic entrepreneuring system, and an adaptive human community." Consequently, it is not surprising that families residing within such communities look much different than those in mainstream America. This chapter provides a glimpse into the life cycle of the Amish—from birth, to finding a partner in marriage, to retirement and old age.

Small communities, with their distinctive character—where life is stable and intensely human—are disappearing. Some have vanished from the face of the earth, others are dying slowly, but all have undergone change as they have come into contact with an expanding machine civilization. The merging of diverse peoples into a common mass has produced tension among members of the minorities and the majority alike.

*Source: John A. Hostetler, "The Amish Family," *Amish Society* (Baltimore, MD: The Johns Hopkins University Press, 1993), pp. 3, 4, 145–170.

The Old Order Amish, who arrived on American shores in colonial times, have survived in the modern world in distinctive, viable, small communities. They have resisted the homogenization process more successfully than others. In planting and harvest time one can see their bearded men working the fields with horses and their women hanging out the laundry in neat rows to dry. Many American people have seen Amish families, with the men wearing broad-brimmed black hats and the women in bonnets and long dresses, in railway depots or bus terminals. Although the Amish have lived with industrialized America for centuries, they have moderated its influence on their personal lives, their families, their communities, and their values.

The Amish are often perceived by other Americans to be relics of the past who live an austere, inflexible life dedicated to inconvenient and archaic customs. They are seen as renouncing both modern conveniences and the American dream of success and progress. But most people have no quarrel with the Amish for doing things the old-fashioned way. Their conscientious objection was tolerated in wartime, for after all, they are meticulous farmers who practice the virtues of work and thrift.

In recent years the status of the Amish in the minds of most Americans has shifted toward a more favorable position.[1] This change can scarcely be attributed to anything the Amish have done; rather, it is the result of changes in the way Americans perceive their minority groups. A century ago, hardly anyone knew the Amish existed. A half-century ago they were viewed as an obscure sect living by ridiculous customs, as stubborn people who resisted education and exploited the labor of their children. Today the Amish are the unwilling objects of a thriving tourist industry on the Eastern Seaboard. They are revered as hard-working, thrifty people with enormous agrarian stamina, and by some, as islands of sanity in a culture gripped by commercialism and technology run wild. The Amish are a church, a community, a spiritual union, a conservative branch of Christianity, a religion, a community whose members practice simple and austere living, a familistic entrepreneuring system, and an adaptive human community.

Procreation, nurture, and socialization are the major functions of the Amish family. The central role that the family is given in Amish culture can be illustrated in many ways. The family has authority over the individual not only during childhood but also during adolescence and later life. Certain loyalties to parents, relatives, and grandparents may change, but they will never cease. The size of the church district is measured by the number of families (households), not by the number of baptized persons. It is the families that take turns having the preaching service. Maps and directories of settlements made by Amish persons list the households and often the names of the parents, their birth and marriage dates, and the birth dates of the children as well. After marriage it is recognized that the most important family function is childbearing. Parents stress not their own individual rights but their responsibilities and obligations for the correct nurture of their children. They consider themselves accountable to God for the spiritual welfare of their children.

Mate-Finding

The young Amishman's choice of a wife is limited or conditioned by his value system. He must obtain a partner from his own Amish faith, but not necessarily from his own community. Because of minimum contact with Amish young people of other communities and states, marriages in the large settlements have for the most part taken place within the immediate community. The choice of a mate is also governed by the rules of the church. First-cousin marriages are taboo, while second-cousin marriages are discouraged but do occur infrequently. Forbidden in Lancaster Country is marriage to a "Swartz" cousin—that is, to the child of a first cousin.[2]

There are certain exceptions to the rule that marriage must be endogenous with respect to group affiliation. It is always permissible to marry into a more orthodox affiliation if the more liberal party joins the conservative group. Young people intermarry freely among Amish districts and settlements that maintain fellowship with one another.

The occasion that provides the best opportunity for young people to meet is the Sunday evening singing. The singing is usually held at the same house where the morning preaching was held. The youth from several districts usually combine for the singing. This occasion provides interaction among young people on a much broader base than is possible in the single district.

On Sunday evening after the chores are done, the young folks make preparations for the singing. The young man puts on his very best attire, brushes his hat and suit, and makes sure that his horse and buggy are clean and neat in appearance. He may take his sister or his sister's friend to the singing, but seldom his own girlfriend. If he does take his own girl, he will arrange to pick her up about dusk at the end of a lane or at a crossroad.

A singing is not regarded as a devotional meeting. Young people gather around a long table, boys on one side and girls on the other. The singing is conducted entirely by the unmarried. Only the fast tunes are sung. Girls as well as boys announce hymns and lead the singing. Between selections there is time for conversation. After the singing, which usually ends formally about ten o'clock, an hour or more is spent in joking and visiting. Those boys who do not have a date usually arrange for a *Mädel* ("girl") at this time.

Although there are other occasions when young folks get together, such as bees, weddings, and frolics, the singing is the primary occasion for boy-girl association. Both the boy and the girl look upon each other as a possible mate. A boy or girl may "quit" whenever he or she pleases. The usual age for courtship, called *rumspringa* ("running around"), begins for the boy at sixteen, and for the girl between fourteen and sixteen. The onset of courtship is usually not openly discussed within the family or among friends. Excessive teasing by siblings or friends at the wrong time is considered invasive. Respecting privacy, or at least pretending not to know, is a prevailing mode of behavior, even among parents.

Among themselves, young people seldom refer to their boyfriends on girlfriends by first name. The pronoun "he" or "she" is used instead. The terms *beau* and *Kal* ("fellow") are used in general conversation. The term *dating* is used, but has no dialect equivalent.

Besides taking his girl home after the singing on Sunday evening, the young man who has a "steady" girl will see her every other Saturday night. When Saturday evening comes, he dresses in his best; he makes little ado about his departure and attempts to give the impression to his younger brothers and sisters that he is going to town on business.

Before entering the home of his girl, he makes sure that the "old folks" have retired. Standard equipment for every young Amishman of courting age is a good flashlight. When the girl sees the light focused on her window, she knows that her boyfriend has arrived, and she quietly goes downstairs to let him in. The couple may be together in the home until the early morning hours on such occasions. They often play games and enjoy the company of another couple. The clatter of horses' hoofs on hard-surface roads in the early hours of the morning is evidence of young suitors returning home.

The old way of spending time together was for a boy and girl to lie on the bed fully clad. The Amish have no uniform word in their speech for this practice, which to them in earlier times was very ordinary. In English this behavior pattern is known as *bundling*. It is an old custom, having been practiced in Europe and in early American colonies, especially in large, unheated houses. The practice has been sharply condemned by most Amish leaders, though it is defended by some. In the nineteenth century new settlements were started by families that wanted to get away from the practice. Those Amish communities that have assimilated most to the American society have tended to oppose the practice of bundling the most. Groups that have consistently retained their traditional culture with firm and respected sex codes have been least opposed. The practice has disappeared without argument in other areas with the influx of modern home conveniences (living-room suites, etc.) and a wider range of social contacts with the outside world.

Mate-finding takes place in the confines of the little community rather than outside it. Conflict and casualties resulting from mismating are absorbed by the culture. Conflicts are less obvious here than in the greater society. The wedding is a climactic experience for family and community, and the families of both bride and bridegroom take an active part in helping the newlyweds to establish a home.

It is an important task of the family to provide a dowry. Homemade objects and crafts are the usual items. Furthermore, it is understood that each person invited to a wedding will bring a gift for the new couple. These tokens of friendship, which are usually displayed on the bed in an upstairs bedroom, consist of dishes, kerosene lamps, bedspreads, blankets, tablecloths, towels, clocks, handkerchiefs, and small farm tools.

The parents of the bride and bridegroom also provide furniture, livestock, and sometimes basic equipment when the couple moves into their home. For instance, one bridegroom, an only son, had the farm deeded over to him together with the farm machinery and livestock. The bride received from her parents a cow, tables, chairs, a new stove, dishes, bedding, and many other items. The dowry of the bride was in this case not unusual. All mothers by tradition make a few quilts and comforters for each child. These are usually made years in advance so that they will be ready when needed. One housewife made three quilts and two comforters for each child; she had seven boys and three girls.

Married-Pair Living

Social roles are well defined within the Amish family. The force of tradition, religious teaching, and emphasis on the practical help to make it so. Family organization is strictly monogamous and patriarchal. Overall authority tends to belong to the father, but there are varying degrees of practice in specific families. In keeping with a biblical teaching (I Cor. 11:3), the man is the head of the woman just as Christ is the head of the church. The wife has an immortal soul and is an individual in her own right. Although she is to be obedient to her husband, her first loyalty is to God. In marriage husband and wife become "one flesh," a union which is terminated only with death. There is no provision for divorce. The wife follows her husband's leadership and example but decides as an individual whether she is ready for communion. In church council she has an equal vote but not an equal "voice." Should her husband sin to the extent that he is placed under the ban, she, like all members, will shun him. The husband would do the same if his wife were under the ban. Important family decisions typically are joint decisions. The Amish wife participates actively in any decisions to move to a different locality, which was not true of what was called the "corporation wife."[3]

The status of Amish women is positively related to the degree to which they produce economic goods and services essential to the family. Goods produced on Amish farms, such as fruits and vegetables, meat, and dairy products, help to support the family.[4] Women are productive because they are engaged in subsistence agriculture and they also produce children needed for work on the family farm. They preserve large quantities of meat and vegetables for the family. They also make clothing for all the family members. Women who live on farms are accorded greater economic importance than Amish women who live in other settings. The Amish as a whole recognize the important contributions women make. Men cannot farm without wives and vice versa. Although Amish society is acknowledged to be patriarchal, the division of labor is more equal than most outsiders realize. Amish men seldom compliment women, but they daily show how much they esteem them.

Cooperation between husband and wife prevails in differing degrees, depending somewhat on the make-up of the personalities and their adjustment. The line of authority is not rigid, however, as an example will indicate. A man and his wife called at the home of a neighbor to see a bed that was for sale. He remained seated in the buggy while she entered the house and inspected the bed. Undecided, and not willing to commit herself without the encouragement of her husband, she called him. After both had looked at the bed and pondered over the price, she said, "What do you think?" He replied, "You are the boss of the house." After a few gestures that indicated she approved of the purchase, he wrote out a check for the amount asked.

The wife is often consulted when family problems arise, and she exercises her powers in rearing the children, but her husband's word is regarded as final in domestic matters. She is her husband's helper but not his equal. An Amish woman knows what is expected of her in the home, and her attitude is normally one of willing submission. This is not to suggest that there are no exceptions, for the writer has known families where the wife exerted influence out of proportion to the usual pattern. In practice, the farm is the Amishman's kingdom, and his wife is his general manager of household affairs.

Property, whether household goods or farm equipment, is spoken of as "ours" within the family. In actuality, however, any transaction involving the sale or purchase of property is made through the husband or has his approval. Farms are usually owned jointly by husband and wife to ensure legal ownership in case of the death of the husband. In public affairs men are regarded as more fit than women for leadership. Banking, writing checks, and depositing money are done by both in most households. Women and men bid for household items at public sales. The experienced housewife generally has the authority to make decisions pertaining to the house, but husband and wife usually confer with each other before making any large purchases, and the considerate husband will consult his wife before purchasing any household item. The wife generally has a purse of her own that is replenished periodically by her husband for the purchase of household supplies, groceries, and clothing.

Major household expenses or anticipated medical expenditures are usually discussed mutually, and if the wife decides she would like to patronize a certain doctor, her husband is likely to consent. The husband, on the other hand, may purchase farm equipment or livestock without seeking the advice of his wife. The wife often keeps the income from vegetables or produce sold on the farm.

The extent to which the farmer aids his wife in household tasks is nominal. He helps on special occasions such as butchering and cooking apple butter, but he does not help in the routine preparation of food, nor does he wash dishes. At weddings, the men serve as cooks and table waiters with their wives. Guests at an Amish table are often addressed by the husband: "Now just reach and help yourselves."

The wife's duties include care of the children, cooking and cleaning, preparation of produce for market, making clothes for the family, preserving food, and gardening. Typically, washing will be done on Monday, ironing on Tuesday, baking on Friday, and cleaning on Saturday. There are no special shopping nights, as purchases are made in the village store during weekdays. Women and adolescent girls frequently help with the harvest of crops. In one family, each of the older girls manages a team of horses during the summer months. They plow the fields, cultivate the soil, and do the work of adult males. This is exceptional, however, since women are not generally called upon to help with the heavier jobs in farming. It is the woman who sees that the fences, posts, grape arbors, and frequently the trees about the farm buildings are whitewashed in the spring. The appearance of the lawn and the area surrounding the house is largely the responsibility of the wife, and she feels obligated to keep the inside as well as the outside clean and neat in appearance.

The wife aids the husband in chores that are not usually considered household tasks more than the husband helps his wife in household work. In one home, while the men and carpenters were remodeling the barn in anticipation of the oldest son's marriage, the mother arranged to have neighbor women and relatives come for a day to paint the barn's window sashes.

Gardening, except perhaps for the initial spading in the spring, is the sole responsibility of the wife. The Amish wife usually raises a large variety of edibles, often as many as twenty kinds of vegetables. She makes sure that there are plenty of cucumbers and red beets because they are part of the standard lunch at Sunday services. Typical Amish gardens abound with flowers. Some gardens have as many as twenty varieties. Order and cleanliness tend to be distinctive features of Amish gardening. Orchards are a part of the typical Amish landscape, and spraying, if done at all, is the man's job. More often than not, fruits are purchased from commercial sources because expensive equipment for spraying is considered too costly for a small orchard.

Almost all women's and children's clothing is made at home by the wife or her relatives. Food-processing consumes a large part of the wife's time. Meat-curing may be done by the husband, often at the suggestion and according to the plans of the wife.

With regard to the woman's role in religious services, the teaching of the Apostle Paul is literally obeyed: "Let the woman learn in silence with all subjection." In leadership activities, the woman is not "to usurp authority over the man." At baptismal service, boys are baptized before girls. Women never serve as church officials.

Amish parents try to be of one mind when dealing with their children and to discuss any differences between themselves privately and prayerfully. Marriage partners are taught to be considerate of each other and never to disagree in public.

Personal Relationships

The personal relationship between husband and wife is quiet and sober, with no apparent displays of affection. The relationship is in striking contrast to the expectation of a romantic ideal expressed in popular American culture. Patterns of conversation vary among Amish mates, but terms of endearment, or physical gestures of affection, are conspicuously absent.

The husband may address his wife by her given name, or by no name at all. He may merely begin talking to her if he wants her attention. In speaking about his wife to others he may use "she" or "my wife," but rarely her given name. The mother of the family in like manner may refer to him simply as "my husband" or "he."

Irritation between mates is expressed in a variety of ways, but is conditioned by informally approved means of expressing dissatisfaction. As a rule, institutional patterns override personal considerations. Little irritation is observable among the Amish. Displeasure or disapproval is expressed by tone of voice or by gesture. The husband may express disapproval by complete silence at the dinner table, in which case the wife must guess what is wrong. The usual conversation may lag for several days before it is completely restored to a normal level. Harsh and boisterous talk between mates is rare.

Roles of the parents are defined in terms of traditional familial patterns and to some degree by kinship ties. The husband and wife are not only individuals connected by personal sentiments, but as members of a group must maintain the standards and dignity of that group. This tendency toward the consanguineal system compares favorably with the findings of Thomas and Znaniecki in their study of the Polish peasant family, in which, they say, "the marriage norm is not love, but 'respect.' " As they explain:

> The norm of respect from wife to husband includes obedience, fidelity, care for the husband's comfort and health; from husband to wife, good treatment, fidelity, not letting the wife do hired work if it is not indispensable. In general, neither husband nor wife ought to do anything which could lower the social standing of the other, since this would lead to a lowering of the social standing of the other's family. Affection is not explicitly included in the norm of respect, but is desirable. As to sexual love, it is a purely personal matter, is not and ought not to be socialized in any form; the family purposely ignores it, and the slightest indecency or indiscreetness with regard to sexual relations in marriage is viewed with disgust and is morally condemned.[5]

The Polish pattern of marital relationships compares favorably with the Amish. The Amish are in addition very conscious of the biblical pattern: "Wives, submit yourselves unto your own husband, as unto the Lord. . . . So ought men to love their wives as their own bodies. . . . and the wife see that she reverence her husband" (Eph. 5:22, 28, 33).

The Amish are strongly opposed to premarital sex and extramarital affairs, and any transgression among members must be confessed to the church assembly whether or not pregnancy occurs. Males and females have equal responsibility to confess. After a period of punishment (by excommunication), repenting individuals are received back into the church. They are completely forgiven. Pregnancy is not always considered sufficient reason for the offending couple to marry, but if the couple decides to marry, the wedding is held before the birth of the child. If there is no marriage in such cases, the mother may keep the baby or the baby may be adopted by an Amish couple.

Children and Parents

Amish children appear innocent and unspoiled by the things of this world. The birth of a child brings joy to the family and community, for there will be another dishwasher or woodchopper, and another church member. Thus, children are wanted. At no time in the Amish system are they unwelcome, for they are regarded as "an heritage of the Lord."

The first two years of life are happy ones. Baby obtains what he wants. He is given permissive care with great amounts of love from mother, father, brothers, sisters, aunts, uncles, grandfathers, grandmothers, and cousins.

After about the second year, restrictions and exacting disciplines are continuously imposed upon the child until adolescence. He must be taught to respect the authority of his parents and to respond properly to their exactness. The child is considered sinless, since he does not know the difference between right and wrong. It is the duty of parents to teach him this difference so that he will realize his moral inadequacy and choose the "right way" of the Amish religion.

The Amish home is an effective socializing agent that is directed at making the child a mature person in the Amish way of life. Early in life the child learns that the Amish are "different" from other people. Thus, he must learn not only how to understand to play the role at home and in the Amish system but also how to conduct himself in relation to the norms of his "English" neighbors. He cannot have clothes and toys just like the "English" people have. He soon learns to imitate his parents, to take pride in the "difference," and appears no longer to ask "why" until adolescence.

Amish children are raised so carefully within the Amish family and community that they never feel secure outside it. The faces of many Amish boys and girls reflect pure intent, a sincere, honest, cordial, and well-bred disposition. The extraordinary love and discipline they get prepares them well for Amish womanhood and manhood.

Earlier the family was expected to transmit to the child a reading knowledge of German. Today the Amish school aids in this process. The family members may gather about the sitting-room table, each with a German Testament, and take their turns spelling, enunciating the alphabet, and reading. In some families, this exercise is carried out daily in connection with morning and evening prayers. Even preschool children, ages four and five, take their turns by repeating words or syllables as they are pronounced by the family head.

Amish children do not receive regular allowances from their parents. A young person who works a day or half a day for a neighbor is often permitted to keep the earnings, but is expected to save the money. When parents take their children to town they may give them a small sum for buying candy. Early in life parents may provide a "bank" in which to save pennies. The necessity of taking good care of one's clothing and other personal items is strongly emphasized to the child.

Just as the parents are to be examples to their children, so the older children must be good examples to the younger ones. Among children in the family, age is more important than sex in determining authority, accountability, and work. The older ones care for and help the younger children, but they do not punish them physically. Normally, they persuade and wheedle them into obedience. In late adolescence masculine dominance becomes more evident in brother-sister relationships.

Teaching the child to work and accept responsibility is considered of utmost importance. The child begins to assist his parents at the age of four and is given limited responsibility at the age of six. The boy learns to feed the chickens, gather eggs, feed the calf, and drive the horses. The girl is trained to perform small jobs for her mother and to learn early the art of cooking and housekeeping. The role of children and the work performed by each child is well illustrated in the following description of a family of six children, five boys and one girl, between the ages of three and twenty-two.

The girl (aged twelve) enjoys helping her mother with the household duties, especially setting the table and preparing meals. She and her younger brother (aged eight) help their mother with the garden. When the time comes to do the chores, each has a specific assignment, but their duties also overlap. The four oldest children and the father milk 15 cows regularly. The oldest son feeds and beds the horses, hogs, and calves. The second feeds the laying hens, and the third tends the pullets on range and carries wood for his mother. The girl milks three cows, feeds the rabbits, and gathers the eggs. The eight-year-old boy has no regular work assignment but assists his mother or one of the older members of the family. The two older sons frequently help on washday with heavier tasks such as carrying water. The third son has a decided dislike for housework.

In many farm families each child will be given an animal, usually a calf or heifer, which will become exclusively his. The boy or girl will choose and name the animal. Typically this may occur as early as the seventeenth birthday, and the family may gather to watch the young person choose his animal from among the herd. When the animal matures and has a young calf, the calf may be sold and the proceeds will go into the savings account of the child. The fate of the animal is linked to the care and attention it is given by the owner. The child as owner learns the consequences of feeding, neglect, growth, birth, sterility, disease, or death. After the young person marries, the animal is taken to the farm home of the new couple.

In the Amish family, sons who reach the age of twenty-one are paid monthly wages if they are unmarried and continue to work at home. A young man may hire out for the summer, but this practice has almost completely disappeared among those Amish who farm with tractors. Farmers who need assistance frequently request help from a neighbor or a relative for a few days. Single girls occasionally work as maids in other Amish homes. A *Maut* ("maid") among the Amish enjoys the same privileges as a family member would.

The ability of the family to act as a unit in an emergency is illustrated by what happens when the livestock break out. Charles P. Loomis, who worked at an Amish place as a farm hand, describes such an incident. As the family was seated at the suppertable:

> Mattie got up to get some milk and saw that the cows were getting through the gate. She screamed and the whole family dashed to the door. Mother hurriedly put the baby into the carriage. We ran after the 22 cows. The big family encircled them, one girl having run over a mile on plowed ground. We got them back in. They had not been out this spring and were wild. Mother said she had read in books about stampedes in the west. Chris and I put them back in their stanchions after supper. He fed them grain first, but still we had a job. He said, "They're out of practice. When they get to going to the meadow each day they will do better."[6]

Strict obedience to parents is a profound teaching stressed over and over by Amish parents and by the preachers and is a principle based upon several passages in the Bible. An Amish lad who runs away from home, or even an adult who leaves the Amish church, is held guilty of disobedience to his parents.

Amish children, like all children, manifest resentments by pouting or by responding negatively. But when these manifestations are overt, "smackings" are sure to follow either with the palm of the hand, a switch, a razor strap, or a buggy whip. Temper tantrums, making faces, name-calling, and sauciness among youngsters are extremely rare, for the child learns early that his reward for such rebellion is a sound thrashing.

Disputes between boys are perhaps as frequent in Amish as in non-Amish families. The manner of expressing dissatisfaction is mostly verbal, especially among youngsters, but noses occasionally do get broken. Profanity is not permitted, and if discovered by the parents, is usually promptly treated with punishment. Resentment toward a brother or sister is expressed only mildly in the presence of older persons. In the presence of parents, a quarrel may be expressed by silence, hesitancy, or by completely ignoring the situation.

The subject of sex in Amish life is regarded as a purely personal matter. Adults purposely ignore any mention of the subject, especially in the presence of children. Very little sex instruction is given to the ordinary Amish child. In spite of this suppression, the child acquires gradually, piece by piece, an elementary knowledge of the process of biological reproduction. The Amish child most certainly does ask questions about the sexual behavior of animals on the farm. To satisfy his curiosity, the child more often than not talks such matters over with associates his own age. The jokes of young men show that sexual interests have developed long before courtship and marriage. Any remark about sex in private conversation between a boy and girl of courting age is inopportune, but an indecent joke is not uncommon among a group of men.

Food and Table

In the Amish home a "place at the table" is symbolic of belonging. When a place is vacant due to death, marriage, sickness, father's having gone to town, the discipline of the ban, or a runaway child, all are deeply aware of the empty place. The seating is traditionally arranged with father at the end of the table and the boys to his right from youngest to oldest. Mother is seated just to the left or right of father with the girls on her side of the table.

The family table becomes the scene for the evaluation of behavior, for expressing personal likes and dislikes before the group, and for group participation and decision making. Conversation for its own sake is not encouraged. Conversation at breakfast is typically about the work that needs to be done, how and who should do it. The mother may indicate that certain decisions need to be made relative to preparing the brooder house for the chicks, or about the apples that need to be picked. The father may delegate such a task to one of the sons, directing that it be done after school or when there is time. At noon, the absence of the school-age children makes possible a more intimate conversation between parents and older children. A progress report on the work accomplished thus far is often the topic of conversation. Father and mother may evaluate the products of a salesman who called during the morning hours. In the evening the entire family gathers about the table. Silence during this meal is often interrupted by an occasional belch, a question from a child, or the bark of a dog.

Amish women spend much time cooking, baking, and canning foods. They take advantage of the growing season by serving vegetables from the garden and fruits and berries when they are ripe. They use canned foods when necessary and convenient. They also shop in small supermarkets for specific kinds of food. The old-fashioned Amish maintain ice boxes for cooling in the summer. Others have kerosene-operated refrigerators. At the table their portions of food are generous and the flavor is often excellent.

The Amish work hard and eat accordingly. The standard breakfast in Pennsylvania may include eggs, fried scrapple or cornmeal mush, cooked cereal, and often fried potatoes. Bread, butter, and jelly or apple butter are served with every meal. The standard diet is rich in fats and carbohydrates, consisting of potatoes, gravy, fried foods, and pastries. There are traditional foods like home-cured ham, chow-chow, pickled beets, shoo-fly pie, apple dumplings, bean soup, rivel soup, green tomato pie, and stink cheese. The Amish diet is also influenced by contemporary foods like meat loaf, bologna, and pizza. Cakes, pies, and puddings are numerous. Amish gardens are a good source of fresh vegetables, but the Amish tradition of overcooking and oversweetening probably cancels out much of the natural vitamins and minerals. In recent years health foods, vitamins, and food supplements have been much in evidence. Some Amish operate health-food stores.

Family ceremony is minimal, for social order and social roles are clearly defined and effective. According to older Amish informants, the only religious rite observed by a family in bygone days was silent prayer before and after meals. Bedtime prayers were repeated silently in bed. This is the traditional pattern still practiced by the most orthodox groups. Some families kneel together before retiring while the father reads a prayer from the prayer book.[7] Rarely is there a spontaneous audible prayer. The Amish have retained some of the ceremonial practices of the Reformation, such as the use of prayer formularies and prayer books, silent prayer, and Luther's German translation of the Bible.

At mealtime each member at the table repeats silently his memorized meditation. Children, upon reaching the age of puberty or earlier, are expected to say their own prayers. These prayers are memorized, in German, and they may consist of the Lord's Prayer or a prayer of about the same length taken from a prayer book.

Recreation and Leisure

Recreation and leisure are informal and related to work; they are not entered into as pursuits in themselves. Homemade rather than store-bought toys are typically provided. There are certain games which Amish children and young people play. Clapping games are a common form of indoor play among adolescent girls and they are frequently played at informal family visits. They are called "botching." There are several ways of playing. Two people, seated on chairs and facing each other, clap the palms of their hands together alternately, then alternately strike each other's lap until there is a decided loud clap. The feet may be used to keep proper timing. If several participants are efficient, a vigorous contest will ensue to see who can go the fastest. These clappings are sometimes played to the tune of "Darling Nellie Gray" or "Pop Goes the Weasel."

Much of the leisure time of the Amish is spent visiting relatives, the older members of the community, and the sick, and attending weddings in the fall. Easter and Pentecost, observed not only on Sunday but on Monday as well, provide long weekend occasions for visiting. In large settlements where distances to be traveled are as great as forty miles, a family may start early on a Sunday morning and attend church in a neighboring district. They will drive still farther in the afternoon, stop for Sunday evening supper with a family, and continue their journey after supper until they reach their destination.

Weekly auction sales and household auctions are a common form of recreation for many family members. For some boys and men, hunting is a favorite sport in season. Softball is rarely played on Sunday. Young people of courtship age play ball on special weekday holidays such as Ascension Day or Easter Monday. Hiking is a common activity among boys.

The use of tobacco can be classed as another form of pastime. Its use varies from one area to another and with the *Ordnung*. Many districts have officially discouraged its use and will excommunicate a persistent smoker, but conservative groups have tended to have few or no scruples against its use. Among the Lancaster County Amish, who themselves raise tobacco as a cash crop, single and married men, including preachers, use it. In those districts where it is permitted, there is no effort to conceal smoking, except in the case of cigarettes, which are viewed as "worldly." Where forbidden, it is often done secretly. Older men appear to have more of a "right" to chew or smoke than young men. Pipe and cigar smoking is the accepted practice. Modern lighters are used by some. Older informants among the very orthodox Amish say that as far back as they can remember the people have used tobacco.[8] It was formerly common for older women to smoke a pipe and a few of them still do, but this is not done openly.

Quilting

The Amish did not invent the quilting tradition or quilted bedcovers. Quilts are much older than the American frontier. It is believed that the technique goes back at least to ancient Egypt, and the Crusaders found that the quilted shirts used in the Near East made the wearing of armor more comfortable. An inventory from Wales in 1551 lists a quilt, and American women were making quilts in the 1700s.[9] The earliest known inventory listings of quilts among the Amish are in 1831 in Wayne County, Ohio, and 1836 in Mifflin County, Pennsylvania.[10] It was not until the 1880s, apparently, that quiltmaking reached a significant level of popularity among the Amish.[11]

Amish women adopted quilt styles from the larger society but made them in the strong, unprinted colors of their own clothing. By the time the Amish began making quilts, several Amish settlements were well established, including ones in Lancaster and Mifflin counties in Pennsylvania and Holmes County in Ohio. In each of these places, Amish quiltmakers adopted distinctive styles and techniques of quiltmaking, and they continue to take these styles and skills with them as they form new settlements. Colors allowed for quilts reflect the degree of conservatism of a group, with the most conservative groups using the darkest colors.

Quilts are emblems of affection. They symbolize a message of warmth. They are an extension of parental affection to the family, the kin group, and to the wider world. Quilts underscore the importance of the transgenerational family. The patterns, colors, and fabrics are the result of firm boundaries, strong identity, and decisiveness. Inside those boundaries there is warmth and caring. Quiltmaking is a creative family and group enterprise.

Quilting is an important part of the social and family life of Amish women. Within their rules and traditions, it is an artistic expression of individual preference and corporate community life. Like other forms of mutual help such as barn-raisings, frolics, and harvesting, quilting is a festive and enjoyable activity. Amish women make quilts not only for their families but also for the marketplace. With the increasing popularity of quilts as decorative objects and art objects, quilt-making has become a source of economic subsistence for Amish families. Quilts made for sale reflect the tastes of customers, and need not have any relationship to the makers' own quilts.

Amish quilts have become collector's items. Some early quilts are commanding more than $10,000 at art auctions. Not only in the United States but in Europe, Australia, and Asia, Amish quilts are hanging in museums, as well as in the lobbies of large corporations, libraries, and banks.

The Mature Years

Respect for the elders, already obvious among children, is even more pronounced with regard to mature Amish people. All age groups in both sexes revere parents, grandparents, and great-grandparents. The duty to obey one's parents is one of the main themes in Amish preaching. Perhaps the verse most often repeated on this point is one of the Ten Commandments: "Honor thy father and thy mother, that thy days may be long upon the land which the Lord thy God giveth thee" (Exod. 20:12; Eph. 6:2; Col. 3:20).

Not only is there respect for the aged, but authority is vested in the old people. This arrangement naturally lends itself to control of life by the aged. Preservation of the religious ideals and mores is thereby ensured, and the younger people who are inclined to introduce change can be held in check.

A strong consciousness of kinship is peculiarly favorable to gerontocracy, or social control by the older members of society. This control is informal rather than formal, but is, nevertheless, "closer to us than breathing, nearer than hands or feet."[12] The part that old people have "in drawing forth and molding the character and life-policy of every younger person in the kinship group makes the necessity for direct control much less frequent in an isolated culture than in more accessible communities."[13] The relatively integrated community is associated with effective rules imposed by the aged, be they parents or church leaders. Thus deference to age pervades not only familial relationships but also the religious leadership of the group. Furthermore, the counsel of the older bishop or minister carries more authority than that of younger ones.

The Amish farm typically contains two dwellings, one of which is the *Grossdaadi Haus*, which houses the grandparents. At retirement the older couple moves into this house and a married son or daughter falls heir to responsibility for the farm. The grandparents may retain some type of control of the farm until the younger couple demonstrate their ability to manage the farm. The grandparents have not only a separate household unit but a horse and buggy of their own. Instead of two houses, many farms have one dwelling that is large enough to accommodate two separate household operations. When there are no grandparents to occupy these quarters, they are sometimes rented to other Amish people, or occupied by the hired man and his wife. Some of the Amish who retire in or near a village will erect a small barn beside their dwelling so that they can feed and maintain a horse.

By the time they are 60, many Amish have accumulated enough wealth for a satisfactory retirement. Traditionally, the Amish do not accept old-age assistance or public assistance of any kind. Neither do they buy life insurance. Needy older persons are aided by relatives. Should such close relatives be incompetent or unwilling, the church will come to the assistance of the elderly.

The retirement of the father and mother from active life on the farm stabilizes the social organization of the entire Amish community. While the young man is free to make his own decisions, the very presence of the parents on the farm influences the life of the younger generation. The young couple is not obligated to carry out the wishes of the parents, yet an advisory relationship stimulates not only economic stability but also religious integrity.

The final stages of life are characterized by integrity rather than despair. Amish attitudes and practices with respect to aging constitute a sound system of retirement.

Age at Retirement. The age at which Amish retire is not rigidly fixed. Health, family needs, and the inclination of the individual are all considerations in determining the proper time. A couple may retire anytime between the ages of 50 and 70. Moving "off the farm" provides opportunities for the young who need a farm. By providing a farm for their offspring, the older couple advances their standing in the community. They also do not have to choose between full-time work or doing nothing. They continue to work at their own pace, helping their married children to become established on the farm. Many continue to work in small shops of their own.

Prestige. In community and church activities older men and women keep their right to vote, and their influence or "voice" increases. Ordained leaders never retire from their positions. Wives have an important influence on their husbands. Long periods of visiting friends and persons of the same age, and exchanges before and after the preaching service, help to form an informal consensus on any subject.

Housing and Transportation. Private housing is provided in the "grandfather" house, the dwelling unit adjacent to the main farmhouse. This arrangement allows for independence without sacrificing intergenerational family involvement. By having their own horse and buggy, both couples may travel at will. There is no fear of losing a driver's license.

Health and Medical Care. Good nutrition and health care are readily at hand. Years of physical labor and exercise have kept the body active. When health fails, relatives and friends come to visit frequently. There is no stigma attached to being sick. In case of financial need, either the relatives or the church will pay unmet medical bills.

Functional Traditions. By living in their own house, a retired couple can maintain personal customs and living arrangements. This includes furnishings, guest rooms for visitors, shop tools, facilities for making toys for children, quilts, and rugs, and maintaining Amish standards. Old-fashioned ways are preferred and perpetuated voluntarily. The slow rate of technological change allows social bonds to take priority. In an institution for old people or in an apartment, the same sense of living comfortably with an unchanging social structure would not be possible.

Economic Security. Amish retirees are with few exceptions not wealthy. Income, however, is not a serious problem. Economic subsistence is maintained without government aid of any kind. Life earnings, rentals from farms, carpentry, or part-time work provides some income. They do not seek or need counsel with respect to maintaining their human rights. The community's sensitivity to sharing and practicing mutual aid and its abiding interest in the well-being of those in need are great assets to older people.

Social and Family Continuity. Transgenerational contacts are maintained with relatives. There is little problem with loneliness. Older people are assured of meaningful social participation, in work and in community activities, in seasonal frolics, auctions, and in the activities of weddings and holidays. Travel to distant places may also constitute a significant pastime for older people. Contentment with helping the married children, whether in work, in times of sickness, or in crisis, constitutes a basic attitude and expectation. The young ask their parents about farming methods or for advice on rearing children. This does not mean that their advice is accepted, but their views as parents are recognized and respected.

The Amish home is the center of life and place of belonging for all the family members. Home is a place of security. It is a center for decision making with respect to work, play, and exposure to the wider community and to the outside world.

Notes

1. In selecting a theme for the bicentennial of the founding of the United States of America, the *Michigan Farmer* chose to feature the Amish when only a few years previously the state had prosecuted them for maintaining uncertified schools. The narrative was written by an Amish girl, Mary Miller, and appears in the July 1976 issue.

2. The nickname "Swartz cousin" originated with Jacob Swartz, who was excommunicated for marrying Magdalena Stoltzfus (b. June 18, 1832). She was his "first cousin once removed" (the offspring of his first cousin).

3. An observation made by Gertrude E. Huntington in "The Amish Family," in *Ethnic Families in America*, ed. Charles H. Mindel and Robert W. Habenstein (New York: Elsevier Scientific Publishing Co., 1976), p. 307. I am indebted to Gertrude E. Huntington for assistance in clarifying the nature of family structure and roles in Amish society.

4. Julia Erickson and Gary Klein, "Women's Roles and Family Production among the Old Order Amish," *Rural Sociology* 46 (2):1981, 282–96.

5. William I. Thomas and Florian Znaniecki, *The Polish Peasant in Europe and America* (New York: Alfred A. Knopf, 1927), 1: 90.

6. Charles P. Loomis, "A Farmhand's Diary," *Mennonite Quarterly Review* 53 (July 1979): 248.

7. The standard prayer book is *Christenpflicht*. Prayers on pp. 124 and 126 of the book are typically used in the morning and evening.

8. Additional sources on the use of tobacco appear in John Umble, "The Amish Mennonites of Union County, Pennsylvania. Part I: Social and Religious Life," *Mennonite Quarterly Review* 7 (April 1933): 71–96; and in the *Mennonite Encyclopedia*, s.v. "Tobacco."

9. Joseph Harriss, "The Newest Quilt Fad Seems to Be Going Like Crazy," *Smithsonian* 18 (May 1987): 114–24.

10. Eve Wheatcroft Granick, *The Amish Quilt* (Intercourse, Pa.: 1989), p. 25.

11. Ibid. p. 39.

12. Howard Becker and Harry E. Barnes, *Social Thought from Lore to Science*, 3rd ed. rev., 3 vols. (New York: Dover, 1961), 1: 11.

13. Ibid.

African-Americans in the 1990s*

William P. O'Hare, Kelvin M. Pollard, Taynia L. Mann, and Mary M. Kent

The experience of family life varies in every culture by race, class, and gender. This article explores some of that variation for African-American families. Recent decades have seen a number of dramatic changes in African-American households, including an increase in single-parent families and a decline in the proportion of children who live with two parents. Among other things, this article illustrates the interrelationships between race, class, and gender, and the importance of understanding how larger social and economic forces have had an impact upon African-Americans and their family life.

African-Americans—30 million in number in 1991—are the largest and most visible minority group in the United States.[1] Because of their population size, along with their legacy of slavery and legal subjugation, blacks occupy a special niche in U.S. society. We often view the progress of blacks as a litmus test of how open our society really is. Furthermore, as African-Americans become a larger share of the U.S. population, the black experience assumes a greater part of our national character.

Blacks have made significant progress on many fronts since the 1950s and

*Source: William P. O'Hare, Kelvin M. Pollard, Taynia L. Mann, and Mary M. Kent, "African-Americans in the 1990s," *Population Bulletin*, 46, no. 1 (July, 1991).

1960s, when major civil rights legislation was enacted. In general, the education, health, living conditions, and incomes of African-Americans have improved. Many more blacks vote in elections and get elected to public office. But the remarkable progress of the post-World War II era appears to have slowed during the 1980s, even regressed in some areas. And African-Americans still rank below whites on nearly every measure of socioeconomic status.

The gap between the well-being of blacks and whites is continuing evidence of the second-class status of African-Americans. Black infants are twice as likely to die as are white infants. Black children are nearly three times more likely to live in a single-parent family or to live in poverty than are white children. Blacks are only half as likely to go to college; those who earn college degrees have incomes one-third less than do whites with the same education. And, while the number of affluent blacks has skyrocketed over the past decade, the net wealth of black households is only one-tenth that of whites.

Why has the progress of African-Americans slowed? Many observers feel that Ronald Reagan's presidential administration, which dominated national politics during most of the 1980s, was particularly harmful to black socioeconomic advancement, erasing civil rights gains and promoting a general antiminority climate. Others see a myriad of factors that combined to thwart the progress of blacks. Some of these factors have polarized American society in general, widening the gap between rich and poor and chipping away at the middle class. Among African-Americans, opportunities continue to open up for the educated middle class while the urban poor appear stuck in a quagmire of unstable families, intermittent employment, welfare dependence, and the temptations of crime.

This view of black Americans as living within two increasingly separate worlds gained wide acceptance during the 1980s. William Julius Wilson, a sociologist at the University of Chicago who emerged as a major analyst of U.S. blacks in the past decade, argues that economic changes, combined with social and demographic forces within the black community, produced these countervailing trends.[2] Wilson contends that the urban poor became more impoverished and more isolated because the decline of manufacturing and the movement of many blue-collar jobs to suburban areas eliminated a source of relatively well-paying, secure jobs for blacks. Joblessness increased among urban blacks, reducing the pool of marriageable men and undermining the strength of the family. Poverty increased as the number of female-headed households grew.

At the same time, new opportunities for middle-class blacks were generated by the expansion of civil rights. But the movement of the middle class out of the ghettos left "behind an isolated and very poor community without the institutions, resources and values necessary for success in modern society."[3]

This interpretation of the origins of urban poverty drew attention away from racial discrimination as the major barrier to the progress of African-Americans and toward the effects of broad economic, demographic, and social welfare trends. But recent studies provide new evidence that racial discrimination continues to undermine the progress of blacks.

Assessing the well-being of blacks is more difficult now than in the past. Only a few generations ago, 90 percent of African-Americans lived in poverty and racial inequities seemed obvious. Today, the root of the disparities between blacks and whites is harder to discern. Is racism dying, or is it still the primary reason for black underachievement? Why are some blacks moving into the middle and upper classes while others remain in poverty? There is no consensus about the answers to these complex questions. We can, however, sketch a portrait of African-Americans in the 1990s using demographic and socioeconomic data, and shed some light on these complex relationships.

African-American Families

No change in the black community has been more dramatic or more fundamental than the reordering of families and family relationships. In recent years, these changes have prompted many observers to proclaim a crisis in the black family, generally characterized by the growing numbers of poor, female-headed families.

While the vast majority of the 10 million African-American households are family households (that is, the household members are related by birth, marriage, or adoption), only about half the families were headed by a married couple in 1990, down from 68 percent in 1970 and 56 percent in 1980. A much higher percentage (83 percent) of white families are headed by married couples, although this percentage also has slipped over the past two decades.[4]

African-American households are larger than white households, but are slightly smaller than Hispanic households. The average black household contained 2.9 persons in 1990, compared with 2.6 persons for all whites and 3.5 persons for Hispanics. Both African-American and Hispanic female-headed households have one more person, on average, than households headed by white females. Black households also are more likely than white to include adults in addition to a married couple or household head. In 1990, about a third of all black households included other adults, compared with only a fourth of white households.[5]

Changing Marriage Patterns

Marriage and divorce statistics since the 1960s record major shifts in the African-American family. In 1960, 65 percent of black women age 30 to 34 were in an intact marriage. In 1990, only 39 percent were married and living with their husbands. Over the same period, the percentage divorced grew from 8 to 12 percent, and the percentage who had never married grew from 10 to 35 percent. While a similar movement away from marriage occurred among white women, the change was much more dramatic among blacks.

Some analysts explain the decline in marriage among blacks in economic and demographic terms, while others cite more fundamental societal changes that have affected all Americans. The rising divorce rates and increase in the number of persons who choose not to marry may indicate that the institution of marriage itself is weakening. The marketplace and public institutions provide many of the goods and services that previously were the domain of the family. Low fertility rates have curtailed the number of years parents have dependent children living at home. The increased job opportunities for women make marriage less of an economic necessity, and, in the more tolerant climate of modern society, less of a social necessity for women. With a fourth of all children born to unmarried women, even childbearing is no longer confined to marriage. The movement away from marriage can also be seen as a consequence of modernization and urbanization, which has fostered individualism, weakening the family.[6]

Many social scientists focus on the relationship between marriage rates and the relative number of men and women. Women are more likely to marry when the ratio of men to women is high than when there is a relative shortage of men. The rapid rise in the number of births during the baby boom created a "marriage squeeze" in the 1970s and 1980s because there were more women than men in the marrying ages. This caused many young Americans to delay or forego marriage and childbearing.[7] This imbalance of the sexes was more extreme for the black than for the white population. On average, the ratio of males to females at birth is lower among blacks than whites,[8] and black male mortality is relatively high in the young adult ages. Even allowing for an undercount of black men in the census, black women outnumber men in the ages when most people marry and start families, age 20 to 49. Following this reasoning, fewer black women are getting married because there are not enough eligible men available.

In addition to demographic and social factors, economic changes—which eliminated many jobs held by black men in central city areas—and racial discrimination in hiring and firing have pushed many black men to the margins, or completely out, of the labor force. The deteriorating economic position of black men has been blamed for further discouraging the formation of married-couple families. Black men, with low wages and little job security, have difficulty fulfilling the traditional role as the major breadwinner for a family. The rise in female-headed families, whether formed through divorce, separation, or out-of-wedlock childbearing, has been linked to the decline in the ratio of employed black men per black woman.

Several analysts claim that welfare programs designed to aid single-parent families were a disincentive for low-income blacks to marry, although statistical analysis has failed to find a strong association between welfare payment levels and family composition.[9]

Many analysts argue that the modern African-American family has always differed from European-American families and should not be expected to conform to the married-couple pattern. Modern black family structure can be viewed as a legacy of slavery, when marriage among blacks was not recognized legally. Slave families tended to be consanguineal (organized around blood relatives) rather than conjugal (built around a married couple). Some trace this family structure back to the social structure in the African countries from which the ancestors of American blacks came.[10]

There is an ongoing debate as to whether the retreat from marriage among black Americans resulted directly from the disruptive effects of slavery; whether it is only indirectly associated with slavery through the continuing economic marginalization of blacks; or whether black culture and social structure, emanating from African roots, lead to different marriage and family patterns. Recently, social scientists have focused on issues related to the social and economic marginalization of black men to explain the low marriage rates among African-Americans.

Overwhelmingly, blacks still marry other blacks, despite opinion polls showing that interracial marriage has become socially acceptable to a growing percentage of Americans. The percentage of married African-Americans whose spouse is not black has not changed over the past decade. In 1987, only 3 percent of married blacks had a nonblack spouse. In contrast, about 16 percent of married Asians and Hispanics had a non-Asian or non-Hispanic spouse. When African-Americans do marry a nonblack, it is usually the wife who is white, Asian, or of another race.

The Children

African-American children have been most affected by the changes in marital status and family composition that have occurred over the past few decades. The share of black children living with two parents declined from 58 percent in 1970 to 38 percent in 1990.[11] Just over half (55 percent) of black children lived in a single-parent household in 1990, 51 percent with their mother. In contrast, 19 percent of white children lived in single-parent households in 1989—a significant share, but minor compared with the statistic for blacks (see Table 8-1).

Black children are more likely to live with a grandparent than are white or Hispanic children. In 1990, 12 percent of black children lived in households that included their grandparents, compared with only 4 percent of whites and 6 percent of Hispanics.[12]

More than a fourth (27 percent) of all African-American children live with mothers who have never married. The percentage is highest among young chil-

TABLE 8-1

Living Arrangements of Children Under 18 by Race and Ethnic Group, 1990 (numbers in thousands)

	BLACKS		WHITES		HISPANICS[a]	
	Number	Percent	Number	Percent	Number	Percent
Total children	10,018	100.0	51,390	100.0	7,174	100.0
Living with						
Two parents	3,781	37.7	40,593	79.0	4,789	66.8
One parent	5,485	54.8	9,870	19.2	2,154	30.0
Mother only	5,132	51.2	8,321	16.2	1,943	27.1
Father only	353	3.5	1,549	3.0	211	2.9
Other relative[b]	654	6.5	708	1.4	177	2.5
Nonrelative	98	1.0	220	0.4	54	0.8

[a] Hispanics may be of any race.
[b] 463,000 black children and 452,000 white children lived with a grandparent with neither parent present.

Source: Bureau of the Census. *Current Population Reports* P-20, no. 447 (Washington, D.C.: GPO, 1990), table 4.

TABLE 8-2

Characteristics of Black Children and Their Families, 1990

	CHILDREN LIVING IN	
	Two-Parent Households	Female-Headed Households
Median family income (1989)	$31,757	$9,590
Percent of children whose families:		
Are headed by a high school graduate	79.2	66.0
Own their home	55.3	22.3
Live in central cities	49.7	63.6
Live in public housing	6.3	29.8
Have incomes below poverty	18.1	61.1

Source: Bureau of the Census, *Current Population Reports* P-20, no. 450 (Washington, D.C.: GPO, 1991), table 6.

dren: 39 percent for children under age six.[13] One of the major consequences of living in a female-headed family is that such families generally have fewer economic resources than married-couple families. Nearly two-thirds are poor and live in central cities; over one-quarter live in public housing (see Table 8-2). The 3.8 million black children living in two-parent families appear privileged in comparison. Their parents are more educated, earn nearly four times as much money, and are more than twice as likely to own their own home. These stark differences highlight the two separate worlds inhabited by poor and middle-class black children, and suggest that the African-American population will become more polarized as these children mature.

Fertility

Black Americans have had higher fertility than white Americans for the past two centuries. At the height of the baby boom in the mid-1950s, blacks were having an average of 4.4 children per woman, compared with 3.6 among whites. Because of their higher birth rates and younger age structure, a disproportionately high share of U.S. births are black. In 1988, the National Center for Health Statistics registered 671,976 African-American births—17 percent of all births that year.[14] The total fertility rate (TFR), or total number of lifetime births per woman, has remained higher for blacks. The TFR, which provides a good barometer of fertility independent of age structure, was 32 percent higher for blacks than for whites in 1988—2.4 children per woman compared with 1.8 per woman for whites.

There has been remarkable stability in the ratio of black to white fertility rates since 1960: the TFR for blacks has remained one-quarter to one-third higher than the TFR for whites. Fertility levels for blacks and whites fell in tandem during the 1960s and 1970s and have fluctuated similarly during the 1980s. The TFRs for both groups have risen slightly in recent years.[15]

Socioeconomic differences between blacks and whites explain much of the difference in their fertility levels. Birth rates are similar among black and white

FIGURE 8-1

Babies Born Out-of-Wedlock, by Race, 1970, 1980, and 1988

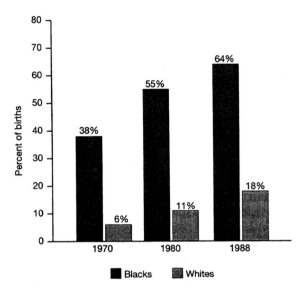

Source: National Center for Health Statistics, *Monthly Vital Statistics Report* 39, no. 4, supplement (1990), table 18; and *Vital Statistics of the United States* 1987 (Washington, D.C.: GPO, 1989), table 1–31.

women with the same level of educational attainment, for example. In 1988, the completed fertility rate of black women age 35 to 44 with some college education was only 4 percent higher than that of their white counterparts. The black rate was 11 percent higher among women with less than a college education.[16] And among low-income families in 1985, white women were more likely to have had a child in the previous year than were black women.[17]

Regardless of the reasons, black fertility remains slightly higher than white fertility. In addition, two glaring disparities in the childbearing patterns of blacks and whites are cause for concern: compared with whites, black babies are nearly four times more likely to be born to a single mother, and three times more likely to be born to a young teenage mother.

In 1988, 64 percent of black babies were born out-of-wedlock, compared with 18 percent of white babies. Birth rates for unmarried women have soared in the 1980s, as shown in Figure 8-1. In fact, the rates have increased faster among whites than blacks. Still, single black women of every age are more likely to have a child than single white women. The disparity is greatest among teenagers. In 1988, unmarried white teenagers age 15 to 17 bore 17 births per 1,000 girls, while unmarried black teenagers bore 74 births per 1,000.

Birth rates for all teenagers have fallen over the past two decades. Between 1970 and 1985, the fertility rate for teenage black girls age 15 to 17, whether married or single, declined from 101 to 70 births per 1,000 girls; for white teenagers, the rate fell from 29 to 24. In the past several years, however, teenage fertility has edged upward. By 1988, birth rates had increased to 77 for black teenagers and to 26 for white teenagers. Throughout the 1980s, however, the gap between black and white teenage fertility remained fairly constant.

The disproportionately high rate of teen childbearing in the African-American community exacerbates many social problems. Health problems, high infant mortality, educational deficiencies, long-term welfare dependency, and poverty are among the consequences risked by teens who have babies. Teenage mothers are more likely to be unmarried, and therefore without the potential income and support a husband could provide. Many analysts also fear that a "cycle" of teenage childbearing may continue into succeeding generations.[18]

Income, Wealth, and Poverty

Black family incomes increased during the 1950s and 1960s, but beginning with the recession in the early 1970s, the income levels for blacks have stagnated. In 1989, the median annual income for black families was $20,200, a 6 percent improvement over 1980 after adjusting for inflation, but slightly below the comparable figure for 1969.[19]

White families, in contrast, continued to increase their incomes during the 1970s and 1980s, albeit at a lower rate than during the expansionary years just after World War II. The ratio of black to white earnings has actually fallen. Black family income was 61 percent that of whites in 1969, but only 56 percent as high as in 1989.

Why have black families lost ground over the past two decades? Demographic factors explain part of the loss. Foremost among them is the growth in female-headed families, which pulled a larger proportion of black families into the lowest income groups. In 1989, black female-headed families had only a third the annual income of black married-couple families, $11,600 compared with $30,700.

Also, the average black family has fewer members in the labor force than white families, 1.51 compared with 1.67 in 1989. This 10 percent difference is explained by the lower participation of blacks in the labor force, higher unemployment rates, and greater percentages of single-parent households among black than white families. Even if blacks and whites held comparable jobs and earned equal pay, the higher number of wage-earners per family for whites would keep their average family income above that for blacks.

Age, Family, and Education Differences

Average income figures also fail to show the vast diversity within the African-American population. While the percentage of low-income families is much greater among blacks, there is also a solid middle class. The plethora of studies on blacks in poverty may give a distorted view of the African-American population.[20] Only a few writers have focused on the middle-class and affluent blacks, yet these groups have increased significantly.[21]

In 1989, 26 percent of black families had incomes below $10,000, 32 percent earned between $10,000 and $25,000, and 42 percent received $25,000 or more per year. Among whites, however, only 8 percent of families had incomes under $10,000, while 69 percent were in the $25,000 or over category.

Income levels differ markedly by educational level, age, and family type. Black married-couple families, for example, increased their earnings during the 1970s and 1980s. By 1989, the median income for blacks had grown to 82 percent that of whites for families in which both husband and wife worked.

In families headed by younger blacks, especially those with a college degree, average income is almost as high for blacks as it is for whites. Among married-couple families where the head of household is 25 to 44 years old and a college graduate, the median income of blacks ($54,400) is 93 percent that of whites ($58,800).[22]

Female-headed families rank at the bottom of the income distribution, but there is considerable diversity even within this group. The extremely low median income of black female-headed households—less than $12,000, compared with nearly $19,000 for white female-headed households—is partially attributable to the lower educational levels and the lower percentages of divorced women among blacks. White women are more likely to obtain a legal divorce, and therefore to receive alimony or child support, an important source of additional income. Among white and black women with similar marital and educational characteristics and who head their families, however, the income differences diminish. Average incomes for families headed by single women who are college graduates are no higher for white than for black families.

While a college education erases some of the income difference between whites and blacks, blacks do not reap the same financial rewards from education as do whites. The average incomes for blacks invariably are lower than for whites, regardless of educational level or geographic area (see Table 8-3). Race

TABLE 8-3

Median Income and Poverty Rates by Education in Three Geographic Areas: Blacks and Whites Age 25-44, 1989

	METROPOLITAN NORTH		METROPOLITAN SOUTH		NONMETROPOLITAN SOUTH	
	Black	White	Black	White	Black	White
Median personal income (dollars per year)						
Less than high school	$5,700	$9,800	$6,000	$8,300	$4,900	$8,200
High school only	13,000	17,000	12,500	15,100	10,000	13,000
Some college	18,100	21,800	17,000	19,000	12,600	16,900
College graduate	26,000	30,100	24,000	29,000	20,000	22,500
Poverty rate (percent)						
Less than high school	51	23	41	26	52	25
High school only	24	6	18	8	24	10
Some college	13	3	13	4	23	6
College graduate	4	2	3	1	6	4

Source: Authors analysis of the March 1990 Current Population Survey.

differences are somewhat smaller in the South than in the North, especially in nonmetropolitan areas where all incomes are lower.

The Future of African-Americans

The history of the black population in the United States is fairly well document-ed, but what does the future hold for these Americans? Many of the forces that will shape the advancement of black Americans have been described above, but it is not clear what the sum of these forces portends.

Many of the trends outlined here suggest that the black population will be more diverse as America moves into the twenty-first century. The economic gap between rich and poor blacks is growing. Many black scholars argue that *race* will lose significance while *class* divisions gain importance. Already, many young blacks who spent most of their lives in post-1960s America see issues differently than their parents, who grew up enduring overt racial oppression.

The middle-class blacks of the future may feel little in common with poor blacks because their experiences will have been dramatically different in so many ways. By the year 2000, every black under age 40 (nearly 60 percent of the black population) will have grown up in the more hospitable post-1960 racial climate.

Yet racism—one of the major forces that led blacks to rely so heavily on one another—is still very much evident. While the attitudes of whites toward blacks have softened a great deal over the past few decades, many still harbor discriminatory attitudes. Indeed, efforts to promote fuller participation of blacks in colleges and the work force have generated claims of reverse discrimination by some whites. Furthermore, the actions of many whites in the voting booth, in hiring, and in decisions of where to live are at odds with the benign attitudes expressed in opinion polls. To confound matters, the rapid growth of Hispanics and Asians may imperil black economic advancement, heighten group tensions, and lead to stronger black cohesiveness. While the future of America's black pop-ulation is uncertain, it is clear that African-Americans will continue to be a high-ly visible feature of the American social and political landscape.

Notes

1. The terms "African-American" and "black" are used interchangeably in this report. The term "white" refers to all whites, including Hispanics, unless specifically stated otherwise. Hispanics may be of any race, but the majority are white.

2. William J. Wilson, *The Truly Disadvantaged: The Inner City, the Underclass, and Public Policy* (Chicago: University of Chicago Press, 1987); and William J. Wilson, *The Declining Significance of Race: Blacks and Changing American Institutions* (Chicago: University of Chicago Press, 1978).

3. Douglas Massey and Mitchell L. Eggers, "The Ecology of Inequality: Minorities and the Concentration of Poverty, 1970–1980," *American Journal of Sociology* 95 (March 1990): 1153–1188.

4. Paul C. Glick, "A Demographic Picture of Black Families," in *Black Families*, ed. Harriette P. McAdoo (Beverly Hills, Calif.: Sage Publications, 1981), p. 108; and Bureau of the Census, "Household and Family Characteristics: March 1990 and 1989," *Current Population Reports* P-20, no. 447 (Washington, D.C.: GPO, 1990), table 1.

5. Bureau of the Census, P-20, no. 447, 1990, op. cit., table 16.

6. Thomas J. Espenshade, "Marriage Trends in America: Estimates, Implications, and Underlying Causes," *Population and Development Review* 11, no. 2 (1985): 193–245; and Charles Westoff, "Fertility Decline in the West: Causes and Prospects," *Population and Development Review* 9, no. 1 (1983): 99–104.

7. Espenshade, op. cit., pp. 232–234.

8. Among white Americans, nearly 106 male babies are born for every 100 female babies, on average. Among African-Americans, 103 males are born for every 100 females. Male mortality is higher than female at every age, further depleting the number of African-American men relative to women. For the 20 to 49 age group, there are only 89 black men for every 100 black women.

9. Wilson 1987, op. cit., pp. 95–100; Jaynes and Williams, op. cit., p. 531; see also Reynolds Farley and Walter R. Allen, *The Color Line and the Quality of Life in America* (New York: Russell Sage Foundation, 1987), p. 170.

10. Farley and Allen, op. cit., p. 171; and Floretta Dukes McKenzie, "Education Strategies for the '90s," in *The State of Black America 1991*, ed. Janet Dewart (New York: National Urban League, Inc., 1991), pp. 95–110.

11. Glick, op. cit., p. 110; and Bureau of the Census, "Marital Status and Living Arrangements: March 1990," *Current Population Reports* P-20, no. 450 (Washington, D.C.: GPO, 1991), table 4.

12. Bureau of the Census, P-20, no. 450, 1991, op. cit., table 4.

13. Ibid., tables 4 and 6.

14. National Center for Health Statistics, "Advance Report of Final Natality Statistics 1988," *Monthly Vital Statistics Report* 39, no. 4, supplement (15 August 1990), table 1.

15. Ibid., table 4.

16. Bureau of the Census, "Fertility of American Women: June 1988," *Current Population Reports* P-20, no. 436 (Washington, D.C.: GPO, 1989), table 2.

17. O'Hare 1987, op. cit., p. 46.

18. Reid, op. cit., pp. 12–13.

19. Bureau of the Census, P-60, no. 168, 1990, op. cit., table 8.

20. Wilson 1987, op. cit.; Jencks and Peterson, op. cit.; Ken Auletta, *The Underclass* (New York: Random House, 1982); Fred Harris and Roger W. Wilkins, eds., *Quiet Riots: Race and Poverty in the United States* (New York: Pantheon Books, 1988); and Nicholas Lemann, *Promised Land: the Great Black Migration and How it Changed America* (New York: Alfred A. Knopf, 1991).

21. Bart Landry, *The New Black Middle Class* (Berkeley, Calif.: University of California Press, 1987); and William P. O'Hare, "In the Black," *American Demographics* 11 (November 1989): 25–29.

22. Bureau of the Census, P-60, no. 168, 1990, op. cit., table 4.

Hispanic Families in the United States: Research Perspectives*

Catherine Street Chilman

While African-American families currently comprise the largest minority group in the United States, by the early part of the next century the Hispanic population will be even larger. Like African-American families, Hispanic families differ from non-Hispanic white families in a number of ways. However, as Catherine Street Chilman argues in this article, it is important to realize that there is also a great deal of cultural diversity within the Hispanic population. Puerto Ricans, Mexican-Americans, Cuban-Americans, and immigrants from Central and South America have different immigration histories and bring with them varying cultural patterns. If we are to begin to understand diversity in family life, we must appreciate this variation within ethnic and racial groups as well.

The impact of the Hispanic population on American society is enormous and diverse, having many implications for family research, professional practice, and public policies. Scholars and professionals need a deeper understanding of the variety of Hispanic individuals and families in this country.

Although it is common to view all Hispanic families in this country as being

*Source: Catherine Street Chilman, "Hispanic Families in the United States: Research Perspectives," in *Family Ethnicity: Strength in Diversity*, ed. by Harriette Pipes McAdoo (Newbury Park, CA: Sage, 1993), pp. 141–163.

similar in values, beliefs, behaviors, resources, and concerns, such sweeping assumptions are seriously erroneous (Andrade, 1982; Cortes, 1980; de Silva, 1981; Frisbie, 1986; Mirandé, 1977; Staples and Mirandé, 1980). These families are far from homogeneous; they represent a number of different national and ethnic origins, vary by social class, speak a variety of dialects, have differing histories, differ in immigration and citizenship status, and live in various regions of this country. . . .

The first part of this chapter provides general immigration and demographic facts about each of the major Hispanic groups in the United States. The second section discusses some of the chief social and psychological research findings regarding these families. . . .

Some Current Issues in Immigration

Until 1945, legal immigration to the United States was mainly governed by an act of Congress of 1924, which was amended in 1952. This used the national origin system, which favored Western Europeans over Asians and Pacific peoples. In general, there was a ratio for each nation in the world that limited immigrants to numbers proportional to the population makeup of the United States in 1920 (for example, about one-fourth of immigrants granted entry were from Great Britain). However, the independent countries of the Western Hemisphere were afforded unlimited entry under this act.

In 1965, new legislation abolished restrictions against Asian and Pacific peoples. However, it imposed limits on immigration from the Western Hemisphere, with a quota of 120,000 persons a year being established. Preference was given to those with occupational skills judged to be needed in this country (LaPorte, 1977).

Because of severe economic and political problems in their own countries, larger numbers of Hispanics have sought to enter the United States than provided for under immigration laws. Thus many illegal aliens have recently entered this country, particularly from Mexico and Central and South America. Portes (1979) holds that the current large waves of illegal immigrants, most of whom are Mexicans, could be prevented from entering the United States, but that business and industry do not want this to occur. These workers are a cheap source of labor, and the fact that they are illegal creates an advantage for their employers, because they are highly vulnerable employees.

The Immigration Reform and Control Act of 1986 offered legal status in the United States or amnesty to illegal aliens who could prove they had resided continuously in this country since before January 1, 1982. More liberal amnesty provisions were developed for agricultural workers. The amnesty program includes sanctions against employers who hire illegal aliens and provisions for stepped-up border patrol and immigration service enforcement agents. The goal is to deter further illegal immigration while offering the protection of legal status to aliens who have lived here since before January 1, 1982 (Applebome, 1988).

Aliens applying for jobs had to apply for amnesty by the end of August 1987 to be hired for work that year, but applications were low and only about half of the estimated 2 million illegal aliens in this country had applied for amnesty by January 1, 1988, even though the deadline for such application was May 1, 1988. Most observers agree that the major impediment to this application was fear that families would be broken up, because some members of a number of families lacked documentary proof that they had lived continuously in the United States since before January 1, 1982. In fact, it is probable that many family members did not live in this country before 1982 and that of those who were here at that early date, a number probably had moved back and forth across the border. Attempts were made in Congress in 1987 to amend the legislation to protect family unity and grant amnesty to all family members if some members had gained amnesty or were eligible for it, but these amendments failed to pass.

The family issue is but one difficult aspect of the immigration problem. There are powerful economic and political pressures in countries of origin inducing immigrants to cross the border, whether these immigrants can gain legal entry or not. At the same time, many Hispanics south of the United States yearn to enter this country because of the relative economic gains and personal freedoms it appears to offer. Moreover, the long border between the countries is very difficult to police adequately, and a number of U.S. employers desire the cheap labor provided by illegal immigrants who fear discovery and deportation.

It is essential for family researchers, policy and program personnel, and practitioners to recognize the severe problems families face when they have immigrated to this country illegally. As suggested earlier, they are extremely vulnerable to employer exploitation. They also live in constant fear of discovery and are therefore difficult to reach if they need assistance. Further, they are ineligible for public aid and must rely on private sources for help. Immigration, in and of itself, poses a number of problems for families; illegal immigration severely escalates these problems.

Population Characteristics

There are difficulties in defining the term *Spanish origin.* Recognizing that census reports do contain some errors, it is helpful, nonetheless, to consider the data they present. According to these reports, there were more than 12 million persons of Spanish origin in the United States in 1979: 7.3 million Chicanos, 1.7 million Puerto Ricans, 800,000 Cubans, 800,000 Central or South Americans, and more than 1 million persons of other Spanish backgrounds. The total number of Hispanic-origin people in the United States increased by 33 percent between 1970 and 1979, with the fastest-growing group being Mexican—which grew by 62 percent. The majority of Hispanic families live in Arizona, California, Colorado, New Mexico, Texas, Florida, and New York. These families are largely concentrated in 10 of the nation's 305 metropolitan areas, with especially large numbers in New York and Los Angeles.

Age

The median age of the Hispanic population is fairly young when compared with the remainder of the population. This difference in age level is both a result and a cause of the higher fertility rate of Hispanic families. This comparatively youthful age has a number of other implications for public policy, including the likelihood that programs for children and adolescents will have a disproportionate number of Hispanics in them.

Educational Levels

On the average, members of Hispanic families, particularly the elderly, have lower educational levels than any other population group in the United States (U.S. Bureau of the Census, 1980). These lower levels of education for most Hispanics are partly a result of the recent migration of many of them, as well as the poverty and low levels of public education in their former countries. Continuing problems of low educational achievement for many Hispanic-Americans, including children and youth, is a matter of intense concern, especially because it adversely affects their future employment opportunities.

Employment and Income

Racial discrimination is apt to be another important factor in the high rates of unemployment of those Puerto Ricans who have dark skins and are classed as nonwhites—an effect of the African, Indian, and Spanish mix of their native land. Racial discrimination, still present in the United States, often comes as a shock to immigrants who have experienced much less of this in Puerto Rico (M. Delgado, 1987).

Spanish-American men and women are more apt than the rest of the population to be in blue-collar and service occupations. This is especially true for people of Mexican and Puerto Rican origin. Women are more apt than men to be in white-collar occupations. The great majority of Hispanic families live in urban areas today. There has been a massive shift away from farm employment, mostly because of the industrialization of agriculture. However, on average, there has been little advancement in occupational level.

Hispanic women are generally paid at a lower wage level than either white or African-American women. This is also true for those Hispanic men who are in clerical occupations or who are factory operatives. On the other hand, Hispanic men who are in professional or managerial fields earn more, on average, than black men in these occupations but considerably less than white males.

As of the 1980 census, more than 50 percent of all female-headed Hispanic families were below the poverty line, including 72 percent of Puerto Rican families, 49 percent of Chicanos, and 38 percent of other Hispanic families. For all groups, two-parent families with the wife in the labor force had the highest income, and one-parent families had the lowest annual income: about $25,000 for white one-parent families, $15,000 for African-Americans, and $18,000 for Hispanics (U.S. Bureau of the Census, 1983). In general, families with young children had the lowest average annual income in the nation. Overall, a large percentage of the children lived in impoverished families—a shocking and tragic fact. Minority children were in particularly adverse situations: 46 percent of black families with children had incomes below the poverty line. This was the case for 39 percent of Hispanic families and 16 percent of white families. . . .

Marital Stability

The 1980 census data for five southwestern states show that rates of marital stability are about the same for Mexican-Americans, Cuban-Americans, and Anglo-Americans, with divorce and separation rates of about 25 percent for these groups (U.S. Bureau of the Census, 1980). However, both blacks and Puerto Ricans experienced rates of about 40 percent. Mexican-Americans and Cuban-Americans had a far lower remarriage rate than did Anglos, but the reasons for this are unknown. Interestingly, Mexican-American divorce rates rise with higher levels of education for women, though the reverse tends to be true for Anglos (except for those women with graduate educations). Frisbie (1986) speculates that Mexican-American women with higher levels of education tend to become more acculturated to American patterns and are, therefore, more accepting of separation and divorce; however, this may be an overly simple explanation.

Precise data regarding unmarried parenthood among Hispanic-Americans tend to be missing. However, studies of unmarried adolescent mothers reveal that Hispanic girls are fairly similar to other adolescent women (*Family Planning Perspectives*, 1983). Although premarital chastity has been emphasized within the culture, this norm has been drastically eroded in recent years. Thus nonmarital intercourse and pregnancy have become increasingly common. Although the parents of pregnant teenage girls usually consider illegitimate childbearing a serious problem, they tend to welcome the baby into the family if the young woman decides to keep her child and not get married—a decision she frequently makes.

Fertility

According to the 1980 census, Hispanic women had higher birth rates than did either blacks or Anglos; however, those rates have been declining somewhat in more recent years. For example, only a little more than one-third of the women aged 15 to 44 had three or more children in 1980, compared with almost half of this group in 1970. Estrada (1987) notes that these high rates are caused by a number of factors: the youthful age structure of the Hispanic-American population, large families and high fertility rates of incoming immigrants, and traditional, though fading, negative attitudes toward birth control. These attitudes are partly associated with the fact that the huge majority of Hispanic-Americans are Catholic.

Large families are most likely to be characterized by low levels of employment, education, and income. This is found for such families in most parts of the world. Therefore, although these data can be interpreted as the consequence of high fertility, analyses also show that high fertility is a result of little education, unemployment, and poverty and the hopelessness, alienation, and lack of medical care they often engender (Chilman, 1968, 1983). High fertility also tends to go with low levels of modernization and a predominantly agricultural society (Chilman, 1968). There is evidence that the birth rate for Hispanic-American families is currently declining in association with rising levels of education, urbanization, and employment of Hispanic women. Increased availability of low-cost, high-quality family planning services also has been helpful, although addition of Spanish-speaking personnel to the professional staffs of such service agencies is frequently needed (J. Jones, 1985).

Language

The vast majority of Hispanics in this country are bilingual. Two-thirds of those who speak Spanish report that they also speak English well or very well (Estrada, 1987). A recent Institute of Social Research survey of Mexican-American households in the Southwest and Midwest revealed that the majority of adults interviewed spoke both English and Spanish. There was general consensus among the respondents that the speaking of Spanish was very important. Most thought there ought to be bilingual education in the schools. There was a generally strong feeling of ethnic identity, with many of the younger members of the population showing a particularly enthusiastic movement in this direction (Arce, 1982).

Many of the elderly and recent immigrants speak only Spanish, and many Hispanics, in general, chiefly speak Spanish within the family. As with other immigrant groups, it is common for the children to learn English before the parents do and for family members who are mainly confined to the home (often the elderly and mothers of young children) to speak English far less well than those who are in school or employed. This can create a number of disruptive family problems and is another indication that professionals who seek to work with Hispanic families should be bilingual, so that they can converse directly with all family members (Bernal, 1982; Falicov, 1982; Garcia-Preto, 1982).

Variations by National Origin

In the discussion that follows, emphasis is placed on the family-related cultural patterns of various Hispanic-American groups. There are two reasons for this emphasis: (a) most of the associated research and clinical observations reported in the literature emphasize cultural patterns and (b) these patterns are important in affecting individual and family behaviors, although not as important as much of the literature, including the following discussion, would suggest.

It is essential to recognize that cultural patterns by themselves do not determine an individual's behavior, although they may strongly affect his or her values, attitudes, and norms. Each person's behavior is also strongly affected by her or his temperament, special abilities and limitations, physical condition, age, life situation, and total developmental experience within the family and elsewhere. Moreover, the behavior of families is an outcome of the interaction of the individuals within them, plus the family's size, structure, history, developmental stage, and total situation—as well as cultural patterns.

Thus these patterns constitute one of a number of complex factors that affect familial behaviors and those of family members. For instance, Baca Zinn (1980) perceptively wrote that cultural values are important in family life, but should be studied in social context. They become fully meaningful only when they are related to historical, economic, residential, and other structural factors. Although they are important dimensions of families, they do not by themselves determine, or fully explain, family organization. Rather, one needs to study actual behaviors of families as well as their expressed beliefs (Baca Zinn, 1980, pp. 68–69). One also needs to take into account the economic resources of a family. For instance, members of an extended family may live together out of economic need rather than preference. Younger relatives may provide support for aging kin—again, more because of necessity than because of cultural norms.

The historical background of a people also influences the behavior of its members in a number of subtle and not-so-subtle ways. Among other things, history, including legends, affects the self-image of group members as well as their perceptions of people of other national origins. Thus brief historical sketches of various Hispanic groups are provided below.

Puerto Ricans

Puerto Rico was a Spanish colony from the time of its discovery by Columbus in 1493 until the United States invaded and annexed it in 1898 during the Spanish-American War (Fitzpatrick, 1981; Garcia-Preto, 1982). Although Puerto Rico gained increasing control over its own affairs during the next half century, becoming a commonwealth in 1952, real political control over the island remains in the United States today. This fact has spawned understandable resentment among Puerto Ricans, with some groups agitating for complete independence, some for statehood, and others for continued collaboration with the United States and the resulting benefits of this partnership, perceived by some as outweighing the costs. These varying positions naturally affect the attitudes of Puerto Ricans who come to the United States; it can be expected that a number would continue to harbor antipathy toward this country, with resulting barriers to acculturation.

As a people, Puerto Ricans are of many colors, from completely Negroid to completely Caucasian, and they must face the difficult problem of racial prejudice in the United States (Fitzpatrick, 1981). Poverty has been widespread in Puerto Rico, a central reason for the large migration to the continental United States. Cultural patterns are highly variable, affected by the kind of occupation pursued, the region of the island (such as isolated rural areas, farm villages, or urban areas), and social class status. Fitzpatrick (1981) cites a number of studies of family life and socialization in Puerto Rico, but most of them were carried out during the 1950s and 1960s and are therefore now rather out of date. There seems to be almost no research regarding Puerto Rican family life in this country. Thus in their discussions of the topic, both Garcia-Preto (1982) and Fitzpatrick (1981) tend to rely chiefly on clinical observations.

According to Garcia-Preto (1982), the dignity of the individual and respect for each person, regardless of her or his status, is of basic importance to most Puerto Ricans. This also pertains to respect for authority within the family as well as elsewhere. "The rules for respect are complex. For instance, Puerto Ricans think that a child who calls an adult by his or her first name is disrespectful. To make direct eye contact with strangers, especially women and children, is also unacceptable" (Garcia-Preto, 1982, p. 172). Garcia-Preto writes further that Puerto Ricans strongly favor self-control and an appearance of calm; they tend to attribute stressful situations to external factors and to express stress indirectly through somatic complaints.

Traditionally, Puerto Ricans place a high value on the family's unity, welfare, and honor. Emphasis is on commitment to the group, rather than the individual, and on familial responsibilities, including obligations to and from the extended family.

The double standard of sexual morality has been instilled as a basic value, with emphasis on modesty and virginity in women, sexual freedom among men, and, simultaneously, the obligation of men to protect the honor of the women in the family. This double standard has been considerably eroded in recent years, owing to the impact of changing cultural patterns in the United States and in Puerto Rico itself. Clearly defined sex roles have been common, but this pattern is changing, especially as more and more women find employment outside the home.

Parent-youth conflicts are observed by clinicians to be common among Puerto Rican families in the United States, especially among recent immigrants. As often happens with immigrants, traditional family values and roles are frequently challenged by children and adolescents as they seek to become completely "Americanized" in our highly individualistic, competitive society. As parents feel they are losing control, they often become more authoritarian, emphasizing responsibility, obedience, and respect toward the family. This tends to escalate the conflict, which may become particularly intense and harmful because the support of a homogeneous neighborhood and extensive family network is generally lacking—aids that had been of important assistance in their former island home (for further details, see Fitzpatrick, 1981; Garcia-Preto, 1982).

The above observations concerning Puerto Rican cultural patterns should be viewed with a certain amount of skepticism, especially with regard to Puerto Rican families in this country. As noted earlier, cultural patterns vary from group to group within Puerto Rico and also within the United States. The latter variation is strongly affected by the reasons, timing, and conditions of immigration and the region of the United States to which the immigrants came. For instance, the existence of large Puerto Rican communities within New York City and the constant movement back and forth, to and from the island, tend to reduce ready acculturation and shifts from more traditional family roles. This movement has a deep impact on the family, as it reinforces many links to the island and fosters continuous dismantling and reconstruction of family life (Rodriguez, Sanchez, and Alers, 1980). Puerto Ricans who have moved to other regions, such as in the Midwest, less readily find compatriots and may, therefore, take on American ways, including egalitarian family patterns and individualism, more quickly. However, they may also suffer more from a sense of loneliness and isolation.

As indicated earlier, Puerto Ricans, on the average, tend to have more economic, occupational, familial, and educational problems than other Hispanic groups in this country. The reasons are unclear, but such problems are probably a result of such factors as the poverty in Puerto Rico, from which they have fled; poor economic and social conditions in New York City, where most of them live; racism; lack of facility in the English language; perhaps, in some cases, a search for the more generous public assistance grants in New York as against Puerto Rico; and slow acculturation to this country because of frequent travel back and forth to the homeland.

A large percentage of Puerto Ricans in this country receive public assistance. This is partly a result of their ready eligibility for this aid because they are citizens of the United States, an outcome of Puerto Rico's status as a commonwealth of this country. This status also makes it possible for them to move readily to the U.S. mainland without immigration restrictions. Their citizenship status, in sum, confers certain privileges on them and makes them different from other Hispanic groups seeking entry to, and citizenship in, this country.

Mexican-Americans

Most Mexicans are of mixed Spanish and Indian descent. Their national heritage goes back many centuries to Indian civilizations that existed before the arrival of the Spanish explorers in the early 1500s. During the seventeenth, eighteenth, and nineteenth centuries, Spain extended its rule over the region that is now Mexico, California, and the southwestern United States. Mexico finally obtained its independence from Spain in 1821, but it was a weak country with little control over its vast territory (Kraus, 1959).

The rule by the United States over what is now the American Southwest and was previously part of Mexico dates only from the Mexican War of 1848— a war that ended in victory for the United States and the acquisition of lands that now include Arizona, California, Nevada, Utah, and Wyoming. Texas, which had recently (1835) won its independence from Mexico, was annexed by the United States in 1844. Thus, for a number of Mexicans in this country, their roots in what is now American soil far predate the arrival of the Anglos (Falicov, 1982). It is natural that Indian-Spanish heritage remains strong and that many continue to have feelings of resentment toward the United States. Although some Mexican-Americans have been in this country for many generations, the majority are either first- or second-generation immigrants.

Resentment toward this country has been perpetuated and, at times, strengthened by discriminatory and often exploitative behaviors by some Anglo-Americans toward many Mexicans in the United States and toward Mexico itself (Alvirez, Bean, and Williams, 1981). However, this resentment is mixed with admiration and envy of this country, which, potentially at least, offers many more opportunities than Mexico does for economic advancement.

At different time periods there have been large waves of Mexican immigration to the United States for political reasons (for example, flight from the violence of the Mexican Revolution of 1910) and for economic reasons (for example, the flight from crushing poverty and unemployment in Mexico in recent years). Most Mexican-Americans in the United States continue to suffer discrimination today, with limited access to good housing, education, and jobs. They are often exploited by employers, especially if they are illegal immigrants. They also have high rates of both unemployment and early school leaving.

Although most Mexican-Americans live in the Southwest, some have migrated to other parts of the country. For instance, some have lived in midwestern cities for three generations or more. As in the case of other immigrant groups, those who live near the borders of their "mother" country are less likely to acculturate readily than those who live far from their native land. For example, Mexicans who live in Chicago are more apt to become Americanized quickly than are those who live in southern Texas.

Much more has been studied and written about the family patterns of Chicanos (the appellation that many of today's Mexican-Americans prefer) than any other Hispanic group in the United States. Earlier research tended to assume that Mexican and Mexican-American life family patterns were essentially the same. It was generally believed that Hispanics were all highly familistic, with authoritarian, patriarchal patterns, including machismo for males and submissiveness for females. It was also held that premarital virginity and high fertility norms were characteristic of these families.

Andrade (1982) has summarized numerous studies and reports that an exaggerated supermother figure emerges from a summary of impressions of Mexican-American women: the unceasingly self-sacrificing, ever-fertile woman without aspirations for herself other than to reproduce. Andrade comments that several of the investigations from which this interpretation emerged were carried out in rural settings by Anglos, many of whom were males, unfamiliar with the culture or the situation they were investigating. Notably, almost all of these studies investigated lower-class samples, thus confounding ethnicity with socioeconomic status. Moreover, samples tended to be small and nonrandom (Andrade, 1982, p. 229).

Both Andrade (1982) and Mirandé (1977, 1979) emphasize that early writings about Hispanic family patterns (especially those about the Chicanos) were quite erroneous in stressing lack of egalitarian behaviors between husbands and wives. Mirandé (1979, p. 474) proposes that the concept of the all-dominant and controlling Chicano male is largely mythical. He criticizes unfounded psychoanalytic interpretations that interpret the machismo concept as a pathological defense against the Mexican-American male's feelings of inadequacy engendered by the adverse effects of discrimination and poverty. Mirandé also stresses that there are many kinds of Mexican-American families, with differing culture patterns. These patterns vary in accordance with recency of immigration, place of residence, socioeconomic status, degree of intermarriage with other ethnic groups, age, urbanization, and employment of women outside the home.

According to Mirandé (1979), more recent studies have shown an egalitarian family pattern in the behaviors of urban as well as rural Chicano families. One Mexican-American study project found, in both Los Angeles and San Antonio, that the families were not patriarchal, as had been frequently assumed (Grebler, Moore, and Guzman, 1973). Rigid differentiation of sex role tasks was lacking, and both men and women shared in homemaking and child rearing as needed. However, fathers tended to have a stronger role outside the family, and mothers were usually the dominant persons in the day-to-day matters of child rearing and homemaking—a point also made by Baca Zinn (1980). See also Cromwell and Cromwell (1978), Hawkes and Taylor (1975), and Staton (1972) for generally similar findings.

Mirandé (1977) describes the Chicano woman as the center of the family and the mainstay of the culture. As with many other ethnic groups, the mother tends to perpetuate the language and values of the "old country" and is usually a source of warmth and nurturance within the home.

The father is seen as the authority figure in many Chicano families. He is usually warm in his relationships with younger children, but more controlling as they get older. He often appears to be aloof and uninvolved in the details of family matters. Although he is seen by himself and others as the family leader who has power, the culture also includes a strong sense of related paternal responsibility.

Children are taught to carry family responsibilities, to prize family unity, and to respect their elders. However, the peer group becomes very important to adolescent boys as they grow older. Traditionally, girls stay at home with their mothers until marriage, but Chicanas (Mexican-American females) today are struggling for greater equality with both men and Anglos. They wish to keep their ethnic identity, but they also desire more flexibility in family and other roles.

The culture also emphasizes the family as a basic source of emotional support, especially for children. Support is provided not only by the parents, but also by grandparents, uncles, aunts, cousins, and friends. For example, although there has been a great deal of rural-urban migration among Hispanic populations, it appears that many Chicanos continue to live in comparatively large, intact kinship units where there are extensive networks of relatives who are helpful and supportive (Arce, 1982). No sharp distinction is made between relatives and friends, with the latter being considered as virtually kin if a close relationship has been formed. The term *compadrazo* is often used for this relationship. However, the pattern of close extended family relationships tends to fade among third- and fourth-generation families and among those who are upwardly mobile (Alvirez et al., 1981).

Bean, Curtis, and Marcum (1977) carried out an analysis of 1969 data from 325 Mexican-American couples who were members of a stratified sample in the Southwest. They found, among other things, that couples with egalitarian relationships were highest in their marital satisfaction—hardly a surprise. In general, the authors found little to support the concept that Mexican-American families have cultural patterns that are different from those of Anglo families and unique, culturally related sources of marital satisfaction. This point is also made by Zapata and Jaramillo (1981), who compared a small sample of Anglo families to Mexican-American ones in two southwestern cities. They found that differences in perceived family roles and alliances pertained far more to differences in socioeconomic status than to ethnicity.

Vega, Patterson, et al. (1986) provided helpful information regarding selected family patterns of a group of southwestern urban Mexican-American and Anglo parents with fifth- and sixth-grade children (N = 147 in each group). Using the Family Adaptability and Cohesion Scale II (Olsen, Russell, and Sprenkel, 1982), observers rated these families for the above characteristics. They also used an acculturation scale developed by Cuellar, Harris, and Jasso (1980). As might be expected, Vega, Patterson, et al. (1986) found that levels of acculturation varied for the Mexican-Americans according to their length of residence in the United States and their socioeconomic status.

Cuban-Americans

Cuban-Americans have a rather different background and immigration history than either Puerto Ricans or Mexican-Americans. . . . Cuba had been a colony of Spain for hundreds of years before the intervention of the United States in 1898, following an insurrection of some Cuban groups against oppressive Spanish domination. American motivations for intervention were mixed: Some liberal groups supported the Cuban cause of independence from Spain, but more powerful groups were swayed by their economic and political interests in this strategic island (Dulles, 1959).

After victory in the Spanish-American War, the United States established a strong political hold on Cuba, inducing rebellions, especially on the part of those people who were victims of the one-crop sugar economy and land ownership by the very few. The Cuban revolution of 1959 brought Castro and a predominantly socialist government into power and created fear and resistance in the United States, especially among those who, correctly or incorrectly, equated the Castro government with Soviet intrusion into the Western Hemisphere. At the present time, barely contained conflict between the United States and Cuba continues. One result of this conflict has been differing waves of immigration from Cuba to this country (Bernal, 1982; Dulles, 1959).

Many of the first wave of Cuban immigrants made a poor adjustment to the United States, partly because of their own troubled and disadvantaged backgrounds (Bernal, 1982). A serious public policy issue has arisen concerning government plans to deport some of those Cubans who have criminal records and the resistance of many to being deported. Cuban immigrants have settled chiefly in metropolitan areas such as Miami, New York, and Chicago. Although the different immigrant groups vary enormously in a number of ways, they also share a general cultural heritage.

Although formal research regarding Cuban-American families seems to be lacking, Bernal (1982) presents a summary of largely clinical observations. The traditional Cuban emphasis on familism, including the extended family, appears to be much like that found in other Hispanic countries. According to Bernal, the double standard of sexual morality, along with the concept of male dominance, has prevailed in Cuban culture as well. However, as shown above concerning Mexican and Puerto Rican families in the United States, when women work outside the home, egalitarian values and behaviors tend to emerge.

Bernal cites several small studies from the 1970s to the effect that younger and second-generation Cubans become acculturated to the United States more quickly than older or first-generation immigrants. As in reports regarding Puerto Rican families and immigrant families from many countries, the cultural differences between children and their parents often lead to youthful rebellions, authoritarian parental reactions, and considerable family stress. Bernal observes further that Cubans tend to regard themselves as a special people, perhaps because of their homeland's strategic political and economic importance to other nations over the centuries. This sense of being special may lend a feeling of superiority to some Cubans, with allied attitudes of chauvinism, racism, and classism, which may be viewed by some observers as arrogance and grandiosity. However, as in the case of Puerto-Rican Americans, more research about Cuban-American families is needed before much can be said about the ways in which they are like or different from other families in this country.

Immigrants from Central and South America

Very little has been written about the family patterns of other Hispanic immigrants. According to L. Cohen (1977), two-thirds of the immigrants from Central and South America during the 1970s were women. Most had children whom they left behind with their maternal grandmothers. These women often came on student or tourist visas or crossed the border illegally. They frequently had kin and friends who helped them come into this country and find work. They were afraid to bring their young children with them, and often dreaded returns home to visit for fear they could not reenter the United States.

These women were usually never married, separated, divorced, or widowed. They had a harder time than men in getting employment because of both sex and ethnic discrimination (L. Cohen, 1977). Despite low wages, most sent money home to help their families. They found it hard to bring their children to this country because it is difficult to gain permission for immigration of whole families to the United States. Much more needs to be learned about immigrant families in the United States from many parts of Central and South America, but there appears to be limited research about them. . . .

Some Implications for Research

As we have seen, there has been relatively little research devoted to Hispanic-American families. Most studies have focused on selected marital attitudes and behaviors of Mexican-American couples. The majority of these studies have looked at what significant differences, if any, are to be found between these couples and their Anglo counterparts, especially in matters pertaining to traditional male-dominant behaviors and segregated, rigidly defined sex roles. No significant differences between groups have been found, and it seems that these particular questions do not need further general exploration with respect to Mexican-Americans. However, they might well be asked in studies of particularly problem-laden subgroups, as well as Puerto Rican, Cuban, and other Hispanic families in this country, with the appropriate use of demographic controls.

Research has far from answered a number of other questions that might be raised about Hispanic family relationships, including further exploration of the impact on marital and parent-child relationships of recent immigration, extended families, unmarried parenthood, divorce, remarriage, unemployment, substance abuse, and family violence.

Much more needs to be known about Hispanic child-rearing beliefs, attitudes, goals, and behaviors with respect to the various ethnic and social class groups and in association with child development outcomes in such areas as school achievement, parent and child satisfaction, crime and delinquency, and youth employment. . . .

References

ALVIREZ, D., BEAN, F., & WILLIAMS, D. (1981). "The Mexican-American Family." In C. H. Mindel and R. W. Habenstien (eds.), *Ethnic families in America: Patterns and variations* (2nd ed., pp. 269–292). New York: Elsevier.

ANDRADE, S. (1982). "Social science stereotypes of the Mexican American woman: Policy implications for research." *Hispanic Journal of Behavioral Science*, 4, 223–243.

APPLEBOME, P. (1988, January 3). "Amnesty requests by aliens decline." *New York Times*, pp. 11, 12Y.

ARCE, C. (1982, March). "Maintaining a group culture." *ISR Newsletter.*

BACA ZINN, M. (1980). "Employment and education of Mexican-American women: The interplay of modernity and ethnicity in eight families." *Harvard Educational Review*, 50, 47–62.

BEAN, F. D., CURTIS, R., and MARCUM, J. (1977). "Families and marital status among Mexican Americans." *Journal of Marriage and the Family*, 39, 759–767.

BERNAL, G. (1982). "Cuban families." In M. McGoldrick, J. K. Pearce, and J. Giordano (eds.), *Ethnicity and family therapy* (pp. 186–207). New York: Guilford.

CHILMAN, C. (1968). "Fertility and poverty in the United States." *Journal of Marriage and the Family*, 30, 207–227.

CHILMAN, C. (1983). *Adolescent sexuality in a changing American society: Social and psychological perspectives for human services professions.* New York: John Wiley.

COHEN, L. (1977). "The female factor in resettlement." *Society*, 14(6), 27–30.

COONEY, R. S., ROGLER, L. H., HURRER, R., and ORTIZ, V. (1982). "Decision making in Puerto Rican families." *Journal of Marriage and the Family*, 44, 621–631.

CORTES, C. (1980). *The Cuban experience in the United States.* New York: Arno.

CROMWELL, V. L., and CROMWELL, R. E. (1978). "Perceived dominance in decision making and conflict resolution among Anglo, Black, and Chicano couples." *Journal of Marriage and the Family*, 40, 749–759.

CUELLAR, I., HARRIS, L., and JASSO, R. (1980). "An acculturation scale for Mexican American normal and clinical populations." *Hispanic Journal of the Behavioral Sciences*, 2, 199–217.

DELGADO, M. (1987). "Puerto Ricans." In *Encyclopedia of social work* (vol. 2, pp. 427–432). Silver Spring, MD: National Association of Social Workers.

DE SILVA, E. (1981). *Survival and adjustment skills to the new culture: Working with Hispanic women who have settled in the United States.* Paper presented at the National Conference on Social Welfare, San Francisco.

DULLES, F. (1959). *The United States since 1865.* Ann Arbor: University of Michigan Press.

ESTRADA, L. (1987). "Hispanics." In *Encyclopedia of social work* (vol. 1, pp. 730–739). Silver Spring, MD: National Association of Social Workers.

FALICOV, C. (1982). "Mexican families." In M. McGoldrick, J. K. Pearce, and J. Giordano (eds.), *Ethnicity and family therapy* (pp. 134–163). New York: Guilford.

Family Planning Perspectives. (1983). vol. 15(4), 197.

FITZPATRICK, J. (1981). "The Puerto Rican family." In C. H. Mindel and R. W. Habenstein (eds.), *Ethnic families in America: Patterns and variations* (2nd ed., pp. 189–214). New York: Elsevier.

FRISBIE, W. (1986). "Variations in patterns of marital instability among Hispanics." *Journal of Marriage and Family Therapy*, 48, 99–106.

GARCIA-PRETO, N. (1982). "Puerto Rican families." In M. McGoldrick, J. K. Pearce, and J. Giordano (eds.), *Ethnicity and family therapy* (pp. 164–186). New York: Guilford.

GREBLER, L., MOORE, J. W., and GUZMAN, R. (1973). "The family: Variations in time and space." In L. Duran and H. Bernal (eds.), *Introduction to Chicano studies: A reader.* New York: Macmillan.

HAWKES, G., and TAYLOR, M. (1975). "Power structure in Mexican and Mexican-American farm labor families." *Journal of Marriage and the Family*, 37, 806–811.

HETHERINGTON, M., COX, M., and COX, R. (1978). "The aftermath of divorce." In J. Stevens and M. Mathews (eds.), *Mother-child, father-child relationships.* Washington, DC: National Association for the Education of Young Children.

JONES, J. (1985). "Fertility-related care." In H. P. McAdoo and T. Parkam (eds.), *Services to young families* (pp. 167–206). Washington, DC: American Public Welfare Association.

KRAUS, M. (1959). *The United States to 1865.* Ann Arbor: University of Michigan Press.

LAPORTE, B. (1977). "Visibility of the new immigrants." *Society*, 14(6), 18–22.

MIRANDÉ, A. (1977). "The Chicano family: A reanalysis of conflicting views." *Journal of Marriage and the Family*, 39, 747–756.

MIRANDÉ, A. (1979). "Machismo: A reinterpretation of male dominance in the Chicano family." *Family Coordinator*, 28, 473–479.

OLSEN, D., RUSSELL, C., and SPRENKEL, D. (1982). "The circumplex model of marital and family systems: VI. Theoretical update." *Family Process*, 22, 69–83.

PORTES, A. (1979). "Labor functions of illegal aliens." *Society*, 14(6), 31–37.

RODRIGUEZ, C., SANCHEZ-KORROL, V., and ALERS, J. (1980). *The Puerto Rican struggle: Essays on survival.* New York: Puerto Rican Migration Research Consortium.

STAPLES, R. & MIRANDÉ, A. (1980). "Racial and cultural variations among American families: An analytic review of the literature on minority families." *Journal of Marriage and the Family*, 42, 887–904.

STATON, R. (1972). "A comparison of Mexican and Mexican-American families." *Family Coordinator*, 21, 325–329.

U.S. Bureau of the Census. (1980). *Persons of Spanish Origin in the United States: March 1979* (Current Population Reports, Series P-20, no. 354). Washington, DC: Government Printing Office.

U.S. Bureau of the Census. (1983). *Characteristics of the population below the poverty level*

(Current Population Reports, Series P-60, no. 138). Washington, DC: Government Printing Office.

VASQUEZ, M., and GONZALEZ, A. (1981). "Sex roles among Chicanos." In A. Baron, Jr. (ed.), *Explorations in Chicano psychology* (pp. 50–70). New York: Praeger.

VEGA, W. A., KOLODY, B., and VALLE, J. (1986). "The relationship of marital status, confidant support, and depression among Mexican immigrant women." *Journal of Marriage and the Family,* 48, 597–605.

VEGA, W. A., PATTERSON, T., SALLIS, J., NADER, P., ATKINS, C., and ABRAMSON, I. (1986). "Cohesion and adaptability in the Mexican American and Anglo families." *Journal of Marriage and the Family,* 48, 857–867.

WALLERSTEIN, J. (1985). "The over-burdened child: Some long-term consequences of divorce." *Social Work,* 30, 116–123.

YBARRA, L. (1982). "When wives work." *Journal of Marriage and the Family,* 44, 169–177.

ZAPATA, J., and JARAMILLO, P. (1981). "Research on the Mexican-American family." *Journal of Individual Psychology,* 37, 72–85.

Day-to-Day Living*

Mark Robert Rank

Like the effects of culture and race, social class can have a dramatic impact upon family dynamics. Mark Robert Rank demonstrates this vividly through interviews with families who are poor and on welfare assistance. Life is characterized as a struggle, filled with frustration and deprivation. This in turn puts considerable strain and stress upon families and their interrelationships. As the title of his book implies, these are households that are "living on the edge." This chapter provides a sense of what it is like for families to face the daily challenges of living in poverty, while simultaneously trying to subsist on the limited help provided by welfare programs.

> There's lots of nights that I go to bed and I lay awake and wonder how I'm gonna pay the bills. Because gas and electric is high. The telephone is high. And everything's going up instead of down. They keep everything up so high. It makes you wonder if you can make it through the month. When I take my check to the bank, I feel this way—I'm putting this check in the bank but it isn't gonna be my money. The bills are gonna have that money, not me.
> —*Elderly woman living on food stamps and social security*

Public assistance programs provide a bare minimum on which to live. They are not intended to raise a family's standard of living above the poverty line, only

Source: Mark Robert Rank, "Day-to-Day Living," from *Living on the Edge: The Realities of Welfare in America* (New York: Columbia University Press, 1994), pp. 51–61.

to provide limited assistance to particular categories of people. What is it like to live on welfare and in poverty on a day-to-day basis?

The Constant Economic Struggle

Perhaps most apparent when one listens to welfare recipients describe their daily lives and routines is the constant economic struggle that they face. This includes difficulties paying monthly bills, not having enough food, worrying about health care costs, and so on. The amount of income received each month is simply insufficient to cover all these necessary expenses. Having talked with dozens of families, having seen the daily hardships of recipients, having felt their frustrations and pain, I have no doubt that these families are indeed living on the edge.

This economic struggle is typified by the experience of Mary Summers. A fifty-one-year-old divorced mother, Mary and her two teenage daughters have been on public assistance for 11 months. She receives $544 a month from AFDC and $106 a month worth of food stamps. After paying $280 for rent (which includes heat and electricity), she and her daughters are left with $370 a month (including food stamps) to live on. This comes to approximately $12 a day, or $4 per family member. While this may seem like an implausibly small income for any household to survive on, it is quite typical of the assistance that those on welfare receive.

Mary turned to the welfare system because she had been unable to find work for two years (this in spite of a rigorous search for a bookkeeping or accountant's position, jobs she has held in the past). She comments, "This is probably about the lowest point in my life, and I hope I never reach it again. Because this is where you're just up against a wall. You can't make a move. You can't buy anything that you want for your home. You can't go on a vacation. You can't take a weekend off and go and see things because it costs too much. And it's just such a waste of life."

I asked Carol Richardson to describe what her day-to-day problems were. Having lived in poverty for most of her 45 years—Carol and her five children have received welfare on and off for 20 years—she can be considered an expert on the subject: "Making ends meet. Period. Coming up with the rent on time. Coming up with the telephone bill on time. Having food in the house. It looks like we've got enough now. I got food stamps last month. Otherwise we would be down and out by now. It's just keepin' goin' from day to day. Carfare, busfare, gas money...."

... Joyce Mills described her feelings about applying for public assistance. At the time of the interview, she was no longer receiving AFDC. I asked her about her most pressing problems. Although she was working full-time in a clerical position, and although she was receiving $81 a month from the food stamp program, she was clearly having a difficult time surviving economically:

> I think it's just trying to make ends meet. I don't think I go out and spend a whole lot of money, not like I'd like to. I'd like to be able to fix the kids' rooms up nice

and I haven't been able to. And if I do have the money, it's always something else that comes up. It's really frustrating. Then when I think, if my husband were not incarcerated and working with the job that he had, God, we could, both of us, be raking in very close to a thousand dollars a month. And it just makes me so mad. I've been juggling bills around trying to make ends meet. Now my muffler is off of the car and I gotta get that fixed.

I've been using that car very little since this happened this week. If it wasn't for this car, I would have had the money for Tommy's violin. And last night it just comes to a head, and I just released my tensions through tears. And thank God the kids were sleeping. It's so frustrating when you're trying to lead a normal life, but you can't do it. And then I was trying to think, "Well, if I get this in this month. If I can take so much out of this from the savings account. . . ." There was a time where I could have done that, but now I'm down to nothing. And this past check, it was down so low that I didn't have anything. I got paid and that week it was gone. It was all gone. So it was hard. I had to resort to borrowing.

Perhaps most revealing is her remark "It's so frustrating when you're trying to lead a normal life, but you can't do it." For many recipients, particularly those with children, this expresses in a nutshell their economic frustrations and the dilemmas they face.

Trying to lead a "normal" life under the conditions of poverty is extremely difficult. For example, Marta Green describes how not having a car for transportation severely restricts the kinds of activities she can do with her children, particularly during the wintertime.

In the winter we don't go anywhere. Because it's very hard without a car. I always had a car until last winter. It was very hard. Because we had to wait there sometimes twenty minutes for the bus. And with the kids and the very cold days, it's very hard. I only took them out last winter once, besides the Saturday afternoons that we go to church.

One Sunday, they had some free tickets to go to the circus. And I only had to buy my ticket. They both had theirs free. The circus was at seven. And it was done by ten. And we were waiting for the bus until eleven thirty that Sunday night. In the middle of the winter. And then finally we started walkin' home. We walked all the way home. We made it home by twelve thirty. They were tired and almost frozen. And then I thought, this is it, no more. So we really don't go very much anywhere.

As a result of daily economic constraints, the diversions open to welfare recipients must be quite simple and inexpensive. Going for walks, visiting friends or relatives, playing with their children, watching television, and reading are the types of activities available to provide some enjoyment and diversion for recipients during their otherwise hard times.

Ironically, those who have the fewest economic resources often pay the most for basic necessities, frequently of inferior quality. Take Marta Green as an example. Without access to an automobile, Marta often shops at a small neighborhood grocery store that charges higher prices for food than do larger supermarkets. In addition, the selection and quality of food items are generally worse than the offerings of the large chains. Without a bank account, Marta has to pay to cash her government checks and to make other monetary transactions. Her winter utility bills also run higher because she cannot afford better-quality housing with improved insulation. This pattern has been found repeatedly among the poverty-stricken (Caplovitz 1963; Jacobs 1966; Beeghley 1989; Maital and Morgan 1992).

The hard times and daily problems are succinctly summarized by 46-year-old Alice Waters, who is on SSI as a result of cancer and whose husband died of emphysema: "Day-to-day problems? No money, that's number one. No money. Bein' poor. That's number one—no money."

The End of the Month

Food stamp and AFDC benefits, received monthly, are usually not enough to provide adequately throughout a particular month. Many recipients find that their food stamps routinely run out by the end of the third week. Even with the budgeting and stretching of resources that recipients try to do, there is simply not enough left. Tammy and Jack Collins describe the process:

Tammy: Mainly it's towards the end of the month, and you run out of food stamps and gotta pay rent. Tryin' to find enough money to buy groceries. It's the main one.

Q: When that comes up, do you turn to somebody to borrow money, or do you just try to stretch what you've got?

Tammy: I try to stretch. And sometimes his ma will pay him for doin' things on the weekend for her, which will help out. She knows we need the money.

Jack: We collect aluminum cans and we got a crusher in the basement and we sell them.

Q: What happens when you run out of food?

Tammy: That's when his ma helps us.

Recipients often rely on some kind of emergency assistance, such as food pantries or family and friends, to help them through. Such networks provide an important source of support. Of the food pantries I visited, all reported that the numbers of people coming in for emergency food supplies increased dramatically during the last ten days of each month.

I asked Carol Richardson if she ran out of food, particularly at the end of the month.

Carol: Yeah. All the time.

Q: How do you manage?

Carol: We've got a food pantry up here that they allow you to go to two times a month. They give you a little card. And in between those times, we find other food pantries that we can get to. We've gone to different churches and asked for help all the time. And we get commodities at the end of the month. Cheese and butter. And then we usually get one item out of it, which helps an awful lot.

Borrowing from friends or relatives is another end-of-the-month strategy. We asked Rosa and Alejandro Martinez, an elderly married couple, about this. Rosa responded, "Sometimes we're short of money to pay for everything. We have to pay life insurance, mine and his. We have to pay for the car. We have to pay the light. And we have to pay the telephone. And there are a lot of expenses that we have to pay. And sometimes we can't meet them all. And between the month, I borrow, but I borrow from my friends to make ends meet."

Others deal with the financial squeeze at the end of the month differently. For example, Clarissa and John Wilson, a married couple in their thirties, rely on extra money from a blood plasma center to help them through. I asked them if they had bills which they are unable to pay.

Clarissa: Yeah, that's just frustrating. When you know that you can't pay your bills, and where are you gonna get the money to pay them. If you don't pay 'em, they're gonna always be with you. And that's just frustrating.

John: That's the main reason that we're always going to University Plasma. That's the main reason. To keep up . . .at least try to keep up, some of the bills. If the bills weren't a problem, we wouldn't go every week like we do.

Clarissa: Sometimes I don't see why we're gettin' the aid check because it still doesn't meet our needs—half of our needs. Maybe forty percent of it, I'd say.

In short, at the end of the month, the economic struggles that recipients face loom even larger. Even the basic necessities may be hard to come by.

A Set of Dominoes

For welfare recipients, there is little financial leeway should any unanticipated expenses occur. When nothing out of the ordinary happens, recipients may be able to scrape by. However, when the unexpected occurs (as it often does), it can set in motion a domino effect touching every other aspect of recipients' lives. One unanticipated expense can cause a shortage of money for food, rent, utilities, or other necessary items. The dominoes begin to fall one by one.

Unanticipated expenses include items such as medical costs and needed repairs on a major appliance or an automobile. During these crises, households must make difficult decisions regarding other necessities in their lives. I asked Cindy and Jeff Franklin to describe how they deal with these kinds of problems.

Cindy: Well, I think it's running out of money. (*Sighs.*) If something comes up—a car repair or (*pause*) our refrigerator's on the fritz. . . . We have enough money for a nice, adequate, simple lifestyle as long as nothing happens. If something happens, then we really get thrown in a tizzy. And I'd say that's the worst—that's the worst.

> *Jeff:* Yeah, 'cause just recently, in the last month, the car that we had was about to rust apart. Sort of literally. And so we had to switch cars. And my parents had this car that we've got now, sitting around. They gave it to us for free, but we had to put about two hundred dollars into it just to get it in safe enough condition so that we don't have to constantly be wondering if something's gonna break on it.
>
> *Cindy:* I think that sense of having to choose—the car is a real good example of it—having to choose between letting things go—in a situation that's unsafe, or destituting ourselves in order to fix it. Having to make that kind of choice is really hard.

When welfare recipients must make these types of choices, it is seldom because they have budgeted their finances improperly. Rather, they simply do not have enough money to begin with, often not enough to cover even the basic monthly expenses. Among the poverty-stricken, this is a major recurring problem. Public assistance programs help, but they just do not provide enough. Households are forced routinely to make hard choices among necessities.

One particularly difficult choice facing some households in wintertime is choosing between heat or food—the "heat-or-eat" dilemma. A three-year study done by the Boston City Hospital showed that the number of emergency room visits by underweight children increased by 30 percent after the coldest months of the year. In explaining the results, Deborah Frank, who led the study team, noted, "Parents well know that children freeze before they starve and in winter some families have to divert their already inadequate food budget to buy fuel to keep the children warm" (*New York Times*, September 9, 1992). An underweight child's ability to fight infection and disease becomes even more impaired when that child is also malnourished.

Tammy and Jack Collins described earlier how they are pushed to stretch their food supplies and to juggle their bills, particularly at the end of each month. When asked about her children's needs, Tammy responded, "Their teeth need fixing. That's the worst. See, our insurance doesn't cover that. And we've got one that needs an eye checkup that we can't get in to get done because the insurance don't cover that." If they decide to get their children's teeth fixed or eyes examined, the Collinses know they will have to make some hard choices as to which bills not to pay or which necessities to forgo. The dominoes thus begin to fall.

Consequences and Effects

Much has been written about the negative consequences of poverty. The poor suffer from higher rates of disease and crime, experience more chronic and acute health problems, pay more for particular goods and services, have higher infant mortality rates, encounter more dangerous environmental effects, face a greater probability of undernourishment, and have higher levels of psychological stress (Schiller 1989).

As mentioned earlier, hunger is a real consequence of poverty. Many of the families I talked to admitted that there were times when they and their children were forced to go hungry and/or significantly alter their diets. Running out of food is not uncommon among those who rely on public assistance.[1]

A widow in her sixties, Edith Mathews lives in a working-class, elderly neighborhood. When she received $45 worth of food stamps a month, they were not enough to provide an adequate diet (she was subsequently terminated from the program for not providing sufficient documentation). Edith suffers from several serious health problems, including diabetes and high blood pressure. The fact that she cannot afford a balanced diet compounds her health problems. She explains:

> Toward the end of the month, we just live on toast and stuff. Toast and eggs or something like that. I'm supposed to eat green vegetables. I'm supposed to be on a special diet because I'm a diabetic. But there's a lotta things that I'm supposed to eat that I can't afford. Because the fruit and vegetables are terribly high in the store. It's ridiculous! I was out to Cedar's grocery, they're charging fifty-nine cents for one grapefruit. I'm supposed to eat grapefruit, but who's gonna pay fifty-nine cents for one grapefruit when you don't have much money? But my doctor says that that's one thing that's important, is to eat the right foods when you're a diabetic. But I eat what I can afford. And if I can't afford it, I can't eat it. So that's why my blood sugar's high because lots of times I should have certain things to eat and I just can't pay. I can't afford it.

Similarly, Edith is often forced to reuse hypodermic needles to inject insulin. While she is aware that this could be dangerous, she feels she has little choice: "And then those needles that I buy, they cost plenty too. Twelve dollars and something for needles. For a box of needles. And you're only supposed to use 'em once and throw 'em away. But who could afford that? I use 'em over, but they said you shouldn't do that. Sometimes they get dull and I can't hardly use 'em. But I just can't afford to be buying 'em all the time. It's outrageous the way they charge for things."

Nancy Jordon was asked about not having enough food for her three children. In her mid-thirties, Nancy had been receiving public assistance for two months. Her income from working as a cosmetologist was simply too low to survive on as a single parent. She explains that not having enough money for food has had physical consequences not only upon her children but upon her as well:

Nancy: Well, as long as I got money. If not, I have to resort to other measures. It's a sad thing but a woman should never be broke because if she's got a mind, and knows how to use it, you can go out in the streets. Which is the ultimate LAST resort is to go to the streets. But at a point in a woman's life, if she cares anything about her children, if she cares anything about their lifestyle, they'll go. Matter of fact, some would go to the streets before they would go to aid.

Q: Have you had to do that, in the past, to feed your kids?

Nancy: A couple of times yes.

In addition to suffering from hunger, recipients may let health problems go unattended until they became serious, live in undesirable and dangerous neighborhoods, or face various types of discrimination as a result of being poor. But perhaps the most ubiquitous consequence of living in poverty and on public assistance is the sheer difficulty of accomplishing various tasks most of us take for granted: not being able to shop at larger and cheaper food stores because of lack of transportation and so paying more for groceries; having to take one's dirty clothing on the bus to the nearest laundromat with three children in tow; being unable to afford to go to the dentist even though the pain is excruciating; not purchasing a simple meal at a restaurant for fear it will disrupt the budget; never being able to go to a movie; having no credit, which in turn makes getting a future credit rating difficult; lacking a typewriter or personal computer on which to improve secretarial skills for a job interview. The list could go on and on.

These are the types of constraints experienced day in and day out by most of the people I saw and spoke with. The barriers facing the poor are often severe, apparent, and ongoing. They represent an all-pervasive consequence of living in poverty. Even the little things in life can become large. Recall Marta Green's difficulties when she took her children to the circus. Or consider the time the utility company shut off the Collins's gas: Tammy and Jack found that simply giving their children baths became a formidable task. Tammy explains: "They used to shut our gas off during the summer. And then I had no hot water for bathin' the kids. I had to heat it on the stove downstairs and carry it up to the bathtub. That was the worst times. I had an electric stove. I used to sit a big pan on top of it, and heat it."

For Cindy and Jeff Franklin, economic problems have turned what many of us would consider insignificant decisions into major quandaries.

> *Jeff:* I mean there's times when I'm taking the bus, and I have to wonder can we really afford to take the bus this morning?
>
> *Cindy:* Right now, today, we've got just over a dollar. And three dollars in food stamps. And that's all we've got till the end of the month, till the end of the month. That's fairly unusual because the car ate up so much money this month. Usually we manage our money better than that. But we really have to think. I mean, it's not just thinking about whether or not you can afford to go to a movie, but you have to think about can the kids and I stop and get a soda if we've been out running errands. It's a big decision, 'cause we just don't have much spending money.

Living in poverty and on public assistance is a harsh, ongoing economic struggle that becomes more acute by the end of the month. There is very little slack in the rope. When an unanticipated event leads to economic stress, entire lives suffer, domino fashion. Everyday life is complicated by a variety of negative physical consequences, including the difficulty of carrying out the most basic tasks. As Mary Summers commented at the beginning of this chapter, "This is where you're just up against a wall. You can't make a move."[2]

Notes

1. Several studies attempting to document the extent of hunger in America (e.g., Brown and Pizer 1987, the Food Research and Action Center 1991, and Cohen, Burt, and Schulte 1993) have found that those on public assistance routinely run out of food at the end of the month. In addition, the Food Research and Action Center report estimated that 4.7 million children under the age of 12 in the United States go hungry at some point during the month, typically near the end.

2. Or, as William Cobbett the English journalist, essayist, and politician of the late eighteenth and early nineteenth centuries wrote, "To be poor and independent is very nearly an impossibility."

References

BEEGHLEY, LEONARD. 1989. *The Structure of Social Stratification in the United States.* Boston: Allyn and Bacon.

BROWN, J. LARRY and H. F. PIZER. 1987. *Living Hungry in America.* New York: New American Library.

CAPLOVITZ, DAVID. 1963. *The Poor Pay More: Consumer Practices of Low-Income Families.* New York: The Free Press.

COHEN, BARBARA E., MARTHA R. BURT, and MARGARET M. SCHULTE. 1993. "Hunger and Food Insecurity among the Elderly." Project Report. Washington, D. C.: The Urban Institute.

Food Research and Action Center. 1991. *Community Childhood Hunger Identification Project: A Survey of Childhood Hunger in the United States.* Washington, D. C.: Food Research and Action Center.

JACOBS, PAUL. 1966. "Keeping the Poor Poor." In Leonard H. Goodman, ed., *Economic Progress and Social Welfare*, pp. 159–184. New York: Columbia University Press.

MAITAL, SHLOMO and KIM I. MORGAN. 1992. "Hungry Children Are a Bad Business." *Challenge* 35: 54–59.

SCHILLER, BRADLEY R. 1989. *The Economics of Poverty and Discrimination.* Englewood Cliffs, N. J.: Prentice Hall.

Shattered Dreams*

Lillian B. Rubin

This selection is taken from Lillian B. Rubin's book, Families on the Fault Line: America's Working Class Speaks about the Family, the Economy, Race, and Ethnicity. *In this chapter she examines what has happened to the working-class family and to their dreams as a result of the downturn in the economy over the past 20 years. Like her earlier book,* Worlds of Pain: Life in the Working-Class Family, *Rubin utilizes in-depth interviews with working-class households to illustrate how social class impacts upon family dynamics.*

"Used to be you worked hard, you figured you got someplace. Not anymore," says 38-year-old George Karvick, a white father of three who worked for years in an automobile parts factory and now has a job in the maintenance division of a real estate management company. "We did everything we were supposed to do—worked hard, saved some money, tried to raise our kids to be decent law-abiding people—and what do we get?" he asks, his words biting, his eyes burning with indignation. "The goddamn company goes belly-up and look at me now."

"Maintenance, they call it; I'm nothing but a goddamn janitor," he says, spit-

---

ting out the words as if they sear his tongue. "I worked hard to get where I was, and it's damn hard to go backward."

It is, indeed, "damn hard to go backward," harder still to believe in a future when things might be different again. "Life's never been some kind of a picnic, but now, every day there's more bad news," says George's wife, Anna. "It's so scary. I worry all the time. How bad will it get? It's like you work your whole life to be something, you know, so your kids will grow up and be something, and look what happens. Now I don't know; what are we working for now?"

The hope that sustained working-class people through bad times 20 years ago, the belief that if they worked hard and played by the rules they would eventually grab a piece of the American dream, has been shattered. And with good reason. The 1973 recession marked the beginning of a long decline for American workers—a slide whose worst effects were obscured by the rise of two-income families and cushioned by the spending binge of the 1980s. By the time that decade was gone, the government had more than tripled the national debt, and the IOUs of both industry and consumers had more than doubled.[1]

In the 1990s the bill came due. But when the economy slumped this time, there were no reserves, nothing to break the fall—not in industry, not in the government, not in personal checking or savings accounts. Instead, both the nation and its people were left with a ruinous load of debt that required drastic cutbacks in both the public and private sectors. For industry this meant a dramatic restructuring of American business that took millions of jobs, at least half of which are gone for good, according to the best estimates of labor experts and the executives heading up the corporate makeovers.[2] Even the service sector, which saw fairly high levels of growth during the 1980s and which provided a paycheck—although a less than satisfactory one—for workers displaced from manufacturing, has suffered a shakeout that no one expects to end soon.[3]

Reflecting on these changes in the economy, Janet Norwood, the former U.S. Commissioner of Labor Statistics, said: "We've never been in a situation quite like this. It used to be that when we had a recession, everyone waited to be rehired. But the psychology now is that many of these jobs are not going to come back."[4]

For many younger workers who are trying to get a foothold on the ladder, therefore it's not going backward that worries them but whether there's any possibility of moving forward. "It's not like it was when my folks were my age," complains Ed Demovic, a 25-year-old white stock clerk, married four years with two small children. "My parents didn't have it easy, and neither did Linda's. I listen to my dad talk; he didn't have any gravy train, but there was a chance to get ahead. You know, if you were willing to work hard, you could do okay. When one of us kids complained, he'd always tell us how we were living a lot better than he did when he was a kid, so we had no gripes coming. Not anymore! I'm not going to be able to say that to my own kids. From where I stand, it looks like we're going to be worse off. And God knows how bad things'll be by the time their turn comes."

The changed realities of the job market, the belief—a reasonable one until recently—that a college education would pay off heavily in increased lifetime earnings, has sent working-class youth into the college classroom in larger numbers than ever before.

Yet our optimistic statistics about the benefits of a college education obscure fundamental truths about class and gender differences. In 1990 men with four years of college earned, on average, $44,554 a year compared to $28,043 for male high-school graduates. Women college graduates, however, earned only $28,911—virtually the same as men who only went to high school—while women with high-school diplomas earned $18,954—nearly $10,000 less than men with the same education.[5]

The same income tables that show an increase in earnings of college graduates over those with four years of high school make no distinction between the kind of low-prestige school a working-class youth is likely to attend and the elite college or university that educates the child of a professional family. But it's clear to anyone who is not blinded by our myth of classlessness that the education is superior and the opportunities for mobility greater with a degree from Harvard or Princeton than one from Clearview State. If the average earnings of college graduates were broken down by school—which would, by and large, reflect a breakdown by class—the annual income of the Clearview graduate would be significantly less than the one from Princeton. As I wrote in *Worlds of Pain*, "Even when the children of working-class families go to a four-year college, most go to schools that, at best, will track them into lower-middle-class jobs through which they will live lives only slightly better than their parents'."[6]

Ironically, even that meager promise has now been broken. As of the late 1980s over 3 million people with some college education were working at full-time jobs that paid less than $11,000 a year.[7] By now that number undoubtedly is considerably higher. And even those college graduates who have enjoyed the prosperity their education promised now face diminished prospects. From 1979 to 1989, for example, the average earnings of people with a college degree rose by 2 percent after adjustment for inflation. Over the next three years these same college graduates saw their wages drop by 1.6 percent.[8]

At the same time that wages were falling, the average cost of a college education at a four-year public institution—the only kind a working-class student can possibly afford—soared from $599 a year in 1975 to $2,006 in 1990, while funds for student aid decreased. At those prices, a working-class youth needs not only a high level of motivation but a job, a student loan, and a room at home with mom and dad. "I couldn't go to school if I didn't live at home," explained Susanna Dionne, a black 19-year-old student and part-time worker. "I work twenty-four hours a week, and I've got some student loans, but it's not enough to pay for rent and food. Mostly between my job and my loan, I have enough to pay for my tuition and books and have a little left over for clothes and expenses like that. I'm lucky, though; I've got it better than a lot of my friends. I only pay my parents board, no rent."

With all her "luck," by the time Susanna graduates from college she'll be between $10,000 and $12,000 in debt with no certainty of the kind of job her degree would have bought in rosier economic times. If she goes on to graduate or professional school, she'll add another $8,000 or so to her debt burden. Asked how she expects to pay off such debts, she answers worriedly, "I don't know; I worry about it all the time. I'd like to go to social work school and get my master's, but I get scared when I think about owing all that money. But the problem is, when I read the paper and see how hard it is to get a decent job, then I think maybe I have to. I mean, what choice will I have? Go to college all these years for some stupid job at Kmart?"

In an economy where unemployment is high, where media headlines announce that college graduates face the "worst job market in thirty years,"[9] and where the wages of the college educated haven't kept up with inflation for the last several years, Susanna and her peers have something to worry about. "I feel like I can't win, and I keep wondering what I'm doing," she continues. "I'm going to owe all this money and if I have to go to graduate school to get a decent job, it'll be even more. How am I ever going to pay it back? No matter what I do, I'll be in debt for years and years. What am I going to do, live with my parents forever so I can pay off my debts?"

Susanna's parents brood, too. "How's she going to pay off all the money she'll owe?" asks her father, Raymond, a 45-year-old semiskilled worker. "What kind of a way is that to start out a life, having such big debts?" Her mother, Louise, a 40-year-old clerical worker, seconds her husband's words and adds her own concerns as well: "Don't get me wrong," she warns. "I don't want to push my kids out the door, but I've been mom for a long time. My oldest son's got a job and a girlfriend, but he still lives here because he doesn't make enough money to get married and move out. And I've got another girl coming up behind Susanna. What's going to happen if these kids can't get off on their own like grown children are supposed to do? How long do we have to turn our lives over to them?" she asks, looking intently at me, as if expecting an answer.

It's a question that troubles many parents today as, in this era of decreasing wages and rising unemployment, more than a quarter of all adults under 35 are living under the parental roof.[10] True, as I said earlier, adult children in working-class families have always lived at home until they married. But until recently, they generally married in their teens, as the working-class women and men I interviewed 20 years ago did. Today, however, with so many young people deferring marriage into their twenties and beyond, their presence in the household becomes a noticeable burden to parents who are ready to move on to the next stage of life. "Our parents didn't have a chance to get tired of us being around," laughs Regina Whitehead, a white 47-year-old receptionist. "I was eighteen, just out of high school, and Danny was nineteen, almost twenty, I guess, when we got married. It's different today. With kids not wanting to get married, and they can't afford to live on their own, they hang around a long time, and it's like you wonder when you're going to get to live your own life."

For the mothers, especially, almost all of whom work full-time outside the home, the full nest, not the empty one, is the problem. "We've got two of my kids still living with us. They're good kids; I even like having them here sometimes," continues Regina. "But it's hard; there's always something extra to do, lots of extra laundry all the time, things like that. And you know, if it was just me and my husband, I wouldn't be worrying so much all the time about what to cook for supper. It's a lot different when you've got them around. I come home from work, and there's always some kind of mess to clean up. Just once before I die I'd like to know what it's like to come home and the house would be just the way I left it," she concludes with a sigh.

Women like Regina Whitehead not only have a different sense of themselves than their mothers did, but a different set of expectations for this stage of life. Two decades ago many of the young families I met left their children in a grandmother's care while mother went off to a part-time job. It's true that these grandmothers usually were paid for their child-care services. But it was also a labor of love, something grandmothers expected to do, indeed would have been glad to do without charge if their financial situations permitted. Today, however, grandma is likely to have her own full-time job. "I sometimes feel guilty because I can't help my kids out like my mother helped me," says Regina. "But I can't work and take care of the grandbabies, too."

It isn't just that she can't, however; it's also that she doesn't want to. "You say you 'can't,' which suggests it's what you'd like to do if you could afford to stay home," I remark.

She laughs. "Guess you caught me there, didn't you? Don't get me wrong, I love being grandma, but my life's important to me, too, and so is my job. It may not be some big-time job like yours, but I like doing it."

Even fathers, most of whom cling to the old traditions more tightly than mothers—especially for their daughters—are ready for their adult children to leave the nest. "It's one thing you don't want the kids out on their own when they're eighteen, nineteen. But twenty-five?" exclaims Dan Whitehead acerbically. "If my girls had tried to leave when they were eighteen, I would have broken their legs. But I don't know; now I think: *Christ, how long?* I mean, what I really want is for them to get married and settle down in a place of their own. But if they're not going to do that, well, I don't know, maybe it's time for them to go anyway."

In all families an adult child living at home poses a dilemma: How will these adults, who are also and always parent and child, relate to each other? What happens to the old family rules? What kind of responsibilities can parents expect the children to assume? These are difficult issues for families to resolve. But for middle-class families the return of adult children doesn't create the kind of economic burden that working-class parents experience, nor does it generally mean a change in their life plans.

For the older families in this study, retirement—or if not actual retirement, some other significant life change, such as a move from the city to the country—is high on the list of things they dream about, talk about, plan for. "All I've been thinking about is retiring and getting out of this stinking city," says Walt Mobley, a 53-year-old white security guard. "My wife and me, we talk about it all the time."

But as their children continue to need their help, such talk comes to seem more like a fantasy than a realistic plan for the future. "Crazy, isn't it?" he continues. "Here we are with the kids all grown up; we should be making our plans. But what happens? I can't because I have to take care of them. My son's got a shitload of debts from college, so he can't go anywhere until he pays some of that off. That bum my daughter was married to walked out on her, so now she's here with her two kids. God knows when she'll get her life together again."

It isn't only the needs of adult children, however, that stand in the way of the older generation realizing its dreams. Few working-class families have the kind of pensions or investments that would allow them to retire in reasonable comfort. Their largest and most significant asset is the house they live in, the house that they always assumed would provide the nest egg for their old age. "The one thing we knew we had was the equity in this house; it was our security blanket." But after years of rising property values, most of these families awakened one day to find that their homes had lost a sizable portion of their value. According to a report in *The Wall Street Journal*, home equity dropped an unprecedented 16.6 percent in 1990, causing a decline in average household net worth for only the second time since World War II.[11]

In Southern California, the site of the greatest and most sustained level of housing price appreciation in history, the bust has been so severe that in one three-month period during 1992, nearly 18 percent of homes sold for less than their purchase price.[12] A figure that would be much higher if most sellers hadn't taken their houses off the market rather than suffer the loss. "We paid $240,000 for this place seven years ago," says May Yau, a 49-year-old Asian office worker who lives in a small city near Los Angeles. "A couple of years later, it was worth over $300,000. If we had sold even two, three years ago, when we first thought about it, that's what we could have gotten. Now it's too late; the best offer we've had was $215,000. So we're stuck here for a while anyway." Unfortunately for the Yaus and others like them, it may be a very long while, since California housing economists predict that home prices will plunge another 20 percent before leveling off.[13]

Translated into human terms, this means, among other things, that plans for the future have to be reconsidered. "Work's so damn slow, it'd be a good time to call it quits and get out of here," says Don Lermen, a 55-year-old white mechanic. "But with the economy the way it is, nobody's buying houses in this city right now. We had the place up for sale for eight months and didn't have a nibble. The real estate agent said when a place hangs around that long, it gets stale. So we took it off the market. You know, even if we could sell it right now, with prices what they are—so low, I mean—we wouldn't get enough out of it. So it comes down to, I can't afford to retire."

Equally important, it means also that people who felt safe in their affluence now experience themselves at risk. "Until a couple of years ago, I had this plan," explains Paul Terrones, a 50-year-old white appliance repair man. "We've got some savings, see, some investments that could bring in some money. So I figured we'd sell this house, and buy a little place up in the mountains. I don't mean where the tourists go; some small town where you could buy something cheap so I could put the rest of the money from the house into something that would bring in some more income. Between that, and maybe I'd do a few odd jobs on the side—you know, building or fixing things for people in town—we could live a good life. But no more; I can't even think about it anymore. This house is down about 25 percent in the last two years. And with interest rates where they are, you've got to be a lot richer than I'm ever going to be to live off investments.

"So what am I going to do now? Hell, I don't know, and I don't like not knowing. Me and my wife, we both feel kind of nervous all the time now, you know, uptight about what's going to happen, how we'll manage. Christ!" he explodes, slamming his fist against the arm of his chair. "I thought we had it made, and look at us all of a sudden worrying about what's going to happen tomorrow."

It's one of the great ironies of this era that while the older generation worries about falling housing prices, their children find themselves priced out of the housing market. Twenty years ago a young working-class family had a chance of making the dream of owning a home come true. "It's what we worked for, to have a nice house for the kids to grow up in," explains Serena Wycoff, a 45-year-old white hairdresser. "It was hard; we were young, and we had babies right away. And it took quite a few years for my husband to settle down in a job. He floated around at first, trying this and that. But when he saw nothing else really worked, he got on at Ford, and he's been there ever since. God willing, he'll stay there until he retires. But with the economy the way it is and everybody getting laid off, you can't be sure of anything these days, can you?" she concludes, shaking her head as if to push the unwanted thoughts away.

The Wycoffs' house, like the homes of most working-class people of their generation, is small, unpretentious, modestly furnished, the pride of ownership visible in the many loving little touches that say: *This is mine, the achievement of a lifetime.* But even the falling prices and lowered mortgage rates haven't brought such a home within the reach of most young working-class families.[14] Those in the top income tier might be able to support the mortgage payments, but the down payment is a daunting obstacle. In the last two decades, therefore, the proportion of young families who own their own homes dropped from 51.4 percent to 44.3 percent,[15] while the average age of first-time home buyers leaped astonishingly—from 27 to 35 in the ten years between 1980 and 1990.[16]

The few families in this study who have managed to become homeowners have been forced into the very low end of the housing market, which means that their houses have even less space and fewer comforts than the unassuming homes in which they grew up. "Believe me, I didn't grow up in no mansion, but it was a lot nicer house than this one, bigger, too," says Luanne Roberts, a 31-year-old white cashier, who surveys her living room with a critical eye.

Or the only housing they can afford is in distant fringe cities, leaving them with long commutes that add not only to the daily stress but also to the time pressure that husbands and wives both complain about so bitterly. "The driving back and forth is a killer; traffic's murder," explains Burt Reimerson, a 33-year-old white warehouse worker who lives in a small city on the edge of a metropolitan area in the Midwest. "I get off work at 5 and don't get home until 6, 6:30. By then I'm dead beat. But can I just take a load off and take it easy? Hell, no. First there's the kids; then the wife's always got something for me to do. Christ, there's no time to live; it's work and shit, that's all, work and shit. But what can I do? No way could we afford a house closer to the city—no way."

Stress and time, however, aren't the only expenses of the commute to suburb or exurb. When the Reimersons lived in the city, Burt's wife, Leona, was a secretary making over $20,000 a year. Now with the mortgage payment higher than the rent they used to pay and the additional expense of a long-distance commute, her earnings are more important to the family economy than ever before. But being so far away from the children proved to be too anxiety provoking. "At first we thought I'd commute, too, like Burt does," she explains. "I tried it for a couple of months, but it didn't work. It's not good for both of us to be over an hour away from the kids. I worried the whole time I was gone. Suppose they need something? Or one of them gets sick? Or maybe it's snowing and I can't get home. Burt didn't like it either, so we talked and decided I should quit and look for something closer to home."

But she hasn't been able to find a comparable job in or near the town where they now live. "I guess there never were that many places to work around here, but with the recession and nobody's hiring and companies going out of business and all . . .," she explains, her words trailing off, her hands thrust forward, palms up in a gesture of helplessness. "I looked and looked but I couldn't find a secretary's job like the one I had, and things were getting tighter and tighter. We needed the money real bad, so I couldn't hold out anymore. I gave up and took this job in the bakery, working for $4.50 an hour. Can you believe it?" she asks, shaking her head and pausing to let the words sink in. Then she continues, a note of pride in her voice: "I worked my way up after about a year, so now I manage the shop. But I still only get $6.25 an hour, not near what I was making before. It's something like $8,000 a year less. Boy, what a difference that would make in our life right now. This move cost us so much, I sometimes wonder whether it was worth it. We both do," she concludes wistfully.

Yet the Reimersons and the others like them are the lucky ones. For the rest, the dream of owning a home seems like a mirage. "It pisses me off," exclaims Dale Streets, a 29-year-old black UPS driver. "I grew up in a house, but I don't think my kids will. And I'm one of the lucky ones. I got a steady job; I make a pretty good living, and with what my wife brings in, we're doing okay. But you've got to be rich to buy a house these days, and that ain't going to happen," he concludes unhappily.

It's true that with housing prices so high buying a home is a problem for young families in any class. But parents in the middle-and upper-income brackets are far more likely than those below to be able to offer all or part of a down payment to their children. For the working-class young, such outside help rarely is available. "Have you seen the prices of houses around here?" asks Delia Johnson, a black 28-year-old bridge toll taker. "I'm not talking about anything fancy, just a plain old little house. Even with both of us working as hard as we can, we're never going to be able to save enough to buy one. I mean, we talk about it; we even go out looking sometimes. But it's not going to happen. Where would we ever get the money for a down payment?" she asks, her body slumping in discouragement.

It's not only while they're alive that middle-class parents help out their adult children, but after they die as well. No one talks much about this nearly taboo subject, but the prospect of an inheritance is a reality of life that most young middle-class adults don't forget.[17] For it provides both a financial and a psychological safety net to know that one day they'll come into enough money to ease at least some of their financial burdens. The working-class young see no possibility for such relief. Indeed, most of them will be lucky if they don't have to support their parents in their old age.

In addition to whatever help or inheritance they may get from their well-off parents, the adult children of middle- and upper-middle-class families earn more money, therefore have far more options than those in the working class. In her inquiry into the downward mobility of middle-class baby boomers, Katherine Newman writes at length about the housing misfortunes of young adults who grew up in an affluent town in New Jersey. Unable to afford homes in the community of their childhood or its stylish equivalents, they settle for housing in less prosperous towns, where houses are smaller than those they're accustomed to; community services, conveniences, and comforts are fewer; and neighbors are more diverse.

"Communities that have lower housing costs often lack the amenities that make a well-heeled community like Pleasanton so desirable: parks, pools, and the like," writes Newman. "They are also more likely to be mixed income towns where racial and class tension is in the air. Whatever the current economic status of Pleasanton's boomers, there is no escaping the fact that they were raised in a lily-white town, where the schools were good, and the diction, worldview, and style of the middle to upper-middle class became part and parcel of their personalities. People raised in Pleasanton stick out when they 'integrate' these modest communities and often find they have little in common with their older, less educated neighbors. Housing, it seems, is not all they were after: a community of like-minded souls is no less important and it may be a long time in coming," Newman concludes.[18]

Small wonder that working-class families are so irate today. They watch the neighborhoods they love being taken over by people who "stick out," who are contemptuous of them and their lifestyle, and worst of all, who move there as a last resort and for whom the need to do so is one of life's misfortunes. For what to Newman's middle-class families seems like deprivation would be a gift of abundance to the working-class families in this study. Indeed, it's at least partly the migration of young professional middle-class families into these communities that has priced the working class out. For the older families who live in these neighborhoods, there's some benefit. As the professionals move in and gentrify the area, property values go up. But the children of the working-class will suffer the cost, since they'll never by able to buy a house in the neighborhood they grew up in.

The parents of the young families in this study watch the struggle of their adult children in pain and puzzlement. "What happened?" they ask themselves. "Where did it all go wrong?" they wonder. They did what was expected, willingly sacrificing their own comforts and gratifications in their earlier years in the belief that it would ensure a better, easier life for their children in the later ones. Hasn't this been the unique and quintessential American promise—that each generation would surpass the one before it? "You always expected that you'd sacrifice but it would be worth it because your kids will have it better than you did," says Leona Reimerson's mother, a 49-year-old sales clerk whose husband, Joe, has worked on the assembly line for 23 years. "What else did you work all your life for?"

For the parental generation—men and women who are old enough to have been wage earners 20 years ago—nothing seems to make much sense anymore. When they were their children's age, median family income (in 1972 dollars) hovered around $12,000 a year; now it has nearly tripled to just over $34,000. For those who managed on $12,000 two decades ago, the idea that they could make over $30,000 and still feel poor is almost impossible to comprehend. As Mike Fillman, a white 49-year-old machinist, exclaimed: "Dammit, I don't get it. Between me and the wife we make $38,000 a year, and we're always behind. I remember when I thought that was a fortune. If anybody'd ever told me I wouldn't be rich on that kind of money, I'd have told him he was nuts. Back when I was making twelve or thirteen grand a year, I used to think if I could just get up to twenty I'd have it made. Now thirty-eight doesn't make it. How do you figure it?"

It is hard indeed to "figure it," to integrate the fact that dollars no longer mean the same thing, that he can make what once seemed like "a fortune" to him and still have trouble paying the bills. He knows that everything costs more, that taxes are higher, that they take a bigger cut out of his paycheck now than they did before. He has heard and read enough to know that after taking inflation into account, his $38,000 isn't worth much more than his $12,000 was two decades ago. And he knows, too, that the average pay for men in his line of work fell by about 4 percent in 1991.[19]

But this cognitive knowledge lies alongside a deeply embedded sensibility born in the past, making it difficult to incorporate fully the new reality. So when he comes up against the economic squeeze he feels in the present, he's caught, not quite able to understand why he's hurting financially when the numbers tell him he *ought* to feel rich. Just so, when he sees his grown children unable to make it on incomes that would have seemed grand when he was their age, the picture doesn't make sense. "I don't get it, that's all; I just don't get it. It's all unreal; nothing makes any sense anymore. How did we get to this place in this country? What the hell's gone wrong?"

Partly what's gone wrong is that while the numbers seem large, when inflation is factored in, adults 35 and younger earn less now than people in the same age group did 30 years ago. Moreover, although federal income taxes haven't risen substantially, and in some cases may even be less than they were before, other taxes—such as state income taxes, payroll taxes, property taxes, sales taxes, social security, and various local taxes and use fees—have taken an increasing share of the weekly paycheck of most workers.

During the 1960s, for example, real wages were increasing by 1 or 2 percent a year, while taxes were taking about one-third of the extra income. So long as people were improving their living standard, the tax burden wasn't an issue.

But in the 1970s real wages began to stagnate or decline at the same time that many taxes were increasing, which meant that taxes were taking a greater portion of people's already diminishing income—a situation that laid the basis for the tax revolts that in recent years have made headlines in communities across the country.

But while the increasing tax burden is the manifest target of working-class anger, the discontinuity between past and present realities sustains and nourishes their discontent. "At first when I started to work it seemed like we were making so much money," says Mike's wife, Marlen. "I mean, $38,000! That's a lot, isn't it? We really felt rich, like now we could have all those nice things we couldn't afford before. We bought a new refrigerator—the old one was *really* old—and new carpet and a sofa for the living room, things like that. And Mike bought a new car. It was the first brand-new car he ever bought. We tried to help out the kids, too; they were having a real hard time. Then all of a sudden, the bills piled up on us. Sure, it was easy to charge all that stuff, but pretty soon we were having trouble paying the interest on our credit cards. We learned pretty fast that we weren't rich," she concludes ruefully.

The result has been a peculiar disjunction between the belief that they ought to be affluent juxtaposed against the end-of-the-month shortfall, leaving people perplexed and uncertain about just how to feel and whom to blame. "What the hell's happening to this country?" they shout. "Nothing makes sense anymore," they cry. But since no one lives comfortably in a world in which "nothing makes sense," they make sense in whatever way they can, which often means blaming "them." Sometimes "they" are an abstraction—the government, the politicians, the bureaucrats, the feds, the Congress. But there's little satisfaction in raging against these distant, lifeless, and immovable bodies. So they turn instead on those in their line of vision—the aliens in their midst, most of whom these days are people of color.

Notes

1. By the time the 1990s came into view, the $286 billion annual interest on the $3.1 trillion national debt was the third largest expense in the federal budget. Between 1980 and 1990, U.S. industry increased its debt from $1.4 trillion to $3.5 trillion, while consumer debt rose from $1.4 trillion to $3.7 trillion (*Time*, January 13, 1992).

2. After a step round of cutbacks in the middle of the 1990–1992 recession, for example, the CEO of Eastman Kodak explained: "If it were just the recession, we would be hiring these people back again. And we aren't going to do that." At about the same time, when Xerox announced a 20 percent cut in its work force, the chairman of the company said that the economic slump was only speeding up cost-cutting plans that were already in place (quoted in *The New York Times*, December 16, 1991).

3. The end of the cold war and the defense cuts that are sure to follow mean that at least a million more defense industry jobs probably will be slashed over the next several years.

4. Quoted in *Time*, July 20, 1992.

5. *Statistical Abstract*, U.S. Bureau of the Census (1992), Table 713, p. 454.

6. Rubin, *Worlds of Pain*, p. 209.

7. Bennett Harrison and Barry Bluestone, *The Great U-Turn: Corporate Restructuring and the Polarizing of America* (New York: Basic Books, 1988), p. 127.

8. *The Wall Street Journal*, May 14, 1992.

9. *San Francisco Examiner*, March 1, 1992.

10. The most recent statistics from the U.S. Census Bureau show that 27 percent of adults under 35 live with their parents. Separating out those between the ages of 18 and 24, the bureau estimates that the figure has risen from just over 40 percent three decades ago to more than 50 percent today (*The New York Times*, February 12, 1993). But all these figures can be no more than estimates, since these young people are transients, tending to move in and out as both their economic fortunes and their tolerance for family living rise and fall.

11. *The Wall Street Journal*, March 18, 1992.

12. *The Wall Street Journal*, October 13, 1992.

13. Ibid.

14. Until the most recent decline, the inflationary spiral of the last two decades sent the median price of a starter home up 21 percent at the same time that real income of young working-class families *declined* by anywhere from 12 to 20 percent. From 1979 to 1989, workers with a high-school diploma saw their wages decline by 9.8 percent, while the wages of high-school dropouts fell by 17.3 percent. Over the next three years, the decline continued, falling another 2.2 percent and 3.9 percent, respectively (*The Wall Street Journal*, May 14, 1992).

15. *The New York Times*, October 20, 1991. In southern California, the land of sunshine and single-family dwellings, home ownership has declined to 54 percent of all households, a rate well below the 64 percent in the nation at large (*The Wall Street Journal*, October 12, 1992). Focusing on the generation that came of age in the Reagan era, Newman, *Declining Fortunes*, p. 32, reports that only 15 percent of families in this age group owned their own homes in 1990, compared to 23 percent in 1973.

16. *San Francisco Chronicle*, November 29, 1991. Newman, *Declining Fortunes*, p. 38, notes that "only 9 percent of the nation's renters are able to afford a home"—a figure that includes all races. The figures for African-American and Latino families are even more bleak: 98 percent of both these groups can't afford a median-priced starter home.

17. See "Waiting for the Windfall," *Time*, January 18, 1993, for an examination of the effects of inheritance on the baby boom generation. According to this article, the share of total household net worth derived from inheritances and family gifts rose from 47 percent in 1962 to 71 percent in 1989.

18. Newman, *Declining Fortunes*, p. 123.

19. "Employment and Earnings," U.S. Department of Labor (December 1991), Table C-2, pp. 90–91. This figure assumes an inflation factor of 4 percent in 1991.

References

HARRISON, BENNETT, and BARRY BLUESTONE. *The Great U-Turn: Corporate Restructuring and the Polarizing of America.* New York: Basic Books, 1988.

NEWMAN, KATHERINE S. *Declining Fortunes.* New York: Basic Books, 1993.

RUBIN, LILLIAN B. *Worlds of Pain: Life in the Working-Class Family.* New York: Basic Books, 1976. New paperback edition with new introduction, 1992.

U.S. Bureau of the Census. *Statistical Abstract of the United States: 1992* (112th ed.). Washington, D. C.: U.S. Government Printing Office, 1992.

Wife*

Susan A. Ostrander

Few studies have looked at families of the upper class. Susan A. Ostrander in her book, Women of the Upper Class, *examines such households through interviews with wives in wealthy families. As in the previous two readings, we can clearly recognize the impact that social class has upon family dynamics. Upper-class membership influences the role expectations that wives and husbands have of each other, family decision making, and specific dissatisfactions. But in addition, Ostrander also points to the similarities these women have with wives in other social classes. As she notes, "These similarities powerfully illustrate the subordinate position of women in society and the importance of gender frameworks as explanations for women's position in society. Even in the most privileged class, women lack freedom, independence, and influence over family decisions relative to men."*

He expects me to make a nice home to come to, to be a cheery companion, to be ready to go on vacations when he wants to. He expects me to go along with what he wants to do. . . .

*Source: Susan Ostrander, "Wife," from *Women of the Upper Class* (Philadelphia: Temple University Press, 1984), pp. 37-69.

He wanted to move to the country, and I didn't so we moved to the country.

My husband never asks me what I think. He just tells me how its going to be.

They could be traditional wives anywhere. They could be sitting in working-class bungalows, cramped city apartments, or suburban tract houses. But they aren't. The first woman, Mrs. Smythe . . . arrived late for our interview, coming from a luncheon for the Friends of the Metropolitan Opera Association held at a nearby estate. Her uniformed maid ushered me to a sunroom to await her arrival. Mrs. Smythe's family is old enough and wealthy enough to have the library of an established local university named after them. . . .

Mrs. Carpenter (the woman who had recently moved to the country) spoke with me in the plush blue and gold surroundings of her intown woman's club. The club's membership is invitational and limited to the oldest and wealthiest families in the city. She is the retiring president of the club. Mrs. Cooper, (the woman whose husband never asked her what she thought) was speaking specifically about decisions having to do with the company of which he is the president. The company is owned by her family, not his, and carries her family name—a name known to virtually every family in America. . . .

Much of what these women described as the meaning of upper class focused on the basic differences of their lives and the lives of other people. But as they talked about themselves as wives, their descriptions were strikingly similar to those of women in other classes. How do they see their responsibilities as wives? What are their expectations of themselves in that role?

Expectations

The upper-class women I spoke with centered their lives around their husbands and their husbands' work and adapted themselves to the men's needs, performing what Jessie Bernard has called the "stroking" function. The stroking function, according to Bernard, consists of showing solidarity, giving help, rewarding, agreeing, understanding, and passively accepting.

Mrs. Haines, for example, a young wife who mentioned as an aside toward the end of the interview that her husband was regularly out of town from Monday through Friday on business, remarked: "You have to be your husband's biggest booster. You have to make him feel good. He does not appreciate it if he comes home and I'm exhausted. I've got to be ready to find out what his week was like. He comes first, and I have to bend my life to fit his."

Mrs. Lane is an extremely protective wife in her fifties. Her husband heads one of the city's oldest and most prestigious shipping firms: "He's the brain in the family and it's my role to see that he's at his best. I've subjugated everything to that. When he comes home in the evening, this house must be perfectly quiet. I've told everyone the phone must not ring after five o'clock. He wants me to be pleasant, pretty, and relaxed. I can't dare cry in front of him or show any emotion. I never bring a problem to him, except during forty-five minutes set aside on Sunday mornings for that purpose. I keep a list." When asked about her husband's responsibilities to her, Mrs. Lane conveyed the sense that the question had never occurred to her. "Oh, I think he's perfect," she said. "He's kind and considerate. . . ."

Mrs. Atherton. . .emphasized a protective role: "It's little things I do. . .like taking the telephone off the hook when he's home. He's so tired and he needs to relax. If he wants a sweater, I think I'm better equipped to go upstairs and get it. I used to try to protect him too much. There was never any dissention or anger in this house. I make life as comfortable as possible for my husband." She was the only woman who spoke of the sexual aspect of her responsibilities as wife, noting "sexual compatibility" as a part of making life comfortable for her husband. She added the importance of her looking attractive, saying, "When we go out, I like to know I will look as good as I can. . . ."

Mrs. Sharpe spoke of the importance of just being there, being attentive, as part of her stroking role. She said, "I try not to go to meetings in the evening and leave him alone." Mrs. Wilson also noted the importance of simply being available to her husband: "I'm here when he wants to blow up, when he wants me to listen."

Women of wealth and privilege, like women of other social classes, are expected as wives to accommodate to their husbands' emotional and other needs. Upper-class wives speak of their responsibilities to make their husbands feel good, to protect them from personal and family problems, to make life comfortable for them, to be loving and attractive partners, and simply to be available in case the men want something. They also speak of subjugating their own needs to those of their husbands. This mode of accommodation is the primary way in which upper-class women are clearly subordinate to their husbands. This mode runs throughout the other expectations of themselves as wives.

The women I spoke with take it for granted that they are solely responsible for "running the house." Though this expression does not mean doing the actual housework, which is the primary responsibility of women from other classes. Upper-class women are fully responsible, indeed perhaps more so, than wives of other classes for making sure that there is food on the table; clean and pressed clothes in the closets and dresser drawers of the various members of the family; and that the house is generally pleasant, clean, and in good order at all times. And, like other women, they do some complaining about that. The difference is that women of the upper class are far less responsible for actually cooking the meals, washing the laundry, and running the vacuum cleaner.

All of the women I spoke with have some kind of household help, although the extent of help varies and live-in help is by no means typical. Thus "running the house," for upper-class women, could be seen in the context of a statement made by Mrs. Holt. When asked how she and her husband divide up household responsibilities, she said, "When you have someone else to do the work, there's not much dividing up to do." And Mrs. Atherton said of herself and other women of her social group: "Very few of us are doing mundane household chores. If I chose, I wouldn't have to lift a finger around the house. I like to cook when I have the time, but I think I enjoy it because I know I don't have to do it."

Upper-class women are not personally responsible for performing housework. They make decisions about how others, whose labor is purchased, perform the housework. For example, Mrs. Wilson spoke of planning, not cooking, meals; of ordering, not actually buying, foods. It is certainly the case, however, that the level of expectation in terms of what is done and how it is done is much higher.

Mrs. Clarke, for example, a rather harried young mother of three spoke poignantly of her husband and his long hours away from home, saying: "He wants a certain quality in his life. He likes the house well taken care of." Her earlier comment about her husband's time away from home reflects another expectation of wives who run the households for men who essentially run the nation's business. It is the expectation that the men will be absent much of the time. . . .

Mrs. Haines's husband is away five days a week; Mrs. Hammond's husband had been out of the country for the better part of five years setting up an overseas branch of the firm he now heads; and Mrs. Vincent's husband "worked abroad for months at a time." These women are examples of upper-class wives running their households in complete isolation from their husbands. Other studies have found this rigid division of responsibilities between husbands and wives in upper economic groups, though they have not noted the extent to which husbands are often absent. A study done by sociologists Blood and Wolfe 20 years ago concluded that "the more successful the husband is in his occupation, the less the wife can count on his help at home."[1] Helen Hacker concurs, saying "traditionally, the roles of husband and wife in the upper class are clearly separated."[2]

Most upper-class wives know that they can enhance their husbands' position by running the house and by protecting their husbands from domestic concerns. Since the women take care of the domestic front, the men are free to concentrate their energies on business and community activities. Mrs. Cooper put this particularly succinctly: "If a man's home life is happy, he can put his all into being a dynamo in the business world." When asked how she helps her husband with work, Mrs. Harper said: "I help just by not upsetting him and keeping the house running. . . ."

Several other women said that they help their husbands' careers by simply doing whatever is necessary for their husbands to be happy and successful in work, and by adjusting their own lives to their husbands' desires. Mrs. Haines (the young wife whose husband was out of town five days out of every seven) said: "We've been married eight years and he's always traveled. Usually he's away Monday through Friday. I've adjusted to it. I've learned to fill my days. I feel he's a better husband when he's doing what he does. I've learned to keep busy during the week, because when he comes home he doesn't want to go out much. I've molded my life to his."

Most of the women mentioned that they are also responsible for their families' "social arrangements," though only the newcomers spoke of an obligation to entertain in order to advance their husbands' position. Women from old established families seem to feel that the men can make it on their own merits and do not need this kind of help from their wives. Mrs. Haines feels she is "fortunate to be married to a man who says that if he can't make it on his own, my being able to whip up a Beef Wellington is not going to help him. He considers [entertaining] frosting on the cake."

Entertaining clients or prospective associates is, thus, not seen by upper-class couples as a way to climb the ladder of success. These are men and women born to privilege, and social striving is not necessary. It is assumed that the men will acquire the top positions due them in a matter of time. Business entertaining among the old upper class, therefore, is more a demonstration of having already attained the most powerful positions in the corporate hierarchy, rather than a means of achieving those positions—as might be the case with rising young executives from other socioeconomic classes. . . .

"Making social arrangements" is a broader social form than "entertaining." It is one of the ways that upper-class women construct and maintain the social fabric of upper-class life. . . . The women see to it that the social network of "congenial" people is kept in good order. Mrs. Clarke, for example, said that her husband expects her to have "people around that he enjoys, to do things with." Mrs. Harper, a mother of five (whose husband is a partner in one of the city's oldest corporate law firms) said: "When he's worked hard all day and he calls up and says let's get a tennis game together, I do it. He'd get upset if I didn't. . . . If he wants me to organize a party, I have to get it done. If he calls me in the middle of the morning and wants to have a party the next day, I've got to do it."

Making social arrangements supports the exercise of power in the business world. Since the woman is responsible for arranging the man's social as well as home life, the man is free to concentrate all his energies on the nation's economic affairs. As Mrs. Hall concluded, "The wife takes care of social arrangements and leaves the husband to business."

Being available to travel with their husbands on business trips is the first of three expectations related directly to their husbands' work. The importance of this responsibility of upper-class wives was expressed by Mrs. Harper: "I have to be available and ready [to travel]. If he wants to go on a trip, I'd better be ready. My theory is that if I'm not available he'll find someone else who is. . . ."

Business travel by upper-class couples enhances national class networks. The importance of such travel and the need for women to be available to go along are reflected in discussions of the advantages of volunteer work. . . . Volunteer work they explained, provides them with the flexible schedules necessary to accompany their husbands on his business trips.

Another task of upper-class wives is to be a "sounding board" for their husbands' business concerns. The women spoke repeatedly and with resonating sameness of the importance of this role. They described explicitly how passive listening and acceptance, not active participation, was wanted of them. Mrs. Harper said bluntly, "I listen, and I keep my mouth shut." Similarly, Mrs. Vincent thought that her husband is "just looking for a sounding board, not real advice."

Though these kinds of comments were typical, a few of the women did think they had at times given useful advice. Mrs. Sharpe spoke of her husband's unhappiness in a former job: "I urged him to leave and to go to another company. He's much happier now. . . ."

Some of the women also talked about their role in the socialization of younger executive wives—women married to the men who work for their husbands. Mrs. Lane. . .said: "Whenever a new executive wife comes along I give her quite a lecture on ceasing to be an emotional person. She should never be nervous or cross. These men can't take that. She should always be prompt and ready to go." Mrs. Lane has recently found that the younger wives were not as willing as they used to be: "I find the newer wives want to be people. They feel they have as many rights as their husbands. They say they could never do what I ask, that they're equals."

Socializing young wives did not always mean teaching them to conform to husbands' demands. Recognizing the difficulties caused by the frequent moving that is part of corporate life, two of the women—both newcomers—had opposed their own husbands on this issue. Mrs. Atherton, speaking of one young wife whose husband had been offered a promotion and a transfer in the firm headed by Mr. Atherton, said, "Large companies sometimes move their executives indiscriminately without much concern with what it's going to be like for the rest of the family. For big daddy, it's a step up the ladder. Some of the people in my husband's firm have had promotions offered and the man has turned them down because his wife objected. One I know had grown children and good friends here and a new home. She didn't want to leave. I was supportive to her in her decision. My husband would have felt it was none of my business, and he didn't know I was involved. . . ."

In regard to expectations of wives, then, these upper-class women describe a general mode of accommodation and a number of specific tasks. The general mode consists of adjusting, "molding," their own lives to the lives of their husbands—a mode that is inevitably one of subjugation. In terms of tasks, they are expected to run the house and shield their husbands from mundane household and family concerns. They free the men to concentrate all of their energies on their work, work that sometimes necessitates long absences from home. The women are also responsible for making the social arrangements that support the fabric of upper-class life.

Tasks directly related to their husbands' work are the need to travel with their husbands on business trips and to serve as sounding boards for their husbands' business concerns (only rarely giving real advice). The wives of men who head business firms may also be called upon, or take it upon themselves, to socialize the wives of new men hired into the firm. These tasks reflect a rigid division of labor between men and women of this class, which differs somewhat in content but not substantially in form from the division of men and women in other socioeconomic classes.

The wives' tasks reflect not only the division of labor, or social differentiation, but also a clear subordination of the women to the men, a social stratification based on gender. This is particularly true of the expectations that wives be accommodating, adaptive, available. This general mode makes it difficult, if not impossible, for the women to have life agenda independent of the men. This mode of subjugation seems inherent in all the tasks for which the women are responsible. They not only run the house, they do so in a way that shields their husbands from any concern over what goes on there; they do so even when he is away from home for extended periods of time. They not only make the social arrangements, they make them on short notice and at their husband's request. They not only travel with their husbands on business—a task that surely has its pleasant aspects—but they do so also on short notice, which means that their own schedules must be open and flexible. They not only are available to listen to their husbands talk about business problems, they also learn, for the most part, to hold their tongues and not give any real advice. This evidence of gender stratification, and subjugation of upper-class women calls attention to the need for a gender as well as a class conceptual framework for understanding these women's lives.

Decisions and Money

Gender as well as class stratification was evident as the women talked about family decision making. Major decisions were described as changes in place of residence, childrens' schooling, husbands' job, or the wife's decision to take paid employment or return to school. These decisions were made, most women said confidently, by themselves and their husbands together. Some of the women, however, qualified this. Mrs. Smythe, implying basic agreement with her husband on most issues, said: "If he thinks it's a good idea, it doesn't take too long for me to think so too. He can usually convince me he's right."

Mrs. Holt implied the use of feminine wiles: "I think the woman often has her way of getting what she wants. Some of her decision making may not seem so obvious. [My husband and I] have had our share of disagreements." Mrs. Lane claimed that since her and her husband's views were essentially the same, making decisions was an almost automatic joint venture: "I have a very brilliant husband, and I tend to have the same views as he does, to repeat what he says. But we make decisions together, and I think he respects my opinion. . . ."

Although the women claimed almost universally that they made decisions "together" with their husbands, it appeared that in fact, the husband had the decision-making power in the family. When important, recent decisions were analyzed, the power structure of the family was clearly gender stratified, with the men in a position of dominance: their wills prevailed in important decisions. Mrs. Appleton's statement is indicative of this phenomenon. Her husband had just changed jobs, and she reported that they had made the decision "together." When I asked her what would have happened if she had actively opposed the job change (which she did not like because it was going to mean more entertaining of clients and less time spent with her husband), she laughed and said, "He probably would have said 'so what!' "

Mrs. Crowell, whose husband had recently been promoted, gave the "partnership" answer in response to my question of how decisions were made. She then went on to offer: "I don't think he would have refused [the promotion] even if I'd said I absolutely don't want you to take it. He came home a few weeks ago and told me he'd be doing more traveling even though he knew I wouldn't like it."

Such evidence suggests that upper-class women, like women of other social classes, have less equalitarian marriages in terms of family decision making than they, themselves, believe. Lillian Breslow Rubin found this same false belief about equalitarian decision making in her study of working-class couples. She reports that "most people said 'fifty-fifty.' Yet, when one pushes the question a little further the illusion is quickly dispelled. Almost all agree: the husband has veto power over a decision."[3]

I was interested in the fact that upper-class husbands dominate family decision making. Studies of women and families in other classes have found that power over money is a primary factor in deciding how much of a voice the women have. Upper-class women have substantial inheritances independent of their husbands. How, therefore, are the husbands able to maintain their power? For an answer to this question, I began to look at the issue of money and its link to family power.

When asked about their own money and what it meant to them, the women readily acknowledged its effect on their lives. They spontaneously offered comments about the effect that having their own money has on their relationships with husbands. Mrs. Bennett, an elderly widow, said: "I had my own money and made decisions about investing without consulting my husband. It was very important to me. It's hard to have to ask your husband for money."

Mrs. Hall, who had married down in class, said: "I have my own money. [My husband] insisted on paying the household bills. My money went for fripperies like horses. He set himself up a goal that he was going to earn as much money as I had. It's very important for me to have my own money." She went on to say that she had recently begun handling her own money: "I didn't used to do my own accounts. I was being very childlike. My husband's secretary did my accounts. After a while I didn't like that. I wanted to be able to buy things without its going through my husband's office. I didn't want everyone to know how much everything cost. So now I handle my own accounts, and I enjoy it immensely. . . ."

Mrs. Sharpe (a woman from one of the city's oldest and wealthiest first families) said: "The household money is mostly mine, partly his. My mother left me a large sum of money. I've been able to give gifts I otherwise couldn't have." She did not, however, make her own investment decisions: "I don't want to make investment decisions. I'd rather have my husband do that. He asked me about it. . . ."

Mrs. Cooper (whose husband heads a company bearing her family name) remarked: "I get a household allowance from my husband's bank account, though I can't say I don't have money of my own. It's in a savings account, and it goes for special things. Most of it is invested. My daughter is about to be married, and I know my husband had some financial problems recently, so it's nice not to have to go to him and say I need some extra in my allowance. . . ."

Most of the women, as their comments indicate, fully enjoy having their own money and recognize the freedom and independence it gives them. A few, however, said that having their own money is of little importance to them. They claimed that since their husbands do not use money as a source of power, having their own money doesn't make that much difference to them. Mrs. Martin who spoke of "doing her share" in raising the children and of "being a good companion" as her responsibility as a wife said of financial matters: "Since I don't have a tightwad for a husband, having money of my own hasn't made much difference to me. I don't really think about it."

Mrs. Hammond (whose husband had been out of the country for the better part of five years setting up an international branch of his firm) said that she pays "all the bills from a joint account. I could have inherited some money from my mother but I persuaded her to pass me for the children. I don't feel the need for money of my own for personal security. I never think about it. . . ."

A direct link between money and family decision making was made by Mrs. VanHague, the only woman who professed to be the major decision maker in her marriage. This elderly dowager, now a widow, responded to my question about major money decisions, saying: "I made most of the decisions because he figured it was my money."

The relationship of economic power to financial decision making is also evident in the cases of three women with whom I was able to trace actual, recent decisions. The husbands of women who do not control their own money appear to have the major share of the power. Mrs. Appleton (who laughingly said that her husband would have paid little attention to her objections to his new job) reported that although she does have some money of her own, she sees her husband in the traditional role of "provider": he pays all of the household bills, and she appears to know little of financial matters. Mrs. Crowell (who said that she did not think her husband would have turned down his promotion even if she had absolutely opposed it, and who is contemplating enrolling in graduate school in special education) indicated that although she has some money of her own, she "would like to be more independent. It's part of the reason why I want to work."

Mrs. Carpenter and her husband had recently moved to a large country estate. When I asked her how they had decided on the move, she answered without cracking a smile: "He wanted to move to the country, and I didn't. So we moved to the country." Later in the interview she said of household finances: "He gives me a household allowance. If I need more usually it's quite a scene. I send him to the store so he knows how much things cost. Then he comes home and says he sees what I mean about the prices. Or sometimes I'll be cagey about it and give him hot dogs or hamburgers until he asks how much of a raise I want. . . ."

In sum, it appears that having control over their own money is as important for upper-class wives as it is for wives in other social classes. This is especially true when it comes to having a say in family decisions. Whether the husband is a cab driver, a clerk, or a chairman of the board, the women's voices are heard more loudly in homes where they are economically independent. In households where having money of her own makes little difference, the wife sees her husband as an exceptional man—a man who recognizes his wife's contribution to the family in her own right, provides her with an allowance comparable to a "salary," and does not ask questions about how she spends it. When wives are expected to justify their expenditures and to make elaborate appeals for increases, the scenes in the upper-class households are very much the same as those in any other household. This was evident from the women's descriptions of "finagling it," like Mrs. Carpenter who sent the husband to the grocery store, or serving him budget meats for several days in a row.

It is difficult for wives to have to ask their husbands for money; and women who have to do so are inevitably in a position of subordinance. If the husband checks up on how his wife spends the money he gives her, it is cause for resentment on both sides. Even when he is "good about it," the women are aware that they are "lucky"—a word that implies the lack of control on the woman's part and the recognition that if he were not "good about it," there wouldn't be much she could do.

At least some of the women are displeased about their lack of an equal voice in family decisions and see a link between this and their financial control. I then wondered how the women's control or lack of control over their own money relates to the division of household labor. I found that the women who are economically self-reliant, due to an inheritance or a salary, seem to have different ideas about family and household responsibilities than the women who rely economically on their husbands. Women who manage their own money had less traditional views about their roles as wives.

Mrs. Hoight, whose husband's expectations for her are rigid, described with some guilt her unwillingness to go along with his wishes: "He'd like it if I stayed home more than I do and was more supportive. I should devote myself to being interested in the things he is. I do feel a lot of guilt about my housekeeping. My husband says he would like more order, more meals on time. It could become a major conflict, but it never has." When I asked her how she and her husband manage money, she replied: "I have a small income from my father-in-law. The money I have is my own to manage. I buy and sell my own stocks. I make my own decisions about investments."

Mrs. Ames also expressed nontraditional views about her responsibilities as a wife. She sees it as her role to "bring love and joy, to do my part on the team. I've always been a liberated woman, as independent as I wanted to be." Like Mrs. Hoight, she has money of her own that she uses to her advantage: "I pay the bills, often out of my own money. The women I know who married a husband with no money of their own are far more subservient than I've been. I mentioned it to one of my friends once and she said, 'Don't forget he's buying everything I have. I wouldn't have anything if it weren't for him, so I have to do it his way.' Those women are in a completely different situation from mine."

Mrs. Spears (the only woman who had had a full-time, paid professional career for some years) described her relationship with her husband as follows: "[My husband and I] have a partnership. We don't have distinct roles. I think that's because I've always worked. . . ."

Mrs. Howe was the only woman who indicated that she had made some real changes in how tasks got done at home. In regard to finances, she said: "I am fortunate to have a supplementary income, and if I didn't, I would really miss it. It gives me a definite independence. . . ."

In contrast to these women who manage their own money are the women who speak of their husbands' lack of involvement at home. Mrs. Holt. . .said of household finances: "I pay the bills, but it's his money."

Mrs. Lane is a stirring and extreme illustration of how a wife's financial dependence affects her behavior. She is the executive wife so protective of her husband that the phone dare not ring after five o'clock, and so intimidated by him that she only dares to discuss problems during the weekly 45 minutes set aside for that purpose. At the end of the interview, when asked how she would categorize her family's social position, Mrs. Lane described her own financial position before her marriage: "My family lost everything in the crash of '29. But it's all worked out, because I married well."

Virtually all of the women I spoke with—unlike Mrs. Lane—had inherited their money from their own families. But the issues of money, power, and division of labor are not simply related to *having* their own money (which is taken for granted among these women) but rather to controlling and managing it. Like. . .Mrs. Sharpe, most of the women had given up control of their inheritances, turning them over to their husbands to manage. This appears to be a largely unquestioned gender expectation of upper-class women—though a few. . .had questioned it.

Why are these women—who have the economic base to exert greater power in families than women more objectively economically dependent on husbands—so subordinate to the men of their class? Searching my data for evidence of their own recognition of their subordinate position, I looked first at the dissatisfaction the women had regarding their home and family responsibilities.

Dissatisfactions

I did not ask the women directly about their satisfaction or dissatisfaction with their role as wives. What they chose to tell me, therefore, was unsolicited and in the context of other questions. Not suprisingly, it was often emotionally charged as well. Their husbands' frequent traveling was a matter of particular displeasure, especially when there were small children to consider.

Mrs. Wilson, who was born into an old family and married somewhat down in class, said when I asked her how she had helped her husband in his work: "He's a compulsive worker. Once he went out of town four days a week, for a year. I was home with three kids, and it was pure hell. Nobody to talk to. I just had to hang in there. I don't think men realize how much women contribute to the family." When asked how she and her husband divided up responsibilities at home, she said: "Being a wife carries much the same responsibilities as being a mother. My husband's just one of the children. He doesn't have a lot of responsibility around the house. The next generation isn't going to accept that. Men are living in a fool's paradise. I never have time to really think, and I don't think I've ever talked to anyone as I have to you [in this interview]. I'm always running up and down. A woman's time is cut into little tiny segments. I really do resent it. Women don't have many choices. . . ."

Mrs. Howe, a young wife with school-age children answered my question about how she had helped her husband's career by saying: "He's worked every Saturday for as long as I can remember. I don't like it, and he knows I don't like it. I feel it places tremendous strain on the family. He also has to travel a lot and work evenings. A few years ago he was always late for dinner, and I finally put my foot down and said you can't keep a family together without sharing time. . . ."

Mrs. Atherton, whose children were grown, responded to the question of how she and her husband divided up responsibilities: "He traveled a great deal [when the children were younger], so I was put in the role of both mother and father. I was angry and resentful."

In a variation on this theme, Mrs. Hall objected to her husband's expectations that she travel *with* him on business. She recognized that his demands affected whatever efforts she might make to have an independent life or serious work of her own: "If I started traveling with him, then whatever I would be involved in would be for nothing. If you travel all the time with your husband, then you've got to cancel your own appointments. That says that your appointments aren't important, that your work doesn't mean anything."

Like Mrs. Hall, several of the women expressed dissatisfaction that their work outside the home is not respected or supported by husbands. This is true of both volunteer work and paid work. . . . Many of the women reported that husbands fear their taking paid jobs, which is seen as a reflection of the men's inability to provide financially. At this economic level, such a phenomenon is surprising. It speaks to the power of traditional gender roles—in this case, man as provider—even when the economic class renders such roles unnecessary.

Mrs. Carpenter's husband, for example, was particularly negative about her chairing several local boards: "It would have been an affront to my husband for me to get a job, a sign that he couldn't support me in the manner to which I was accustomed. I was furious at first, but if you love somebody you don't defy them, so I just sulked." At the same time, she has refused to lessen her extensive volunteer activities, saying with icy calm: "If he doesn't like it, he can go to hell. Marriage is a compromise, and that's something he can compromise on. . . ."

Some women said that their husbands objected to their working outside the home because it would mean that they would be less available or would interfere with their husbands' own work schedules or other interests. Mrs. Carnes, who had recently taken a part-time paid job, said of her husband: "He does notice that I'm preoccupied sometimes, and he doesn't like that. He'd like me to be a homebody, but he's given up on that long ago. He knows it's not for me, and he's generally supportive."

Mrs. Langdon's husband had posed economic as well as social reasons for opposing his wife's thoughts of paid work: "[My husband] has said that my taking a job would mean that we would have to give up a lot of the things I would like to do, and as long as we don't need the money he thinks it's foolish. He feels I'm being more personally rewarded for [the volunteer work] I'm doing. He would probably also figure out what it would mean for him in taxes."

Mrs. Harper, whose husband was very supportive of her volunteer work, described his attitude toward her taking a paid job: "I think he'd like it fine as long as it didn't interfere with his schedule. . . ."

The very few women who had paid jobs or were in school full-time at the time of the interview all reported that their husbands were supportive. For example, Mrs. Spears (who claimed that she and her husband had a "partnership" rather than "distinct roles") is a full-time academic. Nonetheless, she offered: "Still, I do feel the overall running of the house is my responsibility." She also described her frustration at having her own accomplishments ignored: "Almost nobody knows what I do. Sometimes it makes me angry. I still go places where they introduce everybody at the speaker's table, and I'm there because of my husband, and they don't even bother to find out if I do something besides be his wife. They could at least ask. . . ."

It appears, then, that upper-class wives share with their counterparts in other social classes husbands who may object to their work involvements outside the home, whether in unpaid community activities, paid jobs, or schooling. Some studies of this issue report that ". . .the public's attitude toward working wives [has] gone from the unacceptable exception to the approved norm."[4] A recent study claims that 75 percent of husbands now support the right of married women to be employed.[5] Rubin, however, presents evidence (1976) of negative attitudes of working-class husbands toward their wives working outside the home;[6] and studies continue to report that wives take major responsibility for their households even when working outside.[7] The upper-class women I spoke with are well aware of this. They know that they need the support of their husbands to make changes in their work lives; and when they contemplate such changes, they seem to expect that they will continue to be responsible for runing the house—or making the decisions about its running. They also seem to expect that their husbands will not make any major adjustments in their own lives. This is a source of dissatisfaction among upper-class women, just as it is among women of other classes.

Studies by Jessie Bernard and Anne Locksley, among others, have shown that wives are generally less satisfied and more frustrated with their marital relationships than their husbands.[8] And upper-class women, like women of other socioeconomic levels, have not been very successful in changing the gender-based divisions of tasks at home. Only one of the women I spoke with, Mrs. Howe, had actually been able to change the way she and her husband handle home responsibilities. A dynamic young community leader, who describes herself as an "equaliterian," she spoke with assurance and style: "How we divide things up has changed a lot over the past few years. I used to feel it was all my responsibility. Now we all pitch in and do our share. I taught [the children] to do it, and gradually my husband just picked it up. We did talk about equalizing roles in the family, because it was important to me that [the children] grow up with this."

Mrs. Howe is decidedly the exception to the rule among upper-class women. Even in this most priviledged class—among women who have substantial money of their own, who can hire other women to do the everyday, nitty-gritty housework, and who are their husbands' class equals—gender stratification is clearly evident, and change is minimal. Why?

One source of subordinance among upper-class women—as a general mode of accommodation and in family decision making—is the class tradition of women turning over their inheritances to their husbands to manage. When the women give up the control of their money, they give up the freedom to order their own lives and the ability to speak with an equal voice in family decisions. This is not surprising. Low economic power has long been shown to be related to low decision-making power in families in other social classes.[9] Why, then, do upper-class women give up control of their money? The interviews indicate that they know the control of their own money is related to their position relative to husbands. The simplest answer, therefore, is probably subscription to traditional gender roles and traditional gender role socialization. In our culture, the male role dictates that men be the primary economic providers and decision makers: it is primarily their job to earn and control the money. Upper-class women, by turning their inheritances over to their husbands, are simply adhering to this general expectation within their class.

Traditional gender role expectations do not, however, tell the whole story. There is a more unique class explanation for this common practice of upper-class women. In order for upper-class wives to challenge their husbands' traditional economic role and its associated power in the family, they would have to ultimately challenge the men's economic role outside the family. These husbands are, after all, the men who manage the nation's business and financial affairs. It would mean a great deal, therefore, for wives to handle the family financial affairs. Mrs. Harper explained why she handed over her inheritance to her husband to manage, saying, "That is his field. He's in corporate finance." Mrs. Atherton said simply, "When it comes to investments, he's more qualified than I."

In other words, the women would ultimately have to challenge the men's class position in society in order to manage their own money. Upper-class men. . .exercise the dominant economic and political power in the society. It is unlikely that they would relinquish such power in their own families or that their wives would be able to seriously challenge it. Sociologist Helen Hacker. . . , has claimed that since upper-class men have so much power in the wider society, they also have more power than other men at home in their marriages and families.[10]

There are other, less monumental, reasons why upper-class women do not significantly alter their position relative to their husbands. Certainly one factor is the presence of household help. Recall the comment of Mrs. Holt. When I asked how she and her husband divide household responsibilities, she said, "When you have someone else to do the work, there's not much dividing up to do. . . ." Unlike women of other classes, upper-class women can ease their household responsibilities with paid help. The impetus to alter their role at home is therefore less urgent.

Another factor is that women of the upper class, unlike their counterparts in other socioeconomic classes, are exempt from the economic necessity of working. This exemption is both an advantage and a disadvantage. Upper-class women need not take just any job to support themselves, and their children are not threatened by the feminization of poverty that is increasingly plaguing women and children today. But since they do not have to work, they lack that impetus to change their subordinate position at home. (Ironically, the upper-class husband may not have to work, for economic reasons, either; but he inevitably maintains an office outside the home and engages in some sort of work activity. And, according to the women I spoke with, he generally expects his wife to plan her time so his activities are not interfered with.)

Summary and Conclusions

The upper-class wife bears many similarities to traditional wives in other social classes. These similarities powerfully illustrate the subordinate position of women in society and the importance of gender frameworks as explanations for women's position in society. Even in the most priviledged class, women lack freedom, independence, and influence over family decisions relative to men.

Upper-class women, like other women, experience dissatisfaction with their role as wives—with its expected mode of accommodation, unequal voice in family decisions, and sole responsibility for home and family. But the obstacles they confront to changing their role are class-based and very different from the obstacles experienced by women in other classes.

Although the personal descriptions and expressions of the role of the upper-class wife do not differ greatly from those of wives in other classes, the societal consequences are very different. A major consequence of upper-class wives' activities is to support the economic position of their husbands at the very top of society's hierarchy. As long as upper-class wives assume an accommodative and supportive function at home and in the community, their upper-class husbands are free to devote their full energies to managing the economic and political affairs of the society and to perpetuating the dominance of the upper class. As Dorothy Smith suggests, by supporting their husbands as individuals, upper-class women indirectly support and uphold the class structure.[11]

This view of the upper-class family as a central perpetuator of its own privilege is, of course, not a new one. In a study done over 40 years ago, Warner and Lunt said that "...the upper class family...is a potent mechanism for maintaining the class system.... [It] maintains the values [of the class] and organizes the relations of its members."[12] Twenty-five years ago, Baltzell called attention to the importance of the traditional role of women in enhancing the continuity of the upper-class family—approving the fact that upper-class women are less likely than other women to have paid jobs. He asserts that this traditional position of women is an index of family stability, and he adds that, "On the whole, career women do not add to the stability of the home."[13] In contrast to the changes occurring in families of other classes, there has been little apparent change in the upper-class family. The great stability of the upper-class family was evidenced in a study of continuities and discontinuities in upper-class marriages by Paul Blumberg in 1975. Replicating a 1947 study by Hatch and Hatch, Blumberg found that "although tremendous forces have shaken American society in past generations, the upper class has retained itself remarkably intact, and, having done so, is perhaps the most untouched group in American life."[14]

To the extent that upper-class women are supportive of and subjugated by this traditional family structure—with its rigid division of labor between the sexes and its traditional subordination of women—the function of the upper-class family is reinforced. As the primary social form for the orderly transmission of power and privilege from generation to generation, the family confines the women who preserve it.

Notes

1. Robert O. Blood, Jr., and Donald M. Wolfe, *Husbands and Wives* (New York: Free Press, 1960), p. 35.

2. Helen Mayer Hacker, "Class and Race Differences in Gender Roles," in *Gender and Sex in Society*, ed. Lucille Duberman (New York: Praeger, 1975), p. 138.

3. Lillian Breslow Rubin, *Worlds of Pain* (New York: Basic, 1976), p. 110.

4. Susan Kinsley, "Women's Dependency and Federal Programs," in *Women into Wives*, ed. Jane Roberts Chapman and Margaret Gates (Beverly Hills, Calif.: Sage, 1977), p. 80.

5. Andrew Cherlin and Pamela Barnhouse Walters, "Trends in the United States in Men's and Women's Sex-Role Attitudes: 1972 to 1978," *American Sociological Review* 46 (Aug. 1981): 455.

6. Rubin, *Worlds of Pain*, p. 176.

7. Joseph Pleck, "Men's Family Work," *Family Coordinator* 29, no. 4 (1979): 94–101.

8. Jessie Bernard, *The Future of Marriage* (New York: Bantam, 1972); Anne Locksley, "On the Effects of Wives' Employment on Marital Adjustment and Companionship," *Journal of Marriage and the Family* 42 (May 1980): 337–346.

9. Blood and Wolfe, *Husbands and Wives*; F. Ivan Nye and Lois W. Hoffman, eds., *The Employed Mother in America* (Chicago: Rand-McNally, 1963).

10. Hacker, "Class and Race Differences," p. 138.

11. Dorothy Smith, "Women, the Family, and Corporate Capitalism," *Berkeley Journal of Sociology* 20 (1975–1976): 80–82.

12. W. Lloyd Warner and Paul S. Lunt, *The Social Life of a Modern Community* (New Haven, Conn.: Yale University Press, 1941), p. 252.

13. E. Digby Baltzell, *Philadelphia Gentlemen: The Making of a National Upper Class* (Glencoe, Ill.: Free Press, 1958), p. 162.

14. Paul M. Blumberg and P. W. Paul, "Continuities and Discontinuities in Upper Class Marriages," *Journal of Marriage and the Family* 37, no. 1 (Feb. 1975): 75.

New Realities
of the American Family*

Dennis A. Ahlburg and Carol J. De Vita

The structure of the family has changed dramatically over the past 30 years. The title of this reading, "New Realities of the American Family," is indicative of these changes. The authors use demographic data from the U.S. Census Bureau to quantify the degree and manner in which American families have been evolving. These include changes in the patterns of marriage and divorce, birth rates, single parenthood, and the living arrangements of family members. In addition, the authors argue that this diversity of family structures entails different sources of strengths and problems for families. As Ahlburg and De Vita conclude, "Recognizing the diversity of American families and addressing the complexity of their needs must lie at the heart of the debates on family issues."

The family has changed so much in just a few decades that it is difficult for individuals and social institutions to keep up. Men and women who were raised in the 1950s and 1960s when television programs such as *Ozzie and Harriet* and *Father Knows Best* epitomized the image of the American family are now likely to find themselves in family situations that look and function very differently.

*Source: Dennis A. Ahlburg and Carol J. De Vita, "New Realities of the American Family," *Population Bulletin,* 47, no. 2 (August, 1992).

Families today most likely have two or fewer children; there is a good chance that the mother is employed outside the home; and the odds of divorce before the children are grown are about 50–50.

The breadwinner-homemaker model with husband and wife raising their own biological (or adopted) children was once the dominant pattern. Today, many family forms are common: single-parent families (resulting either from unmarried parenthood or divorce), remarried couples, unmarried couples, step-families, foster families, extended or multigenerational families, and the doubling up of two families within the same home. Women are just as likely to be full- or part-time workers as full-time homemakers.

If ordinary people sometimes find themselves puzzled about how to respond to (or interpret) the new family patterns, so are the experts. Family patterns are so fluid that the U.S. Census Bureau has difficulty measuring family trends. Most large-scale, nationally representative surveys cannot readily tell us what proportion of husband-wife families are stepfamilies; how adopted or foster-care children are faring; distinguish roommates from couples who are living together as unmarried partners; or measure the extent of family support networks for elderly persons who live alone.

Workplace policies often lag behind the new family arrangements, as the movement to pass "parental leave" or "family leave" policies suggests. Family health insurance, which is often provided through the workplace, may cover only married husband-wife partners and their off-spring, not cohabiting couples. Gay and lesbian advocates have questioned the fairness of these restrictions based on the premise that the living arrangements of gays and lesbians function much the same way as married-couple families. Stepfamilies may encounter a maze of bureaucratic red tape in trying to establish whose children are covered by which insurance policy. Family law—particularly the advent of no-fault divorce law, joint child custody, and inheritance and estate planning—has slowly evolved to try to accommodate the new fluidity of marital and family arrangements.

As a consequence, few social institutions have received as much attention and scrutiny as the American family. The family unit forms the cornerstone for U.S. social policy, and the economic well-being of the family often serves as a barometer for measuring the well-being of the nation. Given the importance of the family, it is not surprising that current statistics on the formation and structure of American families have been viewed with alarm:

> The marriage rate fell almost 30 percent between 1970 and 1990;
> The divorce rate increased by nearly 40 percent during this same period;
> Over one-quarter of all births in 1990 were to unmarried mothers, compared with one in ten in 1970; and
> About half of all children today are expected to spend some part of their childhood in a single-parent home.

Demographic trends are key to this evolution. Marriage, divorce, widowhood, remarriage, and childbearing patterns have changed dramatically since the 1950s and have radically altered the size and composition of the American family. Young people are marrying at older ages and more are foregoing marriage altogether. Marriage is less permanent. People are more likely to divorce, although remarriage rates are high. Women are having fewer children and generally waiting until older ages to have them. But more births are occurring outside of marriage, and more children are being raised in single-parent homes. Intertwined with demographic factors are economic changes—the stagnation of men's wages, the loss of manufacturing jobs, increased competition in global markets—that have contributed to the difficulties of raising and sustaining families.

This report will discuss the social and demographic trends that contribute to the changing composition and economic status of the American family. It will describe the various types of families that are prevalent today and project their numbers into the future.

The United States is not alone in experiencing such far-reaching demographic change. Family patterns in the United States reflect broad social and demographic trends that are occurring in most industrialized countries around the world. Low marriage and fertility rates and high divorce and nonmarital birth rates are seen in many other industrialized nations. Although every country has its own social and political traditions, Americans can learn important lessons by studying how other nations are responding to these changes.

Defining Households and Families

The U.S. Bureau of the Census carefully distinguishes between a *household* and a *family*. Households are defined as all persons who occupy a housing unit such as a house, apartment, single room, or other space intended to be living quarters. A household may consist of one person who lives alone or several people who share a dwelling. A family, on the other hand, is two or more persons related by birth, marriage, or adoption who reside together. This definition does not measure family ties that extend beyond the immediate housing unit. Yet, family members who live outside the home often help older people, young couples, and single parents maintain their independence and meet family responsibilities.

While all families form households, not all households are families under Census Bureau definitions. Indeed, the growth of the nonfamily household (that is, persons who live alone or with unrelated individuals) is one of the most dramatic changes to occur during the past 30 years. In 1960, 15 percent of all households were nonfamily households; by 1991, 30 percent were nonfamily units, and by the year 2000, 31 percent may be nonfamily households. Nonfamily households are a diverse group. They may consist of elderly individuals who live alone, college-age youth who share an apartment, cohabiting couples, individuals who delay or forego marriage, or those who are "between marriages." While these individuals may not reside within an officially designated family unit, most have family ties beyond their immediate household. What is more, given the aging of the U.S. population and current patterns of marriage, divorce, childbearing, and widowhood, nonfamily households are expected to account for a growing share of the housing market well into the twenty-first century.

Types of Families

While the share of family households has declined in the past 30 years, the structure of American families has grown more complex. A popular image of the American family is a married couple with two or more children in which the husband is the sole source of family income and the wife stays at home to attend to family matters. The demographic reality is that in 1991 just over one-third of all families (37 percent) consisted of a married couple with children—regardless of the number of children or the labor force status of the wife—and only one in five married couples with children fits the popular stereotype described above.

Although 70 percent of households contain a family unit, family composition is quite diverse. They include: married couples with children, married couples without children, single-parent families headed by a woman, single-parent families headed by a man, and other family units, such as siblings living together, an unmarried daughter living with her aging mother, or grandparents raising grandchildren. Just under half of all families have children, but there is considerable variation in these family arrangements.

Married Couples with Children

Despite our changing lifestyles, married couples with children continue to be a prominent family pattern. But even within this model there are two distinct types: the intact biological family and the stepfamily or blended family that may include adopted children. Most married-couple families with children are intact biological families (77 percent in 1985, the last available estimate), but 19 percent had one or more stepchildren, and 2 percent had one or more adopted children.[1] Although over 80 percent of stepfamilies are white, the odds of being in a stepfamily are twice as great for African-Americans as for whites. Thirty-five percent of all black married-couple families in 1985 were stepfamilies, compared with 18 percent for whites. The vast majority of stepchildren in married-couple families live with their biological mother and stepfather. Demographer Paul Glick estimates that one out of every three Americans is now a stepparent, a stepchild, a stepsibling, or some other member of a stepfamily. If current trends continue, the share will rise to nearly half by the year 2000.[2]

Combining and blending families is not always easy and does not necessarily mitigate differences between family types. Compared with stepfamilies, intact biological families tend to involve marriages of longer duration, have more children, are somewhat more likely to have only one parent in the labor force, and have higher family income.[3] Blended families may also generate conflict and tension, particularly for children, which is sometimes seen as a factor in the high divorce rates among remarriages.

Married Couples without Children

Forty-two percent of all families in 1991 consisted of married couples without children. But again, there are distinct differences within this category. Some of these couples might be called *preparents* (those who have not yet had children);

others may be *empty nesters* whose children are grown and have left the family home; while others may be *nonparents* either by choice or because of infertility problems. Among married couples without children in 1991, about 15 percent of the women were under age 35, suggesting a possible delay in childbearing. Indeed, over half of all married women younger than 35 who were childless in 1990 reported that they expected to have a child at some point in the future.[4] This figure rises to over 80 percent for married women in their twenties. On the other hand, half of all married couples without children had a woman age 55 or older. Many women of this age group are the mothers of the post-World War II baby-boom generation and probably have adult children who live elsewhere.

The aging of the baby-boom generation (born 1946–1964) will affect the growth of families without children. While many younger baby boomers (born 1957–1964) are still in the preparent stage of family life and are likely to become parents in the not-too-distant future, older baby boomers (born 1946–1956) who currently have children at home will soon be entering the empty nest phase. Projections by Decision Demographics show that married couples without children are likely to represent 43 percent of all families in 2000 if current trends in family formation remain unchanged.

Single-Parent Families

Nearly one in eight families was headed by a single parent in 1991, double the proportion in 1970. Women were five times more likely than men to be raising a family alone in 1991, and African-Americans were almost three times more likely than whites to be single parents. Single-parent families represented one in five white families with children, one in three Hispanic families with children, and six in ten black families with children. Changing patterns of marriage, divorce, remarriage, and the rise in births to unmarried women have contributed to the growth of single-parent families. "About half of today's young children will spend some time in a single-parent family, most as a consequence of divorce . . ." writes demographer Larry Bumpass. "Furthermore, this is not just simply a transitional phase between a first and second marriage. The majority will reside in a mother-only family for the remainder of their childhood."[5]

Living Arrangements of Children, Young Adults, and Elderly

The growing diversity of U.S. family life in the 1990s is most apparent in the living arrangements of children, young adults, and older persons. These groups have experienced the most dramatic change.

Children

One quarter of all children (or 16.6 million children) in 1991 lived with only one parent—double the percentage of 1970 and almost triple that of 1960. Minority children were most affected by this change. In 1960, two-thirds of African-

American children lived in two-parent homes; by 1980, less than half (42 percent) did so, and by 1991, only one-third (36 percent) were in a two-parent family. The number of Hispanic children in one-parent homes almost doubled between 1980 and 1991, reaching 2.2 million (or 30 percent) of all Hispanic children. High divorce rates and out-of-wedlock childbearing contributed to this trend.

But difficult economic times have also resulted in more families "doubling up," that is, sharing a common household together. Since 1970, the share of children who live in their grandparents' home has risen from 3 percent to 5 percent in 1991. These data reflect children (and their parents) who live in the home of the grandparent, not arrangements whereby grandparents move in with their adult children and grandchildren. About 3.3 million children lived in their grandparents' home in 1991. African-American children are three times more likely than white children to live with grandparents (12 percent versus 4 percent, respectively). About 6 percent of Hispanic children live with grandparents.

In most cases, one or both parents are present in the household. For half of these households, only the mother is present; in 17 percent, both parents are present. The "doubling up" of two-parent families within the grandparents' home increased during the 1980s (13 percent in 1980) as families responded to difficult economic conditions. In 28 percent of these households, neither parent is present, however, and grandparents are solely responsible for their grandchild.

Young Adults

The transition from being a dependent in the parental home to establishing an independent household has become increasingly complex and diverse. Compared with the 1970s, more young adults (ages 18 to 24) are living at home with their parents, more are living alone or with roommates, and fewer are maintaining married-couple family households of their own. Over half (54 percent) of all 18- to 24-year-olds lived with their parents in 1991—up from 47 percent in 1970. Some of these young adults never left the family home after completing high school; others are college students who live at home at least part of the year. Even by ages 25 to 34, about 12 percent of young adults in this age group were at home with their parents—up from just 8 percent in 1970. Inflationary pressures, the rising cost of housing, slower wage growth, the increased cost of higher education, and the repayment of student loans are seen as important factors that have kept young adults at home with their parents. Less than half (48 percent) of adults under age 35 were the head (or spouse of the head) of a separate family household in 1991.

For those who can afford it, living alone or with roommates has also become increasingly common. So, too, has cohabitation—that is, living with someone in a sexual union without a formal marriage. Three million households in 1991 had cohabiting couples, nearly 60 percent of whom were under age 35. Cohabitation has increased sixfold since 1970 when only 500,000 households had cohabiting couples. Only opposite-sex couples are counted in these figures, so these data underestimate the extent of cohabitation in the United States today.[6]

About one-third of all cohabiting, opposite-sex couples in 1991 had children under age 15 present in their homes, but far more cohabiting couples are parents. By one estimate, almost half of cohabiting couples have children either living with them or living elsewhere with a custodial parent.[7]

Cohabitation is often seen as a prelude to marriage. Although only 5 percent of women ages 15 to 44 were cohabiting with a male partner in 1988, one-third had done so at some time in the past.[8] One-quarter of white women, one-quarter of Hispanic women, and nearly one-third of black women had lived with their first (or only) husband before marriage. Among single persons who plan to cohabit in the future, more than 80 percent said that cohabiting allows couples to make sure they are compatible before getting married. At least one of the partners expects the arrangement to result in marriage in 90 percent of cohabitations.[9] Respondents may be overly optimistic, however: 55 percent of first cohabiting unions of white women and 42 percent of those of black women resulted in marriage.[10]

It is important to note that the rise in cohabitation has helped to offset much, although not all, of the fall in marriage rates.[11] If we expand our notion of "marriage" to include legal marriage *and* cohabitation, there has been little decline in the institution of marriage in the United States.

Elderly

Often overlooked in the discussion of families is the living arrangements of older persons. The majority (54 percent in 1991) of persons age 65 and older are in married-couple households. But this fact masks considerable differences in living arrangements by the age and sex of the older person. It also masks the role that the extended family network plays in the support and care of older individuals.

Three out of four men ages 65 and older lived with their wife in 1991, whereas less than half (40 percent) of older women lived with their husband. Because women tend to live longer than men, there are more older women than older men. Most older women live alone, particularly after age 75. This is likely to increase the need for assistance from family, friends, or social agencies as failing health or chronic disabilities rob older individuals of their independence. In general, older women are twice as likely as older men to live with other family members, although by age 85, the difference narrows somewhat. About 5 percent of all persons age 65 and older were living in institutions, such as nursing homes, in 1990.

Outlook for the American Family

The American family is like a patchwork quilt—composed of many patterns yet durable and enduring even when it becomes frayed around the edges. Despite the diversity and fragmentation of family patterns that have emerged over the past 40 years, most Americans continue to regard the family as a central component of their life. They may no longer live in the seemingly well-ordered family world of the 1950s, but they are struggling to understand and adapt to the new realities of family life.

Making predictions about the future course of the American family is a hazardous business. The scope and magnitude of change in our marriage, divorce, and childbearing patterns have been enormous, making a total reversal of these trends seem unlikely. Yet assuming that future change will continue at the same rapid pace witnessed over the past 20 or 30 years is also an unlikely scenario. While most people will marry and continue to regard the two-parent family as the preferred norm, considerable variation will exist, depending on social and economic conditions.

In the short run, demographic factors suggest a slower pace of change in family patterns during the 1990s. The baby-boom generation, the largest generation in U.S. history, is in the prime childbearing/child-rearing ages. For the next ten years, there is likely to be little change in the overall share of families with children. But the composition of those families—whether single-parent, blended, multigenerational, or intact nuclear families—is likely to shift and change with time. Although we know that single-parent families are at greatest risk of living in disadvantaged situations, we have relatively little knowledge of the stepfamily or blended-family model. Because divorce and remarriage rates continue to be at relatively high levels, these reconstituted families are (and will continue to be) a dominant force in the life of many children. What is more, we need to understand how these families function in regard to older relatives: will members of stepfamilies feel the same sense of responsibility and obligation toward assisting older relatives as individuals who grew up in intact nuclear families? The answer to this question is likely to shape our public policy options and strategies.

In the long run, as we move into the twenty-first century, two demographic trends will strongly influence the structure of American family life. First, the aging of the population—that is, the continued growth in the size and share of the older population—will increase both the number of households without children and the number of persons who live alone. This trend may raise concern over public commitment toward school bond referenda or other public expenditures for children's programs. On the other hand, an increasing number of frail elderly who live alone will require more supportive services in an era when adult daughters hold jobs and are not as readily available as earlier generations to be caregivers. The political struggle over the allocation of scarce resources will almost inevitably be seen in terms of generational conflict and trade-offs. But a better understanding of the mutual supports and interdependencies that extend beyond the nuclear family will be a key part of meeting this challenge.

Second, the U.S. minority population is large and growing, and this fact places a special spotlight on children in need. By the year 2000, one in three school-age children will be from a minority population, compared with about one in four today. Child poverty rates, however, are two to three times higher for minority children than for non-Hispanic whites, and minority children are at greater risk of growing up in disadvantaged circumstances. Neglecting the needs of the next generation can only undercut America's investment in its own economic future.

Valuing the family should not be confused with valuing a particular family form. Indeed, family life in the 1990s will be marked by its diversity. As blended families become the norm, the responsibilities of family members become more complex, more ambiguous, and more open to dispute. Social legislation (or "pro-family" policies) narrowly designed to reinforce only one model of the American family is likely to be shortsighted and have the unintended consequence of weakening, rather than strengthening, family ties. Recognizing the diversity of American families and addressing the complexity of their needs must lie at the heart of the policy debates on family issues.

Notes

1. Louisa F. Miller and Jeanne E. Moorman, "Married-Couple Families with Children," *Current Population Reports* P-23, no. 162 (1989): table B.

2. See Jan Larson, "Understanding Stepfamilies," *American Demographics* (July 1992): 36–40.

3. Jeanne E. Moorman and Donald J. Hernandez, "Married-Couple Families with Step, Adopted, and Biological Children," *Demography* 26, no. 2 (May 1989): 267–277.

4. Martin O'Connell, "Late Expectations: Childbearing Patterns of American Women for the 1990's," Studies in American Fertility, *Current Population Reports* P-23, no. 176 (1991): table H.

5. Larry L. Bumpass, "What's Happening to the Family? Interactions Between Demographic and Institutional Change," *Demography* 27, no. 4 (1990): 485.

6. U.S. Bureau of the Census, "Marital Status and Living Arrangements: March 1991," *Current Population Reports* P-20, no. 461 (1992): table 8.

7. Larry L. Bumpass, James A. Sweet, and Andrew Cherlin, "The Role of Cohabitation in Declining Rates of Marriage," *Journal of Marriage and the Family* 53, no. 4 (November 1991): 913–927.

8. See Kathryn A. London, "Cohabitation, Marriage, Marital Dissolution, and Remarriage: United States, 1988," *Advance Data from Vital and Health Statistics*, no. 194 (Hyattsville, MD: National Center for Health Statistics, 1991): 1–3.

9. Bumpass, "What's Happening to the Family?" p. 487.

10. London, "Cohabitation," p. 2.

11. Bumpass, "What's Happening to Be Family?" p. 488.

Exiles from Kinship*

Kath Weston

As Kath Weston argues in this chapter from her book, Families We Choose: Lesbians, Gays, Kinship, *gays and lesbians have often been portrayed as reject-ing "the family" and as willing exiles from kinship. Yet Weston poignantly illustrates that same-sex relationships can and do produce family ties. Her dis-cussion raises a key issue regarding definitions of the family (brought up in the first reading by Goode), and the ramifications of such definitions. Furthermore, she discusses the repercussions that lesbians and gays often face when they disclose their sexual identity.*

> Indeed, it is not so much identical conclusions that prove minds to be related as the contradictions that are common to them.
>
> —Albert Camus

Lesbian and gay San Francisco during the 1980s offered a fascinating opportuni-ty to learn something about how ideologies arise and change as people lock in conflict, work toward reconciliation, reorganize relationships, establish or break ties, and agree to disagree. In an apartment on Valencia Street, a young lesbian reassured her gay friend that his parents would get over their initially negative

*Source: Kath Weston, "Exiles from Kinship," Families We Choose: Lesbians, Gays, Kinship (New York: Columbia University Press, 1991), pp. 21–41.

reaction if he told them he was gay. On Polk Street, a 16-year-old searched for a place to spend the night because he had already come out to his parents and now he had nowhere to go. While two lovers were busy organizing an anniversary party that would bring blood relations together with their gay families, a woman on the other side of the city reported to work as usual because she feared losing her job if her employer should discover that she was mourning the passing of her partner, who had died the night before. For every lesbian considering parenthood, several friends worried about the changes children would introduce into peer relationships. For every eight or nine people who spoke with excitement about building families of friends, one or two rejected gay families as an oppressive accommodation to a heterosexual society.

Although not always codified or clear, the discourse on gay families that emerged during the 1980s challenged many cultural representations and common practices that have effectively denied lesbians and gay men access to kinship. In earlier decades, gay people had also fought custody battles, brought partners home to meet their parents, filed suit against discriminatory insurance policies, and struggled to maintain ties with adoptive or blood relations. What set this new discourse apart was its emphasis on the kinship character of the ties gay people had forged to close friends and lovers, its demand that those ties receive social and legal recognition, and its separation of parenting and family formation from heterosexual relations. For the first time, gay men and lesbians systematically laid claim to families of their own. Here I examine the ideological transition that saw "gay" and "family" change from mutually exclusive categories to terms used in combination to describe a particular type of kinship relation.

Is "Straight" to "Gay" as "Family"
Is to "No Family"?

For years, and in an amazing variety of contexts, claiming a lesbian or gay identity has been portrayed as a rejection of "the family" and a departure from kinship. In media portrayals of AIDS, Simon Watney (1987:103) observes that "we are invited to imagine some absolute divide between the two domains of 'gay life' and 'the family,' as if gay men grew up, were educated, worked and lived our lives in total isolation from the rest of society." Two presuppositions lend a dubious credence to such imagery: the belief that gay men and lesbians do not have children or establish lasting relationships, and the belief that they invariably alienate adoptive and blood kin once their sexual identities become known. By presenting "the family" as a unitary object, these depictions also imply that everyone participates in identical sorts of kinship relations and subscribes to one universally agreed-upon definition of family.

Representations that exclude lesbians and gay men from "the family" invoke what Blanche Wiesen Cook (1977:48) has called "the assumption that gay people do not love and do not work," the reduction of lesbians and gay men to sexual identity, and sexual identity to sex alone. In the United States, sex apart from heterosexual marriage tends to introduce a wild card into social relations, signifying unbridled lust and the limits of individualism. If heterosexual intercourse can bring people into enduring association via the creation of kinship ties, lesbian and gay sexuality in these depictions isolates individuals from one another rather than weaving them into a social fabric. To assert that straight people "naturally" have access to family, while gay people are destined to move toward a future of solitude and loneliness, is not only to tie kinship closely to procreation, but also to treat gay men and lesbians as members of a nonprocreative species set apart from the rest of humanity (cf. Foucault 1978).

It is but a short step from positioning lesbians and gay men somewhere beyond "the family"—unencumbered by relations of kinship, responsibility, or affection—to portraying them as a menace to family and society. A person or group must first be outside and other in order to invade, endanger, and threaten. My own impression from fieldwork corroborates Frances FitzGerald's (1986) observation that many heterosexuals believe not only that gay people have gained considerable political power, but also that the absolute number of lesbians and gay men (rather than their visibility) has increased in recent years. Inflammatory rhetoric that plays on fears about the "spread" of gay identity and of AIDS finds a disturbing parallel in the imagery used by fascists to describe syphilis at mid-century, when "the healthy" confronted "the degenerate" while the fate of civilization hung in the balance (Hocquenghem 1978).

A long sociological tradition in the United States of studying "the family" under siege or in various states of dissolution lent credibility to charges that this institution required protection from "the homosexual threat." Proposition 6 (the Briggs initiative), which appeared on the ballot in California in 1978, was defeated only after a massive organizing campaign that mobilized lesbians and gay men in record numbers. The text of the initiative, which would have barred gay and lesbian teachers (along with heterosexual teachers who advocated homosexuality) from the public schools, was phrased as a defense of "the family" (in Hollibaugh 1979:55):

> One of the most fundamental interests of the State is the establishment and preservation of the family unit. Consistent with this interest is the State's duty to protect its impressionable youth from influences which are antithetical to this vital interest.

Other antigay legislative initiative campaigns adopted the slogans "save the family" and "save the children" as their rallying cries. In 1983 the *Moral Majority Report* referred obliquely to AIDS with the headline, "Homosexual Diseases Threaten American Families" (Godwin 1983). When the *Boston Herald* opposed a gay rights bill introduced into the Massachusetts legislature, it was with an eye to "the preservation of family values" (Allen 1987).

Discourse that opposes gay identity to family membership is not confined to the political arena. A gay doctor was advised during his residency to discourage other gay people from becoming his patients, lest his waiting room become filled with homosexuals. "It'll scare away the families," warned his supervisor (Lazere 1986). Discussions of dual-career families and the implications of a family wage system usually render invisible the financial obligations of gay people who support dependents or who pool material resources with lovers and others they define as kin. Just as women have been accused of taking jobs away from "men with families to support," some lesbians and gay men in the Bay Area recalled co-workers who had condemned them for competing against "people with families" for scarce employment. Or consider the choice of words by a guard at that "all-American" institution, Disneyland, commenting on a legal suit brought by two gay men who had been prohibited from dancing with one another at a dance floor on the grounds: "This is a family park. There is no room for alternative lifestyles here" (Mendenhall 1985).

Scholarly treatments are hardly exempt from this tendency to locate gay men and lesbians beyond the bounds of kinship. Even when researchers are sympathetic to gay concerns, they may equate kinship with genealogically calculated relations. Manuel Castells's and Karen Murphy's (1982) study of the "spatial organization of San Francisco's gay community," for instance, frames its analysis using "gay territory" and "family land" as mutually exclusive categories.

From New Right polemics to the rhetoric of high school hallways, "recruitment" joins "reproduction" in allusions to homosexuality. Alleging that gay men and lesbians must seduce young people in order to perpetuate (or expand) the gay population because they cannot have children of their own, heterosexist critics have conjured up visions of an end to society, the inevitable fate of a society that fails to "reproduce."[1] Of course, the contradictory inferences that sexual identity is "caught" rather than claimed, and that parents pass their sexual identities on to their children, are unsubstantiated. The power of this chain of associations lies in a play on words that blurs the multiple senses of the term *reproduction.*

Reproduction's status as a mixed metaphor may detract from its analytic utility, but its very ambiguities make it ideally suited to argument and innuendo.[2] By shifting without signal between reproduction's meaning of physical procreation and its sense as the perpetuation of society as a whole, the characterization of lesbians and gay men as nonreproductive beings links their supposed attacks on "the family" to attacks on society in the broadest sense. Speaking of parents who had refused to accept her lesbian identity, a Jewish woman explained, "They feel like I'm finishing off Hitler's job." The plausibility of the contention that gay people pose a threat to "the family" (and, through the family, to ethnicity) depends upon a view of family grounded in heterosexual relations, combined with the conviction that gay men and lesbians are incapable of procreation, parenting, and establishing kinship ties.

Some lesbians and gay men in the Bay Area had embraced the popular equation of their sexual identities with the renunciation of access to kinship, particularly when first coming out. "My image of gay life was very lonely, very weird, no family," Rafael Ortiz recollected. "I assumed that my family was gone now—that's it." After Bob Korkowski began to call himself gay, he wrote a series of poems in which an orphan was the central character. Bob said the poetry expressed his fear of "having to give up my family because I was queer." When I spoke with Rona Bren after she had been home with the flu, she told me that whenever she was sick, she relived old fears. That day she had remembered her mother's grim prediction: "You'll be a lesbian and you'll be alone the rest of your life. Even a dog shouldn't be alone."

Looking backward and forward across the life cycle, people who equated their adoption of a lesbian or gay identity with a renunciation of family did so in the double-sided sense of fearing rejection by the families in which they had grown up, and not expecting to marry or have children as adults. Although few in numbers, there were still those who had considered "going straight" or getting married specifically in order to "have a family." Vic Kochifos thought he understood why:

> It's a whole lot easier being straight in the world than it is being gay. . . . You have built-in loved ones: wife, husband, kids, extended family. It just works easier. And when you want to do something that requires children, and you want to have a feeling of knowing that there's gonna be someone around who cares about you when you're 85 years old, there are thoughts that go through your head, sure. There must be. There's a way of doing it gay, but it's a whole lot harder, and it's less secure.

Bernie Margolis had been sexually involved with men since he was in his teens, but for years had been married to a woman with whom he had several children. At age 67 he regretted having grown to adulthood before the current discussion of gay families, with its focus on redefining kinship and constructing new sorts of parenting arrangements:

> I didn't want to give up the possibility of becoming a family person. Of having kids of my own to carry on whatever I built up. . . . My mother was always talking about she's looking forward to the day when she would bring her children under the canopy to get married. It never occurred to her that I wouldn't be married. It probably never occurred to me either.

The very categories "good family person" and "good family man" had seemed to Bernie intrinsically opposed to a gay identity. In his fifties at the time I interviewed him, Stephen Richter attributed never having become a father to "not having the relationship with the woman." Because he had envisioned parenting and procreation only in the context of a heterosexual relationship, regarding the two as completely bound up with one another, Stephen had never considered children an option.

Older gay men and lesbians were not the only ones whose adult lives had been shaped by ideologies that banish gay people from the domain of kinship. Explaining why he felt uncomfortable participating in "family occasions," a young man who had no particular interest in raising a child commented, "When families get together, what do they talk about? Who's getting married, who's having children. And who's not, okay? Well, look who's not." Very few of the lesbians and gay men I met believed that claiming a gay identity automatically requires leaving kinship behind. In some cases people described this equation as an outmoded view that contrasted sharply with revised notions of what constitutes a family.

Well-meaning defenders of lesbian and gay identity sometimes assert that gays are not inherently "antifamily," in ways that perpetuate the association of heterosexual identity with exclusive access to kinship. Charles Silverstein (1977), for instance, contends that lesbians and gay men may place more importance on maintaining family ties than heterosexuals do because gay people do not marry and raise children. Here the affirmation that gays and lesbians are capable of fostering enduring kinship ties ends up reinforcing the implication that they cannot establish "families of their own," presumably because the author regards kinship as unshakably rooted in heterosexual alliance and procreation. In contrast, discourse on gay families cuts across the politically loaded couplet of "profamily" and "antifamily" that places gay men and lesbians in an inherently antagonistic relation to kinship solely on the basis of their nonprocreative sexualities. "Homosexuality is not what is breaking up the Black family," declared Barbara Smith (1987), a black lesbian writer, activist, and speaker at the 1987 Gay and Lesbian March on Washington. "Homophobia is. My Black gay brothers and my Black lesbian sisters are members of Black families, both the ones we were born into and the ones we create."

At the height of gay liberation, activists had attempted to develop alternatives to "the family," whereas by the 1980s many lesbians and gay men were struggling to legitimate gay families as a form of kinship. When Armistead Maupin spoke at a gathering on Castro Street to welcome home two gay men who had been held hostage in the Middle East, partners who had stood with arms around one another upon their release, he congratulated them not only for their safe return, but also as representatives of a new kind of family. Gay or chosen families might incorporate friends, lovers, or children, in any combination. Organized through ideologies of love, choice, and creation, gay families have been defined through a contrast with what many gay men and lesbians in the Bay Area called "straight," "biological," or "blood" family. If families we choose were the families lesbians and gay men created for themselves, straight family represented the families in which most had grown to adulthood.

What does it mean to say that these two categories of family have been defined through contrast? One thing it emphatically does *not* mean is that heterosexuals share a single coherent form of family (although some of the lesbians and gay men doing the defining believed this to be the case). I am not arguing here for the existence of some central, unified kinship system vis-à-vis which gay people have distinguished their own practice and understanding of family. In the United States, race, class, gender, ethnicity, regional origin, and context all inform differences in household organization, as well as differences in notions of family and what it means to call someone kin.[3]

In any relational definition, the juxtaposition of two terms gives meaning to both.[4] Just as light would not be meaningful without some notion of darkness, so gay or chosen families cannot be understood apart from the families lesbians and gay men call "biological," "blood," or "straight." Like others in their society, most gay people in the Bay Area considered biology a matter of "natural fact." When they applied the terms "blood" and "biology" to kinship, however, they tended to depict families more consistently organized by procreation, more rigidly grounded in genealogy, and more uniform in their conceptualization than anthropologists know most families to be. For many lesbians and gay men, blood family represented not some naturally given unit that provided a base for all forms of kinship, but rather a procreative principle that organized only one possible *type* of kinship. In their descriptions they situated gay families at the opposite end of a spectrum of determination, subject to no constraints beyond a logic of "free" choice that ordered membership. To the extent that gay men and lesbians mapped "biology" and "choice" onto identities already opposed to one another (straight and gay, respectively), they polarized these two types of family along an axis of sexual identity.[5]

The chart below recapitulates the ideological transformation generated as lesbians and gay men began to inscribe themselves within the domain of kinship. What this chart presents is not some static substitution set, but a historically motivated succession.[6] To move across or down the chart is to move through time. Following along from left to right, time appears as process, periodized with reference to the experience of coming out. In the first opposition, coming out defines the transition from a straight to a gay identity. For the person who maintains an exclusively biogenetic notion of kinship, coming out can mark the renunciation of kinship, the shift from "family" to "no family" portrayed in the second opposition. In the third line, individuals who accepted the possibility of gay families after coming out could experience themselves making a transition from the biological or blood families in which they had grown up to the establishment of their own chosen families.

Moving from top to bottom, the chart depicts the historical time that inaugurated contemporary discourse on gay kinship. "Straight" changes from a category with an exclusive claim on kinship to an identity allied with a specific kind of family symbolized by biology or blood. Lesbians and gay men, originally relegated to the status of people without family, later lay claim to a distinctive type of family characterized as families we choose or create. While dominant cultural representations have asserted that straight is to gay as family is to no family (lines 1 and 2), at a certain point in history gay people began to contend that straight is to gay as blood family is to chosen families (lines 1 and 3).

What provided the impetus for this ideological shift? Transformations in the relation of lesbians and gay men to kinship are inseparable from sociohistorical developments: changes in the context for disclosing a lesbian or gay identity to others, attempts to build urban gay "community," cultural inferences about rela-

FIGURE 14-1

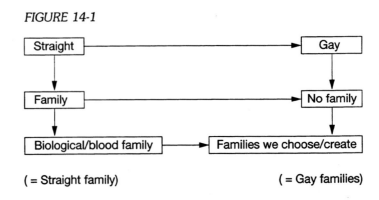

(= Straight family)   (= Gay families)

tionships between "same-gender" partners, and the lesbian baby boom associated with alternative (artificial) insemination. If Pierre Bourdieu (1977) is correct, and kinship is something people use to act as well as to think, then its transformations should have unfolded not only on the "big screen" of history, but also on the more modest stage of day-to-day life, where individuals have actively engaged novel ideological distinctions and contested representations that would exclude them from kinship.

Deck the Halls

Holidays, family reunions, and other celebrations culturally categorized as family occasions represent everyday arenas in which people in the Bay Area elaborated discourse on kinship. To attend was to catch a glimpse of history in the making that brought ideological oppositions to life. During the season when Hanukkah, Christmas, New Year's, and Winter Solstice converge, opportunities abounded to observe the way double-sided contrasts like the one between straight and gay families take shape. Meanings and transformations appeared far less abstract as people applied and reinterpreted them in the course of concrete activities and discussion. Their emotional power suddenly became obvious and inescapable, clearly central to ideological relations that have been approached far too cognitively in the past.

In San Francisco, gay community organizations set up special telephone hotlines during the holidays to serve as resources for lesbians and gay men battling feelings of loneliness or depression. At this time of year similar feelings were common in the population at large, given the tiring, labor-intensive character of holiday preparations and the pressure of cultural prescriptions to gather with relatives in a state of undisturbed happiness and harmony. Yet many gay people considered the "holiday blues" a more acute problem for themselves than for heterosexuals because disclosure of a lesbian or gay identity so often disrupted relations with straight relatives. The large number of gay immigrants to the Bay Area ensured that decisions about where to spend the holidays would make spatial declarations about family ties and family loyalties.

As Terri Burnett, who had grown up on the East Coast, saw it:

> Most people move out here so that nobody will find out. And then they're out all over the place here, but they would *never* go back home. That's one of the reasons why we see so many people depressed at Thanksgiving and Christmas. Because they can't be themselves. They have to go back to households in which they pretend to be all these other people. It's living a schizophrenic existence. And so many people here in San Francisco live a total lie. And this is supposed to be the liberation haven.

For those whose sexual identity was known to biological or adoptive relatives, conflicts over gaining acknowledgment and legitimacy for relationships with lovers and others they considered gay family was never so evident as on holidays. When Chris Davidson planned to return to her childhood home in the Bay Area for the holidays, she worried about being caught in the "same old pull" between spending time with her parents and time with her close lesbian friends. That year she had written her parents a letter in advance asking that they confront their "possessiveness" and recognize the importance of these other relationships in her life. Another woman regarded her parents' decision to allow her lover in their house to celebrate New Year's Day together with "the family" as a sign of growing acceptance. Some people had decided to celebrate holidays with their chosen families, occasionally inviting relatives by blood or adoption to join the festivities. One man voiced pride in "creating our environment, our *intimate* environment. I have an extended [gay] family. I have a lot of friends who we have shared Christmas and Thanksgiving with. Birthdays. Just as you would any other extended family."

In the field I spent Christmas eve with my lover and six other lesbians. All of us were known to the two women who had invited us to their home, but neither my lover nor I had met any of the others previously. Earlier in the year, my partner and I had begun to develop a multistranded family relationship with our hosts, Marta Rosales and Toni Williams.

That night the eight of us had gathered together to combine support with celebration at a potentially difficult time of year, goals that each woman seemed to weigh differently in accordance with her total kinship situation. Everyone was conscious of how the holiday was supposed to proceed: "extended family" would assemble in one place, momentarily putting aside the cares of day-to-day life in favor of eating, reminiscing, enjoying, exchanging gifts, and catching up on family gossip. We were also acutely aware that such gatherings help define family membership, just as purposeful exclusion on holidays can alienate family ties.

Different backgrounds and political orientations did not prevent us from raising similar questions about such occasions. If your parents or siblings reject you because you are a lesbian, does spending the holidays with gay family offer an equal, second-best, or better alternative? What do you miss about celebrating with straight family? Is there anything *to* miss? Would it be a good idea to bring a lover to visit biological or adoptive relatives for the holidays? If she decides to come along, is it worthwhile to try to explain why your "friend" is so important to you? If you have a partner and are lucky enough to have both straight families accept you, whose relatives should you spend the holiday with? How accepting would they have to be to invite them to spend a holiday at your home?

This was the first Christmas Marta and Toni had spent "alone together," a phrase each kept repeating as though the wonder of it would never sink in. Other years they had made the trip to southern California, where both maintained ties to blood kin. The two of them planned to spend a quiet Christmas morning in their own apartment, but wanted to share their mixed sense of excitement and loss with a group of their closest friends the evening before. As though to provide a counterpoint to the emotions Toni and Marta were experiencing, one of their guests left before dinner to catch a plane to New York City where her parents lived. Although she intended to stay there only overnight, due to work obligations, she wanted to be with her family for the holiday.

Her departure triggered a passionate debate about why she would want to do such a thing. "Her mother's crazy—totally nuts," one of the women who knew her reported. "She's never gonna have a good time there. I don't see why she's going." Another complained that parents expect their gay kids to do all the traveling, continuing to treat them as single whether or not they have a partner. "They might ask a lover to come along, if they're accepting," someone commented. "Yeah, but you still have to go there—it's hard to get them to come here." One after another, women spoke about how they had always "gone home" with high expectations (for love, understanding, a "good connection" with relatives), only to have their hopes shattered within the first few hours. Rhetorically, someone asked why we keep trying, why we keep going back. Another woman entered the conversation to question the tendency to continue calling the place where a person grows up "home." "As far as I'm concerned," she said, "*this* is home." A sense of shared experience filled the room with brief silence, drawing this group of relative strangers close.

With dinner in the oven, Toni and Marta joined us to add their stories about the frustrations of Christmas past when they had shuttled back and forth between relatives in the southern part of the state. Most of Marta's relatives knew they were lovers and often invited them to visit, but Toni's parents had forbidden Marta to enter their house after discovering the lesbian nature of their relationship years ago. Marta was feeling proud of her lover for "standing up" to her parents for once: "She says, 'I'm not going home, 'cause Marta and I want to spend Christmas together. And the day you guys can have her home for Christmas, I'll be home.'" "Still," Toni said to the group at large, "don't you miss being with them? Your parents and all?" "Sure," responded a woman who was out to her biological family and found spending time with them relatively unproblematic. "Like hell," came the quick rejoinder from a woman sitting in the corner near the fireplace. "Forget it, let's eat," said another. "Then let's open the presents!" As the group drifted toward the room at the back of the apartment where a long table had been set up, the conversation turned to the scents of cinnamon and roast turkey wafting in from the kitchen. Moments later we were sitting down, our glasses raised in a toast. "To being here together." And the refrain: "Together."

When a celebration brought chosen relatives into contact with biological or adoptive kin, family occasions sometimes became a bridge to greater integration of straight and gay families. Those who felt rejected for their sexual identities, however, could experience holidays as events that forced them to ally with one or the other of these opposed categories. The feeling was widespread that, in Diane Kunin's words, "[gay] people have to make some really excruciating choices that other people are not faced with." Because contexts such as holidays evoked the more inclusive level of the opposition *between* two types of family, they seldom elicited the positive sense of choice and creativity associated with gay families. Instead, individuals too often found themselves faced with the unwelcome dilemma of making an either/or decision when they would have preferred to choose both.

Kinship and Procreation

Since the time of Lewis Henry Morgan, most scholarly studies of familial relations have enthroned human procreation as kinship's ultimate referent. According to received anthropological wisdom, relations of blood (consanguinity) and marriage (affinity) could be plotted for any culture on a universal genealogical grid. Generations of fieldworkers set about the task of developing kinship charts for a multitude of "egos," connecting their subjects outward to a network of social others who represented the products (offspring) and agents (genitor/genetrix) of physical procreation. In general, researchers occupied themselves with investigations of differences in the ways cultures arranged and divided up the grid, treating blood ties as a material base underlying an array of cross-cultural variations in kinship organization.

More recently, however, anthropologists have begun to reconsider the status of kinship as an analytic concept and a topic for inquiry. What would happen if observers ceased privileging genealogy as a sacrosanct or objective construct, approaching biogenetic ties instead as a characteristically Western way of ordering and granting significance to social relations? After a lengthy exercise in this kind of bracketing, David Schneider (1972, 1984) concluded that significant doubt exists as to whether non-Western cultures recognize kinship as a unified construct or domain. Too often unreflective recourse to the biogenetic symbolism used to prioritize relationships in Anglo-European societies subordinates an understanding of how particular cultures construct social ties to the project of cross-cultural comparison. But suppose for a moment that blood is not intrinsically thicker than water. Denaturalizing the genealogical grid would require that procreation no longer be postulated as kinship's base, ground, or centerpiece.

Within Western societies, anthropologists are not the only ones who have implicitly or explicitly subjected the genealogical grid to new scrutiny. By reworking familiar symbolic materials in the context of nonprocreative relationships, lesbians and gay men in the United States have formulated a critique of kinship that contests assumptions about the bearing of biology, genetics, and heterosexual intercourse on the meaning of family in their own culture. Unlike Schneider, they have not set out to deconstruct kinship as a privileged domain, or taken issue with cultural representations that portray biology as a material "fact" exclusive of social significance. What gay kinship ideologies challenge is not the concept of procreation that informs kinship in the United States, but the belief that procreation *alone* constitutes kinship, and that "nonbiological" ties must be patterned after a biological model (like adoption) or forfeit any claim to kinship status.

In the United States the notion of biology as an indelible, precultural substratum is so ingrained that people often find it difficult to take an anthropological step backward in order to examine biology as symbol rather than substance. For many in this society, biology is a defining feature of kinship: they believe that blood ties make certain people kin, regardless of whether those individuals display the love and enduring solidarity expected to characterize familial relations. Physical procreation, in turn, produces biological links. Collectively, biogenetic attributes are supposed to demarcate kinship as a cultural domain, offering a yardstick for determining who counts as a "real" relative. Like their heterosexual counterparts, lesbians and gay men tended to naturalize biology in this manner.

Not all cultures grant biology this significance for describing and evaluating relationships. To read biology as symbol is to approach it as a cultural construct and linguistic category, rather than a self-evident matter of "natural fact." At issue here is the cultural valuation given to ties traced through procreation, and the meaning that biological connection confers upon a relationship in a given cultural context. In this sense biology is no less a symbol than choice or creation. Neither is inherently more "real" or valid than the other, culturally speaking.

In the United States, Schneider (1968) argues, "sexual intercourse" is the symbol that brings together relations of marriage and blood, supplying the distinctive features in terms of which kinship relations are defined and differentiated. A relationship mediated by procreation binds a mother to a daughter, a brother to a sister, and so on, in the categories of genitor or genetrix, offspring, or members of a sibling set. Immediately apparent to a gay man or lesbian is that what passes here for sex per se is actually the *hetero*sexual union of two differently gendered persons. While all sexual activity among heterosexuals certainly does not lead to the birth of children, the isolation of heterosexual intercourse as a core symbol orients kinship studies toward a dominantly procreative reading of sexualities. For a society like the United States, Sylvia Yanagisako's and Jane Collier's (1987) call to analyze gender and kinship as mutually implicated constructs must be extended to embrace sexual identity.

The very notion of gay families asserts that people who claim nonprocreative sexual identities and pursue nonprocreative relationships can lay claim to family ties of their own without necessary recourse to marriage, childbearing, or child rearing.[7] By defining these chosen families in opposition to the biological ties believed to constitute a straight family, lesbians and gay men began to renegotiate the meaning and practice of kinship from within the very societies that had nurtured the concept. Theirs has not been a proposal to number gay families among variations in "American kinship," but a more comprehensive attack on the privilege accorded to a biogenetically grounded mode of determining what relationships will *count* as kinship.

It is important to note that some gay men and lesbians in the Bay Area agreed with the view that blood ties represent the only authentic, legitimate form of kinship. Often those who disputed the validity of chosen families were people whose notions of kinship were bound up with their own sense of racial or ethnic identity. "You've got one family, one biological family," insisted Paul Jaramillo, a Mexican-American man who did not consider his lover or friends to be kin.

> They're very good friends and I love them, but I would not call them family. Family to me is blood. . . . I feel that Western Caucasian culture, that it's much more broken down, and that they can deal with their good friends and neighbors as family. But it's not that way, at least in my background.

Because most individuals who expressed this view were well aware of the juxtaposition of blood family with families we choose, they tended to address gay kinship ideologies directly. As Lourdes Alcantara explained:

> I know a lot of lesbians think that you choose your own family. I don't think so. Because, as a Latin woman, the bonds that I got with my family are irreplaceable. They can't be replaced. They cannot. So my family is my family, my friends are my

> friends. My friends can be *more important* than my family, but that doesn't mean
> they are my family. . . . 'Cause no matter what, they are just friends—they don't have
> your blood. They don't have your same connection. They didn't go through what
> you did. For example, I starved with my family a lot of times. They *know* what it
> is like. If I talk to my friends, they will understand me, but they will never feel the
> same.

What Lourdes so movingly described was a sense of enduring solidarity arising
from shared experience and symbolized by blood connection. Others followed a
similar line of reasoning (minus the biological signifier) when they contended that
a shared history testifies to enduring solidarity, which can provide the basis for
creating familial relationships of a chosen, or nonbiological, sort.

In an essay on disclosing a lesbian or gay identity to relatives, Betty Berzon
(1979:89) maintains that "from early on, being gay is associated with going against
the family." Many people in the Bay Area viewed families as the principal medi-
ator of race and ethnicity, drawing on folk theories of cultural transmission in
which parents hand down "traditions" and identity (as well as genes) to their children.[8] If having a family was part of what it meant to be Chicana or Cherokee
or Japanese-American, then claiming a lesbian or gay identity could easily be
interpreted as losing or betraying that cultural heritage, so long as individuals
conceived kinship in biogenetic terms (cf. Clunis and Green 1988:105; Tremble
et al. 1989). Kenny Nash had originally worried that coming out as a gay man
would separate him from other African-Americans.

> Because I related to the black community a lot as far as politics, and . . . unfortu-
> nately, sexual politics in some parts of the black movement are not very good. Just
> as there is this continuing controversy about feminism and black women in the
> women's movement. It's a carry-over, I think, into [ideas] about gay people, gay men
> and lesbians. Because there are some people who think of [being gay] as the antithe-
> sis of building strong family institutions, and that's what we need: role models for
> people, bringing up children, and all that stuff.

Condemnations of homosexuality might picture race or ethnicity and gay identity as antagonists in response to a history of racist attributions of "weak" family
ties to certain groups (e.g., blacks), or in response to anything that appeared to
menace the legacy of "strong" kinship bonds sometimes attributed to other categories of people (e.g., Latinos, Jews). In either case, depicting lesbian or gay
identity as a threat to ethnic or racial identity depended upon the cultural positioning of gay people outside familial relations. The degree to which individuals
construct racial identity *through* their notions of family remains a relatively unex-
plored aspect of why some heterosexuals of color reject gay or lesbian identity
as a sign of assimilation, a "white thing."

Not all lesbians and gays of color or whites with a developed ethnic identity took issue with the concept of chosen families. Many African-Americans, for
instance, felt that black communities had never held to a strictly biogenetic interpretation of kinship. "Blacks have never said to a child, 'Unless you have a mother, father, sister, brother, you don't have a family' " (Height 1989:137).[9] Discourse
and ideology are far from being uniformly determined by identities, experiences,

or historical developments. Divergent perceptions of the relation between family ties and race or ethnicity are indicative of a situation of ideological flux, in which procreative and nonprocreative interpretations vie with one another for the privilege of defining kinship. As the United States entered the final decade of the twentieth century, lesbians and gay men from a broad spectrum of racial and ethnic identities had come to embrace the legitimacy of gay families.

From Biology to Choice

Upon first learning the categories that framed gay kinship ideologies, heterosexuals sometimes mentioned adoption as a kind of limiting case that appeared to occupy the borderland between biology and choice. In the United States, adopted children are chosen, in a sense, although biological offspring can be planned or selected as well, given the widespread availability of birth control. Yet adoption in this society "is only understandable as a way of creating the social fiction that an actual link of kinship exists. Without biological kinship as a model, adoption would be meaningless" (Schneider 1984:55). Adoption does not render the attribution of biological descent culturally irrelevant (witness the many adopted children who, later in life, decide to search for their "real" parents). But adoptive relations—unlike gay families—pose no fundamental challenge to either procreative interpretations of kinship or the culturally standardized image of a family assembled around a core of parent(s) plus children.

Mapping biological family and families we choose onto contrasting sexual identities (straight and gay, respectively) places these two types of family in a relation of opposition, but *within* that relation, determinism implicitly differentiates biology from choice and blood from creation. Informed by contrasting notions of free will and the fixedness often attributed to biology in this culture, the opposition between straight and gay families echoes old dichotomies such as nature versus nurture and real versus ideal. In families we choose, the agency conveyed by "we" emphasizes each person's part in constructing gay families, just as the absence of agency in the term "biological family" reinforces the sense of blood as an immutable fact over which individuals exert little control. Likewise, the collective subject of families we choose invokes a collective identity—who are "we" if not gay men and lesbians? In order to identify the "we" associated with the speaker's "I," a listener must first recognize the correspondence between the opposition of blood to choice and the relation of straight to gay.

Significantly, families we choose have not built directly upon beliefs that gay or lesbian identity can be chosen. Among lesbians and gay men themselves, opinions differ as to whether individuals select or inherit their sexual identities. In the aftermath of the gay movement, the trend has been to move away from the obsession of earlier decades with the etiological question of what "causes" homosexuality. After noting that no one subjects heterosexuality to similar scrutiny, many people dropped the question. Some lesbian-feminists presented lesbianism as a political choice that made a statement about sharing their best with other women and refusing to participate in patriarchal relations. In everyday conversations, however, the majority of both men and women portrayed their sexual identities as either inborn or a predisposition developed very early in life. Whether or not to act on feelings already present then became the only matter left to individual discretion. "The choice for me wasn't being with men or being a lesbian," Richie Kaplan explained. "The choice was being asexual or being with women."

In contrast, parents who disapproved of homosexuality could convey a critical attitude by treating gay identity as something elective, especially since people in the United States customarily hold individuals responsible for any negative consequences attendant upon a "free choice." One man described with dismay his father's reaction upon learning of his sexual identity: "I said, 'I'm gay.' And he said, 'Oh. Well, I guess you made your choice.'" According to another, "My father kept saying, 'Well, you're gonna have to live by your choices that you make. It's your responsibility.' What's there to be responsible [about]? I was who I *am.*" When Andy Wentworth disclosed his gay identity to his sister:

> She asked me, how could I *choose* to do this and to ignore the health risks . . . implying that this was a conscious, "Oh, I'd like to go to the movies today" type of choice. And I told her, I said, "Nobody in their right mind would go through this *hell* of being gay just to satisfy a whim." And I explained to her what it was like growing up. Knowing this other side of yourself that you can't tell anybody about, and if anybody in your family knows they will be upset and mortified.

Another man insisted he would never forget the period after coming out when he realized that he felt good about himself, and that he was not on his way to becoming "the kind of person that they're portraying gay people to be." What kind of person is that? I asked. "Well, you know, wicked, evil people who *decide* that they're going to be evil."

Rather than claiming an elective gay identity as its antecedent, the category "families we choose" incorporates the meaningful *difference* that is the product of choice and biology as two relationally defined terms. If many gay men and lesbians interpreted blood ties as a type of social connectedness organized through procreation, they tended to associate choice and creativity with a total absence of guidelines for ordering relationships within gay families. Although heterosexuals in the Bay Area also had the sense of creating something when they established families of their own, that creativity was often firmly linked to childbearing and child rearing, the *pro* in procreation. In the absence of a procreative referent, individual discretion regulated who would be counted as kin. For those who had constructed them, gay families could evoke utopian visions of self-determination in the absence of social constraint. Of course, the contextualization of choice and creativity within the symbolic relation that opposes them to blood and biology itself lends a high degree of structure to the notion of gay families. The elaboration of gay kinship ideologies in contrast to the biogenetic symbolism of straight family illustrates the type of structured relation Roman Jakobson (1962) has called "the unexpected arising from expectedness, both of them unthinkable without the opposite."

Certainly lesbians and gay men, with their range of backgrounds and experiences, did not always mean the same thing or advance identical cultural critiques when they spoke of blood and chosen families. Ideological contrasts utilized and recognized by all need not have the same significance for all.[10] Neither can an examination of ideology alone explain why choice should have been highlighted as an organizing principle of gay families. Only history, material conditions, and context can account for the specific content of gay kinship ideologies, their emergence at a particular point in time, and the variety of ways people have implemented those ideologies in their daily lives. In themselves, gay families comprise only a segment of the historical transformation sequence that mapped the contrast between straight and gay first onto "family/no family," and then onto "biological family/families we choose." Gone are the days when embracing a lesbian or gay identity seemed to require a renunciation of kinship. The symbolic groundwork for gay families, laid during a period when coming out to relatives witnessed a kind of institutionalization, has made it possible to claim a sexual identity that is not linked to procreation, face the possibility of rejection by blood or adoptive relations, yet still conceive of establishing a family of one's own.

Notes

1. See Godwin (1983) and Hollibaugh (1979).

2. For an analysis that carefully distinguishes among the various senses of reproduction and their equivocal usage in feminist and anthropological theory, see Yanagisako and Collier (1987).

3. On the distinction between family and household, see Rapp (1982) and Yanagisako (1979).

4. On relational definition and the arbitrariness of signs, see Saussure (1959).

5. For Lévi-Strauss (1963b: 88), most symbolic contrasts are structured by a mediating third term. Apparently conflicting elements incorporate a hidden axis of commonality that allows the two to be brought into relationship with one another. Here sexual identity is the hidden term that links "straight" to "gay," while kinship mediates the oppositions further down in the chart. This sort of triadic relation lends dynamism to opposition, facilitating ideological transformations while ensuring a regulated, or structured, relationship between the old and the new.

My overall analysis departs from a Lévi-Straussian structuralism by historically situating these relations, discarding any presumption that they form a closed system, and avoiding the arbitrary isolation of categories for which structuralism has justly been criticized in the past (see Culler 1975; Fowler 1981; Jenkins 1979). The symbolic oppositions examined in this chapter incorporate indigenous categories in all their specificity (e.g., straight versus gay), rather than abstracting to universals of increasing generality and arguably decreasing utility (e.g., nature versus culture). Chronicled here is an ideological transformation faithful to history, process, and the perceptions of the lesbians and gay men who themselves identified each opposition included in the chart. For the deployment of these categories in everyday contexts, read on.

6. Notice how the contrasts in the chart map a relationship of difference (straight/gay) first onto a logical negation (family/no family, or A/NA), and then onto another relation of difference (biological [blood] family/families we choose [create], or A:B). On the generative potential of dichotomies that are constituted as A/B rather than A/NA, see N. Jay (1981: 44).

7. See Foucault (1978) on the practice of grouping homosexuality together with other nonprocreative sex acts, a historical shift that supplanted the earlier classification of homosexuality with adultery and offenses against marriage. According to Foucault, previous to the late eighteenth century acts "contrary to nature" tended to be understood as an extreme form of acts "against the law," rather than something different in kind. Only later was "the unnatural" set apart in the emerging domain of sexuality, becoming autonomous from adultery or rape. See also Freedman (1982: 210): "Although the ideological support for the separation of [erotic] sexuality and reproduction did not appear until the twentieth century, the process itself began much earlier."

8. See di Leonardo (1984), who criticizes the transmission model for its lack of attention to the wider socioeconomic context that informs the ways people interpret the relation of kinship to ethnicity.

9. See also Joseph and Lewis (1981: 76), Kennedy (1980), McAdoo (1988), and Stack (1974). For a refutation and historical contextualization of allegations that African-Americans have developed "dysfunctional" families, or even no families at all, see Gresham (1989).

10. Abercrombie et al. (1980) lay out many of the objections to treating culture as a shared body of values and knowledge determinative of social relations. For theoretical formulations critical of the assumption that ideology mechanically reflects a more fundamental set of material conditions, see Jameson (1981), Lichtman (1975), and R. Williams (1977). For different approaches to examining the influence of context, embodiment, and power relations on the formulation and interpretation of cultural categories, see Rosaldo (1989), Vološinov (1973), and Yanagisako (1978, 1985).

References

ABERCROMBIE, NICHOLAS, STEPHEN HILL, and BRYAN S. TURNER. 1980. *The Dominant Ideology Thesis.* Boston: Allen & Unwin.

ALLEN, RONNIE. 1987. "Times Have Changed at the *Herald.*" *Gay Community News* (June 28–July 4).

BERZON, BETTY. 1978. "Sharing Your Lesbian Identity with Your Children." In Ginny Vida, ed., *Our Right to Love: A Lesbian Resource Book,* pp. 69–74. Englewood Cliffs, N.J.: Prentice Hall.

———— 1979. "Telling the Family You're Gay." In Betty Berzon and Robert Leighton, eds., *Positively Gay,* pp. 88–100. Los Angeles: Mediamix Associates.

BOURDIEU, PIERRE. 1977. *Outline of a Theory of Practice.* New York: Cambridge University Press.

CASTELLS, MANUEL, and KAREN MURPHY. 1982. "Cultural Identity and Urban Structure: The Spatial Organization of San Francisco's Gay Community." In Norman I. Fainstein and Susan S. Fainstein, eds., *Urban Policy Under Capitalism,* pp. 237–259. Beverly Hills, Calif.: Sage.

CLUNIS, D. MERILEE, and G. DORSEY GREEN. 1988. *Lesbian Couples.* Seattle: Seal Press.

COOK, BLANCHE WIESEN. 1977. "Female Support Networks and Political Activitism: Lillian Wald, Crystal Eastman, Emma Goldman." *Chrysalis* 3: 44–61.

CULLER, JONATHAN. 1975. *Structuralist Poetics: Structuralism, Linguistics and the Study of Literature.* Ithaca, N.Y.: Cornell University Press.

DI LEONARDO, MICAELA. 1984 *The Varieties of Ethnic Experience: Kinship, Class, and Gender Among California Italian-Americans.* Ithaca: Cornell University Press.

FITZGERALD, FRANCES. 1986. *Cities on a Hill: A Journey Through Contemporary American Cultures.* New York: Simon & Schuster.

FOUCAULT, MICHEL. 1978. *The History of Sexuality.* vol. I. New York: Vintage.

FOWLER, ROGER. 1981. *Literature as Social Discourse: The Practice of Linguistic Criticism.* Bloomington: University of Indiana Press.

FREEDMAN, ESTELLE B. 1982. "Sexuality in Nineteenth-Century America: Behavior, Ideology, and Politics." *Reviews in American History* 10: 196–215.

GODWIN, RONALD S. 1983. "AIDS: A Moral and Political Time Bomb." *Moral Majority Report* (July).

GRESHAM, JEWELL HANDY. 1989. "The Politics of Family in America." *The Nation* (July 24–31): 116–122.

HEIGHT, DOROTHY. 1989. "Self-Help-A Black Tradition." *The Nation* (July 24–31): 136–138.

HOCQUENGHEM, GUY. 1978. *Homosexual Desire.* London: Alison & Busby.

HOLLIBAUGH, AMBER. 1979. "Sexuality and the State: The Defeat of the Briggs Initiative and Beyond." *Socialist Review* 9(3): 55–72.

JAKOBSON, ROMAN. 1962. *Selected Writings*. The Hague: Mouton.

JAMESON, FREDERIC. 1981. *The Political Unconscious: Narrative as a Socially Symbolic Act*. Ithaca: Cornell University Press.

JAY, NANCY. 1981. "Gender and Dichotomy." *Feminist Studies* 7(1): 38–56.

JENKINS, ALAN. 1979. *The Social Theory of Claude Lévi-Strauss*. New York: St. Martin's Press.

JOSEPH, GLORIA I., and JILL LEWIS. 1981. *Comon Differences: Conflicts in Black and White Feminist Perspectives*. Garden City, N.Y.: Anchor/Doubleday.

KENNEDY, THEODORE R. 1980. *You Gotta Deal With It: Black Family Relations in a Southern Community*. New York: Oxford University Press.

LAZERE, ARTHUR. 1986. "On the Job." *Coming Up!* (June).

LÉVI-STRAUSS, CLAUDE. 1963b. *Totemism*. Boston: Beacon Press.

MCADOO, HARRIETTE P. 1988. *Black Families*. 2d ed. Newbury Park, Calif.: Sage.

MENDENHALL, GEORGE. 1985. "Mickey Mouse Lawsuit Remains Despite Disney Dancing Decree." *Bay Area Reporter* (Aug. 22).

RAPP, RAYNA. 1982. "Family and Class in Contemporary America: Notes Toward an Understanding of Ideology." In Barrie Thorne with Marilyn Yalom, eds., *Rethinking the Family*, pp. 168–187. New York: Longman.

ROSALDO, RENATO. 1989. *Culture and Truth: The Remaking of Social Analysis*. Boston: Beacon Press.

SAUSSURE, FERDINAND DE. 1959. *Course in General Linguistics*. New York: McGraw-Hill.

SCHNEIDER, DAVID M. 1968. *American Kinship: A Cultural Account*. Englewood Cliffs, N.J.: Prentice Hall.

_____ 1972. "What is Kinship All About?" In Priscilla Reining, ed., *Kinship Studies in the Morgan Centennial Year*. Washington, D.C.: Anthropological Society of Washington.

_____ 1984. *A Critique of the Study of Kinship*. Ann Arbor: University of Michigan Press.

SILVERSTEIN, CHARLES. 1977. *A Family Matter: A Parents' Guide to Homosexuality*. New York: McGraw-Hill.

SMITH, BARBARA. 1987. "From the Stage." *Gay Community News* (Nov. 8–14).

STACK, CAROL B. 1974. *All Our Kin: Strategies for Survival in a Black Community*. New York: Harper & Row.

TREMBLE, BOB, MARGARET SCHNEIDER, and CAROL APPATHURAI. 1989. "Growing Up Gay or Lesbian in a Multicultural Context." In Gilbert Herdt, ed., *Gay and Lesbian Youth*, pp. 253–264. New York: Haworth Press.

VOLOŠINOV V. N. 1973. *Marxism and the Philosophy of Language*. New York: Seminar Press.

WATNEY, SIMON. 1987. *Policing Desire: Pornography, AIDS, and the Media*. Minneapolis: University of Minnesota Press.

WILLIAMS, RAYMOND. 1977. *Marxism and Literature*. New York: Oxford University Press.

YANAGISAKO, SYLVIA J. 1978. "Variance in American Kinship: Implications for Cultural Analysis." *American Ethnologist* 5(1): 15–29.

_____ 1979. "Family and Household: The Analysis of Domestic Groups." *Annual Review of Anthropology* 8: 161–205.

_____ 1985. *Transforming the Past: Tradition and Kinship among Japanese Americans*. Stanford: Standford University Press.

YANAGISAKO, SYLVIA JUNKO, and JANE FISHBURNE COLLIER. 1987. "Toward a Unified Analysis of Gender and Kinship." In Jane Fishburne Collier and Sylvia Junko Yanagisako, eds., *Gender and Kinship: Essays Toward a Unified Analysis*, pp. 14–50. Stanford: Stanford University Press.

Dating*

Martin King Whyte

While the first third of this reader focused upon variation among families, this section turns to the family cycle. As individuals move through the life course, they experience a number of family-related transitions. The formation of families can be considered a process, and dating is the first stage in the process leading to the transition from singlehood to the married state. Martin King Whyte's chapter examines how mate selection and dating have been changing in this country. He uses data to map trends in patterns of variables such as dating, going steady, premarital sex, and engagement. Whyte's work points out that studying social change in dating is a complex process in which we must look at both continuities and change.

One of the most intriguing questions about mate choice in America is how the nature of dating has changed over time. We know surprisingly little about this question. Our American "dating culture" gives popular approval to young people pairing off with various romantic partners, without adult supervision and without defining those partners necessarily as potential mates. We think this dating culture evolved gradually during the latter part of the nineteenth century and

*Source: Whyte, Martin King. *Dating, Mating, and Marriage.* (New York: Aldine De Gruyter) Copyright (c) 1990 by Walter de Gruyter, Inc., New York.

early in the twentieth century. Prior to that time, pairing off was more subject to direct adult supervision and was interpreted more in terms of the immediate goal of choosing a mate. The venues available for such pairing off were relatively limited compared to present times, and for middle-class couples, at least, the dominant practice was for the male to visit the female in her home. Terms such as "courting" and "keeping company" were used for such activity, and the archaic tone of such terms today conveys how much change has occurred in premarital relations.

The exact reasons for the emergence of a dating culture are still being debated. Some scholars place major emphasis on factors such as growing affluence and a proliferation of recreational venues aimed at the young, longer periods of schooling in predominantly coeducational schools, and the growth of forms of employment which took adults away from the home and therefore made it more difficult for parents to supervise the leisure time activities of their adolescent children. Others stress the rise of individualistic and consumption- and market-oriented philosophies, which provided subtle underpinnings for new modes of recreational romance and "playing the field." Some writers have even placed major stress on technological innovations—on the development of the automobile in the twentieth century (and of the bicycle in the nineteenth), and of accompanying innovations such as drive-in movies, which helped to free young daters from the scrutiny of their parents. But so little research has been done on the topic of the emergence of the dating culture in America that it is difficult to be specific about how and when it evolved in different segments of our society (see Burgess and Wallin 1953, Chap. 3; Fass 1977; Rothman 1984; Modell 1983).

It is clear at least that major parts of what we associate with the process of dating were already widely accepted in the period after World War I. The more recent evolution of dating in America is almost as much *terra incognita* as the earlier origins of this practice, however (but see Ehrmann 1959; Burchinal 1964; Gagnon and Greenblat 1978). While conducting this research, I occasionally asked friends and acquaintances how they thought dating had changed, and I usually got only the vaguest of replies. Most people felt that dating today was very different from the days when their parents were young, but they were unable to state precisely what had changed, with one or two exceptions. The major change people are aware of is that sexual intercourse is a more common part of dating activities than in the past. In addition premarital cohabitation is becoming more and more widespread. From these changes some people generalize that a process of liberalization (or moral decay, depending on your point of view) must characterize the evolution of dating in America. According to this viewpoint, over the years parents have lost control, and young people have started dating earlier, have begun sexual activities at younger ages, have more casually tried and discarded large numbers of dating partners, and in general have experienced a variety of romantic and sexual experiences, so that marriage itself is viewed as less special than it once was. But these are hunches, rather than conclusions based on concrete evidence.

In this chapter data are presented to check a variety of hunches about our contemporary American mate choice process. There are two primary reasons why such data are of interest. First, the topic of continuity and change in premarital relations is a "blank spot" in the study of social change in America. We know something about recent trends in such aspects of family life as marriage ages, divorce rates, and fertility levels, but . . . we don't know much about what has happened to dating behavior. So there is some intrinsic interest in finding out how aspects of dating have or have not changed, and how any trends detected in this realm relate to broader social changes occurring in American society. The second reason for interest in dating trends concerns . . . the link between premarital relations and marital success. Dating is an activity with a variety of purposes. For young people just beginning to participate in this activity, dating may be seen primarily or exclusively in recreational terms, devoted simply to testing one's attractiveness to the opposite sex and having fun, as the term "dating game" implies. However, eventually dating relationships tend to become more sustained and serious, and at some point dating begins to be seen more directly in terms of the goal of selecting a mate. . . . For this reason a central question of interest in the current study is whether some kinds of experiences in the dating stage are more conducive to a "wise" choice of a mate and subsequent marital success than others. If we can detect consistent trends over time in dating experiences, and if we find that the trends discovered are potentially threatening to marital success (or for that matter, are potentially conducive to marital success), we will have built a logical link between such dating trends and our "big question," the health of American marriage as an institution. Although the final testing of ideas about the impact of dating experiences on marital outcomes will not occur until later . . . I want to consider here a variety of arguments about how these earlier experiences might be expected to have an important impact one way or the other.

How might variations in the timing and intimacy of dating be important? Quite contrary claims have been made in previous writing on this topic. On the one hand, there is what might be called the "educational" or, perhaps more appropriately, "marketplace learning" conception of dating. According to this conception, which might be considered the "orthodox" rationale for our dating culture, making a "wise" selection of a mate requires a considerable amount of knowledge and experience. Even though at one level Americans believe that marriage should be based upon love, and that in the best of circumstances, "love conquers all," still at another level we recognize that it doesn't make sense to rush to the altar with the first person who makes your heart beat faster. Rather, through dating, which provides an opportunity for explorations into romantic intimacy without requiring rapid escalation toward marriage, you can acquire knowledge of what sort of person you are attracted to and what sort of person you might be suited to when it comes time to eventually choose a marital partner. Through experience with a series of dates and steadies, you can gain awareness that will help you make a better choice of someone you might be able to live with "happily ever after."

While this conception might suggest a highly rational process, in which individuals gradually develop a detailed mental "check list" that they will use to screen dating partners to see if they might be suitable marriage targets, this need not be the case. Rather, it might be assumed that this sort of "comparison shopping" experience penetrates to a subconscious level, so that when one meets "Mr. Right" or "Ms. Right" the appropriate strong romantic attraction will be triggered spontaneously, leaving no need to consult a trait check-list.[1] The implication of these ideas, in terms of marriage, is that the emergence and elaboration of our dating culture was a "good thing." In general, according to this conception, individuals who have gained more experience in the dating stage, by having dated more individuals and by having the opportunity to consider a wider range of potential marriage partners, should be able to make a better choice when it comes time to select someone to wed.

But numbers of dates, steadies or marital prospects, are not the only consideration, according to this scenario. Another logical implication is that the better you get to know any one dating partner, and indeed the more the level of intimacy with that partner approaches what would occur once you marry, the better able you will be to judge whether that partner would be suitable as a spouse. So not only experience with a variety of dating partners, but also development of a high level of premarital intimacy with at least some of them, is seen as part of the useful learning process made possible by our dating culture. This sort of argument may be recognized as one that sexually active or even cohabiting young people use to try to calm their anxious parents: "After all, mom and dad, it wouldn't make sense to marry without knowing how sexually compatible we are and how we could get along on an intimate, day-to-day basis, would it?" So according to this justifying rationale, tendencies toward more prolonged dating with more partners, and toward intimacy with the most serious partners, should be conducive to "good" mate choice decisions. In contrast, individuals who start dating late, who only date one or a few individuals, and who head for the altar without getting to know their eventual spouses quite intimately should be more likely to make "bad" decisions and end up unhappily married.

This view on the positive functions of dating variety and premarital intimacy has not gone unchallenged. In addition to objections based on moral and religious grounds, there are a number of criticisms from a more pragmatic viewpoint. Critics pose a number of reasons for doubting that dating variety and intimacy help individuals to make a wise choice of an eventual spouse, as assumed by the "marketplace learning" scenario. One of the major criticisms attacks the assumption that through dating and progressively higher levels of intimacy you become better prepared for an eventual choice of a mate. In part the objection to this view concerns the idea that having had alternative romantic partners, including very intimate ones, does not, in fact, prepare you very well to make the exclusive and life-long commitment to a spouse that marriage is supposed to entail. In other words, rather than preparing you to feel that you have selected Mr. Right, extensive dating experiences may lead to a painful awareness of alternatives foregone, with a "grass is greener on the other side of the fence" sentiment always present in the back of your mind. As one prominent study of American high schools in the 1950s stated the matter:

It seems unfortunate that so much of adolescents' energies must be spent in cultivating skills that serve them only at one point in life—in playing the courtship game.
These skills and habits may be impediments to happiness in later life. The "love of
the chase" may linger after marriage for both male and female, making married life
less content (Coleman 1961, p. 123).

If this alternative view is correct, then individuals who have had more limited dating experiences, and perhaps those who married their first sweethearts,
should end up with the most satisfactory marriages, exactly the opposite of the
prediction one is led to by the marketplace learning scenario.

There are additional criticisms of our dating culture that approach the matter from other angles. One version argues that the problem with the marketplace
learning conception is that it makes false assumptions about what really motivates
people in the dating stage. Critics question whether dating as it is normally practiced really provides for the kind of useful learning that the conventional rationale assumes. An alternative view is captured by the term, the "dating game." In
this view other elements besides trying to find out who one would be suited to
tend to dominate dating in America. In particular, concern to display popularity
or to gain certain romantic and possibly sexual favors from partners leads young
people to put on false fronts (what Douvan and Adelson [1966] call "dating personalities") in order to impress dates and potential dates. With each individual
manufacturing artificiality in order to impress their date, neither is in a very good
position to learn what their partner is really like or whether they might be a suitable choice for a longer-term relationship.

The best-known version of this criticism comes from the work of Willard
Waller, who coined the term, "rating and dating," to convey the idea that competition among students for popularity dominates dating behavior and completely negates the kind of learning process that the orthodox scenario assumes takes
place. (See Waller 1937 and the discussion in Lasch 1977, Chapter 3. For a critique of Waller's ideas, see Gordon 1981.) According to Waller, individuals are
not motivated to date those who might be most suited to them, but those who
are most likely to be defined as a "good date" or a "good catch" by peers. In
such an environment, even if you could accurately assess the characteristics of
your romantic partner by piercing through the superficiality of that partner's "dating personality," you would still end up dating the wrong person for the wrong
reasons. When it comes time to pick a marriage partner, it will be very difficult
to "switch gears" and select someone who is uniquely suited to your own needs
and personality. In this version of the criticism of the marketplace learning scenario, extensive dating is at least not very conducive to a wise marital decision,
if not actually being counterproductive.

Still other criticisms of our dating culture raise additional and somewhat
related points—that early dating and early intimacy may lead to a younger age
at marriage or may produce powerful emotions and urges that completely close
out any sort of rational consideration of suitability. In either case the result is not
likely to be a level-headed choice of a mate and a wise decision about when to
marry. The resulting marriage is not likely to be as successful as one based upon
a more gradual and constrained entry into premarital intimacy. High levels of

absorption into dating and romantic concerns may also interfere with school learning and occupational training, resulting in poorer job placement and lower income, outcomes that will create considerable stress on a marriage relationship.[2]

Here, additional views on both sides of the issue could be discussed, but the general situation should be clear by now. There exist two conflicting arguments about whether various features of dating and premarital intimacy are conducive to marital success or not. The conventional rationale for our dating culture assumes that length of dating experience, variety in dating partners, and extensiveness of premarital intimacy are all useful preparations for a successful marriage. In the various criticisms of this scenario, it is argued that the opposite may more often be the case—that extensive dating and premarital intimacy may interfere with making a suitable choice of a marital partner.... These alternative points of view will not be tested [here] ... but they form the background within which to consider what changes are visible in the dating experiences of women in our Detroit sample.

In the pages that follow, concrete evidence is offered to replace the speculations described earlier on whether the timing and nature of dating have changed. Our survey allows us to investigate whether various guesses about the evolution of dating in America over the last half century or so are accurate. Has everything become more free-wheeling in American dating, or are such claims incorrect? Since we interviewed women retrospectively about their dating experiences spanning a period of more than 60 years, we can begin to shed some light on what the actual changes in dating have been.[3]

In examining changes in dating patterns in the Detroit sample, I categorize the women we interviewed in terms of their years of marriage ... rather than by age. By categorizing women by the year in which they first married I am, of course, ignoring the fact that the dating history these women are describing took place prior to their wedding, and that some women spent longer times in the dating stage than others. I simply want to establish whether women who married at successive points in time had similar or different experiences in their prior dating stage. In much of this analysis, it will be sufficient to divide respondents into three large groups, each representing a 29-year time span of entry into marriage. These will be referred to as three major "marriage generations": those who were prewar brides, marrying in the years 1925–44 (N = 66); those who entered marriage during the "baby boom" years of 1945–1964 (N = 180); and those recent marriage cases who first wed during the years 1965–84 (N = 209).[4]

These categories, while nicely dividing the years of first marriage of the sample into three even slices, have the virtue of corresponding roughly to three different historical environments that are recognized in much previous writing on the American family. The first generation encompasses major disruptions brought on by the Great Depression and by World War II, which produced trials of strength for most American families (see Elder 1974). The second generation produced not only an unexpected baby boom, but also a high tide of general "familism" in American social life, with earlier and more universal marriage than before, a declining and then relatively stable divorce rate, the zenith of the "housewife syndrome" in America, and the explosion of life in suburbia—themes conveyed in the popular media of the time and in such popular television programs as *Father Knows Best.* The third marriage generation encompasses a retreat from this familistic ethos, with declining birth rates, increasing divorce rates, and the rise of the feminist and sexual liberation movements. So the divisions in terms of which most comparisons will be made are not totally arbitrary.

At times I will want to use a finer time breakdown. Occasionally categories that divide women by their year of marriage into twelve groups, each of them five years in length, will be used, and I will refer to these groups as "marriage cohorts," (those who first married before 1929, in 1930–34, 1935–39, etc.). In places I will use the actual year of marriage to get the most detailed picture of trends. This chapter is concerned simply with determining trends in behavior in the dating stage. . . .

Dating and Going Steady

The first question of interest is at what age women started dating in various periods. A direct question in a written supplement to our questionnaire asked women to report their age at the time they went on their first date, and it turns out, based on their replies, that there has not been any clear trend over time in the age of starting dating.[5] There is no clear correlation between marriage year and the age of first date, and in all three generations the median age at the time of the first date was 16. So in this respect, at least, in recent years women do not seem to be starting the dating process earlier.[6]

At this point it should be noted that the age at which women in our sample first married did change over time, but not in a simple fashion. As we know from many other studies of American marriage, ages of marriage dropped gradually during the twentieth century until the mid-1950s, and since then they have been going up again (see, for example, the discussion in Cherlin 1981). In the Detroit sample this curvilinear pattern is also visible. In the prewar generation, the median age at first marriage was 21, then it dropped among baby-boom era brides to 20, and among recent cases it has risen again to 21.[7] The crude generational breakdown used here hides some of the recent increase; in the two final marriage cohorts (involving women who married after 1975) the mean age at marriage was over 23 years, matching national trends. The curvilinear trend in marriage ages, combined with the stable estimated age of beginning dating, means that the average number of years of potential dating—between the time of the first date and getting married—was about five years for women in the prewar cohorts, decreased to about four years during the baby-boom years, and is now back to five years or more. This changing length of time spent in the dating stage should be kept in mind when we consider other trends in dating behavior.

One other feature of the marriage ages in the Detroit sample should be noted. The ages of first marriages of the women we interviewed covered a very wide range, from 14 to 60! Even though there has been substantial publicity given to recent research claiming that women who pass the "prime marriage ages" may never succeed in marrying (see Bennett and Bloom 1986),[8] our data provide some support for the old saying that "it's never too late." Overall, 5 percent of the women in our sample first married at age 30 or later, and in addition to our champion who first married at age 60, there was another woman who finally made it to the altar at age 50. Both of these examples of the "never too late" phenomenon were wed in the late 1970s, indicating continued hope recently for women past the prime marriage ages.[9] So despite current concern that women who don't marry early may forfeit their chances, our data hint that the social convention that women should marry before it gets "too late" may be weakening.

Even though the age of starting dating has not gotten steadily earlier, other features of dating experience have changed. We asked our respondents to estimate how many different individuals they had ever gone out with on a date. The prewar brides on the average reported dating only 4–7 males, whereas the baby boomers estimated dating 10–14 and the youngest women in our sample gave figures averaging 12–15 males. It is possible that these figures exaggerate the trend, since older women may have forgotten some of the males they dated (and younger women may be more prone to brag by inflating the number they dated). Still, we suspect that there is a real trend underlying these figures, with younger women having had more dating partners before they married.[10]

The fact that women who married in more recent times report more males ever dated does not mean that "playing the field" has become more common than "going steady." Our respondents were asked about both their age at the time when they first went steady and about the number of "steadies" they had. It turns out that the age of starting to go steady has decreased steadily over time. Among prewar marriage cases, the median age of starting to go steady was 18, among baby-boom era brides it was 17, and among recent marriage cases the average age had dropped to 16. Whereas it was once common for young women to play the field for a couple of years before starting to go steady, in recent decades going steady starts almost immediately.

The number of individuals the average woman goes steady with before marriage has also increased somewhat in recent cohorts. Among prewar marriage cases a slight majority of women—55 percent—had not had any other steady boyfriends aside from the men they married. But this was true of only 34 percent of the women in the baby-boom marriage generation and only 25 percent of the women who married after 1965. In other words, the phenomenon of "marrying one's first sweetheart" seems less and less common, although it was still the pattern for one quarter of the youngest women in the sample. As one might expect, the average number of males ever gone steady with shows a corresponding increase, from 2.7 for the prewar generation through 3.5 for baby-boom era brides to 3.6 for the youngest respondents. (These averages include the eventual first husband.) Together these figures show that while dating itself has not begun earlier in recent times, "serious dating" in the form of going steady begins earlier now. Since starting to go steady is seen by most as quite separate from preparing to marry, the fact that this stage begins earlier is not incompatible with our finding that women in this youngest generation ended up having had both more dates and more steady boyfriends prior to marriage than their older counterparts.[11]

How did parents react and adapt to these changes in dating behavior? Did they increasingly give their offspring free rein to do as they pleased in regard to the opposite sex? We don't have the best possible measures to answer these questions. We did ask our respondents the following two questions: "Did your parents ever try to influence who you went out with?" "Did they ever tell you they didn't want you to go out with a particular person?" It turns out that there is not a significant difference in the responses of women of different generations to these questions. In all three generations about half of our respondents reported that their parents had tried to influence who they went out with, and of those whose parents had played such a role, about three-quarters reported parents trying to forbid them going out with particular individuals. Unless we believe that the older women in our sample are selectively "forgetting" about such parental obstruction—a pattern that does not appear particularly plausible—these responses lead us to believe that parents have not significantly altered their concern about who their daughters go out with.[12]

In some cases this parental involvement and concern may even be expressed in some less subtle ways. For example, in one of our pretest interviews we asked a respondent how her parents conveyed to her that they were unhappy with the man she was dating. She replied that her mother pulled out a gun from a drawer, pointed it at her, and told her that if she tried to go out the door for her scheduled date she would shoot her dead![13] On the other hand, the figures from our survey indicate that about half of even the older women felt that their parents gave them complete freedom to go out with anyone they wanted to. So our primary conclusion is that the women we interviewed reported a substantial and fairly constant (across generations) level of autonomy to make their own decisions about whom to date.

Premarital Sex

So far the picture we get is of a dating process that has changed only modestly. Reported parental supervision of dating has not changed much, and dating does not begin any earlier. However, going steady begins earlier, and both the number of males dated and the number of steadies have somewhat increased. But what of premarital sexual activity? Hasn't there been more of a revolution there? We asked a number of questions about this aspect of the dating process, but many of them were indirect. In other words, we didn't ask our respondents whether they had ever had sex before they got married. Instead, we asked them to report the age at which they first had sexual intercourse. By comparing their answers to this question with our data on the ages at which they got married, we can make a rough estimate of the proportion of women in the sample who engaged in premarital sex. It is a conservative estimate, since those women who lost their virginity in the weeks or months leading up to their wedding and who did not have another birthday before walking down the aisle would, according to this calculation, be classified incorrectly as virgins at marriage. So this measure will somewhat underestimate the proportion of nonvirgins at marriage. But since we are concerned here with comparisons across generations, this method should still give us a fairly clear picture of trends.

When we examine the proportion of the sample who had their first sexual experience at a younger age than when they were married, we do find a dramatic change across generations. Among the prewar brides, only 24 percent had already lost their virginity, according to our rough estimate. For the baby-boom era brides this figure increases to 51 percent, and in the post-1965 cases to 72 percent. So the premarital loss of virginity has changed from being the experience of only a minority of women to that of the large majority of women. If we look at finer time divisions, the recent trend is even more striking. The percentage of nonvirgins at marriage, as computed by this method, increased from 56 percent among those married in the years 1965–69 to 67 percent among those who married in 1970–74, and then to 85 percent among those who married in 1975–79 and 88 percent among those who married in the years 1980–84. Keep in mind that these figures probably underestimate the extent of premarital sex in all generations. In other words, according to our estimates, it is probably the case that less than 10 percent of those women in the Detroit area who were marrying in the mid-1980s were still virgins.[14] Clearly a sexual revolution has taken place. From a situation in which "nice girls don't" we have moved to a new era in which "most girls do."

Is sexual experience beginning ever earlier, or is part of the increase in premarital sex simply due to the delay in marriage ages of women in recent years? From reports on the age of first sexual experience we can examine this question. In general, our figures point to sex not only becoming more common prior to marriage, but beginning at an earlier age. In the prewar generation the median age of first sexual experience was about age 20. Among baby-boom era brides it dropped to about age 19, and in recent marriage cases to about age 18.[15]

One further implication of these trends is clear. Formerly, it was the case that most women who engaged in premarital sex did so with their eventual husbands. Indeed, more than half of the women in both the Kinsey survey (Kinsey et al. 1953) in the 1940s and the Hunt survey in 1970 (Hunt 1974) who were not virgins at marriage had only had sex with their eventual husbands. This pattern has been interpreted as indicating that not only an exclusive romantic relationship (i.e., going steady), but even some sort of commitment to marry is seen by most women as necessary before they will engage in premarital sex (for those who do, in fact, lose their virginity prior to marriage). Hunt also argued, by comparing the similarity of the figures from his survey and from Kinsey's (see Hunt 1974, p. 151) that this situation had not changed over time, in spite of a major increase in premarital sexual activity among females.

However, our findings point to change, rather than continuity, in this realm. As women have reached increasing levels of intimacy at earlier ages, and with partners with whom there may be no explicit commitment to marry, it has become more likely that a woman will have had other sexual partners before her husband. We asked our respondents how old they were when they first started dating their eventual husbands, and by comparing this piece of information with their reports on their age when they first had sex, we can calculate an estimate of the proportion of respondents who had had sex already with another partner before their eventual husbands.[16] According to this calculation, the percentage of women who had other sexual partners prior to their eventual husbands rose from 3 percent among our prewar brides to 17 percent for brides of the baby-boom era, and then to 33 percent among brides in the most recent generation.[17] As with our premarital sex estimates, if we examine more detailed time divisions, the recent increase is even more striking. Comparing the four marriage cohorts within our final marriage generation (those marrying in 1965–69, 1970–74, 1975–79, and 1980–84), the percentage of women who we estimate had prior sexual partners is 17 percent, 31 percent, 41 percent, and 51 percent. So not only are women who are virgins at marriage becoming increasingly scarce, but women who have lost their virginity before they start dating their eventual husbands are more and more the norm.

This trend does not imply necessarily that casual sex or sex with a variety of partners in the same time span is becoming accepted for women, either in attitudes or in behavior. We did not ask more detailed questions in this realm, so we cannot tell what proportion of our respondents engaged in premarital sex in anything other than an exclusive romantic setting (i.e., at least going steady).[18] But since an increasing proportion of women are having several steady relationships before they settle on a man to marry, and since sexual activity is increasingly accepted within a steady relationship, the net result is an increase in women whose sexual initiation precedes meeting and starting to date the man they will eventually marry.

Mapping Trends

From the various trends reviewed so far we can now construct profiles of how the average timing of the various stages in dating has changed across the generations in our sample. In the prewar generation dating began, on the average, at about age 16; going steady followed a couple of years later, at age 18; and the first sexual experience followed at age 20 or so. However, for the majority of women sex began with marriage, at about age 21, rather than before.[19] In the baby-boom era, dating still began at about age 16, going steady followed at 17, and the first sexual experience two years later, at age 19. Still about half of the women, however, did not begin sexual relations until they married, and marriage occurred relatively early, below age 20 for half of the women in that generation. For the most recent generation in our sample, again dating began at age 16, but going steady began soon afterward, while these women were still 16. Then sexual relations began at about age 18, on the average, or about 3 years before the average woman in this generation married. So the primary change in the dating process is not in beginning the whole process earlier, but in reaching deeper levels of intimacy at earlier stages in the dating process. Therefore, since the median age of first dating the eventual husband remained at about 18 for all three generations, the chart shows that intimacy was increasingly occurring not only prior to marriage, but prior to starting dating the first husband.[20]

The most dramatic expression of intimacy during the dating stage is pre-marital cohabitation, where a couple lives together as husband and wife, but without the benefit of matrimony. We know from studies by the U.S. Census Bureau and others that cohabitation has been increasing in recent years (see Spanier 1983; Eekelaar and Katz 1980), but to date there are few studies that can tell us what proportion of people do at some point live together before getting married. We asked about this directly, although again we do not have a perfect measure. The question used was, "Did you and your husband live together before you got married?" Responses to this question might slightly understate the extent of cohabitation, since women who lived with some other male before marriage but did not cohabit with their eventual spouse would not be counted as having cohabited. (Also some women, of course, might not admit to having cohabited.)

The shift across cohorts in responses to this premarital cohabitation question is particularly dramatic. No women who married before the early 1950s admitted to having cohabited prior to marriage. Then among the cohorts who married between 1955 and 1974, between 5 and 10 percent cohabited. But in the final two marriage cohorts, the rate skyrockets—to 32 percent for those marrying in the period of 1975–79 and then to 40 percent for those marrying in the years 1980–84. So cohabitation prior to marriage is now approaching becoming a majority phenomenon in the complex urban area that Detroit represents.[21] If this trend continues, and is duplicated in other places in the United States, then we can expect to see not only premarital sex but living together before marriage increasingly accepted as a normal part of the dating and mating process in American society.

At this point the reader may well wonder whether AIDS and other sexually transmitted diseases are not changing this situation fundamentally. There has been considerable discussion in the mass media of a new conservatism in American family life and sexual behavior generally in the 1980s, and even some advocates arising for what is called "the new celibacy." Could such general trends, and fear of contracting AIDS in particular, reverse the trends described here and produce an increase in the proportion of women (and perhaps also men) who remain virgins until marriage? Certainly it is not inconceivable that the trend toward premarital intimacy can be reversed, since this appears to have happened before in American history. Researchers have uncovered evidence suggesting that the current sexual revolution is the second in our history, rather than the first. An earlier major increase in premarital sexuality occurred at the end of the eighteenth century and early in the nineteenth century, but was followed by a retreat toward increasing premarital chastity during the Victorian era in the latter part of the nineteenth century (see Smith and Hindus 1975). Could this reversal be repeated as America approaches the end of the twentieth century?

It would be nice if I could answer this question using data from the Detroit survey, but unfortunately we did not ask any questions in this survey about such things as fear of venereal disease. In any case, the timing of our interviews was such that fear of AIDS could not have been a major concern during the premarital years of the women we interviewed, since the disease had only been identified in the early 1980s. So my thoughts on this issue are largely speculative, rather than based on evidence from the Detroit survey.[22] At the time that I write these lines I see no clear signs that the trend toward premarital intimacy is being reversed. Insofar as unmarried individuals do not dismiss the danger of AIDS as irrelevant to them, because it is confined largely to "special" populations—drug addicts, homosexuals, and hemophiliacs—they are likely to become more cautious about "casual sex." But unless and until AIDS is seen as making greater inroads into the heterosexual population, individuals are not likely to feel that premarital sex in the context of an exclusive relationship with a steady or a future spouse is very dangerous.

Whether or not this perception is accurate or foolish, it seems to me that the dominant trend that emerges from the Detroit interviews—sexual intimacy incorporated into the dating and mating sequence as part of a romantic and exclusive relationship—is likely to continue to be interpreted as "safe sex." Popular attitudes toward premarital sexuality in this context remain quite liberal. Perhaps the AIDS scare may contribute to some greater hesitancy about beginning sexual activity, and therefore to an increase in the average age of the first sexual experience, and unmarried couples may more regularly choose condoms as their preferred means of birth control. But I do not anticipate any significant trend toward rising virginity at marriage unless AIDS spreads much more widely into the general population. The previous and long-standing convention that women, at least, might lose status and harm their chances for attracting a desirable marriage partner by giving up their virginity prior to marriage has been demolished, and I see no sign that this convention is being revived.

Approaching Marriage

For most Americans, even though dating initially begins without any clear connection to mate-selection, the eventual goal is to find someone to marry. Since we only interviewed women who had been married we have no direct evidence on the point; however, other research indicates that the increasing availability of premarital sex and cohabitation have not weakened the popularity of marriage as an institution. Very few individuals see our more liberal contemporary sexual mores as providing an acceptable alternative to marriage.[23] But has the way in which people select a partner changed? For instance, do people rush into marriage more nowadays? Is a formal engagement stage less common today than in the past? We asked a number of questions that allowed us to look at some features of the final stage of the dating process—the stage of selecting a suitable marriage partner and preparing to walk down the aisle.

One question that intrigued us was whether there had been any change in the number of "serious marital prospects"—the number of men that the average woman ever thought about marrying before she settled on her eventual husband. We asked respondents directly, "Before you married your (first) husband, were there any other men you seriously considered marrying?" (If so) "How many were there?" It turns out that change in this area has been slight. In the prewar marriage generation only 35 percent of all respondents had other "serious prospects."

In the baby-boom generation the comparable figure was 47 percent, and among recent marriage cases 46 percent. There is a slight indication of an increase in the likelihood of having given other men serious consideration, but the trend is not statistically significant.

For those who did have other prospects, there is also not much sign of change in the number of alternatives considered. The mean number of other prospects considered is between 1.2 and 1.4 for each generation, with no clear trend. In spite of the tendency we have already commented on for going steady and sexual intimacy to begin at earlier ages, when women come to the process of actually selecting a spouse, they do not have a larger number of choices in recent years. Most women still go to the altar with the only man they seriously considered marrying, and even those who considered another usually had only one alternative. (But for the record, in our sample one woman claimed to have given five other men serious consideration.)[24]

We also inquired about how women first met their husbands. We were interested in whether they had met directly or whether they had been introduced. Allowing for some crudeness in the question, due to the possibility that "introduction" could have been defined in various ways by different respondents, still it is striking that there has been little change across generations in this aspect of mate choice. In the three major generations 58 percent, 54 percent and 58 percent of the women reported having met their spouse directly, so there is no clear trend visible.

We also examined more specifically how the couple had first met. In a follow-up to our initial question about whether the couple had met directly or had

TABLE 15-1

Generational Differences in First Meeting

How the Couple First Met	MARRIAGE GENERATION		
	1925–1944	1945–1964	1965–1984
Introductions:	42.4%	46.1%	41.6%
Of which:			
By parents, older kin	2.8	3.9	2.4
By siblings, same age kin	12.7	11.2	11.0
By other kin	.2.8	2.8	0.5
By friends, other nonkin	18.4	27.6	25.8
Blind date	5.7	0.6	1.9
Direct Meeting:	57.6	53.9	58.4
Of which:			
Known since childhood	0.0	2.8	1.4
In neighborhood	8.2	7.3	4.0
In church, church activity	3.3	1.7	1.9
In organization, club	4.9	1.1	1.0
In school, school activity	13.2	11.8	14.0
At work	11.5	10.6	14.0
At party, dance, wedding	0.0	7.9	5.3
At bar, dance hall	3.3	1.7	4.8
In public, chance meeting	13.2	7.9	10.6
Vacation, amusement spot	0.0	1.1	1.4
(N)	(66)	(180)	(209)

been introduced, we asked who had done the introducing, or where the couple had first met. The responses to these open questions are reported in Table 15-1. Just as there has been no clear change in the balance of introductions versus direct meetings, these figures do not show any statistically significant overall trends. However, a few features of these percentages might be highlighted. First, in all generations introductions by friends and other nonfamily members were more common than introductions provided by family members, and a slight trend toward fewer family introductions is visible in the younger generations in the table. Blind dates are also less often mentioned by those in younger generations. We recorded no cases at all of the much talked about modern replacements of the blind date—couples matched via computer dating or through classified personal ads. The neighborhood where one grew up, church activities, and clubs and other organizations are all somewhat less common as arenas for finding mates in the younger generations than in the oldest generation, and work organizations and parties and dances have become somewhat more promising venues.

It is rather difficult to put such data on how the couple first met in any kind of interpretive perspective, since we lack systematic data on this question

TABLE 15-2

Comparative Data on How Couples First Met

HOW THE COUPLE FIRST MET	CURRENT STUDY	CT 1949–1950	FRANCE 1959	ENGLAND 1969	USSR 1962
Introductions	43.4%	39.6%	17.0%	12.4%	8.7%
Of which:					
By family	16.3	n.a.	6.0	)	3.3
				12.4*	
By friends, nonkin	25.2	28.7	11.0	)	5.2
Blind date	2.0	10.9	n.a.	n.a.	n.a.
Direct Meeting:	56.6	60.4	83.0	87.6	91.5
Of which:					
From neighborhood, childhood	7.5	12.4	22.0	6.7	9.0
Church, church activity	2.0	2.4	n.a.	2.2	n.a.
Organization, club	1.6	1.9	6.0	n.a.	n.a.
School, school activity	13.1	7.0	)	4.5	17.5
			13.0*		
Work	12.2	12.4	)	14.6	21.0
Party, dance, wedding	5.8	12.4	17.0	32.6	5.7
Bar, dance hall	3.3	n.a.	n.a.	4.5	27.2
Public place, chance meeting	10.0	11.9	15.0	6.7	2.3
Vacation, amusement spot	1.1	n.a.	10.0	12.4	5.0
Other	n.a.	n.a.	n.a.	3.4	3.8
(N)	(455)	(715)	(1646)	(1037)	(500)

n.a. = not available * = combination of category above and below

Sources:
Current study: respondents from all marriage generations together.
CT: white couples who married in New Haven in 1949–50, as identified by marriage licenses (both marrying for first time only), from Hollingshead 1952.
France: results of a national survey of married men and women reported in Girard 1974, p. 98.
England: results of a national survey of married men and women under 45, reported in Gorer 1971, p. 265 (percentages recomputed to total 100).
USSR: newly married couples identified through marriage registrations in Leningrad, as reported in Kharchev 1965.

for other times and places. I have attempted in Table 15-2 to piece together some figures from other studies that are somewhat comparable to ours. However, differences in samples, question wording, and coding procedures make this comparison almost impossible, and so any conclusions reached here can be only tentative. But several contrasts in these figures seem apparent. First, introductions of various kinds are more commonly mentioned in our data than in the other studies, although this may be an artifact of our asking about it directly.[25] Schools and places of work are the next most common places of meeting in our sample and are more common venues than in the French and English studies, but less common than in the Soviet study cited. Parties, dances, bars, and other places of entertainment seem less common meeting places in our study than in the European samples examined in the table.

Given the imprecision of this comparison, it is hard to know what to make of specific details. But two general observations do seem to be important. First, the similarities of our figures and those computed by Hollingshead from his study of New Haven marriages in 1949–50 do lend weight to the idea that there is an identifiable and relatively stable pattern by which marital partners are first brought together in America. Second, in a majority of cases the circumstances are other than those focused on in most of the mate-choice literature. Most research on mate choice in America is conducted among students and carries the implicit, if not explicit, assumption that schools and colleges are where most pairing off goes on in America. But only about one-eighth of our sample met directly in school or school activities.[26] Popular writings on finding a mate focus not only on schools, but also on the workplace, on computer dating, on singles bars, and on vacation spots of the "Club Med" variety (see Godwin 1973; Mullan 1984). But these also are routes to mate choice used by only a small proportion of our sample to find a spouse. It would appear that future research on mate choice in America should look more in-depth at the introduction process, whether by family or friends, as the primary route to finding a spouse in our society. And other locales besides schools and offices deserve greater attention as well.

Perhaps our American ideology in regard to mate choice has blinded us in this realm. We are a society that believes in freedom of mate choice, and the idea of an arranged marriage is odd and repulsive. From this viewpoint it is only a short step to assuming that most couples in America should and do meet on their own. But in fact our data indicate that nearly half of all couples meet first via somebody else's introduction, rather than directly, and that the percentage who meet in this way has not changed much across generations. Of course, those doing the introducing are rarely the sort of hired matchmakers lampooned in "Fiddler on the Roof." Still, informal introductions turn out to be a very important, and a little studied, aspect of the dating and mating process in American society today.

We also investigated the "propinquity question." It is a standard theme of textbooks on American marriage that a large proportion of those who marry lived only a few blocks apart before they started dating (see, for example, Udry 1971, pp. 185–6). After all, without an arranged marriage system, people have to meet and get to know potential spouses, and your chances of doing so are much higher if you live near a prospect than if you live very far away. (Even if you meet via an introduction, it is unlikely that you will be introduced to a person living at a great distance.) Recent studies hint that propinquity—the closeness of prior residence—may no longer be so important a factor in mate selection in recent years. With more automobiles, increased college attendance, greater geographical mobility via jobs, and other developments, one can cast one's mate choice "net" somewhat wider. We asked our respondents how far apart they and their first husband had lived when they first started dating.[27] The median distance at the time of the first date as computed from this measure fluctuated somewhat, but did show a slight upward trend. In our prewar generation of women the median distance apart was three miles, and this increased to four miles for those in the baby-boom generation and five miles for women marrying since 1965. So there is some evidence for the view that propinquity is a somewhat less binding constraint than in the past, but still the fact that half of all recent brides lived less than five miles away from their future husbands when they started dating is notable.

Once they have found "Mr. Right," how long do women date him before they marry? Our data on this point are rather crude—we only have the age of the woman when she started going out with her eventual spouse and her age at the time she married, rather than a direct question about the number of months that she dated him. But our data suggest that here there has not been much change in the final stage of dating. The median number of years spent dating the eventual husband was two years in all three generations. In this case, the median is a somewhat misleading statistic, and the mean number of years spent dating the eventual husband shows the same curvilinear trend we saw earlier in examining marriage ages—the averages were 2.5 years, 2.2 years, and 2.6 years for the three generations.[28] There has been some change over time, but there has not been a consistent tendency toward either hasty or delayed marriages. These figures provide no evidence that the average woman was "rushing into marriage," since even in the baby-boom era when such hastiness was the subject of much public criticism, most women waited for two years or more before heading for the altar. In recent times, there are modest signs of further caution and delay before deciding to tie the knot.

If we consider the question of a formal engagement there is also not much sign of change. The great majority of women in all generations were formally engaged before they married. The figures for our three major generations were 85 percent, 89 percent, and 90 percent who had been engaged, and the slight increase here is not statistically significant. However, not all of those who considered themselves formally engaged received an engagement ring. And the proportion of women who reported receiving an engagement ring is higher in more recent generations—only 55 percent of prewar brides received a ring, but 71 percent of baby-boom era brides and 74 percent of recently married women did. Evidently, these figures provide testimony more to the increasing success of the diamond industry in promoting their products (see Epstein 1978) than to changes in underlying American mate-choice customs. Assuming recollections are accurate, there has been a rather slight increase in the length of time spent in the engagement stage. The median number of months spent engaged is 8 for both the prewar generation and the baby-boom era brides, but 11 among those marrying since 1965.[29]

In various preceding sections of this chapter trends in the percentage of women in our sample who have had various premarital experiences were considered.... The data show that in the prewar generation, only getting engaged was a majority experience. Since then, having had other serious marital prospects and getting engaged have only become slightly more common, but having had other steadies besides the eventual husband and having engaged in premarital sex have become much more common experiences, such that they are now part of the "premarital regime" of the large majority of women when they marry. Additionally ... both having had other sexual partners prior to dating the eventual husband and having cohabited with the eventual husband prior to marriage are rapidly becoming more common, and may well be majority phenomena for Detroit area women by the time this book is published.... Intimacy has become "normal" prior to the walk to the altar.

Conclusions

This chapter started by asking whether everything about the dating process in America has been getting earlier and more casual. The simple answer to this question is no. But that simple response is not very enlightening. In the preceding pages we have discovered both impressive continuities in dating behavior across generations and startling changes.

The major change in the dating regime that our data attest to is that premarital intimacy of various kinds—going steady, engaging in premarital sex, living together before marriage, having known other sexual partners before the husband—is occurring earlier, and to a higher proportion of young women, than in the past. The fact that more is involved in this trend than simply increasing premarital sexual activity leads me to refer to this as an "intimacy revolution," rather than simply a sexual revolution.[30]

This is really a striking set of changes in many ways. These trends testify, among other things, to dramatic alterations in the expectations surrounding the behavior of unmarried women, and to a decline in the sexual double standard. In earlier decades in this century premarital intimacy by males was often seen tolerantly as "sowing wild oats." No such tolerance existed for unmarried females. Virginity was seen as a prerequisite for a "good marriage," and young women who lost their virginity or simply developed a reputation of being fickle or "loose" placed their prospects on the marriage market in great jeopardy. As a result, young women tended invariably to become categorized, or stigmatized, into two groups: the "nice girls" who didn't (engage in premarital sex), and the "easy girls" who did. Young males anxious to sow their wild oats provided lots of attention for the "easy girls" as well as for professional prostitutes, but when it came time to select a girl for marriage they usually turned, instead, to one of the "nice girls."[31]

Clearly the situation has changed markedly. Young females are generally not expected to be virgins at marriage anymore, and engaging in sex or even having lived with a male prior to marriage no longer seems to harm a woman's chances of making a suitable marriage. (We have no data in this study on expectations, but from our figures it is clear that males who require a bride to be a virgin face an increasingly difficult search process.) It is probably the case that females are still more likely to be criticized than males for "sex without feeling" or for having more than one sexual partner at any particular time. In this sense some division between "nice girls" and "easy girls" still exists. But the categories have been redefined so that "nice girls" include those who are intimate, sexually and otherwise, but only in the context of an exclusive, romantic relationship. Promiscuity now has a narrower meaning of casual sex or sex that is not exclusively with one partner, rather than premarital sex per se. The assumptions that used to loom heavily over women—that intimacy before marriage indicated that as a wife she would be dissatisfied or unfaithful—no longer hold, for better or for worse.

This change clearly forms part of a more general process of alteration in the status of women relative to men. We should note, though, that we don't feel that the women's liberation movement was primarily responsible for these changes. The timing is simply wrong. The women's liberation movement began to be a noticeable force in America in the mid-1960s, but the "intimacy revolution" clearly was underway well before that time. The same comment could be made about explanations of the sexual revolution in terms of the invention of the "pill" and other modern contraceptive devices and liberalized abortion rights. Again, the changes toward greater and earlier premarital intimacy were clearly underway even before the pill and legal abortion became available. Feminism and birth control options may have helped to accelerate changes that were already underway, changes that some analysts believe began even earlier than the time-span of our data, perhaps in the late nineteenth century (see Kinsey et al. 1953; Smith 1973; Degler 1974; Rothman 1984).

Our data don't speak directly to the reasons for this century-long pattern of change, but I would argue that factors such as increasing commercialization and affluence (particularly the rising financial autonomy of young people), growing privatization of family life and the decline of community controls, the assimilation of immigrants and the weakening of ethnic family controls, and the influence of Sigmund Freud's ideas on sexuality played more of a role in fostering the intimacy revolution than recent phenomena such as the pill and the women's liberation movement. (See Smith and Hindus 1975; Shorter 1971.) This "intimacy revolution" is one of the most dramatic symbols of the decline in conventions. . . . Expectations that intimacy will be postponed until at least engagement, if not marriage, have fallen by the wayside in the face of a logic that says that whatever one does in an exclusive, romantic relationship must be "all right."

Part of the picture we have seen in this chapter is an "intimacy revolution" taking place in the lives of unmarried females over the last 60 years. However, our data also show us another side of the picture, a side in which there is much continuity with the past. Dating does not apparently start earlier than it used to. Parents still seem to hover at the sidelines, worrying about who their youngsters will go out with and whether they will make a "suitable" choice for a marriage partner. And even though premarital intimacy is much more common today, dating has not become an endless stage, or a replacement for marriage. For the vast majority of young people, intimacy in the dating stage serves simply as a further preliminary to the selection of a mate. The process of mate selection seems to be invested today with the same deliberation and ceremony as in the past. Most women end up selecting a mate from only one or two serious prospects. And 90 percent of them get formally engaged, and more of them than in earlier generations receive an engagement ring symbolizing their commitment. Both the dating stage and the engagement stage with the man they plan to marry are as long or longer, on the average, as was the case in earlier generations.

These elements of continuity modify our judgment about what has changed in the dating process. Startling as the inroads of intimacy into the process are, they don't add up to a fundamental alteration or challenge to the nature of "courting" in America. This increasing intimacy has not undermined, but has been incorporated into, a dating and mating sequence whose basic goals remain the same as before. The primary goal of this activity—to find a suitable mate—has not changed, although the rules about what one may do along the way have clearly been modified.

The basic argument I am making, then, is that the changes in the dating process are less revolutionary than they might at first appear. Even premarital cohabitation, shocking as it may be to the traditionally minded, has come to be viewed as just one more stage in a sequence that will eventually lead to the altar. But the changes that have occurred in the dating process raise important questions. The implications of the intimacy revolution for moral and religious concerns will not be dealt with here, for they are not the proper terrain for a sociologist. But the sociologist can consider the social consequences implied by such changes, and in particular the consequences for those marriages which are formed at the end of this transformed dating process. Are those marriages likely to be better or worse as a result of increased premarital intimacy?

In some sense the intimacy revolution that our figures document is the logical culmination of our system of free mate choice based upon dating. Under the "marketplace learning" conception described earlier, it is assumed that the best mate selection is an informed selection, and that making such a selection requires familiarity with alternatives and also quasimarital intimacy with serious marriage prospects. According to this concept, the more constrained mate selection environment prior to the intimacy revolution was less sensible and more risky, a sentiment conveyed vividly by Sir Thomas More in *Utopia* when he compares mate selection unfavorably with buying a horse:

> . . . when you're choosing a wife . . . you're unbelievably careless, you don't even bother to take it out of its wrappings. You judge the whole woman from a few squares inches of face, which is all you can see of her, and then proceed to marry her—at the risk of finding her most disagreeable, when you see what she's really like (quoted in MacFarlane 1985, p. 166).

When this sort of argument is pursued to its limits, premarital sex, cohabitation, and even sex with other potential marital prospects, can be seen not only as acceptable, but even as valuable preparation for a successful marriage.

Yet not only moralists, but many social scientists, raise questions about whether this intimacy revolution is a "good thing." As discussed earlier, these critics argue on a number of grounds that the kinds of changes that have been documented in this chapter—increasing numbers of dating partners, earlier pairing off with a steady boyfriend, and rising premarital sexuality—are not the building blocks of strong and satisfying marriages, and may in fact lead to more brittle conjugal bonds. . . .

Notes

1. In subsequent portions of this study I will no longer include references to both male options and female options, as in this passage. Instead I will refer to females dating and mating males, since our data come from interviews with married women. However, in most instances this is just a convenient shorthand, and the logic presented could apply to the male side of the dating game as well as to the female side. Some readers may find the use of marketplace terms and analogies offensive when talking about love and marriage. However, it is now a commonplace that the process of mate choice is in all societies governed by conditions in the "marriage market," even though the nature of what is exchanged in that market and who is in charge of making the exchanges differs from one society to another. (See the discussion in Goode 1964.) Therefore this study will often make use of such marketplace analogies.

2. The extreme version of this phenomenon is when premarital intimacy leads to pregnancy and a hasty, "shotgun" wedding. In the usual case the academic and career preparation of both the husband and wife are adversely affected, although the wife is affected more seriously.

3. My inquiry here focuses on changes in dating as an ongoing institution. As noted earlier, some analysts have argued that dating is on the decline or is even dying out (see Murstein 1980). I see no evidence from our research of any such dramatic change.

4. Four of our respondents had missing information in regard to their year of marriage, leaving 455 cases for analysis here. As noted earlier, only the year of first marriages, and dating experiences prior to such marriages, are considered here.

5. The actual wording used was, "How old were you when you first went on single dates?" The insertion of the word *single* was meant to convey the idea that we didn't want them to consider instances of going out with a mixed sex group of friends, with no pairing off as a couple. But we did not offer respondents a specific definition of what a date was, instead leaving it up to them to interpret the term as they chose. In general respondents did not seem to have trouble knowing what the term meant, or for that matter with being able to respond to other terms we used, such as "going steady."

6. This conclusion differs from that offered by some authors—see Gagnon and Greenblat (1978). Sociological studies done in America in earlier times occasionally pointed to the age of the onset of dating being younger than our data show. Burgess and Wallin (1953, p. 119) found that the median age of first date reported by their well-educated sample of Chicago-area engaged couples interviewed in 1937–1939 was 15, and in a study of youths in a small midwestern town in the next decade Hollingshead found that more than 90 percent of youths of both sexes had dated by the end of their fifteenth year (Hollingshead 1949, p. 225), implying an even younger median age at the onset of dating. A national survey of high school seniors conducted in 1960 also computed a median age at first date for females of about 15 (Bayer 1968, p. 629). Of course, with our sample the process of recall may produce an upward bias in our estimates from older respondents, but if so, one would have to conclude that the age of starting dating has gotten steadily later, rather than earlier. I have not been able to think of any explanation, in terms of bias in our estimates, which would be consistent with the idea that the actual age of beginning dating has gotten earlier in more recent years.

7. There is a minor complication to this pattern. The earliest cohort in our sample has the youngest average marriage age. The median marriage age computed for cohort one is 17. However, due to the small number of cases involved (five), and to what is technically called "sample truncation bias"—the fact that our sample upper age limit of 75 excluded women who married in the 1920s at older ages—we consider this pattern spurious and ignore the marriage age figures for our first cohort. We use medians in these calculations rather than means because the distribution of marriage ages is highly skewed. The median indicates the age by which 50 percent of the cases considered (e.g., women in our prewar marriage generation, minus the first cohort within that generation) had

a given experience, while the mean is simply the arithmethic average of the ages at which each woman in that group of cases had the experience. The mean ages of first marriage for our three generations (again, minus the first cohort who married prior to 1930) are 20.5, 20.5, and 22.

8. In a June 2, 1986, *Newsweek* magazine story based on this research it was claimed that a 40-year-old woman's probability of marrying was "less than her chances of being shot by a terrorist." Subsequently, these researchers acknowledged that their projections were inaccurate, and projections by the U.S. Census Bureau yielded substantially higher estimates. For example, the latter estimates were for never married women who were college graduates, between 32 and 41 percent of those aged 35 could still expect to marry, and between 17 and 23 percent of those aged 40 could still expect the same. See the discussion in Cherlin forthcoming, Chapter 5.

9. Of course, there is an age truncation bias problem that prevents us from saying whether such unusually late first marriages are more or less common in recent times. Women who first married at such unusually late ages in the 1950s and earlier would presumably be deceased and not available for interview. It might also be noted that from other information in our questionnaire we know that the interviewee who first married at age 60 was still a virgin at marriage. Apparently there are other things besides getting married for which it is never too late.

10. Part of the increase is due to the later ages of marriage of recent years, giving women more time to meet a variety of dating partners. However, both the relatively late marriage ages of our oldest women, and the fact that our early-marrying baby-boom era brides reported a relatively higher number of males dated (10–14, on the average) than prewar brides, indicate that this trend is not simply a consequence of changing marriage ages.

11. Burgess and Wallin's study of middle-class, engaged couples interviewed in the late 1930s showed both an earlier age of going steady (76 percent by age 16) and fewer women with no other steadies than their eventual husband (30.7 percent) than our older marriage generations show (Burgess and Wallin 1953, pp. 120, 127). I do not have a ready explanation for this divergence, but it does provide an additional piece of evidence against the view that everything is starting earlier and getting more casual in recent years.

12. There are, of course, problems of both vagueness and recall that make our conclusions here tentative. Young people may not be aware of some of the more subtle ways parents try to influence their dating patterns, and over time the less blatant instances may drop from memories. One study by Sussman interviewed parents in the New Haven area in 1950, rather than their offspring, and found more than 80 percent of them reported active efforts to try to influence who their youngsters went out with (see Sussman 1953). Of course, the apparent constant level of parental involvement and concern about the dating patterns of their daughters may conceal a declining ability of parents to actually influence their offspring, which in turn produces increasing resignation among parents.... In some respects the younger women in our sample were more likely to "marry out" of their ethnic or religious group than were the older women, which may give some indication that actual parental influence on mate-choice decisions has declined somewhat.

13. The ending of the story is also interesting. I presume that she resisted going out the door immediately, but she did keep seeing the man her parents disliked and eventually married him. Obviously, she lived to tell the tale.

14. A 1970 survey using a national sample found that sex before marriage had increased from 31 percent among the oldest women in the sample to 81 percent among the youngest (see Hunt 1974, p. 150).

15. Data collected by Zelnick and Kanter from national samples of teenage females indicate that through the 1970s premarital sexual intercourse was becoming much more common, but that the average age of first intercourse was declining only slightly—from 16.4 years of age in their 1971 sample to 16.2 years in their 1979 sample (see Zelnick and Kanter 1980). These figures look much younger than those we have computed for our recent marriage cases, but they cannot be compared directly, since Zelnick and Kanter's study would not include cases who began intercourse only after their teens or at marriage, as ours does.

16. Again this may be a somewhat conservative estimate because, as with our general premarital sex estimate, women who had sex with another partner and then started dating their eventual husbands before passing another birthday would not be detected by this method as having had sex prior to dating their husbands.

17. Or, to look at things in another way, we can consider only those women who we calculate had sex before marriage. Of those women, the proportion in our three marriage generations who we estimate had their first sex prior to starting dating their eventual husbands is 13 percent, 32 percent, and 46 percent. Or, to make the comparison with the Kinsey and Hunt studies clearer, the proportion of women who had premarital sex who did so only with their eventual husbands dropped from 87 percent to 68 percent and then 54 percent.

18. Opinion polls overwhelmingly support the view that the permissiveness in regard to premarital sex extends to exclusive romantic relationships, but not to casual or multiple relationships (see the discussion in Hunt 1974).

19. Since the figures in the chart report average, or median ages, they give the appearance of sexual relations beginning for most women prior to marriage, even for the first marriage generation. This appearance can be attributed to the fact that rarely, if ever, does a woman delay her first sexual experience until a year or more after her marriage. So the age of first sex figures are truncated or limited by the age at marriage, while there is no comparable lower limit. Thus the median age computation for first sex ends up being lower than for age at marriage, even though most women were not beginning sex until marriage in this first generation.

20. If we use an alternative average tendency statistic, the mean, in place of the median, the typical age of first starting to date the eventual husband can be seen actually increasing within our sample—from 18.2 to 18.5 and then 19.5 in our three marriage generations. Use of means would make the same point as clearly—with age of first sex changing from occurring about two years after starting dating the eventual husband for the oldest generation (20.2 versus 18.2) to occurring before starting dating the husband among the most recent marriage generation (19.0 versus 19.5).

21. A few figures on cohabitation elsewhere allow us to put these figures in perspective. National survey data from England yield figures of 3 percent premarital cohabiters among those who married in 1966, 10 percent among those marrying in 1971–1975, and 19 percent among those marrying in the late 1970s. In France, the increase is said to be from 17 percent of those marrying in 1968–69 to 44 percent of those marrying in 1976–1977, and in Denmark and Sweden premarital cohabitation is claimed to already be a majority phenomenon (see Freeman and Lyon 1983, pp. 57–9). A recent study in Finland and Soviet Estonia found that about 70 percent of the newly married Finnish and Estonian couples had lived together prior to wedlock (see Haavio-Mannila and Rannik 1987). Several recent North American studies based on couples who married in the late 1970s or early 1980s yield estimates higher than ours, thus implying that premarital cohabitation has become a majority phenomenon already. Watson (1983) studied 84 couples in Victoria, Canada and computed a figure of 64.3 percent premarital cohabiters, and DeMaris and Leslie (1984) in a study of 309 recently married couples in Gainesville, Florida computed a figure of 71 percent premarital cohabiters. Gwartney-Gibbs (1986) studied marriage license applicants in a county in Oregon and determined that the percentage of couples who had cohabited prior to marriage had risen from 13 percent in 1970 to 53 percent in 1980. One possible explanation for the higher estimates in these other studies is that they are based on samples that include remarriages as well as first marriages, unlike the Detroit area estimates. Previous studies indicate that premarital cohabitation is more common among the formerly married than among those who have never married.

22. In commenting on this issue I can rely to some extent on the results of surveys I have taken over the years among students in my family sociology courses at the University of Michigan.

23. To be sure, marriage ages have risen in recent years, and as more people delay entry into marriage some of them may end up never marrying. Popular attitudes have changed, making a life without marrying more acceptable (see Thornton and Freedman 1983). However, to a considerable extent the rise in marriage ages and increase in the projected number of individuals who may never marry are only returning American Society to patterns that were common earlier in our history, after a highly atypical period in the baby-boom era of unusually young and nearly universal marriage. Compared to many other advanced industrial countries, America still has relatively young marriage and a high marriage rate. However, one portion of the American population represents a possible exception to the argument that the availability of alternatives has not produced a general tendency to avoid marriage entirely, and that is the black population. From a pattern in the past in which blacks tended to marry earlier than whites and in equal or greater proportions, the period since the 1960s has seen a dramatic reversal and a rising trend toward both late marriage and nonmarriage for blacks (see Espenshade 1985).

24. A few other studies on this issue yield figures similar to ours. A study of three generations of married women in the Columbus, Ohio, area in 1949 yielded figures ranging from 24 percent to 42 percent who had one or more other marital prospects, with a slight tendency for such prospects to be more common among the youngest generation of women (see Koller 1951). An English national survey in 1969 found that 30 percent of the married women interviewed had other serious marital prospects. But in the latter study older women were more likely to have had other prospects than younger women (see Gorer 1971, pp. 22–23). One study in France in 1959 reveals a different picture, with 65 percent of the women interviewed there claiming to have had other serious prospects (see Girard 1974, p. 156). To cite a case at the opposite extreme, in a sample of ever-married Chinese women in the city of Chengdu who were interviewed for a research project on which the author is currently collaborating, only 6 percent of the respondents said that they had had other prospects besides the man they eventually married (see Whyte forthcoming).

25. In other studies, if respondents were just asked how or where they had met their spouse, they might mention a place of first meeting even when an introduction had led to that meeting.

26. However, the "introduction by friends" category may also conceal cases of introductions that took place within a school or college context.

27. This was an open question, and answers were coded in tenths of a mile, with a city block treated as equal to one-tenth of a mile.

28. The fact that median figures given here do not correspond to what one might assume (with the apparent courting intervals of 3, 2, and 3 years) is attributable to the difference between computing separate medians for the two ages involved versus subtracting the ages first and then computing a single median figure.

29. In Hollingshead's study of white couples who married for the first time in New Haven in 1949–1950, 84 percent of the women had received an engagement ring, 89 percent had had an engagement stage, and 10.3 months was the average length of engagement (with 28 months the average of the dating and engagement stages together). See Hollingshead 1952, p. 310.

30. Earlier writers discussed some stages in the development of this intimacy revolution which our survey did not examine. For example, the rise in the incidence of petting within the context of dating from the 1920s onward was the subject of much commentary. See, for example, Kinsey et al. 1953; Hunt 1974; Fass 1977.

31. For documentation of this syndrome in earlier times, see Whyte (1943); Hollingshead (1949); Schulman (1977).

References

BAYER, ALAN. 1968. "Early Dating and Early Marriage." *Journal of Marriage and the Family* 30: 628–32.

BURCHINAL, LEE G. 1964. "The Premarital Dyad and Love Involvement." Pp. 623–74 in *Handbook of Marriage and the Family*, Harold Christensen, ed. Chicago: Rand McNally.

BURGESS, ERNEST W. and PAUL WALLIN. 1953. *Engagement and Marriage*. Chicago: Lippincott.

CHERLIN, ANDREW. 1981. *Marriage, Divorce, Remarriage*. Cambridge: Harvard University Press.

CHERLIN, ANDREW. forthcoming. *Marriage, Divorce, Remarriage*, rev. ed. Cambridge: Harvard University Press.

COLEMAN, JAMES S. 1961. *The Adolescent Society*. New York: The Free Press.

DEGLER, CARL N. 1974. "What Ought to Be and What Was: Woman's Sexuality in the Nineteenth Century." *American Historical Review* 79: 1467–90.

DeMARIS, ALFRED and GERALD R. LESLIE. 1984. "Cohabitation with the Future Spouse: Its Influence upon Marital Satisfaction and Communication." *Journal of Marriage and the Family* 46: 77–84.

DOUVAN, ELIZABETH and JOSEPH ADELSON. 1966. *The Adolescent Experience*. New York: John Wiley.

EEKELAAR, JOHN M. and SANFORD N. KATZ, eds. 1980. *Marriage and Cohabitation in Contemporary Societies*. Toronto: Butterworths.

EHRMANN, WINSTON. 1959. *Premarital Dating Behavior*. New York: Henry Holt.

ELDER, GLEN H., JR. 1974. *Children of the Great Depression*. Chicago: University of Chicago Press.

EPSTEIN, EDWARD J. 1978. *Cartel*. New York: Putnam.

ESPENSHADE, THOMAS J. 1985. "The Recent Decline in American Marriage: Blacks and Whites in Comparative Perspective." Pp. 53–90 in *Contemporary Marriage: Comparative Perspectives on a Changing Institution*, K. Davis, ed. New York: Russell Sage.

FASS, PAULA S. 1977. *The Damned and the Beautiful*. New York: Oxford University Press.

FREEMAN, MICHAEL and CHRISTINA M. LYON. 1983. *Cohabitation without Marriage*. Aldershot: Gower.

GAGNON, JOHN H. and CATHY S. GREENBLAT. 1978. "Rehearsals and Realities: Beginning to Date." Pp. 106–118 in *Life Designs: Individuals, Marriages, and Families*, John H. Gagnon and Cathy S. Greenblat, eds. Glenview, IL: Scott Foresman.

GIRARD, ALAIN. 1974. *Le Choix du Conjoint.* Paris: Universities Presses of France.

GODWIN, JOHN. 1973. *The Mating Trade.* Garden City: Doubleday.

GOODE, WILLIAM J. 1964. *The Family.* Englewood Cliffs: Prentice Hall.

GORDON, MICHAEL. 1981. "Was Waller Ever Right? The Rating and Dating Complex Reconsidered." *Journal of Marriage and the Family* 43: 67–76.

GORER, GEOFFREY. 1971. *Sex and Marriage in England Today.* London: Nelson.

GWARTNEY-GIBBS P. A. 1986. "Institutionalization of Premarital Cohabitation." *Journal of Marriage and the Family* 48: 423–34.

HAAVIO-MANNILA, ELINA and ERKKI RANNIK. 1987. "Family Life in Estonia and Finland." *Acta Sociologica* 30: 355–69.

HOLLINGSHEAD, AUGUST B. 1949. *Elmtown's Youth.* New York: Wiley.

HOLLINGSHEAD, AUGUST B. 1952. "Marital Status and Wedding Behavior." *American Sociological Review* 17: 308–11.

HUNT, MORTON. 1974. *Sexual Behavior in the 1970s.* Chicago: Playboy Press.

KINSEY, ALFRED C., WARDELL B. POMEROY, CLYDE E. MARTIN, and PAUL H. GEBHARD. 1953. *Sexual Behavior in the Human Female.* Philadelphia: Saunders.

KOLLER, MARVIN R. 1951. "Some Changes in Courtship Behavior in Three Generations of Ohio Women." *American Sociological Review* 16: 367–70.

LASCH, CHRISTOPHER. 1977. *Haven in a Heartless World.* New York: Basic Books.

MACFARLANE, ALAN. 1986. *Marriage and Love in England: Modes of Reproduction 1300–1840.* New York: Basil Blackwell.

MODELL, JOHN. 1983. "Dating Becomes the Way of American Youth," Pp. 91–126 in *Essays on the Family and Historical Change*, Leslie P. Moch and Gary D. Stark, eds. College Station: Texas A&M University Press.

MULLAN, BOB. 1984. *The Mating Trade.* London: Routledge and Kegan Paul.

MURSTEIN, BERNARD L. 1980. "Mate Selection in the 1970s." *Journal of Marriage and the Family* 42: 777–92.

ROTHMAN, ELLEN K. 1984. *Hands and Hearts: A History of Courtship.* New York: Basic Books.

SCHULMAN A. K. 1977. "The War in the Back Seat." Pp. 150–57 in *The Family: Functions, Conflicts, and Symbols*, P. Stein, J. Richman and N. Hannon, eds. Reading: Addison-Wesley.

SHORTER, EDWARD. 1971. "Illegitimacy, Sexual Revolution, and Social Change in Modern Europe." *Journal of Interdisciplinary History* 2: 237–72.

SMITH, DANIEL S. 1973. "The Dating of the American Sexual Revolution." Pp. 321–35 in *The American Family in Social-Historical Perspective*, ed. Michael Gordon, New York: St. Martin's Press.

SMITH, DANIEL S. and MICHAEL HINDUS. 1975. "Premarital Pregnancy in America, 1640–1971: An Overview and Interpretation." *Journal of Interdisciplinary History* 4: 537–70.

SPANIER, GRAHAM B. 1983. "Married and Unmarried Cohabitation in the United States: 1980." *Journal of Marriage and the Family* 45: 97–111.

SUSSMAN, MARVIN B. 1953. "Parental Participation in Mate Selection and Its Effect upon Family Continuity." *Social Forces* 32: 76–81.

THORNTON, ARLAND and DEBORAH FREEDMAN. 1983. "The Changing American Family." *Population Bulletin* 38: 1–43.

UDRY, J. RICHARD. 1971. *The Social Context of Marriage.* 2nd ed., Philadelphia: Lippincott.

WALLER, WILLARD. 1937. "The Rating and Dating Complex," *American Sociological Review*, 2: 727–37.

WATSON, ROY. 1983. "Premarital Cohabition vs. Traditional Courtship: Their Effects on Subsequent Marital Adjustment." *Family Relations* 32: 139–47.

WHYTE, MARTIN KING. forthcoming. "Changes in Mate Choice in Chengdu." In *Social Consequences of Chinese Economic Reforms*, Deborah Davis and Ezra Vogel eds., Cambridge: Harvard University Press.

WHYTE, WILLIAM F. 1943. "A Slum Sex Code." *American Journal of Sociology* 49: 23–31.

ZELNIK, MELVIN and JOHN F. KANTER. 1980. "Sexual Activity, Contraceptive Use, and Pregnancy among Metropolitan-area Teenagers: 1971–79." *Family Planning Perspectives* 12: 230–37.

Beginning Sex in the Close Relationship*

Susan Sprecher and Kathleen McKinney

In the previous selection, Whyte illustrated some historical changes in the process of dating. This chapter by Susan Sprecher and Kathleen McKinney focuses particularly upon sexual behavior. Rather than describing historical patterns, they move to the micro-level and examine the sexual scripts for men and women as they become involved in intimate relationships. The research they review outlines some of the factors in the decision-making process as to when a couple does or does not become sexually involved. They examine a number of important contemporary issues, including a discussion about AIDS between sexual partners.

In this chapter we discuss how the sexual aspect of the close relationship begins. Questions we address . . . include: How important is the first sexual intercourse experience to the couple? What are the possible sexual pathways on which couples travel? What factors affect the relationship partners' decisions to become sexually involved? How do partners actually initiate sex, and what happens when one partner is ready for sex and the other is not? We also consider whether couples today discuss AIDS and safe sex practices before they become sexually involved.

*Source: Susan Sprecher and Kathleen McKinney, "Beginning Sex in the Close Relationship," in Sexuality (Newbury Park, CA: Sage, 1993), pp. 43–66.

The First Time

The "first time" for heterosexual couples usually is thought of as the first time they have sexual intercourse. Some heterosexual couples and all homosexual couples, however, give special significance to the first time for other types of intimate sexual behaviors, such as oral-genital sex. Although the first intercourse experience during adolescence or young adulthood (the transition from virgin to nonvirgin status) has been the focus of much research (topics examined include age at which it occurs, degree of affection experienced for the partner, reactions to the event, and whether it is discussed with others), very little research has examined the first time for particular couples and how this event is experienced in the relationship. Here we review the limited research on the first time for the couple.

The Sexual Script for the First Time

Imagine that Shelley and Mike, who met at a party . . . began a dating relationship and are now at a stage in their relationship when they are about to have sexual intercourse for the first time. A common myth is that sex is a spontaneous act. According to sociologists (e.g., DeLamater, 1989; Gagnon, 1990; Gagnon and Simon, 1973; Reiss, 1989), however, sexual partners follow a *sexual script*, which they have learned from society. A couple's first sexual intercourse experience and later sexual interactions are influenced by the following aspects of the sexual script:

> *Who:* They have chosen a person of about the same age and of the opposite sex (or of the same sex for those who are homosexual). The person is also likely to be from their "field of eligibles"—for example, someone with a similar background (Kerckhoff, 1974).
>
> *Where:* The couple is likely to have sex in a private location. For example, couples often have sex in a bedroom.
>
> *When:* They wait until they have been dating for a while. They also have sex at the end of an evening date.
>
> *Why:* They have sex to express love for each other. They also find it pleasurable.
>
> *What behaviors and in what sequence:* Couples are likely to engage in a particular sequence of sexual behavior. They begin with passionate kissing, move to breast and genital touching, perhaps have oral-genital sex, and then have sexual intercourse (Geer and Broussard, 1990; Jemail and Geer, 1977).

Of course, not all couples adhere exactly to all aspects of society's common sexual script. Couples also may develop their own idiosyncratic, relationship-specific sexual scripts, which tend to continue throughout their relationship.

The Significance of the First Time

The first sexual encounter often is considered to be a *significant event* or *turning point* in the couple's relationship. Baxter and Bullis (1986) defined a *turning*

FIGURE 16-1

Example of Turning Points in a Developing Relationship

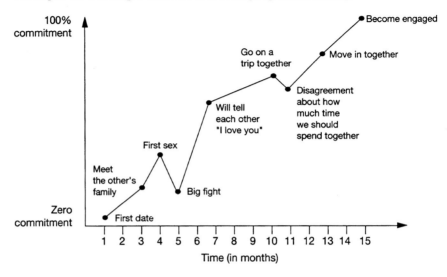

point as any event associated with change, either positive or negative, in the relationship. They used the Retrospective Interview Technique (RIT) (see Huston, Surra, Fitzgerald, and Cate, 1981), which asks relationship partners to identify all of the turning points in the relationship and to plot those points on a graph similar to the one in Figure 16-1. The x axis represents time in the relationship, and the y axis represents an index of commitment, such as an estimate of the likelihood of marriage or the degree of commitment. Figure 16-1 depicts a typical individual in a college relationship and indicates that the first sexual experience has a positive effect (after a brief downturn) and increases the person's commitment. Baxter and Bullis (1986) found that events associated with "passion," such as first sex, were among the events having the greatest positive effect on commitment. The graph in Figure 16-1 is for one member of the couple. His or her partner may have a different perception of the occurrence, timing, and effects of the turning points in their relationship.

Significant events, such as first sex, usually are remembered with vivid detail ("flashbulb memory") months and years later. Harvey, Flanary, and Morgan (1986) investigated the memories of a sample of middle-aged adults for the most emotionally significant relationship they had experienced. They reported, "Across subjects, the theme of first sexual encounter turned out to be a predominantly salient memory for both sexes (reported in over 50 percent of all subjects)" (pp. 367–368).

Pathways to the First Time

In the not so distant past, many couples waited until they were married before having sexual intercourse. For example, Kinsey (Kinsey, Pomeroy, Martin, and

Gephard, 1953) found that among the women in his study who were born before 1900, 73 percent did not have sex until they married. Today, some couples, like their great-grandparents (or at least their great-grandmothers) wait for marriage, but most couples have sex at some point on the *dating continuum* (Adams, 1986), which includes the stages of casual dating, serious dating, and engaged.

Researchers have categorized couples according to how soon in the relationship they have sex. Christopher and Cate (1985b) had each partner of 54 dating couples complete Bentler's (1968a, 1968b) Sexual Involvement Scale (which asks about 21 sexual behaviors ranging from *one minute continuous lip kissing* to *mutual oral manipulation of genitals to mutual orgasm*) for four significant points in their relationship. These four points were first date, casually dating, considering becoming a couple, and perceiving themselves as a couple. With this retrospective information, Christopher and Cate identified the following four sexual pathways:

> *Rapid-involvement couples (7 percent):* These couples had sex very early in the relationship, often on the first date.
>
> *Gradual-involvement couples (31 percent):* These couples reported a gradual increase in sexual behavior over the four stages of dating.
>
> *Delayed-involvement couples (44 percent):* These couples tended to delay sexual involvement until they considered themselves to be a "couple."
>
> *Low-involvement couples (17 percent):* These couples were still not very sexually intimate at the time they felt like a couple.

Earlier, Peplau et al. (1977) developed a typology of sexual pathways, based on the Boston Dating Couples Study. . . . They delineated three groups of couples, based on the timing and occurrence of sex. These couples were "early-sex" couples (41 percent of their sample), who had sex within the first month of dating; "later-sex" couples (41 percent of the sample), who did not have sex until they had been dating at least one month; and "abstaining" couples (18 percent of the sample), who had not had sex at the time of the investigation.

The Sexual Decision-Making Process

What factors determine whether a couple has sex early in the relationship or waits until later? Couples must decide when they are ready to have sex, and they are likely to weigh several factors in this decision. Some researchers have studied the sexual decision-making process by asking virgins or abstaining couples why they have not yet had sex. Other researchers have surveyed young adults who have made the decision to engage in premarital sex and have asked why they had sex, particularly their reasons for the first time.

Reasons for Not Having Sex

Two types of virgins have been identified, and they give different reasons for not having premarital sex. D'Augelli and her colleagues (D'Augelli and Cross, 1975;

D'Augelli and D'Augelli, 1977) distinguished between adamant virgins and potential nonvirgins. *Adamant virgins* have made the decision not to engage in premarital sex because they strongly believe that intercourse should be saved for marriage; that is, they adhere to the abstinence standard.... Adamant virgins are influenced strongly by their families and religion. For example, a view expressed by one adamant virgin is: "Premarital intercourse is simply wrong. It should be saved for marriage—marriage is more than a piece of paper. Sex belongs in marriage, according to society" (D'Augelli and D'Augelli, 1977, p. 58). *Potential nonvirgins* say they have not had sex because they have not been in the right situation or in love enough. They also have a fear of pregnancy. They say, however, that they are open to the possibility of engaging in premarital sex. In an extension of this earlier research, Herold and Goodwin (1981) found that adamant virgins were most likely to give moral or religious beliefs as the primary reason they remain virgins. Conversely, potential nonvirgins rated having not met the right person as the major reason for their virginity status.

Whereas the above research focused on why individuals remain virgins, other research has examined why partners decide not to have sex in a particular dating relationship (regardless of whether they had sex in previous relationships). The woman usually controls the level of sexual activity in heterosexual relationships; that is, if a couple has been together for several months but has not had sex, it is usually because the female partner is not ready yet. In their study of dating couples, Peplau et al. (1977) asked the men and women in the 42 abstaining couples (18 percent of the sample) to rate the importance of four reasons for not having engaged in sex. "Partner does not wish to have sexual intercourse at the present time" was judged to be an important reason by 64 percent of the men but by only 11 percent of the women. Women were more likely than men to rate "It is against my moral or religious convictions" as an important reason (31 percent for women, 11 percent for men). Almost half of both men and women rated fear of pregnancy as a major reason, and 22 percent of the women but only 14 percent of the men said that it was too early in the relationship.

Today, there is a new reason to avoid premarital sex. Young people receive the message from parents, public health officials, Magic Johnson, and even billboards ("Virgin. Teach your kids it's not a dirty word.") that sex can be dangerous because of AIDS. Some evidence exists that AIDS may be a new reason to abstain from sex. Leigh (1989) asked men and women from the San Francisco area (76 percent heterosexuals, 24 percent homosexuals or bisexuals) to rate the importance of various reasons for not having sex. Fear of AIDS was rated by the participants as the most important reason. Of the four different groups surveyed (heterosexuals and homosexuals of both genders), homosexual men rated it highest in importance, and homosexual women rated it lowest in importance.

Motives for Being Sexually Active

Sex for the first time in a particular relationship, though usually a passionate act, typically occurs after some planning and thought. Both partners in the couple have to decide whether they want to make their relationship a sexual one and how soon to do so. Many couples discuss the decision to have sex before it occurs (Randolph and Winstead, 1988). They may consider several factors in their decision to have sex for the first time.

Christopher and Cate (1984, 1985a) developed a scale, called the Inventory of Sexual Decision-Making Factors, to measure factors that might be considered in the decision to have sex for the first time in a relationship. Students who had previously had sexual intercourse were asked to indicate how important each of 43 items was in their decision to have premarital intercourse for the first time with their most recent sexual partner (data reported in Christopher and Cate, 1984). Students who had not previously had sex were asked to indicate how important each factor would be in their decision to have sexual intercourse with their ideal partner for the first time (data reported in Christopher and Cate, 1985a).

In an analysis of the data from the nonvirgins, Christopher and Cate (1984) found four general reasons underlying the decision to have sex for the first time. These were as follows:

1. *Positive Affection/Communication*   Example items: "Love for partner," "Number of dates with partner prior to intercourse," "Possibility of eventual marriage."
2. *Arousal/Receptivity*   Example items: "Participant's physical arousal immediately prior to intercourse," "Partner's physical arousal immediately prior to intercourse," and "Receptivity of participant to partner's sexual advances."
3. *Obligation and Pressure*   Example items: "Participant's feeling of obligation to have intercourse with partner," "Partner's pressure on participant to have intercourse," "Number of participant's friends engaging in intercourse."
4. *Circumstantial*   Example items: "Participant's preplanning to increase chance of intercourse," "Amount of alcohol/drugs consumed by partner," "Date was a special event."

Christopher and Cate (1984) compared men and women on their scores on the above four factors. Two gender differences emerged in the importance attached to these reasons for engaging in sex for the first time within a particular relationship. Positive Affection/Communication items were rated as more important by women than by men, whereas Obligation/Pressure items were rated as more important by men than by women. The researchers also compared groups, who differed on level of prior sexual experience, on the importance attached to the above factors. Positive Affection/Communication was rated as more salient in the sexual decision-making process of the sexually inexperienced subjects than of the sexually experienced subjects, whereas Arousal/Receptivity was judged to be more important by the highly experienced subjects. Similar findings emerged in the data from the students who had not had sexual intercourse and who rated each item according to what they expected would happen once they did become sexually active (see Christopher and Cate, 1985a). Women were more likely than men to rate relationship issues (e.g., love for partner) as a salient issue in their sexual decision-making process for a future first sexual intercourse experience. The virgins in the Christopher and Cate (1985a) study also were asked what level of commitment they anticipated to have with their partner before having sexual intercourse for the first time. The options listed were as follows: casually dating, seriously dating, engaged, and married. Subjects who expected to have sexual intercourse with a partner for the first time at the casual dating stage rated physical arousal and circumstantial factors as more important and relationship factors as less important than other subjects, particularly as compared to those subjects who anticipated first sexual intercourse at marriage.

One common finding in the research on motives people have for sex is that love is a more important sexual motivation for women than for men, whereas men are more motivated than women to have sex out of lust or physical release. Consider the exchange in Box 16-1, which introduced a chapter in Symons's (1979) book on the evolution of human sexuality (p. 286):

BOX 16-1

Diane Keaton: "Sex without love is an empty experience."

Woody Allen: "Yes, but as empty experiences go, it's one of the best."

As reported above, Christopher and Cate (1984, 1985a) found that women scored higher on the Positive Affection/Communication items. In another study (Carroll et al., 1985) men and women were asked the open-ended question, "What would be your motives for having sexual intercourse?" Typical responses given by females were "To show my love for my partner and to feel loved and needed" and "My motives for sexual intercourse would all be due to the love and commitment I feel for my partner." Males were more likely than females to answer with such responses as "need it" and "to gratify myself." Whitley (1988, as reported in Leigh, 1989) asked men and women, "What was your most important reason for having sexual intercourse on the most recent occasion?" He reported that 51 percent of men but only 9 percent of women gave lust/pleasure reasons, whereas 51 percent of women but only 24 percent of men gave love/emotion reasons.

In the study of San Francisco adults that was introduced in the previous section, Leigh (1989) also asked her respondents to rate how important several reasons were for *having sex*. The three reasons rated as most important by the respondents were as follows: for pure pleasure, to express emotional closeness, and to please partner. Men were found to give more importance than women to all of the following reasons: pleasure, pleasing one's partner, conquest, and relief of tension. Women gave more importance than men to only one reason: to express emotional closeness. Some differences also were found between the homosexual and heterosexual respondents. "Heterosexuals rated reproduction, emotional closeness, and pleasing one's partner as more important than did homosexuals, and homosexuals rated conquest and relief of tension more highly than did heterosexuals" (p. 203). No differences were found between homosexual men and women.

Another study, however, suggests that these particular gender differences in sexual motivations may be limited to young adults. Sprague and Quadagno (1989) surveyed adults aged 22 to 57 years. Among the younger adults in the sample, women were motivated to engage in sex to express love, whereas men were motivated by physical factors. These gender differences, however, were reversed among the older adults in the sample. These findings support the belief that although a man is at his sexual peak around age 20, a woman's desire is strongest in her mid to late thirties.

Whereas research has shown that young women attach more importance than men to love as a reason to have sex, and young men attach more importance than women to physical reasons, these gender differences are not very large. Men also have sex for love, and women get physical pleasure from sex. It is interesting, though, to speculate on what might have been found had these studies been conducted 150 to 200 years earlier. The gender differences probably would have been even more pronounced, particularly concerning the physical motive for sex. The image we have acquired of the Victorian (nineteenth century) middle-class woman is passionless. During the Victorian era, it was assumed that women did not get pleasure from sex. Degler (1974), a historian, described the story of a nineteenth century young English woman who asked her mother how she should behave on her wedding night. The mother advised her to "lie still and think of the Empire" (p. 467). Reiss and Lee (1988) reported that an American medical doctor told his medical class in 1883, "I do not believe one bride in a hundred, of delicate, educated, sensitive women, accepts matrimony from any desire for sexual gratification; when she thinks of this at all, it is with shrinking, or even with horror, rather than with desire" (Parven, 1883, p. 607). A study that was uncovered at the Stanford University archives, however, suggests that Victorian women may have been more sexual than this image suggests. The survey was conducted by Dr. Clelia Mosher. Her survey, which may have been the first sex survey, was conducted during the period from 1892 to 1920, with 45 well-educated, middle-class women. A majority of the women felt desire for sex, and many of the women reported usually experiencing an orgasm. An example comment written by a woman: "The desire of both husband and wife for this expression of their union seems to be the first and highest reason for intercourse" (Degler, 1980, p. 264).

Now that we have discussed the *why* of first sexual encounters in close relationships, we will discuss *how* sex gets initiated and *by whom.*

The Initiation and Negotiation of Sex

Sex, and particularly the first experience of intercourse, does not just happen. The precursors of sex include nonverbal and verbal cues of sexual interest and intent. Furthermore, the pathways to sexual involvement have misperceptions and misunderstandings. These are the issues discussed in this section.

Flirting in Public Places

Social scientists have observed the process by which men and women send each other nonverbal signals that suggest they would like to begin or advance their intimate contact. In one study, Perper and Fox (1980) spent hundreds of hours in singles bars on the East Coast, watching how men and women meet for the first time and, in some cases, leave the bar together. From their observations of the nonverbal behavior in the singles bars, Perper and Fox (1980) concluded that successful flirtation depends on negotiating several escalation points. At each escalation event, the flirtation either escalates upward toward greater intimacy, or the budding romance ends.

The first escalation stage is *approach*. One person approaches the other, and the person approached must respond in some way, such as by moving toward the approaching person or by tilting his or her head. The second stage is *swivel and synchronize*. In this stage the two swivel to face each other and begin to synchronize their movements (he raises his glass, and then she raises hers). The third stage is *touch*. One partner touches the other, and the other must respond positively for the relationship to continue. The researchers found that the women were more likely than the men to touch first.

From in-depth interviews conducted with a smaller sample of men and women, Perper and Fox (1980) also found that the women were more aware than the men of what occurred during flirtation. For example, the women could point to specific behaviors that they had done to attract the attention of a man. Men, on the other hand, were more oblivious to the sequence of behaviors that resulted in the man and woman leaving the bar together.

Another observational study of flirting was conducted by Moore (1985), who recorded nonverbal acts engaged in by women that resulted in a man's attention within 15 seconds after the behavior. In her first study, she identified 52 distinct behaviors that females engaged in that seemed to result in male attention. Some of the more common flirting behaviors were the smile, laugh, room-encompassing glance, short darting glance, head nod, primp, lean, and solitary dance. . . . In a second study, Moore observed women in four different settings for nonverbal solicitation. The average number of flirting acts per woman during an hour of observation was 70.6 in a singles bar, 18.6 in a snack bar, 9.6 in a library, and 4.7 in a woman's meeting. Moore also found that women who engaged in more nonverbal solicitation behaviors were more likely to be approached by men.

Misperception of Sexual Intent

Although both men and women at singles bars, parties, and other social settings may flirt with others to show romantic or sexual interest, sometimes people are not flirting but only are being friendly. Their friendly behavior may be misinterpreted as flirting or seductive behavior. It has been stated that "in American society it is difficult to distinguish friendly cues from sexual cues" (Abbey, 1991, p. 96).

Several years ago, Abbey (1982) began an article with an account of an event that had occurred to her. She wrote:

> One evening the author and a few of her female friends shared a table at a crowded campus bar with two male strangers. During one of the band's breaks, they struck up a friendly conversation with their male table companions. It was soon

apparent that their friendliness had been misperceived by these men as a sexual invitation, and they finally had to excuse themselves from the table to avoid an awkward scene. What had been intended as platonic friendliness had been perceived as sexual interest (p. 830).

To examine whether this misinterpretation of female friendly behavior occurs, Abbey (1982) conducted a laboratory experiment in which a male subject and a female subject interacted for five minutes while they were observed through a one-way mirror by another male and female. After the conversation, the subjects judged the conversation, as well as each other. The observers also judged the subjects. Abbey was interested particularly in how the interacting subjects were judged on the adjectives *flirtatious, seductive*, and *promiscuous*. Abbey found support for her hypothesis that men interpret women's friendliness as sexual interest. The female subject was seen as more promiscuous and seductive by male subjects and observers than by female subjects and observers. Males also attributed more sexual intent to the male subject than did the females. Another gender difference found was that males were more sexually attracted to the female subject than the females were to the male subject.

The basic finding that men are more likely than women to see the world through "sexual glasses" (e.g., Abbey, 1982) has been replicated in several other studies. Abbey, Cozzarelli, McLaughlin, and Harnish (1987) found that males had higher ratings than females of a woman's sexual interest regardless of what the woman was wearing (revealing or nonrevealing clothing) and regardless of whether she was pictured (in a photograph) as interacting with another female or with a male. Saal, Johnson, and Weber (1989) suggested that men's perceptions (misperceptions) of women's flirtatious behaviors may occur in a variety of organization settings, including business and academic settings. Shotland and Craig (1988) demonstrated that males are capable of differentiating between sexually interested behavior and friendly behavior but that males perceive more situations as sexual than do females. They concluded that men have a lower threshold than women for labeling friendly or interested behavior as having a sexual intent. For other research on gender differences in sexual intent, see Abbey and Melby (1986) and Sigal, Gibbs, Adams, and Derfler (1988).

Whereas most of the above studies were conducted in the laboratory (with photographs, videotapes, or subjects interacting in structured situations), Abbey (1987) conducted survey research with undergraduate students to examine the prevalence of misperceptions of sexual intent in real-world settings (at least the real-world setting of college). The college students completed a questionnaire about their experiences with misperceptions of sexual intent. The key question asked was, "Have you ever been friendly to someone of the opposite sex only to discover that she or he had *misperceived* your friendliness as a sexual come-on; you were just trying to be nice but she or he assumed you were sexually attracted to him or her?" She found that about two-thirds of the students reported that this had happened on at least one occasion. The average number of incidents for those reporting at least one incident was 4.8. More women (72 percent) than men (60 percent) reported an episode of misperception of sexual intent. The most common location for a misperception was a party.

Abbey (1987) reported that most of the incidents of misperception were brief and nontraumatic. She described the typical experience for a woman in the following way:

> Within the last six months a casual friend touched or kissed her while they were talking at a party. She told him she was not interested in him in "that way." He kept trying or acted as if nothing had happened. No sex occurred; they eventually went their separate ways but remained friends (p. 190).

Sexual Initiation Strategies in Private

Although a couple's initial contacts and flirting behaviors often occur in public locations, once the partners are at the point of actually initiating sex, they are typically in a private location. Not surprisingly, observational studies of the initiation strategies used in actual sexual encounters are nonexistent. Thus our knowledge of what moves are made and which gender typically makes them are based on self-report data only.

Self-report data suggest that early in the relationship, men are more likely than women to initiate sex (this does not change much later in the relationship ...). For example, DeLamater and MacCorquodale (1979) interviewed a random sample of students and nonstudents from Madison, Wisconsin, and found that approximately 40 percent of the respondents said the man usually initiated sexual intercourse, whereas less than 5 percent of the sample said the female typically initiated sexual activity. (Over half of the respondents reported that both partners initiated sexual intercourse.) Grauerholz and Serpe (1985) reported that men feel more comfortable than women initiating sex, and this was true regardless of the type of relationship (e.g., with someone known well or with a stranger). Furthermore, Gaulier, Travis, and Allgeier (1986, as reported in Allgeier and Royster, 1991) found that men are more likely than women "to describe themselves as attempting to move toward greater sexual intimacy and to arouse the partner" (p. 137).

How do men and women initiate sexual activity? McCormick (1979) asked young men and women to describe how they would attempt to have sex with someone to whom they were attracted. Both men and women preferred to use indirect strategies for initiating sex. *Seduction*, an indirect strategy, was the strategy most preferred by the subjects. This term refers to sexually stimulating the dating partner to get the date to want to have sex. Other indirect strategies the subjects reported that they would be likely to use included *sitting closer* and *holding hands.* Jesser (1978) found that the most common strategies both men and women said they would use to try to persuade a partner to have sex were *touching* (snuggling, kissing, etc.) and *allow hands to wander. Ask directly* was the third most common strategy checked (from a list of 20 possible strategies).

In another study, Perper and Weis (1987) asked female college students in the United States and Canada to write an essay describing how they would seduce a man to whom they were attracted. The major proceptive strategies ("female behavior patterns which initiate or maintain sexual interactions") identified by Perper and Weis were (a) environmental/situational strategies (dressing in a seductive way, offering the man a drink, creating a romantic setting), (b) verbal strategies (engaging in sexy/romantic talk, giving compliments, asking for sex), and (c) nonverbal strategies (eye glances, cuddling close, touching, kissing). Although the women's actual behaviors were not examined, the researchers believed that the detail and length of the essays written suggested that women may be more proceptive in sexual interaction than had been assumed in the past. Consider, for example, the essay written by one woman interviewed by Perper and Weis (1987):

> I attempt to influence the mood of my date by suggesting that we go somewhere quiet, relaxing, and secluded. If my date likes this suggestion, I usually let him suggest the place in order to get a better idea of where his head is. If he asks for suggestions as to where to go, I inevitably suggest MY PLACE!
>
> Once we've gotten settled wherever we decided to go I try slipping in compliments whenever I can. These compliments are usually about my date's physical appearance and how it/they turn me on, e.g., your eyes have such a mysterious gleam, they are really captivating; or, your smile is so warm and comforting it just makes me melt. Then after careful evaluation of my date's reaction to all of this I proceed in one of two ways: (a) If his response is positive then I escalate the level of intimacy through more intense eye contact and more but subtle body contact. This is almost always sufficient to eventually make my date suggest or attempt sex; (b) If his response is either negative or apparently indifferent I will back off a bit and wait for him to make the next move. If he takes too long to do this to suit me, I'll try putting on romantic or soft music and suggesting we dance or I'll offer a body massage to sort of break the ice. I find hoping and praying useful at this point (p. 468).

Although the previous studies asked participants to report what they would do in an imaginary situation, Christopher and Frandsen (1990) examined the sexual influence strategies that men and women actually used on their last date. Undergraduate students completed a 48-item Sexual Influence Tactics Scale. For each item, subjects responded on the basis of tactics they used during any sexual encounter that may have occurred during their last date. Factor analysis of the 48 items indicated four general influence strategies, labeled by the investigators as *Antisocial Acts* (e.g., verbally or physically threatened my partner, made my partner feel guilty, pleaded), *Emotional and Physical Closeness* (e.g., told partner how much I loved him or her, acted seductively, did something special for my partner), *Logic and Reason* (e.g., asserted my authority, used logic, insisted on the level of sexual involvement, compromised with my partner), and *Pressure and Manipulation* (e.g., used alcohol and/or drugs to more easily influence my partner, manipulated my partner's mood, I talked fast and told white lies). Men were significantly more likely than women to have used pressure and manipulation, but no gender differences were found in the use of the other influence strategies. Both men and women reported that they were more likely to engage in the behaviors emphasizing emotional and physical closeness than the behaviors included in any of the other three factors. Furthermore, of the four sexual influence strategies, emotional and physical closeness was related most strongly to level of sexual activity, which suggests that "these techniques were successful at increasing sexual involvement" (p. 98).

Resistance Strategies

Dating partners do not always have similar expectations and desires for sexual involvement in the relationship. Traditionally males have preferred to have sex early in the relationship, whereas women have preferred to wait. Many years ago, Ehrmann (1959) stated that women have "negative control" in their relationships through their refusal of sex. Women also have been called the "gatekeepers" to the couple's sexuality (Peplau et al., 1977). When partners have different sexual goals and desires, it is likely that one partner (usually the female, in heterosexual relationships) occasionally will have to engage in rejection strategies in response to the sexual initiation attempts of the partner. Researchers have found that women feel more comfortable than men in saying no to a partner who wants sex (e.g., Grauerholz and Serpe, 1985; Zimmerman, Sprecher, Langer, and Holloway, 1992) and also are perceived to be more likely to say no (e.g., McCormick, 1979).

How do men and women say no or signal that they are not interested? One way a person can avoid unwanted sex is to avoid situations in which sex might occur. For example, some women say they would avoid sex by avoiding a private or intimate situation and by not engaging in proceptive (e.g., flirting) behaviors with a man (Perper & Weis, 1987). One 19-year-old woman from the Perper and Weis (1987) study wrote:

> Try to keep your distance as much as possible. No body contact whatsoever. Gear your conversation toward mundane topics, such as the weather, the place you're at, etc. Act really uninterested. The point will come across. No invitations back to your apartment, just a thank you and good-bye (p. 471).

But what happens when an intimate setting cannot be avoided and a sexual advance is made by one partner and the other does not want sex? Research suggests that direct (verbal) strategies are more common than indirect (nonverbal) strategies when resisting sex (McCormick, 1979). What if *you* are the one making the sexual advances and the other rejects you? What type of rejection strategy would be easier to take? Imagine yourself in the following situation: You are alone with someone you find attractive in a sexual-romantic way. You move very close to him or her, hoping that this move will communicate your sexual desire. Now further imagine that this other person is not interested and resists your sexual initiation attempt. Which of the following strategies would you most prefer that your partner use to turn you down?

> *"Change channel" strategy (diversion):* Your partner pretends not to notice your move and asks you to change the channel on television.
> *"Not good" strategy:* Your partner moves away from you and says, "I'm sorry, this just would not be good for our relationship."
> *"Not attracted" strategy:* Your partner moves away and says, "I'm sorry, I just don't feel sexually attracted to you."
> *"Not ready" strategy:* Your partner moves away and says, "I'm sorry, I just don't think I'm ready for this right now."

Metts, Cupach, and Imahori (1992, p. 8) identified the above four rejection strategies after reviewing earlier literature on sexual initiation and refusal and conducting a pilot test with undergraduate students who were asked how they would resist unwanted sex. They conducted an experiment in which subjects read a scenario similar to the one above and then provided their reactions to the rejection. Different versions of the scenarios were created. The "not ready" and "not good" strategies were perceived by the subjects to be more appropriate than the other two strategies. The "not attrracted" strategy was considered to be the most direct but also the most constraining (e.g., unexpected, discouraging, embarrassing). All of the rejection strategies were perceived to be more appropriate and less constraining if the relationship was described as a "friendship" rather than as a dating relationship or as ambiguous ("casual friendship that held the prospect of potentially developing into a dating relationship"). Finally, male and female subjects had different reactions to being rejected. Females believed, to a greater degree than males, that being sexually rejected would be constraining; that is, they thought it would be uncomfortable, unexpected, discouraging, and embarrassing. These authors discussed how sexual rejection can often be problematic because the person who resists the sexual advances must make sure that the other gets the message ("I don't want to have sex"), yet at the same time he or she is likely to try to avoid harming the relationship and the other's self-esteem.

Sexual Miscommunication

It has been suggested that in their rejection strategies, women are sometimes saying, "Please persist." Female token resistance to sex seems to be a part of the script for the first sexual interaction. Muehlenhard and Hollabaugh (1988) examined whether there is any credence to the common belief that women offer token resistance to sex—that is, they say no even though they mean yes. To examine this notion, the authors asked a group of female undergraduate students how often they had been in the following situation:

> You were with a guy who wanted to engage in sexual intercourse and you wanted to also, but for some reason you indicated that you didn't want to, although you had every intention to and were willing to engage in sexual intercourse. In other words, you indicated "no" and you meant "yes" (p. 874).

The authors found that, of the 610 female participants in their study, 240 (39 percent) had engaged in token resistance at least once and more than half of these 240 women had done this more than once. (A similar percentage, 37 percent, was found by Muehlenhard and McCoy, 1991.) In the Muehlenhard and Hollabaugh study, women also were asked to rate in importance 26 possible reasons for saying no when they meant yes. The reasons most frequently cited for engaging in token resistance to sex were practical ones, such as not wanting to appear promiscuous. In research conducted by Sprecher, Hatfield, Potapova, Levitskaya, and Cortese (1992), token resistance to sex was examined in three countries: the United States, Russia, and Japan. In the United States sample, 38 percent of the women said yes to a question similar to the one presented above (note that this is nearly the same percentage found by Muehlenhard and Hollabaugh, 1988). The percentage of women who had engaged in token resistance to sex was slightly higher for the Russian women (59 percent) but approximately the same in the Japanese sample (37 percent) as was found in the United States sample.

In our research, we also examined whether men sometimes say no when they mean yes. Although cultural stereotypes suggest that men are always willing to say yes to sex, we found that a large number of men in all three countries had engaged in token resistance to sex. The percentages for the male respondents in the three countries were 47 percent for the United States, 48 percent for Russia, and 21 percent for Japan.

Saying no but meaning yes is not the only form of sexual miscommunication. Sometimes individuals may do just the opposite: They may say yes but mean no. In other words, they agree to have sex despite the fact that they do not want it. How common is this form of miscommunication? The respondents in our cross-cultural study also were asked:

> Has the following situation ever happened to you? You were with a person who wanted to engage in sexual intercourse and you did *not* want to, but for some reason you indicated that you did want to. In other words, you indicated "yes" and you meant "no." Has this ever happened to you?

Women in the United States had the highest rate of consent to unwanted sex (44 percent), as measured by the above item. The percentages found for the other groups were United States men, 33 percent; Russian women, 23 percent; Russian men, 33 percent; Japanese women, 15 percent; and Japanese men, 16 percent.

Negotiating Safe Sex Behavior

At the beginning of this chapter we introduced the notion that much of sexual behavior, particularly initial sexual behavior, is scripted; that is, people are like actors following a script provided to them. According to this perspective, very little of their sexual behavior is truly spontaneous. The question we discuss in this last section of this chapter is, "To what degree have couples incorporated safe sex behavior into their sexual script?" We discuss two ways that couples can be cautious in the early stages of the relationship: (a) talking about their sexual histories and about AIDS, and (b) requesting that condoms be used.

Talking About Sexual Histories and AIDS

In romantic or potentially romantic couples, talk about previous sexual relationships may traditionally have been considered to be a taboo topic, something that was off-limits for discussion (Baxter and Wilmot, 1985). Research has shown, however, that many modern couples do talk about their previous sexual relationships. For example, in the Boston Dating Couples Study, Rubin and his colleagues (e.g., Rubin, Hill, Peplau, and Dunkel-Schetter, 1980) asked the partners in the 231 dating couples how much they disclosed on 18 different topic areas. One of these topics was "The extent of my sexual experience previous to my relationship with my partner." Fifty-seven percent of both men and women said they had engaged in "full" disclosure on this topic, and slightly more than one-third of the men and women said they had disclosed "some." Only about 10 percent said they had practically no disclosure. At the time Rubin and his associates conducted their study, however, talk about previous sexual relations was an act of self-disclosure and did not have any significance as a safe-sex behavior. Thus, *when* the partners discussed their sexual histories was not an issue; they probably revealed this information after intimacy had developed. Today, however, young adults are receiving the message from health officials and parents that they should ask a potential partner about his or her sexual history *before* having sex.

Recent survey studies conducted with young adults show that only some young heterosexual adults are asking the recommended questions of their partners. For example, Edgar, Freimuth, Hammond, McDonald, and Fink (1992) reported that a majority of a sample of sexually active men and women were not confident that they knew the number of their partner's previous sexual relationships. In a sample of 100 dating couples, Sprecher (1991) found that only about half of the sample responded that they were at least slightly more likely to ask their current partner about his or her previous sexual contacts because of the threat of AIDS.

The results of one study suggest that other strategies for seeking information about a partner's sexual past might be used before direct questioning. In a sample of college students, Gray and Saracino (1991) found that only 27 percent of the students said they are likely to ask a new sexual partner how many previous sexual partners they have had. A majority of the students (60 percent) said they are likely to "try to guess" whether a new partner had been exposed to AIDS. Metts and Fitzpatrick (1992) discussed other techniques that might be used to reduce uncertainty about a partner's previous sexual history. In addition to the strategy of interrogation (asking the partner directly), the other strategies that might be used include self-disclosing to get the partner to reciprocate, asking others in the social network about the partner, and observing the partner in certain situations to see how he or she responds.

Although a person may ask a potential partner about his or her sexual history, the person may not get the entire truth. Cochran and Mays (1990) surveyed 655 college students from Southern California and found that among the 196 sexually active men and 226 sexually active women in the study, 20 percent of the men and 4 percent of the women would lie about the results of an HIV-antibody test, and 47 percent of the men and 42 percent of the women would underestimate the number of previous partners.

Some couples do not talk about sexual histories but may talk about AIDS more generally. For example, Sprecher (1991) found that approximately three-fourths of dating partners in one sample said they had talked to their partner about AIDS. Bowen and Michal-Johnson (1989) found that 56 percent of a college sample reported that they talked about AIDS in a relationship. Cline, Johnson, and Freeman (1992) (also discussed in Cline, Freeman, and Johnson, 1990) further examined the nature of talk about AIDS in dating relationships and identified four groups:

> *Safe-sex talkers (21 percent of the sample):* These individuals reported that they talked with their sexual partner about AIDS as it applied to their relationship. For example, they talked about sexual histories, condom use, and AIDS prevention within the context of their relationship.
>
> *General AIDS talk (43 percent):* These individuals talked about AIDS topics but not in the context of their own relationship.
>
> *Nontalkers (32 percent):* These individuals reported that they had not discussed AIDS with a sexual partner and did not desire to do so.
>
> *Want-to-be talkers (5 percent):* These individuals reported that they had not discussed AIDS with their partner but wanted to.

Incorporating Condoms into the Sexual Script

How do people get the message across to their partner that they want to use condoms? As discussed by Metts and Fitzpatrick (1992), Adelman (1991), and others, expressing to a partner one's desire for the use of condoms may be difficult because it may suggest that one does not trust the partner or may send a message about one's own sexual behavior outside the relationship. Adelman (1991) suggested that play and humor be used in requests for condom use. Research conducted by Edgar and Fitzpatrick (1988) suggests that gay men may be particularly adept at discussing condom use.

One recent study (Metts and Cupach, 1991) examined how women would ask their partner to use condoms. Females read a scenario that went like this:

> Tonight you have a date with a man to whom you are attracted. You have dated before, but have not had sex with him. From things he has said, you gather that before dating you, he dated several women during the past year. He has been showing sexual interest in you and you are aroused by him, but you have avoided having intercourse with him so far. You anticipate that tonight might be the first time you have intercourse with him. You want to practice "safe sex" but suspect that he might not automatically wear a condom. How would you go about getting him to wear a condom? What would you say? What would you do to achieve your objective; that is, what steps would you go through to get him to wear a condom, even though he may resist? (p. 12).

Half of the women received the above version, and half received a similar version except that it said the man had been dating one woman exclusively for a year. (Data also were gathered from males about resistance to condom requests.)

The most common technique that females listed for seeking condom use in their male partner was the direct request ("If you want to have sex with me, you must wear a condom"). This finding may seem incongruent with the more general finding, as discussed earlier in this chapter, that indirectness is common in sexual negotiations (e.g., McCormick, 1979; Perper and Weis, 1987). Commenting on this, Metts and Cupach wrote: "Review of the plans in their entirety reveal that the direct request seldom appears alone, but is typically preceded by at least one other more subtle element (e.g., hinting/joking, ingratiation) and often followed by more remedial elements (e.g., providing and assisting with a condom)" (p. 18). Thus a sequence of verbal and nonverbal behaviors probably is involved in the request for condom use and in its acceptance.

Summary

We discussed in this chapter how two people move from being attracted to each other to being sexual partners. For some couples the path is smooth and relatively free of obstacles, but other couples may encounter misperceptions, misunderstandings, and miscommunications on the way to sexual intimacy. The stages of becoming sexually involved are based on one or both members planning, scheming, and taking initiative. Although traditionally the male has been the initiator and planner, the research reviewed in this chapter suggests that women also often play a proceptive role in sexual initiation, although their strategies may be more subtle and less direct than men's. Furthermore, today, women increasingly are taking the assertive role in talking about sexual histories and requesting that condoms be used. . . .

References

ABBEY, A. (1982). "Sex differences in attributions for friendly behaviors: Do males misperceive females' friendliness?" *Journal of Personality and Social Psychology*, 42, 830–838.

ABBEY, A. (1987). "Misperceptions of friendly behavior as sexual interest: A survey of naturally occurring incidents." *Psychology of Women Quarterly*, 11, 173–194.

ABBEY, A. (1991). "Misperceptions as an antecedent of acquaintance rape: A consequence of ambiguity in communication between men and women." In A. Parrot and L. Bechhofer (eds.), *Acquaintance rape: The hidden crime* (pp. 96–111). New York: John Wiley.

ADAMS, B. N. (1986). *The family: A sociological interpretation.* Orlando, FL: Harcourt Brace Jovanovich.

ADELMAN, M. B. (1991). "Play and incongruity: Framing safe-sex talk." *Health Communication*, 3, 139–155.

ALLGEIER, E. R., and ROYSTER, B. J. T. (1991). "New approaches to dating and sexuality." In E. Grauerholz and M. Koralewski (eds.), *Sexual coercion: Its nature, causes and prevention* (pp. 133–147). Lexington, MA: Lexington.

BAXTER, L. A., and BULLIS, C. (1986). "Turning points in developing romantic relationships." *Human Communication Research*, 12, 469–493.

BAXTER, L. A., and WILMOT, W. W. (1985). "Taboo topics in close relationships." *Journal of Social and Personal Relationships*, 2, 253–269.

BENTLER, P. M. (1968a). "Heterosexual behavior assessment—I, males." *Behavior Research and Therapy*, 6, 21–25.

BENTLER, P. M. (1968b). "Heterosexual behavior assessment—II, females." *Behavior Research and Therapy*, 6, 27–30.

BOWEN, S. P., and MICHAL-JOHNSON, P. (1989). "The crisis of communicating in relationships: Confronting the threat of AIDS." *AIDS and Public Policy*, 4, 10–19.

CARROLL, J. L., VOLK, K. D., and HYDE, J. S. (1985). "Differences between males and females in motives for engaging in sexual intercourse." *Archives of Sexual Behavior*, 14, 131–139.

CHRISTOPHER, F. S., and CATE, R. M. (1984). "Factors involved in premarital sexual decision-making." *Journal of Sex Research*, 20, 363–376.

CHRISTOPHER, F. S., and CATE, R. M. (1985a). "Anticipated influences on sexual decision-making for first intercourse." *Family Relations*, 34, 265–270.

CHRISTOPHER, F. S., and CATE, R. M. (1985b). "Premarital sexual pathways and relationship development." *Journal of Social and Personal Relationships*, 2, 271–288.

CHRISTOPHER, F. S., and FRANDSEN, M. M. (1990). "Strategies of influence in sex and dating." *Journal of Social and Personal Relationships*, 7, 89–105.

CLINE, R. J., FREEMAN, K. E., and JOHNSON, S. J. (1990). "Talk among sexual partners about AIDS: Factors differentiating those who talk from those who do not." *Communication Research*, 17, 792–808.

CLINE, R. J. W., JOHNSON, S. J., and FREEMAN, K. E. (1992). "Talk among sexual partners about AIDS: Interpersonal communication for risk reduction or risk enhancement?" *Health Communication*, 4, 39–56.

COCHRAN, S. D., and MAYS, V. M. (1990). "Sex, lies, and HIV." *New England Journal of Medicine*, 322, 774–775.

D'AUGELLI, J. F., and CROSS, H. L. (1975). "Relationship of sex guilt and moral reasoning to premarital sex in college women and in couples." *Journal of Consulting and Clinical Psychology*, 43, 40–47.

D'AUGELLI, J. F., and D'AUGELLI, A. R. (1977). "Moral reasoning and premarital sexual behavior: Toward reasoning about relationships." *Journal of Social Issues*, 33, 44–66.

DEGLER, C. (1974). "What ought to be and what was: Women's sexuality in the nineteenth century." *American Historical Review*, 79, 1467–1490.

DEGLER, C. (1980). *At odds: Women and the family in America from the Revolution to the present.* New York: Oxford University Press.

DELAMATER, J. D. (1989). "The social control of human sexuality." In K. McKinney and S. Sprecher (eds.), *Human sexuality: The societal and interpersonal context* (pp. 30–62). Norwood, NJ: Ablex.

DELAMATER, J. D., and MACCORQUODALE, P. (1979). *Premarital sexuality: Attitudes, relationships, behaviors.* Madison: University of Wisconsin Press.

EDGAR, T., and FITZPATRICK, M. A. (1988). *Southern Speech Communication Journal*, 53, 385–405.

EDGAR, T., FREIMUTH, V. S., HAMMOND, S. L., McDONALD, D. A., and FINK, E. L. (1992). "Strategic sexual communication: Condom use resistance and response." *Health Communication*, 4, 83–104.

EHRMANN, W. W. (1959). *Premarital dating behavior.* New York: Holt.

GAGNON, J. H. (1990). "The explicit and implicit use of scripting perspective in sex research." In J. Bancroft, C. M. Davis, and D. Weinstein (eds.), *Annual review of sex research* (vol. 1, pp. 1–43). Mt. Vernon, IA: Society for the Scientific Study of Sex.

GAGNON, J. H., and SIMON, W. (1973). *Sexual conduct: The social sources of human sexuality.* Hawthorne, NY: Aldine.

GAULIER, B., TRAVIS, S. K., and ALLGEIER, E. R. (1986). *Proceptive behavior and the use of behavioral cues in heterosexual courtship.* Paper presented at the Annual Meeting of the Midcontinent Region of the Society for the Scientific Study of Sex, Madison, WI.

GEER, J. H., and BROUSSARD, D. B. (1990). "Scaling heterosexual behavior and arousal: Consistency and sex differences." *Journal of Personality and Social Psychology*, 58, 664–671.

GRAUERHOLZ, E., and SERPE, R. T. (1985). "Initiation and response: The dynamics of sexual interaction." *Sex Roles*, 12, 1041–1059.

HARVEY, J. H., FLANARY, R., and MORGAN, M. (1986). "Vivid memories of vivid loves gone by." *Journal of Social and Personal Relationships*, 3, 359–373.

HEROLD, E. S., and GOODWIN, M. S. (1981). "Adamant virgins, potential nonvirgins and nonvirgins." *Journal of Sex Research*, 17, 97–113.

HUSTON, T. L., SURRA, C., FITZGERALD, N. M., and CATE, R. (1981). "From courtship to marriage: Mate selection as an interpersonal process." In S. Duck and R. Gilmour (eds.), *Personal relationships 2: Developing personal relationships* (pp. 53–88). New York: Academic Press.

JEMAIL, J. A., and GEER, J. H. (1977). "Sexual scripts." In R. Gemme and C. Wheeler (eds.), *Progress in sexology* (pp. 513–522). New York: Plenum.

JESSER, C. J. (1978). "Male responses to direct verbal sexual initiatives of females." *Journal of Sex Research*, 14, 118–128.

KERCKHOFF, A. C. (1974). "The social context of interpersonal attraction." In T. L. Huston (ed.), *Foundations of interpersonal attraction* (pp. 61–78). New York: Academic Press.

KINSEY, A. C., POMEROY, W. B., MARTIN, C. E., and GEPHARD, P. H. (1953). *Sexual behavior in the human female*. Philadelphia: W. B. Saunders.

LEIGH, B. C. (1989). "Reasons for having and avoiding sex: Gender, sexual orientation, and relationship to sexual behavior." *Journal of Sex Research*, 26, 199–209.

McCORMICK, N. B. (1979). "Come-ons and put-offs: Unmarried students' strategies for having and avoiding sexual intercourse." *Psychology of Women Quarterly*, 4, 194–211.

METTS, S., CUPACH, W. R., and IMAHORI, T. T. (1992). "Perceptions of sexual compliance-resisting messages in three types of cross-sex relationships." *Western Journal of Speech Communication*, 56, 1–17.

METTS, S., and FITZPATRICK, M. A. (1992). "Thinking about safer sex: The risky business of 'know your partner' advice." In T. Edgar, M. A. Fitzpatrick, and V. S. Friemuth (eds.), *AIDS: A communication perspective* (pp. 1–19). Hillsdale, NJ: Lawrence Erlbaum.

MOORE, M. M. (1985). "Nonverbal courtship patterns in women: Context and consequences." *Ethology and Sociobiology*, 6, 237–247.

MUEHLENHARD, C. L., and HOLLABAUGH, L. C. (1988). "Do women sometimes say no when they mean yes? The prevalence and correlates of women's token resistance to sex." *Journal of Personality and Social Psychology*, 54, 872–879.

MUEHLENHARD, C. L., and McCOY, M. L. (1991). "Double standard/double bind: The sexual double standard and women's communication about sex." *Psychology of Women Quarterly*, 15, 447–461.

PARVEN, T. (1883). "Hygiene of the sexual functions." *New Orleans Medical and Surgical Journal*, 11, 92–95.

PEPLAU, L. A., RUBIN, Z., and HILL, C. T. (1977). "Sexual intimacy in dating relationships." *Journal of Social Issues*, 33, 86–109.

PERPER, T., and FOX, V. S. (1980, April). *Flirtation behavior in public settings*. Paper presented at the meeting of the Eastern Region of the Society for the Scientific Study of Sex, Philadelphia, PA.

PERPER, T., and WEIS, D. L. (1987). "Proceptive and rejective strategies of U.S. and Canadian college women." *Journal of Sex Research*, 23, 455–480.

RANDOLPH, B. J., and WINSTEAD, B. (1988). "Sexual decision making and object relations theory." *Archives of Sexual Behavior*, 17, 389–409.

REISS, I. L. (1989). "Society and sexuality: A sociological explanation." In K. McKinney and S. Sprecher (eds.), *Human sexuality: The societal and interpersonal context* (pp. 3–29). Norwood, NJ: Ablex.

REISS, I. L., and LEE, G. R. (1988). *Family systems in America* (4th ed.). New York: Holt, Rinehart & Winston.

RUBIN, Z., HILL, C. T., PEPLAU, L. A., and DUNKEL-SCHETTER, C. (1980). "Self-disclosure in dating couples: Sex roles and the ethic of openness." *Journal of Marriage and the Family*, 42, 305–317.

SPRAGUE, J., and QUADAGNO, D. (1989). "Gender and sexual motivation: An exploration of two assumptions." *Journal of Psychology and Human Sexuality*, 2, 57–76.

SPRECHER, S. (1991). "The impact of the threat of AIDS on heterosexual dating relationships." *Journal of Psychology and Human Sexuality*, 3, 3–23.

SPRECHER, S., HATFIELD, E., POTAPOVA, E., LEVITSKAYA, A., and CORTESE, A. (1992). *Sexual miscommunication: Saying no when meaning yes and saying yes when meaning no.* Manuscript submitted for publication.

SYMONS, D. (1979). *The evolution of human sexuality.* New York: Oxford University Press.

WHITLEY, B. E. (1988, August). *College students' reasons for sexual intercourse: A sex role perspective.* Paper presented at the 96th Annual Meeting of the American Psychological Association, Atlanta, GA.

ZIMMERMAN, R., SPRECHER, S., LANGER, L. M., and HOLLOWAY, C. D. (1992). *Which adolescents can't say "no" to unwanted sex in a dating relationship?* Manuscript submitted for publication.

Mate Selection: Finding and Meeting Partners*

Mary Ann Schwartz and BarBara Marliene Scott

People in the United States have an ideology which reinforces the idea that we make many individual choices in everyday life. One of the most personal and individual choices made throughout the life course is the selection of a mate. As Mary Ann Schwartz and BarBara Marliene Scott illustrate in this reading, however, our "choices" are severely constrained by social factors. A complex set of social norms guides who we see as attractive and appropriate as a marital partner.

"There's supposed to be more women than men, so where are they?" "I know there are a lot of good men out there—you just have to know where to find them." Do these comments sound familiar to you? Increasingly over the last decade single women and men looking for "Ms. Right" or "Mr. Right" have lamented the mounting problem of finding or meeting someone to date or marry. And, once they meet, how does each one know that the other is the right person? What attracts them to each other? How people meet and where, how or why they are attracted to each other and not someone else are some of the most basic questions surrounding mate selection.

---

*Source: Mary Ann Schwartz/BarBara Marliene Scott, *Marriages and Families: Diversity and Change,* (c) 1994, pp. 127–135, 142. Reprinted by permission of Prentice-Hall, Englewood Cliffs, New Jersey.

The Marriage Market and the Pool of Eligibles

Throughout our history various romantic theories of love and mate selection have suggested that when the time is right we will meet "Prince Charming" or a "fair maiden" without much effort on our part. Most such notions imply that mate selection is a rather unsystematic and random event determined by the "luck of the draw" or by a power higher than ourselves.

In reality, meeting prospective mates, choosing partners, developing a dating relationship, and falling in love are not random activities but are all predictable and are structured by a number of social and demographic factors. For example, if you are a female college student in a dating relationship, without meeting you or your partner we could predict fairly accurately many things about your partner. For example, he is probably a college student like you (or he has already completed college or attended college at some prior time), he is probably of the same racial or ethnic background and social class as you, he is probably a little taller than you, a few years older, and as religious or spiritual as you are. We might even predict that he is similarly attractive as you. (And if he isn't you probably will not have a lasting relationship; research shows that we are attracted to and tend to marry people who have a similar level of physical attractiveness.) Most likely the two of you are similarly intelligent.

Likewise, if you are a male student in a dating relationship the same predictions apply, with a few differences: Your partner is probably your age or one to five years younger, and she is probably your height or shorter. Although we may not be 100 percent correct, for many of you we are probably very close.

The point here is that we have not randomly guessed about the characteristics of people who date and marry. Rather, we have used the knowledge that sociologists have provided us about the principles of homogamy, endogamy, and exogamy in mate selection. In the following discussion we define these principles and describe how they apply to mate selection in the United States.

Marriage Market

Historically, sociologists have described mate selection in terms of a marriage market. That is, they use the analogy of the commercial marketplace to explain how we choose the people we date, mate, live with, and marry. The marriage market concept implies that we enter the mate-selection process with certain resources and we trade these resources for the best offer we can get. In this sense, the marriage market is not a real place but a process.

Regardless of how we choose mates, as exchange theory suggests, some sort of bargaining and exchange probably takes place. For example, in societies and subcultural groups where marriages are arranged by someone other than the couple, the parent or matchmaker carefully tries to strike the best possible bargain. Large dowries—sums of money or property brought to the marriage by a female—are often exchanged for valued characteristics in a male, such as high status. Indeed, valued resources like dowries can also act to make up for a person's supposed deficiencies. Thus, if a woman is considered unattractive but has a large dowry, she might be able to exchange the dowry for a highly prized mate. Although the idea of swapping or exchanging resources in mate selection may seem distant and applicable only in those cultures in which marriages are arranged, this process is very much a part of mate selection in the United States.

Although the nature of the marital exchange has changed, the market has not been eliminated. Despite some improvements in their bargaining position, women remain at a disadvantage vis-à-vis men in the mate-selection marketplace. Although women have entered the labor force in record numbers and become increasingly independent, their actual earnings are far below that of their male counterparts, as is their ability to earn. Furthermore, many of the traditional resources that women could offer, such as child care, housework, and sexuality, can be obtained by men outside marriage and thus have less value in the marriage market. Women are further disadvantaged by the sexual double standard attached to aging: As women age they are considered to be unattractive and undesirable by men.

Does this description of the marital marketplace sound cold, calculating, and unromantic? Even if we are uncomfortable with the idea, most of us engage in the exchange of various personality and social characteristics in our quest for a mate.

Pool of Eligibles

Theoretically, every unmarried person in the United States is a potential eligible mate for every other unmarried person. Realistically, however, not every unmarried person is equally available or accessible to every other unmarried person. The people whom our society has defined as acceptable marriage partners for us form what sociologists call a pool of eligibles. For almost all of us, the pool of eligibles consists of people of the same race, class, and educational level as ourselves. With amazing consistency, we are very much like the people we meet, fall in love with, and marry—far more so than can be attributed simply to chance. Sociologists refer to this phenomenon as homogamy: the tendency to meet, date, and marry someone very similar to ourselves in terms of important or desirable characteristics.

Two of the most common sets of social rules governing mate selection and the pool of eligibles are exogamy and endogamy. Exogamy refers to marriage outside particular groups. So, our pool of eligibles is first narrowed by society's exogamous norms. The most common exogamous norms in the United States are those that prohibit us from dating or marrying someone who is a family member or who is of the same sex. . . . The incest taboo is a universal norm that narrows our pool of eligibles by eliminating close blood relatives. Regarding same-sex partners, people of the same sex are considered to be socially unacceptable mates and are also excluded, at least theoretically.

The opposite of exogamy is endogamy, marriage within a particular group. Endogamous norms can be formal, such as the laws in many U.S. states prior to 1967 that prohibited interracial marriage. Most, however, are informal. For example, social convention dictates that we marry someone near our own age.

Freedom Versus Constraint in Mate Selection

Our freedom to choose a mate is restricted by cultural norms that sort people according to race, ethnicity, religion, social class, residence, and related factors. The romantic belief that mate selection is based on love and that we freely choose our mates notwithstanding, these factors best predict who meets, dates, falls in love with, and marries whom. Let's look at how our pools of eligibles are loosely or closely organized around these factors. Although all of these factors are interrelated, we will examine each one separately. Two of the most important factors are the marriage squeeze and the marriage gradient.

The Marriage Squeeze

Why do you think some people who want a mate and are actively looking cannot connect? Why do women complain more often than men about having difficulty finding a mate? Is there someone out there for all of us, no matter what resources we have to offer? Or will some of us not find a mate no matter how hard we look? In reality there is not someone out there for everyone. If those people being advised to "sit tight and wait" are women born after World War II they may be waiting for a very long time. Demographic data reveal that at any given time in the United States since World War II, there has been a greater number of women than men who are eligible for marriage and looking for a partner. Sociologists have defined this imbalance in the ratio of marriage-aged men to marriage-aged women as a marriage squeeze, where one sex has a more limited pool of eligibles.

Although demographers predicted that the marriage squeeze would reverse itself by the mid-1980s, this did not happen. In the 1990s the marriage squeeze continues to limit the range of choices of mates for women, although its impact is experienced differently across race and age and even geographic location. African-American women, it seems, are particularly vulnerable to the marriage squeeze. . . . Among African Americans [there is a] historically low sex ratio. . . . According to Staples (1991), this low sex ratio will continue to deny large numbers of African-American women a comparable mate. The lower life expectancy for black men (it is lower than for white males and all females), coupled with the increasing numbers of young black men who are victims of homicides and the disproportionate numbers who are incarcerated, has contributed to the current low sex ratio (Lindsey, 1990). By the time African-American women reach 18 years of age they begin to outnumber African-American males; the comparable age for white women is 32 (Spanier and Glick, 1980). The result of this is a seriously restricted field of eligibles for African-American women.

Not only is the marriage squeeze more evident for some racial and ethnic groups than for others, but it is also more evident in some geographic areas and for some age groups. For example, for every 100 unmarried 37-year-old women in Minneapolis, there are 46 eligible men; in St. Louis, the number is 45. In contrast, cities like Houston, San Diego, and San Francisco rank as some of the better marriage markets for women, with more than 70 eligible men for every 100 women (Westoff and Goldman, 1988:39–44). . . .

An even more notable feature of the marriage squeeze is the age factor. In most U.S. metropolitan areas, at all ages over 25 the number of unmarried women significantly exceeds the supply of eligible men. As women get older, the shortage of men becomes more pronounced. For example, single women aged 25 to 29 face a shortage of eligible mates of almost 25 percent (77 eligible men for every 100 eligible women). For women aged 35 to 39 the sex ratio drops to 48 eligible men per 100 eligible women, and by the time women reach ages 45 to 49, the number is 38 (Westoff and Goldman, 1988). Thus, as women age they become more likely to feel the marriage squeeze.

The Marriage Gradient

Another factor that affects the availability of eligible mates in the marriage market is the marriage gradient. In most cultures, including the United States, informal norms require women to marry men of equal or higher social status. Numerous studies of U.S. mate selection and marriage bear out this pattern. For example, only about 33 percent of women with four or more years of college marry men with less education, whereas 50 percent of men with four or more years of college marry less-educated women (Westoff and Goldman, 1988). The tendency to marry upward in social status is referred to as hypergamy; marriage downward is known as hypogamy. Thus, in most cultures, women practice hypergamy, and men practice hypogamy.

As we have already indicated, hypergamy is much more descriptive of American mate selection than hypogamy. When men marry outside their social-class level, they more often marry downward than upward. Furthermore, the higher a man's occupational level, the more likely he will marry downward. Conversely, when women marry outside their social class, they most often marry upward. This pattern of marriage gives rise to a phenomenon we call the marriage gradient. Because women marry upward and men marry downward, men at the top have a much larger field of eligibles than do men at the bottom. The reverse is true for women: Women at the top have a very small pool of eligibles, whereas women on the bottom have a much wider range of men to choose from. This pattern therefore works to keep some of the highest-status women and lowest-status men from marrying. Although the description here is of marital patterns, the same general trend has been found to operate prior to marriage as well. This tendency has been called by some a *dating* or *mating gradient.*

Although the marriage gradient traditionally provided most women with upward mobility, this is not necessarily the case today. The increasing economic independence of some women has made marriage less of a mobility mechanism. Because of the shortage of men (real or perceived), many women are dating and marrying downward instead of upward. For example, a woman with a college degree was heard to say: "If I could find a kind plumber with a sense of humor, I'd marry him."

As with the marriage squeeze, the marriage gradient is very prominent for African-American women. One study (Staples, 1981) found that as income level rises, so does the number of men who are married and living with their wives. In contrast, African-American women who have a college degree are the least likely of all African-Americans to have married by the age of 30. And the African-American men least likely to marry or remarry are those with less than a high school education. A fundamental problem for middle-class or high-status African-American women is that men who have a similar status are either already married or are seeking a younger mate. Thus, the largest number of African-American men in their pool of eligibles are those with a lower status. Therefore, educated African-American women who are interested in a mate often must date or marry down.

Moreover, with the increasing number of marriages that are now ending in divorce and the high proportion of remarriages, the marriage gradient can be seen operating in second marriages as well. As in other examples, women tend to be most vulnerable to the marriage gradient. Researchers Jerry Jacobs and Frank Furstenberg (1986), for example, found that when women, particularly those with children, remarried, they tended to marry downward instead of upward.

Race

Some of the most important norms in mate selection in the United States revolve around race and ethnicity. Dating, mate selection, and marriage are probably most endogamous and homogamous in terms of race. We currently have little reliable data on the number of contemporary couples who date interracially. We do know that about 98 percent of marriages in this country occur within the same racial group (Bovee, 1993). Although marriage is not an exact barometer of who dates whom because all dating does not result in marriage, it can give us some indication of who chooses whom as a mate. . . .

Social Class

Sociologists typically measure class using a composite scale consisting of level of educational attainment, occupation, and level of income. As we have seen, much of our behavior is affected by our location in the status hierarchy. People who share a similar social-class background tend to share common interests, goals, lifestyles, and general behavior. These kinds of compatibility of interest and general homogamy are the bases of intimate relationships. As with race, Americans mate with people from their own socioeconomic class with far greater frequency than could be expected simply by chance. This is especially true among the upper classes of all races. It has often been observed that the upper classes expend more efforts to control the mate selection of their offspring than do other classes because they have much more to lose if their children marry outside their social class (Ramu, 1989). Even on those occasions when a person marries someone of a different race, ethnicity, religion, or age group, the couple will most likely be from the same social class.

Because social researchers do not agree on the nature and number of social classes in U.S. society, it is difficult to determine accurate statistics on class endogamy. We know, however, that courtships and marriages tend to be highly endogamous for such class-related factors as education and occupation. Educational homogamy is most observable for women with four or more years of college, who tend to marry men with comparable or higher levels of education, and for men who have never attended college (Rawlings, 1978).

Age

Are you involved in a relationship with a person who is much older or younger than you? Do you know others who are? What about your parents? Is your mother older or younger than your father? When you see a much younger woman with an older man do you think: "Gee, she must be looking for a father figure." or "My God. He's robbing the cradle"? Age norms represent yet another important constraint on our freedom to choose a mate. Although no laws require us to date, live with, or marry people within our age group, informal norms and pressures operate to keep mate selection fairly homogamous in terms of age. Most Americans mate with people from a closely related age group. For most of us this means that we date and marry people roughly within two to five years of our own age. Although the sanctions for dating or marrying someone very much older or younger (within the law) than oneself are mild, most people adhere to the age custom in selecting a mate. In later marriages or remarriages, age differences are likely to be a little wider, although they continue to follow the general pattern of age homogamy.

Religion

How important is religion in your choice of a partner? Several studies conducted over the years have found that people tend to select partners who are religiously similar to themselves (see, for example, Kerckhoff, 1976; Glenn, 1982; Shehan, Bock, and Lee, 1990). As with race, many of these studies deal primarily with marriage; nonetheless, we can assume some degree of congruency between whom people date and whom they marry. Thus, religious homogamy is yet another factor that limits our pool of eligible mates.

Sex and Gender

When discussing factors that limit our pool of eligible mates we cannot overlook sex. . . . Heterosexuality is the norm in mating, dating, and mate selection in the United States. Most Americans are so socialized into a heterosexual frame of reference that it is outside their scope of reality even to consider a same-sex relationship as an alternative. So important is the value of heterosexuality to many

Americans that exogamous norms regulating this behavior have been encoded into law to ensure that people mate heterosexually. The stigma attached to same sex relationships, legal constraints, and the physical abuse that such couples frequently experience ("gay bashing") can act as deterrents for some people who might otherwise choose a partner of the same sex.

Other Factors That Affect Mate Selection

As we have seen, mate selection in the United States is an individual decision yet many social and structural barriers and limitations act to constrain our freedom to choose a partner. Besides race, class, age, religion, and sex, these barriers can also include propinquity and family and peer pressure. Let us take a brief look at these factors.

Propinquity

We have already touched on the subject of propinquity and its role in mate selection, particularly as we discussed racial and ethnic homogamy. *Propinquity* is a term used by sociologists to denote proximity or closeness in place and space. Traditionally, Americans met, were attracted to, and married people who lived in the same community. This factor of residential proximity in mate selection was first introduced in a pioneering study of mate selection conducted by James Bossard in 1932. In his study of who married whom in the city of Philadelphia, Bossard found that more than half the couples who applied for marriage licenses lived within 20 blocks of each other. One-sixth lived only a block apart, and one-third lived within five blocks of each other. Subsequent research has reported similar results. Although we are no longer tied to our local communities in the way we were before mass transportation and the mass production of the automobile, residential propinquity continues to contribute to homogamy in mate selection.

Residential propinquity is closely tied to many of the factors we have already discussed: social class, race, sexual orientation, and to a lesser degree religion. Historically, people of the same general social characteristics have tended to live close together. For example, most, if not all, U.S. cities are racially and ethnically segregated, and many are class-segregated as well. It is not unusual to go to a city and find very distinct racial or ethnic communities: the African-American community, Little Italy, Chinatown, Greektown. These residential patterns increase the likelihood that we will meet, date, and marry people of similar social backgrounds.

Obviously propinquity is not limited to place of residence. In a mobile society such as ours, propinquity operates as much, if not more, in schools, the workplace, places of entertainment, and other institutions as we increasingly move out of our communities for a good portion of each day. Nevertheless, the probability of meeting someone and establishing an intimate relationship still depends on the likelihood of interacting with that person.

Family and Peer Pressure

Consider the following scenario:

> I am working on a doctorate; my boyfriend has never attended college. We love each other, but my family and friends insist that I should break off with him because he is not on my level. I think they might be right because sometimes even I am embarrassed by the way he speaks and carries himself. I feel so pressured by them. Can love overcome the prejudices of society?

Stated another way, this woman's question could well be: Can love overcome the pressures of family, friends, or peers? Who is or is not acceptable to parents and other relatives is of importance to most Americans. Parents in particular exercise direct and indirect influence on whom we meet and develop relationships with. Parents influence our choice of mate from the moment we are born through their teaching, their example, where they choose to live, which schools they send us to, and so forth. How, where, and when we are brought up has a profound impact on our views and decisions concerning marriage and family. Additionally, the closer we are to our parents and kin, the more likely we will consider their views.

Peers, too, can be powerful forces in both whom we meet and whom we decide to date or pair with. If our peer relationships are significant and close, we are far more likely to consider our friends' views and feelings about the people we date and marry. . . .

Personal Qualities and Mate Selection

. . . Social factors such as those we have just discussed act as an initial screening. Once our pool of eligibles is determined, other factors come into play, such as the personal qualities or characteristics of the people we meet and consider as potential mates. The personal qualities we consider cover a wide range that includes physical appearance, lifestyles, ability to communicate, values and attitudes, personality, and family background, to name but a few. Probably the most important, at least initially, is physical appearance, because first impressions are often based on whether or not we find a person attractive. In addition, first impressions are often lasting impressions. In the discussion that follows we take a brief look at attractiveness and companionship as classic examples of personal qualities that critically affect mate selection.

Attraction

What does "Ms. Right" or "Mr. Right" look like? All of us have some image, vague though it may be, of who our ideal mate will be. Usually this image includes both physical and personality features, and we consciously or unconsciously rate or compare potential mates in accordance with these images. These ideas and images do not develop in a vacuum; rather, they are shaped in large part by the society in which we live. For most Americans, physical appearance is one of the most important ingredients in mate selection. Whether we admit it or not, how someone looks has a considerable impact on whether we choose that person as a friend or lover.

Researchers have found a number of interesting points about physical attractiveness and its influence on mate selection. One key point is that we tend to think we are better looking than other people do. Furthermore, men are more likely than women to exaggerate their appearance, whereas less-attractive females are more accurate in their self-evaluations. This is true, no doubt, because women get far more feedback about their appearance than men do. In any event, once people meet and dating begins, personality characteristics become important considerations, although attractiveness does not decline in importance (Patzer, 1985).

Dating and marriage relationships tend to be endogamous for physical attractiveness. Various studies have documented our general tendency to look for and end up with partners whose attractiveness is roughly equivalent to our own (Stroebe, Insko, Thompson, and Layton, 1971). Some of the physical similarities between people who become couples are probably the products of race and class endogamy. Some, however, are also probably a function of our definitions of what is physically appealing, including our assessment of where we fit in society's general definition of physical attractiveness.

Companionship

Despite the increasing divorce rate, some demographers are predicting that many people who have married in recent times will likely stay married to the same person for the next 50 years or more unless death or divorce intervenes (Ramu, 1989). If they are correct, then qualities such as compatibility and companionship are critically important in mate selection. It is essential to choose a mate with whom we can communicate; enjoy sexually and socially; and depend on for friendship, support, and understanding. The presence or absence of these attributes can have a tremendous impact on the quality and longevity of the relationship. Ramu (1989) identifies communication and sexual adjustment as the two most crucial personal attributes that contribute to companionship in an intimate relationship. These attributes are complex and depend on a number of factors: the partners' intellectual compatibility, their sensitivity and empathy toward each other, each partner's ideas about the other's sexual behavior, similarity in social class and other important social characteristics, and the importance to both partners of sexual relations in marriage.

The Life Cycle and Mate Selection

The desire to date or participate generally in the mate-selection process does not begin and end with youth. The fact that many people are delaying marriage until later ages, coupled with the large and increasing divorce rate, better health, and an extended life expectancy, mean that an increasing number of older adults will enter or reenter into dating relationships, and some of them will look for a permanent mate. In some ways these older adults resemble their younger counterparts. They seek partners for companionship, for long- and short-term commitments, and to share their life with. They feel a need for emotional care and the same type of mutual aid that many younger couples share. They frequently differ, however, in terms of the ultimate goal of mate selection. Although many older adults say that they would like to remarry, few of them actually do. Many of them are independent and self-sufficient, and they want to remain that way. . . .

Summary

Mate selection refers loosely to the wide range of behaviors and social relationships that individuals engage in prior to marriage that lead to short- or long-term pairing. It is an institutionalized feature of social life and can be found in some form in all human societies, although the exact processes that are followed vary widely from one society to another. In the United States, the mate-selection process, particularly for first marriages, is highly youth-centered and competitive. . . .

The process of mate selection can be viewed sociologically as a sequential or filtering process that stresses homogamy and endogamy. Mate selection in U.S. society is mediated by a range of structural and social factors: the nature of the marriage market, the marriage squeeze and marriage gradient, propinquity, race, class, sex, age, religion, education, family and peers, and cultural ideals about beauty and worth. Due to the impact of these factors we are very much like the people we meet, fall in love with, and marry—far more so than can simply be attributed to chance. . . .

References

Bossard, James. 1932. "Residential Propinquity as a Factor in Mate Selection." *American Journal of Sociology* 38: 219–24.

Bovee, Tim. 1993. "Interracial Marriages Now 1 in 50." *The Times-Picayune* (February 12): A1,A8.

Glenn, Norval D. 1982. "Interreligious Marriage in the United States: Patterns and Recent Trends." *Journal of Marriage and the Family* 44: 555–66.

Jacobs, Jerry, and Frank Furstenberg. 1986. "Changing Places: Conjugal Careers and Women's Marital Mobility." *Social Forces* 64: 714–32.

Kerckhoff, Alan C. 1976. "Patterns of Marriage and Family Formation and Dissolution." *Journal of Consumer Research* 2: 262.

Lindsey, Linda. 1990. *Gender Roles: A Sociological Perspective.* Englewood Cliffs, NJ: Prentice Hall.

Patzer, Gordon L. 1985. *The Physical Attractiveness Phenomena.* New York: Plenum Press.

Ramu, G. N. 1989. "Patterns of Mate Selection." In K. Ishwaran, ed., *Family and Marriage: Cross-Cultural Perspectives,* 165–78. Toronto, Canada: Wall and Thompson.

Rawlings, S. 1978. "Perspectives on American Husbands and Wives." Current Population Reports, Series P-23, no 77. Washington, DC: U.S. Bureau of the Census.

SHEHAN, C. L., E. W. BOCK, and G. R. LEE. 1990. "Religious Heterogamy, Religiosity, and Marital Happiness: The Case of Catholicism." *Journal of Marriage and the Family* 52: 73–79.

SPANIER, GRAHAM B. and PAUL C. GLICK. 1980. "Mate Selection Differentials between Whites and Blacks in the United States." *Social Forces* 53: 707–25.

STAPLES, ROBERT. 1981. *The World of Black Singles: Changing Patterns of Male/Female Relations*. Westport, CT: Greenwood Press.

———, ed. 1991. *The Black Family. Essays and Studies*, 4th ed. Belmont, CA: Wadsworth.

STROEBE, WOLFGANG, C. A. INSKO, V. D. THOMPSON, and B. D. LAYTON. 1971. "Effects of Physical Attractiveness, Attitude Similarity, and Sex on Various Aspects of Interpersonal Attraction." *Journal of Personality and Social Psychology* 18: 79–91.

WESTHOFF, CHARLES F., and NOREEN GOLDMAN. 1988. "Figuring the Odds in the Marriage Market." In J. Gipson Wells, ed., *Current Issues in Marriage and the Family*, 39–46. New York: Macmillan.

The Good-Provider Role: Its Rise and Fall*

Jessie Bernard

This article by Jessie Bernard illustrates both the importance of a historical perspective and the central role played by gender when we try to understand the complexities of marriage in the modern world. She argues that the concept of the good provider as a specialized male role emerged with the growth of a market economy. As the spheres of men and women became separated, so did the definitions of men's and women's appropriate roles. She explores some of the aspects of this role, and the ways in which role definitions are changing as both women and men are involved in the market economy outside of the home.

The Lord is my shepherd, I shall not want. He sets a table for me in the very sight of my enemies; my cup runs over (23rd Psalm). And when the Israelites were complaining about how hungry they were on their way from Egypt to Canaan, God told Moses to rest assured: There would be meat for dinner and bread for breakfast the next morning. And, indeed, there were quails that very night, enough to cover the camp, and in the morning the ground was covered with dew that proved to be bread (Exodus 16:12–13). In fact, in this role of good

*Source: Jessie Bernard, "The Good-Provider Role: Its Rise and Fall," *American Psychologist* (January, 1981), pp. 1–12. Copyright 1981 by the American Psychological Association. Reprinted by permission.

provider, God is sometimes almost synonymous with Providence. Many people like Micawber, still wait for him, or Providence, to provide.

Granted, then, that the first great provider for the human species was God the Father, surely the second great provider for the human species was Mother the gatherer, planter, and general factotum. Boulding (1976), citing Lee and DeVore, tells us that in hunting and gathering societies, males contribute about one-fifth of the food of the clan, females the other four-fifths (p. 96). She also concludes that by 12,000 B.C. in the early agricultural villages, females provided four-fifths of human subsistence (p. 97). Not until large trading towns arose did the female contribution to human subsistence decline to equality with that of the male. And with the beginning of true cities, the provisioning work of women tended to become invisible. Still, in today's world it remains substantial.

Whatever the date of the virtuous woman described in the Old Testament (Proverbs 31:10–27), she was the very model of a good provider. She was, in fact, a highly productive conglomerate. She woke up in the middle of the night to tend to her business; she oversaw a multiple-industry household; *her* candles did not go out at night; there was a ready market for the high-quality linen girdles she made and sold to the merchants in town; and she kept track of the real estate market and bought good land when it became available, cultivating vineyards quite profitably. All this time her husband sat at the gate talking with his cronies.

A recent counterpart to the virtuous woman was the busy and industrious shtetl woman:

> The earnings of a livelihood is sexless, and the large majority of women . . . participate in some gainful occupation if they do not carry the chief burden of support. The wife of a "perennial student" is very apt to be the sole support of the family. The problem of managing both a business and a home is so common that no one recognizes it as special. . . . To bustle about in search of a livelihood is merely another form of bustling about managing a home; both are aspects of . . . health and livelihood (Zborowski and Herzog, 1952, p. 131).

In a subsistence economy in which husbands and wives ran farms, shops, or businesses together, a man might be a good, steady worker, but the idea that he was *the* provider would hardly ring true. Even the youth in the folk song who listed all the gifts he would bestow on his love if she would marry him—a golden comb, a paper of pins, and all the rest—was not necessarily promising to be a good provider.

I have not searched the literature to determine when the concept of the good provider entered our thinking. The term *provider* entered the English language in 1532, but was not yet male sex typed, as the older term *purveyor* already was in 1442. Webster's second edition defines the good provider as "one who provides, especially, colloq., one who provides food, clothing, etc. for his family; as, he is a good or an adequate provider." More simply, he could be defined as a man whose wife did not have to enter the labor force. The counterpart to the good provider was the housewife. However the term is defined, the role itself delineated relationships within a marriage and family in a way that added to the legal, religious, and other advantages men had over women.

Thus, under the common law, although the husband was legally head of the household and as such had the responsibility of providing for his wife and children, this provision was often made with help from the wife's personal property and earnings, to which he was entitled:

> He owned his wife's and children's services, and had the sole right to collect wages for their work outside the home. He owned his wife's personal property outright, and had the right to manage and control all of his wife's real property during marriage, which included the right to use or lease property, and to keep any rents and profits from it (Babcock, Freedman, Norton, and Ross, 1975, p. 561).

So even when she was the actual provider, the legal recognition was granted the husband. Therefore, whatever the husband's legal responsibilities for support may have been, he was not necessarily a good provider in the way the term came to be understood. The wife may have been performing that role.

In our country in colonial times women were still viewed as performing a providing role, and they pursued a variety of occupations. Abigail Adams managed the family estate, which provided the wherewithal for John to spend so much time in Philadelphia. In the eighteenth century "many women were active in business and professional pursuits. They ran inns and taverns; they managed a wide variety of stores and shops; and, at least occasionally, they worked in careers like publishing, journalism and medicine" (Demos, 1974, p. 430). Women sometimes even "joined the menfolk for work in the fields" (p. 430). Like the household of the proverbial virtuous woman, the colonial household was a little factory that produced clothing, furniture, bedding, candles, and other accessories, and again, as in the case of the virtuous woman, the female role was central. It was taken for granted that women provided for the family along with men.

The good provider as a specialized male role seems to have arisen in the transition from subsistence to market—especially money—economies that accelerated with the Industrial Revolution. The good-provider role for males emerged in this country roughly, say, from the 1830s, when de Tocqueville was observing it, to the late 1970s, when the 1980 census declared that a male was not automatically to be assumed to be head of household. This gives the role a life span of about a century and a half. Although relatively short-lived, while it lasted the role was a seemingly rocklike feature of the national landscape.

As a psychological and sociological phenomenon, the good-provider role had wide ramifications for all of our thinking about families. It marked a new kind of marriage. It did not have good effects on women: The role deprived them of many chips by placing them in a peculiarly vulnerable position. Because she was not reimbursed for her contribution to the family in either products or services, a wife was stripped to a considerable extent of her access to cash-mediated markets. By discouraging labor force participation, it deprived many women, especially affluent ones, of opportunities to achieve strength and competence. It deterred young women from acquiring productive skills. They dedicated themselves instead to winning a good provider who would "take care of" them. The wife of a more successful provider became for all intents and purposes a parasite, with little to do except indulge or pamper herself. The psychology of such dependence could become all but crippling. There were other concomitants of the good-provider role.

Expressivity and the Good-Provider Role

The new industrial order that produced the good provider changed not so much the division of labor between the sexes as it did the site of the work they engaged in. Only two of the concomitants of this change in work site are selected for comment here, namely, (a) the identification of gender with work site as well as with work itself and (b) the reduction of time for personal interaction and intimacy within the family.

It is not so much the specific kinds of work men and women do—they have always varied from time to time and place to place—but the simple fact that the sexes do different kinds of work, whatever it is, which is in and of itself important. The division of labor by sex means that the work group becomes also a sex group. The very nature of maleness and femaleness becomes embedded in the sexual division of labor. One's sex and one's work are part of one another. One's work defines one's gender.

Any division of labor implies that people doing different kinds of work will occupy different work sites. When the division is based on sex, men and women will necessarily have different work sites. Even within the home itself, men and women had different work spaces. The woman's spinning wheel occupied a different area from the man's anvil. When the factory took over much of the work formerly done in the house, the separation of work space became especially marked. Not only did the separation of the sexes become spatially extended, but it came to relate work and gender in a special way. The work site as well as the work itself became associated with gender; each sex had its own turf. This sexual "territoriality" has had complicating effects on efforts to change any sexual division of labor. The good provider worked primarily in the outside male world of business and industry. The homemaker worked primarily in the home.

Spatial separation of the sexes not only identifies gender with work site and work but also reduces the amount of time available for spontaneous emotional give-and-take between husbands and wives. When men and women work in an economy based in the home, there are frequent occasions for interaction. (Consider, for example, the suggestive allusions made today to the rise in the birth rate nine months after a blackout.) When men and women are in close proximity, there is always the possibility of reassuring glances, the comfort of simple physical presence. But when the division of labor removes the man from the family dwelling for most of the day, intimate relationships become less feasible. De Tocqueville was one of the first to call our attention to this. In 1840 he noted that:

almost all men in democracies are engaged in public or professional life; and . . . the limited extent of common income obliges a wife to confine herself to the house, in order to watch in person and very closely over the details of domestic economy. All these distinct and compulsory occupations are so many natural barriers, which, by keeping the two sexes asunder, render the solicitations of the one less frequent and less ardent—the resistance of the other more easy (de Tocqueville, 1840, p. 212).

Not directly related to the spatial constraints on emotional expression by men, but nevertheless a concomitant of the new industrial order with the same effect, was the enormous drive for achievement, for success, for "making it" that escalated the provider role into the good-provider role. De Tocqueville (1840) is again our source:

The tumultuous and constantly harassed life which equality makes men lead [becoming good providers] not only distracts from the passions of love, by denying them time to indulge in it, but it diverts them from it by another more secret but more certain road. All men who live in democratic ages more or less contract ways of thinking of the manufacturing and trading classes (p. 221).

As a result of this male concentration on jobs and careers, much abnegation and "a constant sacrifice of her pleasures to her duties" (de Tocqueville, 1840, p. 212) were demanded by the American woman. The good-provider role, as it came to be shaped by this ambience, was thus restricted in what it was called upon to provide. Emotional expressivity was not included in that role. One of the things a parent might say about a man to persuade a daughter to marry him, or a daughter might say to explain to her parents why she wanted to, was not that he was a gentle, loving, or tender man but that he was a good provider. He might have many other qualities, good or bad, but if a man was a good provider, everything else was either gravy or the price one had to pay for a good provider.

Lack of expressivity did not imply neglect of the family. The good provider was a "family man." He set a good table, provided a decent home, paid the mortgage, bought the shoes, and kept his children warmly clothed. He might, with the help of the children's part-time jobs, have been able to finance their educations through high school, and, sometimes, even college. There might even have been a little left over for an occasional celebration in most families. The good provider made a decent contribution to the church. His work might have been demanding, but he expected it to be. If in addition to being a good provider, a man was kind, gentle, generous, and not a heavy drinker or gambler, that was all frosting on the cake. Loving attention and emotional involvement in the family were not part of a woman's implicit bargain with the good provider.

By the time de Tocqueville published his observations in 1840, the general outlines of the good-provider role had taken shape. It called for a hard-working man who spent most of his time at his work. In the traditional conception of the role, a man's chief responsibility is his job, so that "by definition any family behaviors must be subordinate to it in terms of significance and [the job] has priority in the event of a clash" (Scanzoni, 1975, p. 38). This was the classic form of the good-provider role, which remained a powerful component of our societal structure until well into the present century.

Costs and Rewards of the Good-Provider Role for Men

There were both costs and rewards for those men attached to the good-provider role. The most serious cost was perhaps the identification of maleness not only with the work site but especially with success in the role. "The American male looks to his breadwinning role to confirm his manliness" (Brenton, 1966, p. 194).[1] To be a man one had to be not only a provider but a *good* provider. Success in the good-provider role came in time to define masculinity itself. The good provider had to achieve to win, to succeed, to dominate. He was a bread*winner.* He had to show "strength, cunning, inventiveness, endurance—a whole range of traits henceforth defined as exclusively 'masculine' " (Demos, 1974, p. 436). Men were judged as men by the level of living they provided. They were judged by the myth "that endows a money-making man with sexiness and virility, and is based on man's dominance, strength, and ability to provide for and care for 'his' woman" (Gould, 1974, p. 97). The good provider became a player in the male competitive macho game. What one man provided for his family in the way of luxury and display had to be equaled or topped by what another could provide. Families became display cases for the success of the good provider.

The psychic costs could be high:

> By depending so heavily on his breadwinning role to validate his sense of himself as a man, instead of also letting his roles as husband, father, and citizen of the community count as validating sources, the American male treads on psychically dangerous ground. It's always dangerous to put all one's psychic eggs into one basket (Brenton, 1966, p. 194).

The good-provider role not only put all of a man's gender-identifying eggs into one psychic basket, but it also put all the family-providing eggs into one basket. One individual became responsible for the support of the whole family. Countless stories portrayed the humiliation families underwent to keep wives and especially mothers out of the labor force, a circumstance that would admit to the world the male head's failure in the good-provider role. If a married woman had to enter the labor force at all, that was bad enough. If she made a good salary, however, she was "co-opting the man's passport to masculinity" (Gould, 1974, p. 89) and he was effectively castrated. A wife's earning capacity diminished a man's position as head of the household (Gould, 1974, p. 99).

Failure in the role of good provider, which employment of wives evidenced, could produce deep frustration. As Komarovsky (1940, p. 20) explains, this is "because in his own estimation he is failing to fulfill what is the central duty of his life, the very touchstone of his manhood—the role of family provider."

But just as there was punishment for failure in the good-provider role, so also were there rewards for successful performance. A man "derived strength from his role as provider" (Komarovsky, 1940, p. 205). He achieved a good deal of satisfaction from his ability to support his family. It won kudos. Being a good provider led to status in both the family and the community. Within the family it gave him the power of the purse and the right to decide about expenditures, standards of living, and what constituted good providing. "Every purchase of the family—the radio, his wife's new hat, the children's skates, the meals set before him—all were symbols of their dependence upon him" (Komarovsky, 1940, pp. 74–75). Such dependence gave him a "profound sense of stability" (p. 74). It was a strong counterpoise vis-à-vis a wife with a stronger personality. "Whether he had considerable authority within the family and was recognized as its head, or whether the wife's stronger personality . . . dominated the family, he nevertheless derived strength from his role as a provider" (Komarovsky, 1940, p. 75). As recently as 1975, in a sample of 3,100 husbands and wives in ten cities, Scanzoni found that despite increasing egalitarian norms, the good provider still had "considerable power in ultimate decision-making" and as "unique provider" had the right "to organize his life and the lives of other family members around his occupation" (p. 38).

A man who was successful in the good-provider role might be freed from other obligations to the family. But the flip side of this dispensation was that he could not make up for poor performances by excellence in other family roles. Since everything depended on his success as provider, everything was at stake. The good provider played an all-or-nothing game.

Different Ways of Performing the Good-Provider Role

Although the legal specifications for the role were laid out in the common law, in legislation, in legal precedents, in court decisions, and, most importantly, in custom and convention, in real-life situations the social and social-psychological specifications were set by the husband or, perhaps more accurately, by the community, alias the Joneses, and there were many ways to perform it.

Some men resented the burdens the role forced them to bear. A man could easily vent such resentment toward his family by keeping complete control over all expenditures, dispensing the money for household maintenance, and complaining about bills as though it were his wife's fault that shoes cost so much. He could, in effect, punish his family for his having to perform the role. Since the money he earned belonged to him—was "his"—he could do with it what he pleased. Through extreme parsimony he could dole out his money in a mean, humiliating way, forcing his wife to come begging for pennies. By his reluctance and resentment he could make his family pay emotionally for the provisioning he supplied.

At the other extreme were the highly competitive men who were so involved in outdoing the Joneses that the fur coat became more important than the affectionate hug. They "bought off" their families. They sometimes succeeded so well in their extravagance that they sacrificed the family they were presumably providing for to the achievements that made it possible (Keniston, 1965).[2]

The Depression of the 1930s revealed in harsh detail what the loss of the role could mean both to the good provider and to his family, not only in the loss of income itself—which could be supplied by welfare agencies or even by other family members, including wives—but also and especially in the loss of face.

The Great Depression did not mark the demise of the good-provider role. But it did teach us what a slender thread the family hung on. It stimulated a whole array of programs designed to strengthen that thread, to ensure that it would never again be similarly threatened. Unemployment insurance was incorporated into the Social Security Act of 1935, for example, and a Full Employment Act was passed in 1946. But there proved to be many other ways in which the good-provider role could be subverted.

Role Rejectors and Role Overperformers

Recent research in psychology, anthropology, and sociology has familiarized us with the tremendous power of roles. But we also know that one of the fundamental principles of role behavior is that conformity to role norms is not universal. Not everyone lives up to the specifications of roles, either in the psychological or in the sociological definition of the concept. Two extremes have attracted research attention: (a) the men who could not live up to the norms of the good-provider role or did not want to, at one extreme, and (b) the men who overperformed the role, at the other. For the wide range in between, from blue-collar workers to professionals, there was fairly consistent acceptance of the role, however well or poorly, however grumblingly or willingly, performed.

First the nonconformists. Even in colonial times, desertion and divorce occurred:

> Women may have deserted because, say, their husbands beat them; husbands, on the other hand, may have deserted because they were unable or unwilling to provide for their usually large families in the face of the wives' demands to do so. These demands were, of course, backed by community norms making the husband's financial support a sacred duty (Scanzoni, 1979, pp. 24–25).

Fiedler (1962) has traced the theme of male escape from domestic responsibilities in the American novel from the time of Rip Van Winkle to the present:

> The figure of Rip Van Winkle presides over the birth of the American imagination; and it is fitting that our first successful home-grown legend should memorialize, however playfully, the flight of the dreamer from the shrew—into the mountains and out of time, away from the drab duties of home . . . anywhere to avoid . . . marriage and responsibility. One of the factors that determine theme and form in our great books is this strategy of evasion, this retreat to nature and childhood which makes our literature (and life) so charmingly and infuriatingly "boyish" (pp. xx–xxi).

Among the men who pulled up stakes and departed for the West or went down to the sea in ships, there must have been a certain proportion who, like their mythic prototype, were fleeing the good-provider role.

The work of Demos (1974), a historian, offers considerable support for Fiedler's thesis. He tells us that the burdens thrust on men in the nineteenth century by the new patterns of work began to show their effects in the family. When "the [spatial] separation of the work lives of husbands and wives made communication so problematic," he asks, "what was the likelihood of meaningful communication?" (Demos, 1974, p. 438). The answer is, relatively little. Divorce and separation increased, either formally or by tacit consent—or simply by default, as in the case of a variety of defaulters—tramps, bums, hoboes—among them.

In this connection, "the development of the notorious 'tramp' phenomenon is worth noticing," Demos (1974, p. 438) tells us. The tramp was a man who just gave up, who dropped out of the role entirely. He preferred not to work, but he would do small chores or other small-scale work for a handout if he had to. He was not above begging the housewife for a meal, hoping she would not find work for him to do in repayment. Demos (1974) describes the type:

> Demoralized and destitute wanderers, their numbers mounting into the hundreds of thousands, tramps can be fairly characterized as men who had run away from their wives. . . . Their presence was mute testimony to the strains that tugged at the very core of American family life. . . . Many observers noted that the tramps had created a virtual society of their own [a kind of counterculture] based on a principle of single-sex companionship (p. 438).

A considerable number of them came to be described as "homeless men" and, as the country became more urbanized, landed ultimately on skid row. A large part of the task of social workers for almost a century was the care of the "evaded" women they left behind.[3] When the tramp became wholly demoralized, a chronic alcoholic, almost unreachable, he fell into a category of his own—he was a bum.

Quite a different kettle of fish was the hobo, the migratory worker who spent several months harvesting wheat and other large crops and the rest of the year in cities. Many were the so-called Wobblies, or Industrial Workers of the World, who repudiated the good-provider role on principle. They had contempt for the men who accepted it and could be called conscientious objectors to the role. "In some IWW circles, wives were regarded as the 'ball and chain.' In the West, IWW literature proclaimed that the migratory worker, usually a young, unmarried male, was 'the first specimen of American manhood . . . the leaven of the revolutionary labor movement'" (Foner, 1979, p. 400). Exemplars of the Wobblies were the nomadic workers of the West. They were free men. The migratory worker, "unlike the factory slave of the Atlantic seaboard and the central states, . . . was most emphatically 'not afraid of losing his job.' No wife and family cumbered him. The worker of the East, oppressed by the fear of want for wife and babies, dared not venture much" (Foner, 1979, p. 400). The reference to fear of loss of job was well taken; employers preferred married men, disciplined into the good-provider role, who had given hostages to fortune and were therefore more tractable.

Just on the verge between the area of conformity to the good-provider role—at whatever level—and the area of complete nonconformity to it was the nongood provider, the marginal group of workers usually made up of "the under-educated, the under-trained, the under-employed, or part-time employed, as well as the under-paid, and of course the unemployed" (Snyder, 1979, p. 597). These included men who wanted—sometimes desperately—to perform the good-provider role but who for one reason or another were unable to do so. Liebow (1966) has discussed the ramifications of failure among the black men of Tally's corner. The black man is:

> under legal and social constraints to provide for them [their families], to be a husband to his wife and a father to his children. The chances are, however, that he is failing to provide for them, and failure in this primary function contaminates his performance as father in other aspects as well (p. 86).

In some cases, leaving the family entirely was the best substitute a man could supply. The community was left to take over.[4]

At the other extreme was the overperformer. De Tocqueville, quoted earlier, was already describing him as he manifested in the 1830s. And as late as 1955 Warner and Ableglen were adding to the considerable literature on industrial leaders and tycoons, referring to their "driving concentration" on their careers and their "intense focusing" on interests, energies, and skills on these careers, "even limiting their sexual activity" (pp. 48–49). They came to be known as workaholics or work-intoxicated men. Their preoccupation with their work even at the expense of their families was, as I have already noted, quite acceptable in our society.

Poorly or well performed, the good-provider role lingered on. World War II initiated a challenge, this time in the form of attracting more and more married women into the labor force, but the challenge was papered over in the 1950s with an "age of togetherness" that all but apotheosized the good provider, his house in the suburbs, his homebody wife, and his third, fourth, even fifth, child. As late as the 1960s most housewives (87 percent) still saw breadwinning as their husband's primary role (Lopata, 1971, p. 91).[5]

Intrinsic Conflict in the Good-Provider Role

Since the good-provider role involved both family and work roles, most people believed that there was no incompatibility between them or at least that there should not be. But in the 1960s and 1970s evidence began to mount that maybe something was amiss.

De Tocqueville had documented the implicit conflict in the American businessman's devotion to his work at the expense of his family in the early years of the nineteenth century; the Industrial Workers of the World had proclaimed that the good-provider role which tied a man to his family was an impediment to the great revolution at the beginning of the twentieth century; Fiedler (1962) had noted that throughout our history, in the male fantasy world, there was freedom from the responsibilities of this role; about 50 years ago Freud (1930/1958) had analyzed the intrinsic conflict between the demands of women and the family on one side and the demands of men's work on the other:

Women represented the interests of the family and sexual life, the work of civilization has become more and more men's business; it confronts them with ever harder tasks, compels them to sublimations of instinct which women are not easily able
to achieve. Since man has not an unlimited amount of mental energy at his disposal, he must accomplish his tasks by distributing his libido to the best advantage.
What he employs for cultural [occupational] purposes he withdraws to a great extent
from women, and his sexual life; his constant association with men and his dependence on his relations with them even estrange him from his duties as husband and
father. Woman finds herself thus forced into the background by the claims of culture [work] and she adapts an inimical attitude towards it (pp. 50–51).

In the last two decades, researchers have been raising questions relevant to
Freud's statement of the problem. They have been asking people about the relative satisfactions they derive from these conflicting values—family and work.
Among the earliest studies comparing family—work values was a Gallup poll in
1940 in which both men and women chose a happy home over an interesting
job or wealth as a major life value. Since then there have been a number of such
polls, and considerable body of results has now accumulated. Pleck and Lang
(1979) and Hesselbart (Reference Note 1) have summarized the findings of these
surveys. All agree that there is a clear bias in the direction of the family. Pleck
and Lang conclude that "men's family role is far more psychologically significant
to them than is their work role" (p. 29), and Hesselbart—however critical she is
of the studies she summarizes—believes they should not be dismissed lightly and
concludes that they certainly "challenge the idea that family is a 'secondary' valued role" (p. 14).[6] Douvan (Reference Note 2) also found in a 1976 replication
of a 1957 survey that family values retained priority over work: "Family roles
almost uniformly rate higher in value production than the job role does" (p. 16).[7]
    The very fact that researchers have asked such questions is itself interesting.
Somehow or other both the researchers and the informants seem to be saying
that all this complaining about the male neglect of the family, about the lack of
family involvement by men, just is not warranted. Neither de Tocqueville nor
Freud was right. Men do value family life more than they value their work. They
do derive their major life satisfactions from their families rather than from their
work.
    It may well be true that men derive the greatest satisfaction from their fam-
ily roles, but this does not necessarily mean they are willing to pay for the benefit. In any event, great attitudinal changes took place in the 1960s and 1970s.
    Douvan (Reference Note 2), on the basis of surveys in 1957 and 1976,
found, for example, a considerable increase in the proportion of both men and
women who found marriage and parenthood burdensome and restrictive. Almost
three-fifths (57 percent) of both married men and married women in 1976 saw
marriages as "all burdens and restrictions," as compared with only 42 percent and
47 percent, respectively, in 1957. And almost half (45 percent) also viewed children as "all burdens and restrictions" in 1976, as compared with only 28 percent
and 33 percent for married men and married women, respectively, in 1957. The
proportion of working men with a positive attitude toward marriage dropped
drastically over this period, from 68 percent to 39 percent. Working women, who
made up a fairly small number of all married women in 1957, hardly changed

attitudes at all, dropping only from 43 percent to 42 percent. The proportion of working men who found marriage and children burdensome and restrictive more than doubled, from 25 percent to 56 percent and from 25 percent to 58 percent, respectively. Although some of these changes reflected greater willingness in 1976 than in 1957 to admit negative attitudes toward marriage and parenthood—itself significant—profound changes were clearly in process. More and more men and women were experiencing disaffection with family life.[8]

"All Burdens and Restrictions"

Apparently, the benefits of the good-provider role were greater than the costs for most men. Despite the legend of the flight of the American male (Fiedler, 1962), despite the defectors and dropouts, despite the tavern habitués "ball and chain" cliché, men seemed to know that the good-provider role, if they could succeed in it, was good for them. But Douvan's (Reference Note 2) findings suggest that recently their complaints have become serious, bone-deep. The family they have been providing for is not the same family it was in the past.

Smith (1979) calls the great trek of married women into the labor force a subtle revolution—revolutionary not in the sense of one class overthrowing a status quo and substituting its own regime, but revolutionary in its impact on both the family and the work roles of men and women. It diluted the prerogatives of the good-provider role. It increased the demands made on the good provider, especially in the form of more emotional investment in the family, more sharing of household responsibilities. The role became even more burdensome.

However men may now feel about the burdens and restrictions imposed on them by the good-provider role, most have, at least ostensibly, accepted them. The tramp and the bum had "voted with their feet" against the role; the hobo or Wobbly had rejected it on the basis of a revolutionary ideology that saw it as enslaving men to the corporation; tavern humor had glossed the resentment habitués felt against its demands. Now the "burdens-and-restrictions" motif has surfaced both in research reports and, more blatantly, in the male liberation movement. From time to time it has also appeared in the clinicians' notes.

Sometimes the resentment of the good provider takes the form of simply wanting more appreciation for the lifestyle he provides. All he does for his family seems to be taken for granted. Thus, for example, Goldberg (1976), a psychiatrist, recounts the case of a successful businessman:

> He's feeling a deepening sense of bitterness and frustration about his wife and family. He doesn't feel appreciated. It angers him the way they seem to take the things his earnings purchase for granted. They've come to expect it as their due. It particularly enrages him when his children put him down for his "materialistic middle-class trip." He'd like to tell them to get someone else to support them but he holds himself back (p. 124).

Brenton (1966) quotes a social worker who describes an upper-middle-class woman: She has "gotten hold of a man who'll drive himself mad to get money, and [is] denigrating him for being too interested in money, and not interested in music, or the arts, or in spending time with the children. But at the same time she's subtly driving him—and doesn't know it" (p. 226). What seems significant about such cases is not that men feel resentful about the lack of appreciation but that they are willing to justify their resentment. They are no longer willing to grin and bear it.

Sometimes there is even more than expressed resentment; there is an actual repudiation of the role. In the past, only a few men like the hobo or Wobbly were likely to give up. Today, Goldberg (1976) believes more are ready to renounce the role, not on theoretical revolutionary grounds, however, but on purely selfish ones:

> Male growth will stem from openly avowed, unashamed, self-oriented motivation. . . . Guilt-oriented "should" behavior will be rejected because it is always at the price of a hidden build-up of resentment and frustration and alienation from others and is, therefore, counterproductive (p. 184).

The disaffection of the good provider is directed to both sides of his role. With respect to work, Lefkowitz (1979) has described men among whom the good-provider role is neither being completely rejected nor repudiated, but diluted. These men began their working lives in the conventional style, hopeful and ambitious. They found a job, married, raised a family, and "achieved a measure of economic security and earned the respect of . . . colleagues and neighbors" (Lefkowitz, 1979, p. 31). In brief, they successfully performed the good-provider role. But unlike their historical predecessors, they in time became disillusioned with their jobs—not jobs on assembly lines, not jobs usually characterized as alienating, but fairly prestigious jobs such as aeronautics engineer and government economist. They daydreamed about other interests. "The common theme which surfaced again and again in their histories was the need to find a new social connection—to reassert control over their lives, to gain some sense of freedom" (Lefkowitz, 1979, p. 31). These men felt "entitled to freedom and independence." Middle-class, educated, self-assured, articulate, and for the most part white, they knew they could talk themselves into a job if they had to. Most of them did not want to desert their families. Indeed, most of them "wanted to rejoin the intimate circle they felt they had neglected in their years of work" (p. 31).

Though some of the men Lefkowitz studied sought closer ties with their families, in the case of those studied by Sarason (1977), a psychologist, career changes involved lower income and had a negative impact on families. Sarason's subjects were also men in high-level professions, the very men least likely to find marriage and parenthood burdensome and restrictive. Still, since career change often involved a reduction in pay, some wives were unwilling to accept it, with the result that the marriage deteriorated (p. 178). Sometimes it looked like a no-win game. The husband's earlier career brought him feelings of emptiness and alienation, but it also brought financial rewards for the family. Greater work satisfaction for him in lower paying work meant reduced satisfaction with lifestyle. These findings lead Sarason to raise a number of points with respect to the good-provider role. "How much," he asks, "does an individual or a family need in order to maintain a satisfactory existence? Is an individual being responsible to himself or to his family if he provides them with little more than the bare essentials of living?" (p. 178). These [are] questions about the good-provider role that few men raised in the past.

Lefkowitz (1979) wonders how his downwardly mobile men lived when they left their jobs. "They put together a basic economic package which consisted of government assistance, contributions from family members who had not worked before and some bartering of goods and services" (p. 31). Especially interesting in this list of income sources are the "contributions from family members who had not worked before" (p. 31). Surely not mothers and sisters. Who, of course, but wives?

Women and the Provider Role

The present discussion began with the woman's part in the provider role. We saw how as more and more of the provisioning of the family came to be by way of monetary exchange, the woman's part shrank. A woman could still provide services, but could furnish little in the way of food, clothing, and shelter. But now that she is entering the labor force in large numbers, she can once more resume her ancient role, this time, like her male counterpart the provider, by way of a monetary contribution. More and more women are doing just this.

The assault of the good-provider role in the Depression was traumatic. But a modified version began to appear in the 1970s as a single income became inadequate for more and more families. Husbands have remained the major providers, but in an increasing number of cases the wife has begun to share this role. Thus, the proportion of married women aged 15 to 54 (living with their husbands) in the labor force more than doubled between 1950 and 1978, from 25.2 percent to 55.4 percent. . . . Fewer women are now full-time housewives.

For some men the relief from the strain of sole responsibility for the provider role has been welcome. But for others the feeling of degradation resembles the feeling reported 40 years earlier in the Great Depression. It is not that they are no longer providing for the family but that the role-sharing wife now feels justified in making demands on them. The good-provider role with all its prerogatives and perquisites has undergone profound changes. It will never be the same again.[9] Its death knell was sounded when, as noted above, the 1980 census no longer automatically assumed that the male member of the household was its head.

The Current Scene

Among the new demands being made on the good-provider role, two deserve special consideration, namely, (1) more intimacy, expressivity, and nurturance—specifications never included in it as it originally took shape—and (2) more sharing of household responsibilities and child care.

As the pampered wife in an affluent household came often to be an economic parasite, so also the good provider was often, in a way, a kind of emotional parasite. Implicit in the definition of the role was that he provided goods and material things. Tender loving care was not one of the requirements. Emotional ministrations from the family were his right; providing them was not a corresponding obligation. Therefore, as de Tocqueville had already noted by 1840, women suffered a kind of emotional deprivation labeled by Robert Weiss "relational deficit" (cited in Bernard, 1976). Only recently has this male rejection of emotional expression come to be challenged. Today, even blue-collar women are imposing "a host of new role expectations upon their husbands or lovers. . . . A new role set asks the blue-collar male to strive for . . . deep-coursing intimacy" (Shostak, Reference Note 4, p. 75). It was not only vis-à-vis his family that the good provider was lacking in expressivity. This lack was built into the whole male role script. Today not only women but also men are beginning to protest the repudiation of expressivity prescribed in male roles (David and Brannon, 1976; Farrell, 1974; Fasteau, 1974; Pleck and Sawyer, 1974).

Is there any relationship between the "imposing" on men of "deep-coursing intimacy" by women on one side and the increasing proportion of men who find marriage burdensome and restrictive on the other? Are men seeing the new emotional involvement being asked of them as "all burdens and restrictions"? Are they responding to the new involvements under duress? Are they feeling oppressed by them? Fearful of them?

From the standpoint of high-level pure-science research there may be something bizarre, if not even slightly absurd, in the growing corpus of serious research on how much or how little husbands of employed wives contribute to household chores and child care. Yet it is serious enough that all over the industrialized world such research is going on. Time studies in a dozen countries—communist as well as capitalist—trace the slow and bungling process by which marriage accommodates to changing conditions and by which women struggle to mold the changing conditions in their behalf. For everywhere the same picture shows up in research: an image of women sharing the provider role and at the same time retaining responsibility for the household. Until recently such a topic would have been judged unworthy of serious attention. It was a subject that might be worth a good laugh, for instance, as when an all-thumbs man in a cartoon burns the potatoes or finds himself bumbling awkwardly over a diaper, demonstrating his—proud—male ineptness at such female work. But it is no longer funny.

The "politics of housework" (Mainardi, 1970) proves to be more profound than originally believed. It has to do not only with tasks but also with gender—and perhaps more with the site of the tasks than with their intrinsic nature. A man can cook magnificently if he does it on a hunting or fishing trip; he can wield a skillful needle if he does it mending a tent or a fishing net; he can even feed and clean a toddler on a camping trip. Few of the skills of the homemaker are beyond his reach so long as they are practiced in a suitably male environment. It is not only women's work in and of itself that is degrading but any work on female turf. It may be true, as Brenton (1966) says, that "the secure man can wash a dish, diaper a baby, and throw the dirty clothes into the washing machine—or do anything else women used to do exclusively—without thinking twice about it" (p. 211), but not all men are that secure. To a great many men such chores are demasculinizing. The apron is shameful on a man in the kitchen; it is all right at the carpenter's bench.

The male world may look upon the man who shares household responsibilities as, in effect, a scab. One informant tells the interviewer about a conversation on the job: "What, are you crazy?" his hard-hat fellow workers ask him when he speaks of helping his wife. "The guys want to kill me. 'You son of a bitch! You are getting us in trouble.' . . . The men get really mad" (Lein, 1979, p. 492). Something more than persiflage is involved here. We are fairly familiar with the trauma associated with the invasion by women of the male work turf, the hazing women can be subjected to, and the male resentment of admitting them except into their own segregated areas. The corresponding entrance of men into the traditional turf of women—the kitchen or the nursery—has analogous but not identical concomitants.

Pleck and Lang (1979) tell us that men are now beginning to change in the direction of greater involvement in family life. "Men's family behavior is beginning to change, becoming increasingly congruent with the long-standing psychological significance of the family in their lives" (p. 1). They measure this greater involvement by way of the help they offer with homemaking chores. Scanzoni (1975), on the basis of a survey of over 3,000 husbands and wives, concludes that at least in households in which wives are in the labor force, there is the "possibility of a different pattern in which responsibility for households would unequivocally fall equally on husbands as well as wives" (p. 38). A brave new world indeed. Still, when we look at the reality around us, the pace seems intolerably slow. The responsibilities of the old good-provider role have attenuated far faster than have its prerogatives and privileges.

A considerable amount of thought has been devoted to studying the effects of the large influx of women into the work force. An equally interesting question is what the effect will be if a large number of men actually do increase their participation in the family and the household. Will men find the apron shameful? What if we were to ask fathers to alternate with mothers in being in the home when youngsters come home from school? Would fighting adolescent drug abuse be more successful if fathers and mothers were equally engaged in it? If the school could confer with fathers as often as with mothers? If the father accompanied children when they went shopping for clothes? If fathers spent as much time with children as do mothers?

Even as husbands, let alone as fathers, the new pattern is not without trauma. Hall and Hall (1979), in their study of two-career couples, report that the most serious fights among such couples occur not in the bedroom, but in the kitchen, between couples who profess a commitment to equality but who find actually implementing it difficult. A young professional reports that he is philosophically committed to egalitarianism in marriage and tries hard to practice it, but it does not work. He even feels guilty about this. The stresses involved in reworking roles may have an impact on health. A study of engineers and accountants finds poorer health among those with employed wives than among those with nonemployed wives (Burke and Wier, 1976). The processes involved in role change have been compared with those involved in deprogramming a cult member. Are they part of the increasing sense of marriage and parenthood as "all burdens and restrictions"?

The demise of the good-provider role also calls for consideration of other questions: What does the demotion of the good provider to the status of senior provider or even more coprovider do to him? To marriage? To gender identity? What does expanding the role of housewife to that of junior provider or even coprovider do to her? To marriage? To gender identity? Much will of course depend on the social and psychological ambience in which changes take place.

A Parable

I began this essay with a proverbial woman. I close it with a modern parable by William H. Chafe (Reference Note 5), a historian who also keeps his eye on the current scene. Jack and Jill, both planning professional careers, he as doctor, she as lawyer, marry at age 24. She works to put him through medical school in the expectation that he will then finance her through law school. A child is born during the husband's internship, as planned. But in order for him to support her through professional training as planned, he will have to take time out from his career. After two years, they decide that both will continue their training on a part-time basis, sharing household responsibilities and using day-care services. Both find part-time positions and work out flexible work schedules that leave both of them time for child care and companionship with one another. They live happily ever after.

That's the end? you ask incredulously. Well, not exactly. For, as Chafe (Reference Note 5) points out, as usual the personal is also political:

> Obviously such a scenario presumes a radical transformation of the personal values that today's young people bring to their relationships as well as a readiness on the part of social and economic institutions to encourage, or at least make possible, the development of equality between men and women (p. 28).

The good-provider role may be on its way out, but its legitimate successor has not yet appeared on the scene.

Notes

1. Rainwater and Yancy (1967), critiquing current welfare policies, note that they "have robbed men of their manhood, women of their husbands, and children of their fathers. To create a stable monogamous family we need to provide men with the opportunity to be men, and that involves enabling them to perform occupationally" (p. 235).

2. Several years ago I presented a critique of what I called "extreme sex role specialization," including "work-intoxicated fathers." I noted that making success in the provider role the only test for real manliness was putting a lot of eggs into one basket. At both the blue-collar and the managerial

222222222

levels, it was dysfunctional for families. I referred to the several attempts being made even then to correct the excesses of extreme sex role specialization: rural and urban communes, leaving jobs to take up small-scale enterprises that allowed more contact with families, and a rebellion against overtime in industry (Bernard, 1975, pp. 217–239).

3. In one department of a South Carolina cotton mill early in the century, "every worker was a grass widow" (Smuts, 1959, p. 54). Many women worked "because their husbands refused to provide for their families. There is no reason to think that husbands abandoned their duties more often than today, but the woman who was burdened by an irresponsible husband in 1890 usually had no recourse save taking on his responsibilities herself. If he deserted, the law-enforcement agencies of the time afforded little chance of finding and compelling him to provide support" (Smuts, 1959, p. 54). The situation is not greatly improved today. In divorce child support is allotted in only a small number of cases and enforced in even fewer. "Roughly half of all families with an absent parent don't have awards at all. . . . Where awards do exist they are usually for small amounts, typically ranging from $7 to $18 per child" (Jones, 1976, abstract). A summary of all the studies available concludes that "approximately 20 percent of all divorced and separated mothers receive child support regularly, with an additional 7 percent receiving it 'sometimes': 8 percent of all divorced and separated women receive alimony regularly or sometimes" (Jones, 1976, p. 23).

4. Even though the annals of social work agencies are filled with cases of runaway husbands, in 1976 only 12.6 percent of all women were in the status of divorce and separation, and at least some of them were still being "provided for." Most men were at least trying to fulfill the good-provider role.

5. Although all the women in Lopata's (1971) sample saw breadwinning as important, fewer employed women (54 percent) than either nonemployed urban (63 percent) or suburban (64 percent) women assigned it first place (p. 91).

6. Pleck and Lang (1979) found only one serious study contradicting their own conclusions: "Using data from the 1973 NORC (National Opinion Research Center) General Social Survey, Harry analyzed the bivariate relationship of job and family satisfaction to life happiness in men classified by family life cycle stage. In three of the five groups of husbands . . . job satisfaction had a stronger association than family satisfaction to life happiness" (pp. 5–6).

7. In 1978, a Yankelovich survey on "The New Work Psychology" suggested that leisure is now becoming a strict competitor for both family and work as a source of life satisfactions: "Family and work have grown less important than leisure; a majority of 60 percent say that although they enjoy their work, it is not their major source of satisfaction" (p. 46). A 1977 survey of Swedish men aged 18 to 35 found that the proportion saying that the family was the main source of meaning in their lives declined from 45 percent in 1955 to 41 percent in 1977; the proportion indicating work as the main source of satisfaction dropped from 33 percent to 17 percent. The earlier tendency for men to identify themselves through their work is less marked these days. In the new value system, the individual says, in effect, "I am more than my role. I am myself" (Yankelovich, 1978). Is the increasing concern with leisure a way to escape the dissatisfaction with both the alienating relations found on the work site and the demands for increased involvement with the family?

8. Men seem to be having problems with both work and family roles. Veroff (Reference Note 3), for example, reports an increased "sense of dissatisfaction with the social relations in the work setting" and a "dissatisfaction with the affiliative nature of work" (p. 47). This dissatisfaction may be one of the factors that leads men to seek affiliative-need satisfaction in marriage, just as in the nineteenth century they looked to the home as shelter from the jungle of the outside world.

9. Among the indices of the waning of the good-provider role are the increasing number of married women in the labor force; the growth in the number of female-headed families; the growing trend toward egalitarian norms in marriage; the need for two earners in so many middle-class families; and the recognition of these trends in the abandonment of the identification of head of household as a male.

Reference Notes

1. Hasselbart, S. *Some underemphasized issues about men, women, and work.* Unpublished manuscript, 1978.

2. Douvan, E. *Family roles in a twenty-year perspective.* Paper presented at the Radcliffe Pre-Centennial Conference. Cambridge, Massachusetts, April 2–4, 1978.

3. Veroff, J. *Psychological orientations to the work role: 1957–1976.* Unpublished manuscript, 1978.

4. Shostak, A. *Working class Americans at home: Changing expectations of manhood.* Unpublished manuscript, 1973.

5. Chafe, W. *The challenge of sex equality: A new culture or old values revisited?* Paper presented at the Radcliffe Pre-Centennial Conference. Cambridge, Massachusetts, April 2–4, 1978.

References

BABCOCK, B., FREEDMAN, A. E., NORTON, E. H., and ROSS, S. C. *Sex discrimination and the law: Causes and remedies.* Boston: Little, Brown, 1975.

BERNARD, J. *Women, wives, mothers.* Chicago: Aldine, 1975.

BERNARD, J. Homosociality and female depression. *Journal of Social Issues,* 1976, 32, 207–224.

BOULDING, E. Familial constraints on women's work roles. *SIGNS: Journal of Women in Culture and Society.* 1976, 1, 95–118.

BRENTON, M. *The American male.* New York: Coward-McCann, 1966.

BURKE, R., and WEIR, T. "Relationships of wives' employment status to husband, wife and pair satisfaction and performance." *Journal of Marriage and the Family,* 1976, 38, 279–287.

DAVID, D. S., and BRANNON, R. (eds.). *The forty-nine percent majority: The male sex role.* Reading, Mass.: Addison-Wesley, 1976.

DEMOS, J. "The American family in past time." *American Scholar,* 1974, 43, 422–446.

FARRELL, W. *The liberated man.* New York: Random House, 1974.

FASTEAU, M. F. *The male machine.* New York: McGraw-Hill, 1974.

FIEDLER, L. *Love and death in the American novel.* New York: Meredith, 1962.

FONER, P. S. *Women and the American labor movement.* New York: Free Press, 1979.

FREUD, S. *Civilization and its discontents.* New York: Doubleday-Anchor, 1958. (Originally published, 1930.)

GOLDBERG, H. *The hazards of being male.* New York: New American Library, 1976.

GOULD, R. E. "Measuring masculinity by the size of a paycheck." In J. E. Pleck and J. Sawyer (eds.), *Men and masculinity.* Englewood Cliffs, N.J.: Prentice Hall, 1974. (Also published in *Ms.,* June 1973, pp. 18ff.)

HALL, D., and HALL, F. *The two-career couple.* Reading, Mass.: Addison-Wesley, 1979.

JONES, C. A. *A review of child support payment performance.* Washington, D.C.: Urban Institute, 1976.

KENISTON, K. *The uncommitted: Alienated youth in American society.* New York: Harcourt, Brace & World, 1965.

KOMAROVSKY, M. *The unemployed man and his family.* New York: Dryden Press, 1940.

LEFKOWITZ, B. Life without work. *Newsweek,* May 14, 1979, p. 31.

LEIN, L. "Responsibility in the allocation of tasks." *Family Coordinator,* 1979, 28, 489–496.

LIEBOW, E. *Tally's corner.* Boston: Little, Brown, 1966.

LOPATA, H. *Occupational housewife.* New York: Oxford University Press, 1971.

MAINARDI, P. "The politics of housework." In R. Morgan (ed.), *Sisterhood is powerful.* New York: Vintage Books, 1970.

PLECK, J. H., and LANG, L. "Men's family work: Three perspectives and some new data." *Family Coordinator,* 1979, 28, 481–488.

PLECK, J. H., and SAWYER, J. (eds.), *Men and masculinity.* Englewood Cliffs, N.J.: Prentice Hall, 1974.

RAINWATER, L., and YANCY, W. L. *The Moynihan report and the politics of controversy.* Cambridge, Mass.: M.I.T. Press, 1967.

SARASON, S. B. *Work, aging, and social change.* New York: Free Press, 1977.

SCANZONI, J. H. *Sex roles, life styles, and childbearing: Changing patterns in marriage and the family.* New York: Free Press, 1975.

SCANZONI, J. H. "An historical perspective on husband-wife bargaining power and marital dissolution." In G. Levinger and O. Moles (eds.), *Divorce and separation in America.* New York: Basic Books, 1979.

SMUTS, R. W. *Women and work in America.* New York: Columbia University Press, 1959.

SNYDER, L. "The deserting, non-supporting father: Scapegoat of family non-policy." *Family Coordinator*, 1979, 38, 594–598.

TOCQUEVILLE, A. DE. *Democracy in America.* New York: J. & H. G. Hangley, 1840.

WARNER, W. L., and ABLEGGLEN, J. O. *Big business leaders in America.* New York: Harper, 1955.

YANKELOVICH, D. "The new psychological contracts at work." *Psychology Today*, May, 1978, pp. 46–47; 49–50.

ZBOROWSKI, M., and HERZOG, E. *Life is with people.* New York: Schocken Books, 1952.

A Speed-up in the Family*

Arlie Hochschild with Anne Machung

The previous selection examined male role definitions in a world where work and family are in separate spheres. As more and more women are economically active, however, role definitions are changing. Arlie Hochschild and Anne Machung point out that while women have entered the labor force, men's participation in work at home has not changed as quickly. The result is that women who work outside of the home have a "second shift"—a set of responsibilities in the household when they come home after a full day at work. These responsibilities are still defined as women's work. As this selection illustrates, one result is that the juggling of work and family responsibilities becomes defined more as a women's than a men's issue.

She is not the same woman in each magazine advertisement, but she is the same idea. She has that working-mother look as she strides forward, briefcase in one hand, smiling child in the other. Literally and figuratively, she is moving ahead. Her hair, if long, tosses behind her; if it is short, it sweeps back at the sides, suggesting mobility and progress. There is nothing shy or passive about her. She is confident, active, "liberated." She wears a dark tailored suit, but with a silk bow or colorful frill that says, "I'm really feminine underneath." She has made it in a man's world without sacrificing her femininity. And she has done this on her own. By some personal miracle, this image suggests, she has managed to combine what 150 years of industrialization have split wide apart—child and job, frill and suit, female culture and male.

When I showed a photograph of a supermom like this to the working mothers I talked to in the course of researching this book, many responded with an outright laugh. One day-care worker and mother of two, ages three and five, threw back her head: "Ha! They've got to be *kidding* about her. Look at me, hair a mess, nails jagged, twenty pounds overweight. Mornings, I'm getting my kids dressed, the dog fed, the lunches made, the shopping list done. That lady's got a maid." Even working mothers who did have maids couldn't imagine combining work and family in such a carefree way. "Do you know what a baby *does* to your life, the two o'clock feedings, the four o'clock feedings?" Another mother of two said: "They don't show it, but she's whistling"—she imitated a whistling woman, eyes to the sky—"so she can't hear the din." They envied the apparent ease of the woman with the flying hair, but she didn't remind them of anyone they knew.

The women I interviewed—lawyers, corporate executives, word processors, garment pattern cutters, day-care workers—and most of their husbands, too—felt differently about some issues: how right it is for a mother of young children to work a full-time job, or how much a husband should be responsible for the home. But they all agreed that it was hard to work two full-time jobs and raise young children.

How well do couples do it? The more women work outside the home, the more central this question. The number of women in paid work has risen steadily since before the turn of the century, but since 1950 the rise has been staggering. In 1950, 30 percent of American women were in the labor force; in 1986, it was 55 percent. In 1950, 28 percent of married women with children between six and seventeen worked outside the home; in 1986, it had risen to 68 percent. In 1950, 23 percent of married women with children under six worked. By 1986, it had grown to 54 percent. We don't know how many women with children under the age of one worked outside the home in 1950; it was so rare that the Bureau of Labor kept no statistics on it. Today half of such women do. Two-thirds of all mothers are now in the labor force; in fact, more mothers have paid jobs (or are actively looking for one) than nonmothers. Because of this change in women, two-job families now make up 58 percent of all married couples with children.[1]

Since an increasing number of working women have small children, we might expect an increase in part-time work. But actually, 67 percent of the mothers who work have full-time jobs—that is, 35 hours or more weekly. That proportion is what it was in 1959.

If more mothers of young children are stepping into full-time jobs outside the home, and if most couples can't afford household help, how much more are fathers doing at home? As I began exploring this question I found many studies on the hours working men and women devote to housework and child care. One national random sample of 1,243 working parents in 44 American cities, conducted in 1965–66 by Alexander Szalai and his co-workers, for example, found that working women averaged three hours a day on housework while men averaged 17 minutes; women spent 50 minutes a day of time exclusively with their children; men spent 12 minutes. On the other side of the coin, working fathers watched television an hour longer than their working wives, and slept a half-hour longer each night. A comparison of this American sample with 11 other industrial countries in Eastern and Western Europe revealed the same difference between working women and working men in those countries as well.[2] In a 1983 study of white middle-class families in greater Boston, Grace Baruch and R. C. Barnett found that working men married to working women spent only three-quarters of an hour longer each week with their kindergarten-aged children than did men married to housewives.[3]

Szalai's landmark study documented the now familiar but still alarming story of the working woman's "double day," but it left me wondering how men and women actually felt about all this. He and his co-workers studied how people used time, but not, say, how a father felt about his 12 minutes with his child, or how his wife felt about it. Szalai's study revealed the visible surface of what I discovered to be a set of deeply emotional issues: What should a man and woman contribute to the family? How appreciated does each feel? How does each respond to subtle changes in the balance of marital power? How does each develop an unconscious "gender strategy" for coping with the work at home, with marriage, and, indeed, with life itself? These were the underlying issues.

But I began with the measurable issue of time. Adding together the time it takes to do a paid job and to do housework and child care, I averaged estimates from the major studies on time use done in the 1960s and 1970s, and discovered that women worked roughly 15 hours longer each week than men. Over a year, they worked an *extra month of twenty-four-hour days a year.* Over a dozen years, it was an extra year of 24-hour days. Most women without children spend much more time than men on housework; with children, they devote more time to both housework and child care. Just as there is a wage gap between men and women in the workplace, there is a "leisure gap" between them at home. Most women work one shift at the office or factory and a "second shift" at home.

Studies show that working mothers have higher self-esteem and get less depressed than housewives, but compared to their husbands, they're more tired and get sick more often. In Peggy Thoits's 1985 analysis of two large-scale surveys, each of about 1,000 men and women, people were asked how often in the preceding week they'd experienced each of 23 symptoms of anxiety (such as dizziness or hallucinations). According to the researchers' criteria, working mothers were more likely than any other group to be "anxious."

In light of these studies, the image of the woman with the flying hair seems like an upbeat "cover" for a grim reality, like those pictures of Soviet tractor drivers smiling radiantly into the distance as they think about the ten-year plan. The Szalai study was conducted in 1965–66. I wanted to know whether the leisure gap he found in 1965 persists, or whether it has disappeared. Since most married couples work two jobs, since more will in the future, since most wives in these couples work the extra month a year, I wanted to understand what the wife's extra month a year meant for each person, and what it does for love and marriage in an age of high divorce.

My Research

With my research associates Anne Machung and Elaine Kaplan, I interviewed 50 couples very intensively, and I observed in a dozen homes. We first began interviewing artisans, students, and professionals in Berkeley, California, in the late 1970s. This was at the height of the women's movement, and many of these couples were earnestly and self-consciously struggling to modernize the ground rules of their marriages. Enjoying flexible job schedules and intense cultural support to do so, many succeeded. Since their circumstances were unusual they became our "comparison group" as we sought other couples more typical of mainstream America. In 1980 we located more typical couples by sending a questionnaire on work and family life to every thirteenth name—from top to bottom—of the personnel roster of a large, urban manufacturing company. At the end of the questionnaire, we asked members of working couples raising children under six and working full-time jobs if they would be willing to talk to us in greater depth. Interviewed from 1980 through 1988, these couples, their neighbors and friends, their children's teachers, day-care workers and baby-sitters, form the heart of this [analysis].

Inside the Extra Month a Year

The women I interviewed seemed to be far more deeply torn between the demands of work and family than were their husbands. They talked with more animation and at greater length than their husbands about the abiding conflict between them. Busy as they were, women more often brightened at the idea of yet another interviewing session. They felt the second shift was *their* issue and most of their husbands agreed. When I telephoned one husband to arrange an interview with him, explaining that I wanted to ask him about how he managed work and family life, he replied genially, "Oh, this will *really* interest my *wife.*"

It was a woman who first proposed to me the metaphor, borrowed from industrial life, of the "second shift." She strongly resisted the *idea* that homemaking was a "shift." Her family was her life and she didn't want it reduced to a job. But as she put it, "You're on duty at work. You come home, and you're on duty. Then you go back to work and you're on duty." After eight hours of adjusting insurance claims, she came home to put on the rice for dinner, care for her children, and wash laundry. Despite herself her home life *felt* like a second shift. That was the real story and that was the real problem.

Men who shared the load at home seemed just as pressed for time as their wives, and as torn between the demands of career and small children. . . . But the majority of men did not share the load at home. Some refused outright. Others refused more passively, often offering a loving shoulder to lean on, an understanding ear as their working wife faced the conflict they both saw as hers. At first it seemed to me that the problem of the second shift was hers. But I came to realize that those husbands who helped very little at home were often indirectly just as deeply affected as their wives by the need to do that work, through the resentment their wives feel toward them, and through their need to steel themselves against that resentment. Evan Holt, a warehouse furniture salesman . . . did very little housework and played with his four-year-old son, Joey, at his convenience. Juggling the demands of work with family at first seemed a problem for his wife. But Evan himself suffered enormously from the side effects of "her" problem. His wife did the second shift, but she resented it keenly, and half-consciously expressed her frustration and rage by losing interest in sex and becoming overly absorbed with Joey. One way or another, most men I talked with do suffer the severe repercussions of what I think is a transitional phase in American family life.

One reason women take a deeper interest than men in the problems of juggling work with family life is that even when husbands happily shared the hours of work, their wives felt more *responsible* for home and children. More women kept track of doctors' appointments and arranged for playmates to come over. More mothers than fathers worried about the tail on a child's Halloween costume or a birthday present for a school friend. They were more likely to think about their children while at work and to check in by phone with the baby-sitter.

Partly because of this, more women felt torn between one sense of urgency and another, between the need to soothe a child's fear of being left at day care, and the need to show the boss she's "serious" at work. More women than men questioned how good they were as parents, or if they did not, they questioned why they weren't questioning it. More often than men, women alternated between living in their ambition and standing apart from it.

As masses of women have moved into the economy, families have been hit by a "speed-up" in work and family life. There is no more time in the day than there was when wives stayed home, but there is twice as much to get done. It is mainly women who absorb this "speed-up." Twenty percent of the men in my study shared housework equally. Seventy percent of men did a substantial amount (less than half but more than a third), and 10 percent did less than a third. Even when couples share more equitably in the work at home, women do two-thirds of the *daily* jobs at home, like cooking and cleaning up—jobs that fix them into a rigid routine. Most women cook dinner and most men change the oil in the family car. But, as one mother pointed out, dinner needs to be prepared every evening around six o'clock, whereas the car oil needs to be changed every six months, any day around that time, any time that day. Women do more child care than men, and men repair more household appliances. A child needs to be tended daily while the repair of household appliances can often wait "until I have time." Men thus have more control over *when* they make their contributions than women do. They may be very busy with family chores but, like the executive who tells his secretary to "hold my calls," the man has more control over his time. The job of the working mother, like that of the secretary, is usually to "take the calls."

Another reason women may feel more strained than men is that women more often do two things at once—for example, write checks and return phone calls, vacuum and keep an eye on a three-year-old, fold laundry, and think out the shopping list. Men more often cook dinner *or* take a child to the park. Indeed, women more often juggle three spheres—job, children, and housework—while most men juggle two—job and children. For women, two activities compete with their time with children, not just one.

Beyond doing more at home, women also devote *proportionately more* of their time at home to housework and proportionately less of it to child care. Of all the time men spend working at home, more of it goes to child care. That is, working wives spend relatively more time "mothering the house"; husbands spend more time "mothering" the children. Since most parents prefer to tend to their children than clean house, men do more of what they'd rather do. More men than women take their children on "fun" outings to the park, the zoo, the movies. Women spend more time on maintenance, feeding and bathing children, enjoyable activities to be sure, but often less leisurely or "special" than going to the zoo. Men also do fewer of the "undesirable" household chores: fewer men than women wash toilets and scrub the bathroom.

As a result, women tend to talk more intently about being overtired, sick, and "emotionally drained." Many women I could not tear away from the topic of sleep. They talked about how much they could "get by on" . . . six and a half, seven, seven and a half, less, more. They talked about who they knew who needed more or less. Some apologized for how much sleep they needed—"I'm afraid I need eight hours of sleep"—as if eight was "too much." They talked about the effect of a change in baby-sitter, the birth of a second child, or a business trip on their child's pattern of sleep. They talked about how to avoid fully waking up when a child called them at night, and how to get back to sleep. These women talked about sleep the way a hungry person talks about food.

All in all, if in this period of American history, the two-job family is suffering from a speed-up of work and family life, working mothers are its primary victims. It is ironic, then, that often it falls to women to be the "time and motion expert" of family life. Watching inside homes, I noticed it was often the mother who rushed children, saying, "Hurry up! It's time to go," "Finish your cereal now," "You can do that later," "Let's go!" When a bath is crammed into a slot between 7:45 and 8:00 it was often the mother who called out, "Let's see who can take their bath the quickest!" Often a younger child will rush out, scurrying to be first in bed, while the older and wiser one stalls, resistant, sometimes resentful: "Mother is always rushing us." Sadly enough, women are more often the lightning rods for family aggressions aroused by the speed-up of work and family life. They are the "villains" in a process of which they are also the primary victims. More than the longer hours, the sleeplessness, and feeling torn, this is the saddest cost to women of the extra month a year.

Notes

1. U.S. Bureau of Labor Statistics, *Employment and Earnings, Characteristics of Families: First Quarter* (Washington, D.C.: U.S. Department of Labor, 1988).

2. Alexander Szalai, ed., *The Use of Time: Daily Activities of Urban and Suburban Populations in Twelve Countries* (The Hague: Mouton, 1972), p. 668, Table B. Another study found that men spent a longer time than women eating meals (Shelley Coverman, "Gender, Domestic Labor Time and Wage Inequality," *American Sociological Review* 48 [1983]: 626). With regard to sleep, the pattern differs for men and women. The higher the social class of a man, the more sleep he's likely to get. The higher the class of a woman, the less sleep she's likely to get. (Upper-white-collar men average 7.6 hours sleep a night. Lower-white-collar, skilled and unskilled men all averaged 7.3 hours. Upper-white-collar women average 7.1 hours of sleep; lower-white-collar workers average 7.4; skilled workers 7.0 and unskilled workers 8.1.) Working wives seem to meet the demands of high-pressure careers by reducing sleep, whereas working husbands don't.

3. Grace K. Baruch and Rosalind Barnett, "Correlates of Fathers' Participation in Family Work: A Technical Report," Working Paper no. 106 (Wellesley, Mass.: Wellesley College Center for Research on Women, 1983), pp. 80–81. Also see Kathryn E. Walker and Margaret E. Woods, *Time Use: A Measure of Household Production of Goods and Services* (Washington, D.C.: American Home Economics Association, 1976).

What Does Family Mean?*

Norval D. Glenn

The opening selection in this reader contrasted ideal and reality in family life. This piece by Norval D. Glenn echoes this issue. He presents data indicating that what Americans say about family life is very different than what they do, particularly in the area of marriage. Glenn uses public opinion data to contrast the ideal with the reality, and again raises an issue discussed in several other articles in this book—"Is the family in decline?"

If you believe what Americans say about their values, then families are doing fine. In survey after survey, traditional relationships among parents, children, and siblings are identified as the most important aspect of life. Families are seen as more important than work, recreation, friendships, or status. Researchers have been asking Americans about their families for over half a century, and Americans have always replied that the family takes priority over everything else in their lives.

But if you watch what Americans do, traditional family relationships are in trouble. If current divorce rates continue, about two out of three marriages that begin this year will not survive as long as both spouses live. The proportion of

---

Source: Norval D. Glenn, "What Does Family Mean?" *American Demographics* (June, 1992), pp. 30, 34, 36, 37. Reprinted with permission. (c) June 1992, *American Demographics,* Ithaca, New York.

American adults who are married is decreasing, the share of out-of-wedlock births has soared, and most children under age 18 will spend part of their childhood living with only one parent.

In other words, Americans continue to say they embrace traditional family values—but their family relations have changed dramatically. Why has this happened? What are the consequences?

What Americans Say

Surveys taken in 1971 and 1989 show how little expressed attitudes toward the family have changed. In the earlier study, the Quality of Life Survey conducted by the Institute for Social Research at the University of Michigan, people were asked to rate 12 goals, including "an interesting job," "a large bank account," "having good friends," and "a happy marriage." Three-quarters of those responding rated "having a happy marriage" as extremely important, while 70 percent gave that rating to "being in good health," and 69 percent rated "having a good family life" the same. In contrast, only 38 percent said that "having an interesting job" was extremely important.

A more recent survey shows similar results. In the 1989 Massachusetts Mutual American Family Value Study, family-related variables such as "respecting one's parents," "respecting one's children," "being able to provide emotional support to your family," and "having a happy marriage" ranked far above more individually centered goals. For example, such goals as "being financially secure," "earning a good living," "having a rewarding job," "having nice things," and "being free from obligations so I can do whatever I want to" were reported to be relatively unimportant.

Among American high school seniors, family values were on top in both the 1970s and the 1980s. "Having a good marriage and family life" ranked first for all students from 1976 through 1986. Three-quarters of all seniors rated it extremely important in both years. Only "being able to find steady work," "having strong friendships," and "finding purpose and meaning in life" came close in importance.

Studies that interview the same people every few years show that family tends to become even more important in the years following high school graduation. The National Longitudinal Study of High School and Beyond found that high school boys, on average, considered "being successful in work" and "having steady work" somewhat more important than "having a happy family life." But four years after graduation, the same respondents rated "having a happy family life" first.

Other surveys indicate that having a happy family life really is the key to overall happiness. Satisfaction with family life was highly correlated with overall life satisfaction in the 1971 Quality of Life Survey: after family, satisfaction with marriage and satisfaction with financial situation ranked high as predictors of overall life satisfaction. But a poor marriage may be worse than no marriage at all. Bad marriages wreak havoc on happiness; people who do not characterize their marriage as "very happy" report the lowest overall happiness of any category of people, according to the General Social Surveys conducted by the National Opinion Research Center.

The link between strong family ties and overall happiness indicates that family should be more important than anything else. But the truth is that many if not most Americans will sacrifice traditional family ties for activities they claim are less important. It is common for Americans to let the pursuit of more individualistic goals interfere with their family life, even when doing so is clearly contrary to their best interests.

What They Do

What is responsible for the gap between professed family values and life choices? Some of it is probably due to economic, technological, and demographic trends that make it harder for families to stay together. But the surveys indicate that shifting ideas about the family are also driving the changes. In the 1990s, new values are colliding with notions of family stability.

Probably the most important recent change in attitudes about the family has been a decline in the ideal of marital permanence. You can see this decline in the Study of American Families, which interviewed the same sample of mothers at four different dates. In recent years, it found a sharp increase in the percentage of women who said parents who do not get along should split up rather than stay together for the sake of the children. This percentage went from 51 in 1962 to 82 in 1985.

Of course, an increased acceptance of divorce may not imply a weakening of family values. Some analysts argue that the decreased willingness to tolerate unsatisfactory marriages reflects the importance that people now place on marriage. Indeed, the change might be seen as the weakening of one family value and the strengthening of another to replace it.

Previous generations of Americans saw marriage as an institution to be joined and supported. But today, most people value marriage primarily for what they personally can gain from it, not for what it does for their children, extended family, or community. The goal of "having a happy marriage" currently ranks well above "being married to the same person for life" and even farther above simply "being married." Such a ranking indicates that Americans value marriage primarily as a means to individual happiness. Their tendency to value it for any other reason has seen a substantial decline in recent years.

Other surveys have shown an increase in expressed negative attitudes toward marriage. This is not surprising, in view of the fact that Americans' propensity to marry and remarry has declined in recent years. According to the Americans View Their Mental Health Surveys, the percentage of respondents who said that marriage changes a person's life in positive ways went from 43 in 1957 to 30 in 1976. Meanwhile, negative responses increased from 23 percent to 28 percent.

The importance people attach to marital happiness has almost certainly increased in recent years, but attaining marital happiness has become less likely. That gap may account for some of the growth of negative attitudes about marriage. The share of Americans who are still in their first marriages after ten years and who rated those marriages "very happy" has declined substantially. It was 46 percent among those who married in the mid-1960s, but 33 percent of those who married in the middle to late 1970s, according to the General Social Surveys. The proportion of all married Americans who said their marriages were "very happy" also declined.

Negative attitudes toward parenthood have also increased since World War II, according to the Mental Health Surveys. In 1957 and 1976, parents were asked how having children affects a person's life. Positive responses decreased from 58 percent to 44 percent, while negative responses increased from 22 to 28 percent.

Values that emphasize materialistic gain and individual achievement have also increased, at least among young Americans. The share of high school seniors who said "having lots of money" was extremely important grew from 15 percent in 1976 to 28 percent in 1986, and those who ranked "being successful in my line of work" as extremely important grew from 53 percent to 61 percent, according to the University of Michigan's Monitoring the Future Surveys.

Likewise, the proportion of first-year college students who said that "to be very well-off financially" was a very important or essential life goal went from 40 percent in the early 1970s to 70 percent in 1985, according to surveys taken by the American Council on Education and UCLA.

Americans may be more materialistic and achievement-oriented than they are willing to admit. The same respondents who ranked "having nice things" and "being financially secure" near the bottom of a list of "most important" priorities were asked, in the 1989 Massachusetts Mutual Study, to imagine that they were 38 years old and were offered a new job requiring more work hours and less time with their families. The hypothetical job would provide higher rewards, including greater prestige and more pay. Almost one-third said that their acceptance of such an offer would be "very likely," and an additional one-third said it would be "somewhat likely." Not a single one of the 1,200 respondents said it would be "very unlikely."

The evidence is clear. When personal and family goals conflict, many people who express strong support for family values do not live up to those values.

Bridging the Gap

While most Americans express positive views of their own families, they do not hesitate to point out problems in the family next door. Only 6 percent of the respondents in the Massachusetts Mutual survey rated American family life in general "excellent," compared with 54 percent who rated it "only fair" or "poor." Sixty-two percent said family values in this country had gotten weaker, while only 14 percent said stronger. An overwhelming majority (85 percent) said Americans value material things more than family. And only 5 percent predicted that America's family life would be "excellent" in 1999; 59 percent said it would be "only fair" or "poor."

The same people who hold a dim view of America's family life express satisfaction with their own families. Although the Massachusetts Mutual survey respondents rated family life "only fair," 71 percent claimed they were "extremely satisfied" or "very satisfied" with their own family life.

The same gap shows up when you ask Americans about the state of marriage as an institution. Almost two-thirds of the married respondents to the recent General Social Surveys rate their own marriages "very happy," but most of the respondents to each of the several Virginia Slims Women's Opinion Polls said they thought the institution of marriage was weaker than it was ten years earlier. In 1986, one-third of the high school seniors included in the Monitoring the Future Survey agreed with the statement that "One sees so few good or happy marriages that one questions it as a way of life."

One reason for this skewed picture of American family life may be the media's emphasis on negative trends and events. Another is that people tend to deny the extent of problems in their own families. Indeed, other evidence on the prevalence of family problems suggests that the survey respondents' negative perception of other families may be more accurate than their reported positive feelings about their own family life.

The recent confusion surrounding the American family as an institution should be telling us something. While it may be the temporary outcome of major shifts in our social environment, the rift between word and deed is important. Trend-spotters who predict the resurgence of the traditional American family may be engaging in wishful thinking.

Many authorities on the American family still believe that family life is basically healthy and that family values are as strong as ever. But this positive view is largely based on a literal interpretation of people's responses to family-value questions on polls and surveys. A growing minority of family watchers are looking at family-related behavior and taking a less sanguine view. References to "the decline of the family," long common among political and religious leaders, are now frequent in academic literature.

Decisions that address domestic needs must be based on a clear understanding of the complex relationship between values and family life. Americans need to resolve the inconsistency between their actions and their stated values.

Marriages That Last*

Francine Klagsbrun

The previous article suggests that the marital bond is more fragile than in the past. Nonetheless, many marriages are long and satisfying for both partners. What kinds of things help a marriage to survive in a world where women's and men's roles are changing and divorce rates are high? This is the question examined by Francine Klagsbrun in this chapter.

Durability, a psychiatrist said to me, is its own proof of a good marriage. That is, the fact that a marriage has lasted for many years is the ultimate statement about its ability to satisfy the partners, no matter what the marriage might look like from the outside. I do not agree with that assessment. Marriages may last a lifetime yet be filled with hatred. Why do they continue? Often for financial reasons—a woman (less often a man) cannot afford to walk out, so dependent is she on her husband's economic support, especially when there are children in the picture. Or for security—as bad as it is inside a marriage, fear of the outside, the unknown, keeps a couple bound together, even in their unhappiness. Many women, in addition, still feel that they must get their status and position in society from their husbands. Giving up that position means giving up their identity as Mrs. Somebody, leaving them insecure and vulnerable. . . .

Two marital therapists in California who have studied marriage among the elderly, James A. Peterson and Marcia Lasswell, classify long marriages in which the couple gain little enjoyment from one another but are resigned to living together as "survivor marriages," as opposed to "creative marriages," in which there is continual satisfaction and excitement. Like all such labels, these are somewhat oversimplified. Most marriages that endure include "survivor" times and "creative" times. Even the most creative marriage has its lulls and dead spots, and many seemingly shallow marriages are built around more complex emotions and attachments than meet the eye. Yet some marriages do simply survive, with little joy and little heat, and these can be distinguished from more satisfying long marriages. . . .

Marriages that last because they are satisfying to both partners, marriages in which couples can give positive rather than negative reasons for staying together, are usually more complex than those entrenched ones that just go on. These are the marriages that stay together both "because of" and "in spite of"—because of the emotional riches the marriage provides and in spite of difficulties that arise. . . .

What are the characteristics of long, satisfying, happy marriages? . . . There is no formula, no single recipe that when used in the right proportions will produce the perfect marriage, or even a working one. Rather, there are certain abilities and outlooks that couples in strong marriages have, not all of them at all times, but a large proportion a good part of the time. They fall, it seems to me, into eight categories:

1. An ability to change and tolerate change. Change is inevitable in marriage as in life. Partners become involved in work and pull back from work; children are born, go to school, leave home; spouses age, get sick, drop old interests, take on new ones, make new friends, live through the sorrows of old ones; parents get old and die; couples move from apartments to houses and back to apartments, from one town to another. Changes bring anxieties and disequilibrium. Yet in the strongest marriages, each partner is able to make "midcourse corrections, almost like astronauts," as one psychiatrist put it. That is, they are able both to adapt to the change that is happening in the marriage or in the other partner and, when called for, to change themselves.

Couples whose marriages have lasted 15 years or more have lived through some of the most rapid and overwhelming social change in modern history. These people married at a time when marriage had a set form, when husbands knew that their work was to provide for the family and wives knew that theirs was to care for the home and children. During the course of these marriages, the world turned upside down. Marriage was ridiculed as a dying if not dead institution, to which almost any "alternative" was better for the "growth" of the individual. Husbands who played out the traditional roles they had been taught as children were now seen as "insensitive," dictatorial "patriarchs," while wives were "oppressed" in "stifling" marriages. And along with the rhetoric of a changing society came real change, a new emphasis on a woman's right to seek her own work outside her home and on a man's responsibility—and right—to shift some of his energies and time away from the outside to the inside of his home and to his family. The changes brought chaos to many marriages that had started out one way and then found all the premises on which they had been built cut out from under them.

In the marriages that have remained strong and viable, partners have had the flexibility to pick up what was useful to them from the barrage of slogans and confusions of "facts," and change their marriages and themselves to incorporate new ideals that made sense to them. Even the marriages that have kept the most traditional forms, as many have, have had to make concessions to the mood of the times, if not within the marriage itself then in the couple's outlook and their attitudes toward their children. The Flahertys, one of the most conventional couples interviewed, maintained that Peggy Flaherty's place was in her home, and her work the work of running the family finances and caring for her husband. Yet they strongly encouraged their two daughters to develop occupations—one is a dental technician, the other a nurse—and to continue working after they had families of their own. (True, these are typically "women's" occupations, but the very idea of a married woman working had once been anathema to Tom Flaherty.) Although practicing Catholics themselves, they have succored and supported one daughter who is divorced, recognizing, they said, that she had a right to rid herself of a bad marriage and seek her own happiness.

Much greater changes have taken place in the couples who have shifted their life patterns as social values have shifted. The women who have gone to work or back to school years into their marriages have come to see themselves as different beings than they were in their earlier days. They have not discarded their old selves; they have developed a different part of them. But in doing so they have changed their marriages. Their husbands have accommodated to those changes—some more willingly than others—and in doing so, many have changed themselves. They have changed the way they behave by taking on household tasks they would not have dreamed of touching when they first married, and by rearranging their schedules to make room for their wives' schedules. More important, they have changed inwardly, many of them, truly acknowledging their wives' strivings, ambitions, and accomplishments outside their homes. One tiny manifestation of these changes in long marriages are the numbers of no-longer-young men I see at dinner parties automatically getting up to clear the table or serve a course while their wives sit and chat with guests. They are not self-consciously carrying out some carefully formulated contract. They have incorporated this domestic behavior into their way of being. For them, such acts are not merely gestures; they represent an inner change.

But there is an attitude toward change in long marriages that goes far beyond the social issues. There is this: People who stay happily married see themselves not as victims of fate, but as free agents who make choices in life. Although, like everyone else, they are influenced by their own family backgrounds, for the most part they do not allow their lives together to be dominated by their earlier family lives apart. Because they choose to be married to one another, a choice they make again and again, they are open to changing themselves, pulling away from what *was* in order to make what *is* alive and vital. In other words, as much as they are able to, they try to control their lives, rather than drifting along as the patsies of destiny.

A man whose marriage had gone through a rough time for a while spoke about his decision not to leave even when the couple's troubles reached their worst. "Had I left," he said, "I would have missed out on something good. There's a sense of optimism in staying married and watching this incremental change going on. You think, 'Well, some things have changed a little; I'm going to stick around to see what will happen next. . . .' "

In the best of marriages, change takes place in a context. It is contained within the boundaries of the marriage as both parties have known it. Within those boundaries each partner acts and reacts, bending to the changes in the other and in the world outside. And even while they change and sway, couples recognize that some things cannot change and should not change—and that leads to the second characteristic of long-term marriages, and its major paradox.

2. An ability to live with the unchangeable, which means to live with unresolved conflict when necessary. The simultaneous acceptance of change and of lack of change in long marriages is summed up by the words of a shopkeeper, married 38 years: "You have to know when to holler and you have to know when to look away."

A statement made by many couples when asked about the "secrets" of their happy marriage was, "We don't expect perfection," or some variation thereof. They would go on to explain that their marriage had areas that were far from perfect, qualities in one another that they wish could have changed but they have come to recognize as qualities that will never change. Still, they live with those unchangeable, and sometimes disturbing, qualities, because, as one woman said, "The payoff is so great in other areas." We have been so bombarded with advice books and articles about "solving" problems and "overcoming" adversity, about "improving" our marriages and becoming "ideal" mates that we often forget that it is possible also just to let things be, without solution or improvement.

On a superficial level, I think of a woman who described her misery early in her second marriage because of her husband's unbelievably ear-shattering snores. Night after night she lay awake listening to his nasal roars and wondering how she was going to survive this marriage. For a while she tried slipping out of bed in the middle of the night to sleep in the living room. But she didn't sleep well there, and, anyhow, she wanted to be in bed with her husband. Then she prevailed upon him to seek medical help to control the snoring. The doctors had nothing to offer, and the night sounds continued unabated. Finally, she stopped complaining and bought some ear plugs. They do not block out the noise completely, but they help. The snoring problem, she has decided, will never be solved, the plugs make it possible for her to live with it as best she can, and that is as much as she can do.

On a more serious level, long-married couples accept the knowledge that there are some deep-seated conflicts—about personality differences, habits, styles of dealing with things—that will never be solved. In the best of situations, they stop fighting about those issues and go about their lives instead of wasting their energies on a constant, fruitless struggle to settle differences "once and for all." Not long ago, at a time when marriage was under perpetual attack, this very quality of marriage, its imperfectability, was at the crux of the arguments against it. People spoke of marriage as a form of "settling" for something less than ideal, as "compromising" with what one wanted from life. Yet this ability to live with the imperfect is, it seems to me, the essence of maturity. Mature people are able to accept the limitations life places on them and work around them. And in the "working around," in finding ways to live with difficulties, they may experience some of the most creative moments of living.

Couples who get pleasure from their marriages often say that they do so because they focus on the strengths of the marriage, not its weaknesses, on compatibilities rather than dissonances. With that outlook they are able to enhance what is good so that it becomes the core of the marriage while the negatives cling only to the periphery. . . .

3. An assumption of permanence. Most marriages, first, second or later, begin with the hope and expectation that they will last forever. In the marriages that do last, "forever" is not only a hope, but an ongoing philosophy. The mates do not seriously think about divorce as a viable option. Certainly there are "divorce periods," times of distancing and anger, but even if divorce itself crosses the minds of the couple, it is not held out as an escape from difficulties. One can argue, with some truth, that couples married more than ten or fifteen years ago don't think about divorce because it was not as prevalent a part of our culture in earlier days as it is now. But that's not the complete story. Many couples married during those earlier days have divorced, and for many younger couples permanence is a built-in component of marriage, as it had been for their parents.

This attitude that a marriage will last, *must* last (not because some religious authority or family member says so, but because the marriage is that important to the couple), tempers a husband's and a wife's approach to conflicts and imperfections. They see the marriage as an entity in itself that must be protected. Or as family therapist Salvador Minuchin said, "A marriage is more than the sum of its parts. In marriage, one plus one doesn't equal two; it forms something different, something that is much more than two." And for the sake of that "something" that is the marriage, these couples are willing to make compromises and sacrifices when necessary. In today's terminology, they are committed to the marriage as well as to one another.

The commitment, however, is *not necessarily equal* at all times. In marriage after marriage, I had the impression that one partner more than the other was the "keeper of the commitment." One usually seemed more willing to give in after a fight or more prone to compromise to avoid the fight altogether and hold the marriage on a steady keel. That partner may have been the more dependent one, but was just as likely to be the stronger and more mature one, the one more able to swallow pride, break stalemates, and see the other's point of view. But I also had the impression that the caring and dedication to the marriage was strong enough on the part of both partners that when the "commitment keeper" pulled back, or refused to be the conciliator on some issue, the other moved in and took over that role. . . .

It should be pointed out that the commitment to marriage by long-married couples is usually a commitment not only to a relationship, but also to marriage as an institution. Mae West's famous remark that "marriage is an institution, and who wants to live in an institution" makes sense when the institution is seen as a static, stifling edifice. But to couples who value marriage, it is regarded as an institution that adds stability and order to life, transmits ideals from one generation to the next, and provides a structure within which a woman and a man can entrust their souls to one another, knowing that they will be sheltered and protected by its permanence.

4. Trust. This is a word used again and again by couples, and it means many things. It means love, although people tend to use the word "trust" more often than they use "love." In part this is because "love" is an overused word, and one whose romantic meanings have overshadowed the deeper, more profound meaning of the love that binds married people. In larger part it is because feelings of love may wax and wane in the course of a marriage—in times of anger, for example, few people can keep in touch with those feelings—but trust is a constant; without it there is no true marriage. Trust also implies intimacy, or, rather, it forms the base for the closeness that couples in good marriages have established. But couples use the word *trust* more readily than *intimacy* or *love*. And I believe they do because *trust* sums up much of the dynamic of a marriage, the back-and-forth interaction from which everything else grows. Trust in marriage allows for the sense of security and comfort that mark long and satisfying unions. Trust also makes possible the freedom marriage provides, the freedom and "right," in the words of psychiatrist Aaron Stein, "people have to be themselves and have their own feelings." Each partner trusts the other with his or her core self, trusts that that self will not be ridiculed or violated, trusts that it will be nurtured and protected—safe. And in that safety lies a special kind of freedom.

Intimacy, as I have said, is built around the trust partners allow themselves to have in one another. Once that trust exists, there is no set form intimacy must assume. I cannot say that every couple in a strong marriage communicates with one another as openly as the much-publicized communication ideals of our society would have them. Some do. Some are open and loose with one another, ventilating feelings and sensations freely. In other families, one partner, or both, may be more closed off, less able or willing to pour out heartsounds. But these marriages have their own ways of being intimate, which grow from the trust between partners. It may be that one partner is the expansive one while the second is more silent, relying on the other for emotional expressiveness. Or it may be that both act somewhat restrained in revealing sensitivities, yet they understand one another and feel comfortable with the more limited interchanges they have. I found many styles of relating among long-married couples, and no one seemed better than another as long as each couple was satisfied with their own style.

The trust that lies at the heart of happy marriages is also the foundation for sexual enjoyment among partners. When mates spoke about sexual loving, they almost always spoke about trusting feelings that had expanded over the years. "Sex is richer and deeper for us," said one woman. "We trust each other and we're not ashamed to get pleasure." Trust is also the reason invariably given for a commitment to monogamy, as in "I may be tempted, but I wouldn't want to violate our trust." When a partner has had a fling or brief affair, trust is the reason most often offered for having ended it or for avoiding further extramarital involvements. In short, trust is regarded by many couples as the linchpin of their marriage.

5. A balance of dependencies, which is another way of saying a **balance of power**. I prefer *dependency*, even though *power* is a sexier word, with its implied comparison between marriage and politics. I prefer *dependency* because it better conveys the way couples see and regard one another. They speak of needing each other and depending on each other, and in doing so, they are not speaking about the weaknesses of marriage, but about its strengths. In the best of marriages, partners are mutually dependent; interdependent is another way of saying that. They are aware of their dependencies and not ashamed to cater to them, acknowledging openly their debt to one another.

A person who best expressed the positive benefits of dependency in a marriage was a widow, a political person, who had gained prominence in her community for holding office at a time when few other women had. Her husband of 30 years, an attorney, had died about a year earlier. "First," she said, "there are the small dependencies. You know, how do I look in this dress or should I wear this belt or that one? Then there are the bigger things. My husband was an enabler—he helped me to be what I could be and what I was by encouraging me. And he opened my eyes to new things. For example, a new Supreme Court decision would come out and it would become an instant part of our lives because he would have all sorts of opinions about it that we would discuss and eventually I would incorporate. Now I'm not always sure what I think about some of the decisions being handed down. It's not that I lost part of myself by depending on him for this kind of thinking; it's that I would never have developed this interest to begin with. You have just so much time, energy and intellect, and it's so good to be able to depend on your spouse to fill in the gaps. Our dependencies enriched both our lives."

There has been a great emphasis on egalitarian marriages in recent years, marriages in which both spouses share economic earnings and power and both share household duties. Let us hope these marriages increase in number. However, an impression that grows out of this emphasis on economic egalitarianism is that emotional egalitarianism automatically follows and that by contrast, in traditional marriages the dependencies are all one-sided: the woman depends totally on the man. This is not what I found among couples in solid, long marriages. Mates in nontraditional marriages as well as those in more traditional ones shared emotional dependencies. Rarely were husband and wife equally dependent on one another at any particular point. Rather, the dependencies tipped back and forth during the course of a marriage, each spouse nurturing the other as needed, so that over time, a balance was established, and that balance kept the marriage strong and stable. . . .

6. An enjoyment of each other. Wives and husbands in satisfying long marriages like one another, enjoy being together, and enjoy talking to each other. Although they may spend evenings quietly together in a room, the silence that surrounds them is the comfortable silence of two people who know they do not *have* to talk to feel close. But mostly they do talk. For many couples conversations go on continually, whether the gossip of everyday living or discussions of broader events. And they listen to one another. I watched the faces of people I interviewed and watched each listening while the other spoke. They might argue, become irritated, or jump in to correct each other, but they are engaged, and rarely bored.

They enjoy each other physically also, and sexual pleasures infuse many marriages for years and years. I could sense a sexual electricity between some partners. A different kind of warmth emanated from others, a feeling of closeness and affection. They held hands, they touched, they smiled and they spoke of sex as "warm and loving," as one woman said, "maybe not the wildness of our early marriage, but very pleasing."

They laugh at each other's jokes. Humor is the universal salve and salvation, easing tensions and marriage fatigue. "If you can laugh about it," everyone said, "you know it will be all right." And for them it is.

They find each other interesting, but they do not necessarily have the same interests. And that was a surprise. Far fewer couples than I expected spoke about sharing interests or hobbies. Typical of many others were the Augustines, who confessed, almost guiltily, their different interests:

"I'm afraid if you're looking for answers to long marriages, this is not the place," said Marie Augustine.

"Why not?" I asked.

"Because we don't share everything the way you're supposed to."

"I'm not sure you're supposed to. What don't you share?"

"Interests. For example, he likes to sit when we're on vacations and I like to run."

"And I like music and she likes the theater," Tony Augustine joined in.

"He can spend hours studying old coins. And I can spend hours catching up on weeks of newspaper reading," Marie continued.

"What do you do about these differences?"

"We work out arrangements that suit both of us," Marie answered. "With vacations, for example, one summer we run, meaning we travel and run around a lot and that makes me happy, and the next summer we sit. We go to a resort or rent a house in the country where we can look at the view, and that makes him happy."

"We also give each other space, as the kids say," Tony added. "Sometimes I'll go up to the room in our attic and devote all evening to listening to music alone."

"It's odd," Marie said. "I can walk into that room and he'll just be sitting there, and I'll say, 'What are you doing?' and he'll say, 'I'm listening to music.' Well, that's not me, just sitting and doing nothing, listening to music. But I'll go to concerts with him. We go to many concerts because of him."

"And I go to the theater because of her. But we don't say it that way as if we're sacrificing for each other. We go together because we like being together and actually, we each get our own kind of enjoyment out of the other's interests."

"Yes," agreed Marie. "We would never say, in terms of vacations, for example, 'Okay, I'll go run while you go sit.' That wouldn't be any fun for us."

Some other couples make fewer concessions to one another's interests. They might take separate vacations or go to movies or lectures with friends rather than with one another, and they find that for them that separation works better than forcing themselves to put in time at activities that one or the other hates. And for some married people, having separate interests makes each more interesting to the other. . . .

But if sharing interests is not a prerequisite for a rewarding marriage, sharing *values* is. Values refer to the things people believe in, the things they hold dear and worthy. The philosopher Bertrand Russell explained their importance in marriage well when he wrote, "It is fatal . . . if one values only money and the other values only good works." Such a couple will have trouble getting along, let alone enjoying one another's interests or ideas.

Mates who feel well-matched share a common base of values even when they disagree about other things. One couple described having their biggest arguments about money. He loves to spend whatever they have on clothes, records, and the theater; she watches every cent, wearing the same dress again and again. Yet they had an instant meeting of minds when it came time to buy a cello for their musically gifted daughter. They bought the best they could afford, even using a good part of their savings, because they both valued their child's music education above anything else money could buy. Another couple, who love antique Oriental ceramics, think nothing of living in a dingy, run-down apartment while they spend their modest earnings on beautiful ceramic vases that they track down and buy together.

For some couples, religion is the value that informs everything else in life. Those couples were in a minority among the families I interviewed, as they are a minority in our secular society. But those who did value religion considered it the strongest bond in their lives, and many attributed the happiness and stability of their marriages to that bond. I found it interesting that marriages in which both partners valued religion, even if the partners were of different faiths, had fewer conflicts over religious issues than same-faith marriages in which only one felt a religious commitment, especially if the other partner was disdainful of religion.

For all marriages, sharing values enhances the intimacy and mutual respect spouses feel, adding to their enjoyment of one another.

7. A shared history that is cherished. Every couple has a story, and couples in long marriages respect their own stories. They are connected to each other through those stories, and even the sadnesses they shared are a valued part of their history. "Our life is like a patchwork," one woman said. "We pull in red threads from here and blue threads from there and make them into one piece. Sometimes the threads barely hold, but you pull hard at them and they come together, and the patchwork remains whole."

The attachment couples have to their histories is not necessarily a sentimental or nostalgic attachment, but an affectionate one that sees significance in the past and in all the times spent together. George Gilbert said it nicely. His marriage, with one of the most troubled histories of all, had been filled with the traumas of manic-depressive illness and alcoholism until some years ago when he made himself stop drinking and his illness was brought under control by medication. "You know," he said, "you talk about this and you talk about that, and it sounds so chaotic, the alcohol and the rest. But still, in the midst of it all there were good times. In 1970, at the height of my drinking, we went to Cape Cod with our three sons and we got an acre of land. We put out a camper and we rented a canoe and we had a glorious time. Sure, when you reflect you think of the bad things—the flashing lights and the arms wrapped around the porcelain in the bathroom when you're hung over and sick. But there was so much else, even then. There was still a lot of fun, still a lot of humor, still a lot of good loving for both of us. . . ."

People in long marriages value their joint history. When their ties in the present get raggedy, they are able to look to the past to find the good that they shared, rather than give in to the disillusionments of the moment. Their sense of history also gives them a respect for time. They know, by looking backward, that changes take time and that angers vanish with time, and they know that there is time ahead for new understandings and new adventures.

8. Luck. It has to be said, because everyone said it. With it all, the history and the trust, the willingness to change and to live without change, people need a little bit of luck to keep a marriage going.

You need luck, first of all, in choosing a partner who has the capacity to change and trust and love . . . And you need a little luck in the family you come from and the friends that you have. A horrendous family background in which parents abuse their children or offer no love can set up almost insurmountable obstacles to the ability to sustain a marital relationship. Yet there are couples in long, happy marriages who did have devastating backgrounds. Often they were able to break the patterns they had known because of the encouragement of an aunt or an uncle, a grandparent, a teacher, a friend. They were lucky in finding the support they needed.

Then, you need a little luck with life. A marriage might move along happily and smoothly enough until a series of unexpected events rain down on it. A combination of illnesses or job losses, family feuds or personal failures might push the marriage off-course, when without these blows, it could have succeeded. Every marriage needs some luck in holding back forces that could crush it.

These aspects of luck may be out of our power to control. But the good thing about luck is that it is not all out of our control. Many people who considered themselves happy in marriage also spoke about themselves as being lucky. Since they seemed to have the same share of problems and difficulties as anyone else, sometimes even more than their share, I came to think that luck in marriage, as in life, is as much a matter of attitude as of chance. Couples who regard themselves as lucky are the ones who seize luck where they are able to. Instead of looking outside their marriage and assuming the luck is all there, in other people's homes, they look inside their marriage and find the blessings there. They are not blind to the soft spots of their marriages—nobody denied difficulties; they just consider the positives more important. So they knock wood and say they are lucky. And I guess they are. They have grabbed luck by the tail and have twisted it to their own purposes. . . .

On its most immediate level, marriage expands us because it nurtures and protects in a way that nothing else does. Because of the security a good marriage provides, it allows each partner the courage to take risks, to venture into the unknown, to stretch as far as one can in the outside world, knowing that there is a place to come home to, a safe place with room enough to be oneself.

Marriage adds depth to one's being, the depth and understanding that come from looking into oneself in order to understand another. A woman, a professor of philosophy, newly married, described marriage as "even harder than philosophy." It was hard, she said, because it forced you to confront yourself, to sort out what you believe and care about, what you consider important and what trivial. "You could run away," she said. "You can get a divorce and run away when things get really hard. But you still have to confront yourself. If you run away, you run into yourself."

Marriage is filled with challenges, not least of which is the challenge of simultaneously being a whole person and being part of the larger entity that is the marriage. Meeting the challenge means living for oneself but also living outside of oneself. It means being selfish sometimes and selfless at others, and becoming a more complex human being in the process of trying to find a balance between the two.

To be married is to be connected to a past and a future, to be a family with private jokes and special stories, to have secret codewords and rituals. "There's a kind of tenderness that comes from living a long time with somebody," said a woman, "realizing that they are not going to live forever and neither are you but you are in this life together. With all the millions of people around, you're still going to try to make things good for that one person. There's a kind of gentleness that comes after a while, not having everything just happen but finding out what pleases somebody, and making that happen. . . ."

Not everybody needs to be or should be married. Plenty of people have rich and splendid lives without marriage. . . . Marriage has its faults, God knows. It has its pains and tediums, its rages and despair. But when it works, it has its moments: of adventure and passion, of calm contentment, of companionship and of profound love. Married people think nothing can compare to those moments.

The His and Hers Transition*

Jay Belsky and John Kelly

One of the themes woven throughout many of the readings in this collection is how gender is important in shaping the family experience. For over a decade, Jay Belsky has been involved in a research project which examines child development, marriage, and parenting processes. This research has led him to conclude that the transition to parenthood is a different experience for women and men—and that these differences are shaped both by culture and biology. In this chapter, he and John Kelly examine some of these differences, focusing particularly upon issues of household division of labor, concerns about finances, difficulties in the relationship, attitudes about work and career, and the social isolation which can result from the birth of a child.

Most popular magazine articles about the transition to parenthood contain a singular peculiarity: They describe the struggles, problems, and tumult of this period as something "we" endure, as if new mothers and fathers are exposed in equal measure to its stresses and chaos. But as anyone who is already a parent knows, the reality is different. Men and women experience the transition to par-

*Source: From *The Transition to Parenthood: How a First Child*... by Jay Belsky, Ph.D. and John Kelly. Copyright (c) 1994 by Jay Belsky, Ph.D. and John Kelly. Use by permission of Delacorte Press, a division of Bantam Doubleday Dell Publishing Group, Inc.

enthood in such dramatically dissimilar ways that within a very short period of time "we" becomes "me."

I was reminded of this fact dozens of times throughout our study, most memorably during a conversation with a couple who was then nine months into parenthood. As the husband proceeded to paint a glowing picture of life with baby, his wife, who was sitting next to him on the sofa, began fidgeting with annoyance. Yes, the man conceded, the bills did pile up faster these days, and yes, sometimes the baby's crying became irritating. But chores and sleep were not the big problems he had expected them to be. "Overall," he said, "things are turning out surprisingly well." At that point his wife, who was now practically vibrating with annoyance, exploded. "Your transition may be going surprisingly well," she snapped, "but believe me, mine isn't!"

Behind this common husband-wife perceptual gap lay some profound differences in biology, upbringing, and perhaps even evolutionary programming. To state the obvious, men and women are very different. And once the baby arrives, these differences usually produce such widely different priorities, needs, and perspectives that in most marriages, not one but two transitions develop, a His and a Hers.

The two transitions are united by a common set of gratifications. Men and women alike report that parenthood makes them feel better about themselves, their parents, and the larger world. Men and women alike also find the baby irresistible. Also uniting the two transitions is a common set of concerns. In nearly equal degrees new mothers and fathers worry about all of the new work and financial pressures the baby creates and about how parenthood will affect their relationship with each other as well as their work.

What begins to divide the two transitions is each parent's different biological relationship to the new child. While men and women become parents at the same time, they don't become parents in the same way. Most of the profound changes that occur during the transition, especially in its early phase, happen to the woman—and that makes her transition much more tumultuous than her husband's. Some of this tumult is good; indeed, some of it approaches ecstasy. "Women have babies all the time," said one [research] Project mother, "but when you have one of your own, you feel like no one has ever done it before. You think, 'I have created life.'" The love affair with her new creation adds to the new mother's ecstasy. One recent study found that love at first sight is experienced by two-thirds of all new mothers.[1] Another study found that the only two people who hold their gaze longer than a pair of lovers are a mother and her new child. Even women who are determined not to be swept off their feet by the baby often are. I remember one Project mother, a successful attorney, who had approached parenthood with some ambivalence, telling me later, "I never dreamed I could love anyone like this."

Some of the tumult, however, is bad. In the weeks and months immediately following the baby's birth, many women suffer from chronic fatigue and exhaustion. Several recent studies suggest that new mothers may also suffer from anxiety, depression, and low self-esteem. To some extent these two phenomena are related. Fatigue and physical weakness create a vulnerability to sharp and unpredictable mood swings. But a great deal of the new mother's emotional upheaval arises from her unique relationship to the baby. For example, many women find their feelings toward the child so powerful that they start to become all-consuming. The woman cannot think of anything but the baby, and sometimes she finds it hard to remove herself from his presence. Doubts about parental competence also stalk many new mothers. Having brought this wonderful new child into the world, the woman wonders whether she is capable of giving him the love and understanding he needs.

Worries about self are another common feature of the mother's transition. A University of Minnesota study indicates that when a new mother is not worrying about her exhaustion, parental competence, or emotional volatility, she is worrying about the physical changes the baby has produced in her. "Loss of figure" and "general unhappiness about appearance" were two of the top five transition complaints of women in a University of Minnesota study. Reflecting this sentiment was the remark of one of our Project mothers, who said to me one day with more than a hint of ruefulness in her voice, "I look like a potato."

The father's transition is not free of upheaval and tumult either. There is some evidence that new fathers worry even more than new mothers about work and money. And to varying degrees, new fathers also worry about fatigue, intrusive in-laws, chores, and what their wives are enduring. On occasion new fathers even suffer from physical discomfort. While we did not encounter any cases of sympathetic pregnancy, two University of California investigators, Carolyn Pape Cowan and Philip Cowan, reported that several men in their transition study gained weight and complained of vague aches and pains in the months prior to the birth of the new child.

On the whole, though, life in His transition is more even-keeled. Paternal love is slower to take flight. In a recent survey 70 percent of new fathers reported that it took them weeks and months, not hours, to form a strong attachment to the baby. And that love is also easier to control. According to Milton Kolchuck of the University of Massachusetts, new fathers spend an average of ten to fifteen minutes per day in play with a new son or daughter. There are also fewer lows in His transition. While a new mother's stress levels continue to rise throughout the first year after the baby's birth, we found that the new father's stress leveled off after the first month. But there are fewer highs too. In another recent survey, only 1 percent of new fathers described the baby's first step as a "big thrill," compared with 17 percent of new mothers. Another common feature of His transition seems to be guilt. When investigators asked a group of new fathers, "Should child care be shared equally?" 74 percent said yes. But when asked, "Do you share child care equally with your wife?" only 13 percent replied yes.

Our Transition

The different characteristics of the His and Hers transitions give new mothers and fathers different priorities and needs. Bearing and caring for a child absorbs tremendous amounts of maternal energy; working full-time on top of it, as over 50 percent of new mothers currently do, absorbs still more. So one chief priority of Her transition is a reasonably equitable division of labor. The new mother wants a husband who will relieve her fatigue by taking an active role with home and baby—to be her partner, not just a helper. Spousal understanding and empathy are also important to her. The new mother wants a husband who understands her profound attachment to the baby well enough to know why she may sometimes neglect him emotionally and physically to be with that baby. Just as important, the new mother also wants a spouse who understands how powerful and hard to control her feelings toward the baby are and who helps her to regain her emotional balance.

Another priority of the mother's transition is emotional involvement. The new mother wants to feel that in his own way her husband is as involved in the transition and in their new family as she is. Translated into day-to-day terms, this means that she wants a spouse who will sit and listen when she wants to talk about her doubts, anxieties, and frustration; who will play with and care for the baby instead of returning him to her in ten minutes; and who will check the refrigerator to see if the family needs anything *before* he goes to the store. To repeat, what she fundamentally desires is a partner, not a helper.

The principal priority of His transition is work. Most men are brought up to believe that ensuring a family's financial security is a husband's primary responsibility. And even in this relatively egalitarian age this belief continues to exercise a powerful tug on new fathers; some begin to work longer hours or take a second job after the baby's arrival. Absent the physical and emotional upheaval of the mother's transition, however, most of the father's other priorities remain, in modified form, what they were in prebaby days. While he recognizes that the workload has increased dramatically and that the baby has become the chief priority in the marriage, a new father continues to want some affection and attention for himself, a reasonably active social life, and some freedom to pursue his hobbies and sports and to see his friends.

The chief hallmark of couples who transform the His and Hers transition into the Our transition is the ability to reconcile the conflicting priorities of their individual transitions. The husband does this by recognizing that his wife's need for physical and emotional support far outweighs any needs he may have and by surrendering some of his autonomy and stepping deeper into the marriage to provide her with that help and support. The wife does it by recognizing that her husband's wish for some attention and affection also represents a legitimate desire and by learning how to control her feelings about the baby so that she can meet him at least halfway on these desires. She also does it by recognizing that he will see the support he offers differently than she does and by meeting him halfway on this issue by giving him some of the gratitude he expects for his commitment to her and their new family.

Typically in homes where the two transitions become one, the major new-parent concerns such as who does what? how do we spend our money? how often do we go out? and who makes the career sacrifices for the baby? are solved in a mutually satisfactory manner. But the hundreds of small acts of self-sacrifice, consideration, and understanding that are necessary to produce these agreements also give such homes another characteristic: mutual empathy. The husband and wife become so attuned to each other that when differences do arise, they respond as Laurie Cowte did when husband Tom complained of being sexually ignored. Laurie, who had had a baby three months earlier, had legitimate reason to turn Tom's complaint aside. But she knew it was his way of saying, "I feel emotionally ignored." So she decided to put aside her fatigue and do something that would make Tom feel very attended to. A few nights later, when he stepped out of the shower, Tom found a naked Laurie standing in the bathroom waiting for him.

Traditionally two roadblocks have been thought to hinder a couple's journey to the Our transition. . . . Differences in upbringing do give men and women contrasting ideas of what it means to be a parent, and differences in biology contribute to a different relationship and feelings toward the baby. But if the findings of Dr. Jane Lancaster, a University of New Mexico anthropologist, are accurate, couples may also face a third obstacle on the road to the Our transition.

In a recent paper Dr. Lancaster argues that one other reason new parents often do not see eye to eye on chores, money, and work is that evolution has programmed men and women to prioritize parenting in different ways. The origin of this programming lies in each sex's reproductive abilities. Dr. Lancaster believes that a woman is "wired" to pull a man into the family because her limited reproductive capacity—she can only produce so many eggs per month and so many children during her fertile years—means that each child represents an enormous biological investment to her. Hence, the woman is programmed to protect her child in any way she can, most notably by getting as much help and support from her mate as she can.

According to Dr. Lancaster, the reason men often resist the woman's demand to settle in is that their reproductive capacities have produced quite a different kind of evolutionary programming. A man can continue reproducing well into his seventies and emits millions of sperm in a single ejaculation. Therefore he is "wired" to regulate his biological investment in any single child because that child represents only one of hundreds of potential offspring.[2] It is important to emphasize that Dr. Lancaster's view does not mean that a man cannot form a strong attachment to any one single child or that when a woman complains of not getting enough help, it is because she is under the influence of some obscure, atavistic impulse and not because she is not getting enough help. But if Dr. Lancaster is right, then the disagreements today's parents have about money, chores, and careers may simply be the latest manifestation of an ongoing argument between the sexes that stretches back a million years to the African savanna, where the first human parents arose.

What Divides Us

New parents disagree about many things, but when they fight, they usually fight about one of five things: division of labor, money, work, their relationship (who is responsible for the hole that has opened up in it), and social life (are we getting out enough). These five issues are so big, important, and all-pervasive, they might be said to constitute the raw material of marital change during the transition. Quite simply, couples who manage to resolve these issues in a mutually satisfactory way generally become happier with their marriages, whereas those who do not become unhappier. In order to understand how these five issues operate in a couple's relationship, it will help to know more about the issues themselves and how biology, upbringing, and perhaps evolution have conspired to make men and women see them so differently.

Chores and Division of Labor

On the whole, husbands and wives agree that this is the major stress of the transition. They also agree that while they expected the baby to create a lot more work, that expectation did not prepare them for what they actually encountered. One of our Project mothers compared the difference to "watching a tornado on TV and having one actually blow the roof off your house."

Some recent figures explain why the reality of a baby's impact is so much greater than the expectation. Typically nonbaby tasks, such as dishwashing, increase from once or twice a day to four times, laundry from one load a week to four or five, shopping from one expedition per week to three, meal preparation from twice a day to four times, and household cleaning from once a week to usually once a day. Nursing chores add further to the workload. On average a baby needs to be diapered six or seven times and bathed two or three times per day, soothed two or three times per night and often as many as five times per day. His helplessness also transforms once-simple tasks into complex, time-consuming ones. "These days," said one new father, not bothering to hide his exasperation, "going out for ice cream is like planning a moon shot. First I have to check Alex to see if he's wet. Then I have to wrestle him into his clothes, then into the stroller. Next I have to pack an extra diaper in case he wets himself and a bottle in case he starts acting up."

Compared with his 1960s counterpart, a man like this father is notably more involved in baby and household chores. Studies show that on average, 30 years ago a man devoted 11 hours per week to home and baby, while today he devotes 15 or 16 hours. But this 3- to 4-hour increase has not significantly alleviated the new mother's burden. Even in a home where a woman works full-time, we found that her contributions to child care, such as diapering, feeding, and bathing, often exceed her husband's by nearly 300 percent. Or to put it another way, for every three diapers he changes, she changes eight. The new mother's contribution to household chores also increases during the transition, usually by about 20 percent.

One of the major changes that has occurred within Her transition over the past 15 years is the way women themselves view this division of labor. What was acceptable for earlier generations of new mothers is not acceptable for new mothers of this generation. A combination of factors, including maternal employment, feminism, and egalitarianism, has made today's woman expect and feel entitled to a significant amount of help from a man. By the same token, men have not been untouched by the winds of change either. Men today want to be more involved with home and child, and they also realize that their wives shoulder burdens their own mothers never dreamed of shouldering.

Yet despite these changes, when men and women sit down to discuss who does what, they usually end up sounding like a Project couple I interviewed several years ago:

> *Husband (with some self-congratulation):* "My dad is always telling me and my brother he never changed a diaper in his life. I change them all the time, and I think I'm a better parent and a better husband for it."
>
> *Wife (after husband left the room):* "David knows his father never helped his mother, and since he gives me a little help, he thinks he's Mother Teresa. The truth is, I do about eighty percent of everything. You know what really burns me up though? The way David acts when his parents visit. Usually he does a little more then, and of course they think he's wonderful. 'Wow,' his dad keeps saying, 'I never did any of that stuff.' Ohhh, when I hear that, I'd like to take the pair of them . . ."

Why do so many new mothers feel that they don't get the help and support they need? Part of the answer lies in several aspects of His transition that make a man perceive his contribution to home and baby differently than his wife. One is that a man uses a different yardstick to measure his contribution to the division of labor. A wife measures what a husband does against what she does. And because what a man does looks small when measured by this yardstick, the woman often ends up as unhappy and disgruntled as the Project wife above. The man, on the other hand, usually measures his contribution to chores against what his father did. And because by that yardstick his 15 to 16 hours per week represent a 30 to 40 percent increase over what his father did, he often ends up feeling as good about himself and his contribution to the division of labor as the Project father above.

Frequently the man's perception of who does what is also influenced by the fact that at least temporarily, he becomes the family's sole breadwinner. And because this is a role he has been taught to equate with parenting, fulfilling it not only makes a new father feel like he is already satisfying his parental obligation, it also makes the 20 percent he does at home seem like 200 percent to him. How can his wife not appreciate his contribution? The nature of transition chores can also shape a man's perception of the division-of-labor issue. Because his wife is usually more skilled at baby chores, the man sometimes concludes that his help is really not needed. The new father who hops on this train of thought usually gets off at the same station as the Project husband who said to me, "I expected to do more, I really did. But then I started thinking. Since Brenda's breast-feeding Jenny, Brenda should get up with Jenny. Then, pretty soon, 'getting up with Jenny is Brenda's job' became 'Jenny is Brenda's job.'"

It is only a suspicion of mine but on an unconscious level the man's evolutionary programming may also influence his contribution to the division of labor. When today's new father says "I can't stay and help; you know Dan and I always play racquetball on Saturday morning," he may simply be displaying the most up-to-date manifestation of that ancient male impulse—limiting one's investment in the baby.

Sometimes aspects of Her transition can also contribute to an unequal division of labor. For example the yardstick a new mother uses to measure a husband's contribution to chores can produce such maternal disgruntlement and withholding that the man does even less because he does not get the gratitude he feels he is entitled to for surpassing his father's. In addition a woman's significant biological investment in the child can make her so critical of her husband's parenting that without intending to, she drives him away.

I witnessed a dramatic example of this phenomenon at a neighborhood picnic last year. I was talking to another father—a man I'll call Jake—when a scream erupted from a nearby meadow. While we were talking, Jake's two-year-old, Bobby, had wandered off, fallen, and cut his forehead. As Jake comforted him, wife Nora, who had been off getting hot dogs with their older son, appeared. Grabbing Bobby out of Jake's arms, she asked, "What happened?" in a voice full of upset and reproach. Jake told her, then added defensively, "It's only a scratch." Nora, however, was unmollified. "I'm taking Bobby to the nurse," she announced, and proceeded to march off. "Wait," Jake said, running after her, "I'll come with you." "No," said Nora, spinning around. "You stay here. You've already done your work for the day."

As he watched his wife and sons disappear over a hill, I could see Jake struggling with himself. He knew Nora's sharpness was a product of her concern for Bobby, not a personal attack on him. She had simply "lost it" for a moment. Still, the sharpness hurt, and in the end that hurt won out. "Next time let her take the both of them to get a hot dog," Jake said. "I've had it."

Men who find themselves continually criticized for their inadequate diapering, bathing, and dressing skills often end up feeling similarly conflicted. On one level they know that their wives do not really mean to be hurtfully critical; on another level, like Jake, they feel humiliated and often conclude that the best (and safest) policy to adopt vis-à-vis child-care chores is a hands-off policy.

Money Worries

Income among Project couples averaged $25,000 per annum (or about $30,000 in current dollars). This is about the national average for new parents, and it explains why finances are also a major transition issue. Twenty-five thousand dollars does not go very far, particularly when, in addition to covering ongoing expenses such as mortgage and car payments, it has to cover the new expenses created by the baby, who despite his small size can be a formidable consumer. For example, the packages of Pampers or Huggies he goes through every three or four days cost $9.50 to $12.50; the Osh-Kosh jeans and shoes he outgrows every few months cost $20 and $30 if he is one year old and $30 and $40 if he is two. On average his new winter coat costs up to $50; his new stroller anywhere from $80 to $250. Depending on where he lives, his visits to the pediatrician can cost between $25 and $75. If his mother continues to work, child-care costs can run as high as $20,000 per year in some cities.

Most of the disagreements new mothers and fathers have about these expenses arise from another difference between members of the His and Hers transition: Parenting changes men's and women's self-perceptions in very different ways. When a couple joined the Project, one of the first things we asked them to do was play what we called the Penny Game. We gave the husband and wife 15 pennies each and asked them to allot their money to three roles: spouse, worker, and parent, depending upon how closely they identified with these roles. At the start of the transition, women allotted almost as many pennies as men to the worker role—which is to say that mothers-to-be were almost as likely as fathers-to-be to identify themselves as workers. But after the baby's birth a divergence developed. Women (including working women) began allotting more and more of their pennies to the parenting role, men relatively more to the worker role.

The different forms of economic logic that new mothers and fathers develop arise from this divergence in self-perception. Many a man's thinking about money issues is dominated by his worker impulse to conserve and enhance financial resources. A new father frequently works longer hours to increase income and begins cutting back on his own consumption. Now he shuts off the lights when he leaves a room and brings a sandwich to work instead of eating lunch out. Many a woman's economic logic is often shaped by her close identification with the parenting role. New mothers also turn out lights and "brown-bag it" to save money. However, because a mother sees herself first and foremost as a nurturer, the woman's chief concern becomes the baby's well-being. And this often produces economic choices that put her in conflict with her conservation-minded husband.

Exhibit A of this phenomenon was Project wife Betty van der Hovel's decision to have the living-room windows baby-proofed with sliding metal guards two weeks after son Luke's birth. Because husband Ted felt the windows would not pose a hazard until Luke was two or three years old, Betty's decision baffled and annoyed him. "Now on top of everything else I have to find a hundred and fifty dollars to pay for those goddamn guards," he told me one day. "Why couldn't Betty have waited?" But Betty felt that Ted had missed the point entirely. The issue was not money, it was their son's safety. And how could he possibly put economic considerations ahead of that? "Sometimes, you can be such a jerk," I overheard her tell Ted one afternoon during a conversation about the window guards.

Exhibit B of this phenomenon is a disagreement I witnessed one evening at the home of Project couple Tom and Maggie Davis. I was sitting in the kitchen with Tom when Maggie arrived home with a bagful of new baby clothes. "Look at these, Tom," she said, pulling a smock, hat, and booties out of the bag in rapid succession. "Won't Alexis look adorable in them?"

In a transition where conservation is an overriding priority, expensive baby clothes make as little economic sense as sliding metal guards, so Tom reacted to this fashion show the way Ted van der Hovel had to the guards. "Jesus, Maggie, how many times do we have to go through this?" he said. "We just bought a house, we're not making much money, we can't afford to keep buying baby clothes. How many dresses does Alexis need, anyway? She doesn't look in a mirror."

Maggie groaned as if to say, "You don't get it, do you?" And from the perspective of Her transition, Tom had not gotten it. Often for women new baby clothes represent a sensible economic choice because they advance another of the new mother's priorities: social presentation. This is the name given to her desire to present her baby—her creation—to the larger world of family and friends for admiration and praise. And since a $30 Osh-Kosh outfit and a $40 pair of shoes will make her new creation look even more irresistible to that larger world, frequently the new mother believes them to be a sound investment.

One interesting sidelight of the employed-mother revolution is that it may have enhanced the incidence of clothes and toy buying for baby. When men were providing most of the family's income, a mother often had to curb her buying impulse if a husband said, "Enough," because it was money he earned that she was spending. But now that many new mothers have independent sources of income, they feel (within limits of course) that they have a right to spend their money as they choose.

Relationship Difficulties

It is harder to draw a statistical profile of marital estrangement and drift, but several numbers suggest why it is also an important transition issue. One comes from a recent *Parenting* magazine survey that found that new mothers and fathers are twice as likely to kiss the baby as they are each other. A recent University of Michigan study found that the incidence of sexual intercourse drops 30 to 40 percent in the first year after the baby's arrival.

Fatigue, of course, is partly responsible for these changes, and so is the baby, who attracts attention and affection his parents used to direct at each other. But the principal reason new parents touch less frequently is that they feel less connected, less in tune with each other. It is not accidental that one of the most enduring pieces of transition folklore—one that has been passed down from one generation of new parents to the next—is the story of the couple who, on their first night out alone, run out of things to say within five minutes. The sense of drift, estrangement, and loneliness that produces such tongue-tiedness is as much a feature of the transition in most marriages as are money worries and division-of-labor concerns. But once again, differences in upbringing and biology often make men and women blame these problems on very different things.

For men the chief culprit is maternal preoccupation with the baby. While most new fathers expect the baby to become the main priority in the family, many are stunned at how little wifely attention or affection is left over for them. Our Project fathers complained that after the baby's arrival much less interest was shown in their work, hobbies, concerns, or sexual desires. One Project husband described a recent sexual encounter with his wife this way: "Last Sunday, while Ellen and I were lying in bed, I reached over and touched her. She'd been half asleep, but as soon as I put my hand on her breast, she bolted upright, pulled a sheet over her and said, 'Don't. Not now. That's for Jonathan.' Believe me, if I ever had any doubts about her priorities, that incident cleared them up in a hurry."

Often adding to the man's sense of estrangement is the coterie of advisers that surrounds the new mother. While men know why this happens, these figures—who include mothers, sisters, aunts, and other female relatives and friends—possess nurturing skills a man often does not. Their sudden importance in a wife's life often makes a husband feel shunted aside and unimportant. A University of Minnesota study found that while in-laws were not among the top five transition complaints of new mothers, they were the number-one complaint of new fathers, many of whom singled out mothers-in-law and sisters-in-law as sources of alienation and estrangement. "Sometimes I wonder if anyone remembers I'm still here," a Project father said to me one day.

When women talk about transition-time loneliness and estrangement, their chief culprit is what I call male self-focus. Because of upbringing and perhaps biology as well, a man's emotional energy and attention all too frequently tend to flow inward toward his own concerns and needs. Shared experiences which pull a man outside of himself and force him to concentrate on his partner's needs can sometimes disrupt this flow. But because none of the transition's major events absolutely require male participation—a man does not have to be in the delivery room if he does not want to be, for example—often the new father's focus remains relatively undisrupted. As before the baby's arrival, he continues to be preoccupied with his own wants and needs.

An example of how this self-focus can contribute to maternal estrangement and disaffection is a story a Project wife told me about a visit to her husband's parents six weeks after her child's birth. "I'd had a cesarean," the woman said, "so Norman carried Natasha into the house. But he was so concerned about getting to the TV set and the football game that the minute he got through the door, he practically threw her on the floor. He didn't take her out of her baby seat or unwrap her blanket; he didn't ask me what I wanted. He didn't do anything except vanish. Sometimes I wonder whether he realizes the two of us even exist."

An encounter another Project wife had with male self-focus left her feeling even more estranged and alienated. One night about three months after daughter Sarah's birth, mother Jill was standing in front of the bedroom mirror in her bra and panties when she happened to catch a glimpse of husband, Michael, examining her from the opposite side of the bedroom. The look on his face so horrified her that Jill rushed to the closet for a bathrobe. When she told one of our female observers about this incident, Jill said it confirmed what she had already begun to suspect about Michael: He was so wrapped up in what he wanted—"a perfect little beauty queen of a wife"—he had no understanding of or sympathy for what she was going through.

The association men make between work and parenting also contributes to maternal loneliness and estrangement. Just at the point when a new mother wants her husband home by her side, this association will often make the husband pull himself out of the family and immerse himself more deeply in his work. "I know Ralph means well," one of our wives told me, "but I don't understand why he only equates parenting with money. It's important, but right now having him here is a lot more important to me than the few extra dollars his overtime brings in."

Career and Work

At the Project's start in 1982, 30 percent of our wives were employed in the baby's first year, and most held traditionally female jobs. They were beauticians, nurses, teachers, and clerks. Most also worked for a traditionally female reason: Their families could not get by without their paychecks. At the Project's conclusion in 1988, maternal employment stood at 45 percent, and now our employed mothers included more professional women, such as accountants, lawyers, and office managers. An increasing number of our women also looked upon their work, whatever they did, as a career or as the steppingstone to one. Our data closely mirror national trends, which show that between 1970 and 1990 the number of employed mothers with young children almost doubled, from 30 percent to 53 percent.

This change in maternal employment has fueled another equally momentous change. For reasons of both ideology and need, over the past decade more and more employed mothers have come to embrace the notion of egalitarian role sharing. While today's employed mother expects parity or near parity on division of labor, her adherence to this ideal often leads her to expect something much deeper—marital parity. She expects her partner to share emotional responsibility for their child and family and to share in career sacrifices if they have to be made. Not every woman who goes to work embraces egalitarianism, of course, but enough do to have created another potent source of divisiveness between members of the His and Hers transitions.

Some men share their wives' egalitarianism. During the Project, we encountered a number of committed male egalitarians, and interestingly the ones most steadfast in their commitment to this ideal tended to be alike.... For the most part they were low-key, usually nonideological (i.e., they did not have any special intellectual commitment to either egalitarianism or feminism), extremely secure, and often domestically skilled. Also noteworthy, they were all deeply in love with their wives. However, these husbands represented the exception. The norm among Project husbands—and I strongly suspect among husbands in general—is a man in transition. This individual also loves his wife and wants to support her, especially when she holds a paying job. But because he has a lingering allegiance to certain aspects of the traditional male role, he is often psychologically and emotionally unprepared to be the full partner his wife wants and expects.

Take chores. The woman's desire for parity or near parity on the division-of-labor issue frequently causes conflict because it bumps into the transitional man's belief that while a husband should contribute, a wife should remain first among equals in the nursery, kitchen, and laundry room. The working mother's belief that emotional responsibility for child and home should be shared also frequently causes conflict. Unlike his father or grandfather, a transitional man will bathe and diaper the baby. But like them he believes, or at least acts as if he believes, that chores that involve assuming emotional responsibility for home and child, such as scheduling pediatrician's visits, overseeing child-care arrangements, and making out shopping lists, are a woman's work—whether she has a job outside the home or not.

Career conflicts are also common between this man and his wife because his view of himself as the family's principal breadwinner (whatever the reality of the situation) produces an expectation that career sacrifices are also his wife's job. One area where this expectation caused a great many problems for Project mothers was when they had to work late. Usually if a man's desk was clear at five, he would agree to pick up the baby at the sitter or child-care center. However, if it wasn't—even if there wasn't anything terribly pressing on it—he would generally say, "No, I can't. I have to work too. You'll just have to make other arrangements."

Social Isolation

The weeks immediately following the baby's birth are a whirlwind of social activity. But sometime around the end of the first month the congratulatory calls and visits begin to taper off, and that is when the stress of social isolation really starts to make itself felt. Among Project participants, recreational activities in the form of visits to movies, restaurants, and friends' homes declined by 40 percent during the first year of the transition. And several findings from the *Parenting* magazine study suggest that their experience is the rule, not the exception. More than half the survey respondents reported that they did not go out at all during the first six months after the baby's birth unless a relative was able to sit. Even after the first year more than 81 percent had yet to spend a weekend alone, and 91 percent to take a vacation of five or more days alone.

On the whole, new mothers tend to suffer more from isolation than fathers, and new stay-at-home mothers suffer most of all. Said one such mother, "Sometimes it gets so bad, I find myself actually dreading Kate's naps. But when she's up, I spend most of my time wishing I had another adult here to talk to." Work protects men from this kind of desperate isolation. But the lack of date nights, parties, vacations, and extracurricular activities such as Saturday afternoon racquetball takes its toll on them too. In conversations we found men and women equally likely to complain about feeling isolated and cut off. But we also found that like the other major transition stresses, this one is perceived very differently by the two sexes.

Men generally take the position of Mike Evans, one of our Project husbands, who felt that the principal reason for his and wife Phoebe's isolation was what he called Phoebe's obsession with the baby. "She won't leave him alone," Mike complained one day. "I know mothers are supposed to be devoted to their babies, but Phoebe's gone way overboard. Every time David hiccups, she makes a federal case out of it. She won't eat unless he's on her lap or leave him if she thinks the slightest thing is wrong. Last week, an hour before we were supposed to go to the movies, Phoebe marched into the living room and announced that she'd just canceled the sitter. She thought David was coming down with a cold and didn't want to leave him. I went ballistic. We've been out exactly three times in the last eight months."

When I talked to Phoebe Evans a few days later, she was still feeling vaguely guilty about this incident. "I know sometimes I overfocus on David," she admitted, "but it's taken me a while to recognize that and also to recognize that it won't change unless I make an effort to change it." But like most women Phoebe also felt that a major factor in the Evans's isolation was her husband's attitude. "Mike's always telling me, 'Come on. Let's go out, let's go out,' and I want to, but I say no because I'm too exhausted. And that's Mike's fault. He barely lifts a finger to help me."

What Unites Us

"One day, when Michela was four months old, I had an incredible experience with her. She'd been crying and I was trying to soothe her, but nothing worked. So finally, out of desperation, I began singing 'Row, Row, Row Your Boat' very softly. All of a sudden the tears stopped, her eyes got shiny and as big as nickels, and her little mouth formed into a perfect 'O.' She was straining every ounce to focus on me. No one had ever looked at me that intently before—as if I were the sun, moon, and stars all wrapped up in one. It made me so happy, I took Michela's little hand in mine and began waltzing her round and round the kitchen."

This story from a Project mother indicates what is wrong with the portrait of the transition I've painted over the last 15-odd pages—it leaves out all the good parts. If becoming a parent were an endless conflict about money, chores, work, the relationship, and social activity, babies would be a lot rarer than they are. But of course it is not an endless conflict. Along with the tumult, the exhaustion, the loneliness, and hurt feelings there are also moments of sublime happiness, moments when the new parent literally begins dancing with joy. And for the most part what sets new parents to dancing is the same. Among Project husbands and wives there was as much agreement about the transition's gratifications as there was about its stresses. But just as men and women perceive the stresses differently, often they also perceive its gratifications differently.

Take what everyone agrees is the transition's most exquisite gratification: the baby himself. Often when new mothers talk about why he is so wonderful, they speak the language of love. They say the baby has introduced them to a new dimension of this feeling, one they did not know—had not dreamed—existed before. Project mothers tried to explain the uniqueness of this love in many different ways. Some attempted to delineate its parameters in words, and often the words they chose were ones people use when they are trying to describe a profound spiritual awakening. Women talked about being seized by an "all-embracing," "all-encompassing" love. Other mothers employed metaphors to describe the specialness of what they felt. Said one Project woman, "Tilly's opened a door in me I didn't even know was there." Still others described the transforming effect of their new feelings. "The love that flows through Adam's eyes when I hold him makes me tingle," said one mother, while another compared her baby's smile to a "magic wand" that "chases my blues away." We also had a fair amount of new mothers who believed that human language had not yet invented words powerful enough to describe what they felt. "I love Cynthia more than words can say," declared one mother when I asked her to describe how she felt about her new baby.

While new fathers are also set to dancing by the baby, they usually dance more slowly and for different reasons. We had a few men who were as swept away by love as any new mother. Representative of this group was the man who said, "I can't fully express the feelings of love I have for Michael. He's a magnificent blessing. He's increased the love I receive and the love I give." But most new fathers are swept away by the baby for more traditional male reasons. Many look upon him as a terrific new playmate. A number of Project fathers echoed the sentiment of the man who described his new son as being "more fun than TV." Even more men seem to see the baby as a wonderful new cement that strengthens their feelings toward wife and family. "I feel much more deeply committed to my marriage now," said one new father.

While men and women used different verbal styles to describe their feelings about baby, when they talked about him, I noticed that they both used the same facial expression: They smiled.

Changes in feeling about oneself ranks as the second major transition gratification. At one point or another almost all of our mothers and fathers reported that parenthood had made them feel more mature, more grown-up. But these words meant different things to men and to women. Usually when a man used them, he meant that he felt more responsible about his work. Sometimes this would lead him to devote more hours to it; other times, to begin looking at it in a new way. Instead of seeing it simply as a source of revenue, now the new father would begin to look at his job as part of a larger life plan. As the child grew, the family's income needs would increase; did his job offer an opportunity for advancement? And even more important, his family would need a secure source of income. Did his present job provide that security?

New mothers also equated maturity with responsibility. But when a woman talked about responsibility, usually she meant the responsibility of shaping and molding a new life. Many women reported that motherhood made them behave more sensibly. "I used to be a real speed demon," said one woman. "But not anymore. Since Amy's birth, I don't think I've gone more than 45 miles per hour. My husband can't believe it. But now that she's a part of my life, I don't feel I can afford to take risks anymore." Other women reported that their new sense of responsibility had awakened them to larger concerns. "I never paid much attention to environmental issues," one of our mothers told me one day. "I figured I don't live in Brazil, so why should I worry about the rain forest, and I'm not an Eskimo, so why should I worry about the whales? But Eddie's changed that. These things are a part of the world he's going to live in, and I want to make sure that when he's grown-up, they're still there for him to enjoy."

The new sense of family that the baby creates ranks as a third major transition gratification for most new parents. And interestingly it is one that mothers and fathers experience in the same way. When we asked Project participants why the baby enhanced their sense of family, men were as likely as women to cite the same reasons. One was that the new child had given the husband and wife what they had not had before: a biological connection. One Project father spoke for many of our study participants when he said, "Since the baby, I feel a lot closer to my wife emotionally and spiritually because she's not just my partner anymore. She's the mother of my child." The need to pull together to meet the demands of the transition can also enhance a couple's sense of being part of the same unit. "Suddenly you realize if you're going to survive this thing intact," said one woman, "the two of you are going to have to learn to work together in a new way, and that creates a tremendous sense of unity." The remark of another Project participant hints at a third reason why the baby often enhances a couple's sense of family: "When I was a little girl," she said, "we used to spend every summer on the Jersey shore. Since Jane's birth Everett and I have spent a lot of time talking about the traditions we want to create for our new family."

In interviews Project participants singled out one other aspect of the transition as being particularly gratifying: It brought them closer to their own parents. Sometimes this bond arose from empathy. Now that they were parents themselves, participants said they had a better appreciation of what their parents had given them and what they had gone through to give it. Said one man, "Being a dad myself, I realize what a good job my parents did with me and how much I owe them." A Project mother added, "It took me twenty-eight years, but I'm finally beginning to understand all the sacrifices my mom and dad made for me."

Other times the new bond with one's own parents was generational. Suddenly the mother and father felt linked in a great family chain that stretched back into some unknown past and now forward into the baby's future. Being part of this chain evoked powerful feelings in a new parent. A particularly dramatic case in point was the Project father who ended a five-year dispute with his father after his daughter's birth. The two men had not spoken since having a falling-out over the family business. "I felt my father had behaved very pigheadedly," the man said, "and I was angry at him. But after Natalie's birth I felt it was time to put our dispute aside. We're all part of the same family, and it would be silly to allow a business disagreement to continue disrupting the family. So I gulped hard and called him."

One of the things that became clear early in the Project is that couples who are able to focus their attention on what unites them and produce mutual joy usually end up at the end of the transition with a better, happier marriage. I think the reasons for this are fairly self-evident. The transition gives a couple dozens of new and potentially much deeper points of connection. There is the baby and the new biological link he creates between husband and wife; there is the new sense of unity, of family they experience as they join together to nurture him; and there is also the enormous satisfaction of knowing that you and your partner are growing together and growing in the same direction. However, in order to take advantage of these new points of connection, a couple first must learn how to deal with the new differences and divisions the transition also creates. . . .

Notes

1. The one-third of mothers who do not form an instant attachment to the baby do eventually form a strong attachment. It just takes them a little longer to fall in love.

2. Some data from the recent mate-selection research tends to support Dr. Lancaster's theory. For men in all cultures the top priority in a mate is physical attractiveness, and while women may blame this preference on male shallowness, Dr. David Buss of the University of Michigan thinks the deeper impulse behind it is male reproductive needs. In order to spread his nearly inexhaustible seed, a man needs a fertile woman. And since for Ancient Man the two most reliable and ubiquitous markers of female fertility were youth (for obvious reasons) and physical attractiveness (because it indicates good health), Dr. Buss argues that over time evolution has programmed men to prefer young, pretty women. The qualities women prize in a mate also fit their reproductive needs. The high priority they put on wealth and status in a mate (and this preference also occurs in all cultures), reflects the female's need to secure resources to protect her large biological investment in the baby. The relatively low priority women put on male beauty points to the fact that a man of almost any age can get a woman pregnant.

Growing Up Takes Time*

Penelope Leach

Throughout this century popular theories about child development have swung back and forth between approaches which focus upon the importance of culture and parental involvement, and perspectives which place more emphasis upon the biological determinants of human growth. Penelope Leach argues that at least among middle-class parents in modern industrial societies, we have become obsessed with achievement to the point of pushing infants from the moment they are born. She suggests that the pendulum needs to swing back in the other direction and we must realize the biological constraints upon the growth and development of infants. Rather than worry about how a child compares to statistical standards of "normal" development, Leach suggests that parents should enjoy each child as he or she grows and changes. Early indicators of advanced skills do little to predict later achievement, and parents must learn that "growing up takes time."

At a party, late on and liquored, a father describes the results of his two-year-old son's routine developmental assessment and ends, " 'Coming along nicely' just won't do and 'average' is an insult. I don't want him to be average, I want him to be best."

All parents everywhere want the best for their growing children, but parents in Western societies are particularly inclined to confuse that with making them *be* the best. Once children reach adolescence, such parents cheer (or yell) for them to make the grades, pass the exams, and get into the jobs or colleges that usher in adult success. Even while their children are babies, many parents find it hard to accept that the best a child can have is every possible, peaceful opportunity for optimal personal development, and "the best" he or she can be, at any time, is the person that development has produced. Too many Western parents treat the few testable benchmarks of aspects of development as measures of "progress," emphasizing what babies can *do* rather than glorying in the people they are becoming.

All age groups have been invited to the party. A smiley baby girl is carried from adult to adult, and after the obligatory "Isn't she lovely?" almost everyone asks, "How old is she now?" Two older babies crawl among the crowd; one uses the couch to pull himself to a standing position and the mother of the other quickly points out to anyone who will listen that her baby—who does not do that yet—is "younger than he looks." A three-foot person pushes over a two-foot person and someone remarks that she is "old enough to know better" while, over in the corner, smothered but admiring laughter greets the child who thanks his hostess for a "'ceptionally nice party." *How* old is he now? Just as the adults seem unable to interact with each other until each knows what the other "does" ("He works on Wall Street but I'm just a mother, I'm afraid") so they seem unable to relate to any child until he or she has been slotted into an age bracket. The parents are not surprised; exact answers—"three months and four days," "four next week"—trip smoothly off their tongues. Their children's position on the calendar is never far from their consciousness, being used, from the beginning, to judge the legitimacy of their needs, the appropriateness of their demands, and the adequacy of their progress. A new baby's cries at 3 A.M. say she is hungry but it is the calendar that says whether or not she ought to be. An older baby crawls across the floor or gets to his feet, and again it is the calendar rather than his face that tells his parents how to react. If he is "only" six months or nine months old they will be triumphant; if he is "already" twelve or eighteen months old their dominant emotion will be relief at this evidence that their beloved baby is catching up. Catching up with what or whom? With "age norms" from a book or developmental chart, with the expectations of a day-care center or grandparent or with the "superior" performance of a niece or neighbor who, horror of horrors, is younger than he is? This father's frankness may have been unusual but his sentiments are not.

It is not surprising that parents demand excellence from their offspring. Rearing children is a major pragmatic and narcissistic investment. All parents expect a return on it and all returns relate to children's performance. There is always a bargain between the generations although its existence is not always acknowledged or its nature understood. In times and places where the work of even very young children has economic value, and grown ones are obligated to support their aging relatives, outsiders see an obvious pragmatic return for parents and often underestimate or ignore the narcissistic return which is part and parcel of it. In modern postindustrial regions, where economic resources flow from parents to children rather than the other way around and parents may face peak financial commitments to children (such as college fees) just as their earning power dwindles towards compulsory retirement, the absence of a pragmatic return on procreation throws the narcissistic return into high relief, though insiders usually deny it. Citizens of "advanced nations" like to believe that they have babies for altruistic rather than selfish reasons. But when parents across the globe are asked why they have children, what their children are for, all their answers are remarkably similar. We all have children for ourselves and our pleasure. We all want them to make us feel good, to raise our self-esteem and self-respect and therefore the esteem and respect accorded to us by others. In order to make parents feel good, children must succeed according to whatever cultural values are locally prevalent, and it is here, in the nature of the success that will make people proud to be parents, that the real differences lie. Children may succeed in their parents' eyes by contributing to family survival or prosperity with labor, marriage, or procreation; by honoring gods, ancestors or traditions; by fulfilling a range of duties and obligations to other people, implicit in their names or membership of the group into which they were born. But for those steeped in the ethos of the postindustrial West, the dominant values are primarily individualistic and competitive.

Our children have not only a right but a duty to fulfill their "personal potential." Membership on the team is fine, but being its leader is better. And whatever our particular code of ethics and morals, ends justify such a wide range of means that "let the best person win" easily elides into "one who wins is the best," according to a lexicon that often equates personal initiative with sharp practice.

For parents living here and now, then, within that broad value system, a desire for children to achieve not only individual excellence but excellence relative to others is readily understandable. Nevertheless, their determination to demonstrate it from day one in an endless series of nursery comparisons is unfortunate. The evaluation of childish accomplishments by the speed with which they are achieved, rather than by their quality, range or utility, contradicts much of what is known of the nature of human development and is demonstrably counterproductive.

Child development is a process, not a race. In the first years each infant recapitulates the evolutionary stages that produced humanity, so major landmarks like walking and talking are important and exciting. But that does not mean that it is necessarily better to reach them faster and pass them sooner. The modern infant *is* human and therefore *will* become a biped and communicate in speech. She is not a better example of her species because she does these things at an earlier age than average, nor does infant precocity predict adult excellence. We behave as if the child who walks earliest will run fastest, as if exceptionally early single words predict meaningful later sentences and as if children's prospects as intelligent, independent, and socialized people can be improved by speeding them through age-appropriate illiteracy, dependence, or incontinence. It is not so, and there is abundant research evidence to prove it, even though much of it is based on testing procedures that do indeed measure performance against the calendar.

Developmental tests for infants try to cover the whole child by considering his development in each of several areas. "Motor development" covers progress towards walking and beyond, via those best-known milestones: sitting alone, crawling, and standing. "Language" covers progress towards fluent, grammatical speech via listening, responding to, and understanding the speech of others, and via communicating in sounds, labeling familiar objects with names, using single words and phrases. "Social development" ranges from smiling in the first weeks and give-and-take games in the first months to self-care in the second year, while "cognitive development" (often misconstrued as a baby IQ test) attempts to assess aspects of thinking and reasoning via play tasks with standardized objects. The child's score in each area is related to the average of scores achieved by large samples of other children of the same chronological age, and his individual result is then presented as an age score. Children always produce a scatter of scores from area to area. A ten-month-old may perform at thirteen-month level on motor items, at eleven-month level on verbal items, and at the nine-month level on social or cognitive items. Does that mean that he is "advanced" in walking and talking and "behind" in social skills? Yes and no. The scores may be valid for today (though nobody can know whether the performance he gave was the "best" he could give or merely the best he felt like giving at this particular time and with this particular person) but that does not mean that they are a valid statement of his development even relative to the other infants whose scores make up the norms. If that child is tested again six months later he will again produce a scatter of scores but it will probably be a different scatter. Now, at sixteen months, he performs all motor items at sixteen-month level so that he is no longer "advanced" but "average" in motor development. His verbal development has also "dropped back" and he now tests out at the thirteen-month level, which is below rather than above his chronological age, but both his social and his cognitive scores have risen to scores of sixteen months and eighteen months, respectively. Test him yet again when he is two and the natural peaks and lags of development will probably produce equally unpredictable scores.

Babies are born already programmed with a map of the long and complex route towards maturity and beyond, and with the drive to travel along it. The route is the same for every child in the world but the scale of the map is too small to show the millions of minor roads and scenic routes, diversions and disasters, roadblocks and resting places that make each developmental journey unique within unimaginable human diversity. Just as a road map states total distances between major cities but neither predicts nor prescribes individual journey times, so the developmental map is confined to neurobiological distances between sequential landmarks. Babies cannot dance before they run, run before they walk, walk before they stand, or stand before they sit. But exactly how long each one will spend at or between these stage points on the track nobody can know. Nobody should care, either, because it is not a racetrack and there are no prizes for the one who gets there first nor, barring serious long-term physical problems, penalties for the one who gets there last. Babies do what they have to do when they are ready to do it whether or not adults try to motivate or teach them and even if circumstances seem against them. A heavy plaster cast may delay a baby's first attempts to pull herself to her feet but it will not long delay her walking because, if she is developmentally ready to walk when that cast is removed, she will make up for any lost time by spending less on the preliminaries. Released from casts and sitting position at twelve months, some such babies pull themselves to supported standing, cruise around furniture, let go to stand alone, and then walk independently before they are fifteen months old. It should not surprise us. Our pushy passion for leg-strengthening floor play, for baby walkers "to give him the feel of his feet" and for spending hours holding small hands while we cry, "Walk to mommy, darling," is a parallel route rather than a shortcut on that map. Navajo Indian babies who had been kept more or less immobile in cradleboards throughout most of their first year walked at exactly the same average age as other American babies reared in California or Boston.

A baby's performance today says very little that is useful about his likely performance next year. As long ago as 1970 the psychologist who developed the most widely used of all infant development scales, the Bayley Mental Development Index, wrote: "The findings of these early studies of mental growth of infants have been repeated sufficiently often so that it is now well established that test scores earned in the first year or two have relatively little predictive validity." But that does not mean that developmental tests are useless; it simply means that we tend to misuse them. Skilled assessment of the development of populations of infants, or of specified subgroups within populations, is an invaluable research tool. Without standardized scores we should never have discovered, for example, that many aspects of the development of groups of infants tested by the Gesell Institute during the 1970s were advanced by almost six months over the development of similar groups, similarly tested, during the 1930s—invaluable findings to policy makers concerned with child care or education. Such testing can also be a potent weapon in the hands of those who seek to establish the ill-effects of specific kinds of deprivation and then to measure the efficacy of intervention programs such as Head Start. It is the testing of individual children that requires such caution. Useful as a way for professionals to screen for difficulties, such as deafness, that might otherwise go undetected for long enough to cause global developmental problems, such testing is a misleading procedure for parents seeking confirmation of their children's "intelligence" or "advancement" and a dangerous tool in the hands of those looking to speed up the "progress" of children whose overall development gives no realistic cause for concern. As Gesell, father of developmental assessment, pointed out, it is not superior performance in one or all fields that differentiates even highly gifted children from others, but a far more nebulous quality of vividness and vitality: "the infant with superior equipment exploits his physical surroundings in a more varied manner, and is more sensitive and responsive to his social environment . . . the scorable end-products may not be far in advance, but the *manner* of performance is superior."

If parents would look at their children's "manner of performance" rather than at *what* is performed or its date on the calendar, they would see individuals in all their complexity rather than in their age bracket, see all the things they do that have never been studied rather than the things they do not yet do and "should," see who they are rather than how they compare with others. Achieving head control, rolling over, sitting up, crawling and standing, for example, are genuine milestones along the road to becoming a biped but while being a biped is a necessary condition for being a person, it certainly is not a sufficient one. When a two-month-old baby begins to roll himself over, he is not just demonstrating an achievement in neuromuscular control, he is experiencing the vital new autonomy of being able to change his own view from the crib or changing table, to release an arm that has been trapped beneath his body or to keep his mother in view as she moves around the room. When he can sit alone he is not just halfway to an upright posture but freed from the restrictions imposed on him by having to lie down or be propped, so that he can more easily reach out for things with his arms and coordinate his hands and eyes in manipulating objects. Being a sitter enormously enriches his interaction with people and playthings. What he does as he sits has real importance; it matters far more than the speed with which he stops "just" sitting and begins to crawl or stand. Continually looking for further accomplishment, parents deprive both themselves and their children of peaceful pleasure in their joint present.

The assumption that children who go fastest go farthest is so deeply entrenched in our society that it is not surprising parents accept it. It is there in the baby books that tell new mothers their babies "ought" to sleep through the night at six weeks old, sit at six months, and read at six years; it is there on the packaging of "educational" toys that say "suitable for ages 9–18 months" and imply that the baby in that age group who disregards them is backward rather than uninterested or busy with other things. And it is there in the time-framed obstacles some child-care workers and teachers set up: "we cannot take your child until he is out of diapers . . ."; "we expect our three-year-olds to know their colors and the days of the week." Talk to individual parents about their children's separate accomplishments, and most will agree that it does not *really* matter if a baby prefers crawling to construction toys, or if a preschool child has learned a lot of nursery rhymes but no colors. But most of them still believe that *overall* "advancement" must be a Good Thing. The angry father we met at the beginning of this chapter certainly did: "He's quick at *everything* and always has been. He walked sooner than most; he talks better; he draws well, washes his own face, does puzzles meant for older kids—you can't tell me he's not bright." Nobody had told him his child was not bright. The pediatrician had told him he was normal and since he wanted to be told his child was a genius, he found that insulting. How he would have envied the father of a five-day-old baby I met last year: "Isn't he really great?" he responded to my congratulations. "The pediatrician told us he was the best baby in the nursery."

All any parent can be told with confidence is that a baby has no apparent developmental difficulties and that is all any parent need hope for. An infant whose development is accelerated in all fields and remains so over a year or more *may* be highly gifted; certainly plenty of gifted adults were rapid developers in infancy, though some were markedly slow. But plenty of "average" adults were rapid developers too. A baby's present "good performance" shows that his or her environment, care, and fortune have been fine—so far—and that she or he is unlikely to be of much below average intelligence when grown up. But average the child may well be. By definition, most people are. What a tragedy if a child's normal abilities when it is time for school disappoint parents because they were convinced they had produced a prodigy and had allowed themselves to think that a prodigy was what they wanted.

Parents have enormous influence over their children but many people misunderstand its nature. Some still see infant development as Watson or James saw it—see babies as "blank slates" for adults to write upon, formless and functionless creatures that must be shaped and cast by adults. Others, culturally adapted to improving on nature, are convinced that any parent who can repair a car or make over a company can surely exert the same kind of power to perfect one small child.

Such misunderstandings put a burden of responsibility onto parents that is like a novice hiker's rucksack: heavy with the latest trendy gadgets, light on basic necessities, and so badly balanced that there is no pleasure in the walk. Parents do not need to shoulder active responsibility for bustling children from helpless newborns to competent people; they can trust the developmental process to move them along at the rate that is appropriate for them. Children do not forever suck instead of eating if nobody weans them, fail to learn language if words are not taught, remain incontinent unless they are "trained," or grow up in ignorance of what is right unless they have been punished for doing wrong. Encumbered with all that unnecessary activism, many parents jettison some of their vital but more passive responsibilities as models, caring companions, unfailing supporters, and facilitators of children's own overall development as individual people. An imbalance between those two reduces parents' pleasure in the whole child-rearing expedition and puts both the child's performance and long-term development at risk. Nobody's baby will starve because granola and broccoli are not forced down her reluctant throat, but a few people's children will later starve themselves in anorexia nervosa because foods and overwhelming concern were forced on them. Nobody's toddler will grow into an aggressive psychopath because he "got away with" biting other toddlers, but a few people's children will still bite others in kindergarten because, bitten back by a parent "to show how much it hurts," they learned the unintended lesson that hurting people is a legitimate way to exert power over them.

Inbuilt sequences of development do not only render parental pressure unnecessary—because children will do what they need to do as and when they are ready—they also make that pressure pointless, or worse, because children cannot do things until they are ready. Like every other mammal, babies and toddlers instinctively protect themselves and their possessions with teeth and claws. In group care with a shared caregiver, physically aggressive behavior makes for chaos and parents press for more socialized ways with outraged cries of "Don't hit—ask" and "Be nice to your little friend." But until the second, or even the third year, children cannot "be nice" to each other on purpose because it takes that long for social and cognitive growth to bring toddlers to awareness of other people's feelings and to compel them to experiment with putting themselves in other people's shoes. Once that awareness takes root, there is much that adults can do to facilitate and encourage the flowering of empathy and related impulse control, but nothing they do before that will hurry the growth of altruism and relieve caregivers of the necessity for protecting their charges from themselves and from each other.

This inbuilt developmental protection from pushing is important because if parents really could accelerate children's achievement of particular goals the results would often be disastrous. Imagine the fate of a one-year-old who really had learned to respect the feelings of other infants and "ask nicely" while they ignored her pacific gestures and snatched at her toys and hair. Or imagine parents who really concentrated on teaching their baby to walk and succeeded in rushing her past that milestone at seven months. Apart from their own glow of pride, what would they have? A baby who walked around rooms before she had mapped them visually, and who met phenomena like steps and dogs from a perilous upright posture without first having come to terms with them from the relative stability of hands and knees.

But the fact that children cannot do what it is developmentally inappropriate for them to do does not protect them from adult efforts to make them. Parental pressure does not have to be successful to be unfortunate. A child's energy and waking hours are limited and the time adults will spend with her is almost always rationed, so the very process of pressuring her to do something she is not ready to do is likely to deprive her of time to do and enjoy what is appropriate. Hours spent in a baby walker cannot also be spent crawling on the floor with toys. Time adults spend holding her hands and exhorting her to walk cannot also be spent cuddling her, showing her things, and telling her she is wonderful. And even if there is, overall, enough of everybody's time for everything, time that is spent orienting infants towards achievements that are still in the developmental future is time wasted, or worse. Look at early potty training. Diapers almost always become family history in the daytime during a child's third year whether the parents start "training" him when he is twelve or twenty-four months old. Wait until he is developmentally ready and the process may take three months; start before he is ready and it will take all the months until he is, plus that same three months. If it takes three extra minutes to pot as well as change a baby-in-training and that is done four times a day, the difference between starting at one year or two is twelve minutes a day for 365 days, which is over seventy hours or almost two working weeks with nothing to show for them except extra stress. And if the stress of that year of unsuccessful/impossible potting has been considerable, the difference may well be even greater because the one-year-old who did not know how to do what the parents wanted has become a two-year-old who does not want to. It is even easier to pressure children into problems with nighttime dryness. Living with a child who wets his bed, night after night, is not easy: how is the mattress to be dried or kept dry? How is the laundry to be coped with? How can the child be taken on vacation or left overnight with friends? Aware that the child wets in his sleep and therefore cannot be blamed for it, parents may try to be understanding and sensitive to his feelings, but they cannot conceal those practical problems or their own desire for the child to change. Enuresis quickly becomes a major factor in his life and self-image. But what made that little boy into a bed wetter? Whatever the complex physiological, genetic, and emotional explanations for his failure to concentrate his urine and hold it through the night, the direct answer to that vital question is simply "leaving off the diapers that kept the bed dry." The calendar may say that a child is three years old; the developmental charts may pinpoint that as the proper age of nighttime dryness, but parents' only real cue to the right timing for their child comes from his personal development. As long as he still wakes with a soaking diaper each morning, putting him to bed without one guarantees a soaking bed. Should diapers that have been prematurely abandoned be reintroduced? While the parents could solve their practical problems that way, a simple reversal seldom solves the problems that pressuring parents have caused their children. That child has been told that he is a "big boy, not a baby who needs diapers anymore"; how will he feel when he finds himself clad as a baby all over again? How do children who have been coached into the very best nursery school and pushed into kindergarten a year early feel when they are kept down to repeat the class the following year? And how do they feel when after months of unavailing home tuition in reading, parents suddenly take the teacher's advice to withdraw and leave literacy to her?

Parents whose own egos are directly invested in children's forthcoming achievements are distracted from enjoying them as they are today and disappointed when they fail to meet their aspirations for tomorrow. That is sad for the parents but it is much worse than sad for the children. Their ego development depends on parental pleasure and approval; to find themselves a disappointment is disastrous. If children are to develop the self-esteem and self-respect that will maximize their fulfillment of their potential, their resilience, and their ability to esteem and respect other people, they need to feel loved, respected, even celebrated, for what they are rather than for what they do. That means that they need to be as sure that extra achievement could not earn them extra love as that failure could not deprive them of the love they have. Unconditional love in infancy and early childhood, from at least one adult who is both consistently available and emotionally involved, seems a mondial prerequisite of mental health throughout life. Putting conditions on that love may be as risky as putting limits on adult availability. Today's families often do both at once.

Children in the postindustrial West have the longest compulsory childhood the world has ever known. With all those years of enforced dependence ahead of them, we have to learn that letting them take their own time over growing up is what is best for them now and what will best help them to fulfill their own potential when they are grown. It will not be an easy lesson. The tyranny of time works powerfully on adults and the more time children take, the more parents must give. As well as seeming to spell progress and promise success, a speedy passage through developmental phases means that parents can quickly be rid of bottles and broken nights, diapers and nightmares, toys and testing, mess and muddle, explanations, exhortations, and endless demands for vigilance, responsibility and love. But all those things are the stuff of childhood. If adults experience childhood as something for children to be put through, and parents to get through, as fast as possible, no child can ever experience their love as belonging by right to the person she is today; it will always seem conditional on her being a different person tomorrow.

"Have yours all left home now? How old are they now?" Only in the lonely peace of the finally emptied nest is there time to realize just how little time it takes children to grow up, and to wonder what the rush was really all about.

Marital Dissolution and Remarriage*

Andrew J. Cherlin

Early conceptualizations of the family life course paid little attention to divorce. As Andrew J. Cherlin's article points out, however, one cannot understand families without an appreciation of patterns of family dissolution and remarriage. As with the earlier article by Whyte, which looked at early transitions in the family life course, Cherlin's work shows that transitions in and out of the married state create complex patterns. After tracing historical patterns of change in marital dissolution, he discusses kinship patterns in families of remarriage and explores the effects of marital dissolution upon family members.

No trend in American family life since World War II has received more attention or caused more concern than the rising rate of divorce. The divorce rate, however, has been rising since at least the middle of the nineteenth century. Figure 24-1 shows the number of divorces per 1,000 existing marriages (after 1920, per 1,000 married women) in every year between 1860 (the earliest year for which data are available) and 1988. These are annual measures, reflecting the particular social and economic conditions of each year. We can see, for example, that

*Source: Reprinted by permission of the publishers from *Marriage, Divorce, Remarriage* by Andrew J. Cherlin, Cambridge, Mass.: Harvard University Press, Copyright (c) 1981, 1992 by the President and Fellows of Harvard College.

FIGURE 24-1

**Annual Divorce Rate, United States. For
1920–1988: Divorces per 1,000 Married Women
Aged 15 and Over; for 1860–1920: Divorces per
1,000 Existing Marriages.**

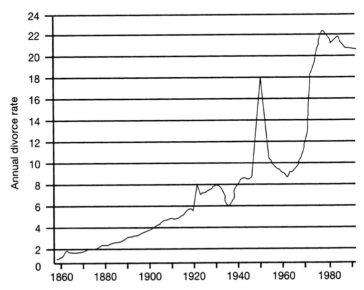

Sources: 1860–1920, Paul H. Jacobson, *American Marriage and Divorce* (New York:
Rinehart, 1959), table 42; 1920–1967, U.S. National Center for Health
Statistics, series 21, no. 24, *100 Years of Marriage and Divorce Statistics*
(1973), table 4; 1968–1987, U.S. National Center for Health Statistics,
Monthly Vital Statistics Report, vol. 38, no. 12, supplement 2, "Advance
Report of Final Divorce Statistics, 1987," table 1; 1988, U.S. National
Center for Health Statistics, *Monthly Vital Statistics Report*, vol. 38, no. 13,
"Annual Summary of Births, Marriages, Divorces, and Deaths: United States,
1989."

the annual rate of divorce increased temporarily after every major war: there is
a slight bulge in the graph following the Civil War, a rise in 1919 and 1920 following World War I, and a large spike in the years immediately after World War
II. We can also see how the Depression temporarily lowered the divorce rate in
the early 1930s: with jobs and housing scarce, many couples had to postpone
divorcing until they could afford to do so.

Ignoring for the moment the temporary movements induced by war and
depression, there is a slow, steady increase in the annual rate of divorce through
the end of World War II. Since the war, however, the graph looks somewhat different. In the period from 1950 to 1960 the annual rates are lower than what we
would expect on the basis of the long-term rise. Then, starting in the early 1960s,
the annual rates rise sharply, so that by the end of the 1970s the rate of divorce
is well above what would be predicted from the long-term trend. After peaking
in 1979, the divorce rate declined slightly in the 1980s; but it is still far above
the levels of the 1960s. Thus if we compare the annual rates from the 1950s with

those from the 1970s and 1980s, as many observers have tended to do, we are comparing a period of relatively low rates with a time of very high rates. The result is to make the recent rise loom even larger than it would if we took the long-term view.

It is true that the rise in annual divorce rates in the 1960s and 1970s was much steeper and more sustained than any increase in the past century; but to gauge the significance of this recent rise, it is necessary to consider the lifetime divorce experiences of adults, rather than just the annual rates of divorce. In Figure 24-2 the dotted line is an estimate of the proportion of all marriages begun in every year between 1867 and 1985 which have ended, or will end, in divorce before one of the spouses dies. Following conventional usage among demographers, I refer to all people marrying in a given year as a "marriage cohort." For recent marriage cohorts, the lifetime record is incomplete, and I have relied on projections prepared by Samuel H. Preston, John McDonald, and James Weed.[1] Any projection, of course, can be undermined by future events, so the importance of Figure 24-2 lies more in the general trends it shows than in its precise estimate for recent marriage cohorts. We can see from the dotted line that the proportion of all marriages in a given year that eventually end in divorce has increased at a faster and faster rate since the mid-nineteenth century. Moreover, the increase has been relatively steady, without the large fluctuations which the annual rates show in times of war or depression.

In order to make the underlying long-term trend clearer, the graph also shows the smooth curve that most closely fits the pattern of change.[2] People who

FIGURE 24-2

Proportion of Marriages Begun in Each Year That Will End in Divorce, 1867 to 1985.

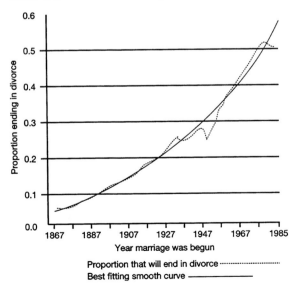

Sources: See notes 1 and 2.

married in the years when the dotted line is above the smooth curve were more likely to become divorced than the long-term historical trend would lead us to expect; people who married in years when the dotted line is below the smooth curve were less likely to become divorced than would be expected. We can see, for instance, that although the annual divorce rates were temporarily low in the early 1930s, more of the people who married just before or during the Depression eventually became divorced than we would expect from the long-term trend. The hardship and distress families suffered when breadwinners lost their jobs irrevocably damaged some marriages, and many unhappy couples later divorced after economic conditions improved enough to allow them to do so. Conversely, Figure 24-2 indicates that the proportion of ever-divorced for those marrying between the end of the war and the late 1950s probably will not reach the expected levels based on the long-term trend. To be sure, a greater proportion of them will divorce than was the case for previous marriage cohorts, but the increase will be modest by historical standards.

On the other hand, for those who married in the 1960s and the 1970s, the increases are likely to exceed what would be predicted by the long-term trend. Couples who married in 1970, for instance, lived the early years of their marriage during a period of very high annual divorce rates. By 1977, only seven years after they had married, one-quarter of these couples had already divorced. In contrast, it was 25 years before one-quarter of those who married in 1950 had divorced. Weed projected that 51 percent of marriages begun in 1970, and 53 percent of those begun in 1976 and 1977, eventually will end in divorce.[3]

Among the most recent marriage cohorts there is yet another turnabout, as Figure 24-2 shows. If divorce rates continue to decline slightly, or even if they remain constant, couples who married in the 1980s will have lower lifetime levels of divorce than the historical record would predict. If these rates continue, the probability of ending a marriage in divorce would rest on a high plateau— Weed projects that 51 percent of 1985 marriages would end in divorce if the rates were to remain close to the level of the mid-1980s. Such a development could mark the end of more than a century of exponential increases in divorce. But it is difficult to tell whether divorce rates will remain stable or begin to rise again. . . . Social scientists can't predict the demographic future very well.

There are other estimates of the proportion of recent marriages that would end in divorce at current rates. At the low end, Robert Schoen estimated that 44.1 percent of married women and 43.9 percent of married men would end their marriages in divorce if recent rates continued.[4] At the high end, Teresa Castro Martin and Larry L. Bumpass, using different data, estimated that up to 64 percent of recent marriages would end in separation or divorce if recent rates continued.[5] Bumpass and Martin included marital separation, noting that about 5 percent of marriages end in separations that are not followed by a divorce. Even so, their predictions are startlingly high. Who is right? All of these demographers are making different assumptions about the future, and all are forced to use imperfect data. I think it's safe to say that about half of all marriages will end in a separation or a divorce if current rates continue.

In sum, although annual measures of divorce often show large fluctuations from year to year or decade to decade, the lifetime proportions ever-divorced for people marrying in a given year have risen in a regular fashion for the past century, with some variations. Those who married during the Depression and those who married in the 1960s and 1970s experienced even higher levels of divorce over their lifetimes than the historical trend would predict. And those who married in the decade or so following the war were the only cohorts in the last hundred years to show a substantial, sustained shortfall in their lifetime levels of divorce. This latter group, of course, includes most of the parents of the baby boomers. Figure 24-2 suggests that the lifetime level of divorce for the baby boom parents was unusually low; for their children it will be unusually high. As for those who married in the 1980s, the incomplete record so far suggests that their levels of divorce may fall below the historical trend, but that still will leave them with a very high rate of marital disruption.

The other way in which a marriage can terminate, of course, is with the death of one spouse. Because mortality rates have declined in the twentieth century, the annual rate of death for married persons has declined at the same time that the annual rate of divorce has been rising. Some demographers have noted that as a result, the total rate of marital dissolution—the number of marriages ending in either divorce or death in a given year per 1,000 existing marriages—hardly changed between 1860 and 1970. From 1860 to 1864 the combined rate was 33.2 dissolutions per 1,000 marriages; in 1970 the combined rate was 34.5.[6] Since 1970, however, the rising rate of divorce has pushed the total dissolution rate above its historical high. The rate peaked at about 41 in the late 1970s and early 1980s; then as divorce rates fell slightly and death rates continued to decline, it fell to 38.7 in 1989.[7] In the mid-nineteenth century, most of the dissolutions in a given year were caused by the death of one spouse, but by the mid-1970s, for the first time in our nation's history, more marriages ended every year in divorce than in death.[8]

Divorces tend to occur at a different stage of family life than deaths, and the two types of dissolution have different consequences for the remaining family members. Most people who divorce do so early in their marriage—about half of all divorces occur by the seventh year of marriage[9]—so that many divorces happen when children are still in the home. In the past, it was common for parents to die while their children were still young, but as mortality rates have fallen, a greater proportion of parental deaths have occurred when the children have already reached adulthood. Consequently, the most important effect on family life of any further fall in death rates will be to extend the "empty nest" stage of marriage after the children leave home. One of the most important effects of the rise in divorce, on the other hand, is to increase the proportion of parents whose marriage is dissolved while their children are still at home. At the rates of the early 1960s, about one-fifth of all children would have experienced the disruption of their parents' marriages before they reached 16, but at the rates of the late 1970s and 1980s, about two-fifths would experience a disruption by age 16.[10]

Most of these disruptions result, at least temporarily, in a one-parent household consisting of a mother and her children, because mothers keep custody of their children in most instances. Among all children not living with two parents in 1990, 79 percent were living with their mother, only 11 percent with their father, and most of the rest with other relatives.[11] As marital disruption increased in the 1970s, so did the number of one-parent households headed by women. In 1990, 6.6 million women headed households that included their own children under 18, more than double the number in 1970.[12] Earlier in the century, it was common for divorcing parents to send their children to live with relatives or for divorced mothers to take their children and move in with kin. Today, however, most currently divorced mothers live alone with their children.[13] About half of the children in one-parent households formed by marital disruption will spend five years in this type of family before their mother remarries or they turn 18.[14]. . .

One other form of marital dissolution to be considered is separation. Most married couples stop living together before they are legally divorced. Some remain separated—without divorcing—for an extended period or even for the rest of their lives. Others separate and then reconcile their differences and resume their marriages. Even for couples who eventually divorce, the process of moving into separate households may be more difficult and traumatic than subsequently obtaining a divorce. Unfortunately, little is known about separation. Unlike marriage and divorce, which are always sanctioned by the state, many separations are informal arrangements between two spouses. Consequently, official records on legal separations, which are incomplete in any case, give an inadequate picture of the number of separations. A 1980 survey in which the Bureau of the Census asked about separation and divorce revealed that most separated people obtain a divorce quickly: 58 percent of women and 63 percent of men within one year, and 77 and 82 percent, respectively, within two years.[15] Separated black women and men, however, are much less likely to obtain a rapid divorce: only 42 percent of women and 53 percent of men were divorced within two years.[16]. . .

Family Life after Divorce

Although social scientists have long been concerned about divorce, they produced little empirical research about its consequences until the 1970s. Since then, they have begun to establish a body of knowledge about its effects on adults and children. On the one hand, recent studies lend qualified support to the view that divorce can be beneficial in the long run for some of those involved. For instance, researchers have produced findings in support of the oft-stated claim that children function better in a single-parent family than in a conflict-ridden nuclear family.[17] On the other hand, the studies also show that divorce is a traumatic process that can cause serious short-term psychological distress. There is evidence that for some adults and children, the harmful effects may be longer lasting.

Developmental psychologists P. Lindsay Chase-Lansdale and E. Mavis Hetherington suggest that the first two years following the breakup of a marriage constitute a "crisis period."[18] During this difficult time adults and children typically face intense emotional upset, continuing family conflict, and adjustments to new living arrangements. When children are involved—as they are in more than half of all divorces—they usually live with their mothers, whose daily routine is often disrupted during the first year after divorce. Hetherington followed for six years a group of middle-class families who had recently divorced and a comparison group of two-parent families. All of the families initially had preschool-aged children. She reported the predominance just after the divorce of a "chaotic lifestyle," as one participant called it, which seemed to persist throughout the first year after divorce and then improve in the second year. Single mothers and their children in the divorced families were more likely to eat pickup meals at irregular times, the children's bedtimes were erratic, the children were more likely to arrive at school late, and so forth.[19]

Saddled with sole or primary responsibility for supporting themselves and their children, single mothers frequently have too little time and too few resources to manage effectively. Robert S. Weiss, after several years of observing single parents, identified three common sources of strain. One is responsibility overload: single parents must make all the decisions and provide for all the needs of their families, a responsibility that at times can be overwhelming. Another is task overload: many single parents simply have too much to do, with working, housekeeping, and parenting; consequently, there is no slack time to meet unexpected demands. A third is emotional overload: single parents are always on call to give emotional support to their children, whether or not their own emotional resources are temporarily depleted.[20]

Moreover, divorced and separated women who are raising children often find that their economic position has deteriorated. Many of those who were not employed in the years preceding their separation have difficulty reentering the job market. Others who were employed find that their wages are too low to support a family. In theory, divorced fathers should continue to help support their children, but in practice only a minority do so adequately. Some avoid a legal agreement altogether: in a 1989 Bureau of the Census survey, 19 percent of all divorced and separated women living with children under 21 reported that they wanted child support but couldn't obtain an award for reasons such as the inability to find their ex-husbands. Even among divorced and separated women who were supposed to receive child support payments, 22 percent reported receiving nothing in 1989. And among those who were fortunate enough to receive any payments in 1989, the average amount received was just $3,322 for the divorced and $3,060 for the separated.[21]

As a result of their limited earning power and of the low level of child support, single mothers and their children often experience a sharp decline in their standard of living after a separation. In the Panel Study of Income Dynamics (PSID), a national study of families who were interviewed annually beginning in 1968, separated and divorced women suffered an average drop of about 30 percent in their standard of living in the year following a marital break-up. Men, in contrast, experienced a rise of 10 to 15 percent because they no longer fully supported their wives and children.[22] Middle-class homemakers suffered the largest average declines. They had agreed to take care of the home and the children full time in return for their husbands' provision of all financial support. When that bargain broke down, they became dependent on meager child support payments and whatever low-paying jobs their neglected labor market skills could command. Among women in the PSID who had above-average family incomes just prior to the separation, 31 percent saw their standard of living in the year after the separation plunge by more than half.[23]

Many single parents, particularly those with low incomes, receive assistance from a network of kin, but the resources of these networks usually are limited and spread thin. Economic pressure on the mother means that she has less time for child care and for her personal life. Harried and overburdened, some single mothers fail to provide the attention and care children need, especially during the first year or two after the separation.

To be sure, life in a single-parent family, despite economic pressures, also has its rewards, foremost the relief from marital conflict. In addition, single parents may gain increased self-esteem from their ability to manage the demands of work life and family life by themselves. They may enjoy their independence and their close relationships to their children.[24] Some writers argue that women are particularly likely to develop an increased sense of self-worth from the independence and greater control over their life they achieve after divorce.[25]

Psychologically, the period following the separation is likely to be very stressful for both spouses, regardless of who initiated the break-up. Both spouses commonly retain ambivalent feelings toward their partners even if they were relieved to have ended an unhappy marriage. For example, Weiss studied adults who came to a series of eight-week discussion and counseling sessions he organized in Boston for persons separated less than one year. Most reported a persistent feeling of attachment to their spouse, a sense of bonding that continued for several months whether the participant had initiated the separation or not. Thus many of the separated adults who attended Weiss's seminars felt an intermittent longing for their husbands or wives and an accompanying anxiety that Weiss labeled "separation distress." Only after the first year of separation did this attachment fade.[26]

Overall, then, the first year after divorce or separation is often a time when the separated spouses experience ambivalence about the separation, increased anxiety, occasional depression, and personal disorganization—even if they were the ones who chose to end their marriages. And it is a time when the income of mothers with custody of their children often drops sharply. Within a year, however, most separated adults have begun the process of reorganizing their lives, although it may take a few years more to establish a stable identity and a new life situation.[27]

Children too experience an initial period of intense emotional upset after their parents separate. Judith S. Wallerstein and Joan B. Kelly studied 131 children from 60 recently separated families who sought the services of a counseling center in Marin County, California. They met with the children at the time of the divorce action and then again eighteen months, five years, and ten years later. At first, according to their study, almost all the children were profoundly upset. Their reactions varied according to age. Preschool children tended to be frightened and bewildered by the separation and to blame themselves for what had occurred; older children often expressed great anger. Adolescents were better able to comprehend the reasons for the divorce, but they often were deeply worried about the effects of the separation on their own future.[28]

A number of studies suggest that the short-term adjustment to divorce is different for boys than for girls. Boys in conflict-ridden families—whether or not a separation has occurred—show more aggressive and antisocial behavior, whereas girls are less prone to do so.[29] Hetherington and others have identified "coercive cycles" between mothers and their preschool sons that can occur soon after a divorce: mothers, who may be overburdened, angry, and depressed, respond irritably to the whining and difficult behavior of their distressed sons, only to aggravate the very behavior they try to quell.[30] Girls appear to adjust to a separation more rapidly and to exhibit more "good" behavior. But there is some evidence that they internalize their distress more and, despite outward adjustment, may suffer from depression or lowered self-esteem.[31]

Less is known about long-term adjustment to divorce. Hetherington found marked improvement in the relations between many of the parents and their preschool children between the first and second year after the divorce. One-half of the mothers and one-fourth of the fathers reported that by two years after the divorce their relationships with their children had improved over the tension-filled last days of their marriages.[32] The majority of the children had resumed normal development. But in one type of family, problems tended to linger: six years after the divorce, when the children in Hetherington's study were ten, mothers who had not remarried reported more loneliness and depression and a lower sense of control over the course of their lives. Their relationships with their sons were more likely to include the ineffective parenting and coercive cycles found between mothers and sons during the crisis period. In contrast, relationships between nonremarried mothers and their daughters were similar to mother-daughter relationships in families in which no divorce had occurred.[33]

Wallerstein paints a very pessimistic picture of long-term adjustment. The older males, who were 19 to 29 at the ten-year follow-up, were said to be "unhappy and lonely" and to have had "few, if any, lasting relationships with young women." Many of the older girls, she and her co-author Sandra Blakeslee stated, appeared well adjusted at first but encountered problems years later. At the ten-year mark, most of the 19-to-23-year-old women were said to be overcome by fear and anxiety at the prospect of making an emotional commitment to a man.[34] But although Wallerstein's clinical study contains many insights, the prevalence of long-term problems in the general population of divorced children almost certainly is lower than she reports for her sample. Families were referred to her clinic for short-term therapy by lawyers, clergy, and occasionally court authorities. Many of the parents had prior mental health problems.[35] In addition, Wallerstein didn't compare her children with a control group of children in families that were not disrupted, so it is difficult to judge how many of the problems exhibited by her subjects are common to all children, whether or not their parents have divorced. Given the nature of the study, then, it is perhaps surprising to discover that nearly half of the children survived the divorce with little or no lasting impairment. Sixty-eight percent of the younger children and somewhat less than 40 percent of the older children were said to be doing well at the ten-year follow-up.

Nevertheless, there is evidence from national surveys that growing up in a single-parent family is associated with diminished chances for a successful adult life. Using data from several national surveys of adults, Sara McLanahan and her colleagues have shown that those who report living in a single-parent family as a child are more likely subsequently to drop out of high school, marry during their teenage years, have a child before marrying, and experience the disruption of their own marriages.[36] Part of the association is due to the lower income in single-parent families, which itself increases the risk of undesirable outcomes such as dropping out of school. But McLanahan estimates that low income accounts for only about half of the story. What is behind the other half isn't clear, but it may include inadequate supervision and discipline by some single parents, the influence of the kinds of disadvantaged neighborhoods that many single parents tend to live in, or other family characteristics that make both living in a single-parent family and experiencing negative outcomes more likely.[37]

Still, most persons who grow up in a single-parent family don't drop out of high school, don't marry as teenagers, and don't have a first child before marrying. For example, McLanahan and Bumpass report that in one national survey of women age 15 to 44, 25 percent of marriages had been disrupted among those who had lived with only one natural parent at age 14, compared to about 14 percent among those who had lived with both parents, controlling for other factors. These percentages can be interpreted in two ways. On the one hand, adults from single-parent families are more likely to experience the disruption of their own marriages. On the other hand, most adults from single-parent families are still in their first marriages. So although growing up in a single-parent family increases the risk of detrimental outcomes later in life, it is not true that most adults who grew up in single-parent families will experience those outcomes.[38]

Nationally representative studies of children produce a similar pattern of findings: the negative effects of divorce are real and persistent, but only a minority experience severe negative consequences. One such study is the 1981 National Survey of Children (NSC), which included a random sample of 227 young adolescents from maritally disrupted families and a larger sample from intact, two-parent families. Paul Allison and Frank Furstenberg found that adolescents who had experienced the divorce or separation of their parents differed only modestly, on average, from those whose parents remained married on a wide variety of outcomes such as school achievement, delinquency, and psychological well-being.

The national surveys provide samples that are much more representative of the average child's experience of marital disruption than do the small-scale studies of white middle-class families that constitute the psychological literature. But the brief, structured interviews in the national surveys cannot yield the kind of in-depth information provided by the intensive, repeated testing and observation of studies such as Hetherington's. Consequently, even with the results of national surveys in hand, there are still no firm estimates of the proportion of children who experience harmful psychological effects from parental divorce. It seems unlikely to me that nearly as many will flounder in the long run as Wallerstein predicts. But taking into account what is known from recent studies, we might conclude that: (1) almost all children experience an initial period of great emotional upset following a parental separation; (2) most return to a normal developmental course within one or two years following the separation, and (3) a minority of children experience some long-term psychological problems as a result of the break-up that may persist into adulthood.

Not all children respond similarly to divorce. There are important differences among children, even within the same family, in temperament and in relations with other family members. Some children are simply more resilient to stress than others. Some manage to find safe niches that insulate them from the trauma of divorce. For example, they may have a special relationship with another adult, or they may be buffered from the conflict by one parent.[39] Furthermore, not all divorces have the same consequences for children. This latter statement might seem obvious, but until recently there wasn't enough research evidence to determine the different pathways that help or hinder children's adjustment to parental divorce.

Nevertheless, I think that two conclusions can be drawn: First, children do better when the custodial parent—usually the mother—can reestablish an orderly and supportive household routine. Hetherington refers to the benefits for children of an "authoritative" parenting style, which combines warmth and involvement with supervision and "moderately high but responsive" control.[40] When the custodial parent can keep the house in order, get the children to school and to bed on time, maintain disciplinary standards consistently but without undue harshness, and provide love and warmth, children can draw support from the parent and from the structure of their daily routine. But carrying out these child-rearing tasks can be difficult for overburdened, financially strapped, emotionally upset single parents. During the crisis period, when the parent may be anxiety-ridden, harried, or depressed and the household may be disorganized, the children lose another pillar—often the last remaining pillar—of support. The custodial parent, then, can help children by functioning effectively as a parent.

Second, children do better when there is less conflict between their parents. This principle applies to intact two-parent homes as well as to families of divorce. In fact, studies show that children living with a single parent show fewer behavioral problems than do children living in homes in which two angry parents argue persistently.[41] When conflict remains after the breakup, children do better if they are shielded from the disputes. If parents can communicate, despite the conflict, and can cooperate on child-rearing tasks, their children benefit. Parents who use their children as pawns or who urge their children to take sides in the battle between the mother and father often increase the child's difficulties.[42]

It is less clear whether children do better, on average, when they have a continuing relationship with both parents after the separation. The Hetherington and Wallerstein studies found that regular visits by the noncustodial parent—usually the father—helped the child greatly.[43] But other recent observational studies have not found this relationship.[44] Moreover, in the 1981 NSC, children who had regular visits with their noncustodial fathers were just as likely as those with infrequent visits to have problems in school or to engage in delinquent behavior or early sexual activity.[45] In any case, the amount of contact between children and their noncustodial fathers is shockingly low. In the NSC, half of the children from maritally disrupted homes who were living with their mothers had not seen their fathers in the last year. Just one-sixth of these children, who were then age 12 to 16, were seeing their fathers as often as once a week.[46] Much of the drop-off in contact occurred in the first two years after the disruption. Why so many fathers fade away is still unclear. Some remarry and form new families; others move away, or their ex-wife and children move away from them; still others may find that frequent visits produce too much guilt and sadness. Whatever the case, most children are deprived of a valuable continuing relationship that might help them develop and adjust. . . .

Remarriage after Divorce

Remarriages have been common in the United States since its beginnings, but until this century almost all remarriages followed widowhood. In the Plymouth Colony about one-third of all men and one-quarter of all women who lived full lifetimes remarried after the death of a spouse, but there was little divorce.[47] Even as late as the 1920s, brides and grooms who were remarrying were more likely to have been widowed than divorced.[48] Since then, however, the increase in divorce and the decline in mortality have altered the balance: by 1987, 91 percent of all brides and all grooms who were remarrying were previously divorced, and 9 percent were widowed.[49] Thus it is only since the Depression that remarriage after divorce has become the predominant form of remarriage. And since the turn of the century, such remarriages have increased as a proportion of all marriages. In 1900 only 3 percent of all brides—including both the never-married and the previously married—were divorced. In 1930, 9 percent of all brides were divorced; and in 1987, 32 percent of all brides were divorced.[50]

In the early 1960s, when the divorce rate began to rise sharply, the remarriage rate for divorced people also rose. This parallel rise was taken to mean that Americans still embraced the institution of marriage, even though many were rejecting their current spouses. In the 1970s, however, while the divorce rate still soared, the remarriage rate fell—and it remained low and relatively stable in the 1980s.[51] Yet we now know that separated and divorced adults were as likely to be living with new partners in the mid-1980s as in 1970—they just weren't as likely to have married them. The National Survey of Families and Households revealed that although there was a 16 percent drop between 1970 and 1984 in the proportion of separated and divorced adults who remarried within five years, there was a 7 percent *increase* in the proportion who formed a union—either by cohabiting or marrying—within five years.[52] In fact, as noted earlier, cohabitation before remarriage is even more common than cohabitation before first marriage: 60 percent of persons who remarried between 1980 and 1987 lived with someone before the marriage—46 percent with only the person they married and 14 percent with someone else.[53]

So union formation after a marital separation is occurring at the same speed as, or even a bit faster than, 20 years ago. The majority of these first unions of divorced people are cohabiting unions. Separated and divorced adults may be rejecting rapid remarriage, but they aren't rejecting living with a partner. And most eventually remarry—about two-thirds of divorced women and three-fourths of divorced men.[54] Blacks, however, are much less likely to make the transition to remarriage than are whites. Only 32 percent of black women and 55 percent of black men remarry within ten years.[55]

When either partner in a remarriage has children from a previous marriage, the structure of the new family can be quite complex. It may include children from the wife's previous marriages, from the husband's previous marriages, and from the new marriage. The children from previous marriages often create links between the household of the remarried parent and the household of that parent's ex-spouse. Stepgrandparents and other quasi-kin may play important roles in the lives of the parents and children. Not all families of remarriage, of course, exhibit the full range of complexity. Still, according to the NSFH, one out of every seven children in a two-parent family was living with a parent and a stepparent.[56]

Conventional wisdom suggests that remarriages should be more successful than first marriages because of the greater maturity and experience of the partners, but the divorce statistics suggest otherwise. During the first several years of marriage, the rate of divorce for remarriages is substantially higher than for first marriages; afterward, the rates are similar. By one estimate, 37 percent of remarriages among women end in a separation or a divorce within ten years, compared to 30 percent of first marriages.[57] Some researchers have linked this higher probability of divorce to the complex family structures of remarriages, while others have argued that the first-married and remarried populations differ in personal characteristics that could influence the risk of divorce. In either case, the expanded families of remarriage after divorce may complicate the lives of remarried adults and their children. . . .

Family Life after Remarriage

For most divorced men and women, living as a single adult is a temporary phase in a process of decoupling and recoupling. As noted . . . [earlier], most divorced persons remarry—about two-thirds of the women and three-fourths of the men. It appears that most people who remarry cohabit with their partners first. Indeed, cohabitation after divorce has become so common that rates of union formation—cohabiting or marital—have remained roughly constant despite declines in the rate of remarriage.

In the United States and other Western societies, remarriage has been the traditional answer to many of the problems faced by single parents. In the Plymouth Colony, for example, it was not unusual for one parent to die before the children reached adulthood. Most of the widows and widowers remarried within a short time, according to a study by John Demos, often within one year. The surviving parent, Demos emphasized, remarried quickly not out of any lack of respect for the deceased spouse but rather because it took two parents to meet the demands of raising a family in the harsh environment of the colony.[58] Today, despite the changes in American society, many divorced parents remarry because they need assistance in similar ways. Remarriage improves the financial situation of a divorced mother and provides another adult to share the household tasks and responsibilities. In addition, remarrying is a way to end the loneliness and isolation many divorced persons experience.

Whereas divorce often weakens the ties between children and their relatives on the side of the noncustodial parent (usually the father), remarriage creates a new set of relationships with a stepparent and his or her kin. When at least one spouse has children from a previous marriage, the family of remarriage can extend far beyond the bounds of the family of first marriage. Stepparents, stepchildren, stepsiblings, stepgrandparents, the new spouses of noncustodial parents, and other kin all may play a role in family life. This expanded set of family relationships in a remarriage can help compensate children for the loss of kin they may suffer after their parents divorce. Children whose custodial parent remarries often seem to inherit not only a stepparent but also a set of stepgrandparents and other stepkin. And since many children retain some contact with their noncustodial parent and grandparents, some children whose parents remarry may have contact with more kin than they did before their father and mother separated. But the introduction of these new relationships can also cause at least temporary problems for parents and children.

When children retain contact with their noncustodial parents, they create links between households; their visits can require communication among the divorced parents, the new stepparent, and the noncustodial parent's new spouse. In practice, most children have only infrequent contact with their noncustodial parent. Nevertheless, the great increases in divorce and remarriage have made these links across households so common that conceptions of family and kinship have been altered. To illustrate, let us consider the case in which a married couple with two children divorces and the wife retains custody of the children, as shown in panel A of Figure 24-3. If we ask the divorced mother who is in her immediate family, she certainly would include her children, but she might well exclude her ex-husband, who now lives elsewhere. If we ask her children who is in their immediate family, however, we might get a different answer. If the children still see their father regularly, they probably would include both their father and their mother as part of their family.[59] And if we ask the ex-husband who is in his immediate family, he might include his children, whom he continues to see, but not his ex-wife. Thus, after divorce, mother, father, and children each may have a different conception of who is in their immediate family. In fact, one can no longer define "the family" or "the immediate family" except in relation to a particular person.

The situation becomes more complicated in a remarriage that involves children from previous marriages. Let us suppose that the mother remarries someone who also has children from a previous marriage and that the mother then has additional children with her new spouse, as diagramed in panel B of Figure 24-3. Now the mother's household contains persons in four different positions—the mother herself, the father/stepfather, the children from her first marriage, and the children from her remarriage. The persons in each of these four positions may have a different conception of who is in their family. The children from the remarriage are likely to include all the members of their household and no one else. The mother's new husband may well include three sets of children: those from his previous marriage, from his new marriage, and from his wife's previous marriage. In reality, few remarriages involve family structures this complex; just 6 percent of remarried couples under age 40 in 1980 had three sets of children.[60] But whenever children are present from previous marriages, multiple definitions arise.

A household formed by divorce or remarriage that involves children from a previous marriage becomes the intersection of an overlapping set of relationships, each of which constitutes an immediate family for one or more members of the household. Although each person in a postdivorce household may have a clear idea of who belongs to his or her immediate family, the definitions of the immediate family are likely to vary widely among persons in the same structural positions in different households.

It also is unclear exactly who a person's more distant relatives are. In many households linked by the ties of broken marriages, there can be considerable

FIGURE 24-3

Kinship Relations and Household Structure after Divorce (A) and after the Mother's Remarriage (B).

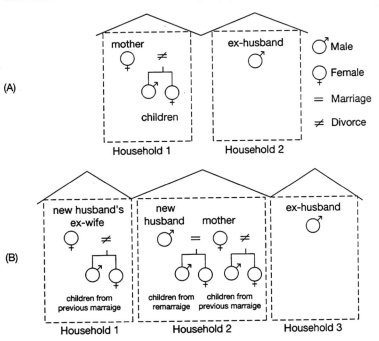

interaction among people whose only relationship is through the broken marriage, such as between a husband's second wife and his ex-wife's second husband. Anthropologist Paul Bohannan has labeled these linked households "divorce chains" and the persons related through the ties of broken marriages "quasi-kin."[61] For example, in panel B of Figure 24-3, the children from the mother's previous marriage might play with the children from her new husband's previous marriage when the husband's children come to visit. Over time, these two sets of children might begin to consider themselves relatives, although they have no formal ties to each other.

In practice, it appears that even ex-spouses who share the task of child rearing often have little to do with each other. Furstenberg and Christine Winquist Nord found surprisingly little coordination and consultation between custodial and noncustodial parents, even when the noncustodial parent saw the child frequently. The dominant style, they state, was more like "parallel parenting" than co-parenting: each parent operated as independently as possible. This strategy served to minimize parental conflict.[62] Similarly, a study of divorced families in Northern California by Stanford University researchers found that, by three-and-one-half years after the separation, the most common pattern of interaction between the parents was "disengaged"—low communication and low conflict.[63]

When at least one spouse has children from a previous marriage, the addition of a new adult to the household alters the entire system of relationships among family members. But our society, oriented toward first marriages, provides little guidance to currently divorced adults, to remarried adults, and to their children as to how they should manage their unfamiliar and complex family lives. The lack of institutionalized—that is, generally accepted—ways of resolving problems is particularly noticeable for the families of remarriages following divorce.[64] To be sure, many aspects of remarried life are similar to life in a first marriage and are subject to established rules of behavior. And remarriage itself is an institutionalized solution to the ambiguous status of the divorced parent. But for remarried adults and their children, day-to-day life includes many problems for which institutionalized solutions are just beginning to emerge.

Consider the problem of what a stepchild who calls his father "dad" should call his stepfather. There is still no general rule, but my observations suggest that the most common answer is to call him by his first name. Note, however, that this practice, if accepted, will institutionalize the ambiguous position of the stepparent. An adult whom a child addresses by his first name is neither a parent nor a stranger. Rather, that adult is more like a friend or a companion. The relationship between stepparents and the stepchildren can vary greatly from family to family. Stepparents must create relationships and negotiate with the biological parents and the stepchildren what each person's rights and obligations will be. Consequently, during the first year or two of a remarriage, adults must work carefully and gradually at establishing a coherent system of relationships among kin, stepkin, and quasi-kin.

The first years of life in a stepfamily are also a time of adjustment for children. Many have adapted painfully but successfully to the departure of the father from the household. The arrival of a stepfather necessitates further adjustment.

One might think that children's psychological well-being would improve quickly, because stepfathers can provide the family with additional income, emotional support, warmth, and discipline. But studies show that the overall level of well-being of children in stepfamilies is about the same as that of children living with their mothers.[65]

Among children who have not yet entered adolescence, the addition of a stepfather to the home appears to create more problems for girls than for boys. In contrast, the behavior of young boys seems to improve, or at least doesn't deteriorate, when their mothers remarry.[66] These sex differences are just the opposite of what occurs, according to the psychological studies at least, when marriages break up and young children remain with their mothers alone: boys show more behavior problems and girls are perhaps more depressed and withdrawn. Hetherington and her collaborators speculate that young girls, who tend to form close relationships with their divorced mothers, may view the stepfather as intruders. Young boys, who are more likely to engage in persistent "coercive cycles" of bad behavior with nonremarried mothers, may benefit from the introduction of a stepfather.

In one study of children aged six to nine in stepfamilies, the authors report that boys were doing better when there was more cohesion and emotional bonding between their mothers and their stepfathers, which presumably reflected a greater integration of the stepfather into the life of the family. But girls were doing better when there was *less* cohesion and bonding between the mother and stepfather. The authors argue that the involvement of the stepfather threatens the close relationship that daughters have developed with their mothers.[67] Moreover, several studies have found evidence that children appear to fare better when they are in the custody of the same-sex parent—boys with their fathers, and girls with their mothers.[68] But fathers have custody of their children rarely and often under special circumstances, such as when the mother is unfit or the father has been unusually involved in child rearing. So it is very risky to generalize from the existing studies of same-sex custody.

A recent study of somewhat older children by Hetherington and her collaborators reported that both boys and girls had persistent difficulties in adjusting to the presence of a stepfather. The researchers followed nine-to-thirteen-year-old children in recently formed stepfamilies for two years. They speculated that the developmental tasks of early adolescence—particularly coming to terms with emerging sexuality and developing a sense of autonomy—may make the addition of a stepfather to the home problematic for boys and girls. It may be unavoidably distressing, they argue, for an early adolescent to think of his or her mother and stepfather as sexually active.[69]

It also appears that the role of the stepmother is more problematic than the role of the stepfather. Stepmothers have more competition from absent mothers than stepfathers do from absent fathers because absent mothers are less likely to withdraw from their children's lives. In the NSC, the small number of children in father-custody homes reported substantially more contact with their absent mothers than did children in mother-custody homes with their absent fathers.[70] It may be more difficult, then, for stepmothers to establish a workable role in the family. And because of the selective nature of father custody, children in stepmother-father families may be more troubled. That is, children sometimes may be sent to live with their fathers when their problems are greater than the mother feels she can deal with. In the National Health Interview Survey, parents in stepmother-father families were more likely to feel that their child needed psychological help than were parents in mother-stepfather families.[71] Regardless, there are far fewer resident stepmothers than stepfathers because most mothers retain custody of their children. In 1985 there were 740,000 children under 18 living with a stepmother and a biological father, compared to 6.05 million children who were living with a biological mother and a stepfather.[72]

Finally, the divorce rate for remarried persons is modestly but consistently higher than for persons in first marriages, largely because of the sharply higher risk of divorce during the first few years. Some observers believe that the rate is higher because the remarried population contains a higher proportion of people who, for one reason or another, are likely to resort to divorce if their marriage falters.[73] Furstenberg and Graham Spanier argue, more specifically, that the experience of divorce makes people more averse to remaining in a second unhappy marriage.[74] These arguments were raised initially in reaction to a hypothesis of mine, namely that many of the difficulties of families of remarriage, including the higher divorce rate, stem from the lack of institutionalized support. Without accepted guidelines, solving everyday problems can engender conflict and confusion among family members.[75] The evidence tying second divorces to the incomplete institutionalization of remarriage is mixed, however, and a lesser aversion to divorce among remarried partners is undoubtedly a factor.[76]

Costs and Benefits

Because of the rise in divorce, more and more people—currently more than 1 million couples per year—are experiencing the distress of marital separation. Yet the process of divorce does benefit many adults who go through it, because it frees them from the tensions of an unhappy marriage. Most divorced persons say that their lives would have been worse had they not separated from their spouses.[77] At least one partner in every disrupted marriage chooses to divorce and, as best we can judge, the benefits of divorce to that partner outweigh the costs. I suspect, however, that few adults who are about to separate are prepared for the intense emotional difficulties that often are experienced by both partners during the first years after separation or for the economic decline that afflicts many mothers. Most divorced adults will spend most of the rest of their lives not living alone or in a single-parent family but in a family of remarriage. Although parents and children in a family of remarriage can have difficulty adjusting to their complex and poorly institutionalized situation, remarriage improves the financial situation of single parents, creates an additional set of kin to supplement the remaining ties to the kin of noncustodial parents, and can provide another stable source of affection and emotional support.

The situation of children whose parents divorce is more problematic. With few exceptions, children do not want their parents to separate. Yet children's problems often precede the breakup; and some of these problems would have occurred even if the parents had stayed together. Several collaborators and I studied the statistical records of national samples of children in the United States and Great Britain who were followed for four or five years.[78] The records contained information on behavior problems, reading and mathematics achievement, and family difficulties for the children, all of whom were living with two married, biological parents at the beginning of the study. We tracked them as they split into two groups as the years passed: those whose parents divorced and those whose parents stayed together. As might be expected, the children whose parents divorced showed more behavior problems and scored lower on reading and mathematics tests than did the children whose parents stayed together. But when we looked backward through the records to the start of the study—before anyone's parents had separated or divorced—we found that the children whose parents would later divorce *already* were showing more problems and doing worse in reading and mathematics. For boys, we found that about half of what appeared to be the effect of divorce could be predicted on the basis of the boy's problems and his family's difficulties before the breakup. For girls, less of the effect could be predicted beforehand.

These findings suggest that the process of divorce often begins well before the parents split up. Children caught in the conflict preceding a divorce tend to develop problems even while both parents are still in the home. Moreover, the findings suggest that some two-parent families may function poorly, due to serious problems of the parents or the children, regardless of whether the parents ever consider divorce. But these troubled families are invisible to the outside world unless the parents split up—at which point we may mistakenly attribute all of the children's problems to the breakup itself.

Does this mean that parents in troubled marriages needn't stay together for the sake of the children? I think that statement, although true at the extreme, is too simplistic. It is probably true that children are better off, as many researchers have claimed, living with one separated parent than living in a home torn apart by intense conflict or abuse. What if, however, the parents are unhappy with their marriage, have lost much of their affection for or interest in one another, but are able to limp along without much hostility or open conflict? No one knows how many divorcing couples are in this situation, and I don't think a divorce under these conditions helps children. Moreover, Wallerstein and Kelly found that some partners in conflict-ridden marriages still were able to share in maintaining a loving and supportive relationship with their children. Even though many of the children in their study doubted that their parents were happily married, even though many were well aware of a long history of difficulties between their parents, very few greeted divorce with relief; most were shocked and distressed at the news that their parents were separating.[79]

I think it is clear that most children do not benefit from divorce. Our U.S. and British study suggests that overall the effect on children of the breakup and its aftermath is negative but modest in size. For example, children whose parents divorced during the study showed about 5 to 20 percent more behavior problems, once their predivorce characteristics were taken into account.[80] A review of 92 studies, by Paul R. Amato and Bruce Kieth, concluded: "Parental divorce (or the factors associated with it) lowers the well-being of children. However, the estimated effects are generally weak."[81] These averages, however, conceal wide variations in children's responses. I think the data suggest that most children suffer only moderately increased difficulties; some do better than before the breakup; and some experience serious, long-lasting problems. There also may be long-term effects that show up only in adulthood. And the evidence reviewed in this chapter suggests that despite the material advantages that a parental remarriage usually provides, remarriage can cause further difficulties in children's adjustment, at least in the short term. . . .

Finally, despite a leveling off of the divorce rate, divorce and remarriage did not become any easier for parents and children—at least as far as I can tell. The widespread sharing of the experience of divorce did not assuage the personal pain adults and children feel when a family breaks up. It did not lead to much improvement in the precarious economic situation many divorced mothers find themselves in. And it could not substitute for the lengthy period of adjustment to the breakup of a family or to the presence of a new stepparent. This lack of progress tempers my optimism about whether it will be easier to manage these transitions a decade from now.

Notes

1. The estimates for 1867 to 1949 are taken from Samuel H. Preston and John McDonald, "The Incidence of Divorce within Cohorts of American Marriages Contracted since the Civil War," *Demography* 16 (Feb. 1979): 1–25; the estimates are based on vital registration and census data. Preston and McDonald estimated the lifetime proportions divorcing for marriages surviving to 1970 by assuming that 1969 divorce and death rates will continue to hold in the future. The data for the 1950 to 1985 cohorts are taken from projections by James Weed, "U.S. Duration of Marriage Tables: A 1985 Update," paper presented at the annual meeting of the Southern Demographic Association, San Antonio, October 1988. Weed's projections are based on the actual experiences of these cohorts through 1985; he assumes that the divorce and death rates of the 1985 period will continue to hold in the future. There is one exception: for his earliest six cohorts, 1950 to 1955, he based projections on 1977 rates. See U.S. National Center for Health Statistics, Vital and Health Statistics, Series 3, no. 19, "National Estimates of Dissolution and Survivorship" (Washington: U.S. Government Printing Office, 1980). Thus, there is a slight discontinuity between 1955 and 1956. Another slight discontinuity is introduced by changing in 1950 from Preston and McDonald's estimate to Weed's more up-to-date projections. I have smoothed the data by plotting three-year moving averages in 1949, 1950, 1955, and 1956.

2. The solid curve in Figure 24-2 is the result of fitting a third-degree polynomial on time to the projected proportions by ordinary least squares regression. A similar procedure for 1867 to 1964 can be found in Preston and McDonald, "The Incidence of Divorce." The fitted values account for 99 percent of the variance in the projected proportions. The regression equation is:

$$ln\ p = -2.865 + .02068T + .00003137T^2 - .000000339T^3\ (R^2 = .992)$$

where p is the predicted proportion divorcing, T is year minus 1867, and ln is the natural logarithm.

3. Weed, "U.S. Duration of Marriage Tables."

4. Robert Schoen, "The Continuing Retreat from Marriage: Figures from 1983 U.S. Marital Status

Life Tables," *Social Science Research* 71 (January 1987): 108–109. Schoen and Weed both relied heavily on information on divorce collected by the U.S. National Center for Health Statistics. But their models differed somewhat: Weed estimated duration-specific probabilities of divorce for marriages, whereas Schoen estimated age-specific probabilities of divorce for individuals. Neither could include separation as an outcome since NCHS does not collect data on separations.

5. Teresa Castro Martin and Larry L. Bumpass, "Recent Trends in Marital Disruption," *Demography* 26 (February 1989): 37–51. Martin and Bumpass use retrospective marital histories collected as part of the June 1985 Current Population Survey by the Bureau of the Census. They adjusted the divorce figures upward to account for what they believe to be underreporting of separation and divorce in Bureau of the Census surveys. It is this upward adjustment, along with the inclusion of separation as an outcome, that makes their estimate so high.

6. Davis, "American Family"; see also Mary Jo Bane, *Here to Stay: American Families in the Twentieth Century* (New York: Basic Books, 1976).

7. In the first edition of this book, I calculated a rate of 40.5 in 1978. This was probably the peak or close to it. The total dissolution rate for marriages in a given year is the sum of the rates of dissolution by death and by divorce. Kingsley Davis calculated the total dissolution rate per 1,000 existing marriages for five-year intervals between 1860 and 1970. See Kingsley Davis, "The American Family in Relation to Demographic Change," in Charles F. Westoff and Robert Parke, Jr., *Demographic and Social Aspects of Population Growth*, Commission on Population Growth and the American Future, Research Reports, vol. 1 (Washington: U.S. Government Printing Office, 1972), Table 8. In order to calculate the rate for the latest available year, one needs three pieces of information: the number of existing marriages, the number of divorces, and the number of deaths of married persons. The first two are readily available. For 1989 the number of existing marriages was obtained from U.S. Bureau of the Census, Current Population Reports, series P-20, no. 445, "Marital Status and Living Arrangements: March 1989" (Washington: U.S. Government Printing Office, 1990). In order to be consistent with Davis's calculation, I took the number of married men (spouse present and spouse absent) as the indicator of the number of existing marriages. The number of divorces in 1989 is reported in U.S. National Center for Health Statistics, Monthly Vital Statistics Report, vol. 38, no. 13, *Annual Summary of Births, Marriages, Divorces, and Deaths: United States, 1989* (Washington: U.S. Government Printing Office, 1990).

The problem, however, is that since 1961 death rates for married persons have not been reported separately. Yet we know that married persons have somewhat lower death rates than unmarried persons. Davis estimated the number of deaths of married persons for 1965 and 1970; I have done so for 1989, using the following procedure. I compared the death rates for married persons by age and sex in 1960 with the death rates by age and sex for all persons in 1960. From this comparison I calculated the ratio of the death rate for married persons to the rate for all persons in each age-sex group. These ratios were typically in the range of 0.8 to 0.9. I then multiplied the death rates for all persons by age and sex in 1989 by the corresponding ratios, thereby adjusting the total death rates in 1989 to reflect the somewhat lower risk of death for married persons. This adjustment assumes that the ratio of the death rates of married persons to all persons has stayed the same for each age-sex group between 1960 and 1989, an assumption that seems reasonable for the purposes of this chapter. I then multiplied each adjusted death rate by the number of married people in the appropriate age-sex group (obtained from Current Population Reports, series P-20, no. 445), yielding an estimate of 975,666 deaths to married persons in 1989. The figures used in calculating the total rate of dissolution were as follows: (1) deaths of married persons in 1989: 975,666; (2) divorces in 1989: 1,163,000; (3) existing marriages in 1989: 55,284,000; (4) deaths per 1,000 existing marriages: 17.6; (5) divorces per 1,000 existing marriages: 21.0; and, finally, (6) total dissolutions per 1,000 existing marriages: 38.7.

8. For the first edition, I estimated that there were 906,300 deaths of married persons in 1978, as opposed to 1,128,000 divorces.

9. James A. Sweet and Larry L. Bumpass, *American Families and Households* (New York: Russell Sage Foundation, 1987).

10. Larry L. Bumpass, "Children and Marital Disruption: A Replication and Update," *Demography* 21 (November 1984): 71–82. Bumpass estimates experience of disruption by age 16 as 22 percent at the rates of 1963–1965 and 43 percent at the rates of 1977–1979 (which were slightly higher than the rates prevalent at the end of the 1980s).

11. U.S. Bureau of the Census, Current Population Reports, series P-20, no. 450, "Marital Status and Living Arrangements: March 1990" (Washington: U.S. Government Printing Office, 1991).

12. U.S. Bureau of the Census, Current Population Reports, series P-20, no. 447, "Household and Family Characteristics: March 1990 and 1989" (Washington: U.S. Government Printing Office, 1991), Table 1; and U.S. Bureau of the Census, Current Population Reports, series P-20, no. 218,

"Household and Family Characteristics: March 1970" (Washington: U.S. Government Printing Office, 1971), Table 1.

13. James A. Sweet, "The Living Arrangements of Separated, Widowed, and Divorced Mothers," *Demography* 9 (February 1972): 143–157.

14. Bumpass, "Children and Marital Disruption."

15. The Bureau of the Census does provide annual information in its Current Population Survey on the number of people who were separated from their spouses at the time of the survey, but the figures are difficult to interpret for two reasons. First, the number of people currently separated depends not only on the rate at which people become separated but also on the rate at which they stop being separated—that is, on how quickly they divorce or reconcile once they have separated. As a result, the number of people currently separated could increase over time merely because separated spouses were taking more time to obtain their divorces, even if the overall rate of divorce were decreasing. Second, demographers suspect that the category "currently separated" is not accurately reported in surveys. The March 1989 Current Population Survey (U.S. Bureau of the Census, *Current Population Reports*, Series P-20, no. 445, "Marital Status and Living Arrangements: March 1989," U.S. Government Printing Office, 1990), for example, reported the following impossible situation: 2,671,000 women were separated from their husbands, but only 1,712,000 men were separated from their wives. It seems likely that some of the so-called separated women had never married their supposed husbands and that some men who actually were separated from their wives reported instead that they had never married.

16. Sweet and Bumpass, *American Families and Households.*

17. See, for example, James L. Peterson and Nicholas Zill, "Marital Disruption, Parent-Child Relationships, and Behavior Problems in Children," *Journal of Marriage and the Family* 48 (May 1986): 295–307.

18. P. Lindsay Chase-Lansdale and E. Mavis Hetherington, "The Impact of Divorce on Life-Span Development: Short and Longterm Effects," in Paul B. Baltes, David L. Featherman, and Richard M. Lerner, eds., *Life-Span Development and Behavior*, vol. 10 (Hillsdale, N.J.: Lawrence Erlbaum Associates, 1990), pp. 105–150.

19. E. Mavis Hetherington, Martha Cox, and Roger Cox, "The Aftermath of Divorce," in J. H. Stevens, Jr., and M. Matthews, eds., *Mother-Child, Father-Child Relations* (Washington: National Association for the Education of Young Children, 1978), pp. 146–176.

20. Robert S. Weiss, *Going It Alone: The Family Life and Social Situation of the Single Parent* (New York: Basic Books, 1979).

21. U.S. Bureau of the Census, Current Population Reports, series P-60, no. 173, "Child Support and Alimony: 1989" (Washington: U.S. Government Printing Office, 1991), Tables 1 and 3. The proportion of never-married women who receive any child support payments is even lower.

22. Saul D. Hoffman and Greg J. Duncan, "What *Are* the Economic Consequences of Divorce?" *Demography* 25 (November 1988): 641–645. Hoffman and Duncan demonstrate convincingly that Lenore J. Weitzman's widely cited estimate of the decline in women's standard of living after the breakup (73 percent, on average) is exaggerated and inconsistent with other figures in her book, *The Divorce Revolution: The Unexpected Social and Economic Consequences for Women and Children in America* (New York: Free Press, 1985). Her estimate of the rise in men's standard of living (42 percent) is almost certainly exaggerated also.

23. Greg J. Duncan and Saul D. Hoffman, "Economic Consequences of Marital Instability," in Martin David and Timothy Smeeding, eds., *Horizontal Equity, Uncertainty, and Economic Well-Being* (Chicago: University of Chicago Press, 1985), pp. 427–467. See Table 14.A.5.

24. Weiss, *Going It Alone.*

25. Janet A. Kohen, Carol A. Brown, and Roslyn Feldberg, "Divorced Mothers: The Costs and Benefits of Female Family Control," in George Levinger and Oliver C. Moles, eds., *Divorce and Separation: Context, Causes, and Consequences* (New York: Basic Books, 1979), pp. 228–245.

26. Robert S. Weiss, *Marital Separation* (New York: Basic Books, 1975).

27. Ibid.

28. Judith S. Wallerstein and Joan Berlin Kelly, *Surviving the Breakup: How Children and Parents Cope with Divorce* (New York: Basic Books, 1980).

29. Chase-Lansdale and Hetherington, "The Impact of Divorce." See also Peterson and Zill, "Marital Disruption."

30. G. R. Patterson, *Coercive Family Process* (Eugene, Oregon: Castalia Publishing Company, 1982).

31. Chase-Lansdale and Hetherington, "The Impact of Divorce."

32. Hetherington, Cox, and Cox, "Aftermath of Divorce."

33. E. Mavis Hetherington, "Family Relations Six Years after Divorce," in Kay Pasley and Marilyn

Ihinger-Tallman, eds., *Remarriage and Stepparenting: Current Research and Theory* (New York: Guilford Press, 1987), pp. 185–205.

34. Judith S. Wallerstein and Sandra Blakeslee, *Second Chances: Men, Women, and Children a Decade after Divorce* (New York: Ticknor and Fields, 1989).

35. Families with children who had severe psychiatric problems were excluded, but parents often entered the study with a long history of psychiatric problems. As Wallerstein acknowledges in an earlier book, nearly 50 percent were "moderately disturbed or frequently incapacitated by disabling neuroses and addictions." Some were "chronically depressed" or "sometimes suicidal." Another 15 to 20 percent were characterized as "severely disturbed," with long histories of mental illness and chronic inability to cope with the demands of life (Wallerstein and Kelly, *Surviving the Breakup*, p. 328). Only a third of the sample were deemed to possess "adequate psychological functioning" prior to the divorce. We are never told what, if any, bearing parents' psychological histories had on their capacity to cope with divorce or to respond to the challenges of being a parent. Wallerstein and Blakeslee express great surprise at how many of the couples had difficulty adjusting to life after divorce, how many entered troubled second marriages, and how many had serious problems as parents. But given their psychological histories, the difficulties should have been anticipated. See Andrew Cherlin and Frank F. Furstenberg, Jr., "Divorce Doesn't Always Hurt the Kids," *The Washington Post*, March 19, 1989, p. C3.

36. Sara McLanahan, "Family Structure and the Reproduction of Poverty," *American Journal of Sociology* 90 (January 1985): 873–901; and Sara McLanahan and Larry L. Bumpass, "Intergenerational Consequences of Family Disruption," *American Journal of Sociology* 94 (July 1988): 130–152.

37. McLanahan summarizes her research findings in the newsletter of the Institute for Research on Poverty at the University of Wisconsin: Sara McLanahan, "The Consequences of Single Parenthood for Subsequent Generations," *Focus* 11 (Fall 1988): 16–21.

38. The .14 and .25 figures are estimates derived from the results in McLanahan and Bumpass, "Intergenerational Consequences," and are only illustrative. The authors also combine the experience of parental marital disruption with the experience of living with a never-married mother; further results suggest that the difference between these two groups is small.

39. E. Mavis Hetherington, "Coping with Family Transitions: Winners, Losers, and Survivors," *Child Development* 60 (1989): 1–14.

40. Hetherington, "Family Relations Six Years after Divorce," and "Coping with Family Transitions."

41. Peterson and Zill, "Marital Disruption."

42. Christy M. Buchanan, "Variation in Adjustment to Divorce: The Role of Feeling Caught in the Middle between Parents," paper presented at the biennial meeting of the Society for Research in Child Development, Seattle, April 18, 1991.

43. Chase-Lansdale and Hetherington, "Impact of Divorce."

44. For a review see Robert E. Emery, *Marriage, Divorce, and Children's Adjustment* (Beverly Hills: Sage Publications, 1988), pp. 85–86.

45. The payment of child support by noncustodial fathers, however, was associated with fewer behavioral problems. See Frank F. Furstenberg, Jr., S. Philip Morgan, and Paul D. Allison, "Paternal Participation and Children's Well-Being after Marital Dissolution," *American Sociological Review* 52 (October 1987): 695–701.

46. Frank F. Furstenberg, Jr., Christine Winquist Nord, James L. Peterson, and Nicholas Zill, "The Life Course of Children after Divorce," *American Sociological Review* 48 (October 1983): 656–668.

47. John Demos, *A Little Commonwealth: Family Life in Plymouth Colony* (New York: Oxford University Press, 1970).

48. Paul H. Jacobson, *American Marriage and Divorce* (New York: Rinehart, 1959).

49. U.S. National Center for Health Statistics, *Monthly Vital Statistics Report* 38, no. 12, supplement, "Advance Report of Final Marriage Statistics, 1987" (Washington: U.S. Government Printing Office, 1990).

50. Ibid.; and Jacobson, *American Marriage and Divorce.*

51. In 1970 there were 180 remarriages per 1,000 divorced women aged 25 to 44; in 1980 the rate was 123; in 1987 it was 129. See National Center for Health Statistics, "Final Marriage Statistics, 1987"; and Larry Bumpass, James Sweet, and Teresa Castro Martin, "Changing Patterns of Remarriage," *Journal of Marriage and the Family* 52 (August 1990): 747–756.

52. Bumpass, Sweet, and Cherlin, "The Role of Cohabitation."

53. Bumpass and Sweet, "National Estimates."

54. Sweet and Bumpass, *American Families and Households.*

55. Ibid.

56. This figure is from unpublished NSFH data kindly provided by James Sweet and Elizabeth

Thomson. The calculation excludes children born to cohabiting mothers and children living with one natural parent and a cohabiting partner.

57. Sweet and Bumpass, *American Families and Households.*

58. John Demos, *A Little Commonwealth: Family Life in Plymouth Colony.*

59. Wallerstein and Kelly, *Surviving the Breakup,* reported that the inclusion of the noncustodial father in the child's view of his family is common when the father continues to see the child.

60. Andrew Cherlin and James McCarthy, "Remarried Couple Households: Data from the June 1980 Current Population Survey," *Journal of Marriage and the Family* 47 (February 1985): 23–30.

61. Paul Bohannan, "Divorce Chains, Households of Remarriage, and Multiple Divorces," in Paul Bohannan, ed., *Divorce and After* (New York: Doubleday, 1970), pp. 127–139.

62. Frank F. Furstenberg, Jr., and Christine Winquist Nord, "Parenting Apart: Patterns of Childrearing after Marital Dissolution," *Journal of Marriage and the Family* 47 (November 1985): 893–904.

63. Eleanor E. Maccoby, Charlene E. Depner, and Robert H. Mnookin, "Coparenting in the Second and Fourth Years Following Parental Separation," unpublished manuscript, Stanford University, 1990. See also Eleanor E. Maccoby and Robert H. Mnookin, *Dividing the Child: Social and Legal Dilemmas of Custody* (Cambridge, Mass.: Harvard University Press, 1992).

64. See my article, "Remarriage as an Incomplete Institution," *American Journal of Sociology* 84 (November 1978): 634–650, from which I draw heavily in this section.

65. See, for example, Nicholas Zill, "Behavior, Achievement, and Health Problems among Children in Stepfamilies: Findings from a National Survey of Child Health," in E. Mavis Hetherington and Joseph D. Arasteh, eds., *Impact of Divorce, Single Parenting, and Stepparenting on Children* (Hillsdale, N.J.: Lawrence Erlbaum Associates, 1988); pp. 325–368.

66. See the following reports on small-scale, intensive studies by psychologists: James H. Bray, "Children's Development during Early Remarriage," in Hetherington and Arasteh, *Impact of Divorce;* Hetherington, "Family Relations Six Years after Divorce;" Eulalee Brand, W. Glenn Clingempeel, and Kathryn Bowen-Woodward, "Family Relationships and Children's Psychological Adjustment in Stepmother and Stepfather Families," in Hetherington and Arasteh, *Impact of Divorce;* and J. W. Santrock, R. A. Warshak, C. Lindberg, and L. Meadows, "Children's and Parents' Observed Social Behavior in Stepfather Families," *Child Development* 53 (1982): 472–480. Two reports on the 1981 National Survey of Children provide at least partial confirmation that girls seem to react more negatively to the introduction of a stepparent than do boys: Paul Allison and Frank F. Furstenberg, Jr., "How Marital Dissolution Affects Children," *Developmental Psychology* 25 (1989): 540–549; and Peterson and Zill, "Marital Disruption." An analysis of the 1981 Child Health Supplement to the National Health Interview Survey, however, found only small differences between girls and boys: Zill, "Behavior, Achievement, and Health Problems."

67. Bray, "Children's Development during Early Remarriage."

68. See Chase-Lansdale and Hetherington, "The Impact of Divorce," for a review.

69. E. Mavis Hetherington and W. Glenn Clingempeel, *Coping with Marital Transitions: A Family Systems Perspective* (in press).

70. Furstenberg et al., "The Life Course of Children of Divorce."

71. Zill, "Behavior, Achievement, and Health Problems."

72. U.S. Bureau of the Census, Current Population Reports, Series P-23, no. 162, "Studies in Marriage and the Family: Married-Couple Families with Children" (Washington: U.S. Government Printing Office, 1989), Table A.

73. See, for example, Terence C. Halliday, "Remarriage: The More Complete Institution?" *American Journal of Sociology* 86 (November 1980): 630–635.

74. Frank F. Furstenberg, Jr., and Graham B. Spanier, "The Risk of Dissolution in Remarriage: An Examination of Cherlin's Hypothesis of Incomplete Institutionalization," *Family Process* 33 (1984): 433–442. See also, by the same authors, *Recycling the Family: Remarriage after Divorce* (Beverly Hills: Sage Publications, 1984).

75. See Cherlin, "Remarriage as an Incomplete Institution."

76. Some support for my position came from a national study of married persons who were interviewed in 1980 and reinterviewed in 1983. The probability of divorce during the interval was higher among remarried couples, and it increased with the complexity of the remarriage. For example, the probability was higher when both spouses had been remarried than when just one had been; and it was higher when stepchildren were present than when they were not. See Lynn K. White and Alan Booth, "The Quality and Stability of Remarriages: The Role of Stepchildren," *American Sociological Review* (October 1985): 689–698.

77. Hetherington, Cox, and Cox, "Aftermath of Divorce"; and William J. Goode, *Women in Divorce* (New York: Free Press, 1956).

78. Andrew J. Cherlin, Frank F. Furstenberg, Jr., P. Lindsay Chase-Lansdale, Kathleen E. Kiernan, Philip K. Robins, Donna Ruane Morrison, and Julien O. Teitler, "Longitudinal Studies of Effects of Divorce on Children in Great Britain and the United States," *Science* 252 (June 7, 1991): 1386–89.

79. Wallerstein and Kelly, *Surviving the Breakup.*

80. Cherlin et al., "Longitudinal Studies of Effects of Divorce."

81. Paul R. Amato and Bruce Kieth, "Parental Divorce and the Well-Being of Children: A Meta-Analysis," *Psychological Bulletin* 110 (1991): 26–46. Quoted at p. 40.

Downward Mobility*

Terry Arendell

The previous article helped chart patterns of demographic change related to marital dissolution. This article explores the economic consequences for 60 mothers and their children after divorce. Thirty years ago, the age group most likely to be found in poverty was the population over 65. Today the age group most likely to be in poverty is below the age of 15. The demographic trends outlined by Cherlin have led to downward mobility for many women and children in this country, and to a pattern which has been called the "feminization of poverty." Terry Arendell looks at this downward mobility and the effects it has on women and children after divorce.

These women had assumed that after divorce they would somehow be able to maintain a middle-class lifestyle for themselves and their children. Those in their twenties and thirties had been confident that they could establish themselves as capable employees and find positions that would provide sufficient incomes. Most of the older women, who had been out of the work force longer, had been less confident about their earning abilities, but they had assumed that the difference between the former family income and their own earnings would be ade-

*Source: Terry Arendell. *Mothers and Divorce: Legal, Economic, and Social Dilemmas*, pages 36–52. Berkeley, CA: University of California Press. Copyright (c) 1986 The Regents of the University of California.

quately compensated for by court-ordered child support and spousal support payments. In fact, virtually all of the women had assumed that family management and parenting efforts, which had kept most of them from pursuing employment and career development while they were married, would be socially valued and legally recognized in their divorce settlements. What had worried them most was not economic difficulty but the possible psychological effects of divorce on themselves and their children. Still, they had believed that they would probably recover from the emotional trauma of divorcing in a matter of months and would then be able to reorganize their lives successfully.

Drastically Reduced Incomes

But even the women who had worried most about how they would manage financially without their husbands' incomes had not imagined the kind of hardship they would face after divorce. All but two of the 60 women had to cope with a substantial loss of family income. Indeed, 90 percent of them (56 out of 60) found that divorce immediately pushed them below the poverty line, or close to it. As wives and mothers, they had been largely dependent on their husbands, who had supplied the family's primary income.[1] Without that source of income, they suffered a drastic reduction in standard of living—an experience not shared by their ex-husbands.[2] Like women generally, they were "declassed" by divorce.

The economic decline experienced by these 60 women, all of whom remained single parents, was not temporary.[3] With caution and careful spending, most could meet their essential monthly expenses. But few had any extra money for dealing with emergencies or unexpected demands, and some continued to fall further behind, unable even to pay their monthly bills. One of them, divorced for nearly eight years, described her experience this way:

> I've been living hand to mouth all these years, ever since the divorce. I have no savings account. The notion of having one is as foreign to me as insurance—there's no way I can afford insurance. I have an old pickup that I don't drive very often. In the summertime I don't wear nylons to work because I can cut costs there. Together the kids and I have had to struggle and struggle. Supposedly struggle builds character. Well, some things simply aren't character building. There have been times when we've scoured the shag rug to see if we could find a coin to come up with enough to buy milk so we could have cold cereal for dinner. That's not character building.

Although they had been living for a median period of over four years as divorced single parents, only *nine* of these 60 women had managed to halt the economic fall prompted by divorce; four of these nine had even managed to reestablish a standard of living close to what they had had while married. Thus the remaining majority—51 women—had experienced no economic recovery. Few had any savings, and most lived from paycheck to paycheck in a state of constant uncertainty. One of them, a woman in her late forties and divorced more than four years, told me:

I can't go on like this. There's no way. I can manage for another year, maybe a year and a half, but no more. I don't have the stamina. It's not that I don't have a job. My problem is money, plain and simple. That's all that counts in this situation.

This group of recently divorced mothers was by no means unique. All female-headed households experience high rates of economic hardship, and the gap in median income between female-headed families and other types of families has actually widened between 1960 and 1983.[4] Part of the reason is obvious: certain fixed costs of maintaining a family—such as utility bills and home mortgages or rent—do not change when the family size declines by one, and many other expenses, such as food and clothing, do not change significantly. Additionally, in most cases when the mother obtained employment, it provided a low income that was substantially reduced by new expenses, such as the costs of transportation and child care.[5]

These women understood how their economic dependency in marriage had contributed to their present economic situation. One of them, who had been married nearly 20 years before divorcing, said:

Money does wonders in any situation. I'm sure women with more education and better jobs don't have situations quite as desperate as mine. But I quit school when I married and stayed home to raise my children.

Unfortunately, they arrived at such understanding the hard way, through experience. Before divorcing, they had expected to receive "reasonable" child support and had thought they could probably find jobs that paid "reasonable" wages. They had only the vaguest understanding of other women's divorce experiences. Thus two of them said:

Friends of mine had ended up divorced with children, and they would tell me some of these things. But I had no empathy at all. I might say, "Gee, that doesn't seem fair" or "Gee, that's too bad." But it never *really* hit me how serious it is until it happened to me. So I think there must be a lot of people out there who don't have the foggiest idea what it feels like.

I had no idea how *much* money it takes. You don't have the [husband's] income, but you still have your family. There's the rub.

Their experiences led them to conclude that in America today, divorced women generally must accept a reduced standard of living. And as women with children, they were keenly aware that only remarriage could offer a quick escape from economic hardship.[6] A mother of three told me:

I have this really close friend. She was a neighbor and often kept my daughter until I got home from school. She and her husband had two darling little kids. One day he just up and left. Surprised us all—he married his secretary eventually. My friend hadn't worked before, so I helped her get some typing skills. She worked for two weeks and said, "No more." She called me and said, "Well, I'm not going through what you did. I'm getting married." That was like a slap in the face. Gosh, did I look that bad? I started to doubt myself. Was I doing that bad a job? Should I have

gone the marriage route? Gone out and gotten a job and then married somebody?
I still wonder about that. Things would have been a lot easier financially. The kids
would have had a father. And I would have done what society looks at favorably.
I don't know. I still don't know what to do.

Economically these women lost their middle-class status, but socially their
expectations of themselves and their children remained the same. They still identified with the middle class, but their low incomes prevented them from participating in middle-class activities. This contradiction created many dilemmas and
conflicts:

I went to a CETA workshop, and I started crying when all they talked about was
how to get a job. A woman came after me in the hallway, and I just bawled. I'd
been searching for a job for months, I had a degree and teaching credential, and
here I was being told how to fill out a stupid job application. And I had three kids
at home that I didn't know how I was going to feed that week and a lovely home
I couldn't afford.

I moved here after the divorce because the school had a particularly good program
for gifted children. Kids were classed by ability and not just by grade level. So my
kid was in a really good spot for what he needed. I didn't realize at the time that
I was the only single parent in that group. One reason those kids can achieve at
that level is because they have a very stable home life, two parents to work with
every child on the enrichment and the projects and the homework. I hate to say
this, but it's all socioeconomic. Every kid in there belonged to a high socioeconomic
group. Oh, they can rationalize that it's not really like that, but it's completely
WASPish, all two-parent families where the mothers don't work. Mothers are available to take kids to music lessons, soccer lessons, gymnastic lessons, and all of that
whenever it's needed. I had to take my son out of that class. I couldn't keep up
the level of activity required of the kids and the parents. The gap was growing
greater and greater. If I'd lived like this a long time, I might have known how to
cope, but this was all new. And it all came down to money.

The women resented their precarious positions all the more because they
knew that their former husbands had experienced no loss in class status or standard of living and could have eased their struggles to support the children:

Five hundred dollars here or there—or taking over the orthodontist's bills—anything
like that would have meant a lot. I don't see why this kid should have to live with
jaw and tooth problems because I got a divorce. His jaw had to be totally realigned,
so it wasn't just cosmetic. His father could easily have paid that monthly [ortho-
dontist] bill and deducted it. That would have made a tremendous difference. But
he wouldn't. By making me suffer, he made his child suffer too.

When the children retained some access to middle-class activities through
involvement with their fathers, their mothers had ambivalent feelings. They were
grateful that their children were not neglected by their fathers and could enjoy
some enriching and entertaining activities with them; but they found their former
husbands' greater financial resources a painful reminder of how little they themselves could provide. One woman, who had to let her child get free meals
through the subsidized school lunch program, despite her many efforts to make
more money, told me this:

His father seldom buys him anything. But his stepmother sometimes does. She can give him all these nice things. She's given him nice books, a stereo headset. I have no idea what her motivation is, but it's a very funny feeling to know that I can't go and buy my son something he would love to have, but this perfect stranger can. And how will that affect my son ultimately? He must know how difficult things are here, and that I'm not deliberately depriving him. But it's kind of ironic—I helped establish that standard of living, but I end up with none of it, and she has full access to it.

Expenses and Economizing

Living with a reduced budget was a constant challenge to most of these women because they had no cushion to fall back on if expenses exceeded their incomes. Their savings were depleted soon after they divorced; only 12 of the 60 women I talked to had enough money in savings to cover a full month's expenses. Most said they had radically cut back their spending.[7] The major expenses after divorce were housing, food, and utilities. The women with young children also had substantial child care expenses, and several had unusually high medical bills that were not covered by health insurance.

Within a short time after their divorces, more than one-third of the women—16 women living in homes they owned and 7 living in rented places—had to move to different housing with their children in order to reduce their expenses. Two of the women had moved more than four times in the first two years after their divorces, always for financial reasons.[8] During marriage, 49 of the 60 women had lived in homes owned with their husbands. After divorce, only nine of them retained ownership of the family home. Of these nine, six were able to acquire ownership by buying out their husbands as part of the community property settlement (five of them only because they were able to get financial assistance from their parents); two retained the home by exchanging other community assets for it; and one received the home according to the dictates of the religion she and her husband shared.

Home ownership brought with it many expenses besides mortgage payments. Several women neglected upkeep and repairs for lack of money. A woman who was in her fifties reported this common dilemma:

I owe $16,000 on this house. I could get about $135,000 for it, so I have a large equity. But it would have taken all of that to get that condominium I looked at, and my payments would still have been about $400 a month. I don't know how I'll be able to keep up the house, financially or physically. The house needs painting, and I can't keep up the yard work. I'd like to move. I'd like a fresh start. But the kids don't want to move, and I can't imagine how I'll handle all of this once they're gone. When the alimony [spousal support] stops, there'll be no way I can manage a move. I'm stuck here now. The mortgage is really low and the interest is only 5 percent.

Two of the mothers reduced expenses by moving their children from private to public schools. Two others were able to keep their children in private schools only after administrators waived the tuition fees. Seven mothers received financial assistance for preschoolers' child care costs, five from private and two from public agencies. One of these women, who worked full-time, had this to say about her expenses:

> I'm buying this house. I pay $330 a month for it. Child care for my two kids runs to almost $500 a month. Since I bring home only a little more than $900, there's no way I could make it without the child care assistance. There'd be nothing left.

About half of these women had economic situations so dire that careful budgeting was not enough, and they continued to fall further behind economically. Those living close to the margin managed by paying some bills one month and others the next. Their indebtedness increased, and opportunities for reversing the situation did not appear:

> I'm so far in debt. Yes indeed. I keep thinking, why should I worry about the bills? I'll never get out of debt! All I can do is juggle. Without my charge cards, my kids would be bare-assed naked. And school is coming up again. What am I going to do for school clothes? And they've all grown fast this year. . . . I probably owe $3,000 on charge cards, and I still owe rent—I haven't paid this month or last. The landlord I have has been very understanding. He's let us go along as best he can. We've been here four years, and he knows what I'm going through. Over the years, he's given me several eviction notices, but this last time he hired a lawyer and everything. I decided I'd just pitch my tent on the capitol mall in Sacramento and say, "Here I am." I've written my congressman again, because I qualify for subsidized housing. But it'll take forever to get any action on that.

For many, however, even the persistent realities of economic hardship could not extinguish middle-class hopes:

> My husband liked really good food and always bought lots and the best. So when he left, it was really hard to cut the kids back. They were used to all that good eating. Now there's often no food in the house, and everybody gets really grouchy when there's no food around. . . . I think I've cut back mostly on activities. I don't go to movies anymore with friends. We've lost $150 a month now because my husband reduced the support. It gets cut from activities—we've stopped doing everything that costs, and there's nowhere else to cut. My phone is shut off. I pay all the bills first and then see what there is for food. . . . I grew up playing the violin, and I'd wanted my kids to have music lessons—piano would be wonderful for them. And my older two kids are very artistic. But lessons are out of the question.

Obtaining credit had been a real problem for many, for the reasons given by this woman, who had worked during the marriage while her husband attended school:

> My kids and I were very poor those first years after the divorce. I had taken care of our finances during marriage. But I didn't have accounts in my own name, so I couldn't get credit. I got a job as soon as I could. I was getting $65 a month for child support and paying $175 a month for rent. Between the rent and the child care and the driving to work, I was absolutely broke. I really didn't have enough to live on. I had no benefits either, with my first job. I was living dangerously, and with children. I could barely pay the basic bills. There wasn't enough money

for food lots of times. I cried many times because there wasn't enough money. I couldn't get any credit. [When I was married] my husband could get any credit he wanted, but it was on the basis of *my* job, which had the higher income. He couldn't even keep his checkbook balanced, but now I'm the one who can't get credit! It was a hard lesson to learn. Now whenever I get a chance, I tell women to start getting a credit rating.

The woman who told me this, incidentally, had managed to overcome initial impoverishment and gain a middle-class income from her job.

Some women regarded personal possessions such as jewelry, furniture, and cars as things they might sell to meet emergencies or rising indebtedness:

I sold jewelry to have my surgery, to pay for the part that wasn't covered. I still have some silver, and I have some good furniture, which could probably bring something. That's probably what I'd do in an emergency, sell those things. What else do people do?

Teenaged children helped by earning money through odd jobs and baby-sitting. Older teenagers changed their college plans, and several entered community colleges instead of universities. One woman's daughter was already in the Navy, pursuing her schooling in languages and working as a translator, and the daughter of another was considering military service as a way of saving money for a college education.

Most women compared their own hardship and forced economizing to the economic freedom enjoyed by their ex-husbands. For example:

I know my ex-husband goes somewhere almost every weekend, and he usually takes a friend along. I wonder how he can do that. How can he go somewhere every weekend? The only way I could do that is find a rich man! I couldn't possibly work enough hours to pay for that much stuff. I'd be doing well to finance a [20-mile] trip to San Francisco!

There were some exceptions to the general pattern of economic decline. Nine of the 60 women had regained some latitude for discretionary spending, though only three of them had managed this economic reversal without help. These nine were a distinct subgroup; the others did not share their higher standards of living or their feelings and approaches to the future. Still, only two of these nine women had not experienced a major decline in income immediately upon divorcing (or separating). One had been living on welfare because her husband's excessive drinking and erratic behavior had prevented him from holding a job; she found employment immediately after separating from him. The other one had been the primary family wage earner during her marriage.[9] Four of the women whose incomes had dropped significantly had managed to stop and even reverse the economic decline very soon after divorce because they were granted temporary spousal support awards and acquired some money and assets from their community property settlement; two of them, who had been divorced after more than 20 years of marriage, also received substantial amounts of money from their parents. Although these four did not experience the degree of hardship shared by the others, they did not fully recover their formerly high income levels and therefore also had to alter their lifestyles. As one of them said:

> Essentially, I took an $80,000 drop in annual income. And I had to borrow again last year. This year I finally sold the house, and that was really the only way I've made it. My change in lifestyle has been *tremendous*. Just my heating and electricity bill for our home was $350 a month. We just barely got by on $2,000 a month. I stopped buying household things; I stopped buying clothes for myself. And I rented out a room in the house. It was a huge house, and that helped out. I let the cleaning woman and the gardener go. I didn't paint. I let the property taxes go until I sold the house and paid them then. I quit taking trips. This house I'm in now has much lower operating expenses. My son doesn't have the same things he'd had. His grandparents buy most of his shoes and clothes now. He used to have lots and lots, so it's been a change for him.

Of the other five women who succeeded in improving their economic situations after a few years, three did so entirely through their own work efforts, and the other two managed with help from their former husbands—one took in the child for more than a year while his ex-wife worked at several jobs, and the other accepted a shared parenting arrangement.

Emotional Responses to Economic Loss

None of the nine women who had experienced substantial economic recovery reported suffering serious emotional changes. Forty-four of the others, however, spoke of frequent struggles with depression and despair. Every one of them attributed these intense feelings, which often seemed overwhelming, directly to the financial hardships that followed divorce. This woman spoke for many others in describing the effects that economic loss had had on her:

> I think about money a great deal. It's amazing. I used to get so bored by people who could only talk about money. Now it's all I think about. It's a perpetual thought, how to get money—not to invest, or to save, but just to live. The interesting thing is that you develop a poverty mentality. That intrigues me. I would never have thought that could happen. But if I had had money, several times in the last year I would have fought what was happening to me in a way I no longer think of fighting. You tend to accept what's coming because there's so much you *have* to accept. You get so you accept everything that comes your way. For example, I accepted at first what I was told about treating this cancer on my face: that the only surgery possible would leave my face disfigured with one side paralyzed. I knew it would ruin any possibility of my teaching if they did that to my face, but I would have just accepted it if a friend hadn't gotten me to go to someone else for consultation. I wouldn't have done that on my own. That's not how I would have behaved at other times in my life. I think it must happen to a lot of divorced women. It was only this year that I realized how strange this has become. I'm educated, I've come through a wealthy phase of my life, and now here I am, being shuttled around and not even fighting. It continues to fascinate me. After a while, you develop a begging mentality in which you'd like to squeeze money out of anybody. I guess I'm somewhere in the realm of poverty. I know there are poorer people, but I'm pretty well down near the bottom. If I were to lose this job—which is

always possible, there's no security to it—I'd be finished. Finished. I'd lose the house. I'd lose everything. There's no way I could survive.

The first year of divorce was traumatic for most, especially because legal uncertainties were mixed with other fears. A vicious circle was common: anxieties brought sleepless nights, and fatigue made the anxieties sharper. Although economic hardship remained, by the end of the first year most of the women had learned to control some of the anxiety surrounding it.[10]

Depression overtook a majority of these women at some time or other. Their feelings of despair over financial troubles were worsened by concerns for their children. One of them said:

> I thought about running away, but who would I have turned my kids over to? I also thought about suicide—especially when the youngest was still a baby and I had so much trouble with child care and it cost me so much. I kept thinking that if I were gone, it would take a major burden off of everybody.

In fact, such despair was a common experience: 26 of the 60 women volunteered that they had contemplated suicide at some time after divorce. They mentioned various contributing factors, such as emotional harassment from their husbands and uncertainty about their own abilities and identities, but all said that economic hardship was *the* primary stress that pushed them to the point of desperation.

One mother gave a very detailed account of her experience with suicidal depression, which occurred at a time when she had been barely managing for several months. She would drag herself to work and then collapse in bed when she got home. When she would get out of bed, she told me, the sight of her ten-year-old son sitting in front of the television set, alone in a cold room and eating cold cereal, would send her back to bed, where her exhaustion and despair would be exacerbated by hours of crying. She went on:

> I came home to an empty house that night—it was February. I had gotten my son's father to take him that weekend so I could go to my class—the one about learning to live as a single person again. I'd hoped that by getting some encouragement, I'd be able to pull myself out of this and find a way to make a better living. About eleven o'clock, I just decided this was no way to live. I couldn't take care of this child. I'd gone to Big Brothers, and they wouldn't take him because he had a father. But his father wasn't seeing him. Family Services weren't any help. The woman there did try to help, I think. She cared. But she'd been married more than twenty-five years and just didn't understand. All I could do in the fifty-minute appointment with her was cry. My attorney wasn't giving me any help or getting me any money. My mother was mad at me—she said it was my fault for leaving my husband.
>
> I just couldn't see it ever being any different, so I decided to kill myself. I'm sure that's not a unique thing. It was the most logical thing in the world. I knew exactly how I was going to do it. I was going to fill the bathtub with warm water and cut my wrists. It would be fine then—that thought was the only thing that made me feel any better. Nothing was as bad as the thought of getting up the next day. So I called my son's father—he was going to bring him back the next day—and I asked him if he thought he could take care of him. I didn't think I gave any evidence [of my feelings] or anything—it wasn't a desperate call for help, or a threat-

ening call, or anything like that, because I'd already made up my mind. I just didn't want him to bring my son in here and find me like that. I wanted him to make some kind of arrangements to take care of him. He didn't say anything on the phone, but in about twenty minutes the doorbell rang. Two young men in blue uniforms were standing there. They wanted to take me to an emergency room. It was a crisis place, they said. They were young and scared themselves and acted like they didn't know what to do.

I guess the shock of realizing how far I'd gone was enough to snap me out of it. I'd spent those twenty minutes [after the phone call] piddling around taking care of some last-minute things, tidying up and so on. It seems that once I made the decision, it gave me such inner peace, such a perfect reconciliation. It seemed the most logical, practical thing in the world. Then their coming stopped me from doing it. I didn't go with them, but they gave me a phone number and told me there were people there who would come and get me anytime.

I've only recently put into perspective what happened. It wasn't so much my inability to cope as it was the convergence of everything in my situation. That person at Family Services did help, actually, when she pointed out that some people who've never had trouble dealing with anything don't know what else to do when they feel like they can't cope. That fit. I'd never had a crisis I couldn't deal with in some way. I'd gotten myself into bad situations before, but I could always see cause-and-effect relationships, and I'd always felt like I could make some changes right away that would change things in my life. In this case, I couldn't figure anything out. I don't even know how to tell you what I thought.

This woman had been divorced before and had not suffered depression; but she had had no child then, no one else for whom she was responsible.

These women who were new to poverty had no ideas about how to cope in their new situations, and they found little help in the society at large. Some of the most desperate were unable to afford professional counseling. One of them said:

At one point during the eviction, I was getting hysterical. I needed help. So I called a program called Women's Stress. Good thing I wasn't really suicidal, because they kept me on hold a long time. They said, "Well, this program is just for women with an alcohol or drug problem. Does that fit you?" I said, "No, but if I don't get help, it will." They said they'd send me a pamphlet, which they did. It cost twenty-five dollars to join. I never did find any help.

The worst personal pain these women suffered came from observing the effects of sudden economic hardship on their children. Here is one woman's poignant account:

I had $950 a month, and the house payment was $760, so there was hardly anything left over. So there we were: my son qualified for free lunches at school. We'd been living on over $4,000 a month, and there we were. That's so humiliating. What that does to the self-esteem of even a child is absolutely unbelievable. And it isn't hidden; everybody knows the situation. They knew at his school that he was the kid with the free lunch coupons.... My son is real tall and growing. I really didn't have any money to buy him clothes, and attorneys don't think school clothes are essential. So he was wearing these sweatshirts that were too small for him. Then one day he didn't want to go to school because the kids had been calling him

Frankenstein because his arms and legs were hanging out of his clothes—they were too short. That does terrible things to a kid, it really does. We just weren't equipped to cope with it.

But the need to cut costs—on food, clothing, and activities for the children—was not the only source of pain. Most of the mothers reported that their parenting approaches changed and that their emotions became more volatile, and even unstable, in periods of great financial stress. Mothers who went to work full-time resented the inevitable loss of involvement in their children's lives:

> I wish I could get over the resentment. [In the first years after the divorce] I spent half the time blaming myself and the other half blaming their father. Because I was so preoccupied, I missed some really good years with them, doing things I'd looked forward to and wanted to do. Those years are gone now.

Some of the mothers also thought the experience of economic hardship after divorce might eventually affect the society at large, as more and more women and children come to share it.[11] For example:

> It's not just the mother [who's affected]. It's a whole generation of kids who don't even know how to use a knife and a fork, who don't sit at a table to eat, who don't know how to make conversation with people of different ages. There are so many awful possibilities, and it's a whole society that's affected. I'm not talking about people who have lived for years in poverty. We planned and lived one way with no idea of the other reality. Then this harsh reality hits, and everything becomes a question of survival. I think it must be different if that's all you've experienced. At least then your plans fit your possibilities—that sort of thing. You can't spend your whole day trying to survive and then care anything about what's going on in the world around you. You really can't. . . . Maybe it's going to take 50 percent of the population to be in this shape before we get change. But some of us have to be salvaged, just so we can fight. We can't all be so oppressed by trying to survive that we can't do anything at all.

Although their despair was worsened by concern for their children, it was the children who gave these women their strongest incentive to continue the struggle:

> Sure, I think about suicide. And I'm a smart lady who's been creative and able to do some things to change our situation. But I'm tired—*tired*. And it's real hard. What keeps me alive is my kid. I may be boxed in, but if I give up, what will happen to her? She doesn't deserve that.

Most of these women also admitted to having lost a sense of the future. A 50-year-old woman, who said she wondered if she would someday become a bag lady, told me:

> That's what I started to say at the beginning—*I don't have a future*. I can sit around and cry about that for a while, but then I have to move on and ask, what am I going to do about it? And there's not much I can do. What career can I start at my age? How do I retrieve all those years spent managing a family?

And another somewhat younger woman said:

> The worst poverty is the poverty of the spirit that sets in when you've been economically poor too long, and it gets to the point where you can't see things turning around.

To avoid this sense of hopelessness, a majority of the 60 women tried not to think about the future and made only short-term plans:

> I learned very quickly that I couldn't think too far into the future or I'd drive myself crazy. The future became, "What will I do next month?" I learned I had to go day to day and just do the best I could. That's been my major technique for coping, and I learned it right away. I've built up some retirement and Social Security through work, thank heavens. But I have to live right now. I just can't think about the future. The worst that can happen is that the state will take care of me, and I'll end up in a crappy old folks' home. But I don't think about that.

Ten of the 60 women—a unique subgroup—said they had not experienced serious depression or despair after divorce. But the reasons they gave simply reemphasize the central importance of economic loss in the lives of divorced women. Four of these ten had various sources of income that protected them from poverty and enabled them to work actively toward improving their situation. Two of them were using income from the divorce property settlement to attend graduate school, and they hoped to regain their former standard of living by pursuing professional careers. Two were receiving financial support from their parents while they sought employment and planned for the possible sale of their homes as part of the property settlement. The remaining six said they were generally optimistic *in spite of* their poor economic positions. Like the others, they found the financial hardships imposed by divorce surprising and difficult to handle; they simply found these hardships easier to cope with than the despair they had known in their marriages.

In summary, these women discovered that the most important change brought about by divorce was an immediate economic decline, which for most of them had not been reversible. Despite their economizing efforts and dramatically altered lifestyles, many of them continued to lose ground financially. In addition, economic circumstances had a powerful effect on their emotional lives. Only a very few escaped feelings of despair and hopelessness. Most found that economic uncertainties fostered depression, discouragement, and despair, and nearly all said they had endured periods of intense anxiety over the inadequacy of their income and its effects on the well-being of their children. Most of them felt trapped in their present circumstances and said they had no sense of the future.

Notes

1. According to Lee Rainwater (1984) and the U.S. Bureau of the Census (1985), the earnings of working married wives contribute only 22 percent of the average family's total income. For this

reason, poverty, which occurs in only one of nineteen husband-wife families and in only one of nine families maintained by a single father, afflicts almost one of every three families headed by a woman.

2. Some other studies that show the adverse economic impacts of divorce on women are Duncan and Morgan (1979); Weitzman (1981, 1985); Spanier and Casto (1979); Eisler (1977); Espenshade (1979); Levitan and Belous (1981); U.S. Commission on Civil Rights (1983); McCarthy (1985). An analysis of the University of Michigan's Panel Study of Income Dynamics, a nationally representative and longitudinal study of 5,000 families, concludes: "Former husbands are better off than their wives. . . . even after adjusting for these transfers [child support and alimony], husbands are still better off than their wives" (Hampton 1974: 169). Another major study found: "It is only the women and children whose standards of living decline even when the father is making payments. . . . Four in five fathers can live at or above the Intermediate Standard Budget" (Chambers, 1979: 48).

3. The University of Michigan Panel Study of Income Dynamics found that the economic decline experienced by women after divorce is not temporary (Duncan and Morgan, 1974, 1976, 1978, 1979; Hill, 1981). Saul Hoffman and James Holmes (1974: 24) state: "Even after adjusting for demographic and environmental variables, female-headed families with children were shown to be two and one-half times as likely to be temporarily poor and twice as likely to be persistently poor as similar families headed by married couples." See also Rainwater (1984); Kamerman (1984); Corcoran, Duncan, and Hill (1984); McCarthy (1985).

4. Between 1960 and 1983, the median income of female-headed families with no husband present dropped by the following percentages: from 61 to 57 percent of the median income of male-headed families with no wife present, from 43 to 41 percent of the median income of married couples, and from 51 to 38 percent of the median income of married-couple families in which the wife was also employed. In 1983, the median income for female-headed families was $11,484; for male-headed families with no wife present, $20,140; for married-couple families, $26,019; and for married couples in which the wife was employed, $30,340 (U.S. Bureau of the Census, 1985).

5. From his Michigan study, David Chambers (1979) concludes that the custodial parent needs 80 percent of the predivorce income to maintain the family's standard of living. The total income of most family units of divorced women and children falls below 50 percent of their former family income. Sweden, in fact, has determined that single-parent families actually need more income than others and provides cash supports that give them incomes comparable to those of two-parent families (Cassetty, 1983).

6. Research supports the common-sense belief that the surest way to reverse the economic decline resulting from divorce is to remarry (Sawhill, 1976; Duncan and Morgan, 1974, 1979; Johnson and Minton, 1982). Do women remarry because they conclude, pragmatically, that being a single woman is too costly, for themselves and perhaps also for their children? Would fewer women remarry if they could successfully support themselves? The answers to such questions will have interesting political implications.

7. Various studies have found that reduced consumption of both goods and services is a major response by divorced mothers to economic decline; for example, see Hampton (1976); Espenshade (1979); Masnick and Bane (1980). They spend much less than divorced men do on food, recreation, clothing, and discretionary items (Masnick and Bane, 1980). According to McCubbin et al. (1980: 866), a 1979 General Mills study reports: "in order to cope with inflation, 75 percent of the single-parent families were cutting back on health-related items (medical care, dental care, etc.)."

8. George Masnick and Mary Jo Bane (1980) note that many single-parent families move several times in two or three years. Buehler and Hogan (1980) note that women and their children frequently move to poorer housing in order to economize following divorce.

9. A . . . study by Lee Rainwater (1984: 84) shows how economic dependency in a previous marriage makes it difficult for a woman to recover economically from divorce: "By the fourth year that they headed their own families, women who had regular work experience before becoming female heads had family incomes equal to 80 percent of their average family income while a wife. Women who had not worked at all had incomes slightly less than half that of their last married years."

10. Various studies argue that the first year or so after divorce is the most stressful and traumatic (Hetherington, Cox, and Cox, 1976; Wallerstein and Kelly, 1979, 1980; Weiss, 1979a, 1979b). Additionally, both Pett (1982) and Buehler and Hogan (1980) found that financial concerns were among the factors that limited divorced mothers' emotional recovery from divorce. None of these studies, however, attempts to distinguish the effects of economic uncertainty from more generalized separation emotions.

11. Michael Smith (1980: 80) concludes from his analysis of the Panel Study of Income Dynamics that no emotional recovery period is evident: regardless of the number of years since their divorce, divorced women had lower community participation and efficacy, as well as a greater sense

of alienation and loss of control over their lives. He states that powerlessness and limited community participation may be viewed as important indicators of the social conditions with which single parents must cope.

References

BUEHLER, C., and J. HOGAN. 1980. "Managerial Behavior and Stress in Families Headed by Divorced Women: A Proposed Framework." *Family Relations* 29 (4): 525–532.

CASSETTY, J. 1983. "Emerging Issues in Child-Support Policy and Practice." In J. Cassetty (ed.), *The Parental Child-Support Obligations.* Lexington, Mass.: Lexington Books.

CHAMBERS, D. 1979. *Making Fathers Pay: The Enforcement of Child Support.* Chicago: University of Chicago Press.

CORCORAN, M., G. DUNCAN, and M. HILL. 1984. "The Economic Fortunes of Women and Children: Lessons from the Panel Study of Income Dynamics." *Signs* 10 (2): 232–248.

DUNCAN, G., and J. MORGAN (eds.). 1974. *Five Thousand Families*, vol. 4. Ann Arbor: University of Michigan Press.

_____. 1976. *Five Thousand Families*, vol. 5. Ann Arbor: University of Michigan Press.

_____. 1978. *Five Thousand Families*, vol. 6. Ann Arbor: University of Michigan Press.

_____. 1979. *Five Thousand Families*, vol. 7. Ann Arbor: University of Michigan Press.

EISLER, R. 1977. *Dissolution: No-Fault Divorce, Marriage, and the Future of Women.* New York: McGraw-Hill.

ESPENSHADE, T. 1979. "The Economic Consequences of Divorce." *Journal of Marriage and the Family* 41 (3): 615–625.

HAMPTON, R. 1974. "Marital Disruption: Some Social and Economic Consequences." In G. Duncan and J. Morgan (eds.), *Five Thousand Families*, vol. 4. Ann Arbor, Mich.: University of Michigan Press.

HETHERINGTON, E., M. COX, and R. COX. 1976. "Divorced Fathers." *The Family Coordinator* 25: 417–428.

HILL, M. 1981. "Some Dynamic Aspects of Poverty." In G. Duncan and J. Morgan (eds.), *Five Thousand Families*, vol. 9. Ann Arbor: University of Michigan Press.

HOFFMAN, S., and J. HOLMES. 1974. "Husbands, Wives, and Divorce." In G. Duncan and J. Morgan (eds.), *Five Thousand Families*, vol. 4. Ann Arbor: University of Michigan Press.

JOHNSON, W., and M. MINTON. 1982. "The Economic Choice in Divorce: Extended or Blended Family?" *Journal of Divorce* 5 (1–2): 101–113.

LEVITAN, S., and R. BELOUS. 1981. *What's Happening to the American Family?* Baltimore, Md.: Johns Hopkins University Press.

MCCARTHY, L. 1985. *The Feminization of Poverty: Report of the Lieutenant Governor's Task Force on the Feminization of Poverty.* Sacramento: State of California.

MCCUBBIN, H., C. JOY, A. COUBLE, J. COMEAU, J. PATTERSON, and R. NEIDLEE. 1980. "Family Stress and Coping: A Decade Review." *Journal of Marriage and the Family* 42: 855–871.

MASNICK, G., and M. BANC. 1980. *The Nation's Families: 1960–1990.* New York: Auburn House.

PETT, M. 1982. "Predictors of Satisfactory Social Adjustment of Divorced Single Parents." *Journal of Divorce* 5 (3): 1–17.

RAINWATER, L. 1984. "Mothers' Contributions to the Family Money Economy in Europe and the United States." In P. Voydanoff (ed.), *Work and Family.* Palo Alto, Calif.: Mayfield.

SAWHILL, I. 1976a. "Discrimination and Poverty Among Women Who Head Families." *Signs* 1: 201–221.

SMITH, M. 1980. "The Social Consequences of Single Parenthood: A Longitudinal Perspective." *Family Relations* 29 (1): 75–81.

SPANIER, G., and R. CASTO, 1979. "Adjustment to Separation and Divorce: An Analysis of Fifty Case Studies." *Journal of Divorce* 2 (3): 241–253.

U.S. BUREAU OF THE CENSUS. 1985. *Statistical Abstract of the United States, 1985. National Data Book and Guide to Sources.* Washington, D.C.: U.S. Government Printing Office.

U.S. COMMISSION ON CIVIL RIGHTS. 1974. *Women and Poverty.* Washington, D.C.: U.S. Government Printing Office.

WALLERSTEIN, J., and J. KELLY. 1979. "Children and Divorce: A Review." *Social Work* (November): 468–475.

WEISS, R. 1979a. *Going It Alone: The Family Life and Social Situation of the Single Parent.* New York: Basic Books.

———. 1979b. "Growing Up a Little Faster: The Experience of Growing Up in a Single-Parent Household." *Journal of Social Issues* 35 (4): 97–111.

WEITZMAN, L. 1981. *The Marriage Contract: Spouses, Lovers, and the Law.* New York: Free Press.

———. 1985. *The Divorce Revolution: The Unexpected Social and Economic Consequences for Women and Children in America.* New York: Free Press.

Families and Aging: Diversity and Heterogeneity*

Vern Bengtson, Carolyn Rosenthal, and Linda Burton

As individuals and families age, there are changes in the issues faced in everyday life. Throughout the industrialized world, recent decades have seen both dramatic increases in longevity and growth in the diversity of families as people age. These changes have had a significant impact upon family life—including new types of family relationships, a multiplication of intergenerational ties, and new meanings attached to different marital statuses in later life. This piece examines some of these changes and paints a portrait of diversity in family life as people age.

Two things in the past 50 years have changed traditional expectations about families and aging in industrialized societies. The first and most familiar are the widespread demographic transitions involving increased longevity, decreased fertility, and attenuated family structures across several generations. The second is an increased diversity in family forms, norms, and behaviors—particularly evident among subgroups in North American society—resulting in significant heterogeneity in the situations of elderly individuals within their family relationships.

*Source: Vern Bengtson, Carolyn Rosenthal, and Linda Burton, "Families and Aging: Diversity and Heterogeneity," in *Handbook of Aging and the Social Sciences, 3rd. ed.* (San Diego: Academic Press, 1990), pp. 263–273, 280.

The purpose of this chapter is to review research reflecting the diversity and heterogeneity of family relationships involving aging individuals. We will review implications of the demographic transition for aging families and evidence for their increasing heterogeneity, emphasizing the necessity of considering the social-structural contexts of family relationships in aging. In the first section we discuss the demographic transitions that will have a significant impact on families and aging in the 1990s. Second, we explore marital patterns with aging, including marital quality, widowhood, divorce, remarriage, and singlehood.

I. The Demographic Revolution and Aging Families

Today's elderly are participants in a quiet revolution in the demography of intergenerational family life. Individuals are growing older in intergenerational families that are quantitatively and qualitatively different from those of their great-grandparents, in terms both of the structure and the duration of family roles and relationships (Cherlin and Furstenberg, 1986; Uhlenberg, 1978; Wells, 1982). Unlike the two- and three-generation families of their predecessors, there is a greater probability that today's elderly will be part of a four- or even five-generation family with fewer members per generation (Hagestad, 1986; Streib and Beck, 1980; Vinovskis, 1977; Wells, 1982). Shanas (1980) estimated that about 50 percent of people over age 65 are members of four-generation families. Hagestad (1988) reported that 20 percent of women who died after the age of 80 were great-great-grandmothers, members of five-generation families.

Moreover, the number of years that aging individuals spend in family roles has increased dramatically. In the early nineteenth century, North American parents and children may have shared 20 to 30 years of life together; grandparents and grandchildren, only a decade (Juster and Vinovskis, 1987; Uhlenberg, 1978). Today's aging parents may be part of their children's lives for over a half a century (Preston, 1984). As grandparents, their ties to adult grandchildren and, perhaps, great-grandchildren may extend beyond 20 years (Barranti, 1985; Hagestad and Burton, 1985).

These changes in family structure and in the duration of roles and relationships can largely be attributed to the joint effects of two demographic trends: (1) the dramatic decline in mortality during the last century—life expectancy has increased approximately 27 years since 1900 (Bengtson, 1986; Gee, 1987; Uhlenberg, 1980; U.S. Bureau of the Census, 1984); and (2) the decline in fertility—the number of children born per female has decreased from 3.7 children in 1900 to 1.8 in 1986 (Connidis, 1989; U.S. Bureau of the Census, 1987; Watkins, Menken, and Bongaarts, 1987). Other features of the demographic revolution that have contributed to changes in the family life of older adults include variations in the timing of fertility, namely teenage childbearing (Burton and Martin, 1987), delayed childbearing (Connidis, 1989) and childlessness (Parke, 1988), and increases in single parenthood and divorce (Bengtson and Dannefer, 1987).

A. Emergence of the "Beanpole Family" Structure

One intergenerational family structure that has become increasingly common in contemporary North American society is what can be described as the "beanpole family," the product of declining mortality and fertility. Also called "verticalization," this occurs through intergenerational extension, when the number of living generations within lineages increases, and intragenerational contraction, when there is a steady decrease in the number of members within each generation (Bengtson and Dannefer, 1987; Hagestad, 1986; Knipscheer, 1988). Verticalization has many implications for the complexity and potential pool of intergenerational relationships as well as for multigenerational living arrangements.

First, in the decades to come, individuals will grow older having more vertical than horizontal linkages in the family. For example, vertically, a four-generation family structure has three tiers of parent-child relationships, two sets of grandparent-grandchild ties, and one great-grandparent-great-grandchild linkage (Hagestad, 1988). Within generations of this same family, horizontally, aging individuals will have fewer brothers and sisters. In addition, at the level of extended kin, family members will have fewer cousins, aunts, uncles, nieces, and nephews (Pullam, 1982).

With the increase in the number of generations in a family, the question arises as to whether there will be a comparable increase in multigenerational households. In the early 1900s, it was fairly common for older individuals to live in three-generation households with their children and grandchildren (Juster and Vinovskis, 1987; Smith, 1986). That pattern, however, has changed dramatically over time. Even though the number of generations per family has increased, today's elderly are more likely either to live alone or with a spouse (Shanas and Hauser, 1974; Treas and Bengtson, 1987). Jackson (1985) noted that the sharing of a multigenerational household is a function of many factors, including age, gender, marital status, health, and race, and not just the number of generations per family; to this should be added what is perhaps the major factor, economic necessity (including housing shortages).

B. Extended Duration of Family Roles and Relationships

Having fewer children and living longer has lengthened the time spent in intergenerational family role statuses (Hagestad, 1981; Hess and Waring, 1980; Riley, 1983). Because of sex differences in longevity, however, the length of time spent in family roles is different for women and men.

Watkins et al. (1987) provide a profile of the changes in duration of intergenerational family roles for women across time. Using simulation models based on mortality, marriage, and fertility rates, they estimate the number of years a woman might have spent with parents over the age 65 and children under age 18 under the demographic regimes prevailing in the United States in 1800, 1900,

1960, and 1980. Their findings have striking implications for the changing roles of aging women in intergenerational families. For example, because of the dramatic increase in the survival of aging parents over time, women in 1980, compared to those in 1800, spent four times the number of years as a daughter with both parents alive. Moreover, the time spent by a woman as the adult child of one or more parents over the age of 65 has increased from approximately seven years in 1800 to 18 years [in] 1980. At the same time there has been a decrease in the average time spent with a child under the age of 18, so that by 1960 the number of years spent with parents over age 65 exceeded years spent with children under age 18.

Gee (1987) reports similar results in an analysis of Canadian census data on birth cohorts from 1860 to 1960. She provided further insight into the connections between adult children and their aging parents by estimating that of children over age 50 in 1960, only 16 percent had a surviving parent, which will increase to 60 percent among the 1960 birth cohort; at age 60, the increase will be from 2 to 23 percent (by the year 2200).

These figures are particularly important in considering implications for family elder caregiving. When women are aged 50 to 60, their parents are typically near or over the age of 80—thus having the highest risk of physical and mental frailty and being more likely to depend on their children. In light of the declines in fertility, the potential size of a caregiver pool for a dependent parent poses a dilemma. Smaller families mean that women may have fewer siblings with whom to share the sometimes considerable burden of a dependent aging parent. Consequently, having fewer children to share caregiving is a trend in conflict with the longer survival of aging parents (Treas and Bengtson, 1987).

Increases in the duration of time spent being a parent and child are not the only intergenerational statuses that have changed for women over time. Since the second half of this century, grandparenthood has emerged as a lengthy period in the life course, distinct from parenthood (Hagestad and Burton, 1985). Increased longevity, coupled with the timing of the transition to grandparenthood, has afforded aging women the opportunity to know their grandchildren as infants, adolescents, young adults, and even as parents (Cherlin and Furstenberg, 1986). Although we lack strong empirical data on when the transition to grandparenthood typically occurs, the median age at entry is estimated to be around 45 (Sprey and Matthews, 1982). Because the average life expectancy for females is currently about 79 years, today's aging female could feasibly spend close to one-half her life as a grandparent.

The length of time women spend as widows is another family status affected by demographic transition. Essentially, the length of time women spend as widows (roughly five–seven years) has remained constant over time (Watkins et al., 1987); however, today's aging women become widows at later ages. With improvements in life expectancy, the fraction of women widowed before 50 has markedly declined (Uhlenberg, 1974), yet widowhood remains much higher at each age for women than for men. For example, 46 percent of women versus 11 percent of men are widows at ages 70 to 74 (Sweet and Bumpass, 1987). These differences are caused by the combined effects of the higher age-specific death rates for adult men, the tendency for men to marry younger women, and the higher remarriage rates of elderly men (Uhlenberg, 1980).

It should be clear that declines in mortality have profoundly affected the length of time women occupy in intergenerational family statuses, but overall the effect has been less striking for men (Hagestad, 1986; Uhlenberg, 1974; Wells, 1982). Because of the life-expectancy differential between men and women—currently, women in the United States outlive men by seven years (U.S. Bureau of the Census, 1984)—most males die before they experience durations in family roles comparable to those of females. Three demographic factors, however, have had a significant impact on the statuses of male parent, husband, and widower: fertility, marriage, and divorce.

Using U.S. Census data, Eggebeen and Uhlenberg (1985) examined the amount of time spent by black and white men in the roles of spouse and parent of young children. Between 1960 and 1980, there was a dramatic reduction in the amount of time men spent in family environments with young children present and a complementary increase in the amount of time spent outside of marriage. Reductions in family role durations have important implications for the connectedness of men to intergenerational family life. Through declining involvement with young children, men will miss out on significant mechanisms that tie them to intergenerational families. Those intergenerational connections may become particularly important to men as they approach old age.

In later life, marriage patterns are the critical determinants of the length of time men spend in the status of widower or as the dependent parent of middle-aged children. Most elderly men are married and live with their spouse (U.S. Bureau of the Census, 1987). In the event that a spouse dies, older men also have a greater likelihood of remarrying because of the significant male/female life expectancy. Moreover, men are less likely to spend a significant difference in amount of time as a dependent parent to their adult children; primarily because older men have spouses who are their primary caregivers (Hess and Waring, 1980).

As the role statuses of men and women in the multigenerational family structure increase in duration, they present new opportunities to form what Turner (1970) called "crescive bonds." These are bonds that evolve over time and are shaped by the accumulation of common experiences and meanings. Husbands and wives, parents and children, grandparents and grandchildren may accrue over 50 years of these shared experiences in each relationship. With fewer family members per generation, individuals have a greater opportunity to invest themselves heavily across a group of kin that is more manageable in size.

C. Diversity in Family Structure and Roles

In addition to the increase in "beanpole" families and changes in the duration of intergenerational family roles for women and men, the demographic revolution also has produced a number of variable patterns in intergenerational family structures and roles. The structures include age-condensed, age-gapped, truncated, matrilineal, and stepfamily models. All types are variable in width and length and reflect distinct family patterns in fertility.

1. *Age-Condensed Intergenerational Patterns* Burton (1985) demonstrated that the occurrence of teenage pregnancy across multiple generations has a three-fold impact on family structure and relationships. First, it creates an age-condensed family structure in which the age distance between generations can be just 15 years. Second, the small distance between generations blurs intergenerational boundaries. For example, the relationship between mothers and daughters was more intragenerationally oriented; essentially, mothers and daughters perceived themselves as being more like sisters than like parent and child. Third, in the majority of families Burton studied, teenage pregnancy sparked early transitions to grandmotherhood that were not welcomed by the respondents (Elder, Caspi, and Burton, 1987). Most of the young grandmothers in the study refused to take on the role of surrogate parent to their grandchild, so the burden of care for the new child was pushed up the generational ladder to the great-grand-mother in the lineage. In most instances, these young great-grandmothers were responsible not only for the care of their great-grandchild, but for their adolescent granddaughter (the child's mother) and their own aged parent, as well.

2. *Age-Gapped Intergenerational Patterns* Whereas teenage pregnancy creates multiple generations with very little age distance between tiers and unclear generation boundaries, delayed childbearing has the opposite effect. When women postpone birth until their mid- to late thirties, particularly if this has been a pattern in the family, a family structure with large age gaps is created. These may have implications for intergenerational relationships. First, parents and grandparents who enter their roles much later in life may not experience their statuses for as long a period of time as have their younger counterparts in other families. Second, the greater age distance between generations may create strains in the development of bonds across the life course, particularly since it may result in women simultaneously experiencing child-rearing problems with their adolescent and caregiving demands from their aging parent (Rossi, 1987). Third, the later in life that one has a child, the fewer children one may have, and the potential caregiver pool for aging parents is even smaller than those in the beanpole family structure and the families with teen mothers.

3. *Childlessness* Childlessness creates the shortest and slimmest lineage structure (Parke, 1988). Establishing intergenerational bonds and the options for receiving care within the family become quite limited for older childless adults. Often, the childless elderly establish bonds with extended or fictive kin. Building such connections, however, may become more difficult as the frequency of kin concomitantly declines with fertility.

4. *Matrilineal Intergenerational Structure* The rise of out-of-wedlock child-bearing suggests yet another form of intergenerational family structure. For example, in 1986, approximately one-half of all births to black women occurred by females who were not married (U.S. Bureau of the Census, 1987). This trend has salience for the roles in which older black women may engage. Older black women may be called upon more often by their daughters to serve as the "other parent" for their children (Burton, 1990). In addition, older women may be more

likely to share a household with their daughters and grandchildren, to assist with child rearing and the economic pressures of single parenthood (Wilson, 1986).

   5. *Stepparenting and Stepgrandparenting* A fifth demographic trend that has created diversity in the intergenerational family life of the elderly is the record-high rate of divorce among their young-adult and middle-aged offspring (U.S. Bureau of the Census, 1987). When the children of elderly parents divorce, it has a marked effect on the intergenerational family life of the aged (Aldous, 1987; Hagestad, 1986). The parents of the adult child who does not receive custody of his or her children are faced with the possibility of not having the same opportunities to be actively involved in the lives of their grandchildren. Moreover, the elderly parents may be forced to restrict important relationships with their former daughter- or son-in-law and their families. If divorce is followed by remarriage, elderly parents are faced with a complex reconstitution of the intergenerational family, and even further complexity emerges when remarriage involves integrating stepchildren into the kinship structure (Matthews, 1987).

II. Couples and Singles in Later Life

A. Marital Status and Its Impact

In later life, a much greater proportion of men than women are married (Sweet and Bumpass 1987, p. 299; see also, Treas and Bengtson, 1987), reflecting the custom for men to marry women younger than themselves, the greater longevity of females than males, and the higher remarriage rates for older men (Treas and VanHilst, 1976). The distribution of marital statuses of the aged is quite diverse across race (Sweet and Bumpass, 1987, p. 300). Among older women, white and Hispanic women are more likely to be married than are black women. Elderly white males have the highest probability of being married, elderly black females the least. Black persons are much more likely to be single, separated, or divorced than are white persons.

   Data from many sources support the conclusion that compared to unmarried elderly, married elderly have higher levels of morale, life satisfaction, mental and physical health, economic resources, social integration and social support, and lower rates of institutionalization (Verbrugge, 1979). Some of the "protective" health impact of marriage is related to two facts: (1) married people are less likely than persons of other marital statuses to engage in high-risk health behaviors (Verbrugge, 1979); and (2) in times of poor health, a spouse provides invaluable care (Shanas, 1979). In addition, older married women are less likely to be poor than are their unmarried peers and more likely to live in their own households (Mindel, 1979).

B. Marriage and Marital Quality in Later Life

The majority of older people rate their marriages as happy or very happy (Stinnett, Carter, and Montgomery, 1972). Many unhappy marriages may have previously ended in divorce, leading to a survivor effect in marriages (Troll, Miller, and Atchley, 1979). Some unhappy marriages survive. Nevertheless, it appears that commitment to spouse and to marriage as an institution and, secondarily, personal characteristics valued in a spouse, are the most important reasons for marital stability (Lauer and Lauer, 1986). Economic stability is no doubt another significant reason people remain married. Other factors important in long-term happy marriages are viewing one's mate as a best friend, liking one's mate as a person, agreeing on life goals, and maintaining humor and playfulness in marriage.

Marital satisfaction seems to vary over the life course. Most recent research suggests a *U*-shaped relationship with age: greater satisfaction is expressed by the young and the old, and less by persons in the middle stages of the life course (Lupri and Frideres, 1981; Spanier, Lewis, and Coles, 1975). Gilford and Bengtson (1979) suggest that there are two orthogonal dimensions to marital satisfaction: a positive interaction dimension, including such activities as working cooperatively, having stimulating discussions, and laughing together; and a negative-sentiment dimension, including sarcasm, disagreements, criticisms, and anger. Examining marital relations in a three-generational sample, they found that with age, negative sentiments declined and positive interaction had a *U*-shaped relation. The marriages of the oldest (grandparent) generation were thus reported to be more satisfactory on both dimensions than those of the middle-aged (parent) generation. Note, however, that among the oldest respondents (aged 71–90) both positive interaction and negative sentiment were low.

Rather than asking whether aspects of marital relationships such as satisfaction increase or decline over time, some scholars have postulated that the long-term relationships of the old may differ in fundamental, qualitative ways from the new relationships of the young. A developmental literature on love suggests that relationships are transformed with time so that the very basis of bonds of affection changes (Levinger, 1974). In this perspective, physical attraction, passion, and self-disclosure are viewed as facilitating the formation of new relationships, but relations are sustained over the long term by familiarity, loyalty, and a mutual investment in the relationship (Reedy, Birren, and Schaie, 1981).

C. Widowhood and Its Consequences

Widowhood is a profound life-course transition, bringing a number of losses and changes at objective and subjective levels (Martin Matthews, 1987). Widowhood has negative effects on health, exhibited in higher rates of depression (Pearlin and Johnson, 1977), mortality (Gove, 1973), and mental illness (Gove, 1979). This may lessen over time, however, with minimal effects in the long run (Ferraro, 1984).

The impact of widowhood is affected by age at widowhood (Morgan, 1976), whether the event is "on time" or "off time," and by gender, social class, race, health, and living environment. Because widowhood has become increasingly synonymous with elderly women, and because the widowhood population is so disproportionately female, almost all research on widowhood in later life has focused on women.

The gender differential in widowhood is pronounced throughout later life: at ages 65 to 69, 34 percent of women are widowed; for men, the figure is 7 percent. At ages 75 to 79, 60 percent of women are widowed but only 18 percent of the men; and at age 85+, 82 percent of women but only 43 percent of men are widowed (Sweet and Bumpass, 1987, p. 298).

Children are key figures in the support systems of the elderly, and this is particularly true of the widowed elderly (Lopata, 1979). The use of children as a resource, however, may be problematic. Exchange relations between adult children and widows, as opposed to married women, are less reciprocal, with the parent in the position of growing dependency (Heinemann, 1983). In addition to dependency related to declining health and income, widowed elderly also may be restricted in their ability to obtain interpersonal rewards. Adult children and grandchildren have other interpersonal sources of rewards but may be the only major source of rewards for the elderly widow (Heinemann, 1983; Matthews, 1979). Perhaps because of the difficulties associated with dependence of children, support from children does not appear to be associated with widows' higher morale. There is some indication, however, that support from peers (friends, neighbors, siblings) is associated with higher morale (Balkwell, 1985; Bankoff, 1983). This finding leads to a consideration of the *principle of substitution* and its limitations.

According to the principle of substitution (Shanas, 1979), elderly persons in need of social support and care receive these supports—in serial order depending on availability—from a spouse, then from a child, then from siblings, other relatives, friends, and neighbors. Johnson and Catalano (1981) point out that this suggests any one person is sufficient to meet the needs of the elderly. Different categories of persons, however, provide somewhat different types of support (e.g., Johnson and Catalano, 1981) and with different levels of commitment, extensiveness, duration, and effectiveness. For example, friends and neighbors share activities and provide companionship, and children appear to be less effective or available sources of these types of social support. Children, on the other hand, provide more extensive instrumental support and do so over a longer period of time. Research thus indicates that although much emphasis in gerontology has been placed on the contributions of adult children, it is important to have diverse social networks that include age/generational peers, whether family or nonfamily.

Widowhood brings about changes in social networks and social participation. Change may occur because the husband is no longer available to provide various kinds of support, because of the loss of a social partner or escort, or because of the threat of dependency associated with widowhood. An important change is the development of social involvement with widowed peers who may be especially helpful to the widow in providing emotional support because they share the same problems and because they do not make her feel like a "fifth wheel" (Lopata, 1979).

The best predictors of adequate social involvement in widowhood are good health and adequate economic resources (Arling, 1976; Atchley, 1975; Ferraro, 1984; Harvey and Bahr, 1974). Education, nonurban residence, and the presence of friends and neighbors with whom to participate in social activities are also important (Arling, 1976).

The broad patterns of widowhood are reasonably evident, but research is needed on variations among different groups. Even among groups often categorized together, there may be important differences. Although there are differences between women and men, there are perhaps greater differences among women themselves because of the cross-cutting influences of income, education, and social class. The urban/rural dimension may also make a difference; elderly rural widows are somewhat advantaged over urban widows, especially on subjective dimensions and some types of contact (Fengler and Danigelis, 1982; Martin Matthews, 1988).

Social class is related to different experiences in widowhood. Since working-class couples tend to live in a sex-segregated world (Lopata, 1979) they experience less disorganization in their lives immediately following widowhood than do their middle-class peers (Lopata, 1973). In the long run, however, middle-class women are advantaged in widowhood, for example, with respect to social integration (Lopata, 1979).

Gender, too, is a differentiator in the experience of widowhood. Some studies indicate widowers experience more negative health problems (Berardo, 1970; Gove, 1973), greater social isolation (Berardo, 1970), more restricted social networks (Martin Matthews, 1988; Wister and Strain, 1986), have fewer emotional ties with families, and are less likely to have a confidant (Strain and Chappell, 1982) than are widows, although other studies suggest no gender differences (Petrowsky, 1976) or that widowers are advantaged on these dimensions (Atchley, 1975). To put these differences in perspective, however, with advancing age and increasing functional limitations, the similarities between widows and widowers become more striking than the differences (Feinson, 1986; Martin Matthews, 1987; Wister and Strain, 1986).

Race and ethnicity are associated with the likelihood of becoming widowed as well as with living arrangements: Pelham and Clark (1987) found that white and black widows tend to live alone, and Hispanic and Asian widows live with others. Hispanic widows had the largest household size and number of offspring, and white widows had the smallest household size and number of offspring. Perhaps because of these differences, Hispanic widows appear to have more active support systems than do white widows (Cantor, 1979; Dowd and Bengtson, 1978; Pelham and Clark, 1987).

D. Divorced Elderly

Uhlenberg and Myers (1981) estimated that between 10 and 13 percent of the elderly population currently have experienced divorce, and that in 1979, only 3.3 percent reported their current marital status as divorced. They noted that the divorce rate among the elderly (2.2 per 1000) is much lower than in younger age groups (40 per 1000). The proportion divorced in the 65 to 74 age group is almost double that of persons aged 75 and older. Furthermore, divorce has increased greatly in all age groups in recent years (Glick, 1979) and is expected to continue to increase (Uhlenberg and Myers, 1981).

Divorced elderly are disadvantaged compared to other elderly with respect to economic situation (Hennon, 1983; Uhlenberg and Myers, 1981), family and kinship relationships (Berardo, 1982; Uhlenberg and Myers, 1981), mortality (Kitigawa and Hauser, 1973), and physical and mental health (Gove, 1973). These negative findings may reflect inadequate social-support networks (Berardo, 1982; Uhlenberg and Myers, 1981). Successful readjustment following divorce in mid-life, and by inference in late life, appears to be related to greater personal resources such as money, education, and strong kinship and friendship networks (Berardo, 1982).

Chiriboga (1982) suggested that older people have a more limited range of options than younger people do following marital breakdown. This is especially the case for women; remarriage is not common, because of the lack of potential partners and the tendency for men to marry younger women.

As a small but growing segment of the older population, the divorced elderly represent one example of diversity among today's elderly. But they are under-researched (Martin Matthews, 1988; Troll et al., 1979). Studies are needed to examine the impact of later-life divorce on the lineage unit and on relations with children and grandchildren. Since most divorced persons remarry, what effect does divorce and remarriage in early or middle adulthood have on parent-child relations in old age? What kind of filial support do noncustodial parents receive in late life? Do stepchildren take on filial responsibility for elderly parents?

E. Remarriage

Remarriage rates among the elderly are low. In 1975, the remarriage rate for widowers was 20 percent, and the rate for widows was 2 percent (Glick, 1979). Remarriage rates are far higher for men than for women (Treas and Van Hilst, 1976). Factors promoting the likelihood of remarriage are good health, adequate financial resources, and having one's friends and relatives support the remarriage (McKain, 1972; Treas and Van Hilst, 1976; Vinick, 1978).

Most older people remarry for companionship (McKain, 1972; Vinick, 1978). Social networks also have a strong influence on remarriage. Among the widowed, couples who remarry usually know each other prior to widowhood or are introduced by a mutual friend or relative (McKain, 1972; Vinick, 1978). Most widowed elderly who remarry have had successful first marriages (McKain, 1972).

F. Singles in Later Life

In the United States, about 4.9 percent of men and 5.4 percent of women aged 65 to 74 have remained single all their lives; in the age group 75 and over, the figures are 3.5 percent of men and 6.2 percent of women (Keith, 1986). The proportion of singles in the older population will decrease as the baby-boom parents, who had unusually high rates of marriage, enter old age. After that, the proportion of singles will increase again, reflecting current trends in which a some-what greater proportion of persons remain unmarried (Gee, 1987). A currently unknown proportion of the single elderly is gay or lesbian, a population almost totally neglected in research (for an exception, see Lee, 1987).

Research on the family life of older people generally has emphasized spousal and parent-child-grandchild relationships—that is, relationships anchored in the family of procreation. Since single elderly never have had these relation-ships available to them, the family relationships of lifelong singles are anchored in the family of orientation. The small amount of existing research on elderly sin-gles suggests that especially for women, family relationships are highly important. They appear to have had somewhat more intensive relationships than their mar-ried peers did with their own elderly parents, aunts and uncles, siblings, nieces, and nephews (Allen and Pickett, 1987; Johnson and Catalano, 1981). It is unclear whether the different kinship networks of singles are mirrored in differences in their wider social networks, for example in greater community involvement, or more contact with friends and neighbors (Ward, 1979).

With the onset of age-related impairment, however, differences in the sup-port networks of singles and marrieds become apparent. In late life, if and when older singles need a high level of instrumental assistance, their kinship networks appear to be less supportive than those of the married or those with children (Johnson and Catalano, 1981). Siblings are vulnerable to age-related health loss-es as well and may experience competing demands from their husbands, chil-dren, and grandchildren. Nieces and nephews or friends may provide help, but such help does not begin to meet the levels of that provided by children (Keith, 1986; Johnson and Catalano, 1981).

The somewhat negative impact in late life of the kinship pattern of singles, however, may be offset by other aspects that appear to equip singles to deal well with the challenges of later life. The overall effect of lifelong singlehood includes having developed qualities of independence, self-reliance, and habituation to liv-ing alone (Johnson and Catalano, 1981). Further, these individuals do not expe-rience the desolation of widowhood or divorce. In later life, the singles are hap-pier (Ward, 1979) and have better physical and mental health (Gove, 1973; Verbrugge, 1979) than divorced and widowed elderly. Compared to marrieds, however, singles experience retirement more negatively (Ward, 1979) and have a higher rate of suicide and institutionalization.

Conclusions

The central conclusion that can be drawn from this literature review is that fam-ily structures, roles, and relationships of contemporary elderly Americans are increasingly diverse. We have suggested that this diversity is a function of the intersection of changing patterns of mortality, fertility, and divorce with structur-al forms: race, socioeconomic status, and gender.

We see this diversity as having several structural manifestations: "beanpole family" structures, the age-condensed families of early childbearers, the age-gapped structures of late childbearers, the truncated configurations of the childless, the matrilineal forms of single parents, and the stepfamily model of those who experience divorce and remarriage. In addition, the duration of family roles has increased differentially for men and for women. Moreover, it appears that the bonds between generations have taken on new meaning as families negotiate the growing number of years they will share together as adults.

References

ALDOUS, J. (1987). "Family life of the elderly and near-elderly" (NCFR presidential address). *Journal of Marriage and the Family*, 49 (2), 227–234.

ALLEN, K. R., and PICKETT, R. S. (1987). "Forgotten streams in the family life course: Utilization of qualitative retrospective interviews in the analysis of lifelong single women's family careers." *Journal of Marriage and the Family*, 49 (3), 517–526.

ARLING, G. (1976). "Resistance to isolation among elderly widows." *International Journal of Aging and Human Development*, 7 (1), 67–86.

ATCHLEY, R. C. (1975). "Dimensions of widowhood in later life." *Gerontologist*, 15, 176–178.

BALKWELL, C. (1985). "An attitudinal correlate of the timing of a major life event: The case of morale in widowhood." *Family Relations*, 34 (4), 577–581.

BANKOFF, E. A. (1983). "Social support and adaptation to widowhood." *Journal of Marriage and the Family*, 45, 827–839.

BARRANTI, C. C. R. (1985). "The grandparent/grandchild relationship: Family resources in an era of voluntary bonds." *Family Relations*, 34, 343–352.

BENGTSON, V. L. (1986). "Sociological perspectives on aging, families, and the future." In M. Bergener (ed.), *Perspectives on aging: The 1986 Sandoz lectures in gerontology* (pp. 237–263). New York: Academic Press.

BENGTSON, V. L., and DANNEFER, D. (1987). "Families, work and aging: Implications of disordered cohort flow for the 21st century." In R. A. Ward and S. S. Tobin (eds.), *Health in aging: Sociological issues and policy directions* (pp. 256–289). New York: Springer.

BERARDO, F. (1970). "Survivorship and social isolation: The case of the aged widower." *Family Coordinator*, 19, 11–15.

BERARDO, F. (1982). "Divorce and remarriage at middle age and beyond." *Annals of the American Academy of Political and Social Science*, 464, 132–139.

BURTON, L. M. (1985). *Early and on-time grandmotherhood in multigeneration black families*. Unpublished doctoral dissertation. University of Southern California.

BURTON, L. M. (1990). "Teenage childbearing as an alternative life course strategy in multigeneration black families." *Human Nature*. (in press).

BURTON, L. M., and MARTIN, P. (1987). "Thematikin der Mehrgenerationenfamilie: Ein Beispiel." *German Journal of Gerontology*, 21, (June).

CANTOR, M. (1979). "The informal support system of New York's inner city elderly: Is ethnicity a factor?" In D. Gelfand and A. Kutzik (eds.), *Ethnicity and aging* (pp. 153–174). New York: Springer.

CHERLIN, A. J., and FURSTENBERG, F. F. (1986). *The new American grandparent*. New York: Basic Books.

CHIRIBOGA, D. A. (1982). "Adaptation to marital separation in later and earlier life." *Journal of Gerontology*, 31 (1), 109–114.

CONNIDIS, I. (1989). *Family ties and aging*. Toronto: Butterworths.

DOWD, J., and BENGTSON, V. L. (1978). "Aging in minority populations: An examination of the double jeopardy hypothesis." *Journal of Gerontology*, 33 (3), 427–436.

EGGEBEEN, D., and P. UHLENBERG. (1985). "Changes in the organization of men's lives: 1960–1980." *Family Relations*, 34, 251–257.

ELDER, G. H., JR., CASPI, A., and BURTON, L. M. (1987). "Adolescent transitions in developmental perspective: Sociological and historical insights." In M. Gunnar (ed.), *Minnesota symposium on child psychology* (vol. 21). Hillsdale, NJ: Erlbaum.

FEINSON, M. J. (1986). "Aging widows and widowers: Are there mental health differences?" *International Journal of Aging and Human Development*, 23 (4), 241–255.

FENGLER, A. P., and DANIGELIS, N. (1982). "Residence, the elderly widow, and life satisfaction." *Research on Aging*, 4 (1), 115–133.

FERRARO, K. F. (1984). "Widowhood and social participation in later life." *Research on Aging*, 6 (4), 451–468.

GEE, E. M. (1987). "Historical change in the family life course." In V. Marshall (ed.), *Aging in Canada* (2nd ed.). Markham, ON: Fitzhenry and Whiteside.

GILFORD, R., and BENGTSON, V. L. (1979). "Measuring marital satisfaction in three generations: Positive and negative dimensions." *Journal of Marriage and the Family*, 41, 387–398.

GLICK, P. (1979). "The future marital status and living arrangements of the elderly." *Gerontologist*, 21 (3), 276–282.

GOVE, W. (1973). "Sex, marital status and mortality." *American Journal of Sociology*, 79, 45–6.

GOVE, W. (1979). "Sex, marital status and psychiatric treatment: A research note." *Social Forces*, 58, 89–93.

HAGESTAD, G. O. (1981). "Problems and promises in the social psychology of intergenerational relations." In R. W. Fogel, E. Hatfield, S. Kiesler, and J. March (eds.), *Aging: Stability and change in the family* (pp. 11–46). New York: Academic Press.

HAGESTAD, G. O. (1986). "The aging society as a context for family life." *Daedalus*, 115, 119–139.

HAGESTAD, G. O. (1988). "Demographic change and the life course: Some emerging trends in the family realm." *Family Relations*, 37, 405–410.

HAGESTAD, G. O., and BURTON, L. M. (1985). "Grandparenthood, life context, and family development." *American Behavioral Scientist*, 29, 471–484.

HARVEY, C. D., and BAHR, H. M. (1974). "Widowhood, morale, and affiliation." *Journal of Marriage and the Family*, 36, 97–106.

HEINEMANN, G. D. (1983). "Family involvement and support for widowed persons." In T. H. Brubaker (ed.), *Family relationships in later life* (pp. 127–148). Beverly Hills, CA: Sage.

HENNON, C. G. (1983). "Divorce and the elderly: A neglected area of research." In T. H. Brubaker (ed.), *Family relationships in later life* (pp. 149–173). Beverly Hills, CA: Sage.

HESS, B. B., and WARING, J. M. (1980). "Parent and child in later life: Rethinking the relationship." In R. M. Lerner and G. B. Spanier (eds.), *Child influences on marital and family interaction* (pp. 445–529). New York: Academic Press.

JACKSON, J. J. (1985). "Race, national origin, ethnicity, and aging." In R. H. Binstock and E. Shanas (eds.), *Handbook of aging and the social sciences* (pp. 264–303). New York: Van Nostrand-Reinhold.

JOHNSON, C. L., and CATALANO, D. H. (1981). "Childless elderly and their family supports." *Gerontologist*, 21 (6), 610–618.

JUSTER, S., and VINOVSKIS, M. (1987). "Changing perspectives on the American family in the past." *Annual Review of Sociology*, 13, 193–216.

KEITH, P. M. (1986). "The social context and resources of the unmarried in old age." *International Journal of Aging and Human Development*, 23 (2), 81–96.

KITIGAWA, E. M., and HAUSER, P. M. (1973). *Differential mortality in the United States: A study in socioeconomic epidemiology.* Cambridge, MA: Harvard University Press.

KNIPSCHEER, C. P. M. (1988). "Temporal embeddedness and aging within the multigenerational family: The case of grandparenting." In J. E. Birren and V. L. Bengtson (eds.), *Emergent theories of aging* (pp. 426–446). New York: Springer.

LAUER, R. H., and LAUER, J. C. (1986). "Factors in long-term marriages." *Journal of Family Issues*, 7 (4), 382–390.

LEE, J. A. (1987). "The invisible lives of Canada's gray gays." In V. W. Marshall (ed.), *Aging in Canada: Social perspectives* (2nd ed., pp. 138–155). Markham, ON: Fitzhenry and Whiteside.

LEVINGER, G. (1974). "A three-level approach to interaction: Toward an understanding of pair relatedness." In T. Houston (ed.), *Foundations of interpersonal attraction.* New York: Academic Press.

LOPATA, H. Z. (1973). *Widowhood in an American city.* Cambridge, MA: Shenckman.

LOPATA, H. Z. (1979). *Women as widows: Support systems.* New York: Elsevier.

LUPRI, E., and FRIDERES, J. (1981). "The quality of marriage and the passage of time: Marital satisfaction over the family life cycle." *Canadian Journal of Sociology*, 6 (3), 283–305.

MARTIN MATTHEWS, A. (1987). "Widowhood as an expectable life event." In V. W. Marshall (ed.), *Aging in Canada: Social perspectives*, (2nd ed., pp. 343–366). Markham, ON: Fitzhenry and Whiteside.

MARTIN MATTHEWS, A. (1988). *Social support among the elderly widowed and divorced: Extended family, friends and neighbors.* Paper presented at the 17th annual meeting of the Canadian Association on Gerontology, Halifax, Nova Scotia, October.

MATTHEWS, S. H. (1979). *The social world of old women.* Beverly Hills, CA: Sage.

MATTHEWS, S. H. (1987). "Perceptions of fairness in the division on responsibility for old parents." *Social Justice*, 1 (4).

McKAIN, W. C. (1972). "A new look at older marriages." *Family Coordinator*, 21, 61–69.

MINDEL, C. H. (1979). "Multigenerational family households: Recent trends and implications for the future." *Gerontologist*, 5, 456–463.

MORGAN, L. A. (1976). "A re-examination of widowhood and morale." *Journal of Gerontology*, 31, 687–695.

PARKE, R. (1988). "Families in life span perspective: A multilevel developmental approach." In M. Heatherington, R. M. Lerner, and M. Perlumutter (eds.), *Child development in the life span perspective.* Hillsdale, NJ: Erlbaum.

PEARLIN, L. I., and JOHNSON, J. S. (1977). "Marital status, life-strains and depression." *American Sociological Review*, 42, 704–715.

PELHAM, A. O., and CLARK, W. F. (1987). "Widowhood among low income racial and ethnic groups in California." In H. Lopata (ed.), *Widows*, (vol. 2), *North America*, 191–222. Durham, NC: Duke University Press.

PETROWSKY, M. (1976). "Marital status, sex and the social networks of the elderly." *Journal of Marriage and the Family*, 38, 749–756.

PRESTON, S. (1984). "Children and the elderly: Divergent paths for America's dependents." *Demography*, 21, 435–457.

PULLAM, T. W. (1982). "The eventual frequencies of kin in a stable population." *Demography*, 19, 549–565.

REEDY, M. N., BIRREN, J. E., and SCHAIE, K. W. (1981). "Age and sex differences in satisfying love relationships across the adult life span." *Human Development*, 52–66.

RILEY, M. W. (1983). "The family in an aging society: A matrix of latent relationships." *Journal of Family Issues*, 4, 439–454.

Rossi, A. F. (1987). "Parenthood in transition: From lineage to child to self-orientation." In J. Lancaster, J. Altman, A. Rossi, and L. Sherrod (eds.), *Parenting across the life span: Biosocial dimensions* (pp. 435–456). Hawthorne, NY: Aldine de Gruyter.

Shanas, E. (1979). "The family as a social support system in old age." *Gerontologist*, 19, 169–174.

Shanas, E. (1980). "Older people and their families: The new pioneers." *Journal of Marriage and the Family*, 42, 9–15.

Shanas, E., and Hauser, P. M. (1974). "Zero population growth and the family of older people." *Journal of Social Issues*, 30, 79–92.

Smith, D. W. (1986). "Accounting for change in the families of the elderly in the United States, 1900–present." In D. Van Tassell (ed.), *Old age in a bureaucratic society* (pp. 87–109). Westport, CT: Greenwood.

Spanier, G. B., Lewis, R. A., and Coles, C. L. (1975). "Marital adjustment over the family life cycle: The issue of curvilinearity." *Journal of Marriage and the Family*, 37, 263–275.

Sprey, J. S., and Matthews, S. H. (1982). "Contemporary grandparenthood: A systematic transition." *Annals of the American Academy of Political and Social Sciences*, 464, 91–103.

Stinnett, N., Carter, L. M., and Montgomery, J. E. (1972). "Older persons' perceptions of their marriages." *Journal of Marriage and the Family*, 32 (3), 428–434.

Strain, L. A., and Chappell, N. L. (1982). "Confidants: Do they make a difference in quality of life?" *Research on Aging*, 4, 479–502.

Streib, G., and Beck, R. W. (1980). "Older families: A decade review." *Journal of Marriage and the Family*, 42 (4), 937–956.

Sweet, J. A., and Bumpass, L. L. (1987). *American families and households*. New York: Russell Sage Foundation.

Taylor, R. J. (1985). "The extended family as a source of support to elderly blacks." *Gerontologist*, 25, 488–495.

Treas, J., and Bengtson, V. L. (1987). "Family in later years." In M. Sussman and S. Steinmetz (eds.), *Handbook on marriage and the family* (pp. 625–648). New York: Plenum.

Treas, J., and VanHilst, A. (1976). "Marriage and remarriage rates among older Americans." *Gerontologist*, 16, 136–143.

Troll, L. E., Miller, S., and Atchley, R. (1979). *Families in later life*. Belmont, CA: Wadsworth.

Turner, R. H. (1970). *Family interaction*. New York: Wiley.

Uhlenberg, P. (1974). "Cohort variations in family life cycle experiences of U. S. females." *Journal of Marriage and the Family*, 36 (2), 284–292.

Uhlenberg, P. (1978). "Changing configurations of the life course." In T. Hareven (ed.), *Transitions: The family and the life course in historical perspective* (pp. 65–98). New York: Academic Press.

Uhlenberg, P. (1980). "Death and the family." *Journal of Family History*, 5 (3), 313–320.

Uhlenberg, P., and Myers, M. (1981). "Divorce and the elderly." *Gerontologist*, 21 (3), 276–282.

U.S. Bureau of the Census (1984). "Demographic and socioeconomic aspects of aging in the United States." *Current Population Reports* (Series P-23, no. 138). Washington, DC: U.S. Government Printing Office.

U.S. Bureau of the Census (1987). "Fertility of American Women: June 1986." *Current Population Reports* (Series P-20, no. 421). Washington, DC: U.S. Government Printing Office.

VERBRUGGE, L. M. (1979). "Marital status and health." *Journal of Marriage and the Family*, 41 (2), 267–285.

VINICK, B. H. (1978). "Remarriage in old age." *Family Coordinator*, 27 (4), 359–363.

VINOVSKIS, M. A. (1977). "From household size to the life course: Some observations on recent trends in family history." *American Behavioral Scientist*, 21, 263–287.

WARD, R. L. (1979). "The never married in later life." *Journal of Gerontology*, 34 (6), 861–869.

WATKINS, S. C., MENKEN, J. A., and BONGAARTS, J. (1987). "Demographic foundations of family change." *American Sociological Review*, 52, 346–358.

WELLS, R. V. (1982). *Revolutions in Americans' lives.* Westport, CT: Greenwood.

WILSON, M. N. (1986). "The black extended family: An analytical consideration." *Developmental Psychology*, 22, 246–256.

WISTER, A. V., and STRAIN, L. (1986). "Social support and well-being: A comparison of older widows and widowers." *Canadian Journal on Aging*, 5 (3), 205–220.

The Family:
Problems and Solutions*

Bert N. Adams

In the popular press as well as the research literature, much of what we read concerning families focuses upon problems. Challenges to the family's stability and strength seem to abound in contemporary society, and many analysts fear that this central institution is on the brink of disaster. This article by Bert N. Adams helps to provide a framework for thinking about problems in family life. His discussion develops a context for considering problems and solutions at both the micro level of family therapy and the macro level of social policy. One of Adams's critical points is that the discussion of family problems takes place within a politically charged environment where values play a central role.

Coming across such a title, one would very likely expect to read about what is wrong with the family today and what should be done about it. That, however, is not the intention of this paper. Rather, I want to raise the issue of what is meant when the *language* of problems and solutions is used. The aim is to stimulate our thinking about the value-ladenness of the institution with which we deal as professionals. I organize this discussion under three possibilities: (a) the

*Source: *Journal of Marriage and the Family,* "The Family: Problems and Solutions," Bert N. Adams; 47:3, pp. 525–529, 1985.

same set of circumstances or conditions may be a problem but also a solution to another problem simultaneously; (b) the objective solution to one person's problem may cause that person, or someone else, another problem; (c) whether a phenomenon is viewed as a problem or a solution may not be an objective reality at all, but may be determined by the observer's values. We examine each of these below.

Problem and Solution

Family therapists are well aware of the fact that within families (and individuals) there may be layers of problems. Thus, one problem may be the solution to another; or if one problem is "solved," it may simply uncover another. My prime illustration is drawn from the small but intriguing literature on *folie à famille*, primarily from Lynn Wikler's summary article on the subject (1980).

Folie à famille is a delusion or psychosis shared by the members of a family. Identified over 100 years ago, it is seldom mentioned in the family literature. Its features include the intimate association of the people; a high level of similarity in the content of the psychosis; and evidence that the people accept, support, and share each other's delusional ideas. The third point is crucial, since a husband and wife might both believe that she is a messenger of God but may never have communicated about this belief. If that were true, this would be two separate individual psychoses—not a shared, or family, delusion.

The most frequent content of a family delusion is *paranoia*, or the family's belief that they are being persecuted. Examples referred to by Wikler include:

> a family that believed it was being sprayed by the neighbors with poisonous gasses, another that thought it was being followed and grossly mistreated by Communists, a third that believed it was being punished by the Catholic Church [1980: 261].

The second most frequent content is *delusions of grandeur*. An example from H. Stierlin, quoted by Wikler, is as follows:

> A woman believed herself to be a messenger of God. . . . He gave her messages about special ways of living which she then communicated to her family. . . . They gave away all of their possessions, built a compartment under a bed, and lived there. Only the woman's mother was allowed to leave the house, and then only to get food. Eventually the landlord learned of this bizarre behavior and asked them to leave. When they ignored his requests, the police were called upon to enforce the eviction. The three clambored out from their hole under the bed wrapped only in sheets and were caught running down the street. The police brought them to a psychiatric clinic [Stierlin, 1973, in Wikler, 1980: 261].

The third most frequent content of *folie à famille* is *wish fulfillment*, and it is an example of this content that is most useful in illustrating problem/solution simultaneity. A family with a six-year-old daughter brought her to a psychiatric clinic, claiming that she speaks and acts normally at home, but that she acts

retarded in public. They want the clinicians to help them get her to "stop playing games" in public. Prior to bringing her for inpatient evaluation, Mary had
been taken to other clinics, where the parents were told that she is severely
retarded. Unwilling to accept the outpatient diagnoses, they instead see these
diagnoses as proof of Mary's capabilities: "she has fooled the clinicians."

Now, as an inpatient, Mary goes through eight weeks of evaluation by a
variety of specialists, with the understanding that the family will remain intensively involved throughout her stay. Father, mother, 18-year-old half sister, and
12-year-old brother all agree that she is perfectly normal but "fakes it" in public.
Before being admitted Mary had never been apart from the family overnight.
During the separation terrible events occurred in rapid succession in her family.
I will quote Wikler at length:

> 1. Two weeks after admission, her father suffered a major heart attack, and was in
> an Intensive Care Unit for two weeks. He was in bed during the whole eight weeks
> Mary was on the psychiatric ward. He had no previous history of medical prob-
> lems. . . .
> 2. Two and a half weeks after Mary's admission, Mary's half sister experienced a
> severe industrial accident in which three of her fingers were totally severed. . . . This
> was the first time there had been any such event.
> 3. Four weeks after Mary's admission, her brother suddenly suffered an outbreak of
> hives and had a series of blackout spells with a loss of memory. His mother
> arranged a neurological examination the results of which were negative . . . [Wikler,
> 1980:264].

As the reports from the specialists were given to the family, uniformly diagnos-
ing her as severely retarded, the mother removed her from the ward, and her
behavior did not change.

This case is invaluable for two reasons. First, the cause of the shared delusion can be recognized. The father is a singularly unsuccessful lawyer, who is
highly dependent on his wife. The wife is highly educated but has not pursued
a career. In addition, when an older brother of Mary's drowned, the mother
showed signs of psychosis. The 18-year-old is a factory worker who has not lived
up to the family model of success or achievement. Thus, the family members are
barely coping with lack of success and negative self- and family images. Now, it
begins to become evident that there is something wrong with the youngest child.
However, the family members are incapable of dealing with a child who has no
hope of achieving even up to minimal family standards. This becomes the "last
straw," and the mother induces the belief that the girl is perfectly normal but
plays games—a belief that comes to be shared by all the family members, since
it meets a need for each of them.

So what of the terrible events that accompanied her hospitalization? The
most plausible explanation is that the time of separation became a time of doubt,
with the result that the other family members began to "self-destruct." As the
delusion began to crack open, the former doubts and insecurities were laid bare.
We are not saying, of course, that a family delusion is not a problem, or that it
should not be treated as such. Rather, the argument is that if a family delusion

is broken open or "solved," the therapist also must be prepared to deal with the problem—the belief or behavior—for which the delusion was a solution.

While this is a somewhat dramatic example, the point is clear: the same family circumstances may be both a problem, objectively defined, and a solution to another problem.

Solution → Problem

The second interrelation between problems and solutions in the family concerns a solution to one problem *producing* another problem, either for the same family member or for someone else. Again, we are not talking here about what people value or perceive as a problem or solution but about the objective situation. Let us illustrate with divorce as an objective problem-producer or solution.[1]

How good is divorce as a solution to individual difficulties? Lenore Weitzman's research shows that a year after divorce, men's income is about 80 percent of the former family income, while their ex-wives' income is about 32 percent (1981: 47). These percentages, Weitzman points out, are predicated on the assumption that men pay the amount of alimony and support determined by the courts—an incorrect assumption, since only some 50 percent of child support is actually paid. Thus, at least in the short run, divorce is a more economically feasible solution for men than for women.

Another body of research, by Stan Albrecht, Sara McLanahan, and others, shows that women replace their marital conflict, companionship, and former couple networks with premarital friends, kin, and a generally active social network. Men, on the other hand, replace their marital problems with postdivorce loneliness—a new problem. They, of course, tend to solve this new problem with early remarriages (Albrecht, 1980; McLanahan et al., 1981).

Senator Jeremiah Denton, introducing the Senate hearings on broken families in 1983, made the following comment: "The unmarried are twice as likely to die of heart disease, twice as likely to die of lung cancer, seven times more likely to die of cirrhosis of the liver, five times more likely to commit suicide, six times more likely to die in an automobile accident. That is consoling to us old married slobs" (U.S. Senate, 1983: 32). His data may very well be accurate, objective, and consoling to him; but a few appropriate controls would have been in order. At the very least, he might have divided his "married slobs" by their degrees of happiness or misery and his unmarried into never married, widowed, and divorced. I am not at all convinced that his *miserable* married "slobs" would be better off on his various physical symptoms than his divorced persons would be; and his distinction is even more questionable for women than for men, Jessie Bernard and others would remind us (Bernard, 1971: 85–98).

Without belaboring the point further, then, an individual solution—such as divorce—is not unmitigated. It will raise other problems for the *same* people. The same, incidentally, can be said for marriage.

Another possibility is that one person's solution may become another's problem. A couple's divorce, as a solution to *their* misery, has ramifications for those around them, especially their children. But what are the ramifications? Let me give you three quotations from the Senate hearings on divorce:

> I have had a number of families in my practice for whom divorce was clearly the best solution for all parties, particularly the children [Peter Wallace in U.S. Senate, 1983: 50].
> Many children emerge from divorce as self-confident, mature, morally compassionate adults, with this fostered by family travail. . . . Children whose parents divorce may come to place a higher value on a stable marriage and home life [Judith Wallerstein in U.S. Senate, 1983: 72–73].
> Actually divorce is nothing more than trading one set of problems for a different set of tragic and often enduring problems, often including the problems associated with father absence. Parent relief often results in children paying the price [George Rekers in U.S. Senate, 1983: 129].

Presumably these experts have the same data at their disposal. Apparently the answer to the question of whether divorce is a solution or a problem for children is: sometimes it is one, sometimes the other, but it is usually a mix. If, after divorce, the parents continue to fight through their children, it can traumatize the children. This, however, may simply be a continuation of predivorce parental conflict, which may already have been devastating for the offspring. In fact, not understanding the dynamics of parental conflict, children often blame themselves for their parents' difficulties. It is noteworthy that children who think they are the "family problem," or the reason for their parents' trouble, may actually be a temporary solution. The reason for this is that parents who are incapable of dealing with their marital differences directly instead may fight through and over their offspring's behavior and lifestyles.

In summary, then, the solution to a problem may very well raise new problems for the same individuals. Or one person's solution may be another's problem. Or, most likely, the issues may be complex for all the parties involved, with problem and solution mixed together. The observer who defines divorce—or nondivorce for that matter—as a problem or solution may be grasping only a part of the objective reality. This brings us to the third and final relationship between problem and solution in the family.

Values as Determinants of Problems and Solutions

Whether a particular datum is seen as indicative of a problem or a solution may not be objective but may simply be determined by what the observer values.[2] A brief quotation from Allan Carlson of the Rockford Institute makes this point. He had two questions: "First, what caused the dramatic breakdown in American family life; and second, why do analysts of the situation give such divergent interpretations to the same raw data?" (Carlson in U.S. Senate, 1983, Part 2: 34). Both, he continues, are a result of the breakdown of the nuclear family *norm*. This observation is correct: whether we see today's changes as problems or solutions to traditional problems depends to a great extent on what we value most. Much of this value issue revolves around the question of whether the individual or the family is primary, or is the building block of society. When the two come in conflict, which should take precedence?

Several quotations will make clear this struggle between individual and family values. At the Senate hearings, Amitai Etzioni, a social scientist, proclaims: "We went too far in promoting ego over relationships and institutions. The time is overdue to stress the need to revitalize both" (Etzioni in U.S. Senate, 1983: 28). Alexander Solzhenitsyn, speaking to a Harvard graduating class, states, "The defense of individual rights has reached such extremes as to make society, as a whole, defenseless against the individual. It is time in the West to defend not so much human rights as human obligations" (Solzhenitsyn, quoted in U.S. Senate, 1983, Part 2: 120). On the other hand, James Ramey, author of *Intimate Friendships* (1976), has been quoted as saying: "The problem is stunted, incomplete human development and opportunity, especially for women. The traditional family has thwarted potentialities and self-sufficiency, and must get out of the way." Well then, is individualism a problem for the family, or is the family a problem for the individual? It depends on what you value most.

Divorce, as discussed here, is not just a mix of objective problems and solutions for the parties involved. For centuries it simply was perceived as a "social problem"—because it broke up families—and was held to a minimum. Now, however, it is often viewed in toto as a problem for the family, or as a solution for the individual. A digression on traditional marriage and the individual might be helpful. Marriage traditionally has been the "wedding" of two incomplete individuals—a male and a female—so that they might, not just sexually but in other ways, complete each other. Linda Haas's study of role-sharing couples is most instructive on marriage and individual independence (1980). Role sharing means sharing equally in decisions, earning responsibility, and domestic chores. Haas found that many of her couple members were teaching each other all the survival skills they knew, so that both would know how to cook, tinker with automobiles and wiring, and so on. Some four years after she did her study, I came across one of the wives from her sample. "How is it going?" I asked. "We are divorced," she answered. Then she explained in one sentence what had happened: "We each became so self-sufficient and 'complete' that when the first major upset in our relationship occurred we looked at each other and said, 'I don't have to put up with this; I don't need you,' and we were gone." We have simply not produced a basis for marital permanence other than mutual dependence. We can think of some, such as mutual appreciation or support of each other's achievements, and may be living in a relationship not predicated on traditional dependence; but as yet a new norm of mutual self-sufficiency cum marriage has not emerged.

Returning to my point, those who value self-sufficient human beings tend to downplay marital permanence, and those who value permanence tend to see self-sufficiency and independence—especially for females—as a problem. Not surprisingly, for example, Harold Voth of the Veteran's Administration testified at the Senate hearings as follows: "The entire nation must carefully examine the effects of the feminist movement on the family. I believe this movement has substantially harmed family life" (Voth in U.S. Senate, 1983: 264). Note the word *harmed* and the earlier term *too far* in Etzioni: these are indicators of what these observers value.

Divorce and gender roles are not the only areas of family life where values strongly bias our interpretations of the *same* data. Spouse abuse is another. In a 1983 article in *Time* magazine, the following comment was made: "In most of the rest of the world, private violence is not considered a high priority social problem" (Anderson, 1983: 18). This, however, does not state the issue strongly enough. In India during the summer of 1983, I was speaking to scholars, public officials, and practitioners about wife abuse as a family problem in the United States. Before I finished my remarks, I was interrupted by an Indian male scholar: "No, no, no, wife beating is not a problem, it is a solution to a problem." The problem of which he was speaking, he explained, is uppity, disobedient women. His fear concerns gender-role changes that are shaking traditional Indian male dominance, and the obvious physical solution to the problem is beating. At this and other times during my stay in India, I was able to sit back and let the Indian male and female professionals argue about whether the role changes occurring in the United States were good or bad, and whether they hoped they would happen in India.

However, we cannot dismiss the value debate about wife beating as strictly an issue elsewhere. There are more than remnants of the same attitude in the United States. Look closely at the opposition to funding for shelters for battered wives, and you will find an undercurrent of male-dominated familism. As one newspaper columnist said, "Some of us still value intact families and broken women more than intact women and broken families."[3] Recent proposals to pay families to keep their elderly in the home or to pay families to keep mothers at home with the children lead me to fantasize on how much agencies or the government should pay to keep battered wives from leaving. . . . But enough of this: the value issue is obvious, and it is of concern when one political group or another talks of familism or individualism as if they have captured the "good values."

So I will close. My final point is that in a day of conflicting and politicized values and norms, and changing intimate behavior, writers and researchers should wear their values on their sleeves. Of course, there are conditions that are problems and solutions simultaneously; and if we are working with such families, we should be cognizant of the problem for which the overt problem also may be a solution. Also, the world of the family is complex and often is a mix of problems and solutions for the same or different members of the unit. We as professionals will continue to act on the best objective information we can get; however, what we label as a problem or a solution may be determined by our priorities, by what we personally value. We cannot hide behind sophisticated methods and pretend that interpretation is unnecessary. We do and should have social and family values that we live and work by, but let us keep them out in the open—wear them on our sleeves—as we go about our work as therapists, educators, policy makers, or researchers.

Notes

1. Many of the references in the next two sections are drawn from *Broken Families*, hearings before the Subcommittee on Family and Human Services of the Committee on Labor and Human Resources, U.S. Senate, 98th Congress. Especially pertinent is Part I: "Oversight on the Breakdown of the Traditional Family Unit, Focusing on the Effects of Divorce, Separation and Conflict within Marriage on Children and on Women and Men," March 22 and 24, 1983.

2. A whole subarea of family study where values and attitudes have determined what has been said is the black family in the United States. Only in the past two decades have Andrew Billingsley, Robert Hill, Robert Staples, Joyce Ladner, Reginald Clark, and others begun to actually *describe* black family life. On the values and ideologies that have bound black family analysis, see Adams, 1978; Johnson, 1974.

3. This quotation, and the one from Ramey above, have been in the author's notes for several years. It is impossible at this point to identify their original sources.

References

ADAMS, B. N. 1978. "Black families in the United States: an overview of current ideologies and research." Pp. 173–180 in D. Shimkin, E. Shimkin and D. A. Frate (eds.), *The Extended Family in Black Societies*. The Hague, The Netherlands: Mouton.

ALBRECHT, S. L. 1980. "Reactions and adjustments to divorce: differences in the experiences of males and females." *Family Relations* 29: 59–68.

ANDERSON, K. 1983. "Private violence." *Time* (September 5): 18–19.

BERNARD, J. 1971. "The paradox of the happy marriage." Pp. 85–98 in V. Gornick and B. Moran (eds.), *Women in Sexist Society: Studies in Power and Powerlessness*. New York: Basic Books.

HAAS, L. 1980. "Role sharing couples: a study of egalitarian marriages." *Family Relations* 29: 289–296.

JOHNSON, L. 1974. "The search for values in black family research." Paper presented to the annual meetings of the National Council on Family Relations, St. Louis (October 24).

McLANAHAN, S. S., WEDEMEYER, N. V., and ADELBERG, T. 1981. "Network structure, social support, and psychological well-being in the single-parent family." *Journal of Marriage and the Family* 43 (August): 601–612.

RAMEY, J. 1976. *Intimate Friendships*. Englewood Cliffs, NJ: Prentice Hall.

STIERLIN, H. 1973. "Group fantasies and family myths—some theoretical and practical aspects." *Family Process* 12: 111–125.

U.S. Senate. Committee on Labor and Human Resources. Subcommittee on Family and Human Services. 1983. Broken Families (Part I: "Oversight on the breakdown of the traditional family unit, focusing on the effects of divorce, separation and conflict within marriage on children and on women and men," March 22, 1983; Part II: March 24, 1983). 98th Congress, 1st session. Washington, DC: Government Printing Office.

WEITZMAN, L. 1981. *The Marriage Contract*. New York: The Free Press.

WIKLER, L. 1980. "*Folie à famille:* A family therapist's perspective." *Family Process* 19: 257–268.

Profiling Violent Families*

Richard J. Gelles and Murray A. Straus

Violence in the family is a social problem that has been gaining greater atten-tion and concern in recent years. In this chapter, Richard J. Gelles and Murray A. Straus provide a profile and understanding into why violence occurs in families. They discuss the manner in which the social organization of the family actually increases the risk of violence, the specific characteris-tics of violent families and individuals, and finally, when and where violence is most likely to occur.

Each incident of family violence seems to be unique—an uncontrolled explosion of rage, a random expression of anger, an impulse, a volcanic eruption of sadism. Each abuser seems a bit different. The circumstances never seem to be the same. In one home a child may be attacked for talking back to a parent, in another the precipitating incident may be a broken lamp. Wives have been beat-en because the food was cold, because the house was cold, because they were cold.

If we reject the notion that violence and abuse are the products of mental illness or intraindividual pathologies, then we implicitly accept the assumption

*Source: Pp. 77–97 in *Intimate Violence*. New York: Simon & Schuster Copyright (c) 1988 by Richard J. Gelles and Murray A. Straus. Reprinted by permission of Simon & Schuster, Inc.

that there is a social pattern that underlies intimate abuse.[1] The public and the media recognize this underlying pattern. Perhaps the most frequently asked question by the press, public, and clinicians who treat cases of domestic abuse is, "What is the profile of a violent parent, husband, wife, family?" ... [H]umans have an innate desire for social order. They want to live in a predictable world. Even though violence in the home is more socially acceptable than violence in the street and thus, to a degree, more orderly, people still want to know what to look for. What are the signs, indicators, predictors of a battering parent, an abusive husband?

A profile of intimate violence must include at least three dimensions. First, we need to examine the social organization of families in general that contributes to the risk of violence in the home. Second, we review the characteristics of families in particular that make certain families high risk for violence. Third, we discuss the temporal and spatial patterns of intimate violence—where and when violence is most likely to occur.

Violence and the Social Organization of the Family

The myth that violence and love do not coexist in families disguises a great irony about intimacy and violence. There are a number of distinct organizational characteristics of the family that promote intimacy, but at the very same time contribute to the escalation of conflict to violence and injury.[2] Sometimes, the very characteristics that make the family a warm, supportive, and intimate environment also lead to conflict and violence.

The time we spend with our family almost always exceeds the time we spend at work or with nonfamily members. This is particularly true for young children, men and women who are not in the work force, and the very old. From a strictly quantitative point of view, we are at greater risk in the home simply because we spend so much time there. But, time together is not sufficient to lead to violence. What goes on during these times is much more important than simply the minutes, hours, days, weeks, or years spent together.

Not only are we with our parents, partners, and children, but we interact with them over a wide range of activities and interests. Unless you live (and love) with someone, the total range of activities and interests you share are much narrower than intimate, family involvements. While the range of intimate interactions is great, so is the intensity. When the nature of intimate involvement is deep, the stakes of the involvement rise. Failures are more important. Slights, insults, and affronts hurt more. The pain of injury runs deeper. A cutting remark by a family member is likely to hurt more than the same remark in another setting.

We know more about members of our family than we know about any other individuals we ever deal with. We know their fears, wants, desires, frailties. We know what makes them happy, mad, frustrated, content. Likewise, they know the same about us. The depth of knowledge that makes intimacy possible also reveals the vulnerabilities and frailties that make it possible to escalate conflict. If, for instance, our spouse insults us, we know in an instant what to say to get even. We know enough to quickly support a family member, or to damage him. In no other setting is there a greater potential to support and help, or hurt and harm, with a gesture, a phrase, or a cutting remark. Over and over again, the people we talk to point to an attack on their partner's vulnerabilities as precipitating violence:

> If I want to make her feel real bad, I tell her how stupid she is. She can't deal with this, and she hits me.
> We tear each other down all the time. He says things just to hurt me—like how I clean the house. I complain about his work—about how he doesn't make enough money to support us. He gets upset, I get upset, we hit each other.
> If I really want to get her, I call her dirty names or call her trash.

We found, in many of our interviews with members of violent families, that squabbles, arguments, and confrontations escalate rapidly to violence when one partner focused on the other's vulnerabilities. Jane, a 32-year-old mother, found that criticizing her husband's child-care skills often moved an argument to violence:

> Well, we would argue about something, anything. If it was about our kids I would say, "But you shouldn't talk, because you don't even know how to take care of them." If I wanted to hurt him I would use that. We use the kids in our fights and it really gets bad. He [her husband] doesn't think the baby loves him. I guess I contribute to that a bit. When the baby start's fussin' my husband will say "Go to your mom." When I throw it up to him that the baby is afraid of him, that's when the fights really get goin'."

It is perhaps the greatest irony of family relations that the quality that allows intimacy—intimate knowledge of social biographies, is also a potential explosive, ready to be set off with the smallest fuse.

The range of family activities includes deciding what television program to watch, who uses the bathroom first, what house to buy, what job to take, how to raise and discipline the children, or what to have for dinner. Whether the activities are sublime or ridiculous, the outcome is often "zero-sum" for the participants. Decisions and decision making across the range of family activities often mean that one person (or group) will win, while another will lose. If a husband takes a new job in another city, his wife may have to give up her job, while the children may have to leave their friends. If her job and the children's friends are more important, then the husband will lose a chance for job advancement or a higher income. While the stakes over which television station to watch or which movie to go to may be smaller, the notion of winning and losing is still there. In fact, some of the most intense family conflicts are over what seem to be the most trivial choices. Joanne, a 25-year-old mother of two toddlers, remembers violent fights over whether she and her husband would talk or watch television:

> When I was pregnant the violence was pretty regular. John would come home from work. I would want to talk with him, 'cause I had been cooped up in the

house with the baby and being pregnant. He would just want to watch the TV. So he would have the TV on and he didn't want to listen to me. We'd have these big fights. He pushed me out of the way. I would get in front of the TV and he would just throw me on the floor.

We talked to one wife who, after a fight over the television, picked the TV up and threw it at her husband. For a short time at least, they did not have a television to fight over.

Zero-sum activities are not just those that require decisions or choices. Less obvious than choices or decisions, but equally or sometimes more important, are infringements of personal space or personal habits. The messy wife and the neat husband may engage in perpetual zero-sum conflict over the house, the bedroom, and even closet space. How should meals be served? When should the dishes be washed? Who left the hairbrush in the sink? How the toothpaste should be squeezed from the tube, and a million other daily conflicts and confrontations end with a winner and a loser.

Imagine you have a co-worker who wears checkered ties with striped shirts, who cannot spell, whose personal hygiene leaves much to be desired. How likely are you to (1) tell him that he should change his habits; (2) order him to change; (3) spank him, send him to his room, or cut off his paycheck until he does change? Probably never. Yet, were this person your partner, child, or even parent, you would think nothing of getting involved and trying to influence his behavior. While the odd behavior of a friend or co-worker may be cause for some embarrassment, we typically would not think of trying to influence this person unless we had a close relationship with him. Yet, family membership carries with it not only the right, but sometimes the obligation, to influence other members of the family. Consequently, we almost always get involved in interactions in the home that we would certainly ignore or make light of in other settings.

Few people notice that the social structure of the family is unique. First, the family has a balance of both males and females. Other settings have this quality—coeducational schools, for instance. But many of the social institutions we are involved in have an imbalance of males and females. Some settings—automobile assembly lines, for instance—may be predominantly male, while other groups—a typing pool, for instance—may be almost exclusively female. In addition to the fact that intimate settings almost always include males and females, families also typically include a range of ages. Half of all households have children under 18 years of age in them.[3] Thus the family, more so than almost any other social group or social setting, has the potential for both generational and sex differences and conflicts. The battle between the sexes and the generation gap have long been the source of intimate conflict.

Not only is the family made up of males and females with ages ranging from newborn to elderly, but the family is unique in how it assigns tasks and responsibilities. No other social group expects its members to take on jobs simply on the basis of their age or their sex. In the workplace, at school, and in virtually every other social setting, roles and responsibilities are primarily based on interest, experience, and ability. In the home, duties and responsibilities are primarily tied to age and gender. There are those who argue that there is a biological link between gender and task—that women make better parents than men. Also, the developmental abilities of children certainly preclude their taking on tasks or responsibilities that they are not ready for. But, by and large, the fact that roles and responsibilities are age- and gender-linked is a product of social organization and not biological determinism.

When someone is blocked from doing something that he or she is both interested in and capable of doing, this can be intensely frustrating.[4] When the inequality is socially structured and sanctioned within a society that at the same time espouses equal opportunity and egalitarianism, it can lead to intense conflict and confrontation. Thus, we find that the potential for conflict and violence is especially high in a democratic and egalitarian society that sanctions and supports a male-dominated family system. Even if we did not have values that supported democracy and egalitarianism, the linking of task to gender would produce considerable conflict, since not every man is capable of taking on the socially prescribed leadership role in the home; and not every woman is interested in and capable of assuming the primary responsibility for child care.

The greater the inequality, the more one person makes all the decisions and has all the power, the greater the risk of violence. Power, power confrontations, and perceived threats to domination, in fact, are underlying issues in almost all acts of family violence. One incident of nearly deadly family violence captures the meaning of power and power confrontations:

> My husband wanted to think of himself as the head of the household. He thought that the man should wear the pants in the family. Trouble was, he couldn't seem to get his pants on. He had trouble getting a job and almost never could keep one. If I didn't have my job as a waitress, we would have starved. Even though he didn't make no money, he still wanted to control the house and the kids. But it was my money, and I wasn't about to let him spend it on booze or gambling. This really used to tee him off. But he would get the maddest when the kids showed him no respect. He and I argued a lot. One day we argued in the kitchen and my little girl came in. She wanted to watch TV. My husband told her to go to her room. She said, "No, I don't have to listen to you!" Well, my husband was red. He picked up a knife and threw it at my little girl. He missed. Then he threw a fork at her and it caught her in the chin. She was bloody and crying, and he was still mad and ran after her. I had to hit him with a chair to get him to stop. He ran out of the house and didn't come back for a week. My little girl still has a scar on her cheek.

You can choose whom to marry, and to a certain extent you may chose to end the marital relationship. Ending a marital relationship, even in the age of no-fault divorce, is not neat and simple. There are social expectations that marriage is a long-term commitment—"until death do us part." There are social pressures that one should "work on a relationship" or "keep the family together for the sake of the children." There are also emotional and financial constraints that keep families together or entrap one partner who would like to leave.

You can be an ex-husband or an ex-wife, but not an ex-parent or an ex-child.[5] Birth relationships are quite obviously involuntary. You cannot choose your parents or your children (with the exception of adoption, and here your choices are still limited).

Faced with conflict, one can fight or flee. Because of the nature of family relations, it is not easy to choose the flight option when conflict erupts. Fighting, then, becomes a main option for resolving intimate conflict.

The organization of the family makes for stress. Some stress is simply developmental—the birth of a child, the maturation of children, the increasing costs of raising children as they grow older, illness, old age, and death. There are also voluntary transitions—taking a new job, a promotion, or moving. Stress occurring outside of the home is often brought into the home—unemployment, trouble with the police, trouble with friends at school, trouble with people at work. We expect a great deal from our families: love, warmth, understanding, nurturing, intimacy, and financial support. These expectations, when they cannot be fulfilled, add to the already high level of stress with which families must cope.

Privacy is the final structural element of modern families that makes them vulnerable to conflict, which can escalate into violence. . . . The nuclear structure of the modern family, and the fact that it is the accepted norm that family relations are private relations, reduces the likelihood that someone will be available to prevent the escalation of family conflict to intimate violence.

We have identified the factors that contribute to the high level of conflict in families. These factors also allow conflicts to become violent and abusive interchanges. By phrasing the discussion differently, we could have presented these factors as also contributing to the closeness and intimacy that people seek in family relations. People who marry and have families seek to spend large amounts of time together, to have deep and long-lasting emotional involvement, to have an intimate and detailed knowledge of another person, and to be able to create some distance between their intimate private lives and the interventions of the outside world.

There are a number of conclusions one can draw from the analysis of the structural factors that raise the risk of conflict and violence in the family. First, there is a link between intimacy and violence. Second is the classic sociological truism—structures affect people. Implicit in the discussion of these factors is that one can explain part of the problem of violence in the home without focusing on the individual psychological status of the perpetrators of violence and abuse. Violence occurs, not just because it is committed by weird, bad, different, or alien people, but because the structure of the modern household is conductive to violent exchanges.

Family and Individual Characteristics Related to Intimate Violence

The structural arrangement of the family makes it possible for violence to occur in all households. However, not all homes are violent. A profile of intimate violence needs to analyze the characteristics of violent individuals and their families.

Volumes could be written inventorying the characteristics that are thought to be related to family violence. The earliest students of child and wife abuse focused on individual personality characteristics.[6] Abusers were described as sado-

masochistic, having poor emotional control, self-centered, hypersensitive, dependent, egocentric, narcissistic, and so on. Later, those who studied violence and
abuse examined social and social psychological factors such as income, education, age, social stress, and social isolation.[7] Other investigators focused on experience with and exposure to violence. Still others chose to study violence from
the point of view of the family level of analysis, examining family size, family
power, and family structure.[8]

Sometimes investigators agree on specific characteristics that are believed to
be associated with violence; other times the findings are contradictory. There is
one thing that researchers agree on—there are a multitude of factors associated
with violence in the home.[9] Despite public clamor for a single-factor explanation,
no one factor—not mental illness, not experience with violence, not poverty, not
stress, and not alcohol or drugs—explains all or most acts of intimate violence.

Abusive Violence Toward Children

Most people who try to explain and understand individual acts of deviant or aber-
rant behavior such as child abuse immediately turn their focus on the perpetra-
tor. Our culture has a definite "individual level" bias when it comes to trying to
explain seemingly unexplainable acts. When someone does something outrageous, weird, or bizarre, our immediate reaction is to look for the answer within that individual. A full understanding of abusive violence, however, requires an
examination of not only the violent parent, but the child and family situation.

If one had to come up with a profile of the prototypical abusive parent, it
would be a single parent who was young (under 30), had been married for less
than ten years, had his or her first child before the age of 18, and was unemployed or employed part time.[10] If he or she worked, it would be at a manual
labor job. Studies show that women are slightly more likely to abuse their children than men. The reason is rather obvious: Women typically spend more time
with children. But, even if mothers and fathers spend equal time with children
(and this is rare), it is the woman who is typically given the responsibility of caring for and dealing with the children.

Economic adversity and worries about money pervade the typical violent
home. Alicia, the 34-year-old wife of an assembly-line worker, has beaten, kicked,
and punched both her children. So has her husband Fred. She spoke about the
economic problems that hung over their heads:

> He worries about what kind of a job he's going to get, or if he's going to get
> a job at all. He always worries about supporting the family. I think I worry about
> it more than he does. . . . It gets him angry and frustrated. He gets angry a lot. I
> think he gets angry at himself for not providing what he feels we need. He has to
> take it out on someone, and the kids and me are the most available ones.

We witnessed a more graphic example of the impact of economic stress
during one of our in-home interviews with a violent couple. When we entered
the living room to begin the interview we could not help but notice the holes
in the living room walls. During the course of the interview, Jane, the 24-year-

old mother of three children, told us that her husband had been laid off from his job at a local shipyard and had come home, taken out his shotgun, and shot up the living room. Violence had not yet been directed at the children, but as we left and considered the family, we could not help but worry about the future targets of violent outbursts.

Stressful life circumstances are the hallmark of the violent family. The greater the stress individuals are under, the more likely they are to be violent toward their children. Our 1976 survey of violence in the American family included a measure of life stress.[11] Subjects were asked if they had experienced any of a list of 18 stressful events in the last year, ranging from problems at work, to death of a family member, to problems with children. Experience with stress ranged from households that experienced no stressful event to homes that had experienced 13 of the 18 items we discussed. The average experience with stress, however, was modest—about two stressful life events each year. Not surprisingly, the greater the number of stressful events experienced, the greater the rate of abusive violence toward children in the home. More than one out of three families that were unfortunate enough to encounter ten or more stressful events reported using abusive violence toward a child in the previous year. This rate was 100 percent greater than the rate for households experiencing only one stressful incident.

Violent parents are likely to have experienced or been exposed to violence as children. Although this does not predetermine that they will be violent (and likewise, some abusive parents grew up in nonviolent homes), there is the heightened risk that a violent past will lead to a violent future.

One of the more surprising outcomes of our first national survey of family violence was that there was no difference between blacks and whites in the rates of abusive violence toward children. This should not have been the case. First, most official reports of child abuse indicate that blacks are overrepresented in the reports. Also, blacks in the United States have higher rates of unemployment than whites and lower annual incomes—two factors that we know lead to higher risk of abuse. That blacks and whites had the same rate of abusive violence was one of the great mysteries of the survey. A careful examination of the data collected unraveled the apparent mystery. While blacks did indeed encounter economic problems and life stresses at greater rates than whites, they also were more involved in family and community activities than white families. Blacks reported more contact with their relatives and more use of their relatives for financial support and child care. It was apparent that the extensive social networks that black families develop and maintain insulate them from the severe economic stresses they also experience, and thus reduce what otherwise would have been a higher rate of parental violence.[12]

Most of the cases of child abuse we hear about involve very young children. There is nothing that provokes greater sadness and outrage than seeing the battered body of a defenseless infant. The youngest victims evoke the most sympathy and anger, best fit the stereotype of the innocent victim, and are more likely to be publicly identified as victims of abuse. The youngest children are indeed the most likely to be beaten and hurt.

However, the myth that only innocents are victims of abuse hides the teenage victim. Teenagers are equally likely to be abused as children under three years of age. Why are the youngest children and teenagers at the greatest risk of abusive violence? When we explain why the youngest children are likely victims the answer seems to be that they are demanding, produce considerable stress, and cannot be reasoned with verbally. Parents of teenagers offer the same explanation for why they think teenagers as a group are at equally high risk.

Among the younger victims of violence and abuse, there are a number of factors that make them at risk. Low birth weight babies, premature children, handicapped, retarded, and developmentally disabled children run a high lifelong risk of violence and abuse.[13] In fact, the risk is great for any child who is considered different.

If you want to prevent violence and abuse, either have no children or eight or nine. This was the somewhat common-sense outcome of our research on family factors related to violence toward children. It is rather obvious that more children create more stress. Why then did we find no violence in the families with eight or nine children? Perhaps people who have the largest families are the kindest, most loving parents. Perhaps they are simply exhausted. A more realistic explanation is that at a certain point, children become resources that insulate a family from stress. A family with eight or nine children probably did not have them all at once. With a two- or three-year gap between children, a family with eight or more children has older children at home to help care for and raise the infants, babies, and toddlers. If there is a truly extended family form in our society, it is the large family with children ranging from newborn to 20 living in the home.

A final characteristic of violent parents is that they are almost always cut off from the community they live in. Our survey of family violence found that the most violent parents have lived in their community for less than two years. They tend to belong to few, if any, community organizations, and have little contact with friends and relatives. This social isolation cuts them off from any possible source of help to deal with the stresses of intimate living or economic adversity. These parents are not only more vulnerable to stress, their lack of social involvement also means that they are less likely to abandon their violent behavior and conform to community values and standards. Not only are they particularly vulnerable to responding violently to stress, they tend not to see this behavior as inappropriate.

Abusive Violence Between Partners

Dale, wife of a Fortune 500 executive, wrote us so that we would know that wife beating is not confined to only poor households. Her husband beats her regularly. He has hurled dishes at her, thrown her down stairs, and blackened her eyes. When her husband drinks, she often spends the night huddled in the backseat of their Lincoln Continental. Marion lives so far on the other side of the tracks, she might as well be on another planet. She and her husband live five stories up in a run-down tenement. Heat is a luxury that they often cannot afford, and when they can afford it, the heat rarely works. Marion's husband has broken her jaw and ribs, and has shot at her on two occasions. The range of homes where wife beating occurs seems to defy categorization. One can pick up a newspaper and read of wife beating in a lower-class neighborhood and then turn the page and read that the wife of a famous rock musician has filed for divorce claiming she was beaten.

If there is a typical wife beater, he is not a rock musician, actor, football player, or business executive.[14] The typical beater is employed part-time or not at all. His total income is poverty level. He worries about economic security, and he is very dissatisfied with his standard of living. He is young, between the ages of 18 and 24—the prime age for violent behavior in and out of the home—and has been married for less than ten years. While he tries to dominate the family and hold down what he sees as the husband's position of power, he has few of the economic or social resources that allow for such dominance; not only does his neighbor have a better job and earn more money than he does, but often so does his wife.

Researchers have found that status inconsistency is an important component of the profile of the battering husband.[15] An example of status inconsistency occurs when a man's educational background is much higher than his occupational attainment—a Ph.D. who drives a taxicab for a living. Status inconsistency can also result when a husband does not have as much occupational or educational status as his wife. Researchers Carton Hornung, Claire McCullough, and Taichi Sugimoto report that contrary to what is generally believed, violence is less common when the wife is at home then when she works. They suggest that status inconsistency explains this finding. Husbands, they note, can be more threatened when their wives work and have an independent source of income and prestige than when they are home and dependent. Conflict and verbal aggression are frequent occurrences in the wife beater's home. Verbal violence and mental abuse are also directed at his spouse. Perhaps the most telling of all attributes of the battering man is that he feels inadequate and sees violence as a culturally acceptable way to be both dominant and powerful.

There is a great tendency to blame the victim in cases of family violence. Battered women have frequently been described as masochistic. The debate over such presumed masochism has raged to the point where a substantial group of psychologists have called for elimination of the diagnostic category "masochist" from the revision of DSM-III, the official description of psychological diagnostic groupings.

There is not much evidence that battered women as a group are more masochistic than other women. There are, however, some distinct psychological attributes found among battered women. Victims of wife beating are often found to be dependent, having low self-esteem, and feeling inadequate or helpless.[16] On the other hand, battered wives have been found to be aggressive, masculine, and frigid. In all likelihood these contradictory findings are the result of the fact that there is precious little research on the consequence of being battered, and the research that has been conducted frequently uses small samples, without comparison groups. This makes generalizing from such research difficult and contradictory findings inevitable.

Another problem with assessing the psychological traits of battered women is the difficulty in determining whether the personalities were present before the battering or were the result of the victimization. . . .

Pregnant women often report being beaten.[17] Pregnancy, however, does not make women vulnerable to violence and battering.[18] When we analyzed the results of the Second National Family Violence Survey we found that age, not pregnancy, is the best predictor of risk of wife beating. Women between the ages of 18 and 24 are more likely to be beaten, whether they are pregnant or not. Women older than 24 years of age are less likely to be beaten.

Although pregnant women are not more vulnerable to violence, the nature of the violent attack does appear to change when a woman is pregnant. One of the first interviews we ever conducted still stands out in our minds. The subject was a 30-year-old woman who had been beaten severely throughout her marriage. The beatings were more severe, and took on a different tone, when she was pregnant: "Oh, yeah, he hit me when I was pregnant. It was weird. Usually he just hit me in the face with his fist, but when I was pregnant he used to hit me in the belly."

Perhaps the most controversial finding from our 1975 National Family Violence Survey was the report that a substantial number of women hit and beat their husbands. Since 1975 at least ten additional investigations have confirmed the fact that women hit and beat their husbands.[19] Unfortunately, the data on wife-to-husband violence have been misreported, misinterpreted, and misunderstood. Research uniformly shows that about as many women hit men as men hit women. However, those who report that husband abuse is as common as wife abuse overlook two important facts. First, the greater average size and strength of men and their greater aggressiveness means that a man's punch will probably produce more pain, injury, and harm than a punch by a woman. Second, nearly three-fourths of the violence committed by women is done in self-defense. While violence by women should not be dismissed, neither should it be overlooked or hidden. On occasion, legislators and spokespersons like Phyllis Schlafly have used the data on violence by wives to minimize the need for services for battered women. Such arguments do a great injustice to the victimization of women.

As we said, more often than not a wife who beats her husband has herself been beaten. Her violence is the violence of self-defense. On some occasions she will strike back to protect herself; on others she will strike first, believing that if she does not, she will be badly beaten. Sally, a 44-year-old woman married for 25 years, recounted how she used violence to protect herself:

> When he hits me, I retaliate. Maybe I don't have the same strength as he does, but I know how to hold my own. I could get hurt, but I am going to go down trying. You know, it's not like there is anyone else here who is going to help me. So . . . I hit him back . . . I pick something up and I hit him.

Marianne does not wait until she is hit. She says she has learned the cues that her husband is about to hit her:

> I know that look he gets when he gets ready to hit me. We've been married for ten years, and I've seen that look of his. So he gets that look, and I get something to hit him with. Once I hit him with a lamp. Another time I stabbed him. Usually I don't get so bad, but I was real fearful that time.

The violence in Marianne's home is not just one way. She has been hospitalized four times as a result of her husband's beatings. Her fears are very real.

The profile of those who engage in violence with their partners is quite similar to the profile of the parents who are abusive toward their children. The greater the stress, the lower the income, the more violence. Also, there is a direct relationship between violence in childhood and the likelihood of becoming a violent adult. Again, we add the caution that although there is a relationship, this does not predetermine that all those who experience violence will grow up to be abusers.

One of the more interesting aspects of the relationship between childhood and adult violence is that *observing* your parents hit one another is a more powerful contributor to the probability of becoming a violent adult than being a victim of violence. The learning experience of seeing your mother and father strike one another is more significant than being hit yourself. Experiencing, and more importantly observing, violence as a child teaches three lessons:

1. Those who love you are also those who hit you, and those you love are people you can hit.
2. Seeing and experiencing violence in your home establishes the moral rightness of hitting those you love.
3. If other means of getting your way, dealing with stress, or expressing yourself do not work, violence is permissible.

The latter lesson ties in well with our finding that stress also leads to an increased risk of violence in the home. One theory holds that people learn to use violence to cope with stress. If this is correct, then stress would be a necessary, but not sufficient, precondition for family violence. In other words, stress alone does not cause violence unless the family members have learned that being violent is both appropriate and also will not meet with negative sanctions. Another theory is that learning to be violent and stress are two independent contributors to intimate violence and abuse.

The sociologists Debra Kalmuss and Judith Seltzer tested these two theories using the data collected for the First National Family Violence Survey.[20] They found that stress and learning are independent contributions to the risk of abusive violence. Moreover, observing and experiencing violence while growing up was a more powerful contributor to the later risk of intimate violence than was life stress.

Lurking beneath the surface of all intimate violence are confrontations and controversies over power. Our statistical evidence shows that the risk of intimate violence is the greatest when all the decision making in a home is concentrated in the hands of one of the partners. Couples who report the most sharing of decisions report the lowest rates of violence. Our evidence goes beyond the statistics. Over and over again, case after case, interview after interview, we hear batterers and victims discuss how power and control were at the core of the events that led up to the use of violence. Violent husbands report that they "need to" hit their wives to show them who is in charge. Some of the victimized wives struggle against domination and precipitate further violence. Other wives tell us that they will actually provoke their husband to violence because they want him to be more dominant. This is not so much a case of the wife being a masochist as it is another example of the conflicts and struggles that occur as couples confront the traditional cultural expectation that the male should be the dominant person in the household. Some couples fight against this prescription, while others fight to preserve it.

No Place to Run, No Place to Hide

Eleanor began to prepare dinner for her two children and her husband. It was evening on a Saturday night in January. While she grilled hamburgers, her husband Albert walked in. An argument began over whether Eleanor had taken Albert's shirts to the cleaners. Eleanor protested she had. Albert said she was lying. Eleanor protested, yelled, and finally said that Albert was drunk so often he never remembered whether his shirts were clean or dirty. Albert lunged at his wife. He pushed her against the stove, grabbed the sizzling burgers, and threw them across the room. He stalked out, slamming the front door behind him. Quiet tension reigned in the house through a dinner of tuna fish sandwiches and some television, and then the children were put to bed. Eleanor went to bed at 11:00 P.M., but could not fall asleep. At around 1:00 A.M. Albert returned home. He was quiet as he removed his clothes and got into bed. Eleanor turned over, her back to Albert. This signaled that she was awake, and another argument began to brew. This time it was over sex. Eleanor resisted. She always resisted when Albert was drunk. Tonight she resisted because she was still angry over the dinnertime argument. Albert lay his heavy arms around Eleanor and she struggled to get free. The quiet, almost silent struggle began to build. Angry whispers, angry gestures, and finally yelling ensued. Eleanor knew that Albert kept a gun in his night table drawer. Once, after a fight, Albert had gone to bed by putting the bullets on Eleanor's nightstand and the gun under his pillow. As the midnight fight escalated, Albert made a gesture toward the night table. For whatever reason, Eleanor thought that this would be the time that Albert would try to shoot her. She dove across the bed, pulled the drawer out of the night table, clawed for the gun as it rattled to the floor, and came to her feet with the gun in her hand. The first shot tore through Albert's right arm, the second slammed into the wall, the third tore away the top of his head. Eleanor stopped firing only after she heard three of four clicks as the hammer struck the now empty cylinders.

This could be a story out of a soap opera or a supermarket newsstand magazine. It is, unfortunately, a story repeated 2,000 times a year. We have focused on the family structure and the individual and family characteristics that increase the risk of violence in specific households. Eleanor's and Albert's story illustrates the situational structure of intimate violence.

It goes without saying that intimate violence is most likely to occur in intimate settings. Occasionally couples will strike one another in the car. Husbands sometimes grab their wives at a party or on the street. Husbands or wives rarely slap their partners in public. The majority of domestic combat takes place in private, behind closed doors. We have known men and women to stifle their anger and seethe while guests are in the home. As the last guest leaves and the door closes, the fight and the violence erupt.

Eleanor and Albert began their path to their lethal confrontation in the kitchen. When we interviewed couples about the location of violence between partners and toward children, more than half said that the violence occurs in the kitchen. The living room and bedroom were the next most likely scenes. Only the bathroom seemed free from conflict and violence—perhaps because most bathrooms are small, have locks, or most likely because bathrooms are places of individual privacy.

Students of domestic homicide report that the bedroom is the most lethal room in the home. The criminologist Marvin Wolfgang reported that 20 percent of *all* victims of criminal homicide are killed in the bedroom.[21] The kitchen and dining room are the other frequent scenes of lethal violence between family members.

After 8:00 P.M. the risk for family violence increases.[22] This is almost self-evident, since this is also the time when family members are most likely to be together in the home. We found that four out of ten cases of domestic violence occur between 8:00 P.M. and midnight. Eight out of ten domestic fights take place between 5:00 P.M. and 7:00 A.M. Early evening fights occur in the kitchen. The living room becomes the likely setting for evening disputes, and the most violent and most lethal altercations break out in the bedroom, late at night.

The temporal and spatial patterns of intimate violence support our notion that privacy is a key underlying factor that leads to violence. Time and space constrain the options of both the offender and the victim. As the evening wears on, there are fewer places to run to, fewer places to hide. When the first fight broke out between Eleanor and Albert, it was about 5:00 P.M. Albert rushed out of the house in a huff—most likely heading for the neighborhood bar. The bar closed at 1:00 A.M., and that was when Albert went home to his final conflict.

A fight that erupts in the bedroom, in the early morning, constrains both parties. It is too late to stalk out of the home to a bar and too late to run to a friend or family member. The bed and the bedroom offer no protection and precious few places to flee or take cover. It is not surprising that so many of the most violent family fights end there.

Common sense would argue that weekends are the most violent time of the week for families. Common sense would not lead one to assume that the most violent times of the year are Christmas and Easter. When we looked at which day of the week violence was most likely to occur, we found that the empirical evidence was in full support of common sense. Weekends are when families spent the most time together and when the potential for conflicts and conflicts of interest is greatest. Not surprisingly, seven out of ten violent episodes we talked about with family members took place on either Saturday or Sunday. Weekends after a payday can be especially violent. Janice, the mother of an infant daughter, told us about the typical weekend fight:

> It starts over money. He gets paid on Friday. So he comes home on Fridays and I ask him for money. I am usually at the stove cooking when he comes home. And, I have no money left. So I asks. This last Friday he said he didn't have no money. I got real mad. I mean, its payday and he has no money? He said he borrowed money and had to pay it back. I said he just must be lyin'. He spends it on booze or gambles it. Other times we fights because he gives me only fifty dollars. I can't feed him and the baby with just fifty dollars. So I got mad and started to yell.

Thus, the days of the week that are the most violent are those that combine the most conflict and violence-producing structural components of family life—time together, privacy, and stress.

Common sense would not suggest that violence is most likely to erupt at times of the year when families celebrate holidays and the spirit of family togetherness. Yet, contrary to common sense, it is the time from Thanksgiving to New Year's Day and again at Easter that violence in the home peaks.

As we conducted our interviews with members of violent homes we heard again and again about violence that occurred around the Christmas tree. Even the Christmas tree became a weapon in some homes:

> I remember one particularly violent time. When we were first married. He was out drinking and he came home stinking drunk. I suppose I must have said something. Well, he took a fit. He started putting his fist through the walls. Finally, he just picked up the Christmas tree and threw it at me.

Another woman recalled her most violent experience:

> He hit me just before New Year's Day. I don't really recall what went on. We argue a lot. This time it might have been about money, or maybe the kids. Anyway, he got fierce. He punched me again and again. I was bleeding real bad. He had to take me to the hospital. It was the worst time of the year I ever had.

Perhaps people have a clearer memory of a violent event if it happens around a holiday. While this is a plausible explanation for our findings, it is not the complete answer. We have examined weekly reports of hospital admissions for child abuse and neglect, and found that the peak times of year for admissions were the period from Christmas to New Year's Day, and again in the spring around Easter Sunday.

A number of factors may contribute to the likelihood of domestic violence and abuse during the Christmas season. This is a time when families can assume tremendous financial burdens. Purchasing Christmas gifts can either take a toll on a family's resources or plunge a family into debt. Stress can also come from *not* buying gifts and presents. If a family cannot afford gifts expected by children, loved ones, and others, this can be extremely frustrating. The holiday season offers a stark contrast between what is expected and what a family can afford.

Holidays also create nonfinancial stress. Christmas and Easter holidays project images of family harmony, love, and togetherness. Songs, advertisements, and television specials all play up the image of the caring, loving, and even affluent family. A family with deep conflict and trouble may see these images in sad and frustrating contrast with their own lives. We know that prison riots are more likely to occur during holiday seasons, as prisoners apparently become stressed about being separated from family and friends during times of the year when such closeness is expected. Clearly, being with family and friends, but having unmet expectations for love and warmth, can also be extremely frustrating.

Time of day and time of year analysis supports the notion that privacy and stress are important structural contributors to domestic violence. Conflict frequently erupts over a stressful event, during a stressful time of the day, or around a stressful time of year. If the eruption takes place in a private setting, and at a time and place where it is difficult to flee or back down, the conflict can escalate into violence. The more privacy, the greater the power difference, and the few options the victim has in terms of getting help or finding protection, the more the violence can escalate.

The saddest and most frustrating aspect of our analysis of the structural, personal, familial, temporal, and spatial dynamics of intimate violence is that our results seem to say that violence in the home is inevitable. Lessons learned as a child set the stage for using violence as an adult. The structural makeup of the modern family is like a pressure cooker containing and escalating stress and conflict. If violence breaks out late at night, on a weekend, or a holiday, victims often have no place to run, no place to hide.

Our profile of violent families is not quite as bleak as it might seem. First, no one structural factor, personal experience, or situation predetermines that all or any family will be violent. Second, families do not live in a vacuum. Family members and people outside of the home can intervene to turn down the heat under the pressure cooker. We have found that friends, relatives, and neighbors can successfully intervene and reduce the pressure that could lead to violence.

Notes

1. Two articles that critique the theory that abuse is the product of mental illness or psychopathology are Richard J. Gelles, "Child Abuse as Psychopathology: A Sociological Critique and Reformulation," *American Journal of Orthopsychiatry* 43 (July 1973): 611–21; and J. Spinetta and D. Rigler, "The Child-Abusing Parent: A Psychological Review," *Psychological Bulletin* 77 (April 1972): 296–304.

2. The organizational characteristics of the family that promote both intimacy and conflict were first described in Richard J. Gelles and Murray A. Straus, "Determinants of Violence in the Family: Towards an Integrated Theory," in Wesley Burr, Reuben Hill, F. Ivan Nye, and Ira L. Reiss, eds., *Contemporary Theories About the Family* vol. 1. (New York: Free Press, 1979), 549–81. These ideas were further developed in Murray A. Straus and Gerald T. Hotaling, eds., *The Social Causes of*

Husband-Wife Violence (Minneapolis: University of Minnesota Press, 1980); and Richard J. Gelles and Claire Pedrick-Cornell, *Intimate Violence in Families* (Beverly Hills, Calif.: Sage, 1985).

3. U.S. Bureau of the Census, *Statistical Abstract of the United States: 1987*, 107th ed. (Washington, D.C.: Government Printing Office, 1986), chart 45; U.S. Bureau of the Census, *Current Population Report*, ser. P-20, no. 411.

4. This is the classic statement of psychological frustration/aggression theory. The theory has been articulated by J. C. Dollard, L. Doob, N. Miller, O. Mowrer, and R. Sears, *Frustration and Aggression* (New Haven, Conn.: Yale University Press, 1939); and N. E. Miller, "The Frustration-Aggression Hypothesis," *Psychological Review* 48, no. 4 (1941): 337–42. A sociological formulation of the notion that blocked goals can be frustrating can be found in Robert K. Merton, "Social Structure and Anomie," *American Sociological Review* 3 (October 1938): 672–82.

5. This idea was first presented by Alice Rossi in her article, "Transition to Parenthood," *Journal of Marriage and the Family* 30 (February 1968): 26–39.

6. See, for example: Vincent J. Fontana, *The Maltreated Child: The Maltreatment Syndrome in Children* (Springfield, Ill.: Charles C. Thomas, 1971); Richard Galdston, "Observations on Children Who Have Been Physically Abused and Their Parents," *American Journal of Psychiatry* 122, no. 4 (1965): 440–43; Leroy G. Schultz, "The Wife Assaulter," *Journal of Social Therapy* 6, no. 2 (1960): 103–12; Brandt F. Steele and Carl B. Pollock, "A Psychiatric Study of Parents Who Abuse Infants and Small Children," in R. Helfer and C. Henry Kempe, eds., *The Battered Child* (Chicago: University of Chicago Press, 1968), 103–47; and S. R. Zalba, "Battered Children," *Transaction* 8 (July–August 1971): 58–61.

7. See Gelles, "Child Abuse"; and David Gil, "Violence Against Children," *Journal of Marriage and the Family* 33 (November 1971): 637–48.

8. See R. Emerson Dobash and Russell Dobash, *Violence Against Wives: The Case Against Patriarchy* (New York: Free Press, 1979).

9. For a review of the factors related to family violence, see Richard J. Gelles, "Family Violence," in Ralph H. Turner and James F. Short, eds., *Annual Review of Sociology*, vol. 11 (Palo Alto, Calif.: Annual Reviews, Inc. 1985), 347–67; Marc F. Maden and D. F. Wrench, "Significant Findings in Child Abuse Research," *Victimology* 2 (1977): 196–224; and Suzanne K. Steinmetz, "Violence Between Family Members," *Marriage and Family Review* 1 (1978): 1–16.

10. The profile that is presented is a statistical profile. It would be incorrect to assume that someone who does not fit this profile would not be an abuser. Similarly, someone who fit the profile is likely to abuse, but is not always an abuser. The profile was developed in Murray A. Straus, Richard J. Gelles, and Suzanne K. Steinmetz. *Behind Closed Doors: Violence in the American Family* (Garden City, N.Y.: Anchor Books, 1980).

11. The survey is reported in Straus, Gelles, and Steinmetz, *Behind Closed Doors*. The measure of stress was adapted from T. H. Holmes and R. H. Rahe, "The Social Readjustment Rating Scale," *Journal of Psychosomatic Research* 11 (1967): 213–18.

12. Straus, Gelles, and Steinmetz, *Behind Closed Doors*; and Noel Cazenave and Murray A. Straus, "Race, Class, Network Embeddedness and Family Violence: A Search for Potent Support Systems," *Journal of Comparative Family Studies* 10 (Autumn 1979): 281–300.

13. A review of child factors that are related to physical abuse can be found in W. N. Friedrich and J. A. Boriskin, "The Role of the Child in Abuse: A Review of the Literature," *American Journal of Orthopsychiatry* 46 (October 1976): 580–90.

14. The profile of wife beaters is a statistical profile and was first presented in Straus, Gelles, and Steinmetz, *Behind Closed Doors*.

15. C. A. Hornung, B. C. McCullough, and T. Sugimoto, "Status Relationships in Marriage: Risk Factors in Spouse Abuse," *Journal of Marriage and the Family* 43 (August 1981): 675–92.

16. Lenore Walker, *The Battered Woman* (New York: Harper & Row, 1979).

17. Richard J. Gelles, "Violence and Pregnancy: A Note on the Extent of the Problem and Needed Services," *Family Coordinator* 24 (January 1975): 81–86.

18. When we analyzed the results of the Second National Family Violence Survey, we did find that the rates of violence and abuse were higher among pregnant women than women who were not pregnant. However, when we controlled for age, the differences disappeared. Women under the age of 24 years old experienced high rates of violence and abuse, but the rates were the same for pregnant and nonpregnant women. Women over 24 years old experienced lower rates of violence, and again, there were no differences between pregnant and nonpregnant women. Thus, the relationship between violence and pregnancy which we first reported in 1975 (Gelles, "Violence and Pregnancy") and which others have reported, turns out to be spurious.

19. Michael David Allan Freeman, *Violence in the Home: A Socio-legal Study* (Farnborough, England: Saxon House, 1979); Richard J. Gelles, *The Violent Home: A Study of Physical Aggression Between Husbands and Wives* (Beverly Hills, Calif.: Sage, 1974); Morgan E. Scott, "The Battered

Spouse Syndrome," *Virginia Medical* 107 (January 1980): 41–43; Suzanne Sedge, "Spouse Abuse," in Marilyn R. Block and Jan D. Sinnott, eds., *The Battered Elder Syndrome: An Exploratory Study* (College Park, Md.: Center on Aging, 1979), 33–48; Suzanne K. Steinmetz, "The Battered Husband Syndrome," *Victimology* 2 (1978): 499–509; Straus, Gelles, and Steinmetz, *Behind Closed Doors;* Mary Warren, "Battered Husbands," in Margaret E. Ankeney, ed., *Family Violence: A Cycle of Abuse* (Laramie, Wyo.: College of Education, University of Wyoming, 1979), 76–78.

20. Debra Kalmuss and Judith A. Seltzer, "A Test of Social Learning and Stress Models of Family Violence." (Paper presented at the annual meetings of the American Sociological Association, New York, 1986).

21. Marvin Wolfgang, *Patterns in Criminal Homicide* (Philadelphia: University of Pennsylvania Press, 1958).

22. This analysis was first presented in Gelles, *Violent Home*, chapter 4.

Sexual Pluralism: Ending America's Sexual Crisis*

Ira L. Reiss

Ira L. Reiss begins his article by stating, "We are the Western leader in HIV/AIDS, rape, teenage pregnancy, sexual abuse of children, and virtually every other sexual problem that one can name. This unwanted leadership is convincing evidence that we must be doing something very wrong in the way we handle sexuality." Reiss explores why this is the case, and what we can do to reduce our leadership role in the above problems. His solution is for our society to adapt what he calls a sexual pluralism ethic. Such an ethic involves toleration, honesty, equality, and responsibility with regard to sexuality. Reiss's arguments are sure to provoke both insights and controversy.

We are the Western world's leader in HIV/AIDS, rape, teenage pregnancy, sexual abuse of children, and virtually every other sexual problem that one can name. This unwanted leadership is convincing evidence that we must be doing something very wrong in the way we handle sexuality. We must not be fully aware of how we are producing these unwanted outcomes or we would be more adept in controlling them. The challenge is to discover, then alter, whatever is blocking our nation's understanding and ability to handle sexual problems.

Source: Ira L. Reiss, "Sexual Pluralism: Ending America's Sexual Crisis," *Siecus Report* (February/March, 1991), pp. 5–9.

A careful study of our sexual customs, over the last few decades, has convinced me that our major problem is our society's inability to build a new sexual ethic, which can serve as a guide for the much wider range of sexual choices that we are called upon to make today. There are many Americans who think that too much of our restrictive sexual past has been violated, but I believe we have kept far too many elements of this dogmatic sexual heritage, and that this is at the root of our present sexual crisis.

Just a few months ago, I published a book in which I spelled out, in-depth, my answer to why we have these self-destructive tendencies, and what changes in our approach to sexuality might rescue America from the disastrous state it is in today.[1] I feel a sense of urgency, because every moment of delay brings harm to the people caught up in these sexual problems. Moreover, the devastating consequences of phenomenally high rates for all sexual problems has made me aware of the need for social scientists, such as myself, to do more than simply describe our problems. In this spirit, I wrote *An End to Shame: Shaping Our Next Sexual Revolution*—as an important step in the search for ways to resolve the sexual problems we now face. I am convinced that the sexual pluralism ethic, described in this article, is the best chance we have for controlling these sexual problems. As I cannot discuss all the issues included in my book, I have chosen to focus on the mythical beliefs associated with abstinence and love, two examples of how we unknowingly produce the very sexual problems that so disturb us.

The Myth of Abstinence as the Safest Standard

Near Minneapolis, where I live, a senior high school is currently embroiled in a debate over whether to permit even the discussion of condom use. Some parents object to the teaching of contraception. They feel that teaching about contraception conveys a conflicting message about abstinence. Such controversy—common in our country—is one aspect of the intolerance of, and lack of guidance from, adult society that confuses sexually active teenagers today. Abstinence is preached in most of our high school sexuality education classes,[2] despite the fact that more than 80 percent of teenagers are nonvirginal before they are out of their teens.[3,4]

It must be borne in mind that the majority of teenagers who eventually have intercourse have been strongly encouraged by their parents, and their schools, to believe in abstinence and to avoid sexual intercourse during their high school years. In addition, and of great importance, is the fact that those who preach abstinence as the "safest" standard to pursue often put down the safety of using condoms and, as is happening in Minnesota and elsewhere, object to such information being given to their children. Many Americans are anxious and timid about preparing young people to make safer sexual choices by legitimizing the use of condoms. They are more comfortable simply seeking to prevent any sexual involvement at all. Therefore, when teenagers do engage in sexual intercourse, they often do not use condoms, and thus are at increased risk for diseases and pregnancy.[5] The fatal error in our approach to teenage sexuality is that we ignore the fact that vows of abstinence break far more easily than do condoms.

In fact, we are so anxious about teenage sexuality, and so brainwashed about teenage abstinence, that almost no one publicly questions whether encouraging high school students to vow abstinence is really a safe goal to pursue. Accordingly, we mistakenly equate vows of abstinence with the reality of abstaining from intercourse. This logical error creates a lethal moral bias: the promotion of "compulsory abstinence" actually increases, rather than decreases, the likelihood of both disease and pregnancy.

After much debate, in late 1988, the Centers for Disease Control (CDC) finally developed a public service announcement for television about condom use. However, the CDC refused to use the word *condom* and no condom was shown in the announcement. Instead, what was shown was a barefoot man, sitting on a chair, slowly putting a sock over his bare foot, while telling viewers that putting on socks would not save their lives, "but there's something just as simple that could." The viewer was supposed to draw the conclusion that this meant using a condom. Only in regard to our sexuality would we communicate in such an incoherent fashion; and, only a people deeply conflicted, who lack a sexual ethic supporting carefully thought out choices, would produce such a television announcement as this.

In no other area of human life would we continue to support a policy—such as the promotion of abstinence—which fails, in most cases, and actually increases the risk of life-threatening consequences by deliberately avoiding any preparation for safer sexual practices. In the name of traditional sexual morality, proponents of compulsory abstinence put the lives of young people at risk, and most parents—themselves so burdened by sexual anxieties—are not even aware that this is happening.

It is also important to consider the dogmatic, undemocratic nature of the promotion of abstinence by our government and schools. Would we tolerate someone coming into our public schools and telling our young people that they should all belong to one particular religion or political party? As democratic pluralists, we understand that there are many acceptable religious and political paths. In this same spirit, we should not tolerate our young people being told that there is only one acceptable sexual lifestyle for them. This is particularly the case when moral dogmatism may place their lives in jeopardy.

HIV Infection and the Myth of Love as Safe

Another illustration of how our restrictive approach to human sexuality promotes sexual problems arises in regard to HIV/AIDS.

Despite the fact that more than 1,000,000 Americans are infected with HIV, and that 100,000 people have already died from AIDS, we still allow our traditional sexual morality to promote very dangerous sexual advice. In our advertisements about preventing HIV infection, one often sees and hears the words: "*If* you have more than one partner, use condoms." Here again, our narrow

Victorian approach to sexuality, sees only stable relations that involve *love* as *good* and *safe*. The result is that those who are in long-term sexual relationships are not encouraged to use condoms. Our concern, however, should be with risk taking, whether it occurs in a love relationship that lasts one year or in a pleasure-centered relationship that lasts one day. Very few "monogamous" couples are comprised of individuals who have never had other sexual partners, or who will never participate in any future actions that risk HIV infection, so not using condoms is dangerous.

Together with Robert Leik, a colleague of mine, I analyzed whether one has a better chance of avoiding HIV infection by focusing on just one or two partners, or by using condoms without reducing the number of partners.[6] The safest practice obviously is to both reduce partners and to use condoms, but due to a love bias, most people do not do both. The answer, from our research is very clear: even under a very wide range of life conditions, it is far safer to have sexual intercourse with 20 partners, if you are carefully using condoms, than it is to have sexual intercourse with one or two partners, if you are not using condoms. This was the result under virtually every conceivable social condition, even when we estimated condom failure rates at between 10 percent and 25 percent.

In support of our findings, other HIV/AIDS researchers have reported that most women who become infected with HIV heterosexually become infected by a partner with whom they have had a long-term involvement.[7] That partner is often an intravenous drug user or someone who became infected by a previous partner. Realistically, having a long-term sexual relationship with a person, who is infected and not using condoms, is the surest way to expose oneself to whatever disease one's partner may have. Condoms, not the stability of a relationship, are the best protection against HIV infection. Nonetheless, our societal bias, in favor of committed premarital sexual relationships, distorts our reasoning, and is now resulting in the infection of women and babies. Instead of promoting condom use, and saving lives, we push sexual dogmas about the safety of premarital love relationships.

Many Americans, particularly women, are raised with what I call the "dirty water" view of sexuality. Sexual intercourse, outside of a love relationship, is viewed as a glass of dirty water that cannot safely be swallowed. However, add the elixir of love to one's sexual involvement, and suddenly the water is purified and one can safely imbibe. This view betrays our inability to accept sexuality as potentially valuable, even when it does not occur in a love relationship. It is also a male-dominated society's way of restricting women's sexuality. Such restrictions are not placed equally on men.

We are in need of an egalitarian sexual ethic that applies equally to both women and men—one that affords us a rational, rather than rigid, basis for making sexual decisions. It is not enough to simply ask how long a sexual relationship has lasted, or if "love" is present. The thoughtless pursuit of abstinence and love endangers our lives, and blocks the development of a more tolerant and realistic sexual ethic to guide our decision making. Myths about [both] abstinence and love are but two of the many ways we unknowingly promote the very sexual problems we seek to avoid.

Western Europeans generally have a more pluralistic, less dogmatic, approach to sexuality—and they do not have a higher proportion of sexually involved teenagers. In addition, they have lower rates of teenage pregnancy and HIV/AIDS.[8,9] They reject the imposition of one sexual standard for everyone. They realize that restrictive sexual standards have, for centuries, been imposed predominantly on women, and not on men, and that they go hand-in-hand with male-dominated societies. We need to realize that one of the key reasons we find it so difficult to reject our Victorian sexual dogmas is that they are rooted in the traditional male dominance that is still so entrenched in our society. All Western societies, including ours, are now attempting to reduce such male dominance. To challenge traditional sexual beliefs is to offer women the same sexual rights that men have enjoyed for thousands of years. It is precisely this change that creates resistance in those who endorse traditional roles as the only right way to live.

Defining Sexual Pluralism: A Democratic Sexual Morality

Pluralism in any area of life asserts that there is more than one morally acceptable way for people to behave. The heart of pluralism is to tolerate a broad range of choices by others and try not to impose one's personal choices on all others. Pluralism is the way Americans approach religion and politics, marriage partners, and occupational and educational choices. We freed ourselves far quicker from the narrow perspectives of past centuries in these areas, but many still believe that in sexuality, there is but one moral path.

Let us be clear. Sexual pluralism does not assert that all forms of sexuality are legitimate—that anything goes. Or, that if it feels good, do it. No, not at all. Sexual pluralism is a moral concept; it is not an invitation to an orgy. Sexual pluralism totally rejects the use of force or manipulation, as in rape and sexual exploitation of children by adults. The best way to ensure that pressure and deception are avoided is to encourage a concern for one's sexual partner; pluralism promotes this by asserting that honesty, equality, and responsibility (HER) are essential ingredients in any sexual relationship. Advising people to "just say no" does not do this. Pluralism offers choices to people, but demands that they take responsibility for making those choices in line with HER principles. Such principles promote *honesty* about each person's sexual goals for the relationship; ask that we treat the other person as having *equal* rights to choose what sexual acts will occur, if any; and insist that both partners take *responsibility* for avoiding unwanted outcomes, like pregnancy and disease. Only if a sexual relationship is honest, equal, and responsible is it acceptable. This should hold, whether one is 26 or 16, and whether one is seeking pleasure, love, or both.

This is in contrast to what sexuality is like, today, in our conflicted culture with its residues of sexual dogma. It is not uncommon for both partners to avoid honesty about their relationship goals for fear of scaring the other person off. One may want sexual contact or love more than the other. Also, there are still many men who take women to dinner and feel that women owe them some sexual satisfaction in return. In addition, the responsibility for protection against pregnancy is still often fully placed upon the woman. Pluralistic couples, who strive for honesty, equality and responsibility in their relationships, practice sexuality in a fashion much more in line with our cultural values.

Pluralism sees sexuality, not composed just of danger, as many traditionalists do, nor composed just of pleasure, as many libertines do. Rather, pluralism sees sexuality as having both danger and pleasure as its components, and insists that each of us make HER decisions on how they should balance out on our personal scales of values. To be a pluralist, we have to learn more about ourselves, and how we personally value the risks and rewards of sexuality. Traditional dogmatic views of sexuality ignore individual differences and fail to promote thoughtful choices. Only when people are given responsibility, can they develop the ability to act responsibly. Therefore, if we want teenagers, and anyone else, to be prepared for sexual choices, we must teach them to believe in HER principles. People will engage in sexual contact, with or without such training, but if we wish to promote more responsible sexuality, the direction we need to take is clear.

Pluralism asks that we make personal choices that suit ourselves, and that we refrain from imposing them upon others. It gives each of us room to grow and change during our lifetime. What we accept sexually for ourselves, today, may well not be what we accept ten years from now. Pluralism points out a legitimate broad area of choice, within which we can personalize and enrich our sexual lives, and yet, at the same time, it discourages us from being oppressive to those who make choices (restrictive or permissive) that differ from ours. Acceptable sexual choices also include different sexual orientations. Any view that endorses "compulsory heterosexuality," for example, would be rejected. All sexual relationships in line with HER principles are fully acceptable.

[An] incident involving [former] White House Chief of Staff John Sununu reveals the dogma that blocks a pluralistic approach to homosexuality. In 1988, when Sununu was governor of New Hampshire, he became involved in a dispute over a manual written for high school sexuality education teachers by the staff of a local family planning clinic. The manual presented homosexuality as an integral part of a gay or lesbian person's identity, and viewed it as normal—a position in accord with that of the American Psychiatric Association. This tolerant approach offended Governor Sununu; he noted that he would not want his children exposed to that view.[10] In addition, Senator Gordon Humphrey (Republican/New Hampshire) strongly condemned the clinic, and sought to stop federal funds for any project that viewed homosexuality as normal. Funding for the clinic's entire program was stopped, including funds for low-income, pregnant women.

The National Organization for Women and the American Civil Liberties Union came to the aid of the clinic, and after six months of bitter debate, the dispute was settled. The agreement stated that no public funds could be used for the production of the controversial manual. Although Governor Sununu expressed his desire for more drastic action, this settlement remained in place.

There is no doubt that a dogmatic, Victorian stance on sexuality, that sees only one right way for everyone, is behind this objection to viewing homosexuality as normal. A pluralistic perspective would have afforded Governor Sununu a way to tolerate for others what he personally could not endorse for himself. Pluralism, instead of spreading bigotry, avoids pain for all involved.

Just think how most Americans would feel if, instead of homosexuality, the issue were religion or race. Historically there were times when we objected to the equal acceptance of different races and religions, but we attempted to pluralize such views. We have tended to forget our democratic principles, however, when it has come to sexuality. Sexual intolerance, a major remnant of our past, is in desperate need of similar enlightenment.

To be a pluralist does not mean that each of us must try all kinds of sexual behaviors. Former Surgeon General Koop is an excellent example of a person who is restrictive in his personal beliefs, yet pluralistic in trying not to impose his beliefs on others. Much to the dismay of President Reagan, he recommended condom use for those who are sexually active, and advised those opposed to abortion (like himself) to encourage research into contraception and to distribute contraceptive advice.[11,12]

People do not become "moral" by simply following some restrictive dogma imposed on them. Some of the most heinous acts in dictatorships around the world have been executed by those "just following orders." Moral actions require individual free choice and awareness of alternatives, not thoughtless, lock-step conformity. Surely, we all know people who avoid having sexual intercourse, who are still dishonest, unequal, and irresponsible in their relationships with others. Likewise, people can be in a love relationship and treat their partner in a dishonest, unequal, and irresponsible fashion. Millions of husbands, who say they love their wives, force sexual contact on them, and many women and men lie to their mates about extramarital affairs. Heterosexuality, virginity, love, and marriage do not make sexuality moral. What makes sexuality moral is measured by the impact the sexual relationship has on oneself and one's partner. This is precisely where pluralism offers its moral guidance: it promotes desirable outcomes through its demand that only HER sexual relationships be acceptable. If we want sexuality to be morally better than it is, we had best stop trying to prevent it, and start preparing our young people for it.

Trends Toward Pluralism Today

Many social forces in our society today are working toward sexual pluralism. Whereas traditional Victorian sexuality flourishes in a male dominant society, sexual pluralism blossoms in a society that treats men and women more equally. One major reason for my prediction of the growth of pluralism is the movement in our country toward greater gender equality. As women have gained more rights in American society, they have demanded to be treated more equally in their sexual relationships. Greater overall economic and political equality for women has meant that they could be more honest about their sexual feelings, more assertive about objecting to forced sexuality, and more confident in requesting that their partners use condoms. These are important changes when we are attempting to reduce high rates of sexual abuse, pregnancy, and disease.

The high economic costs (billions of dollars every year) of our conflicted attitudes toward sexuality, which result in high rates of teenage pregnancy, rape, HIV/AIDS, and child sexual abuse, may also be encouraging people to take a more pluralistic approach to sexuality. If, instead of being so obsessed with preventing sexuality, or of being so conflicted that we cannot act, we work to prepare people to make sound sexual choices, we will more quickly find ways to reduce the immense costs of sexual problems.

In addition, present gross inequalities in our social and economic structures cannot be overlooked, as they make equality in any sexual relationship questionable. Some 13 percent of Americans—32,000,000 people—live in poverty. For those living outside poverty, sexual problems are high by Western standards; but, for those living in inner-city poverty, sexual problems are extremely high, equal to those in Third World countries. Poverty promotes a preoccupation with staying alive and just getting by, and sexual issues such as contraception often take a back seat. By addressing the root causes of poverty, we not only demonstrate compassion, we also help the development of sexual pluralism and the protection it affords against unwanted sexual outcomes.

There are signs that many religions are rejecting the dogmatic standard of compulsory abstinence and male dominance, and are becoming more acceptant of homosexuality. We see this particularly in Episcopalian, Presbyterian, and Unitarian churches, the United Church of Christ, and also in some reform Judaic temples.[13] Moreover, Catholics are as likely as Protestants to use birth control and have abortions, and despite official decrees, are evolving in a more sexually pluralistic direction.[14]

Since the 1989 Webster abortion decision, there has been renewed support for abortion rights, even among politicians. As people have spoken out in favor of sexual pluralism, politicians have gained the courage to pass legislation to eliminate many of the restrictive sexual laws that are still on the legal books. However, far too many laws still criminalize private consensual sexual acts among adults. The difficulties that many states have had in repealing these laws, even in the 1990s, bears witness to the residual power of our Victorian view that sexuality is dangerous, degrading, and dirty.

The parents of today's teenagers are the older baby boomers, who led the sexual revolution which began in the late 1960s. These baby boomers, because of their sexual experiences and higher levels of education, have found it easier to move toward sexual pluralism. They know that they changed our society during the last sexual revolution, but they are also aware that they did not discard enough of their Victorian past to permit them to put in place a new workable sexual ethic. As parents, they want to protect their children, and know from their personal experience that compulsory abstinence does not do that. The inner conflict they feel will spur them on to support a movement toward sexual pluralism, because this will aid in the completion of the sexual revolution begun by them a generation ago.

Our fears of HIV/AIDS, rape, teenage pregnancy, and child sexual abuse are major motivations for discarding failed dogmatic approaches to sexuality, and for promoting HER sexual pluralism. In spite of this, the supports of traditional, male-dominated societies have powerfully opposed such changes. For example, over the past 20 years herpes 2 has spread in America at the rate of more than 500,000 cases a year. Also, millions of women each year have become infected with chlamydia, which for many will mean an inability to bear children. Yet, no one suggested advertising condoms as a preventive measure before the advent of HIV/AIDS, and our television networks, to date, have not accepted condom brand advertisements.

This dogmatic blockage of our own safety and happiness has been in place too long. The cost is immense in human suffering in all sexual problem areas. In the interest of all, we must clearly point out the great harm promoted by our lack of a sexual ethic appropriate for today's society. Old sexual dogmas help produce the sexual problems we face; they do not offer realistic guidance. Conflicts about how to handle our sexual problems could be resolved by working to accelerate the acceptance of sexual pluralism.

People for Sexual Pluralism: A New Focus

If we are to expedite the movement toward sexual pluralism, we must organize our efforts. Accordingly, I proposed in *An End to Shame* that an umbrella organization be formed called People for Sexual Pluralism.[15] Individual members could include those alienated by attempts to impose a traditional sexual outlook on everyone and organizations whose philosophies are compatible with sexual pluralism. SIECUS, in its recent creation of a coalition of 38 national organizations supporting sexuality education, is clearly moving in the direction of building an organization like People for Sexual Pluralism.

The benefits of an organizational focus on an explicit sexual pluralist ethic would be many. First, it would afford each of us a reference group that could be cited as supporting statements made by individuals in favor of sexual pluralism. More parents might be willing to speak out on sexual issues at PTA meetings and in political caucuses, if they could say that they have the backing of a national organization with an explicit sexual pluralist ethic. Such an organization would have political clout, and would encourage elected officials, who personally favor sexual pluralism, to support, speak out, and vote favorably on relevant issues.

One thing, above all else, is clear. If we are to get a handle on our sexual problems, we must resolve our own inner sexual conflicts by jettisoning the Victorian baggage so many Americans unknowingly still carry. Other Western countries have moved further towards sexual pluralism than we have. If we put into place a new philosophy of HER sexual pluralism, I fully believe that by the end of this decade America will be a leader in addressing and solving the sexual problems that so disturb us today. That will be the sexual revolution of the 1990s.

Those strong in pluralistic beliefs must no longer remain silent. We must speak out and let people know about the vast support that exists for democratic pluralism in sexuality. We must speak out in our schools, our churches, our legislatures, our universities, and our homes. We will then be able to discard the somber dogmatism of the past and promote the joys of a more honest, equal, and responsible sexual ethic. Instead of trying to prevent sexuality we must learn to make sexual relationships more moral by incorporating HER values. Is this not a mission worth working for? And is this not the time to pursue it?

Notes

1. Reiss, I.L. *An end to shame: Shaping our next sexual revolution.* Buffalo, NY: Prometheus Books, 1990.

2. De Mauro, D. "Sexuality education 1990: A review of state sexuality and AIDS education curricula." *SIECUS Report,* December 1989/January 1990, 18 (2), 1–9.

3. Pratt, WF. "Premarital sexual behavior, multiple partners, and marital experience." Paper presented at the Population Association of America Meeting, Toronto, Canada, May 3–5, 1990.

4. Sonenstein, FL, Pleck, JH, and Ku, LC. "Patterns of sexual activity among adolescent males." Paper presented at the Population Association of America Meeting, Toronto, Canada, May 3–5, 1990.

5. Studer, M and Thorton, A. "Adolescent religiosity and contraceptive usage." *Journal of Marriage and the Family,* 1987, 49 (2), 117–128.

6. Reiss, IL and Leik, RK. "Evaluating strategies to avoid AIDS: Number of partners vs. use of condoms." *Journal of Sex Research,* 1989. 26 (4), 411–433.

7. Pumento, M. *The myth of heterosexual AIDS: How a tragedy has been distorted by the media and partisan politics.* New York: Basic Books, 1990.

8. Jones, EF et al. *Teenage pregnancy in industrialized countries.* New Haven, CT: Yale University Press, 1986.

9. Centers for Disease Control. "Update: Acquired immunodeficiency syndrome—Europe." *Morbidity and Morality Weekly Report,* 1990, 39 (47), 850–853.

10. *Foster's Daily Democrat,* Dover, NH, April 16, 1988.

11. Koop, CE. *Surgeon General's report of acquired immune deficiency syndrome.* Washington, DC: U.S. Department of Health and Human Services, 1986.

12. Public Television, Channel 2. *The controversial Dr. Koop.* Minneapolis, MN, October 10, 1989.

13. Roof, WC and McKinney, W. *American mainline religion: Its changing shape and future.* New Brunswick, NJ: Rutgers University Press, 1988.

14. Henshaw, SK and Silverman, JH. "The characteristics and prior contraceptive use of U.S. abortion patients." *Family Planning Perspectives,* 1988, 20 (4), 158–168.

15. Reiss, *An End To Shame,* 229–234.

Vanishing Dreams of America's Young Families*

Marian Wright Edelman

An increasingly serious problem faced by young families with children has been the deterioration of income and wages over the past 20 years (also discussed in Reading 11, "Shattered Dreams"). Marian Wright Edelman details these trends. Overall, the median income of young families with children has dropped by one-third between 1973 and 1990, and by 1990, 40 percent of children in young families were poor. Edelman goes on to discuss several of the causes of these changes, and concludes by pointing to some of the solutions.

Americans from all walks of life are profoundly anxious—troubled by what they see around them today and even more by what they see ahead. This anxiety, not only about their own futures but also about the nation's future, is manifested in countless ways: in paralyzing economic insecurity; in an emerging politics of rejection, frustration, and rage; in a growing polarization of our society by race and by class; and in an erosion of the sense of responsibility to help the weakest and poorest among us.

*Source: Marian Wright Edelman, "Vanishing Dreams of America's Young Families," *Challenge* (May–June 1992), pp. 13–19.

But this anxiety about the future is *most* vivid when we watch our own children grow up and try to venture out on their own—struggling to get established as adults in a new job, a new marriage, a new home, or a new family.

It's true that young families always have faced an uphill struggle starting out in life. But today's young families have been so battered by economic and social changes over the past two decades that the struggle has taken on a more desperate and often futile quality.

And as parents of my generation watch many of their adult children founder—failing to find steady, decent-paying jobs, unable to support families, shut out of the housing market and often forced to move back home—they know that something has gone terribly wrong. Often they don't know precisely what has happened or why. But they do understand that these young adults and their children may never enjoy the same opportunities or achieve the same standard of living or security that our generation found a couple of decades ago.

Two Generations in Trouble

Young families with children—those headed by persons under the age of 30—have been devastated since 1973 by a cycle of falling incomes, increasing family disintegration, and rising poverty. In the process, the foundations for America's young families have been so thoroughly undermined that two complete generations of Americans—today's young parents and their small children—are now in great jeopardy. Figure 30-1 captures the poverty rates of those two jeopardized generations:

FIGURE 30-1

Poverty Rates of Families with Children, by Age of Family Head, 1973, 1979, 1982, 1990

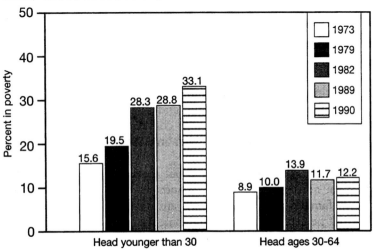

TABLE 30-1

Median Incomes of Families with Children by Age of Family Head, 1973–1990 (in 1990 dollars)

	1973	1979	1982	1989	1990	CHANGE 1973–1990
All families with children	36,882	36,180	31,819	35,425	34,400	– 6.7%
Family head younger than 30	27,765	25,204	20,378	20,665	18,844	–32.1%
Family head age 30–64	41,068	39,978	35,293	39,525	38,451	– 6.4%
Young families' median income as a share of older families' income	68%	63%	58%	52%	49%	

Note: The money incomes of families for all years prior to 1990 were converted into 1990 dollars via use of the Consumer Price Index for All Urban Consumers (CPI-U). The U.S. Bureau of Labor Statistics has generated an alternative price index for the years preceding 1983 that conforms to the current method of measuring changes in housing costs. This index is known as the CPI-UXI. Use of this price index would reduce the estimated 1973 real income by about 7 percent, thus lowering the estimated decline in the median income of young families between 1973 and 1990 from 32 percent to approximately 25 percent. None of the comparisons of median income between various groups of families are affected by these changes.

Young families are the crucible for America's future and America's dream. Most children spend at least part of their lives—their youngest and most developmentally vulnerable months and years—in young families. How we treat these families therefore goes a long way toward defining what our nation as a whole will be like 20, 50, or even 75 years from now.

What has happened to America's young families with children is unprecedented and almost unimaginable.

Adjusted for inflation, the median income of young families with children plunged by one-third between 1973 and 1990 (Table 30-1). This median income includes income from all sources, and the drop occurred despite the fact that many families sent a second earner into the work force. As a result, poverty among these young families more than doubled, and by 1990 a shocking 40 percent or four in ten children in young families were poor.

The past two decades have been difficult for many other Americans as well. But older families with children have lost only a little economic ground since 1973, and families without children have enjoyed substantial income gains. By far the greatest share of the nation's economic pain has been focused on the weakest and most vulnerable among us—young families with children.

This is *not* a story about the current recession, although the recession surely is having a crushing impact on young families. Even comparing 1973 to 1989—two good economic years at the end of sustained periods of growth—the median income of young families with children dropped by one-fourth. Then just the first few months of the recession in 1990 sent young families' incomes plummeting to new depths.

This also is not a story about teenagers. While America's teen pregnancy problem remains tragic and demands an urgent response, only 3 percent of the young families with children we are discussing are headed by teenagers. More than 70 percent are headed by someone aged 25 to 29. The plight of America's young families is overwhelmingly the plight of young adults who are both old enough and eager to assume the responsibilities of parenthood and adulthood, but for whom the road is blocked.

Finally and most importantly, this is *not* simply a story about someone else's children, about minority children or children in single-parent families or children whose parents dropped out of high school.

All Young Families Affected

Huge income losses have affected virtually every group of young families with children: white, black, and Latino; married-couple and single-parent; and those headed by high school graduates as well as dropouts. Only young families with children headed by college graduates experienced slight income gains between 1973 and 1990.

In other words, the tragedy facing young families with children has now reached virtually *all* of our young families. One in four *white* children in young families is now poor. One in five children in young *married-couple* families is now poor. And one in three children in families headed by a young *high school graduate* is now poor. Nearly three-fourths of the increase in poverty among young families since 1973 has occurred outside the nation's central cities. And poverty has grown most rapidly among young families with only one child (Figure 30-2).

There is no refuge from the economic and social shifts that have battered young families with children. We can pretend that they won't reach our children

FIGURE 30-2

Poverty Rates of Children in Young Families, by Characteristics of the Family Head, 1973, 1989, 1990

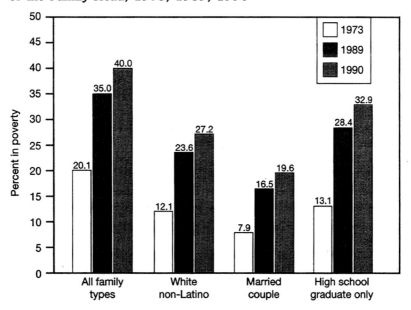

and our grandchildren. We can pretend that those who play by the rules will be okay.

We can pretend, but that will not change the reality—the reality that young families have lost a third of their median income, that two in five American children in young families live in poverty, and that these facts have devastating consequences.

Those consequences include more hunger, more homelessness, more low birth-weight births, more infant deaths, and more child disability. They also mean more substance abuse, more crime, more violence, more school failure, more teen pregnancy, more racial tension, more envy, more despair, and more cynicism—a long-term economic and social disaster for young families and for the country. In virtually every critical area of child development and healthy maturation, family poverty creates huge roadblocks to individual accomplishment, future economic self-sufficiency, and national progress.

Plummeting incomes and soaring poverty and growing gaps based on age and education and race mean more of all these problems, yet many of our leaders seem not to understand why they are occurring. But there is not really a puzzle, when we recognize that the nation has marginalized and pauperized much of two generations of Americans—young parents and young children.

Young families not only lost income in huge amounts, but as the permanence and quality of their jobs deteriorated, they lost fringe benefits like health insurance as well. In the decade of the 1980s the proportion of *employed* heads of young families with children whose employers made health insurance available by paying all or part of the cost dropped by one-fifth. And employers cut back on coverage for dependent spouses and children even more than for workers.

Fewer and fewer young pregnant women have been getting adequate prenatal care because they are poorer and less likely to have adequate insurance or any insurance. And our falling vaccination rates and renewed epidemics of measles and other wholly preventable diseases among preschoolers are being driven by plunging incomes in young families, eroding health insurance coverage, and unraveling government programs.

Falling incomes also have devastated young families in an increasingly expensive housing market. One-third fewer young families with children were homeowners in 1991 than in 1980. Young renter families increasingly are paying astronomical shares of their meager incomes for rent. More and more are doubling up or becoming homeless—in some surveys three-fourths of the homeless parents in this country are under age 30.

Young families are not only suffering from the hunger, housing, health, and other problems that their plummeting incomes have caused. They are suffering as well because they are falling farther and farther behind the rest of the society—imperiling their attachment to the core work force and to mainstream values and threatening their potential to reacquire the American dream in the decades to come.

In 1973 the income of older families with children was not quite one-and-a-half times that of young families with children. By 1990 it was more than double that of the young families.

Combination of Causes

There is no single cause of young families' plight. Instead, they have been pummelled by a combination of profound changes in the American economy; the government's inadequate response to families in trouble; and changes in the composition of young families themselves.

Much of the increase in their poverty is due to economic shifts and to changing government policies that have made it more difficult for young families to obtain adequate incomes. These changes have hurt all young families with children, regardless of their family structure, race or ethnicity, or educational attainment.

Unlike members of earlier generations, young workers today no longer can be confident of finding stable jobs with decent wages, even if they get a high school diploma or spend a couple of years in college. Since 1973, slower growth in U.S. productivity and declines in blue-collar employment made some drop in inflation-adjusted median earnings for young workers inevitable. By last year the average wages of *all* nonsupervisory workers (of all ages) in the private sector fell to their lowest level since the Eisenhower administration.

But the losses have been focused disproportionately on young workers. The median annual earnings of heads of young families with children fell a staggering 44 percent from 1973 to 1990. In other words, in the span of less than a generation this nation nearly *halved* the earnings of young household heads with children (Table 30-2).

These dramatic earnings losses occurred across-the-board. For example, young white families with children were hit as hard as young Latino families: the median earnings of both groups fell by two-fifths. College graduates as well as high school graduates and dropouts lost big chunks of income. But the drop in

TABLE 30-2

Median Annual Earnings of Heads of Young Families with Children, 1973 and 1990 (in 1990 dollars)

	1973	1990	% CHANGE 1973–1990
All heads of young families with children	22,981	12,832	–44
Married couple	25,907	17,500	–33
Male-headed	18,547	14,000	–25
Female-headed	2,073	1,878	– 9
White, non-Latino	25,024	15,000	–40
Black, non-Latino	13,860	4,030	–71
Latino	15,924	9,000	–44
Other, non-Latino	17,664	12,000	–32
High school dropout	15,014	4,500	–70
High school graduate	23,817	14,000	–41
Some college	26,496	18,000	–32
College graduate	31,795	25,721	–19

median earnings for high school dropouts and for young black family heads has been particularly devastating—in each case more than two-thirds.

The erosion in pay levels (due in part to the declining value of the minimum wage) combined with the growth of temporary or part-time and part-year jobs to put a triple whammy on young workers: far lower annual earnings; less secure employment; and less access to health insurance and other employer-provided benefits.

The huge drop in earnings among America's young workers has not received much attention. In part it has been obscured by the almost Herculean work effort of young parents. Many young married-couple families have tried to compensate for lower wages by sending a second worker into the work force. These second earners have softened (but not eliminated) the economic blow. But the growing number of young parents working longer hours or coping with two jobs has placed young families with children under tremendous stress and generated new offsetting costs, especially for child care. Many families, moreover, have two jobs that together provide less security and less support and less access to health care than one good job did a generation ago. This two-earner strategy is totally unavailable, moreover, to the growing number of single-parent families.

Economic Shifts and Family Changes

Today's young families with children look considerably different from those in the early 1970s. They are more likely to be minority families or single parent families. Both groups are more likely to be paid low wages and to be poor than other families. So poverty among young families and children as a whole also rises.

The growth in young female-headed families with children is in part a reflection of changing values. But the economic hardships associated with falling earnings and persistent joblessness among young adults have contributed significantly to falling marriage rates and the increasing rates of out-of-wedlock childbearing. And the fastest growth in out-of-wedlock childbearing has occurred among women in their twenties, not among teenagers, a growth driven in significant part by the earnings free-fall for young adults.

The capacity to support a family has a powerful impact on the marriage decisions of young people. More than two centuries ago Benjamin Franklin wrote: "The number of marriages ... is greater in proportion to the ease and convenience of supporting a family. When families can be easily supported, more persons marry, and earlier in life."

Increases in poverty among young families with children are *not* the result of young Americans having more children. Indeed, young adults have responded to a tightening economic vise by postponing childbearing and choosing to have fewer children. But these attempts to adapt their behavior have been overwhelmed by the far more rapid pace of economic decline and social disintegration they have encountered.

As a result of these economic and social changes, in 1990 a child in a family headed by a parent under age 30 was:

Twice as likely to be poor as a comparable child in 1973;

If living with both parents, two and a half times as likely to be poor as in 1973;

Nearly three times more likely to have been born out-of-wedlock than his counterpart two decades ago;

One-third less likely to be living in a home owned by her family than just a decade ago; and

Three times more likely to see his family pay more than one-half its income for rent.

But despite the devastating suffering these numbers suggest, children in young families have been given less and less government help over the last two decades. They were getting less to begin with—government programs are particularly stingy when it comes to helping younger adults and young children. And in the 1970s and especially the 1980s young families saw programs that might help them cut rather than strengthened and reconfigured to adapt to new realities. As a result, government programs were less than half as effective in pulling young families out of poverty in 1990 as in 1979.

Hard Hit Minority Families

The changes of the last two decades have had a very profound impact on minority young families, especially those that are black. As Table 30-2 shows, the median earnings of the heads of young black families with children fell *71 percent* from 1973 to 1990 (from $13,860 to $4,030 in 1990 dollars). Their total family incomes from all sources fell 48 percent. The *median* income of these young black families is now below the federal poverty line for a family of three. In 1973 it was nearly double that poverty line. *Two out of three* children in young black families now are poor.

This crisis for young black families is contributing mightily to the tearing apart of the black community. This society cannot year after year increase the poverty and isolation and hopelessness of black mothers and fathers and children—it can't keep turning the screws tighter and tighter—without appalling consequences. We see those consequences in the emergency rooms and unemployment lines and prisons and homeless shelters and neonatal intensive care wards and morgues of our cities and our suburbs and rural towns. We see it in the omnipresent violence that destroys so many black lives and leaves blacks and whites alike so fearful. More blacks die from firearms each year in this country than died in the century's worth of despicable lynchings that followed the Civil War. More black men die from firearms every six weeks in Detroit than died in the 1967 Detroit "riot." More black and Hispanic men die from firearms in Los Angeles every two weeks than died in the 1965 Watts "riot."

Frankly, though, I would be skeptical that this nation would attack this cataclysm for young black families were it not for the fact that young *white* families are only a step or two behind in the scope of their economic depression and family disintegration. Perhaps the most important story told in this report is the impact of two decades of this Depression for the young on' three types of families we often assume are insulated from hard times:

> From 1973 to 1990 the poverty rate for children living in young *white* families more than doubled to *27 percent.*
>
> From 1973 to 1990 the poverty rate for children in young *married-couple* families went up two-and-a-half times—to *20 percent.*
>
> And the child poverty rate in young families headed by *high school graduates* went up even faster, to *33 percent.*

In other words, a generation ago white or married-couple young families or those headed by high school graduates were fairly well insulated from poverty. The damage of the last two decades has cut so broadly and deeply that now one in four white children in young families, one in five children in married-couple young families, and one in three children in families headed by young high school graduates is poor.

Private and Public Response

What response do we see to these problems from private and public leadership? Precious little.

Too much of the business community is wholly untroubled by stripping away from millions of Americans the minimum family-supporting wages, fringe benefits, and job security that could help make our families strong again.... The Congress and the administration together persist in keeping defense spending above the levels of the average year in the Cold War—impoverishing our society and the world by arming ourselves not only against real external threats but against weapons-justifying fantasies, while letting the internal enemies of poverty, disintegration, violence, and hopelessness rage unabated. The Congress can't mount the political will to get Head Start—a program universally conceded to be effective and cost-effective—to more than one in three eligible children or to pass the refundable children's tax credit that experts from all parts of the political spectrum think is a minimum first step to tax equity and family economic security.

Finally, far too many of the nation's governors and state and national legislators have responded to budget crunches and political turmoil by scapegoating the poor—trying to bolster their political fortunes by pummeling the welfare recipients whose assistance gobbles up a grand total of 2 to 3 percent of state budgets.

In hard times in the past our society usually has had escape valves—an inherent balance that gave to the powerless help from one institution when others turned their backs—from the federal government when the states were at their worst, from the courts when Congress and the executive were unresponsive. Now we seem to be in an awful time when every institution is competing to pander to the powerful and further penalize the poor.

A Fair Start

In response to the economic plight of America's young families, Congress and the president must take three immediate steps . . . to ensure that every child has a *fair* start, a *healthy* start, and a *head* start.

A *fair start* means renewed and sustained economic growth and enough jobs at decent wages to restore the pact our nation used to have with young families—that personal sacrifice and hard work will be rewarded with family supporting jobs. A fair start also means enactment of a refundable children's tax credit to bolster the incomes of families with children. . . . Such a credit would reduce federal income taxes for middle- and low-income families and help the lowest income families that have no tax liability through a tax refund.

While creating no new bureaucracies, a refundable children's credit would target tax relief and economic support precisely to the group—families with children—that has been hardest hit by declining incomes and rising poverty rates since 1973. . . .

Finally, a fair start means creation of a child support insurance system to give all single parents the chance to lift their families out of poverty through work, ensuring that all children who are not living with both parents receive a minimally adequate child support payment from the absent parent or the government when it fails to collect from the absent parent.

What we *don't* need in this time of great crisis for young families with children is a negative approach rooted in welfare-bashing and welfare cuts that ends up hurting children. Families on welfare are the victims of the recession, not the cause of it. They are victims of budget deficits, not the cause of them. But nearly one-fourth of all young families with children are forced to rely upon Aid for Families with Dependent Children (AFDC) to meet their basic needs, and they are extremely vulnerable to misguided attacks on this essential safety net for children.

Our political leaders know these truths. Yet during an election year too many cannot resist the temptation to direct the public's frustration and anger toward the poorest of poor Americans—those families and children who rely upon welfare for basic income support.

. . . Most of the welfare "reforms" now underway in states are little more than crass attempts to slash state budgets without regard to their impact on families with children. Reducing or stopping benefits to newborns when they are the second or third child in a family, as now proposed by several states, is punitive, pointless, and immoral. Only political leaders who are hopelessly out of touch with the realities of poor families' lives could think that an extra $2.50 per day in welfare benefits would cause teen parents to have a second child, or that reducing the added benefit to $1.25/day (as the governor of Wisconsin and the president now propose for that state) constitutes any serious effort at welfare reform. All they will succeed in doing is taking desperately needed food, clothing, and shelter from infants.

It's time for the president, Congress, and more of our governors to be honest with the American people about the problems facing our economy, our poor families, and our children.

The problem is *not* large numbers of welfare parents trying to "beat the system" by having more children or moving to another state to get higher benefits. The problem is a set of short-sighted, budget-driven welfare rules that make it virtually impossible for parents to work their way gradually off the welfare rolls and a dearth of stable, family-supporting jobs that would allow them to make it on their own.

In many ways, the welfare problem is the same problem facing all young families with children—the result of sharply falling wages, too few job opportunities for those with little education or training, and too little investment in the skills and supports poor parents need to make it in today's economy. And serious solutions begin with a fair start, a healthy start, and a head start for our young families.

A Healthy Start, a Head Start

A *healthy start* means a national health plan to assure insurance coverage for all Americans. Children and pregnant women need basic health care *now*, however. As an immediate step, the president and Congress must extend Medicaid coverage to every low-income child and pregnant woman. And to ensure that this insurance provides real access to essential health services, not merely theoretical coverage, children need universal access to vaccines and increased funding for community health centers, and other public health activities.

A *head start* means full funding of Head Start. A first step in bolstering the productivity of our next generation of workers lies in adequate investments in quality child care and early childhood development. Every dollar invested in good early childhood development programs saves $5.97 in later special education, welfare, crime, and other costs. Yet Head Start still reaches only one in three eligible preschool children. . . . A head start also means passing family preservation legislation that will strengthen and preserve families in crisis so that they can better protect, nurture, and support their own children. So many of these young parents want to be better parents, and with intensive family preservation services they can get the help they need.

These are essential first steps. To reach them and go beyond them, we're going to have to make the president and Congress come to recognize that child and family poverty and insecurity are a national disaster that requires our addressing them with a pittance of the zeal and shared commitment we now apply to digging out after a devastating hurricane or earthquake or confronting a crisis abroad.

Toward the 21st Century: Family Change and Public Policy*

Steven K. Wisensale

This article by Steven K. Wisensale provides us with a glimpse into the future regarding several important trends which will have an increasing impact upon American families. These include the changing structure and composition of families, the family's declining economic status, and the increasing racial diversity and aging of our society. Each of these trends has been touched upon in earlier readings. Wisensale pulls them together to discuss some of their ramifications, and proposes several ideas as to how our society can address them.

Historically, the family has served as the fundamental social unit, producing and raising children, caring for the aged and disabled, and socializing its members in the basic values of individual character development and in the more general responsibilities of citizenship. According to Levitan, Belous, and Gallo (1988), Freud often referred to the family as the basic germ cells of civilization. The family's primary strength lies in the fact that it continues to perform its major functions (sometimes well, sometimes not) despite being subjected to major changes, such as a steady increase in divorce, over the last 20 years. Its primary weak-

*Source: *Family Relations*, "Toward The 21st Century: Family Change and Public Policy," Steven K. Wisensale, 41:4, pp. 417–422, 1992.

ness, on the other hand, can be found in its lack of immunity to external social, economic, and political pressures. That is not to say the family is doomed, but rather that such pressures may weaken it to such an extent that its current functions can no longer be performed effectively. In short, the fear is that our society may lose what it needs most.

Not surprisingly, the perception of the family in terms of strengths, weaknesses, and future prospects varies considerably across a continuum that includes pessimism on one extreme and optimism on the other. The most obvious examples in the literature of the pessimistic viewpoints are Steiner's (1981) *The Futility of Family Policy*, Moynihan's (1986) *Family and Nation*, and Popenoe's (1988) *Disturbing the Nest: Family Change and Decline in Modern Societies*. More optimistic views of the family can be found in Bane's (1976) *Here to Stay: American Families in the Twentieth Century*, Schroeder's (1989) *Champion of the Great American Family*, and Blankenhorn, Bayme, and Elshtain's (1991) *Rebuilding the Nest: A New Commitment to the American Family*. Clustered near the center of the continuum are at least three works that more or less resemble unemotional report cards on the changing nature and current status of the family. Not necessarily pessimistic nor optimistic in tone, these include Cherlin's (1988) *The Changing American Family and Public Policy*, Levitan et al.'s (1988) *What's Happening to the American Family*, and Levy and Michel's (1991) *The Economic Future of American Families*.

But regardless of one's perspective concerning the family, optimists and pessimists alike consistently find common ground on at least three issues. First, they agree that the statistical profile of the U.S. family has changed drastically over the last 20 years. More mothers work, the divorce rate has increased sharply, single parenthood continues to grow, domestic violence is reported more frequently, and more couples postpone marriage longer and have fewer children than previous cohorts. Second, there is also general agreement that economic change has had a dramatic impact on the family. This is particularly true for young, middle-class families who tend not to fare nearly as well as their parents' generation. And third, there is also agreement concerning the nation's changing demographics. The U.S. population is aging and becoming more multiracial. These emerging phenomena will affect both the character and function of the family well into the twenty-first century.

For policy makers, researchers, and family life educators interested in the future of the family, it is imperative that they not only identify major social trends but that they also put forth relevant research questions and specific policy recommendations that are designed to address those trends. The purpose of this article, therefore, is twofold: first, to identify and examine major trends that will affect the family over the next decade and second, to explore several policy options that can be debated and perhaps employed in an effort to address the specific needs of families in the years ahead. To complete this task the article has been divided into four parts. The first three will focus on the changing family, the declining economy, and the dynamics of demographic change. The conclusion, or fourth part, will be devoted exclusively to recommendations.

The Changing Family

While many still harbor images of the traditional family, with the father employed and the mother at home, reality paints an entirely different picture for us. According to the National Conference of State Legislatures (1989), over the past 20 years we have witnessed a steady increase in families without fathers, children without families, and families without homes. More important perhaps is the growing consensus of both researchers and policy analysts alike that even greater challenges await the family in the decades ahead. And, in order to address these challenges, lawmakers in particular must become more knowledgeable about key trends that will impact directly on family life. What follows is a review of some of the major changes occurring within the family and the various policy implications associated with these changes.

Perhaps one of the most dominant changes in family structure has been the steady flow of mothers into the work force. Over 65 percent of women with children aged 3 to 5 years are employed, representing the fastest growing portion of the U. S. labor market (Congressional Research Service, 1987). In 1989, 75 percent of all mothers with children aged 6 to 18 were in the labor force (Gnezda and Smith, 1989), and by 1995 it is predicted that nearly 65 percent of all preschool children and 80 percent of school-age children will have mothers in the work force (Children's Defense Fund, 1989). As a result, families demand more child care services and flexible family leave policies, both of which have been slow in their development and acceptance.

A second major impact on the family has been the extremely high rate of divorce. According to Price (1990), the U.S. divorce rate more than doubled between 1965 and 1979. In 1965, 10.6 of 1,000 married women divorced; in 1979, 22.8 divorced. Today the rate has stabilized at about 22 divorces per 1,000 married women. But still, it is estimated that two of every three new marriages will end in some form of dissolution, and between 40 and 50 percent of children born since 1970 will experience parental divorce (Price, 1990). Moynihan's (1986) prediction concerning children of divorce is even higher at 65 percent. As a result of these changes, which have resulted in more women and children living in poverty, future policies must be more sensitive to divorcing families, particularly with respect to the strict enforcement of child support laws.

A third important change in family structure can be found in the increasing numbers of single-parent households. Though many of these households are created through divorce, an alarming number are produced by teenage pregnancies. The United States reports the highest rates of teenage pregnancy, birth, and abortion in the Western world. Nearly half of all teen mothers give birth out of wedlock and, of these, 93 percent attempt to raise their babies alone (Maggard, 1985). Consequently, most teen parents are confronted with brutal economic realities. For example, 75 percent of single mothers under age 24 live below the poverty line (Maggard, 1985). Put another way, 61 percent of females under age 30 who receive AFDC had their first children as teenagers (National Research Council, 1987). Equally significant, the children of teen parents are at greater risk of health problems, low academic achievement, behavioral problems, and of repeating the cycle and becoming teenage parents themselves (Children's Defense Fund, 1986).

As a result of the growth pattern of single-parent households, policy makers are often forced to attack the problem on several fronts at once. Efforts are clearly needed to prevent the problem through various educational programs as well as treat the problem through a variety of family support policies, including job training, child care, and comprehensive health care coverage. Clearly, if one of the most important predictors of poverty is marital status, then it must be concluded that one of poverty's most effective incubators is the single-parent household. It is this household in particular that demands greater attention from policy makers, researchers, and family life educators.

A fourth change in the structure of the family can be traced to its age composition. Due primarily to a decrease in fertility and an increase in longevity, today's average married couple has more parents than children (Preston, 1984). Predictably, 75 percent of caregivers are female. With an average age of 45, almost two-thirds are married and more than one-third reside with the care recipient. Sometimes referred to as the "sandwich generation," a number of these caregivers are caught between caring for their children and older parents (Congressional Quarterly, 1988). More significantly, projections for the year 2000 indicate that this pattern of informal care will continue and even increase. Therefore, women in particular can expect to spend more years caring for an aging parent than for a dependent child (Brubaker, 1990; Mancini and Blieszner, 1989). In 1900, for example, a woman spent 19 years with a child and only 9 years with a parent. Today, and well into the future, she will spend 17 years caring for a dependent child and 18 years assisting an elderly parent (U.S. House Select Committee on Aging, 1987).

As a result of the aging of the U.S. family (Brubaker, 1990; Mancini and Blieszner, 1989), its younger members will both need and demand more services that are designed to assist them in their caregiving functions. Examples of these include respite care, home health care services, intergenerational family leave policies, and adult day-care programs. To what extent such policies should be initiated by federal or state governments or by the public or private sector continues to be the focus of an ongoing debate.

In addition to the four changes in family life discussed above, there are other important trends that deserve our attention. According to Glick (1990), there has been a rise in age at first marriage from age 20 for women and age 25 for men in 1955, to age 24 for women and 26 for men in 1988. Equally important, perhaps, is the fact that families are also having fewer children. In 1986, for example, when only 65 babies were born per 1,000 women of childbearing age, it marked the lowest birth rate in U.S. history (Wattenberg, 1987).

Another trend concerns the number of young adults choosing to live with their parents. Between 1960 and 1988 the number of 20 to 24-year-olds living with parents rose from 43 percent to 55 percent (Glick, 1990).

Alternative family patterns are also emerging in greater numbers. Between 1970 and 1988 the number of cohabiting couples has increased from .5 million to 2.5 million (Glick, 1990). As a result, our courts and legislative bodies have begun to respond to this trend. In 1990, for the first time in history, the U.S. Census Bureau permitted couples of the same or opposite sex to distinguish themselves from those who are not intimately involved. Thus "unmarried partners" were classified separately from "housemates-roommates." Also, by 1990 at least seven communities had passed domestic partnership laws which allow unmarried couples access to joint medical, health, and dental coverage among other benefits (Heckart, 1990). To date, however, neither the federal government nor the state legislatures have enacted similar laws. But the fact remains that the family is slowly but surely being redefined in legal terms.

Still another trend has been the rapid growth of technology and its corresponding impact on the family, often complicating the decision-making process. Surrogate parenting, the debate over RU 486 and Norplant, access to organ transplants, and the issue of when to preserve and when to end life have all placed the family in the middle of some major controversies that even the U.S. Supreme Court finds difficult to address.

Finally, there are at least two other trends related to families that must be monitored closely: domestic violence and declining access to health care. With respect to the former, Strauss (1990) argues strongly that despite a decrease in child and spouse abuse over the last decade (thanks in part to an increase in the number of shelters), we still need more policies and programs focused on intervention and prevention rather than treatment after the fact. With respect to health care, 37 million people in the United States remain uninsured, many of whom are children in need of basic preventative health services. . . .

But despite these trends and major weaknesses apparent in today's family unit, we should remind ourselves of two points in particular. First, change itself is not necessarily bad. What is bad is to ignore change and thus fail to adopt those policies and programs that are needed most by the family. Second, in the midst of what some would label as depressing times, it may be beneficial to review Orthner's (1991) general assessment. He is quick to remind us that the disabling effects of family change are not cutting evenly across society. The majority of first marriages do not end in divorce, an overwhelming majority of families do not experience spouse or child abuse, most teenage girls do not become pregnant, the majority of students graduate from high school, and most people consider themselves fairly happy in today's world.

In the end, therefore, there are specific soft spots or points of vulnerability within families that need to be addressed by policy makers, researchers, and family life educators far more aggressively today than has been done in the past. In short, careful targeting, rather than a general overhaul, should be the strategy employed to address the needs of changing families.

The Changing Economic Status of Families

While families are obviously changing internally, it cannot be denied that certain external forces are influencing their basic structure and stability as well. This is particularly true with respect to economic forces. Despite an increase in two-paycheck families, real family income has fallen 8.3 percent since 1973 (Levy and Michel, 1991). Further, families with children saw their share of national income drop 20 percent between 1973 and 1984 and workers watched their real earnings drop 10 percent since 1979 (National Conference of State Legislatures, 1989). Clearly, two incomes to support today's families have become the norm. According to the California Assembly Human Services Committee (1987), 35 percent more two-parent families would live below the poverty line if wives were not working.

Young families have been particularly vulnerable to prolonged economic downturn in the United States. Whatever growth that did occur between 1973 and 1986 benefited all U.S. families in all age groups from all regions except young families (National Conference of State Legislatures, 1989). The Children's Defense Fund (1989) reports that while median family income increased by 4 percent for families with a household head of at least 35 years of age, median income fell by 3 percent for families with a 25–35-year-old head of household. For 15 to 24-year-old heads of households, the drop was even more severe, falling 24 percent since 1979. Not surprisingly, single-parent households, which represent one of the fastest growing types of families, are the most economically sensitive to these trends. It has been reported that expenditures exceed income in 25 percent of those households (Hogan, 1990), thus contributing to an ever-widening gap in family income between single-parent and two-parent households.

Another indicator of economic decline in the United States can be found in the statistics concerning the middle class. It is shrinking. During the 1980s, four times as many fell out of the middle class as climbed above it. As a result, the gap between rich and poor is now wider than at any time since the U.S. Census Bureau began collecting such data in 1947 (National Conference of State Legislatures, 1989). Complicating factors even more, the changing composition of families, especially the rise of single-parent households, has resulted in more children experiencing a steady downward shift in economic mobility (Hogan, 1990).

However, no fact concerning the economy is more obvious to the average U.S. consumer than that which concerns the cost of home ownership, long a symbol of middle-class stability. While median-income workers spent 14 percent of their gross monthly income on mortgage payments in 1949, a 1985 worker at the same income level spent an average of 44 percent on the mortgage (National Conference of State Legislatures, 1989). Such findings spawn at least two important questions. First, at prevailing prices and interest rates, will young families be able to afford their first home? And second, if the demand for new homes declines considerably in the years ahead, will current owners see their homes decrease in value? The outcome of such a scenario is significant because, historically, home equity has been the single most important component of net wealth for more than two thirds of those families who own homes (Levy and Michel, 1991).

But families at the lower end of the income scale, those outside the middle class, have been especially hard hit over the past 20 years. Between 1968 and 1993, the poorest 20 percent of families with children witnessed a sharp drop in their share of income from 7.4 to 4.8 percent. And, due primarily to federal and state cuts in human service programs, 4 million more women and children fell into poverty between 1980 and 1984 (National Conference of State Legislatures, 1989). It is not surprising, then, that families with children are the fastest growing group within our nation's homeless population. In 1982 such families comprised 18 percent of the homeless. By 1988, between 28 and 33 percent of the homeless were families, with female-headed, single-parent families comprising the majority of homeless families (Stark, 1988).

The implications of the information presented above are troubling in two respects. First, there is growing inequality between different family types and the gap between rich families and poor families is widening. Single-parent families with female heads are particularly vulnerable in times of economic decline. For single-parent, black families the situation is even more severe. Nearly half of all black children live in poverty (Edelman, 1987). Second, there is also growing inequality between generations of families. More precisely, younger families with children are, in general terms, worse off economically than older families. Each of these points is discussed in greater detail below.

In *The Economic Future of American Families*, Levy and Michel (1991) present a discouraging economic picture of the nation's families. "Income inequality among families with children has increased far more rapidly than income equality among all families," argue Levy and Michel. "In particular, the combination of greater inequality and income stagnation means that the proportion of children in families with incomes below $10,000 has risen from one in ten (in 1973) to one in six today" (p. 4). Since 1969, the year of greatest income equality among families by census measures, income inequality increased gradually in the 1970s and much more sharply in the 1980s, the Reagan years. That is, for every $1.00 received by the poorest one-fifth of families today, the highest one-fifth receive $9.60 (Levy and Michel, 1991). Viewed from an international perspective, income inequality among U.S. families is the greatest among the world's ten most highly industrialized nations (Coder, Rainwater, and Smeeding, 1988).

But not only has there been a widening gap between certain family types, there also has been a shift within income categories that has resulted in some younger families, usually those with children, trading places with older families. For example, while the incomes of elderly families were rising in the 1970s and 1980s, thanks primarily to the expansion of important entitlement programs, families headed by single women, usually low-income families, were growing rapidly. The result was what Levy and Michel (1991) refer to as a sort of "swap" in which elderly families moved from the bottom to the lower middle on the income scale, while their "vacated places" at the bottom were taken by new female-headed families with children. This ongoing phenomenon has also been referred to as the "feminization of poverty" (Rodgers, 1986) and, if these economic patterns continue, argue Levy and Michel (1991), younger families with children will be far less fortunate in the next decade than the two generations immediately preceding them.

With respect to the second point, income inequality between generations, it has become abundantly clear that some cohorts are luckier than others. Works by Kaplan (1987), Light (1988), and Longman (1987) have all reached similar conclusions. That is, members of the "baby boom generation" (those born between 1946 and 1964) are faring far less well than their parents' cohort. More precisely, the parents of the first wave of baby boomers, now in their 60s, experienced a 524 percent increase in their real net wealth during their twenties while baby boomers, now in their forties, experienced an increase of only 34 percent (Levy & Michel, 1991). An important explanation for such a large discrepancy in wealth between two cohorts is that the parents of the baby boomers moved through their twenties in the 1950s and through their thirties in the 1960s. These two decades represent perhaps the most expansive era economically in U.S. history and stand in sharp contrast to the steady economic decline we have experienced since 1970. In short, one cohort has been luckier than the other.

Based on the information presented above, all indications are that the economic future will be far more difficult for younger generations than for the older ones. Younger families in particular will be confronted with lower incomes and decreased net wealth in comparison to older families. But what may be most troublesome is the frightening realization that the unprecedented economic growth this nation experienced in the 1950s and 1960s may never again be repeated. As a result, retarded economic growth will translate into fewer jobs, stagnant wages, lower incomes, decreased net wealth, smaller savings, declining investments, and lower tax revenues. Families as a whole will experience difficulty in moving from a lower to a higher income class and will become even more dependent upon the private sector for jobs and upon the public sector for social services, neither of which will be in abundance. On the other hand, a stronger economy could produce just the opposite effect and, in the process, have a far more positive effect on the general well-being of families, an effect that is similar to a time in the not too distant past.

Shifting Demographics and Generational Equity

As the nation's families wrestle with major changes occurring within the household and adapt to strong outside forces influencing its general well-being, they must also confront two important demographic trends that will carry the nation well into the twenty-first century. Both the country's race mix and age mix are changing at significant rates. How these changes may affect the character and functioning of the family in the years ahead is discussed below.

There is no question that the United States is evolving into a multiracial, multicultural, and multilingual society. In the twenty-first century it is estimated that 33 percent of the country's population will be nonwhite (McCubbin, 1990). The highest concentration of minority families will be Hispanic, followed by blacks, Asian-Americans, and Native Americans. But even more significant are the projections. Between 1980 and 2030 Hispanics are expected to increase in number by 186.8 percent followed by "others" (Native Americans, Asians, Eskimos, and Pacific Islanders) at 78.7 percent, blacks by 68.3 percent, and whites by 24.8

percent ("The 21st Century Family," 1990). In short, we as a nation are changing color.

Such demographic changes as those identified above are especially important with respect to families. Minorities in general, and blacks and Hispanics in particular, tend to have fewer jobs, lower incomes, are more prone to poverty and welfare rolls, have more children, are more susceptible to discrimination, are poorly educated, have higher unemployment rates, and are victimized more frequently by economic downturns than whites (National Conference of State Legislatures, 1989). According to Marian Wright Edelman (1987), today's black children are more likely to be born into poverty, lack access to prenatal health care, have a single mother or unemployed parent, not graduate from high school, and not go on to college than they were in 1980. Similarly, poverty has worsened for Hispanic families as well. Between 1978 and 1987 the poverty rate of married-couple Hispanic families rose from 11.9 percent to 18.1 percent. For blacks, it rose from 11.3 percent to 12.3 percent, and for whites from 4.7 percent to 5.2 percent during the same time period (Center on Budget and Policy Priorities, 1988).

Clearly, minority families are at risk. As their numbers increase, it will be even more imperative in the twenty-first century than it is now for minority youth in particular to become better educated and develop new job skills that will enable them to become both self-sufficient employees and responsible parents. On the other side of the coin, however, policy makers must tear down discriminatory barriers in education and employment and provide opportunities accessible to all regardless of race or ethnic group. For in the end, only a well-educated, fully employed work force is most capable of meeting the needs of its families. It is also this same well-educated and fully employed work force that will be relied upon during the next three decades to support, through Social Security and Medicare taxes, the hoards of baby boomers who will be retiring. Whether or not the younger generation will be able and willing to support the older generation has become one of the most heated policy debates of the 1990s.

According to Paul Light (1988), author of *Baby Boomers*, the year 2016 holds significance for two reasons. First, it will be the seventieth birthday of the baby boom, and second, it marks the fiftieth anniversary of political participation by baby boomers and their thirteenth presidential election. More important, perhaps, if current forecasts hold, the aging baby boomers will be demanding much from their offspring. In fact, argues Light, "The 2016 election may bring the intergenerational conflict many worry about in the present—not between the baby boomers and their parents, but between the baby boomers and their own children" (p. 270).

The reasons for such a conflict between generations can be found in the constantly shifting sands of demographics. Today, for every 100 adults under age 65 there are 20 people over 65. But, by the year 2030 the ratio of old to young will nearly double. For every 100 adults under 65 there will be 40 people over 65. There will also be more over the age of 65 than under 18 (Population Reference Bureau, 1992). Put in other terms, today's Social Security program requires five employees to cover each beneficiary. By the year 2030, however, it is predicted that there will be only 2.5 workers for each Social Security beneficiary (Longman, 1987). Thus, in order to support the old, the young will have to shoulder a very large tax burden as we pass into the twenty-first century.

In the meantime, policy makers are confronted with the following question: How do we invest in the nation's future of retiring baby boomers while meeting the social, economic, and political needs of today? Put more pointedly, in an era of limited resources, should the aged receive a disproportionately large share of those resources in comparison to other groups? These and similar questions have helped to spur on what is now commonly referred to as the "generational equity debate."

Although it is difficult to pinpoint the precise date and time when the debate began, April 4th, 1984, could certainly serve as a more than adequate point of reference. For it was on that date that then Governor Richard Lamm of Colorado stated quite bluntly on ABC's *Nightline* that perhaps too much technology and money was being spent on the elderly during their last years in comparison to the young who have their entire lives before them. Coincidentally or not, a steady stream of articles and speeches followed Lamm's appearance on national television and began to draw attention to the generational equity issue in a way that had not occurred previously.

Beginning with his presidential address ("Children and Elderly: Divergent Paths for America's Dependents") before the Population Association of America in Minneapolis in May of 1984 and combined with his article in *Scientific American* the following December, Samuel Preston (1984) helped to establish the original parameters of the debate. Our society cannot wish away, he stated, the possibility that there is direct competition between the young and the old for society's resources. While expenditure on the elderly can be thought of mainly as consumption, he argued, expenditures on the young are a combination of consumption and investment.

Similarly, Richman and Stagner (1986) followed in Preston's path and also framed the issue in terms of elderly people and children. Writing in *Daedalus* ("Children in an Aging Society: Treasured Resource or Forgotten Minority"), they argued that an aging society poses two possible consequences for U.S. children. On one hand, they may become a treasured resource nurtured all the more for their scarcity and importance to the nation's future. On the other hand, if they are forced to compete with other dependent groups for limited resources, they may come to be regarded as little more than just another needy minority.

Others would join the debate as well. Daniel Callahan (1987), writing in *Setting Limits*, argued strongly that medicine can keep some people alive for a longer period of time than is of any benefit to them. He concluded, therefore, that the United States should consider adopting age-based policies as a means of allocating health care resources across the lifespan. Great Britain, for example, prohibits funding for kidney dialysis for those over age 55. Philip Longman (1987) takes a slightly different approach, arguing that an unfair burden has been placed upon the baby boom generation to support a growing aged population through Social Security and Medicare. Today, contends Longman, expenditures on the aged exceed those on defense and the demand to expand benefits for the elderly will continue well into the next century. Victor Fuchs (1991) is even more specific in his analysis of the situation. U.S. society, he warns, is seriously underinvesting in its children.

Similar points were raised in several editorials in *Newsweek,* and articles in *The Nation, Business Week, The New Republic,* and *Society.* In the meantime, organizations formed and lined up on both sides of the issue. AGE (Americans for Generational Equity) was organized in 1985 to remind policy makers of existing generational inequities. It was quickly countered by the formation of Generations United, a coalition of 90 groups representing all ages that attempts to dispel the belief that the young and old are in conflict over limited government resources.

Often caught in the middle of this debate is the family. In more specific terms, most families are being challenged on two fronts. First, financially it is estimated that two-paycheck families with incomes of over $20,000 will pay more in Social Security taxes than they will receive in benefits when they retire (Longman, 1987). This is in sharp contrast to returns enjoyed by current beneficiaries. For example, a person who retired in 1986 got back his contribution to Social Security within 18 months. Meanwhile, because today's family is heavily taxed to support Social Security beneficiaries, it obviously has less to spend on children (Longman, 1987). Similarly, a political system wedded to expanding entitlement programs for the elderly will have less funds for programs and services needed by families.

On a second front, today's family is being squeezed between two generations that are both in need of care. Not only is child care in greater demand due to two-earner couples and single-parent households, but so, too, is elder care. Nearly 60 percent of women with children under six years of age work outside the home and over half of working mothers return to work before their child's first birthday. At the other end of the scale, almost 62 percent of all women between the ages of 45 and 54 now work, as do 42 percent of those who fall into the 55–64 age bracket (U. S. Bureau of the Census, 1988). It is precisely these two groups of middle-aged females who are most likely to provide the necessary care to a disabled parent. In short, today's demographics dictate that care be provided at both ends of the age scale; almost all forecasts indicate that this pattern will continue in the future.

Recommendations

It has been argued here that the U.S. family is currently being confronted with at least three major challenges. First, the family is changing. What once was viewed as traditional and predictable is no more. Divorce, single-parenthood, cohabitation, and domestic partnership laws have all helped to produce a new family portrait. Second, it was concluded that the economic status of families is on the decline and, unfortunately, the future appears ominous. Young families with children, and especially those headed by females alone, are considered to be the most vulnerable. And third, it is clear that the ongoing demographic changes will continue to have a major impact on families. For not only is the United States changing color, it is also a society that is aging. As a result, in the years ahead, not only will families look different than they do today, they will also have different needs.

In order to address the three major challenges identified here, policy makers, researchers, and family life educators must assume more responsibility and work much harder than they have in years past. It is essential that they propose better policies and programs, ask more relevant research questions, and do a better job of educating the public on important family issues. Presented below are seven recommendations that should be taken into consideration as we continue the ongoing dialogue on the future status of the U.S. family.

First, it is imperative that we recognize that certain family types are more vulnerable than others and, therefore, deserve more attention. The single-parent household headed by a female should be targeted in particular. Stricter enforcement of child support laws, greater access to health care, day care, and family leave programs, commitment to pay equity for women in the labor market, and both job training and more flexible educational programs, especially for high school dropouts, are all needed.

Second, more intergenerational policies should be adopted. Entitlements geared to certain groups based on age or income level fail to assist a majority of our families. Three weeks prior to his death in 1988, Representative Claude Pepper introduced his family policy package to Congress. Long a strong advocate for the elderly, Pepper's venture into intergenerational policy proposals was a significant development that should not go unnoticed. Although portions of it are still being debated, the package included a "Young Americans Act" that parallels the 1965 Older Americans Act and also an intergenerational home health care program. Several states (Connecticut, Maine, New Jersey, and Wisconsin) have since passed intergenerational family leave bills in an effort to address the needs of today's "sandwich generation." But perhaps the best example of an intergenerational policy would be the adoption of some form of national health insurance.

Third, we need a more equitable tax structure that is more fair to families and recognizes their caregiving functions. Tax credits for both child care and elder care should be viewed as profamily policies, not as drains on public revenues. Victor Fuch's (1991) controversial suggestion that our tax policies be employed more aggressively to transfer more resources from high-income to low-income households and to those with children should be placed on the political agenda and opened for debate.

Fourth, corporations must become more sensitive to the needs of families and their actions must originate in the personnel department and not in the office of public relations. Family leave, day care, and adequate health insurance coverage are all needed by today's families. Corporations should do their part to assist them. Although some companies have developed excellent benefit packages for their employees, they are too few in number.

Fifth, researchers in particular must become more involved with the policy-making process. Their questions need to be more relevant and their studies more focused and thus more usable to legislators. This can be accomplished through joint seminars or focus groups in which legislators (and/or their staffs) and university researchers exchange information, needs, and skills.

Sixth, family life educators should devote more time to policy issues and make a stronger effort to educate the general public on the political process. Not only must citizens be made aware of the rapidly changing family, its economic status, and the potential ramifications of ongoing demographic shifts, but skills in lobbying techniques need to be taught as well. This is particularly applicable at the state level where most family policies are formulated and implemented.

Finally, it is important that family issues, and particularly those regarding children, be pushed onto the political agenda during key election years. For far too long the family has been worn on the sleeve of the politician at his/her convenience or simply waved in the face of the U.S. public as if it were little more than a flag. The time is too late and our problems are far too serious for us to tolerate such empty political symbolism in the future.

References

BANE, M. (1976). *Here to stay: American families in the twentieth century*. New York: Basic Books.

BLANKENHORN, D., BAYME, S., and ELSHTAIN, J. (eds.). (1991). *Rebuilding the nest: A new commitment to the American family*. Milwaukee: Family Service America.

BRUBAKER, T. (1990). "Families in later life: A burgeoning research area." *Journal of Marriage and the Family*, 52, 959–981.

California Assembly Human Services Committee. (1987). *The changing American family to the year 2000: Planning for our children's future*. Sacramento: California General Assembly.

CALLAHAN, D. (1987). *Setting limits: Medical goals in an aging society*. New York: Simon and Schuster.

Center on Budget and Policy Priorities. (1988). *Shortchanged: Recent developments in Hispanic poverty, income, and employment*. Washington, DC: Center on Budget and Policy Priorities.

CHERLIN, A. (1988). *The changing American family and public policy*. Washington, DC: The Urban Institute Press.

Children's Defense Fund. (1986). *Welfare and teen pregnancy: What do we know? What do we do?* Washington, DC: Author.

Children's Defense Fund. (1989). *FY 1989: An analysis of our nation's investment in children*. Washington, DC: Author.

CODER, J., RAINWATER, L., and SMEEDING, T. (1988, December). *Inequality among children and elderly in ten modern nations: The U.S. in an international context*. Paper presented at the American Economic Association meetings, New York.

Congressional Research Service. (1987). *Parental leave: Legislation in the 100th Congress* (no. IB86132). Washington, DC: The Library of Congress.

Congressional Quarterly Weekly Report. (1988). "Catastrophic bill is sent to White House." *Congressional Quarterly*, 46 (24), 31–32.

EDELMAN, M. (1987). *Families in peril: An agenda for social change*. Cambridge, MA: Harvard University Press.

FUCHS, V. (1991). "Are Americans underinvesting in their children?" *Society*, 28 (6), 14–22.

GLICK, P. (1990). "Marriage and family trends." In the NCFR Presidential Report, *2001: Preparing families for the future* (pp. 2–3). Minneapolis, MN: National Council on Family Relations.

GNEZDA, M., and SMITH, S. (1989). *Child care and early childhood education policy: A legislator's guide.* Denver, CO: National Conference of State Legislatures.

HECKART, K. (1990). *The broadening definition of the family: Policies concerning domestic partners.* An unpublished manuscript by the School of Family Studies, University of Connecticut, Storrs.

HOGAN, J. (1990). "Economic issues and the family." In the NCFR Presidential Report, *2001: Preparing families for the future* (pp. 14–15). Minneapolis, MN: National Council on Family Relations.

KAPLAN, S. (1987). "The new generation gap: The politics of generational justice." *Common Cause Magazine*, 2, 13–16.

LEVITAN, S., BELOUS, R., and GALLO, F. (1988). *What's happening to the American family?* Baltimore: Johns Hopkins University Press.

LEVY, F., and MICHEL, R. (1991). *The economic future of American families.* Washington, DC: The Urban Institute Press.

LIGHT, P. (1988). *Baby boomers.* New York: W.W. Norton.

LONGMAN, P. (1987). *Born to pay: The new politics of aging in America.* Boston: Houghton-Mifflin.

MAGGARD, H. (1985). *State legislative initiatives that address the issue of teen pregnancy and parenting.* Denver, CO: National Conference of State Legislatures.

MANCINI, J., and BLIESZNER, R. (1989). "Aging parents and adult children: Research themes in intergenerational relations." *Journal of Marriage and the Family*, 51, 275–290.

McCUBBIN, H. (1990). "Ethnic and mixed-race families." In the NCFR Presidential Report, *2001: Preparing families for the future* (pp. 38–39). Minneapolis, MN: National Council on Family Relations.

MOYNIHAN, D. (1986). *Family and nation.* New York: Harcourt, Brace and Jovanovich.

National Conference of State Legislatures. (1989). *Family policy: Recommendations for state action.* Denver, CO: Author.

National Research Council. (1987). *Risking the future: Adolescent sexuality, pregnancy, and childbearing.* Washington, DC: National Academy Press.

ORTHNER, D. (1991). "The family in transition." In D. Blankenhorn, S. Bayme, and J. Elshtain (eds.), *Rebuilding the nest: A new commitment to the American family* (pp. 93–118). Milwaukee: Family Service America.

POPENOE, D. (1988). *Disturbing the nest: Family change and decline in modern societies.* New York: Aldine de Gruyter.

Population Reference Bureau. (1992). *The baby boom entering mid-life.* Washington, DC: Author.

PRESTON, S. (1984). "Children and the elderly in the U.S." *Scientific American*, 250 (b), 44–49

PRICE, S. (1990). "Divorce." In the NCFR Presidential Report, *2001: Preparing families for the future* (pp. 30–31). Minneapolis, MN: National Council on Family Relations.

RICHMAN, H., and STAGNER, M. (1986). "Children in an aging society: Treasured resource or forgotten minority?" *Daedalus*, 115, 171–189.

RODGERS, H. (1986). *Poor women, poor families: The economic plight of America's female headed households.* Armonk, NY: M.E. Sharpe.

SCHROEDER, P. (1989). *Champion of the great American family.* New York: Random House.

STARK, L. (1988). *The new homeless: Women, children, and families. An issues forum on the homeless.* New York: The Association of Junior Leagues.

STEINER, G. (1981). *The futility of family policy.* Washington, DC: The Brookings Institution.

STRAUSS, M. (1990). "Family violence." In the NCFR Presidential Report, *2001: Preparing families for the future* (pp. 26–27). Minneapolis, MN: National Council on Family Relations.

"The 21st century family" [Special issue]. (1990). *Newsweek*, winter/spring.

U.S. Bureau of the Census. (1988). "Over 50 percent of mothers with newborns are in the labor force." *Census and You*, 23 (8), 1–2.

U.S. House of Representatives Select Committee on Aging. (1987). *Exploding the myths: Caregiving in America.* Washington, DC: U.S. Government Printing Office.

WATTENBERG, B. (1987, June 22). "The birth dearth: Dangers ahead?" *U.S. News and World Report*, pp. 56–64.

Process of Family Therapy: Political/Administrative Aspects and Stages of Therapy*

Carl A. Whitaker and William M. Bumberry

Family therapy is one method for attempting to resolve some of the problems found in the previous chapters. As in individual therapy, there are many schools of thought and techniques within family therapy. However, one overriding characteristic of this approach is that the therapist deals with the entire family in attempting to resolve a problem. The family is viewed as an interconnected system. For example, from a family therapy perspective, a child's aggressive behavior would be analyzed not simply as an individual problem, but rather as a result of the way in which the family and its patterns of interaction might foster such behavior. As the authors write, "My intent is to identify the family as the patient. I'm not interested in accepting the black sheep they offer, or the white knight they revere . . . It's the family I make my deal with. The family transcends the sum of the parts." This chapter by Carl A. Whitaker and William M. Bumberry describes in an engaging way the physical process and stages of therapy.

The journey of family therapy begins with a blind date and ends with the empty nest. As with any other kind of relationship, it passes through a number of phas-

*Source: Carl A. Whitaker and William M. Bumberry, "Process of Family Therapy," *Dancing with the Family: A Symbolic Experiential Approach* (New York: Brunner/Mazel, 1988), pp. 53–70. Reprinted with permission from Brunner/Mazel, Inc.

es and struggles along the way. While many of the issues are predictable, the outcome is always in doubt. You don't really know if you're going to make it with a new person.

When you answer the telephone and are asked out by a perfect, or not so perfect, stranger, a complicated sequence of sizing up and testing out typically commences. In addition to finding out how your name and number were discovered, you quickly broach the topics of mutual acquaintances, overlapping interests, and specific plans for the date. If this were to follow the old-fashioned scenario, the woman being asked out would rather carefully size up the prospective suitor and his intentions. If his proposal included a late meeting in a secluded place, she might counter with her own suggestion. Perhaps lunch with three of her best friends at the most public place in town would be her offer. He would then be free to take it or leave it. In any event, she would feel that she had acted wisely.

When initially sought out by a family, the therapist is in a similar dilemma. Do you accept without question the proposal they are making? Do you engage in some give and take to be sure the relationship starts off on acceptable terms? It's my conviction that the therapist must always start off by identifying the proposal of the family, then make any counterproposal he deems fit to get the ball rolling. In fact, I think it's typically advisable to make some kind of counterdemand right off the bat. You need to protect yourself from just being coopted by the family. While there's no need to rigidly dictate an impossible series of conditions, you do need to take a clear position. A two-way political process ensues. This initial appointment-setting telephone exchange sets the tone for what is to follow. This initial struggle is called the Battle for Structure.

Battle for Structure

The key point here is for the therapist to face the need to act with personal and professional integrity. You must act on what you believe. Betrayals help no one. The Battle for Structure is really you coming to grips with yourself and then presenting this to them. It's not a technique or a power play. It's a setting of the minimum conditions you require before beginning.

Mom: Hello, Dr. Whitaker? I'm Mrs. Johnson and would like to talk with you regarding some problems I'm having. My family physician, Dr. Jones, gave me your name.

Carl: Sure. Get your husband and we can set up a time.

Mom: Well, that's not what I had in mind. You see he's a very busy man. Besides, he doesn't really believe in talking about problems.

Carl: It looks like we've got a problem. You see I don't work with individuals.

Mom: Well, wouldn't you see me alone just this first time? That way I could explain the full situation to you.

Carl: No, I'm sorry. I couldn't do that.

Mom: But I haven't really told him I was calling you. It might upset him.
Carl: Sorry.
Mom: But Dr. Jones said you could help me. He specifically gave me your
          name. Now you're saying that you won't help me?
Carl: No, I'm not saying that.
Mom: Then you will see me without my husband?
Carl: No . . . but if you bring him along we could meet.
Mom: Well . . . I'll try. But I can't make any promises.
Carl: That's fine. Neither can I. When you get it organized, we can meet. By
          the way, it would also be important to bring the kids in.
Mom: Now that would really be a mistake. They don't know that Jack and I are
          having a hard time. We don't want to expose them to too much.
Carl: I see them as being important in the family too. It's really necessary that
          they be here.
Mom: I couldn't possibly do that.
Carl: Well, I respect your right to make that choice.
Mom: So you'll see us without the kids?
Carl: No, I didn't say that.
Mom: Okay. Okay. What time do you have free?

Having struggled through this opening snag, therapy has a chance to begin
on a productive note. The most poignant discovery I've made in doing this type
of telephone struggle is that the outcome has more to do with me than with
them. They sense how convinced I am about what I'm saying and respond
accordingly.

If you believe you need a certain grouping before it's worth your time or
their energy to begin, you'll get it. It's not a matter of bullying them. It's an issue
of your letting them know what's important to you. Of course, until you know
what you believe, it's hard to be clear. But beware, excessive flexibility pays off
only for contortionists. You can get two generations, three generations, sometimes
four if you ask. Boyfriends, girlfriends, ex-spouses, current lovers, etc. are all
game if you approach it.

I remember one session attended by an attorney and his wife, ex-wife, and
current girlfriend. It was wild listening to the three women comparing notes on
him for two hours. He was glad to get back to the courtroom.

The Battle for Structure is the period of initial political jousting with the family. I need to establish what Bowen [a well-known family therapist] would call
an "I position" in relation to the family. As they begin to hear and absorb the
conditions and limitations I am presenting, their automatic response is to begin
to piece together their own "we position." While it typically takes time to fully
develop, the initiation of this sort of unifying process is one of the core aspects
of working with families. It is a step in the evolution of a sense of family loyalty or nationalism. At some level, all families do have a sense of loyalty waiting
to be called forth. The more clear emergence of their sense of family identification and pride is not something that needs to be created; the seeds are already
there. It needs only the opportunity to take root and grow.

There are at least two levels to attend to in considering these conditions for therapy. One deals with the reality, factual component—who attends the sessions, who is asked to talk first, what the therapist accepts as a definition of the problem, etc. These decisions are always made (even deciding not to decide is a decision) and merit direct attention by the therapist. Your actual decisions may vary from time to time. They certainly would be expected to vary from therapist to therapist. My own thinking concerning these matters has crystallized over time but remains variable to some extent. These variations tend to reflect my own processes at a deeper level. My beliefs and values dictate what is negotiable and what isn't.

In setting these conditions, I want to engage the family in an interactive process that leads to an experiential exchange. In order for the process of therapy to be impactful rather than merely educational or social, it must consist of real experiences, not just head trips. While education may seem useful, it typically leads only to a more sophisticated way of explaining life, not living it.

The other crucial component in this process is the capacity of the therapist to take seriously his own needs. Becoming a professional martyr by sacrificing yourself to the family is hardly an appropriate model. Giving up or compromising your own beliefs, standards, and needs leads only to therapist burnout. I'm convinced burnout is a side effect of our own failed integrity struggle, not a function of our struggle with them. Your decision to try to turn into what you think they want is your fault.

My standard comment to families of "I'm not really here for you. I'm here for what I can get out of it" is one way of saying I'm not really for hire as a professional prostitute. It lets them know that I will remain the center of my own living. That they need not worry about protecting me. Again, real caring requires distance (caring for self) and the capacity to get personally involved. Unless the core impetus for you is your growth, it degenerates into "helping." Once this occurs all is lost. They become inept and you impotent.

This remark also reflects my belief that if I can get something personal out of my contact with the family, the experience between us will be alive. The aliveness of the experience then also affords them the opportunity to grow. I want to create the conditions where growth is possible, but fully accept that I can't force or orchestrate it.

Joining

The idea of joining is important to consider here. Joining is the process of developing enough of a connection to at least feel that continuing on is worth pursuing. While we often think of it as something the therapist does to a family, I've come to see it as something we do with a family. That is, we engage in some kind of an experience with each other.

The quality of that experience comes from a number of factors. Part of it is the undercurrent sense of how willing we are to get involved with each other. Does the family sense that we have the capacity or even want to get to know them and understand them? Can we really listen? Can we respond in a real, rather than phoney way? Do we sense they are people we're willing to invest in? The personal criteria are endless.

Another factor is the automatic joining that emerges out of a common background, similar experiences, or shared perspectives. This kind of shared essence connotes an increased capacity for empathy. We're not as dependent on mere words to convey the depth of our experience. Of course, this level of connection also carries the built-in dilemma of blind spots and overidentification. I "know" what he means when a farm father talks about being an isolate, or loving the cows. Unfortunately, I may have no sense that there's anything problematic about it. But at least I can get in there.

With this sort of too familiar family, I must also work to discover ways to step away from them and gain some distance. I might play with toys in an absent-minded fashion, take pages of notes to be visually distracted, or work with a cotherapist so I have a "we" to belong to.

Establish a Metaposition

In beginning, my effort is to establish a metaposition in relation to the family. I want them to understand more of what they can expect from me and what I expect from them. This is not designed as a relationship between peers. I want it understood that in my role as a therapist I'm a member of an older generation.

The metaphor of a coach of a baseball team is a good way of describing what the relationship will be. As the coach, I'm really not interested in playing on the team, only in helping them play more effectively. If I allow myself to be seduced into playing first base for them, it will be difficult to return to the metaposition of a coach. They will rightfully expect me to actually make the plays for them.

The more destructive message it gives, however, is that I don't think much of the first baseman they already have. It's a way of saying to them that my way of living is better than theirs. It's a tricky way of trying to convince them to give up on developing their own resources and to buy my brand instead. That kind of sabotage they can do without.

Convening the Clan

One of my ways of concretizing this issue is to try to convene the full clan before starting. Just as it would be foolish for a coach to begin the game without fielding a full team, there is considerable risk in commencing therapy without all the key characters present. The missing members may feel discounted in that they are not considered vital to the overall family functioning. They also typically develop a justifiable sense of paranoia regarding what was said in their absence. When either of these reactions is pronounced, the seeds of sabotage take root. I want the permission of the entire unit to get involved. A concerted effort by any absent family member to undermine the capacity of the family to change typically succeeds.

This guideline of convening the clan represents an effort to create a sense of the family as a unit and to validate the value of each individual member. It also serves to avoid a powerful source of sabotage and forces them to capitulate to my belief that the whole family is the patient. Finally, it minimizes the likelihood that I will be drawn into a position of destructive overinvolvement.

A side effect of this decision is that with the full family present, there is a clear escalation in their level of anxiety. With everyone there, there is no one to talk about behind the back, no one to blame without interpersonal repercussions, and no way to deny what was discussed. This type of anxiety typically makes change more possible.

It seems particularly dangerous to decide to hold the session when the wife-mother or husband-father is absent. For example, meeting without the husband-father is a clear way of auditioning for the part. You're meeting with people already involved in relationships. Therefore, involving yourself in the wife-husband dyad by standing in for him automatically creates a triangle. The kids, too, may see you as a preferable father. This is a strange position for someone interested in being useful to a family, unless of course you're unhappy with your own.

The theoretical notion of an emergent property also enters here. The notion of an emergent property states that you can't really get a sense of an organism by dissecting and examining the component parts. While you can generate ideas and develop hypotheses about the full family based on contact with part of it, the error or distortion factor is unnecessarily elevated. By definition, the level of inference involved is escalated. It brings to mind the story of the three blind men who tried to describe an elephant based on touching only one of the parts. The different perspectives provided by the trunk, ear, and leg are profound. So it is with families.

Perhaps the most disastrous effect of this, though, is what happens to the family. Meeting with less than the full group deprives them of the opportunity for the optimal therapeutic experience. Rather than unifying the family, triangles, alliances, and coalitions are formed.

Beginning with Dad

Early in the initial session there are some additional avenues I pursue. It's my normal style to really commence the interview by asking the father to tell me how the family really works. This follows directly from my belief that men are much less emotionally involved and available than are women. If dad can be prodded to come alive emotionally and become a real human being, it may offer unexpected hope to the entire family. Rather than allowing dad to act like he's the guy who lives next door, I want him to move in.

Carl: So, dad, could you tell me something about the family?

Dad: Sure. We decided to call you because of a problem we're having with our daughter. She's been skipping too much school and it just has to stop.
Carl: That's what your wife said over the phone. She told me a little about that.
        Right now I'm more interested in hearing something about the family and how it operates.
Dad: I'm not sure what you mean.
Carl: If I had asked you to tell me about the Green Bay Packers football team, you'd know what to say. You know, who produces, who doesn't. How well the quarterback and receivers work together. Who is the spiritual/emotional leader.
        I assume you know more about your family than about the Packers.
Dad: I'm still not sure what you want to hear.
Carl: Well, maybe you could start with something about you. You know, what your concerns are. The things you lie awake worrying about at night. What your most personal fears are. Anything that would get us started.

This way of beginning is really more complicated than merely focusing first on dad. It's really about pulling in and engaging the emotional outsiders. By getting them involved, the configuration changes. New potentials are opened. It's standard for me to leave mom and any identified patients for the end. I want to talk with all of the other family members before turning to them.

Expand the Symptoms

The preceding vignette also touches on another early maneuver. Families typically come to therapy with one particular family member manifesting a symptom that has the family concerned. My perspective is that this really should be viewed as a ticket for entry. Never believe the story that this is the only, or even the most significant, issue in the family. My goal is to as quickly as possible expand the picture of what the problems are and why they're here.

It's like beginning a game of poker. It's important for everyone to ante up. Some families do this with relative ease, while others are thoroughly resistant to the very notion. The resistive families are actually more frightened than resistant and it is often stimulating to challenge them in this regard.

Recently, a family of three—mother, father and six-year-old daughter—attended an initial session. The daughter was considered school phobic. Mother was quite obese and father was obviously a hard-driving, type A career man. My initial efforts to expand the family symptom beyond Sarah's school fears were unsuccessful. Dad played dumb, refusing to address any personal concerns and denying any relationship struggles. Mom came to his aid when I pressed about his overdedication to his career. She commented on how proud she was of her husband and his career success. In only a few years he had risen to a powerful position within a respected firm. Even though he worked nearly 75 hours a week and was frequently out late, she had accepted this as the price of success. She closed her statement by adding that her husband was the kind of man who really needed to be immersed in a fast-paced, exciting business world. The following exchange then followed.

Carl: You mean he's totally lost interest in you?
Mom: Well, no, it's not that. It's just that his way of contributing to the family is to make sure that we have everything we need.
Carl: Except a husband and father you mean.
Mom: No. He's a good father.
Carl: (*turning to the daughter*) Sarah, do you think that mommy worries that daddy might be kissing his secretary?
          You know he's gone at work so much. Maybe he gets lonely too.
Sar: No. Daddies don't get lonely. Just mommies, but since mommy has me, she doesn't have to be lonely either.
Carl: Well, I'm sure glad you take such good care of your mommy but I still worry about daddies. It's very hard to tell when they're lonely.

Having laid the groundwork for them to begin to wonder about their relationship, while not pushing for an overt exploration at that moment, I continued the session in a different direction. They naturally returned to the issue of Sarah's refusal to go to school. We danced around the obvious issue of her dedication to mom and her desire to help mom hide from her sense of depression.

Later in the same session, I wanted mom to have the opportunity to really take a look at herself. She was complaining of her inability to play tennis with her high-powered husband because of her weight.

Carl: (*turning to dad*) Do you worry about her weight, too, or do you prefer playing with other partners?
Dad: Of course I'd love to have her pick up the sport, but it's just not possible. It would be dangerous for her to exert herself with so much excess weight.
Carl: So you don't want to feel like you killed her by pushing tennis. I suppose I can understand that.
          How is it that you manage to live with the knowledge that she's slowly committing suicide via her obesity?

The symptom framework has now been expanded. Extramarital affairs, self-destructive overeating, and a relationship gap have been set forth. While they may not really agree with some of these formulations, they leave the session with more to consider. It's not really necessary that they agree. My job was to complicate their initial oversimplification that distorted the family reality.

In addition to merely broadening the symptom constellation, I also strive to change their perspective to an interpersonal viewpoint. When Sarah's school refusal is attached to a protective function with her mother, the picture shifts. It begins to focus on a family issue, not on individual quirks or pathology. By involving dad in mom's overeating, I make this a relationship function, not an indication of lack of willpower.

Another aspect of this work centers on the capacity of the therapist to be "mean." In this context, "meanness" represents both a willingness to be honest in my reaction to them and a refusal to sell out by being artificially nurturing. It's my responsibility to help them take a more courageous look at themselves. Covering up concerns and ignoring problem areas are of no value to anyone. They can get that at home.

In striving to be as honest as I can, my goal is to trigger a real interaction that is not restricted to mere social role-playing. I want it to be more personal. When viewed from this perspective, the more traditional posture of automatic caring can be seen only as being painfully superficial. In order for caring to be real, it must be embedded in a context that is honest. In a backwards kind of way, my "meanness" is a representation of my capacity to care.

By this time the family has been exposed to some of my way of thinking. Another phase of therapy comes to the front. This is called the Battle for Initiative. In this phase, the issue is to push the family to be more proactive. They need to assume more responsibility for what transpires in the therapy.

Battle for Initiative

When you have successfully struggled through the Battle for Structure by establishing your metaposition and conditions for therapy, the process shifts. Now that the family has, in a sense, capitulated to your demands, the risk is that they'll go flat and leave the ball in your court. The next phase, then, is to get them to take responsibility for what happens in therapy. The undercurrent feeling is sometimes, "Okay, Whitaker, you've made us play your way. If you think you're so hot, you fix us." This is dangerous territory. Some may find it appealing to their narcissism, I find it scary and absurd.

It's not unusual for the second interview to begin something like this.

Dad: Well, what should we talk about?
Carl: I'm not really sure.
Dad: Do you have any more questions to ask us? Do you need to know any more information?
Carl: No. No thanks. I feel comfortable like this.
         (*silence*)
Mom: Do you think we should continue where we left off last time, or would you prefer that we move to a new topic?
Carl: It's fine with me either way.
         (*silence*)
Dad: Well, I for one would like a little direction. After all, we're paying you for your expertise, not just to sit there.

Carl: I'm not really interested in telling you what's important for you to talk
          about. You know yourself better than I do.

          My expertise tells me that what I think isn't very important right
          now. What you choose to do with each other is what's crucial.

Dad: What value are you to us then? Why do we need you?

Carl: I'm not sure that you do. I'm here to try to augment your effort to be
          more alive with each other.

          It would be flat-out stupid of me to try to tell you how to live. My
          patterns of living are no more valid than yours. You need to get the game
          started.

At this point in the therapy, the struggle is to get them to take over. To
have the courage to take the initiative to face themselves and not look to the
therapist to do it for them. You need to disrupt the fantasy that you'll make it
all better.

It's often a period accented by tension and anxious silences. I look at it as
the water heating up in the coffeepot before it can percolate. It's not a matter of
the therapist being a nobody. It's an issue of the family becoming a somebody.
They need to grapple with each other. It's an invitation to them to come alive
and stop play-acting.

The issue of their looking to me for a solution, much like the idea that if
someone gave you the "magic words" you'd have it made, can be damaging to
the family. When they consciously place the possibility of change directly in my
hands, they're undermining themselves. I want them to face the reality that
they're the real players, but I offer the comfort that I'm a competent coach.

It's imperative that this learning come about via some sort of experiential
exchange, not via detached teaching. Another way I try to impart this idea is to
never initiate talk about having another session. They need to broach that topic.
They need to jointly decide if they're going to return. If they don't address it,
neither do I. I often push it the other way by refusing to set another appoint-
ment until they go home and talk about it.

Therapeutic Alliance

The successful completion of the Battle for Structure and the Battle for Initiative
forms what I think of as a therapeutic alliance. Only when we've established the
nature of our relationship and they've taken the reins are we ready to go forward. We're now a functional suprasystem.

The whole idea of forming a therapeutic alliance with a family is tricky. My
intent is to identify the family as the patient. I'm not interested in accepting the
black sheep they offer, or the white knight they revere (Be careful! The white
knight is every bit as vulnerable as the black sheep), or even a subsystem as a

valid patient. I'm not even willing to accept them all as patients in serial order. It's the family I make my deal with. The family transcends the sum of the parts.

It's my capacity to always see them as one multifaceted organism, massively interconnected, that permits my alliance with them. While it may not be detectable to an observer, it's been my experience that the family can sense that I'm interested in them as a unit.

This evolves into a phase where the politics become less central. Our connection takes on more of a personal quality. As we're released from this struggle, there is more freedom to be spontaneous and creative. I'm able to access more and more of my internal associations and images. I'm free to be responsive *to* them rather than responsible *for* them. Typically, the family is more accepting of my moves to get more personal, as well as my decisions to separate or move out. I can individuate and belong without too much distortion. They're clearly less dependent and have a better sense of themselves. Our increasing comfort with individuating and joining reflects real growth and marks a more adaptive, healthy system.

It's during this period that the family begins to make some changes. They move forward and are able to risk more without the shield of their presenting problem. Each step they take is important and I want to make sure they realize they did the changing, not me. I try to encourage their movement without directing it.

We might compare experiences, share dreams, etc. My associations become more vivid. For example, when talking with a family about the way dad's anger immediately made everyone go flat, an image popped into my head. "You know, I just had the craziest idea. Do you ever have them, too? The image was that of a giant-sized Cuisinart-type thing labeled 'people grinder.' I assume its function was to do to dad what his anger just did to all of you. Are you planning to get one?"

This led to a much more direct discussion of their fear of dad. Eventually, it wound around to dad not liking the ogre role, but not knowing how to be anything else.

Termination

As the family growth continues, they use more and more of their own resources. They develop the confidence to reject my thinking and begin to more deeply trust their own. They see me as more and more human, with frailties now included. They are free to tease me regarding mistakes or stupid ideas. In effect, they begin to see me as a person, not just a role. They become their own therapist. They assume responsibility for their own living.

Regardless of my sense of impending loss, it's my job to send them off with my blessings. Much like any parent feels when the children leave for college, I experience a sense of loss. But I give them my blessing and they're free to return any time they choose. They don't leave empty-handed though. The impact of the shared therapy experience is interwoven into their life tapestry.

The decision to leave must remain theirs. It's their life. If things have gone well, they leave with more lovingness and more freedom to be real people.

As I sense this phase approaching, I even listen for hints or clues that suggest their readiness to leave. When I detect them, I make them overt. The decision to terminate must be handled with care. It is countertherapeutic to try to interfere with their decision to leave. You must respect their process.

Empty Nest

The new coffee mug that reads, "Life's a bitch. Then you die," sometimes seems appropriate. When the family goes off, there is a sense of loss. We've invested in each other and now experience the pain of separation. While there is often a joyful side, the loss is real.

Since this is such a common part of the life of a therapist, some precautions are in order. Having a professional cuddle group is the best way to ease the pain. When you belong to a group, you're never really alone. It's best to not insist that your family take care of all of these needs. The capacity to separate your professional role from your real life living is essential.

Additional Issues

Establishing the Menu

One of the really exciting aspects of an initial session is that since it's a blind date, no one really knows each other. This allows you to poke and probe around without the sense of it being premeditated. I typically make it a point to venture into a wide range of difficult topics during that first meeting. It's a magic moment of sorts. Families can handle probes about almost anything without clamming up. When you establish these issues as being relevant to living, there is a tacit agreement that we can return to them later. The topics of murderousness, suicidal impulses, sexual impulses, etc. all merit mention. When these primitive issues are established as being normal, they become less toxic.

If you fail to do this early on, you will later encounter more denial and defensiveness. When you ask about mom's homicidal impulses in the tenth session, she suspects you're asking because of something you see in her, not just because you know that all people have such impulses.

Dealing with Impasses

Impasses are inevitable! Periods where you feel stuck and don't know which way to turn are just part of the process.

My favorite way to break through this kind of place is to invite a consultant into the next session. This gives me someone to be united with. It offers binocular vision and gives me space to see things differently. In addition to helping me, a consultant helps the family by ruining their magical fantasy that only I could help them. As they now more clearly see some of my self-doubt, they face the issue of the need to change.

The fresh viewpoint of a consultant often breaks logjams and helps pull the therapist out of a coopted position. Sometimes a real shake-up is in order.

A Father's Rage*

Salvador Minuchin and Michael P. Nichols

In this chapter by Salvador Minuchin and Michael P. Nichols, the method of family therapy is used to address the problem of violence within a specific family (which we saw detailed in the earlier Gelles and Straus reading). This fascinating case study takes us through the process and insights of using a family therapy perspective. The specific act of a father's violence against his son becomes better understood and consequently addressed through an awareness of the underlying family dynamics. For Minuchin and Nichols, it is within the structure of the family that the answers and solutions to a father's violence are found.

I want to tell you a story about a man who hit—and did not want to hit—his children. Reports of family violence call up a certain stereotype: urban poverty, unemployment, drunkenness, brutish men. But it doesn't always happen that way.

Violence is an ugly form of power in the face of which we all feel threatened. The violent person is seen as powerful and menacing. In fact there are

---

two forms of violence. Violence to achieve a goal might be called "coercive violence." But there is another form of violence, "pleading violence," in which the victimizer perceives himself or herself as a victim. In families where there is child abuse or spouse battering, violent men—and sometimes women—often experience themselves as helpless responders to the other person's baiting.

In these circumstances the desperate and uncontrolled attacker pleads for understanding of his or her impossible plight. Regardless of our emotional response to such a distortion of the facts, punitive control of this kind of violent person may only increase the feeling of victimization—and the likelihood of further violence.

The Farrells were an ordinary middle-class family from Vermont. Carter Farrell was in his early forties. After graduating from college and working in Philadelphia as a probation officer for a few years, he returned to his native Vermont to work as a hunting and fishing guide. For $200 a day he would take tired men with jangled nerves from the city into the woods and streams of Vermont to do what he never tired of doing. However, guiding is a chancy occupation. Only the most popular guides make a living at it. Carter lacked the easy, affable manner that might endear him to people who crave conversation as part of the package to restore their spirits. But his great skill at fly-fishing the Battenkill and Mettawee rivers, and his unfailing ability to locate deer in the fall and wild turkeys in the spring, made him highly sought after by serious sportsmen and -women.

At the time I met the family, Carter had retired from guiding and taken a job as a commissioner in the Vermont Department of Fish and Wildlife.

Carter's wife, Peggy, was an elementary school teacher whose experience and good sense made her a perennial choice every time a principal's job opened up in her district. Her answer was always the same: "I'm a teacher, not an administrator." And so, once every five years or so, she avoided the mistake that a lot of people make of trading in a job they love for one with a fancier title.

Peggy and Carter had three children, a girl of 18, a boy of 16, and another girl who was 11. Robin was a senior in high school, Keith was a sophomore, and Tippi was in the sixth grade. They were nice kids, but Carter and Peggy had problems with them.

The Farrell family was referred to me by their therapist, Kate Kennedy, for a consultation. They'd come to her a couple of months previously for discipline problems and then gotten bogged down. Kate, a former student of mine, felt that a consultation would be helpful and convinced the Farrells to come to New York over a weekend.

The Farrell family filed into the room and filled it up. The father, tall and intense, led the rest and sat in the corner chair, farthest from me. He wore blue slacks, a red polo shirt, and a long mustache. Next came his wife, a small, attractive woman with a round face, who sat next to her husband. Her skin was fair and she wore her reddish blond hair cut short. A muted peach-colored blouse set off her gentle features, and contrasted with her husband's strong colors. She was followed by the children, who sat in a row next to their mother. The two teenagers sat at the end, as far away from their father as possible.

I began by asking the parents, "Maybe you can tell me why you've been seeing Kate Kennedy for—how long is it—two, three months?"

"It must be about two months, I think," Mrs. Farrell said. Her voice was mild, not weak but restrained. She was a pretty woman, soft, subdued, and in control.

"Robin and Keith were having trouble," Carter explained. His voice was more forceful than his wife's. "Problems at school and problems at home, getting along."

He was a lean, hard-muscled man with reddish brown hair. In profile his sharp nose and intense look reminded me of a hawk.

"We were having problems with discipline," he said, summing up the situation as he saw it.

"When you say 'we,' you mean both of you?"

"Yes." He nodded.

"With whom, these two?" I asked, pointing to Robin and Keith, the 18- and the 16-year-old.

"With all of them, really," he said. "But primarily these two. Discipline is the main problem—or lack of it, really." He was a stern fellow, patriarchal rather than paternal, and a great believer in rules and regulations. He glanced at his wife and sighed. "We never have devised a good disciplinary program. We just sort of handled it on an ad hoc basis. For any particular situation that arose, why, we did *something*."

Something about this couple's blend of formality and amiability made me want to cut to the point. "Who is the sheriff in the family?"

Carter and Peggy looked at each other in bemused silence. Most parents like to pretend that they share the power, even if that's blatantly untrue. Then Carter said, "I suppose I am."

He got no argument from his wife. And so I asked her, "And are you a deputy sheriff, or are you the attorney for the defense?"

She smiled a small, rueful smile. "Probably—history has been—attorney for the defense." Her husband shifted slightly in his chair. She sat very still.

"And are you a competent or an incompetent sheriff?"

"If I were competent, we wouldn't be here," he said, shrugging slightly.

"So the family has an incompetent sheriff, and a—competent or incompetent attorney for the defense?"

"Unfortunately, I suppose, a very competent attorney for the defense," she said.

"Wow, you *are* in trouble," I said. "This is the worst arrangement that exists."

They laughed and exchanged embarrassed smiles.

They were polite and friendly, but they were approaching me with caution. I knew their problems were serious. Kate told me that the father had fits of rage and sometimes got violent. But they were playing it slow, well-mannered and well-controlled.

I had tried to cut through the formality with a whimsical metaphor, and they had admitted something that would have been very hard to say in plain English.

Then I turned to Robin and Keith. Robin was small and pretty like her mother. She wore a denim jacket over a blue shirt. Her brother was tall and bony, like his father. He had his mother's reddish blond hair, only his was long and parted in the middle. He wore a dark-blue nylon windbreaker over an old white T-shirt. He had the big hands of a man but still looked almost feminine, in that androgynous way of some teenage boys.

"Is mother always on father's back, trying to protect you?" I asked them.

Robin said, "Yes." Her brother nodded.

"That means you must not be learning how to deal with your father—because she's doing your job."

"Well—" Robin began.

Her mother broke in. "That's what I've tried to tell you. If you have a problem with your father, instead of coming to me about it, talk to daddy."

"I see that it is like that," I said. "Because just now mother became your translator."

Robin nodded. She looked young for her age, but she was quick and perceptive.

"So she's helpful like that."

"Well, she only does it with daddy," Robin said. "But that's because—"

"No," I said. "She just did it with me."

"Oh," Robin responded.

"I was talking to you, and she interpreted me to you. Does it bother you, my accent?"

"No." She smiled. "I think it's nice."

"Do you need help to translate?"

"No," she said, still smiling.

I smiled, too, and then turned to Peggy. "Mother, relax."

"I apologize," she said and laughed, seeming not to take offense.

I like it when something like this happens to me in a session, this first immersion in the family's way of being. Mother just told me that I had broken a family rule: I contacted the children without going through her. Perhaps in families where there is a violent man, a strange man has to be checked out before he is admitted. So mother was the gatekeeper. Where was father?

Now I moved to explore the father's isolation, proceeding on the assumption that the counterpart of a mother's overinvolvement would be the father's underinvolvement—that enmeshment and disengagement were part of a mutually reinforcing pattern. If I was wrong, they would correct me.

"So," I said, going back to Robin, "Mother does a good job of protecting you. What kind of trouble do you get into?"

"Well, daddy and I don't get along, and that causes a lot of trouble." She spoke with a strong New England accent, and with the certainty of one who has thought about this. "My father and I don't have any communication at all. Except for like 'Please pass the salt' or something—but we can't talk about anything serious. And we usually don't agree on things."

"Like what?"

"Like anything."

"Like Russia? China?"

She gave me a small, twisted smile, the kind teenagers reserve for adults who ask them to explain themselves. "No, when I say serious things, I mean things that concern me. My problems. Like schoolwork, or with my boyfriend, or *anything*."

"What kind of brute is your father?" I asked, responding to this very polite family with blunt language. I was challenged by the disparity between the image of violence that Kate had described and the pleasant, polite family I was seeing.

The father sat forward, listening carefully to what the daughter he loved but didn't know how to talk to would say.

"Brute?" she said. She sighed. This wasn't easy.

"Is he a primitive kind of person?"

"No, it's not that. He's just real—he's kind of closed up around people. For a long time I don't think he liked to be that involved with us. He's not a bad person. That's just what happened."

"He just doesn't understand people?"

"No, I think he might be scared of people—not physically, but just—I feel like he puts up this barrier for people—well, because they're new, or he just might not be interested in them."

"I see," I said. "Keith, how do you see it?"

"Huh? I'm not sure exactly what you're talking about." Keith was less articulate than his sister and clearly uncomfortable with this conversation about feelings. So I tried to make it easier for him. "Are you having trouble with your father?"

As I spoke to his son, Carter leaned back and rested his elbow on the back of his chair.

"Well, yeah, because we're just two different people," Keith said, as though stating a regrettable but, after all, inevitable fact. "And usually teenagers and fathers just don't get along."

"That's not true," I said. "There are teenagers who *do* get along with their fathers. You are saying *you* don't get along with your father."

Keith nodded.

"And what about your mother? Do you get along with her?"

"Well, yeah," he said, as though it were a strange thing even to ask.

"Why? I thought teenagers didn't get along with their mothers."

"Oh, no," he said. "I can talk to her."

"Can you talk with your mom about things like girlfriends?"

"Sure. I can talk to her about anything."

"Why? That surprises me. When I was your age I talked with my father about these things. Because he had been an adolescent before me, and my mother had never been an adolescent male."

I was beginning to challenge the mother's centrality, but I was doing it with the logic of simple-minded truisms. The logic of my statement was unassailable, making the challenge to the mother invisible.

Then I turned back to Keith's mother. "So how is it you have this insight into young men growing up?"

"I don't know that I have an insight," she said evenly, defending herself against my insinuation. "But I like to let the children know that they can tell me how they feel and that I'll listen, and care, and understand."

Very quickly the father had been identified as the problem in this family. His children couldn't talk to him, and his wife took up the slack. The logic of my questions was to track the father's isolation and the family's anger at him. The logic of my emotions made me protective of the father, the underdog. It's almost a reflex. When one member of the family is an outsider, I gravitate toward that person, hoping to bring him or her back inside the family circle.

"Tippi," I said, turning to the 11-year-old, "Robin said she's been having a lot of trouble. Keith there has difficulty in talking with your father. What about you?"

For the last few minutes she'd been leaning forward on her elbow, looking down, her mind elsewhere. Now she looked up abruptly, surprised and pleased to be asked her opinion.

"Well, I don't have any difficulty talking to either of them." Her accent was even heavier than her brother's and sister's. "But I don't really talk to him," she said, gesturing toward her father, "about things like boyfriends and stuff. I don't guess there's any reason," she said and shrugged.

"And do you talk with your mom?"

"Mm-hmm," she answered. Her expression said, "Why on earth not?"

"Carter, how is it that you manage to talk with Tippi? Apparently she's the only one who feels you can understand her. How did you manage that? How did you succeed in that?"

"Because I realized, when she was still young, that to have a good relationship it needed to start early." He spoke slowly and deliberately, a man measuring his words and controlling his feelings. "So I spent quite a bit of time with Tippi even when she was still a baby."

If he'd known how to ask his older children for their love, if he'd let them know he was open to them, they might have met him more than halfway. But he was too proud or shy to send them any signal they could recognize, and so it never happened.

Something about Carter touched me. He was a gentle man, humble, reticent but longing for contact. He was clearly troubled by his relationship with his children, but he presented himself as calm and unconcerned, friendly but unemotional. One of the themes of Argentinean tangos is that a man with machismo doesn't cry and certainly doesn't let others see him if he does. They must have similar tangos in Vermont.

"Carter, I have a wild guess. I have a feeling that Peggy runs interference between you and the kids. Is that the way it is?"

"That is true . . ." he said hesitantly. "I'm not sure exactly how you mean that. She has been the interceder—the go-between. I don't think that she intended to keep me from the kids, or vice versa. I think that was her idea of how best to handle the fact that I didn't relate all that well to the kids."

I was surprised that he defended his wife. But Carter was an honorable man. He still believed in chivalry. I was concerned that unless I could free this man, he would go the way of the hero of *Billy Budd*, Melville's tragic tale of decency blinded by principle and tongue-tied frustration that turned to violence.

I said, smiling, "They are your children?"

"As far as I know." He smiled back.

"In any case you raised all of them?"

"Well, I raised Tippi; she raised the other two."

"So they are *her* children." Then I returned to Robin, who seemed so perceptive and so honest. "So you have a one-parent family?"

"No, we belong to daddy. It's just that we don't have as close a relationship with him as we do with momma."

"How did that happen, Peggy?"

"I'm sorry?"

"How did that happen? You have three kids, and in my book three kids are a handful, and they usually need two parents. How did it happen that these two have only one parent?"

"Well, that question is not easy to answer." She spoke slowly, under control, like a professional helping person, anxious that I get it right. "One reason is that when Carter and I were young and first beginning to raise a family, we had very different ideas and feelings about how to deal with the children. And rather than working out our differences, I think I took it upon myself to decide how to deal with the children, and to do what I knew was right."

I felt stymied, because I knew that logic can't change a story the family knows to be true. But then absurdity came to my rescue.

"When did you divorce Carter?"

"Pardon?"

"When did you divorce your husband?"

This time she knew what I meant, and was silent.

My question was like a Gypsy fortune-teller's: intuition cloaked in ambiguity. She could have responded any way she wanted. She might have said, "I don't understand." She might have said, "That's crazy."

After a very long minute, she said softly, "About ten years ago."

Again there was silence.

Then Carter turned to face his wife and said, "Longer ago than that."

They looked at each other without saying anything. Then Peggy lowered her eyes.

"Whom did you marry, Peggy, the kids?"

She didn't answer right away. Finally she said, "I don't know. I think I'm still single."

A strange answer. Her fantasy, maybe. She was in fact very much a mother, very involved with her children. But underneath she felt lonely, deprived, and unappreciated. She was alone.

"What happened to you, Carter?"

"With respect to what?"

"With respect to Peggy."

"I don't understand the question," he said in a voice edged with hostility. The more I probed, the more he resisted. Maybe he was afraid to go where he felt me pushing him, or maybe he just wouldn't be pushed.

The Farrells came to therapy for their children. Now, 15 minutes into the session, we were deep into the emptiness between the spouses. Carter was ready to explore his inappropriate disciplining of the children, his out-of-control temper, his violence, maybe even his loneliness. But there were limits. A man doesn't open his bedroom door for the perusal of strangers.

"Well, the question is simple: She divorced you ten years ago—what happened to you? When did you decide you would not invest energy in changing Peggy—in trying to help her understand you?"

"That question is based on a much too simplistic idea of what the relationship was at the time."

"I don't know. Tell me."

"Because, I think, the basic problem arose from my concept of a father's proper role in the family." He spoke with slow, deliberate control. "It had always been my feeling that when the kids got old enough, we would start doing things together—the kids and I. I would become actively involved with them."

This is a common assumption of fathers, though not always stated so openly. Man is the provider, woman the nurturer. Carter thought fatherhood began when the children were old enough to behave and to join him in his activities.

"That means you lent her the kids when they were young, and when they were older you were going to take it over?"

"No, not take it over so much as become part of it. Because up until whatever age this was going to occur, my role as a father was to work and pay the bills—"

"And to let her do the parenting."

"Right. As far as raising the kids and worrying about doctor appointments and nighttime feedings and spankings, and that sort of thing . . ."

"It was her job," I said. Then I asked Peggy, "And you accepted that?"

She furrowed her brow. "I suppose I did for a period of time."

"So you were really a one-parent family. Mother took care of everything. Peggy, why did you accept such a strange arrangement?"

"I didn't know any better," she said with feeling.

"You didn't know how to say, 'Carter, I need you'? It's four words."

She didn't answer.

"He had one function and you had another one?"

Carter nodded. Peggy didn't. "Until Tippi was about three or four years old and I started working, and then I had many functions."

"Did you ever ask Carter for help?"

"Yes," she said softly, and chose not to elaborate. She did not, it seemed, want to criticize him too openly. Not here. Not now. They were alike in that respect.

"And does he help?"

"As we've gotten older he's become more helpful." This was not a ringing endorsement.

"Do you think they need him?"

"Yes, desperately."

"What will you do to give space so that this very tall fellow begins to be able to talk with his dad?"

One of the reasons parenting remains an amateur sport is that as soon as you get the hang of it the children get a little older and throw you a whole new set of problems. In the early years of their marriage, Carter and Peggy's rigid version of the traditional family worked, sort of. But when the children got older and he tried to become involved, there was no room for him.

"Are you very angry at each other?"

Carter said, "No."

"You're not angry with her?" It was hard to believe, but I knew by now it was true. The house rule was: No open acknowledgement of marital conflict.

"No," he said, trying to keep the anger he felt now at me out of his voice.

"I understand that you had been kind of angry at the kids?"

"Yes," he said, and his jaw tensed visibly.

"At whom were you angry—Keith?"

"On occasion, yes. And Robin. And Tippi."

"What Kate Kennedy told me was that you hit Keith—or you hit all of them."

"I hit them, yes."

Slapping the children was part of his idea of acceptable discipline. This was not uncontrolled violence; it was "instrumental." He slapped them to achieve a purpose. But he had also hit them when out of control. He had done wrong and he knew it, and he hated me for bringing it all up again.

"And when you hit Keith, was it Keith alone that you hit?"

When a child's misbehavior infuriates a parent, the real anger is often at the other parent—especially when the two are in conflict over how to deal with the children. My question was an invitation to expand the view of the problem, to explore Carter's response to the children in the context of their being Peggy's children.

He looked puzzled, and so I repeated the question. "Did you hit Keith alone?"

"Yes," he said, meeting my eyes.

"You're certain you weren't really hitting Peggy at the same time?"

"No, I hit myself." Carter was an intelligent man, proud and guilt-ridden, bound by rigid values. He saw himself as at fault and was willing to pay; he wasn't about to blame Peggy for his mistakes, or to let me do so.

"That, I know. What I don't know—"

"No, I did not hit Peggy."

"When you hit Robin, did you hit her alone or did you hit Peggy at the same time?"

"No," he said. "*I did not hit Peggy.*"

He understood, but I wanted to make sure everyone else did. So I asked Keith. "Do you understand what I asked your father?"

"Did it have any effect on momma?"

"Yes. I asked if he was angry at your mom and he hit you instead. Because whenever he deals with you, he deals with mom as well, since you are her children. What do you think?"

"Well," Keith said, "they're adults, and usually whenever they're mad at each other it seems to me they can talk it over."

Keith's parents didn't go around yelling at each other, and so, he assumed, they must be reasonable. This was the myth his parents had taught him. Once you know the family folklore, you don't need to ask questions. But knowing the dangerous extremes the father could reach, I couldn't leave this story unchallenged.

"Carter, I understand that you left home because you were feeling too angry. You left the family for a few weeks?"

"No," he said, "I didn't leave because I was too angry. At the time I left I wasn't angry, but I realized that the frustration caused by my not knowing how to properly discipline the children had gotten out of hand, easily to the point where I would hit them."

"Which incident is clearest in your mind?"

"The clearest incident," Carter began, "is an incident that happened with Keith." Going back to this wasn't easy.

"With Keith? Okay. So why don't you three," I waved my arm to indicate Keith and his parents, "talk a little bit about this incident."

"First of all," Peggy said, "I was not around when it began. I came in when I was called onto the scene." Nobody, it seemed, wanted to bring back that awful moment.

"Okay," I said, trying to sound reassuring, "maybe the three of you can piece it together."

"Which incident is he talking about?" Keith wanted to know.

How many incidents had there been? Could they be separated, or were they really one long incident with interruptions, like a string of sausages?

It was his mother who answered. "When daddy came upstairs with some cigarettes that he said you had gotten into."

No one else was ready to speak.

Then his mother said slowly, "As I was told about the situation by you and other people—Robin and daddy—you were very surprised when he came upstairs with the cigarettes in his hand and pushed them in your face, because you didn't know what he was angry about, or what was going on."

Now Keith remembered. "Well, all I know is Robin and me were talking, and it was at night and it was right before I needed to go to bed. We were talking. And daddy comes storming upstairs and took out a bunch of cigarettes, and me and Robin just looked at each other, real puzzled. And he started smearing 'em all over my face and he grabbed me by the neck and he pushed me up against the wall and he was yelling all kinds of stuff. But I couldn't understand it—I was just about in a state of shock. And I didn't know what in the world was going on. He was choking me, and I couldn't breathe at all—well, hardly. And Robin was crying over there, and I can remember momma coming. But I really didn't know what in the world was going on. It was a weird incident."

Recalling the attack, Keith showed neither anger nor fear, only bewilderment. It was as if his father were more alien than brutal, a man whose ideas and moods were unrelated to anything anyone in his family could understand.

"Continue talking. Because I just want to see how you dealt with that."

Peggy said, "When I came upstairs, I saw Carter with Keith up against the wall, and I started pulling on his arm and told him to let go. And he pushed me away. And I stood there and made sure he let go of Keith. And when he let go, and Keith went into his room, I asked Carter what was going on, and he went downstairs and didn't say anything to me. I had to get the pieces of the story, mostly from Robin. She was the one who was the observer in the situation."

"What did you tell mom?"

"Well, I was just there with Keith when daddy came upstairs. He didn't say anything. He just took the cigarettes out and smeared them in Keith's face and started choking him. And put him up against the wall. And he was saying, 'Well, you haven't learned at all, have you? When are you going to learn to stop stealing from me?' And Keith kept saying, 'I didn't take them,' but daddy kept on."

Robin told the story simply and without embellishment, re-creating the pain and humiliation of the attack. Listening to her, Carter fought the urge to look away. His eyes drifted but he forced himself to look at his family, a proud man determined to face the truth.

And Robin continued. "I don't remember if I went downstairs to get momma or if I just started yelling for her, but she came upstairs. And I was away from daddy, and momma grabbed hold of his arm and told him to stop. And he just kind of flung his arm to push her away. And then he let go, and Keith went into his room. And Tippi was crying in her room, 'cause she heard all this going on."

Father struck son, and two wounds opened, one between father and son, one between husband and wife. Both were unhealed.

After the incident Carter went to his room and packed a suitcase. Then he told his wife that he had to be away on business for a week. He said good-bye and left. When he came back after a week, nobody talked about the incident. It was buried.

Carter's violent explosion frightened everyone in the family and created the need for some kind of decisive action, a ritual of punishment and atonement. And so he left. He walked away. That was his view of the options. The family understood and were afraid to say anything.

I looked at Carter, a good man who could not bend. I felt that it was imperative to help him and the family question the house of values they had constructed on a subterranean fault line that could erupt again at any time. By now I was sure Carter would never hit Peggy, but he was in danger of hurting the kids or himself.

Carter seemed glad to have a chance to explain himself, to get somebody to understand.

"What happened was I found a carton of cigarettes up in my closet that had been opened. Someone had taken a package and tried to glue the carton back together so I wouldn't know one was missing. Now you remember that you had taken cigarettes of mine in the past, and so I assumed it was you. In addition to the fact that you were stealing cigarettes—as I thought—what really made me angry was to think that you thought I was so stupid that I wouldn't know how many packs of cigarettes there were in a carton. That's what really made me so angry—the insult to my intelligence."

When Carter thought his son took him for a fool, indignation swelled up and drove him into a blind rage. As Carter spoke, his wife and daughter listened with their heads down.

Carter continued. "And when I came upstairs with the cigarettes, I was going to say something—I don't know what, I can't remember. But when I got upstairs, and you and Robin were standing there talking, my anger became so great that I couldn't say anything. I *could not say anything* to explain to you."

Something important was going unnoticed here, and I said to Robin, "Ask your dad to explain why he became so angry."

"Why did you get so angry when we were talking?"

"The fact that you two were talking had nothing to do with it. I was angry because someone had come into *my* room, into *my* closet, and stolen something from me."

"I think your father is wrong," I said. "I think he was angry when he saw both of you talking."

"No," Carter said hotly. "The fact that those two were talking had absolutely nothing to do with it."

I repeated my point. "I think your father is wrong."

"Her father is *not* wrong!" Carter looked me straight in the eye, and I could feel his fury.

"Carter," I said firmly, "you are only a father. I am an expert. Later on you will understand what I am saying."

"Perhaps," he said evenly.

I was pulling rank. I felt sorry for Carter—I pitied his isolation, his impotence—but I was frustrated by his certainty and his righteousness.

I turned to Keith and said, "Why didn't you ever ask your father why he became so irrational?"

"Usually—I have lied to him before—and at the time he thought that I was nothing more than a liar, as far as I could see. So I figured there was nothing I could do."

"You figured he was right? Or that he was crazy?"

Keith smiled and shook his head. "He's not crazy."

"He's not crazy? So why couldn't you talk to him?"

"Well, usually, I can't really talk to him about anything like that, anything serious."

"You mean he's heartless?"

"No, he's not heartless. He's just . . ." Again the boy looked perplexed. The impossibility of reconciling the father's strange, stubborn ways with known categories wasn't easy.

I was increasing the emotional intensity of the session. I didn't like the bland logic that was protecting a dangerous and irrational act.

"What about you, Robin? Didn't it surprise you, what your father did?"

"I never thought he would hit Keith."

"Couldn't you ask him, 'What happened, dad?' "

"No, because for the next few weeks I really hated him. I didn't even want to go near him."

"Did you hate him too, Keith?"

"I think so."

"Do you understand what happened, Peggy?"

"No," she said, and there was a lot of feeling in that one little word.

"Did you ask your husband what happened?"

"Yes," she said, "We talked about it afterwards. He told me why he was so angry."

"And did you understand?"

"No, not really."

And so it remained buried. The event, the anger, the guilt, the fear, the hate, the love—all of it. I felt Carter's isolation.

I got up and asked Carter to bring his chair away from the family and next to mine. He did so without hesitation and sat down. I looked at the distance between him and the family and saw that it was not enough. So I asked him to move his chair even farther away, well outside the circle of the group.

Then I said to him, "I understand what happened to you, but it seems nobody in your family does."

"What happened?" he said, curious and wary at the same time.

"What happened to you—" I said, and then got up and moved his chair still farther away from the group, "—that's what happened to you."

He looked at me, and then he looked at his children and his wife, and it was the look of a lonely outsider looking in.

My voice became soft and yearning. "You are an excluded man," I said, putting words to what all of them now could see.

Carter and I talked for several minutes, just the two of us. I was aware that we were talking so softly the rest of the family had to strain to hear. "They are all so round and beautiful," I said. "You are the square peg. You are alone." Then I raised my voice for the family to hear. "So you become brutal because there is an invisible barrier between you and them. They create in you the feeling that they are a unit and you are excluded."

Carter Farrell saw himself as strict, a practitioner of old-fashioned standards. What he didn't see, or didn't fully appreciate, was his rigidity. His wife was an armchair psychologist, protecting his children from their father's incompetent authority. Each was sincere, and they polarized each other into progressively more extreme positions.

Instead of coming together they drifted apart, leaving the mother close and connected to the children and the father outside, raging in pain. When he went upstairs, angry, to talk to his son and found the boy and his sister in animated, friendly conversation, he felt overwhelmed by a sense of rejection and isolation. Feeling shut out and unable to talk to his children, he erupted in a flash of violence.

I asked Carter to rejoin his family, and he moved his chair back to where it had been before, next to Peggy's.

"Why can't you get close to your children?"

"The question is, Why don't I feel that I can get close to my children?" He crossed his legs and leaned back.

"Yes." I wanted to give him room to reenter his family, but he was not an easy man to talk to.

He folded his arms across his chest. "The answer is because of the lack of groundwork that was laid with the children when they were young."

"Carter, it's now. It's going on now."

"Okay, I understand the question. The reason I don't relate to them now, personally—get involved—is because of the antagonism I feel from them."

"Of course."

"I have made overtures, attempts, to let them know that I do understand the problems they're going through. I've been through those problems. I do understand them."

"So why are you so helpless?"

He gave me a look full of hurt and anger and guilt—and I was never more aware of the tangled nature of human emotions.

Beneath his guilt Carter felt the righteous rectitude of the cheated and misunderstood. I was asking him to put aside the bravado of the rooster and the penitence of the guilty to face his helplessness. Only by admitting need and loneliness could he be a full person and a full member of the family.

And then I asked Robin, my "cotherapist," in the family, "Why can't your dad be . . . your dad?"

"Well, after so long of not having him—"

"It's not true you didn't have him. You had him in a particular way."

"But it's very scary to try to accept him with what's happened so recently, because how are we to know it's not going to happen again?" As Robin spoke, her voice took on some of her mother's practiced patience.

"Well, it will happen again—if that's his position at home," I said, pointing to where he had been sitting outside the family circle. "If he needs to knock to enter."

"Peggy, how is it that he became the excluded one? Why can he only act with irrational force to become a father? How did that happen?"

"I think it's a very simple matter of a lack of skill. Because he cares, and he wants to have a good relationship with the children."

The fault was Carter's: He was ineffectual. We had to get away from explanations that focused on Carter's flawed character, and toward an understanding of the tragic flaws in the chemistry of their relationship.

"Talk together about how Carter feels excluded. Who excludes him. And about how that can be changed."

Now Peggy turned to face her husband. "Do you remember this morning when Tippi asked you if you could pick her up a little early from school? So she wouldn't have to go to the class she didn't have her homework for?"

"Mm-hm," he said, wondering what the point was.

"And you said, 'No, Tippi, I'm sorry, I can't help you out.' "

"Mm-hm."

"That was a very good communication with Tippi. Because you let her know how things were, but you also showed her that you cared about how she felt."

"And how did I do that?" he asked.

"When you said, 'I'm sorry I can't help you out.' You let her know you realized that she had a problem—and that you cared that she had a problem—but that this is the way things are. And that's different from the way you very frequently deal with the other children—and others of us, from time to time.

"Like last night, when Keith said he didn't have the dishwasher detergent. And you said something very mean. You said, 'Just because you *want* dishwasher detergent doesn't mean we *have* it.' And I feel like those small distinguishing remarks tell the kids you don't care."

Peggy spoke to Carter like a patient teacher to a slow learner. She wasn't preventing Carter from talking to the children, and she didn't exclude him from the family, but she was the interpreter and judge of their contact. Yet I felt that Peggy was open to change. It was time to bring in the reserves. I moved to the children as helpers.

"Keith, change seats with your mom," I said. Like his father, he readily complied. Keith sat up straight, and his father, sitting next to him, leaned forward, facing me.

"Carter, as long as Peggy takes the position of translating the children to you, they will not know how to talk with you, and you will not know how to talk with them. Talk with Keith."

"I don't like you wearing those pants," he said. This must have been on his mind. It was almost as though he was determined to demonstrate his intolerance.

"Why not?" Keith asked.

"Because they're torn, and I think you should think better of yourself than to go around school wearing a torn pair of pants. I don't want people thinking that my children have to wear ragged clothes."

Keith sat listening to this sudden criticism without complaint, but his eyes lost focus, as though he were enduring yet another meaningless lecture.

When his father finished, he said, "So you're saying when I wear torn pants it makes you look bad?" Like most adolescents, Keith could smell hypocrisy a mile away.

"It makes me look bad, and it makes you look bad."

"As far as you can see. See, I like the way I look. And maybe I like whatever people think of me when I wear these things."

"Is that the only pair of pants you have to wear?"

"It's not the only one I have to wear, but it's the best."

"Those are the best pants you have to wear?"

In the sixties my son's long hair drove me crazy. I knew how Carter felt.

"Oh, yeah, but I've got a lot of those dressy things that I don't really like to wear to school."

"So you'd rather go around wearing rags and have people think whatever you think they think of you than wear nice slacks and have them think you're a nerd because you wear good slacks to school?"

Keith nodded.

The boy and his father had run out of lines.

"That's the end of the conversation," Carter said. "I have no way to understand that."

To Carter his son's ways were written in a foreign tongue. He understood the boy's I-don't-care style of dress as well as he understood Greek. But I didn't want to leave this interchange as a failure of communication. I wanted them to realize that they had talked. Agreement isn't necessary for good communication.

"You see, this was a perfectly good conversation between two cultures. You and your son belong to two cultures that see things differently. It happens that in this crazy culture in which these kids live, ragged pants are in and dressy pants are out. We are old-timers; we don't understand that. He needs to be able to do something to explain that to you. But Peggy is the translator. So they go to her. Meanwhile you remain the square peg and cannot enter.

"Now, Keith, it is your job to explain yourself to your father so he can understand you. And you will need to help him to accept your torn pants."

I got up and went over to Keith and asked, "Would it be better if you tore them more to show your knees better?"

Hoping to detoxify an unnecessary struggle for control with a rigid father, I was playfully trying to expose this ragged style for what it was: a harmless teenage affectation.

Robin giggled. Her mother smiled. Keith sat straight and ripped his pants more so that they really showed his knees. If he was embarrassed he didn't show it. He had his father's ability to stick his neck out.

"That's it," I said. "*That's* it!

"Carter, can you understand that aesthetic? I can't. It's crazy. But that is how these kids think. Your son is a member of an alien culture that thinks knees are beautiful. Who knows?" I said and shrugged.

"Can you explain to your father why that's beautiful?"

"Well . . ." he began.

"Please," his father said.

How could a 15-year-old explain the complex dictates of the adolescent dress code to a father, especially a father too rigid to tolerate his son's need to experiment with becoming his own person? And yet Keith tried.

"It's kind of like it shows that you don't have anything to prove. That you know you're not any better than anybody else. Because you see all these kids always bragging about their Jordaches and whatever. But me and this little society I hang around in—my friends—we just can't stand kids who like to shut out people because they're not as good as them. They're always talking about how expensive their clothes are, and such as that."

"So the people that wear Jordache and jeans like that shut you guys out because you don't wear them?" Carter asked.

Amazingly these two were getting through to each other. First the son was able to say what many adolescents cannot put into words—namely that growing up is about inclusion and exclusion. Now, equally surprising, the father was demonstrating an openness to his son.

"Mm-hm," Keith nodded, not quite used to the strange sensation of communicating with his father.

"Carter, what was your uniform when you were fifteen? How did you show that you belonged?"

There was a long pause. Then Carter turned to face his son. "I didn't. I didn't belong." There was real sadness in his voice. "I didn't belong in the sense that you belong. So I *don't* understand." Not fitting in was an old story for him.

"You did not belong?" I asked.

"No," he said quietly.

"That's a pity. Belonging is very important. You were a loner?"

"Yeah," he said, trying to keep his voice steady.

"Did you ever get a group?"

"When I was eighteen, I suppose."

"How was that? Tell Keith."

Again there was a long pause. "I don't remember exactly how it was, but when I was eighteen your Uncle Jared, and Jamie, and Raymond and I just started hanging around a lot together. We enjoyed each other's company. We were interested in the same things. We had the same off-the-wall sense of humor. We had the same irreverence for society, and old people, and institutions. We just fit together well."

As Carter talked about growing up and the struggle to belong, Peggy listened with obvious compassion.

I turned to Keith. "So that was his torn pants."

Keith nodded thoughtfully.

For Carter it was a revelation to realize that his children could be similar to him in some way; that Keith and he shared the same irreverence for conformity and institutions.

I turned to Carter and said, "When Keith explains it, it's very clear, but he doesn't usually try. They go to you, Peggy."

"And you accept all of that, and so you are a single mother."

I was trying to broaden the focus from Carter's irrational actions to make it a mutual problem with mutual responsibility, but she felt blamed, and she fought back. "I don't really accept it. I deal with it the best I can."

"But," I said, "he feels excluded. He remains outside."

"Only because of his choice."

"No. It's a combined effort. It's not true, Peggy, that it's all his doing. You're all doing it. Robin, you exclude your dad. Keith, you exclude your dad. I don't know about you, Tippi. Do you talk with him or do you think he's just too square?"

"I'm not sure what you mean by square."

"Like I don't know what's happening," Carter volunteered. With Tippi, it seemed, he felt no need to be defensive.

"Tippi, do you think you can teach him?"

I was challenging the "correct way" of doing things. In a rigidly hierarchical family, I was putting the youngest child in charge of her father's education.

"On my own?"

"Yes, on your own. Who else can help you?"

"Keith," she said, looking at her big brother.

"Both of you? Talk with Keith. I think you would be a good teacher because I don't think you would quit. Maybe both of you can imagine some way of helping your dad enter into the [present]. You know, he got stuck in the fifties."

Tippi said, "I don't know how to come up with a solution." Then she turned to her big brother and asked, all earnest, "Do you know any way to teach him how to be hip?"

Keith grinned. "That would be pretty difficult," he said. "Maybe we could just every now and then update him on what's going on."

"But it's . . ." Tippi was truly exasperated. "It's like you could tell him that," she said pointing to Keith's torn pants, "was cool, and he'd know that that's what you were saying, but he wouldn't exactly understand *how* it was cool and *why* it was cool." As far as Tippi was concerned, her father belonged to a different species, *homo adultus*, so the possibility of real shared experience was an *impossibility*.

"So you'd say a shirt with a hole in it is cool, and then he'd get a fishnet shirt. Is that what you're saying?"

"No! I'm saying like why would he *want* to get a fishnet? Because he doesn't hang around people with holes in their shirts or torn pants. It's cool to us 'cause it's accepted. That's like the girl in our school with the blond streak? It looks retarded because nobody else has a blond streak. But if everybody else had it except you, you'd probably get a blond streak like that to be accepted.

And if he hung around everybody that had holes in their pants, eventually he'd probably get a pair of pants and put holes in them."

Tippi was still young enough to speak openly of the need to conform. Some day she would ask questions like, "What is the meaning of life?" But now all she wanted to know was, "Does this look okay?"

"I want you young people to help your father understand people [today]. But you will need to learn how to teach him that, while remaining sensitive to his authority. For him, being an authority is important. Can you do that? It's a hard trick."

Keith nodded. He was willing.

"Yeah? Tippi, what about you? Do you think that you can teach your dad?"

Tippi grinned and nodded. Young and innocent of bitterness, she liked the idea of bringing her father up to date. I was touched, and Carter was smiling.

Then Keith said, "Well, that's the way mom is with us. We can talk together."

"Yes, I know," I said. "But that is what closed father's door."

Then I said to Robin, "Your father was educated with a very different idea of respect and authority. Can you understand that?"

"How he's different? Yes, I can."

"But you didn't."

"No, because I didn't realize at the time that he was so left out, and it was our fault, too."

"It's so easy to see. I could see it in the way you walked into the room and sat down. You three kids sat down next to mom, as far away from your father as possible. Mother sat between you and him, like a protective barrier. It was just so simple."

"I felt like he did it by choice," Robin said, echoing her mother's thoughts.

"He doesn't have any choice," I said. That, of course, was not quite true, but I wanted the children to see their role in this. They already saw their father's.

"I think he's in pain," Peggy said. "Your father becomes frustrated and furious when you don't talk to him. Can't you see that?"

Robin nodded, and her eyes filled with tears.

Only then did I glance at the clock and realize that nearly three hours had gone by. "We will stop now. It's four o'clock."

The Farrells seemed a little startled, too. For three hours we'd been deep into the family's pain, and now it was time to stop. They had to go back to Vermont. Carter and Peggy had to go back to work, and the kids had to go back to school. It was time for the session to end, but I didn't want its momentum to stop.

"I would like to give you three kids a task. See if you can put your heads together and come up with a plan to help your dad connect with you. I don't know how, because I don't know your dad, but I know that he feels alone. He grew up as a loner. And in your home he's still a loner. Can you think what to do to help him? Can you do that?"

All three of them nodded, Tippi most enthusiastically. Then we said good-bye.

Carter and Peggy had very different ideas about how to raise children and, instead of finding a way to come together, they pushed each other farther apart. When Peggy saw Carter picking on the kids for every little thing, it seemed natural to defend them. When she did, it was natural for Carter to feel resentful. And so a pattern was set in motion in which mother and children grew closer and father became increasingly alienated.

In some families this pattern of polarization between parents would lead to a lot of arguments. But Carter and Peggy weren't like that. They kept everything inside. As a result, resentment festered and turned to bitterness. Their divorce was an emotional one, the kind that doesn't show up in the usual statistics.

Carter's unbending sternness masked a personality that feared and despised weakness. He denied loneliness and uncertainty in himself, and he attacked violations of his strict moral code in the behavior of his children. Peggy didn't agree with him, but she could not or would not challenge him directly.

Within this value system there was no flexibility and little room for growth. With time the structure of the family took a destructive spin. Peggy, the good mother, became the full-time teacher, source of all inspiration and understanding, while Carter, who could not challenge Peggy's goodness, saw himself reduced more and more to an outsider looking in, neither a father nor a husband.

And so the Farrells became a caricature of the traditional family: Women nest, men hunt. "When the children get older," Carter and Peggy thought, "there will be space for Carter to become involved." Meanwhile Peggy's job as a mother expanded to the point that there was no space for her to be a wife. "I am still single," she said, denying her role in the family, while in fact she was more and more a mother.

The violence that erupted in the Farrell family was a product of confusion and loss blocked from expression by closed channels of communication. Opening those channels released the pressure and made violence unlikely to recur.

Carter's need to deny and deflect his anger made the whole family prisoners of rage. With access reopened Carter moved toward his wife and children, and toward acceptance. Peggy moved out from between him and the children—toward him. The children did what children do more often than their parents expect; they met him more than halfway.

Starting Right: What We Owe to Children Under Three*

Sheila B. Kamerman

Family policy is a method of dealing with family problems on a macro level. Such an approach centers on designing strategies and programs that will benefit vast numbers of families in need. Sheila B. Kamerman argues in this selection that the family policies of the United States are sorely lacking when it comes to young children and their concerns. As she states, "At this point, the United States has assured our very youngest children neither adequate care outside their homes, nor adequate care within them." Kamerman describes various programs and policies in Europe that she argues could serve as a model for America's policies towards its children.

Were rhetoric a true measure of behavior, the United States would be the most child-centered nation in the world. Our leading child-development experts stress the importance of the first few years of life, and most Americans, when asked, say that the experts are right.... When world leaders gathered in unprecedented number at the United Nations for a World Summit for Children to pledge more resources for child health and welfare, George Bush asserted that "our children are our mirror, an honest reflection of their parents and their world."

*Source: Copyright 1991, New Prospect Inc. Reprinted by permission from *The American Prospect,* Winter 1991.

In fact, the conditions facing many of America's children are a mirror of chronic political ambivalence and stalemate. Over the last 12 years, three national commissions—the ... National Commission on Children, the 1980 White House Conference on Families, and the 1979 National Commission of the International Year of the Child—have been largely ignored, new initiatives were long bottled up in Congress, and by almost every indicator the condition of children has not improved.

Lately, however, we have seen some notable progress. In October, 1990, breaking a long deadlock, Congress and President Bush agreed on a tax and budget package that, despite other cutbacks, increases support for low-income families with young children. The package expands federal grant programs for child care and enlarges funds for Head Start, the highly regarded early childhood education program founded 26 years ago but never fully funded.

The same legislation extends Medicaid significantly by requiring the states to provide coverage for all poor children under age six—a requirement that rises, one year at a time, up to age 18 by the year 2003. In addition, the package includes expanded funds for the Childhood Immunization Program; an enlarged Earned Income Tax Credit for families with children; a small but symbolically important 5 percent tax credit of up to $400 for low-income families with a child under age one; and a new tax credit to help finance health insurance policies covering children of low-income families.

These advances are impressive, even historic. Before uncorking the champagne, however, we need to put the agreement in perspective. One of the key measures, the commitment to expanding Head Start to full coverage, took the form of a promise of future funds. The expansion of another program, Medicaid, is staggered through the decade and even into the next century. These promises could unravel under budgetary pressure. And even with their fulfillment, America's fragmented and means-tested policies affecting children will still lag far behind the more comprehensive and universal family policies of Western Europe. In the same session, Congress was unable to override the president's veto of parental leave legislation. The approved financing for child care is limited, and the expanded tax credits for the working poor appear to be too small to bring about any major reduction in America's high rate of child poverty.

Perhaps most important, the progress that we have made in recent years in reshaping social policy has primarily affected families with children aged three and above. The great challenges we now face concern families with children below age three.

The policy gradually taking shape for the "over-threes" is still only implicit, but the outlines are clear. Increasingly, the American public and its leaders assume that women with children of three and above will be in the labor force and that public subsidies will assist with their child care, at least when family income is modest. Rather than opposing care outside the home, educators and other experts now generally view group experiences as conducive to the psychological development of children aged three to five, as well as to success in school and eventually at work. School districts are expanding preschool programs, first for handicapped, deprived, and poor children, but ultimately to more universal participation. Although part-day kindergarten programs still predominate, a growing number of school districts, prekindergartens, and nursery schools are extending programs to a full school day.

No comparable consensus of public opinion or change in social institutions has yet transformed national policy affecting children under age three and their families. Though millions of mothers of "under-threes" are at work, many Americans—and evidently that includes many policy makers—continue to expect them to be at home full-time. The Family Support Act (FSA) of 1988, our major recent effort at welfare reform, was directed primarily at poor families with children aged three and older. The parental leave legislation adopted by Congress in 1990 would have provided only a brief *unpaid* leave after childbirth; yet even this modest proposal was vetoed by President Bush. Infant and toddler care continues to be in scarce supply.

Many Western European countries offer a vivid contrast. They have developed alternative policies benefiting children under age three, focusing especially on economic support, parental time, and child care. The terms of debate in the United States need to be broadened to include these options for addressing the needs of very young children and their families. If the first years of life are as crucial to subsequent well-being as the experts say they are, we ought to be willing to commit the resources to ensure that good start.

Small Children, Big Problems

Examine the facts of life for America's approximately 11 million children under the age of three, and the need for new measures to address their plight becomes apparent. As the 1980s ended:

> More than half the mothers of under-threes were in the labor force, up from 27 percent in 1970;
> About one in four of the under-threes were living in single-parent (chiefly mother-only) families, up from almost 8 percent in 1970;
> Almost one in four of the under-threes were living in families with incomes below the poverty threshold, the highest poverty rate for any age group.

Despite all the official declarations on behalf of children, one fact stands out above all: The child poverty rate was higher throughout the 1980s than at any time since the middle 1960s, and consistently higher the younger the child.

As might be expected, race, the mother's marital status, and whether or not she holds a job continue to have large effects on children's family circumstances. Black and Hispanic children are most likely to be living in families without their fathers, to have mothers at home rather than at work, and to be living in poverty whether or not their mothers work, although the poverty rate is much higher among those with at-home mothers. Almost one in five white children under three is poor, primarily those in single-parent families.

There has been a dramatic change in how very young children spend their days. Ever greater numbers of the under-threes are cared for outside their homes by caregivers who are not members of their families. One-quarter of the children in this age group (approaching half of the more than 5 million with working mothers) are in the care of an adult other than a relative. A little more than half of this group are cared for in "family day care," largely informal and of unknown quality, while the remainder are in day-care centers.

Programs serving children under age three are in the shortest supply of all child-care services, despite efforts in some states to recruit family day-care providers. Some highly publicized cases of maltreatment and abuse have also provoked extensive concern about the quality of available services. And the price of day care is a big worry for average working parents, who cannot easily afford the $5,000 a year estimated at the end of the 1980s to be the cost for each child under age three at good day-care centers and even, in some places, for family day care.

Thinking Through the Response

The new conditions affecting America's youngest children have elicited a divided and ambivalent response in different quarters of American society and public life.

On one side of the debate, the champions of liberal child policies and gender equality have sought to accommodate, even to facilitate, the changing patterns of work and family life with new government and private-sector policies. In public policy, they have focused primarily on two objectives: increasing support for affordable, good-quality child care and enacting a national policy requiring businesses to provide parental or family leave (formerly known as "maternity" leave) to allow a period for medical recovery after childbirth, followed if possible by some time for parenting, before a return to work. Advocates of reform have also urged other changes in the workplace, such as "flextime" and sick-leave plans to allow parents to care for a sick child, meet daily emergencies, and manage the dual pressures of work and family life.

A countermovement, coming chiefly from the right, has resisted the very premise of these measures. Some conservatives—still committed, however unrealistically, to the traditional view that mothers should stay at home—have opposed new policies that make it attractive for women to be in the labor force and that impose new costs on government and business to enable women to work. At hearings on proposed federal child care legislation in 1989, for example, conservative Republicans argued that rather than subsidize child care costs to encourage mothers to work, the federal government should enact tax credits to subsidize wives to care for their preschoolers at home.

Still others, from the left as well as the right, call for universal child or family allowances or other government subsidies that would support, without bias, whatever choice families made—to use out-of-home child care or for one parent to remain at home rearing the children. These advocates of a more neutral form of child policy have much in common with liberal reformers and feminists, except for their opposition to direct public provision of day care.

Two incidents in October of 1990 crystallized the current national debate over child care. Campaigning for governor of Massachusetts, John Silber set off a furor when he denounced the "overweening materialism" of two-career couples who use child care. Silber went on to declare: "We have a generation of abused children by women who have thought that a third-rate day care center was just as good as a first-rate home."

The same month, Chante Fernandez, a 24-year-old single mother, was arrested in Woodbridge, New Jersey, for leaving her five-year-old daughter unattended in a parked car while she worked the night shift at a local mall. But when the press disclosed that Fernandez had been unable to find any child care and was working hard to support herself and her daughter without any assistance from her former husband, public opinion rallied to her side and all serious charges against her were dismissed.

Silber's comments probably would not have created so great a furor had they not touched a tender point of anxiety, quite literally engendering guilt among the many parents who are genuinely troubled about the day care their children receive. But as the support for Chante Fernandez demonstrated, the public recognizes that for the great majority of women, work is not a "selfish" indulgence, nor is child care a luxury. If some child care is "third-rate," the imperative now is to upgrade it, not to pretend that all families—least of all single-parent ones—can make ends meet with mothers at home.

Yet if most Americans seemed resolved in favor of child care for children age three to five, the debate takes on a different cast for the very youngest children, particularly infants under one year of age. Experts continue to harbor doubts about the developmental effects on infants of out-of-home care. Reviewing the research, a 1990 National Academy of Sciences report concludes there are "unresolved questions concerning full-time care [more than 20 hours a week] in the first year of life." Researchers find that some infants in full-time care display characteristics in interactions with their mothers that are a cause for concern.

But if these tentative findings do raise qualms about out-of-home care for infants, they strengthen the case for a generous extension of the second prong of liberal child care policy: the option of parental leave, extending until children reach their first birthday. In this regard, the United States is almost unique among Western countries in its negligence, not even ensuring a mother opportunity for physical recovery after childbirth, much less providing parent and child some minimum period of time to get started together.

Given the deep moral differences among Americans in their views of child care, as well as the costs of launching new family policies, it will probably not be possible—nor desirable—to arrive at a single, uniform child policy based on homogenous expectations about child rearing. In the United States, child policy will have to provide choices. But reasonable choices are precisely what many American parents do not now have, particularly in the care of children under age three. . . .

Some European Alternatives

Many European countries have been facing similar demographic and social trends as the United States: increasing proportions of mothers in the labor force and of mother-only families, rising use of out-of-home child care, and growing costs for that care. And, like Americans, Europeans are concerned about the time pressures on parenting and child rearing. So they have faced the same knotty problems that acutely affect families with under-threes in America: how to pay for infant and toddler care; how to secure adequate economic support to families with children; how to manage the competing demands of jobs and children.

But the European countries approach these problems with a drastically different set of institutions and assumptions. Primarily after World War II, they established an extensive social "infrastructure" for families with children that includes national health insurance or a national health service; cash benefits given families based on the presence and number of children (child or family allowances); guaranteed minimum child support payments; and often housing allowances for low- and middle-income families as well. This foundation of support is critical to the success of the child-oriented policies they have adopted in recent years.

Child care for children aged two and a half or three to primary school entry is nearly universal in much of Europe. The preschool programs that provide child care usually do so under educational auspices, and the care is free and voluntary to children whose parents want them to attend, regardless of their mothers' employment status.

Child care for the under-threes involves almost as diversified a system as in the United States, including both family day care and center care. The proportion of children under three served by these programs varies from about 10 percent in most of Europe to 33 percent in France and about 50 percent, largely one- and two-year-olds, in Denmark, Finland, and Sweden.

Although the United States does not yet have this array of family policies, this was the *starting point* of discussion in Europe when care of the under-threes emerged as an issue about 10 or 15 years ago.

The motive forces behind new parenting policies, like the policies themselves, have varied from one European country to another. But the policies all share a fundamental value: support for *parental* care for very young children at home for some time following childbirth. And all involve provision of financial support to make this possible. The Europeans seem to be moving toward a two-part policy package: First, they define infant care as care by a parent who is home on a paid and job-protected leave from his or her job for much of the first year following childbirth. And, second, they provide a menu of policy options for care of one- and two-year-olds. The components of the policy package vary significantly in detail but include the following common elements:

A paid, job-protected leave lasting five to six months on average and ranging from a three- to four-month maternity leave to a one-year parental leave, depending on the country;

An extended or supplementary job-protected parental leave for an additional six months to three years, paid as either an earnings-related cash benefit or as a modest flat-rate benefit, designed by various countries either to acknowledge the value of family work and child rearing or to compensate for an inadequate supply of child care services, or both;

The right to work part-time for some time after the post-childbirth leave ends;

An expanded subsidized supply of family day care homes and center care, available at income-related fees to toddler-aged children of working parents.

Countries opt for either a particular policy, a policy varying according to the age of the child (one policy for infant care; another for toddler care), or a diversified policy package with several options. Here are a few illustrations:

A West German parent (overwhelmingly the mother) can stay at home for up to one and a half years after childbirth or work part-time (at her previous place of employment only) and receive very modest financial support. The benefit is helpful for two-parent families primarily as a supplement to family income; it is not adequate to support a single mother at home, unless child support, welfare, or other income also is available.

An employed parent in Austria can stay at home for two years following childbirth, and, beginning with children born in 1990, for a third year, or work part-time until the child is three, and receive close to the wage of an unskilled worker.

A French married mother of three children—for illustrative purposes, let us say they are aged one, three, and six—can stay at home and receive the equivalent of a minimum wage until her baby is three years old. She can also choose to remain at her job with her one-year-old in some form of subsidized child care, probably family day care. Her three-year-old will be in free preschool in any case and her six-year old in first grade. If single and poor, she has still another option that would allow her to stay home until her youngest child is three.

A Swedish working parent can remain at home on a job-protected leave for up to 15 months (soon one and a half years) and receive his/her full pay, or work part time for still longer and receive full pay. (Although mothers take most of the parental leaves, now more than one-quarter of the fathers take at least some time off.) In addition, by 1992, all children aged 18 months and older with working parents are guaranteed a place in subsidized care. Swedish working parents are also guaranteed the right to reduce their working day to six hours until their youngest child is eight.

A Finnish working parent (overwhelmingly mothers) can remain at home until her child is three years old. While her job (or a comparable job) is saved for her for all three years, she receives almost her full wage for one year. A modest cash benefit is available for the other two years. The mother can use the benefit either to supplement family income or to purchase private child care; as an alternative, parents can obtain a guaranteed place in a subsidized public child care center.

These examples are not exhaustive. Several other countries have developed, or are developing, policies resembling one or another of these options.

The European initiatives are driven by diverse motivations and priorities. The French want not only to protect the economic well-being of children in vulnerable families, but also to ensure that women continue to have children even while entering the labor force in ever increasing number. The Germans and

Austrians want to acknowledge and affirm the value of children and "family work." The Finns have shaped their policies out of a concern with the consequences for children of shortages in infant and toddler care, while the demand for women in the labor force was increasing; and they see their policies as supporting the values of parental choice and family work. The Swedes have sought to promote gender equality and children's well-being.

Contrary to American impressions, the European countries with comprehensive child care policies fit no political stereotype. Some of the governments have been conservative, some social democratic, and some coalitions. Their child care policies have continued to advance despite shifts in the political pendulum. Some of these countries are heavily Catholic, others Protestant, some highly secular in recent decades. The countries that have embarked on these experiments include those with high labor-force participation rates for mothers of very young children, and some with low participation. They include some with high unemployment rates and some with low. They include some with very low fertility rates and some with not-so-low rates. And they include some with high rates of mother-only families and some with lower rates.

Clearly, diverse political and economic environments have not prevented the Europeans from achieving a common recognition of the problems facing families with small children. Are there useful policy lessons for the United States in the European examples?

Cultural Diversity and American Policy

It will not be easy to focus policy attention on very young children in the United States. Policy makers disagree about the substantive issues, and many Americans suspect child policy proposals will disproportionately benefit black and other minority children and encourage more out-of-wedlock, minority births. These anxieties and sources of opposition, often latent and unacknowledged, should be confronted openly and answered directly. We are unlikely to make much progress unless we can show that effective family policies are consistent with widely shared values and provide broad benefits across racial and class lines.

Even if we overcome prejudice and racism, however, we face great obstacles to consensus because of the deeply conflicting moral values and cultural practices in America. Some conservatives would support family policy initiatives, but only if they are limited to traditional families. Some feminists are concerned that policies designed to improve conditions for children may have harmful consequences for women. While some conservatives object to providing paid leaves for working mothers, some feminists fear the consequences (lower wages, constricted career paths) for women who take extended leaves.

Given the diversity of values in the United States, what can be done? First, child policy must support parental choice as to whether a mother remains at home to care for her very young child or takes employment in the outside labor market. It also should support choice in the type of child care. Of course, everyone likes the idea of "choice." But real choice requires active support of alternatives, not passive acceptance of the limited options now available to most parents.

All parents—working or not—warrant support in their child rearing. But working parents deserve something more, at least in part because they are paying taxes and contributing to the future Social Security benefits of at-home parents as well. Enabling single mothers to have some time at home without job and income loss, and without having to turn to a stigmatized and inadequate welfare program, is a worthwhile policy goal, as is providing some additional support for those families who maintain traditional roles.

Thus, the goals of any policy agenda for the under-threes should be either to enable at least one parent to remain at home for some time to care for his or her baby, or to enable employed parents to stay at work with support for child care. The policies would include:

> Establishment of a stronger social infrastructure for families with children, including health insurance for all children, available free to those in families with low or modest income, and adequate, affordable housing;
>
> Stronger, family-related income support through one of several avenues: a universal, taxable child allowance (a cash benefit to families with children, based on the presence and number of children in the family), or a child tax credit that is refundable to families with incomes below the tax threshold, or a further expanded earned income tax credit;
>
> A universal one-year job and benefit-protected leave for working parents with prior work history at the time of childbirth (or adoption) paid for as a contributory social insurance benefit at 75 percent of salary up to the maximum wage covered under Social Security;
>
> A reformed, more adequate, nationally uniform AFDC as an option for poor single mothers who fail to qualify for the employment-related parenting benefit, with the requirement that now exists for teen mothers to complete high school, and an additional requirement that these young, single mothers participate in parenting classes;
>
> Increased federal funding for good quality toddler care, both family day care and center care.

Inevitably, questions of cost will influence the debate over child policies. Clearly, we must make choices rather than pretend that the society can do everything at once. Yet we should also remember that countries not as wealthy as ours do all these things.

If it is necessary to start slowly with the under-threes, then the poor, the deprived, and the handicapped are the logical groups to target first. But the European experience offers other, more universal possibilities. Their example provides neither fixed formulae nor final answers, but suggests broad lines for thinking about the path we ought to take. At this point, the United States has assured our very youngest children neither adequate care outside their homes, nor adequate care within them. Recent congressional achievements and new commitments to children should encourage us, however, to reach for the bolder alternatives that our European friends have shown to be practical.

Family Decline
in the Swedish Welfare State*

David Popenoe

David Popenoe takes quite the opposite position than that found in the previous reading. In this article, Popenoe argues that it is precisely the overly generous welfare policies in Sweden which have undermined the strength and stability of Swedish families. These policies have stripped away many of the functions performed by the family, causing it to collapse as a result. According to Popenoe, what is needed in the United States is a more careful balance between well-designed governmental policies, and the strengths of the free market system.

Sweden has much to commend it. Its cities are clean, its countryside beautiful, and its people healthy and long-lived. With no poverty, no slums, and relatively little violent crime and drug abuse, Sweden has to a remarkable degree minimized the extent to which the economic luck of the draw determines the quality of people's lives.

Yet there is one thing about growing up in Sweden today that should give pause even to those sympathetic to the welfare state. There is a strong likelihood that the family has grown weaker there than anywhere else in the world.

---

*Source: Reprinted from: *The Public Interest*, No. 102 (Winter 1991), (c) 1991 by National Affairs, Inc.

What has happened to the family in Sweden over the past few decades lends strong support to the proposition that as the welfare state advances, the family declines. If unchecked, this decline could eventually undermine the very welfare that the state seeks to promote.

The modern welfare state was founded with the goal of helping families to function better as decentralized welfare agencies. It sought to strengthen families, not to weaken them. Over time, however, welfare states have increasingly tended not so much to assist families as to replace them; people's dependence on the state has grown while their reliance on families has weakened. In a classic illustration of the law of unintended consequences, the family under the welfare state is gradually losing both the ability and the will to care for itself.

The impediment to social welfare presented by family decline is often cast in economic terms. If the welfare state is to fulfill its goals, as Danish welfare official Bent Rold Andersen has stressed, its citizens must refrain from exploiting its services to the fullest. There is no economical way for the state to take over all the day-to-day welfare services that the family has long provided its members. Yet in what American social-welfare expert Neil Gilbert has called the "helping hand dilemma," families in the welfare state are penalized by losing the benefits of public care when they provide their own care—whereas they are rewarded with public care when they fail to look after themselves. This is a major component of what some see as the coming economic crisis of the welfare state.

Even more troubling, however, is the possibility of a social crisis. The family in the welfare state may become so weak that it is unable or unwilling to provide the kind of personalized child rearing that it alone can offer.

Marriage and Divorce Rates

The Swedish marriage rate is now the lowest in the industrialized world, and the average age at first marriage is probably the highest. The rate of nonmarital cohabitation, or consensual unions, outranks that of all other advanced nations; such unions, rather than being a mere preclude to marriage (as is more often the case in the United States now), have become a parallel institution alongside legal marriage. About 25 percent of all couples in Sweden today are living in consensual unions (up from 1 percent in 1960), compared with about 5 percent in the United States. The growth of nonmarital cohabitation among childbearing couples has given Sweden one of the highest percentages of children born out of wedlock in the industrial world—over 50 percent of all children, compared with about 22 percent in the United States. It is important to add, however, that—unlike the situation in the United States—very few of these children are born to an "unattached" mother.

The rate of family breakdown in Sweden is more difficult to measure. The Swedish divorce rate, although higher than that of most other European societies, is lower than the American divorce rate. By one estimate, focusing on the cohort born in 1945 and projecting the high divorce rates of the last few decades, the proportion of marriages expected to end in divorce in Sweden is 36 percent, compared with 42 percent in the United States. But the high Swedish rate is surprising from one perspective: many of the factors traditionally associated with divorce in the United States—such as brief courtships and early marriages, teen pregnancies, poverty and income instability, interethnic and interfaith unions, and high residential mobility—are mitigated in Sweden.

The Swedish experience has effectively put to rest the old notion that so-called "trial marriages" would have the desirable effect of cutting the divorce rate. A recent study of Swedish women conducted by the U.S. National Bureau of Economic Research, for example, determined that couples who lived together before marriage had a divorce rate nearly 80 percent higher than those that did not.

In order to divorce one must first marry, and that is precisely what Swedes in large numbers are not doing. The divorce rate, therefore, tells us less and less about the total breakup rate of couples; one must also know the breakup rate of couples who are not married. Such data are hard to come by. To control for casual cohabitation, one Swedish study compared the breakup rates of both married and unmarried couples with at least one child. The dissolution rate of the unmarried couples was nearly three times that of the married couples. It is a reasonable conclusion, based on all available data, that the true "divorce" rate in Sweden—one that takes into account the breakups of both consensual unions and marriages—may surpass that of the United States and be the highest in the Western world.

This family-dissolution rate is reflected in Sweden's high percentage of single-parent families. In 1980 single-parent families amounted to 18 percent of all households with children, compared with 17 percent among American whites. (The total U.S. percentage was slightly higher, because 52 percent of black families had only one parent.) Loosely related to the single-parent family rate are two other rates in which Sweden now leads the world: it has the smallest average household size (about 2.2 persons) and the highest percentage of adults living alone (about 20 percent).

A Waning Social Institution

Many of these statistical indicators of the decline of marriage, the increase of family dissolution, and the rise of nonfamily households point to real changes in the family that are commonly associated with its weakening as a social institution. The following family changes, though harder to measure, support the proposition that the family has declined further in Sweden than in any other Western industrialized nation:

1. *Parental authority.* In Sweden, authority over traditional family concerns has shifted heavily to the state. To give two examples: Sweden became the first nation to pass laws forbidding parents to strike their children, and social workers there have been able to take children away from parents for foster care more easily than in other countries.

2. *Economic dependence of children on their parents.* The economic ties that bind children to their parents elsewhere have largely been supplanted in Sweden by ties between children and the state. For instance, in addition to free or low-cost medical care, public transportation, and education, Sweden virtually guarantees a part-time job to any youth age 16 or over.

3. *Economic interdependence of spouses.* Swedish spouses need have almost no mutual economic obligations. Swedish policy is that each nonhandicapped adult is responsible for his or her own economic well-being. In the early 1970s Sweden did away with the joint income-tax return, and it now permits only individual returns.

4. *Economic care for the elderly.* Swedish families need not provide economic care for their aged members. Sweden probably has the world's lowest percentage of households with extended families.

5. *"Familism" as a cultural value.* Familism refers to the belief in a strong sense of family identification and loyalty, mutual assistance among family members, and a concern for the perpetuation of the family unit; the subordination of the interests and personality of individual family members to the interests and welfare of the family group. Still a strong value in many other advanced nations, familism is remarkably weak in Sweden. Swedish political discussion, for example, seldom focuses on building strong, self-sufficient families. Swedish family legislation is instead almost exclusively concerned with the situation of the individual family member.

The family, then, has probably become weaker in Sweden than anywhere else—certainly among advanced Western nations. Individual family members are the most autonomous and least bound by the group, and the group as a whole is least cohesive. The family carries out fewer of its traditional social functions; these have shifted to other institutions, especially the state and its agencies, which have correspondingly gained in power and authority. The family is smallest in size, least stable, and has the shortest life span; people are therefore family members for the smallest percentage of their lives. In sum, Swedes have apparently become the least willing to invest time, money, and energy in family life. Instead, the main investments are increasingly made in the individual, not in the family unit.

The Roots of Family Decline

Why should the institution of the family have declined further in Sweden than anywhere else? For welfare-state advocates the answer to this question is troubling. Five factors seem strongly associated with Sweden's advanced family decline: the culture of self-fulfillment, economic security, gender-role change, the ideology of the welfare state, and secularism. The part played by economic security and gender-role change is particularly dismaying, inasmuch as they are highly favored policy goals in most industrialized societies. Nevertheless, their role in fostering family decline is clearly implicated by many studies.

Virtually all of the family changes occurring in Sweden—such as the decline in marriage and the high family-dissolution rate—have been evident in every other advanced society in the past few decades. Forces that operate universally appear to have impelled change at a particularly rapid pace in Sweden.

Given the limitations of the social sciences, we will probably never know precisely what forces caused families in advanced societies to undergo the dramatic changes that began in the 1960s. But agreement among family experts is growing that if any one force is to be given causal priority, it is the new cultural emphasis on self-fulfillment—a value that logically opposes familism. Persons motivated by self-fulfillment pursue their own personal interests, whereas persons motivated by familism pursue the collective interests of the family as an institution.

There is no satisfactory way to determine if self-fulfillment per se has become a stronger cultural value in Sweden than elsewhere. But we do have solid information about two other trends that are closely associated with self-fulfillment—growing economic security and changing gender roles.

The Economic Irrelevance of the Family

For most of human history the family was an economic work unit. An economic bond held families together, and ties to a family were ordinarily necessary for sheer physical survival. The changing economic conditions in advanced societies—characterized as they are by widespread personal affluence, welfare safety nets, and the redistribution of income—have seriously attenuated the economic bond of the family. With the growth of personal economic security, the economic bond has largely been replaced by affection.

Compared with economic need, affection is a notoriously fragile basis for family solidarity. In Sweden today it is often financially advisable today to divorce—or better yet, not to get married in the first place, and certainly not to have any children. Thus affluence and economic security have brought higher divorce and lower marriage rates, and have helped to generate low birth rates that are unprecedented.

Personal economic security is probably greater in Sweden than in any other society, and this is due largely to the welfare state. No political goal of the welfare state has loomed larger. The Swedish government takes the view that if the family cannot or does not want to provide for its members, for whatever reason, the government will assume the burden.

On economic grounds alone, therefore, a Swede has little reason to hold a family together, or even to be part of a family. If children and their caretaker parent are left economically disadvantaged through family breakup, for example, the government steps in. The absent parent is forced to pay child support; when this is not possible, the government provides it. The government grants many other subsidies as well, such as for housing, and it has been estimated that the divorced mother in Sweden—in stark contrast to her American counterpart—ends up with about 90 percent of her predivorce standard of living.

If Swedish families don't wish to assume the economic burden of caring for their aging parents—and almost all families do not—the government assumes it for them. If the aged or infirm want to live alone and have no one to care for them, the government provides a homemaker service. Because families below the median income level cannot provide for their members as generously as wealthier families, the government redistributes income from wealthier families to poorer ones.

The result of such policies is that Swedes have become much less economically dependent on their families, and much more dependent on their state. Rather than having to build up and then draw on a pool of family resources over time to meet the needs of family members, families regularly turn over to the state a large portion of their resources in the form of taxes. Resources taken by the state at certain stages of the family's life cycle are then typically given back at other stages.

These economic and social shifts include substantial changes in men's and women's roles. In recent decades, gender roles within families have been changing dramatically, especially with the movement of women—who tend no longer to be full-time homemakers—into the labor market. While undoubtedly bringing many benefits to women, these changes have contributed to family instability in two ways: by reducing the economic dependence of wives on their husbands (that is, by giving women more economic security) and by making marital roles ambiguous. Far from incorporating a set of cultural role prescriptions that is taken for granted, marriage has now become a lifelong bargaining session in which wives and husbands must continually negotiate their roles.

The welfare state has put Sweden in the lead with respect to gender equality. No social goal has been more important to Swedish welfare-state officials in recent decades than the achievement of full equality for women. Although most Swedish women would stress that they have hardly reached full equality with men, by many indicators the Swedish welfare state has been remarkably successful in achieving such equality: Sweden today has probably the smallest percentage of full-time housewives—about 10 percent—of any Western nation, one of the highest percentages of working-age women in the labor force (77 percent in 1983, compared with 62 percent in the U.S.), and the closest correspondence between women's and men's earnings (Swedish women earn about 90 percent as much as Swedish men, whereas the comparable figure is 70 percent in the U.S.).

Welfare-State Ideology

Economic security and gender equality are both established political goals of modern states, goals that appear to weaken families. They are accentuated by, but by no means unique to, the welfare state. In addition to these political goals, the welfare state nurtures a distinctive and pervasive cultural mentality, or ideology, that has antifamily overtones.

Two of the central values of welfare-state ideology are professionalism in human services and egalitarianism in society. These values are strongly held and promoted by the legion of workers who staff the welfare-state bureaucracy. But the family is neither professional nor egalitarian. The cultural dominance of these two values, therefore, poses a special threat to the interests of the family as a unit (as distinct from the interests of individual family members).

Modern professionalism has achieved much by increasing knowledge and refining techniques. But according to many close observers, the great emphasis placed on professional care in Sweden has enfeebled both the confidence and the motivation of "amateur" family members in providing their own care. In the culture of the welfare state, it becomes all too easy for family members to believe that care is best provided by—and should be provided by—government-employed professionals. The argument is that professionals are trained to give the best possible care, and that taxes are paid precisely to purchase such professional care.

To make matters worse, some welfare professionals come to believe that professional care is somehow inherently superior to the care provided by families, and should be substituted for it. The original welfare-state goal—that families should be helped rather than replaced—increasingly is undermined. This is in part the old problem of goal displacement, in which members of an organization become more concerned with perpetuating their organization (and their positions in it) than with meeting its original goals. In this respect the welfare state is no different from other organizations.

Central to the ideology of the welfare state is the belief that care provided by families is not only unprofessional, but also highly inegalitarian in its distribution. Because the family has long limited economic and social equality, it is common for the more dedicated egalitarians among welfare workers to feel ambivalence or even hostility toward it—and especially toward the traditional, patriarchal, bourgeois family.

The bourgeois family is seen as a major root of social problems. In order to destroy it, some welfare-state ideologues are eager to promote alternatives not only to the bourgeois family but to the nuclear family, and to turn over most child rearing to the state.

Adherence to such a radical, individualistic egalitarianism prohibits the state from promoting those family values and arrangements that may in fact be socially preferable. Take, for example, the statement of one Swedish official: "You can no longer speak publicly in Sweden about nuclear families being 'good' because there are now many single parents, and you don't want to make them feel bad." In the same sense, the government cannot reward families that stay together, because this would be regarded as unfair to families that break up. Thus its commitment to equality impels the welfare state to mute its voice on a range of traditional moral issues.

But the welfare state's single-minded pursuit of egalitarianism has perhaps most harmed families by making an implicit pact between the individual and the welfare bureaucracy that excludes the family unit. It is the individual, not the family, who is the welfare state's client and who has the national identification number. Rather than aiming to strengthen the family as a unit, Swedish family policy focuses almost exclusively on helping the individual family member. In the provision of economic and other welfare benefits to each individual, the concerns of the family as a unit—that it be strong, stable, and relatively self-sufficient—are consistently overlooked.

Finally, the lessening of religious belief should be mentioned as another factor associated with family decline. As abundant research in the United States has shown, people who are strongly religious tend to be more familistic and to have a lower divorce rate. Sweden has secularized with startling rapidity in the last half-century, and today is probably the world's most secular society. Less than 5 percent of Swedes regularly attend religious services, and only 50 percent proclaim a belief in God.

Secularism has never been an official policy of the Swedish welfare state. But the ideological climate of the welfare state, with its antipathy to tradition, can hardly be said to be conducive to religious life.

The High Costs of Family Breakdown

Why should modern societies be concerned about a high family-breakdown rate? If Swedes are healthier and more economically secure than ever before, why should Sweden's weakening family system be cast as a problem? If the state is able successfully to pick up the pieces that are left in the wake of family decline, and indeed to improve people's material lot in the process, why is the declining family worrisome? Answers to these questions lie in the social costs that stem from the weakening and the dissolution of families. These costs lie mainly in the economy and in child rearing.

For economic reasons, the welfare state depends heavily on families that can take care of their own, that don't make unnecessary demands on the public purse, and that recognize their responsibilities as well as their rights. But once the welfare state is fully established, such families, unfortunately, appear to become increasingly scarce. The original hope of the welfare state—that families strengthened by state assistance would be better able voluntarily to care for their members—has to some extent been dashed. We have seen this problem in the United States via the "welfare crisis"—growing welfare dependency and skyrocketing welfare costs. Writ large, this becomes the economic crisis of the welfare state.

Welfare-state leaders in European nations, too, have become worried. The Swedish government today, in fact, is in the throes of pruning its welfare-state apparatus, cutting taxes, and asking more of its citizens. Belief that the welfare state is too prominent is now widespread in Sweden, and approval of the long-dominant Social Democratic government—as measured by opinion polls—has fallen to its lowest point in many years, with only about a third of the citizenry indicating support.

The bankruptcy of the welfare state would, of course, be calamitous; but weakened families are unlikely to produce it in the immediately foreseeable future. Such families do, however, cause serious and immediate damage to children. Adults can pick and choose their family ties, but children cannot; adults may improve their lives through family dissolution, but children usually do not;

adults can live in single-person households, but children cannot. Only the most hardened antifamily cynic can really believe that the quality of family life is unimportant for children. Indeed, most people continue to believe that an emotionally rich and secure family life is every child's birthright.

There is no way to know whether parenting has become worse in Sweden in recent years. What can be discerned is a changing social ecology of child rearing that is associated with family decline. Most importantly, parents dissolve their relationships much more frequently than they did before, and children are more often raised by a single parent. The chances that a Swedish child will live continuously to age 18 with both biological parents is now only approximately one in two.

Even without parental breakup, however, important changes in child rearing are occurring. With each passing year, Sweden is drifting further away from the conditions that make for good child rearing. Thus there are fewer families that do many things together (such as eating meals), have many routines and traditions, and provide much interaction between adults and children; children have less regular contact with relatives, neighbors, and the adult world of work; a child can seldom be sure that his parents' marriage will endure; one is less likely to encounter rich family subcultures imbuing the traditional values of responsibility, cooperation, and sharing.

Adults in Sweden no longer need children in their lives, at least for economic reasons. But in social and psychological terms, children need adults as much as ever. Not just any adults, moreover, but parents who are motivated, in the words of psychologist Urie Bronfenbrenner, to provide "enduring, irrational, emotional involvement." In this sense, child rearing is an aspect of human life that the modern propensity to increase efficiency and rationalize procedures cannot improve; it is a cottage industry. What is still required is an abundance of time, patience, and love on the part of caring parents; a bureaucracy cannot provide this. In short, children need strong families.

What ill effects has the changing social ecology of child rearing brought to Sweden? The clearest evidence of a problem is in the data on juvenile delinquency. Swedish delinquency rates rose abruptly during the years of rapid family change and today are among the highest in northern Europe (although the offenses are mostly minor and seldom involve violence). There is also much discussion and some hard data concerning a considerable increase in angst among Swedish youth, with such related problems as depression, suicide, and alcoholism. For the real test, however, we must await the coming to maturity of today's generation of young Swedes.

What Is to Be Done?

Could the United States somehow incorporate the best of Swedish family and welfare policies while avoiding damage to the institution of the family? Many American conservatives believe not; they argue that the welfare state constitutes a single sociopolitical package whose structures cannot be disentangled, and that

America should continue to rely on the market and not become more of a welfare state.

But the market can be just as damaging to the family as the state. This helps account for the fact that the United States and Sweden—the Western world's welfare laggard and welfare leader, respectively—have the world's highest family-dissolution rates. It makes little sense, then, for the United States to think that it is saving the family by refusing to expand its comparatively meager welfare efforts. A middle ground should be sought between state and market; more generous parental-leave policies, for example, would allow parents to integrate work and family more successfully. Reducing the economic uncertainties of life in the United States—without generating the excessive dependence on government found in Sweden—would help the family much more than hurt it. Family conditions in this country have deteriorated so much, in fact, and we are so far behind other nations in providing such basic welfare programs for children as health care and preschool education, that the American adoption and expansion of such programs seem both necessary and inevitable.

In the end, however, family policies—important though they are—remain inadequate to deal with the most serious family problem of the modern world. Public services and facilities alone cannot keep families whole—only people's values can. But values are fragile and must be nourished culturally. Rather than relying on welfare programs to halt family decline, we will instead have to seek more profound ways to mend the torn cultural fabric of modern society.

The Changing Structure of American Families: The Bigger Family Planning Issue*

David T. Ellwood

As the title of this reading suggests, David T. Ellwood examines the changing structure of the American family and its consequences (also described in the earlier readings on family structure variation). Specifically, Ellwood concentrates on the difficult position in which single parents and their children find themselves. He proposes an alternative to the welfare system by formulating policies that would make work pay, and in addition, would strengthen the child support system in this country. Ellwood closes this reading and our collection by noting, "The critical conclusion is that we cannot ignore the changing nature of American families. Policies can and must be designed to do a far better job of coping with the realities of today . . . Our future is at stake."

American families are changing in profound ways. And both public and private policies have lagged far behind the altered realities. Meanwhile, families, and especially children, are suffering. It is time for serious family planning—and I don't mean birth control (although that should play a role).

Some basic facts regarding American families are quite familiar. Everyone

*Source: Reprinted by permission of the *Journal of the American Planning Association*, 59, no. 1 (Winter 1993), pp. 3–8.

knows that Ozzie and Harriet are not typical anymore. But just how far we are from that image often surprises even well-informed observers. Only a third of all households are families with children. The number of single person households rose from less than 13 percent in 1960 to roughly twice that in 1990. But even among families with children, only *19 percent* were two parent households where the father was employed in the labor market and the mother did not work outside the home. Partly the changes are caused by a dramatic increase in the number of working married mothers: In 1960, less than 30 percent of married mothers worked, and now two-thirds of them do.

Still, in my view, the most dramatic and most important changes involve family structure. In 1960, 9 percent of white children were not living with two parents. By 1990, the figure had risen to 21 percent. For blacks the changes were even more dramatic: 33 percent of black children were not living with two parents in 1960; thirty years later 62 percent were not. Yet even these figures understate the extent to which changes influence children. By several estimates, the median child born in the U.S. today will spend time in a single parent home. The problem is not primarily the result of births to teenagers. It is a reflection of higher divorce, less marriage, reduced fertility of married women, and other changes that alter the behavior of all races and classes.

For physical planners, these trends have profound implications. Day-care facilities become critical when fewer parents stay home to care for children. Residential structures need to be designed with Harriet and the kids (sans Ozzie) in mind. Increases in the number of households require more, but smaller housing units. Even more important are the economic and social implications for our children and for our communities. For if the family is becoming less viable economically, our communities and our economic future are in jeopardy.

Why Have Families Changed So Much?

In most popular discussions about family change, welfare receives much of the blame for the altered pattern of family structure. The logic seems solid. Welfare provides single mothers with a means of support. They can afford to have children out of wedlock or to divorce, since the welfare safety net is available. And even if women don't choose to have children to get welfare, welfare may allow them to keep the child if they get pregnant.

Yet academic researchers have been unable to find strong links between welfare and the formation of single parent families. And no careful analyst has claimed that welfare had more than a minor role in the overall growth in single parent families. One reason welfare is so hard to blame has to do with the time series pattern of welfare and family change.

Welfare and food stamp benefits did rise significantly in the 1960s and early 1970s. In 1960, a family of four qualified for an average of $7,652 in welfare benefits (all figures are in 1988 dollars). By 1972, the combination of Aid to Families with Dependent Children (AFDC) and food stamps paid $10,133. And those figures understate the changes, since the Medicaid program had been added and some eligibility provisions relaxed. Caseloads were rising quickly. And family structures were changing.

But the growth in welfare benefits abruptly ended around 1972. Nominal benefit increases all but ceased in AFDC and the real value of benefits began to decline. Inflation eroded benefits so much that the real value in 1988 was back down to $8,019—almost the level it was at in 1960. And many eligibility rules had been tightened considerably. Total public assistance benefits were higher than in 1960, because all recipients got Medicaid and some had some housing and other forms of assistance that were not available in 1980. But there is no doubt that the disposable income available to welfare mothers fell considerably between the early 1970s and 1988. Thus, if welfare had caused family structures to change before the early 1970s, shouldn't the fall in benefits since that time have helped put the genie back in the bottle?

The welfare cutbacks did stop the growth in welfare. But the changes in family structure continued. While the number of black children not living with two parents rose by 2 million, the number of black children on welfare actually declined. If AFDC had been encouraging or even allowing the rapid change in the living arrangements of children, then the fraction of children on AFDC should have risen as fast or faster than the fraction of children not living with two parents. Yet between 1970 and 1988 . . . the fraction of all American children on AFDC held steady, while the fraction of children in single parent families skyrocketed. More sophisticated cross-section or cross-section time-series studies do sometimes find some connection between welfare and family structure, but the magnitude of estimated effects is generally small, when it can be found at all.

Another popular hypothesis is one advanced by renowned sociologist William Julius Wilson and his colleagues. They argue that the decline in the employment of young black men caused marriage to decline sharply in the black community due to the lack of marriageable (employed) men. One might also hypothesize that changing patterns of male earnings could have caused changes in white families.

The changes in employment and earnings of men in the 1970s and 1980s were indeed profound. Just how serious the problem has been can be seen by looking at the earnings of white male high school graduates age 25 to 34—essentially the median American male during the prime family formation years. Earnings for these men fell a remarkable 21 percent, adjusted for inflation, between 1970 and 1990. Indeed, adjusted for inflation, earnings of these men were lower in 1990 than they were in 1960! Younger, less educated, and minority men fared even more poorly. Only the best educated of men under 35 even kept pace with inflation over the 1970s and 1980s.

Yet even these trends don't offer a very good explanation for the altered pattern of families. Marriage rates fell more in both absolute and percentage terms among *employed* black men in the 1970s and 1980s than among the unemployed. Declines in marriage and rises in divorce were virtually identical for 25- to 34-year-old white dropouts, white high school graduates, and whites with higher education, even though the poorly educated fared much, much worse in the labor market over the past two decades. Thus, traditional families were in decline almost as much for the employed and well-educated men as they were for the people devastated by recent economic trends.

There are other plausible explanations: The rise in women's work and earnings may have made women less dependent on men or more desirous of careers other than raising a family. Altered attitudes toward premarital and extramarital sex may have reduced pressure for marriage. Improved birth control methods may have given women more control over fertility and again reduced the need to marry. Conversely a lack of birth control among more sexually active teens may have contributed. Changing mores regarding out-of-wedlock childbearing, easier divorce laws, the "decline of traditional values," all may have played a role.

The unfortunate reality is that no simple answer has yet been found to explain these trends. Almost certainly, changes as profound as those experienced in the past 30 years must reflect a confluence of often mutually reinforcing influences pushing and pulling at the traditional fabric of families.

The fact that we don't know the cause of the changes means we can point to no clear policy to reverse them. Certainly no plausible social policies are likely to make much difference. Tinkering with the welfare system, better education, and availability of birth control, even more tax benefits for two parent families might help somewhat, but single parent families are here to stay. We need to devise policies that understand and address the new realities. At the same time, in acknowledging that we don't know how to reverse the trends, we still ought to focus on policies with incentives that reinforce families, responsibility, and independence.

The Impossible Position of Single Parents

While the changes in family structure may be hard to explain, the implications for the economic well-being of children and families are straightforward. As an increasing number of children in the U.S. are raised in single parent households, the economic position of children will worsen significantly. Single parent families are, on average, much worse off than two parent families. In 1990, the U.S. defined as poor any family of four whose income fell below $13,359 ($10,419 for a family of three). Among children in two parent families the poverty rate was 10 percent. For children in single parent homes, the poverty rate was 55 percent. Of course, some of these differences reflect the mix of people who head such families (single parents typically have lower education, for example), rather than their family structure. Nonetheless, it is very clear that single parent families are in a much more difficult position economically.

All parents, married or single, face a difficult task of nurturing and providing for their children. Yet single parents really only have two choices: They can either work in the marketplace all the time or they can go on welfare. If single parents choose full-time work, they must simultaneously meet the demands of work and the need for child care, the many daily crises involving doctor visits, school holidays, sick children, to say nothing of maintaining a safe and happy household. Women from highly advantaged backgrounds find these demands very heavy. For mothers with a limited education, with little or no work experience, with young children, it can be an almost impossible task. Although most married mothers work, only one-third of them work full time year round. Is it fair or realistic to expect all single mothers to work more than two-thirds of married mothers do?

The only alternative, at present, is welfare. And it is not a very attractive option. No state pays enough in welfare and food stamps to keep a family out of poverty. Adjusting for inflation, benefits are vastly lower than they were 15 years ago. The welfare system frustrates and isolates and humiliates and stigmatizes.

Worse still is the way welfare treats people who try to play by the rules, people who attempt to work their way off of welfare. Welfare benefits are reduced dollar for dollar with earnings. Table 36-1 shows that a woman working full time at the minimum wage would have only $2,400 more in disposable income than if she did not work and collected welfare. That is like working for $1.20 per hour. And one-half of that $2,400 comes from the Earned Income Tax Credit (EITC), which she collects only at the end of the year if she bothers to submit a tax return. On a daily basis, she seems to be working for sixty cents an hour. Even if she can work full time at five dollars an hour, her disposable income is only $3,400 higher and she loses her Medicaid, which is worth several thousand dollars. No wonder administrators in states around the country find that unless a woman is placed in a full-time job paying six dollars an hour or more, with full medical benefits, and low day-care costs, she is likely to come right back onto welfare. It should come as no surprise that only a small fraction (20 to 25 percent) of women leaving welfare actually "earn" their way off. And most of them are the better educated and more experienced women who can command a relatively high wage. Other women try to leave, but there is almost always some setback, often something relatively inconsequential, such as a sick child, which causes them to lose their job and return to welfare.

We would like single parents to support themselves and become self-sufficient, but we have made the task almost impossible. The Family Support Act of 1988 began the movement toward a system that encourages and facilitates self-support rather than seeming to defeat it. But it didn't alter the basic dilemmas inherent in a welfare system. It doesn't make work pay. It doesn't make it possible to support a family on anything less than a full-time job paying at least 50 percent above the minimum wage along with medical benefits. It doesn't ensure that a woman is better off working than on welfare.

Making Work Pay

Low pay is a problem facing many groups, especially women and minorities, but even less well-educated and younger white males have seen major declines in

TABLE 36-1

Earnings, Taxes, Benefits, and Total Income for a Single Parent and Two Children after Four Months at Work in Pennsylvania, January 1991

WORK LEVEL AND WAGE	EARNINGS	DAY CARE	NET TAXES[a]	EITC	WELFARE AND FOOD STAMPS	DISPOSABLE INCOME	MEDICAID?[b]
No work	$0	$0	$0	$0	$7,278	$7,278	Yes
Half time, minimum wage	$4,500	–$1,500	$434	$779	$5,003	$9,215	Yes
Full time, minimum wage[c]	$9,000	–$3,000	$547	$1,235	$1,899	$9,681	Yes
Full time, $5.00/hour	$10,000	–$3,000	$680	$1,235	$1,719	$10,635	No
Full time, $6.00/hour	$12,000	–$3,000	$257	$1,143	$1,376	$11,775	No
Full time, $7.00/hour	$14,000	–$3,000	–$414	$895	$1,060	$12,542	No

[a] Taxes include Social Security, federal, and state taxes. Taxes are sometimes positive due to the earned income tax credit.
[b] Medicaid is the government health insurance program for those on welfare.
[c] Minimum wage rate is $4.50 per hour.

Source: Modeled after a table in Committee on Ways and Means (1990). All figures are approximate.

wages in recent years. Today we guarantee medical care to the welfare poor on public assistance and to those in middle-class jobs. But the working poor often have very little coverage. And day care is often so expensive that it makes little sense for mothers to work. If work does not pay, if low-income workers face greater medical insecurity than those on welfare, should we ask parents to go from being welfare poor to working poor? Would a responsible parent make that choice?

Strategies to make work pay reinforce work, family, and responsibility. The vast majority of working poor families are two parent families. Thus, by helping the working poor we will help support struggling families that might otherwise become single parent ones. We would also help make work a viable alternative to welfare.

I will not focus here on strategies to help the working poor. Briefly they include refundable tax credits to working families to raise take-home pay, ensuring that everyone has medical protection, reducing the cost of day care, and, yes, perhaps even restoring the minimum wage to its level of the 1960s and 1970s adjusted for inflation. (The minimum wage is lower today than it was in 1956.) These are essential first steps in dealing with family change or reducing its incidence. But I would like to focus instead on policies designed to confront the realities that single parents face.

The Forgotten Fathers

All the talk of traditional family values would suggest that mothers *and* fathers would be central to any discussion of children and the future. But the reality is that for single parent families, virtually the entire focus has been on mothers. Mothers are expected to do the entire job of nurturing and supporting the family. Society has done little to encourage or require paternal involvement in the economic and social support of the family.

Recently child support enforcement has begun to get some attention. It is about time. The current system of child support is a disgrace. In 1989, just one single parent in three reported getting any court-ordered child support from the absent parent, and the average amount received was under $3,000. Often the problem is not that the father cannot pay. By several estimates, a truly uniform and universal child support system could theoretically collect up to an additional $10 to $20 billion from fathers.

The current system of child support enforcement fails for many reasons. As currently constructed, it requires actions by all levels of government (federal, state, and local) and it involves deep and frequent intervention by all three branches of government (administrative, legislative, and judicial). It is a system of extraordinary complexity and confusion. Each case is decided individually with heavy involvement by an already overworked judiciary. It may be the only system single mothers hate worse than welfare. Even the most jaded of planners could not stand this system.

A truly reformed enforcement system would have several elements:

Changes in the procedures, responsibility, and incentives for paternity establishment. A single federal or state agency should be given the mission of establishing paternities in all cases as close to the birth as possible. Incentives for both the agency and the mother for getting paternities in place should be strong. The procedures for establishing paternity should be changed to provide for speedy and fair resolution of cases, voluntary acknowledgment of paternity, and early use of blood tests in contested cases.

The burden of enforcement should be removed from custodial parents by eliminating the dual system of child support enforcement. Government currently concentrates primarily on collecting money in cases where the mother is on welfare. In most nonwelfare cases, enforcement is left up to the mother and the courts (though mothers off of welfare can seek help from the government agency charged with collecting money for welfare recipients). Mothers can't be left to negotiate a complex and slow court system, nor should child support enforcement be an afterthought to the welfare system. It ought to be seen as a central element of social policy for all children.

A central registry for collections. All collections should come through a central system so they can be tracked and enforced efficiently. Otherwise enforcement will often be left by necessity in the hands of the mother and the courts.

An improved system of employer withholding. The only effective way to collect child support is through automatic wage withholding. An improved system of withholding, including reporting of child support obligations on the W-4 form and reporting of all new hires would significantly increase collections.

Collection as part of the tax system with failure to pay child support subject to the same penalties and remedies as failure to pay taxes. Payment of child support ought to be as certain as death and taxes. Only if the failure to pay is treated as seriously as failure to pay taxes will we really ensure that money gets paid.

Simplified and improved systems for updating awards. The current system hurts everyone. A vastly simpler system would collect more money and be quicker to recognize changed circumstances (such as unemployment of the father). Ideally this would be primarily an administrative procedure of automatic updates based on the previous year's tax returns of the father and mother or upon petition of either the mother or father.

A vastly improved system of interstate collections. Roughly 30 percent of child support cases are interstate, which are almost impossible to collect. Ideally the system would federalize the entire collection process. Awards might still be set by the state, but collections are best done at the federal level.

Expanded use of administrative law judges and other administrative procedures. The courts are too overburdened to have so much responsibility for child support enforcement. Properly designed administrative or quasi-judicial procedures can expedite the process considerably while still ensuring due process. Such a system would also be able to move quickly to get an award in cases where a mother and father are separated, but uncertain as to whether they will ultimately divorce.

Better information collection. Much more information should be routinely collected including information on the number of children by age for whom paternity has and has not been established, the level of awards and payments for all cases, and the amount owed and unpaid.

In my view the ideal system would involve a federal agency charged with many of the duties now scattered among the states. States would still be responsible for setting divorce settlements, but paternity, child support collection, and award modification could all be done by administrative procedures including administrative law judges under the jurisdiction of a federal agency. Nonetheless, most of these things could be done at the state level, although the problem of interstate cases would remain a very serious one.

An even more neglected area, however, involves finding ways to help and support fathers as they seek to play a role in the lives of their children. Most child support enforcement tools are sticks systems, designed to force fathers to pay support. Until very recently child support enforcement rarely sought to help fathers who were unemployed and unable to pay to get training or to find a job. The Family Support Act of 1988 authorized demonstration projects involving employment and training services for absent fathers who were unable to pay, and these demonstrations have begun. There are a few small programs in a few states. We have years of experience and experimentation with welfare-to-work programs for mothers, yet we have done very little to aid and support the efforts of fathers.

Supporting the efforts of fathers involves more than employment and training services. The larger and more difficult question is how the father can become involved in nurturing their children as well as helping to support them financially. Absent fathers' groups have complained for years that visitation privileges have been denied them, but they are still expected to provide support. I think it is a terrible mistake to link visitation with child support. It is not in the best interests of the child for the mother to be able to bargain away child support to minimize contact with the father.

But that is no excuse for ignoring issues of paternal roles. Real family planners must begin to think about how men can and should be involved in the lives of their children. The issues are extremely complex, given the awkward and often very hostile relationship between the two parents. Some mothers really do not want the father to have any contact with their children. And some fathers express strong desires for increased visitation primarily as a strategy to keep the mother from pursuing child support vigorously. Nonetheless, many children in single parent families may want, need, and deserve real contact with the father. Improvements in child support enforcement need to proceed with haste, but much more research and energy should be devoted to finding better ways to support men who genuinely want to play a constructive role in the lives of their children.

By neglecting fathers we have sent a very damaging signal. Absent fathers have no real responsibility for their children. Fathering a child out of wedlock too often involves no commitments or expectations. Dramatic reforms in child support enforcement are a necessary start. New strategies for paternal involvement are needed as well. Indeed, it is quite possible that we have been neglecting a part of the family equation where policy could have its greatest leverage. We have discovered that making the lives of single parents extremely difficult has not done much to influence family formation. Perhaps if we held fathers more accountable we would get more responsible sexual practices on their part. It is even possible that if men's economic prospects brightened and they were more involved in the lives of their children, marriage would again appear to be an attractive option to both men and women.

Child Support Enforcement and Insurance:
A Real Alternative to Welfare

Improved enforcement and collection procedures could dramatically improve child support collections and benefit both single mothers and their children. But what happens in the cases where the father has low earnings and little child support could be collected immediately? Just as we have a system of unemployment insurance for workers who lose their jobs, we could adopt a kind of child support insurance to guarantee that every youngster gets some minimum child support. Irv Garfinkel of Columbia University, who is rightly credited with developing and pushing this idea in the U.S., calls it "child support assurance."

Suppose a woman with two children could count on just $4,000 in child support annually. Then, a combination of work and child support could easily support this family at the poverty line. Indeed, half-time work at five dollars an hour would be enough to keep a family of three out of poverty in 1992. Full-time work would provide some real security.

A child support enforcement and insurance plan would be designed to place more responsibility for supporting children on absent parents. And when collections from the absent parent fell below some minimum level (because of low earnings of the father, for example), the government would ensure that single mothers still got some child support income. It would change the incentive for the mother to get an award in place, it would change the incentives for work, and it would focus attention on the absent father as a source of support.

Some argue that a minimum child support benefit is simply welfare by another name. But when a woman earns an extra dollar while on welfare, benefits are reduced by a dollar. When she earns an extra dollar while collecting child support, she keeps the whole dollar. Child support will not require trips to the welfare office. There will be no stigma, no reporting, no verification, and no cheating. Perhaps most important, the same uniform system will protect working-class, middle-class, and upper-class families.

Moreover, when the public becomes concerned about the money being spent on insured child support benefits, the rhetoric will become, "Those *fathers* are not pulling their weight, we are paying their child support for them!" The country will be forced to debate workfare for fathers versus training and education. The struggles and responsibilities of fathers will be examined as part of our concern for children in single parent families, just as they should be. Fathers and the paternal role will finally get the attention they deserve. Such a plan has generated support from both the right and the left. . . .

The greatest source of insecurity in America used to be growing old. We dramatically reduced that problem with Social Security, which covers all American families, relates contributions and benefits to earnings, but provides people at the bottom with extra protection. A uniform child support enforcement and insurance plan would do the same. Contributions would be collected from all absent parents, and that money would go directly to the children. And there would be extra protection for those at the bottom.

The most remarkable feature of the system is that it need not cost very much. Most of the payments would come from the absent fathers. For women on welfare, the minimum benefits will simply offset welfare payments and, thus, it costs nothing extra. The only real cost is for people who are off welfare, achieving independence by combining work and child support. Most estimates suggest that the cost of an assured benefit system will be a few billion dollars. And the improved collection system may save more than the insured benefit costs in the long run. If any additional money is spent, it will all be going to women who are working—families who are playing by the rules and trying to provide for themselves. Any additional money spent on supporting the work efforts of fathers would need to be added, but that money too may return in more child support and taxes. Thus, the system will reinforce work, family, and parental responsibility. If we adopted child support enforcement and insurance, we could then begin talking about ways to make welfare truly transitional, perhaps even time limited. But without a child support program we can do very little to reform welfare seriously.

My basic point is not that one plan or another is perfect. Nor is it that one or two policies can deal with the issue. I have not even considered other family issues like parental leave or comprehensive services. The critical conclusion is that we cannot ignore the changing nature of American families. Policies can and must be designed to do a far better job of coping with the realities of today than ones created in the 1930s when few women worked outside the home and when very few homes had one parent who was not a widow. Our future is at stake.